KING CHARLES I

Pauline Gregg began her writing career with books on the social and economic history of England. At the same time she was becoming closely involved in the seventeenth century through her work on the Leveller Movement, which had been the basis of her doctoral thesis. *Free-Born John*, her biography of John Lilburne, the Leveller leader, resulted in a more intensive study of the period which led her to the heart of the struggle – King Charles himself.

Also by Pauline Gregg

Free-Born John (Phoenix Press)

A Social and Economic History of Britain 1760–1980

The Chain of History

The Story of the Main Links in the Chain of Man's Development from the Stone Age to the End of the Nineteenth Century

The Welfare State: an Economic and Social History of Great Britain from 1945 to the Present Day

Oliver Cromwell

Black Death to Industrial Revolution: a Social and Economic History of England

KING CHARLES I

Pauline Gregg

**PHOENIX
PRESS**

5 UPPER SAINT MARTIN'S LANE
LONDON
WC2H 9EA

A PHOENIX PRESS PAPERBACK

First published in Great Britain
by J.M. Dent in 1981
This paperback edition published in 2000
by Phoenix Press,
a division of The Orion Publishing Group Ltd,
Orion House, 5 Upper St Martin's Lane,
London WC2H 9EA

A CIP catalogue record for this book
is available from the British Library.

Printed in Great Britain by
Clays Ltd, St Ives plc

ISBN 1 84212 199 5

To Rosalind and Alan

Contents

Contents

Part III
Personal Rule

Part IV
Conflict

Part V
Civil War

List of Illustrations

Preface

In writing this biography my first debt is to the people of the seventeenth century themselves, who loved words, whose ability to use language was matched by the richness of the medium at their disposal, and whose need to communicate was matched by their ability to do so. To the scholars who have followed, interpreting and re-interpreting, with constantly changing emphasis, I am under a further obligation, particularly, perhaps, to the greatest narrative historian of them all – Samuel Rawson Gardiner. The bibliography at the end of this book indicates part, at least, of my indebtedness to others.

A great deal of my work has been done in the Bodleian Library and once more I would like to record my thanks to that magnificent Library and the splendid staff who unostentatiously and with unfailing good humour meet the demands of harassed authors. To the History Faculty Library of Oxford University, to the British Library and the Public Record Office I am also most grateful. In a special category is Swarthmore College, Pennsylvania. During twelve months' residence in America they allowed me the unrestricted use of their library, including their fine Quaker collection, and I am glad to record my sincere thanks.

I have been helped by many people. Barry Williamson set me on rewarding paths more often, perhaps, than he realized, while his practical help at the Wiltshire Record Office, and elsewhere, has been of the greatest value. Dr Margaret Toynbee generously placed at my disposal her unrivalled knowledge of the portraits of Charles I, a privilege I deeply appreciate. Timothy Wilson, Assistant Keeper in the Department of Medieval and Later Antiquities in the British Museum, most kindly allowed me to use his thesis on Saint George for my section on the Order of the Garter: I am very grateful.

Professor Ivan Roots read my whole manuscript. His discerning eye and his robust approach, combined with his great knowledge of the period, have been of the greatest help to me. At Dent's many people have worked on the production of this book but no one has been more concerned than Peter Shellard, with whom I have been in close contact at every stage: to a patient and understanding publisher I should like to record my thanks.

Above all I want to thank my husband, Russell Meiggs, not only for accepting my relationship with Charles I but for support in every way. His own commitments to the ancient world might have benefited by less intrusion from the seventeenth century.

The notes to the chapters have been kept to a minimum but have been linked to the bibliography in a way which I hope will prove helpful to the reader.

Pauline Gregg
April, 1981

Garsington

Part I
The Prince

1

Duke of Albany

In the year 1600 the affairs of the royal house of Scotland were of absorbing interest to all concerned in the English succession. Queen Elizabeth I had occupied the throne of England for forty-two years, she was sixty-seven years old and childless. Of possible successors James VI of Scotland was favoured by most of those likely to have any influence in the matter. Nothing was said openly, and Elizabeth would not name her successor, but as the new century dawned an elaborate information service was in operation between Scotland and England in which the ceaseless troubles of the turbulent Scottish Court and the ups and down of James's marriage featured prominently. Thus on 20 November 1600, George Nicolson, the English Ambassador to Scotland, wrote from Edinburgh to Sir Robert Cecil, the English Secretary of State, with a series of important announcements:

> On Monday last the King rode to the Queen to Dunfermline and returned yesternight. They never loved better. This night at 11 of the clock the Queen was delivered of a son and word thereof this night at about 3 hours brought to the King. Whereon the King this morning is gone to the Queen and 3 pieces of ordnance shot by this castle in joy of the same.
>
> The Earl and his brother were yesterday hanged on the gibbet in the Market Place here and after quartered by the hangman.

James VI of Scotland was then in his thirty-fifth year; his wife was Anne of Denmark, aged twenty-five, to whom he had been married for eleven years. The baby, their second son and third surviving child of the four who had been born to them, was the future Charles I of England, Scotland, and Ireland.

James's delight was seemingly unfeigned and he found the day of the birth particularly auspicious. 'I first saw my wife', he exclaimed when brought the news, 'on the 19th November on the coast of Norway. She bore my son Henry on the 19th February, my daughter Elizabeth on the 19th August, and now she has given birth at Dunfermline to my second son on the anniversary of the day on which we first saw each other . . . I myself', he added, was 'born on the 19th June'. John Murray, who brought him the news, was rewarded with £16 of Scots money.

James's relief at the ending of the 'Gowrie conspiracy' may have played some part in his joy, for the quartered carcasses that swung on their gibbets in Edinburgh, Stirling and Perth were those of the Earl of Gowrie and his brother, Alexander Ruthven. Gowrie's so-called 'conspiracy' remains a mystery and the degree of Anne's attachment to Alexander Ruthven is uncertain, though she was certainly fond of his sister, Beatrix, who was one of her ladies-in-waiting. Rumours, however, had persisted and only four days before the birth of Charles it was reported that there was 'no good agreement, but rather an open Diffidence between the King of Scots and his Wife', and that many were 'of opinion, that the Discovery of Some Affection between her and the Earle of Gowry's brother . . . was the truest Cause and Motife of all that Tragedy'.

Whatever the truth, it was an ugly episode. The brothers had been killed three months previously in an affray at the Earl's own house instigated, it was rumoured, by James himself. Beatrix Ruthven had been removed from the Queen's service and Anne's third child, a little girl of two, had died at about the same time. Expunging the name of Ruthven 'for ever' and quartering the two bodies was ordered by the Scottish Parliament on 18 November, the day before the Queen's delivery. Such pre-natal disturbance added to the normal uncertainty of birth and survival in the seventeenth century; the new baby was weak and sickly and his mother very ill. James's ebullience was out of tune with the reality at Dunfermline Castle as hasty arrangements were made to baptize the child should it die that night.[1]

In the event Anne recovered and it was again reported on 5 December that 'the King and Queen agree exceeding well'. The baby survived to be given a grander christening on Tuesday December 23 by David Lindsay, Bishop of Ross, in the royal chapel at Holyrood House. His godfathers were the Huguenot Prince de Rohan and his brother Monsieur (later Duke of) Soubise, who were visiting the capital; the godmothers were the Countess of Mar and the Countess of Huntley. The Prince, in a gown of lawn and wrapped in cloth of gold, was carried to the chapel by the Prince de Rohan. Behind them Lord Livingstone bore the baby's robe of royal purple velvet lined with damask, and there followed the Prince's Dames of Honour with the Lord President bearing his crown ducal. As trumpets sounded the procession made its way to the chapel where the King awaited them. The baby, who was held during the service by the Countess of Huntley beneath a magnificent silken pall which had been elaborately worked in gold and silver by his grandmother Mary, Queen of Scots, was baptized Charles. The King then bestowed on him the title of Duke of Albany, traditionally attached to the second son of the King of Scotland, and the heralds proclaimed him Lord of Ardmonoche, Earl of Ross, and Marquis of Ormonde. Celebrations and feasting continued over Christmas, James conferred knighthoods and peerages in his son's honour, while cannon sounded in salute and £100 was thrown to the populace.

Although the Queen received a handsome gift from the King in the form of a New Year's jewel for his 'dearest bedfellow', she did not attend the official christening of Charles but remained at Dunfermline, nursing her resentment and planning, some said, to punish those who had poisoned the King's mind against her. Beatrix Ruthven was not allowed back to her service, though Anne helped her secretly with clothes and money. Six months later Cecil's intelligence was informing him that the Queen of Scotland was scheming to recall one of the exiled Scottish lords, the Earl of Bothwell, to stir up trouble at home, while correspondents in England were writing that the death of Gowrie would be revenged.[2]

James VI of Scotland was the only child of Mary, Queen of Scots, by Henry Darnley, thus inheriting, in double line, the Tudor blood of Henry VII, for Margaret Tudor was the grandmother of both Mary and Darnley – unless, indeed, as some suggested, his mother's Italian secretary, David Rizzio, was his father. But undoubtedly James inherited through his mother the French blood of the Guises and the Stuart blood of the kings of Scotland, while through Darnley he would have been closely related to the families of Angus, of Lennox, and of Douglas. To this mixed heritage was added the Norse and German lineage of James's Danish Queen. Anne was the youngest daughter of Frederick II of Denmark and Norway and of Sophia of Mecklenberg. Of her two brothers the elder had succeeded to the throne as Christian IV at the age of eleven shortly before her marriage;

her younger brother was the Duke of Holst. Anne was not quite fifteen years old when she was brought home to Scotland by James himself, who had been attracted by the fair young beauty whom he saw in a miniature sent from Denmark. The Court and the commercial interests of Scotland favoured the match, for Denmark was a Protestant country, it was not involved in foreign wars or alliances, and its trading connections with Scotland were long-established and beneficial. James's enthusiasm was such that, in somewhat uncharacteristic fashion, he had himself sailed from Scotland to fetch his bride when storms delayed her passage. They were married in Oslo on 23 November 1589, in considerable pomp, but storms again bedevilled their voyage to Scotland. James attributed the inclement weather to black magic, in which at that time he profoundly believed, and the return of the King with his bride in May 1590 was sullied by the trials, torture, and execution of alleged witches.

Anne's Nordic fairness of hair and skin, her slim and graceful figure, gave her a greater beauty in youth than her later portraits imply, and James had her miniature set in one of the green, enamelled heads of his own Order of the Thistle. She was lively and good-natured and at first James and his Court had reason to be pleased with her. But the mounting expenses of her household brought criticism from the Scottish lords, while Anne, a Lutheran, grew tired of Presbyterian austerity. Inevitably she was caught up in the wild and bitter feuding of the Scottish nobility, she was too young to discriminate, and her judgment was not good. It was also inevitable that there should have been rumours, other than those attached to young Ruthven. She 'had a great number of gallants, both in Scotland and England', it was said. But of contemporary stories, apart from the Gowrie affair, the chief is that which concerned the young and bonny Earl of Moray, who was savagely murdered by Huntley in one of the internecine feuds of the Scottish nobility:

> He was a braw callant
> And he rade at the glove;
> And the bonnie Earl o' Murray,
> Oh! he was the Queen's luve.

No details of the affair survive. Anne was sixteen at the time, had been in Scotland for only a year and had as yet no children. There is a similarity in the affairs of Moray and Gowrie in that in each case a man, whose name was associated with the Queen, met violent death in circumstances never fully explained. Another story, which can probably be discounted, is the confidential whispering, long after, of Bedy, a Dane, that *he* was the natural father of Charles.[3] Whether or not there was truth in any of these rumours, James could always be counted on to cover up for his wife. He treated her always with firm and affectionate good sense. Whatever his suspicions he would not have dirty linen washed in public. He had determined to accept Charles as his own son and it cannot be doubted that he was prepared to shield the boy from such indignities as he himself suffered when he was shouted after in Edinburgh streets as 'Jimmy Davidson'.

Against Anne's wishes, but following the custom of the time, their eldest child Henry, a healthy boy born at Stirling Castle on 19 February 1594, had been placed in the care of the family of the Earl of Mar. Elizabeth, another healthy child, was born two years later in Falkland Castle, Fifeshire, and was taken into the family of Lord Livingstone, Earl of Linlithgow. Whatever Anne's intentions with Charles – and she showed much open affection to the sickly little boy – there was an added reason in his very infirmity to put him into care of a trusted guardian. The people chosen to bring him up were Alexander Seton, Lord Fyvie, later Lord Chancellor of Scotland and Duke of Dunfermline, and his wife. Their Roman Catholic sympathies would, James hoped, act as a counter-balance to the Presbyterianism of Mar, placate Anne, and at the same time conciliate the Catholics in England whose support was necessary if his dreams of the English throne were to come true. Dunfermline Castle, the place of Charles's birth and his mother's favourite residence, was the young prince's home for the first three and a half years of his life. It was somewhat gloomy, it was fifteen miles from Edinburgh, but the air was healthier than in the capital and it was outside the rough-and-tumble of the Court. Dame Margaret Stewart, Lady Ochiltrie, was in direct charge of the baby until he was two years old, his 'rokker' (his nurse) was Marioun Hepburn, while Jeane Drummond, third daughter of Lord Drummond and second wife of Robert Ker, first Earl of Roxburgh, was his first governess.

An apochryphal story told in Dunfermline indicates that the King and Queen were there together one night when Marioun Hepburn was heard screaming. 'Hout! tout! What's the matter w'ye, nursie?', cried James, springing out of bed and rushing into the nursery. An old man had appeared in the baby's room and thrown a dark cloak over the child as he lay sleeping in his cradle: 'I'm feared it was the thing that's na canny', gasped the terrified nurse. James interpreted the incident in his own way. 'Gin he ever be king', he said, 'there'll be nae gude a' his reign. The deil has cusen his cloak ower him already'.[4]

When the momentous news reached Edinburgh that Elizabeth I had died and that the succession had been offered to James VI of Scotland, the King left for England without his family. The Queen was pregnant and the King's haste was such that he could neither wait to make careful arrangements for the journey nor visit his children before he left. But he sent nine-year old Henry a copy of his book, the *Basilikon Doron*, which had just been given its first public printing, together with a well-expressed warning against pride in his new position as heir to the English throne: 'a King's sonne and heire was ye before, and no maire ar ye yett'. He left on 5 April 1603, after a tender, public parting from his wife. Anne, with her eldest son at Stirling, her daughter at Linlithgow, and little Prince Charles sick of a fever at Dunfermline, was so distraught that she fell ill and miscarried, writing wildly to James that he was paying no regard to her birth as the daughter of a king. James, in spite of his new responsibilities, was all solicitude and replied with dignity: 'I thank God, I carrie that love and respecte unto you, quhich . . . I ought to do to my wyfe and mother of my children; but not for that ye are a King's daughter for quhither ye waire a King's or a cook's dauchter, ye must be all alike to me, being once my wyfe.'[5] Shortly afterwards he allowed Anne to follow him and she left with Prince Henry on June 2, leaving Elizabeth to follow with her guardians.

Charles had necessarily to stay behind. His general weakness was such that at two-and-a-half he could neither walk nor talk, and his fever persisted. By the end of April, however, Lord Fyvie was able to report to the King and Queen that the fever had abated, though the little boy was still not sleeping well at night. Nevertheless, Lord Fyvie said, 'the greate weaknesse off his bodie, after so lang and hevie seikness, is meikill suppliet be the might and strength off his spirit and minde'. A little later he wrote that the boy 'althocht zit weake in bodie, is beginnand to speik suim words'. He was already wearing coats of white satin, and of yellow satin with white sleeves, he had a scarlet coat and matching hose of French serge, and before he was two he had been given a velvet belt with a dagger at the side. The undersized, delicate little boy, with his mother's pale hair and light complexion, had to rely more even than is usual at two years old upon the help and society of adults, but he played with dolls and soft toys, and he had a rocking horse and a little propelling chair with wheels which helped to strengthen his legs.[6] While rarely alone, it is likely that he was lonely after his family had gone to England.

James was already taking further advice. In spite of the cares and distractions of his new office he sought out a medical officer he could trust – one with recommendations from both Sir Robert Cecil and Gilbert Talbot, Earl of Shrewsbury – and just over a year after his departure from Scotland signed a warrant to Dr Henry Atkins for 50/- a day to attend Duke Charles in Scotland and to bring him to England. The doctor was allowed £100 for the provision of drugs and was to be accompanied by an apothecary, Edward Phillips.

Dr Atkins first saw Charles in one of the great rooms of Dunfermline Castle on the evening of 12 May 1604. The Prince was with Dame Margaret Stewart, who was helping him to walk, for he could still neither stand nor walk unaided. He was not lacking in spirit or guile, however, and was precocious enough to avoid a medical examination that evening by calling for music and himself joining in by imitating the instruments 'with the sound of the trew tune with his high tender voice'. But an examination next day could not be avoided and the doctor reported to the King that the chief trouble was in Charles's joints, the knees, hips and ankles being loose and not yet closed or knit together. He was troubled with scurvy and suffering at the time of Dr Atkins's examination from a looseness of the bowels and a great thirst. His attendants attributed the former, at least, to the fact that he had 'some great teeth breeding'; the thirst could similarly be attributable to a high temperature caused by teething. But the doctor could not confirm this because Charles refused to allow anyone to touch his gums.

About this time Charles had another visitor, Sir Robert Carey, who had brought the momentous news to James of his accession to the English throne. Carey, not an ill-natured man, but a busybody anxious to further his own interests, was thinking of following up his services to the father by services to the son, and he was prompted by more than mere interest when he took stock of the young Prince and decided he was 'a very weake child'. But Dr Atkins soon reported a considerable improvement and there seemed no reason why he should not come south to join his family. The journey was planned with the greatest of care and on 17 July 1604 the cavalcade started. Charles himself travelled in a litter with his faithful nurse, Marioun Hepburn, in attendance, accompanied by Lord and Lady Fyvie, in whose overall charge he would remain until his father had made alternative arrangements. He was escorted by servants and attendants, by a troop of horse, and by trumpeters to herald his coming.

James was at Theobalds in Hertfordshire when he learned that the party had crossed the border and that Charles had set foot for the first time on English soil. The ubiquitous Robert Carey secured the task of escorting the cavalcade to Court, meeting them at Bishop's Auckland. They came via York, Worksop, Wollaton in Nottinghamshire, and Leicester. At Easton Neston, near Towcester in Northamptonshire, the seat of Sir George Fermor, Charles met his parents. Dr Atkins, who had continued to forward his reports during the journey, had pronounced Charles to be in good health with his physical weakness much improved. James showed his gratitude by appointing the doctor one of his physicians-in-ordinary and conveying to him an estate in Surrey with deer to stock it. Charles, however, never showed Atkins favour, although he lived on for twelve years into Charles's own reign. There was, perhaps, some lingering resentment at the examinations he had had to undergo, or, more likely, a feeling that Dr Atkins had, in fact, done less for him than he was able, later, to do for himself, and had exaggerated for his own credit the progress which Charles had made while under his care.

Certainly it was no sturdy child whom Dr Atkins delivered to his parents. Robert Carey recounts how many great ladies came to see the boy with the hope of being granted the influential position of his care. But, said Carey, 'when they did see how weake a child he was, and not likely to live, their hearts were downe, and none of them was desireous to take charge of him.' Nevertheless Carey and his wife, a redoubtable woman, thought they could manage it, and when the Fyvies returned to Scotland towards Michaelmas 1604 the Queen asked Lady Carey to take over the care and keeping of the Duke. 'Those who wished mee no good', said Carey wryly, 'were glad of it, thinking that if the Duke should die in our charge . . . then it would not be thought fitt that wee should remaine in court after.' In the New Year, after making public testimony that the Fyvies had 'carefully and discreetly' governed his son and 'delivered him . . . in . . . good and sound estate', James, on 8 February 1605, gave Carey his official appointment: 'As we have made choice of your wife . . . to have the charge of our second son', he wrote to Sir Robert, 'you will also be tied to residence about our son [and] we authorise you to take charge of his family and see things well ordered about his person.' When, at the end of the year, old Marioun Hepburn, weighed down by her years and the unaccustomed life of the capital, returned home with £100 and a promise of £200 to come, the last link with the old life was severed.

When Charles was put officially in the Carey's charge, a little after his fourth birthday, 'he was not able to go', according to Sir Robert, 'nor scant stand alone, he was so weake in his jointes, and especially his ankles, insomuch as many feared they were out of joint'. A contemporary wrote that 'he was exceedingly feeble in his lower parts, his legs growing not erect, but rapandous and embowed, whereby he was unapt for exercises of activity'. Carey's account does not accord with Dr Atkins's report that Charles could walk up and down a room before he left Dunfermline. In each case self-interest must be taken into account. But Charles's legs were weak enough for the King to want him put in iron boots to strengthen his joints and make walking easier. Lady Carey strenuously opposed the idea and had her way, though Charles wore boots made of Spanish leather and brass, which were more helpful to his weak ankles than ordinary boots or shoes.

It is possible that Charles was suffering from rickets. He was a weak baby at birth and a diet deficiency would have emphasized the symptoms. The description of his limbs, the looseness of the joints, the lack of growth, and the presence of infantile scurvy bear this out. So does the somewhat large head, slightly flattened at the back, which is noticeable in early portraits. Rickets was prevalent in the British Isles in the early seventeenth century and was, indeed, known as 'the English disease'. It was not given a more specific name until 1620 when, as John Aubrey narrates, 'one Ricketts of Newberye, a Practitioner in Physick, was excellent at curing Children with swoln heads, and small legges: and . . . He being so famous for the cure of it, they called the Disease the Ricketts'. Rickets is associated with diet deficiency and lack of sunlight. A child brought up in Dunfermline Castle might well have been deprived of sunlight but a prince's diet would hardly be intentionally deficient, though his food might well have lacked the essential elements of healthy growth. Assuming the normal Scottish custom was followed, Charles was weaned at about a year old, his nourishment until then depending upon the quality of the milk of his wet nurse. After that he was put on a diet of milk or whey thickened with flour, since milk itself was considered merely baby's food, and thereafter rapidly accustomed to broths and bread. It was

11

basically a cereal diet, lacking phosphorus in readily assimilable amounts, with little butter or egg yolk, virtually no vegetables or fruit, and with a deficiency therefore in vitamins D and C which encouraged infantile scurvy. At the same time an excess of carbohydrates promoted a rapid growth in physique out of proportion to the process of calcification, with a resultant weakness in bone structure.[7] It is interesting that James showed symptoms similar, but not so pronounced. James's legs remained somewhat bowed all through his life (though this may have been associated with constant horse-riding) and some of his early portraits, like those of Charles, show the type of head associated with rickets; some of the portraits of Charles's elder brother Henry show the same head-flattening.

As a more efficient alternative to iron boots, the Careys took Charles to 'an Artist for strengthening Limbs, and straitning crooked Bodies', one Edward Stutfeyld, 'a practitioner in bone setting', licensed to practise in 1602 by the Barber Surgeons of London. Charles slowly grew stronger and as he did so his own determination aided his development. Day after day he was on his horse, riding, tilting, jumping. But he remained short in stature and his legs, it seems, failed to grow to their full length, bearing out the analysis that calcification had set in too early. Judging from his armour in the Tower of London he was never more than 5′4″ tall. In an age when people as a whole were less tall than now this was not particularly short. But Charles was always anxious to appear taller than he was and his portraits are so contrived. A slight shortness, a little bowing of the legs, and the hurried walk of the man with short legs – 'when he walked on Foot', wrote a contemporary, 'he rather trotted than paced, he went so fast' – were all that remained of his infantile weakness.

Like his walking, Charles's speech came slowly and with difficulty. He stammered until the end of his life, the effort to form words giving a hesitancy to his speech which could be accounted deliberation, slow-wittedness, or surliness. At one time his father wanted to help by cutting the string beneath his tongue but, again, Lady Carey's influence prevailed. Charles practised talking with pebbles in his mouth but found this no help, preferring the careful formulation of words in his head before pronouncing them.[8] Only at the supreme moment of his life, on trial at Westminster Hall, did his hesitation of speech leave him. Heredity, pre-natal disturbance, childhood worries, the anxiety of physical infirmity, all could have played their part. What tales were told in the nursery of the backward,

difficult child is unknown: his father born shortly after the murder of
Rizzio, his grandfather blown up at Kirk-o'Fields, his grandmother
beheaded by the English, the Gowrie conspiracy associated with his
own birth – all make stories which lose nothing in the telling and
whose effect on a weak and imaginative boy could have been profound. Perhaps in Charles's case his mother's delegation of her role,
though customary, caused more than ordinary deprivation. But
Charles had a strong spirit, as Lord Fyvie had assured his father in
1603. His mother called it obstinacy, and frequently reproved him. So
did the astrologer, Lilly, who spoke of Charles in his infancy as being
'very wilful and obstinate'. Though it would be strange, indeed, if
such an unfortunate heritage as Charles's, coupled with physical
weakness, did not bring difficulties of temperament and temper, yet
the Careys, throughout their long association with Charles, made
no complaint and Marioun Hepburn showed a more than ordinary
devotion and affection to her charge which hardly accords with the
description of him as a perverse and wilful little boy.

When he came to London Charles was established close to his parents
in the Palace of Whitehall in apartments which had been occupied by
Henry, who now moved to nearby St James's Palace. Charles was
acutely conscious of his radiant elder brother and of his enchanting
sister, Elizabeth, who was in the care of Lord and Lady Harington at
Coombe Abbey, two-and-a-half miles north of Coventry. Elizabeth
adored the life of the Court and whenever her parents permitted came
to apartments near the Cockpit within the complex of Whitehall
Palace. Charles became accustomed to a general movement in which
Henry went to Nonesuch and to Richmond, and his mother went to
Hampton Court, where she found the air fresher than in London, or to
the old Palace of Placentia at Greenwich, while the King himself was
already showing the passion for hunting which took him increasingly
away from London to Theobalds or Royston or to some hunting
lodge where the sport was good.

    Of the experiences that affected Charles directly the most impor-
tant was his creation as Duke of York, the customary title of the
second son of the King of England, during the Twelfth Night celebrations of 1605. He had just turned four years old and had been in
England for less than a year. The day before the ceremony he was
invested as Knight of the Bath in company with eleven other nobles of
the King's choice. On both occasions he was carried by an attendant.

After the official inauguration there was a public dinner in the Great Chamber, one table for the little Duke of York and his attendant Earls, another for his fellow Knights of the Bath. That evening there was a great masque in the old Elizabethan Banqueting House, one of the last functions to be held there, attended by the King and the Court, resplendent with foreign dignitaries, and graced by Charles's uncle, the Duke of Holst, who it was noted was 'a lusty reveller'. The performance was *The Masque of Blackness*, notable for the collaboration of Ben Jonson as author and Inigo Jones as choreographer. An idle remark of Queen Anne's that she would like to appear on the stage as a blackamoor had been taken seriously by Jonson who depicted his principal characters as daughters of Niger who sat, the Queen included, in a great scalloped-out sea shell with their faces and their arms up to the elbow blackened. That evening, as usual after such performances, there was a magnificent banquet in the Great Chamber 'which was so furiously assaulted' by the hungry audience – and this, again, was not unusual – 'that down went Table and Tresses before one bit was touched'.[9]

Queen Anne found in the masque the action and display that appealed to her. On her journey south she had been entertained at Althorpe, the home of Sir Robert Spencer, with a fairy masque written specially for the occasion by Ben Jonson, and under her patronage such simple revels were directed into more elaborate and formal channels. The development of the masque itself was due almost entirely to the astounding ingenuity of Inigo Jones. He took the big step of abandoning the dispersed platforms of earlier entertainments and concentrating his action on a single stage where he organized an astonishing series of scenic changes by means of mechanical devices and subtelties in lighting that amazed and delighted his audiences. For nearly forty years, through the reigns of James and Charles, Inigo Jones, with a variety of authors, contrived to keep the masque at the centre of Court life.

The masque was a Court entertainment, devised for and performed by the Court. But plays and professional players were also popular and the theatre played a larger part in Court life than under Elizabeth. James took over the Lord Chamberlain's Men of Elizabeth as The King's Servants, and the Queen and each of their children had a seperate company of players. These and other companies produced a veritable stream of entertainment, particularly over Christmas and the New Year. No fewer than seventeen plays by Shakespeare were performed before King James, often in the presence of his children; they included *Othello*, *King Lear*, *The Tempest* and *Henry V*. *The Merchant of Venice* was played twice at the King's command. In the festive season of 1609/10 as many as twenty-four plays were acted before the King and Queen and their family. The children, in addition, would sometimes watch plays on their own in the Cockpit, which was reserved largely for younger people, where child companies like the Children of Paul's performed.

At the same time literary men not only came to Court, they filled Court office; men like Sir Henry Wotton, Edward Herbert, Sir John Harrington, Sir John Davies and Fulke Greville were the normal contacts of Court life. So were the books they wrote and talked about. John Donne was a friend of the King's – though rather for his theology than for his poetry; Sir Robert Aytoun, the Scottish poet, was secretary to the Queen; Samuel Daniel, and John Florio the translator of Montaigne, were her grooms of the chamber. Chapman, the translator of Homer; Joseph Hall, the satirist; Tom Coryat, writer of highly coloured travel books; Joshua Sylvester, lyric poet and translator were all attached to the household of Prince Henry. Florio was his tutor, both Michael Drayton and Samuel Daniel were under his patronage. Raleigh's *History of the World*, Florio's *Montaigne*, the Authorized version of the Bible, Shelton's translation of *Don Quixote* were all produced during Charles's adolescence. Francis Bacon was prominent in Court and government, Thomas Campion and Henry Wotton were writing lyrics in praise of Princess Elizabeth. James's own library was considerable and he wrote prose and poetry himself, using Charles as transcriber. Anne was fond of music and all the children learned to sing and to play as well as to dance. Painting and drawing figured naturally in their lives both as an art to be cultivated and in the practical necessity of having their likenesses recorded by a Mytens or a Van Somer. Though much of James's Court may be condemned – and was condemned by both his sons – as extravagant and profligate, it brought literature and the arts to Charles in a natural and undemanding way.

2

Duke of York

Life as Duke of York was not much different from before, except that Charles learned to sign his letters York, with a big, curving letter Y. But at Whitehall he was in much closer contact with the outside world than at Dunfermline and there were many children in the circle of the Court where he moved. They played games such as *Rise pig, and go*; *One penny, follow me*; *I pray, my Lord, give me a course in your park*. They played Ducks and Drakes with stones. Just before his fifth birthday occurred a plot which he was old enough to know about, even if not to understand: his father and the whole of the Parliament House, not far from his own residence, were to be blown sky-high by gunpowder placed in the vaults, his brother was to be killed, his sister was to be captured and proclaimed queen. His own fate was uncertain, but one of his serving women, Agnes Foster, was involved. If the religious motivation of the Gunpowder Plot meant little to him he knew that Guy Fawkes himself was hanged and he was impressed by his father's emotional embrace as he cried out that he had been saved by his child's innocence!

More immediately exciting was the fact that about the same time Charles had a permanent tutor of his own. Thomas Murray was a Presbyterian Scot of mild character who held his beliefs moderately, though firmly. He was one of the many young men who had sat at the feet of Andrew Melville, the Scottish Presbyterian teacher and con-troversialist, and had been attached to the Court of James in Scotland. Like many others he came south with the King on his accession to the English throne. Murray was a classical scholar who wrote Latin verses which were well regarded, he was conscientious and, above all, he kept aloof from the competition of Court life. No one could have been better suited to guide the education of the young Duke at this time and he won, and kept, the confidence of both James and Charles. There

16

followed shortly afterwards into Charles's circle Murray's nephew, Will Murray, a bright, extroverted boy, about the same age as Charles. They took lessons together and, in spite of their different temperaments, formed a lifelong friendship.

James was closely concerned with his children's education. When they were small he advised them in a charming letter 'to keep up their dancing privately, though they whistle and sing to one another for music'.[1] He not only wrote to them but expected letters in return in Latin and French as well as English. He took care in choosing tutors whether for drawing, dancing, music, tennis, riding, fencing or formal study. He wrote books on statecraft for his sons' edification and helped to train them in the theological disputation which he valued. Jonson praised him in one of the masques: 'You are an honest, good man, and have care of your bairns!'. Charles's physical weakness encouraged a bent for study and, following his father's example, theology and the classics played a considerable part in his early education. Encouraged by Murray, Charles, like all his family, became an enthusiastic letter-writer. Even before he could write fluently, he would sign with a wavering Charles or York the letters Murray wrote for him. One of the earliest letters – and this was written by Charles himself – was to his father: 'Sweete, Sweete Father', it reads, 'i learne to decline substantives and adjectives, give me your blessing, I thank you for my best man, your loving sone York'.

While Charles learned enough to satisfy his father he knew also how to express some of the hero-worship he felt for his brother. In what is probably his earliest extant letter, written by his tutor but signed Charles, he pours out all the affection, the desire to give, of normal young children. He will keep and cherish for ever a letter that Henry has sent him: 'I will keep it better than all my graith'. He will give Henry anything that he has: 'I will send my pistolles by Maister Newton, I will give anie thing that I have to yow; both my horss, and my books, and my pieces, and my cross bowes, or anie thing that yow would haive. Good Brother loove me, and I shall ever loove and serve yow.' It is clear that Charles's backwardness had not deprived him of any of the normal appurtenances of a young prince. It is also clear that he had a normal boy's wish to show off. 'Pleas your H', he writes a little later, 'I doe keepe your haires in breath (and I have very good sport). I doe wish the King and you might see it.'[2]

Prince Henry, six years older than Charles, was, by common consent, a prince of much excellence. Physically he was all that a prince should be – of middle height (some 5'8"), broad-shouldered, straight-limbed, strong and well-made. His hair was auburn, frown marks on his forehead accompanied a touch of pride about the mouth. If the description of 'a piercing grave Eye . . . a most gracious smile, with a terrible Frown', smacks of the courtier's conventional language, it remains true that his portraits show a very handsome youth of strong character. Some people said he resembled his mother, others his sister. One portrait, at least, shows a face not unlike that of Charles. The early development of the two brothers, however, could not have been more different. While Charles was attending the osteopath, Henry would spend a couple of hours on study and the rest of the day on the heroic pastimes of chivalry – running at the ring, tossing the pike, vaulting, fencing, archery, as well as tennis and golf and, above all, riding. His physical energy was boundless and he would tire his companions long before he became weary himself.

If not academic in the strict sense, Henry had interests over many fields. He listened attentively to sermons, sought discussions with scholars, and welcomed travellers and visitors from abroad with avidity. He was particularly concerned about the possibility of a north-west passage to India and was 'Protector' of the Company of Discoverers of the North-West Passage, incorporated in 1612. At the same time he had a gravity of disposition that was repelled by the extravagances of his father's Court. Within the bounds of a prince's life he followed a routine that was austere in the extreme. Even after he was created Prince of Wales at the age of sixteen he continued, testified his treasurer, 'in his own frugal Courses, suffering almost nothing to pass in his House, or other Affairs, which he himself did not oversee'. He liked plain clothes. Having worn a suit of Welsh frieze for a considerable time and being told it was too mean for him that even a rich suit should not be worn so long, his answer was that he was not ashamed of his country cloth and wished it would last for ever. Both his treasurer and the French Ambassador independently reported his determination. He 'pushes what he undertakes', said the latter, 'with such zeal, as gives success to it'.

Henry's mildness of manner and his gravity are frequently mentioned. He disliked swearing and would never swear himself or take God's name in vain saying 'he knew no Game worthy of an Oath'. Boxes were placed in his various houses where any who swore would be required to pay forfeit for the benefit of the poor. He never omitted prayers before dinner and supper. He would never break his word.

Some of these characteristics are at variance with the picture of the popular, extrovert Prince, a second Prince Hal, so often given. It is likely, indeed, that the developing conscience of adolescence produced an ambivalence which combined the charming athletic extrovert with the serious-minded heir to the throne. That he possessed the rare quality we term 'charisma' there can be little doubt. He had, said a contemporary to whom the modern word was unknown, 'a certain kind of extraordinary unspeakable excellence'.[3]

In spite, or it may be because of his virtues, there was something in Prince Henry that offended his father; perhaps a too obvious reflection on the laxity of the Court, perhaps a too strong insistence on arranging his own affairs in his own way. But none of this affected the devotion of his brother and sister. With Elizabeth he formed a rare friendship. She and Henry wrote regularly to each other when apart and rode daily together when they were near. Henry also expended thought and care on his delicate younger brother, not only giving up his apartments in Whitehall for Charles but lending him horses, allowing him to use his stables, and keeping always a watchful eye on his household. Charles repaid him with affection and hero-worship. Elizabeth was allowed to come to Court for the Christmas and New Year celebrations of 1607/8, when she was eleven, after which she spent some time in and near Whitehall near her parents and her brothers. Here, again, there was an excellence of form and character which not only brought to her feet the young courtiers and poets of her father's Court but won friendship and lasting admiration. As Wotton wrote,

> You meaner beauties of the night,
> That poorly satisfy our eyes
> More by your numbers than your light;
> You common people of the skies,
> What are you when the Moon shall rise?

Close within the circle in which Charles grew up was his father's cousin, Lady Arabella Stuart. By descent she had a claim to the English throne not far inferior to James's own; by her birth and upbringing in England her claim was superior, had she cared to use it. Already a rumoured romance with William Seymour of the Howard line (himself a possible rival to the throne) had been sternly broken by Elizabeth, and shortly after James's succession Arabella was coupled with a plot by Lord Cobham and Sir Walter Raleigh to supplant James himself. Cobham and Raleigh were condemned to death but reprieved to imprisonment in the Tower. To Lady Arabella James was prepared to be gentle; she was welcomed into the family and, although she had little money, she became a well-known figure at Court. She was a strange, fey, feckless creature, her life warped by the heredity that brought her close to the throne, her willpower sapped by the two strong-willed women in whose care she had been brought up – her aunt and her redoubtable grandmother, Bess of Hardwicke. Lasting happiness was thwarted by the impossibility of any marriage whose issue might endanger the succession. It is likely, indeed, that her earlier suspected romance had been a real love affair and that she was nursing a broken heart. At all events, no question of her marriage arose to trouble James until 1610, when she was thirty-five years old. Again it was the Howards who were involved, her suitor being another William Seymour, some twelve years her junior. In spite of warnings, they secretly married and James angrily sent them both to the Tower. They contrived to escape, Arabella in man's costume, but their plans miscarried. Seymour reached France but Arabella was captured in the Channel and brought back to captivity. Sick and distraught she pined away in the Tower a life which had been sad and unfruitful through no fault of her own.

Robert Carr, fellow Scotsman and royal favourite – the page who had run beside James's coach on the journey to London in 1603 and who became Viscount Rochester in 1611 – was another figure familiar to Charles. There were the families of Howard and Essex, in particular the beautiful Frances Howard, daughter of the Earl of Suffolk, whom Henry was said to admire. Seemingly everywhere was the little, gnome-like figure of Robert Cecil, created Earl of Salisbury in 1605, whom Charles soon realized was indispensable to his father's business. Salisbury was one link with Queen Elizabeth. Francis Bacon, Salisbury's cousin, was another. He sat for Ipswich in James's first Parliament and became Attorney General in 1613. The great age of the Sea Dogs and the defeat of the Spanish Armada was linked to the present by no less a person than the colourful Sir Walter Raleigh, whose life was already a legend – casting his cloak for Queen Elizabeth to walk on, buccaneering with Drake and Hawkins, routing the Spaniard, settling Virginia in the New World in the name of the Virgin Queen, seeking gold on the Orinoco, smoking tobacco first brought from America by Drake, making presents to his friends of tobacco pipes with silver bowls, cultivating the curious, new potato crop on his estates in Youghal in Ireland. With all this, he was cultured, widely read and entertaining. 'None but my father', exclaimed Henry referring to Raleigh's imprisonment, 'could keep such a bird in such a cage!' Raleigh admired Henry and dedicated his *History of the World*, which he began in the Tower, to the Prince.

Charles was naturally concerned in the intimate details of family life – the birth of a sister, Mary, in April 1605; of another sister, Sophia, on 25 June 1607 and her funeral the following day; the death of Princess Mary later in the year. On 18 July 1606 he stood with Elizabeth on the waterfront of Greenwich Palace to welcome his uncle, Christian IV of Denmark, though he did not join the party which went to view the fleet in August. It was perhaps fortunate that he was not at the notorious party at Theobalds when James and Christian and most of their guests became completely drunk and the entertainment devised by the unfortunate Earl of Salisbury ended in disarray as guests collapsed, spilling their food and drink over themselves and each other as well as upon the floor and the furniture.[4]

It was a happy family in 1609 when Elizabeth was at Kew in a house of Lord Harington's, Charles at Whitehall, and Henry at Hampton Court. Elizabeth and Henry rode together for a couple of hours each day, they all went to a new shopping centre in the Strand which James called 'Britain's Bourse'. In June of the following year Charles watched with his mother and sister at the watergate at Whitehall as, with great acclaim, Henry arrived by river from Richmond for his inauguration as Prince of Wales. Later Charles sat to observe the ceremony in a special box with his sister, with Lady Arabella – one of her last happy moments with the family – and more than twenty other little boys and girls – 'a very goodly sight', it was said, 'to behold so many little infants of such noble parentage, about the age of nine or ten years'. The ceremony itself was performed in the presence of the assembled Commons and of the Peers of the realm, who marched in order of their rank clad in their rich robes, the climax coming when the Earls of Nottingham and Northampton led the Prince to the throne where he kneeled upon the uppermost step while his patent was read by the Earl of Salisbury. His robes, sword and other regalia were put upon him by the lords who carried them, but the King, taking his son by the hand and kissing him, himself delivered the crown, the staff, the ring and the patent. The King dined that day privately in his chamber, but the Prince of Wales was served in the great hall with the honours of a king.

The following day the customary masque was performed. It was again written by Samuel Daniel, who was proving more accommodating to the ambitious scenic schemes of Inigo Jones than the irascible Ben. In *Tethys Festival* the nine-year-old Charles played his first major role. The Queen played Tethys, Elizabeth the Nymph of Thames, Arabella the Nymph of Trent, ladies of the Court the presiding spirits of other rivers. The scene was a port or haven in which the sea moved gently up and down with many ships riding at anchor. Zephirus appeared within a ring of eight nymphs representing fountains and flanked by two tritons. The little figure, in a short robe of green satin embroidered with golden flowers, with silver wings, a garland of coloured flowers on his golden head, a magnificent bracelet of gold set with rich stones, the gift of his mother, on his bare arm, was the Duke of York. The little girls danced round him. The circle was broken, Charles was given a sword by one of the tritons, he advanced and presented it to his brother, after which he took his place again within the circle of dancers.[5] It was a moment of great pride to the boy. Later in the year they all went to the launching of the *Prince Royal*, a ship whose construction by Phineas Pett they had all, and particularly Henry, followed with intense interest. The launching was unsuccessful, the ship remaining stuck in the slips, and the family returned home. But Prince Henry showed typical determination in returning in the early hours of the following morning to catch the tide at the flood, and saw her successfully afloat.

There is abundant evidence that by this time Charles had conquered his physical infirmity, even if he was not robust. Horses were bought for him, saddlers employed, he played tennis, his dancing and singing lessons continued. On 13 May 1611 he was created Knight of the Garter at Windsor with Thomas, Earl of Arundel and Robert, Viscount Rochester, in a colourful ceremony that made a deep impression upon him.[6] He was getting plenty of air and exercise and his diet now provided abundant protein as well as bread, beer and wine. Breakfast consisted of two kinds of bread, with mutton, chicken and beer. For dinner he was offered a choice of three kinds of bread, ten kinds of poultry or meat, with a sweet to follow and beer or wine to drink. There was a similar choice for supper. On a fish day fish replaced some, but not all, of the meat and poultry. Between meals the Duke was offered beer and bread. Milk and butter appeared but sparingly, a small amount being budgeted for the whole day. Eggs appeared not at all, but old recipes indicate that they were used freely in cooking. It may be assumed that fruit was plentiful. James's love of fruit was notorious – he was suffering from a surfeit of grapes when they went to the launching of the *Prince Royal*. Vegetables may simply not have been thought worth mentioning: they certainly do not figure on the menus of the Duke of York, though they were grown in abundance in market gardens round the capital.[7]

But, notwithstanding his physical development, Charles was becoming more the scholar than Henry. About the time that his brother was being created Prince of Wales and Charles was dancing in *Tethys Festival*, his father was paying over £60 for Charles's books and Charles himself was going through the forms of a public disputation in theology. He was now more frequently with his father than Henry was. He accompanied him to the University of Oxford and when only eleven years old was nominated as Chancellor of Cambridge University – to the annoyance of James who felt that the Duke of York should not be in a position which was subject to competition. The nomination was withdrawn. Henry, recognizing his brother's ability, one day placed the Archbishop of Canterbury's hat, which was lying on a table during an audience with the King, upon his brother's head, saying he would one day make Charles his Archbishop. Charles was furious, snatching the cap from his head and stamping it underfoot.[8] But Henry continued to be an ideal elder brother, and teasing was accompanied by the care first evinced when he gave up his lodging in Whitehall to Charles. He considered it necessary to protect the boy from the disorders of Court life and when he himself was away gave authority to Carey and Thomas Murray to repress any abuses in Duke Charles's household. Charles continued to respond with the greatest affection. 'Most loving Brother', he wrote on 14 March 1611, 'I long to see you, and hope that you will returne shortly, therefore I have presumed to wreat these few lynes to You that I may rest in your favour and ever bee thought Your H. most loving brother and obedient servant.'[9]

Charles's relationship with his mother was close and deeply affectionate. In planning and participating in the masques they were much together, but Charles also came to know the less happy side of her life and marriage. In a Court where the King, with his favourites, his hunting, his didacticism, was paramount, Anne had a diminishing role to play. For one who was 'naturally bold and enterprising', as the Duke of Sully expressed it, this was hard to bear. Although she was Jonson's 'Queen and Huntress chaste and fair' she could not keep up with the King's increasing passion for the chase: 'whensoever your sport and other occasions will suffer you come hither', she once wrote to him sadly, 'you shall be very welcome'. She concluded the letter by 'desyreing to be excused for thus troubling of you in tyme of your sport'.[10] She carefully cultivated her appearance and would wear dresses cut low at the neck and shoulders to display her white skin. There are few accounts of further *amours*. The assertion of Lord Herbert of Cherbury that she cast loving eyes on him is suspect; he was wont to suppose that all women did the same. All accounts agree on her kindness and 'affability'. The Venetian Ambassador found her 'passionately attached' to Charles and to her brother, Christian. In the lighthearted banter they employed she called Charles her 'little servant' and he called her his 'worthy mistress'. When she was ill he wrote to her with gentle raillery and a boy's sense of humour, saying that he was sorry for her illness for many reasons but 'especially because it is troublesome to you, and has deprived me of your most comfortable sight, and of many good dinners, the which I hope by God's grace shortly to enjoy'. And, he adds, 'it may be I shall give you some good recipe, which either shall heal you or make you laugh'. 'Kissing in all humility your most sacred hands', he concludes, 'Your Majesty's most humble and obedient servant, Charles.'[11] He was also fond of his two uncles, particularly of Christian. When, some years later, he heard a rumour of Christian's death, he was very melancholy and would not for some time open the letter which he imagined brought him the news.

When Charles was nearly eleven his household became entirely masculine. The Careys figured less prominently in its control and Lady Carey resumed her old position in the Queen's household. Henry wished a nominee of his own to take the important post of Chief Gentleman of the Bedchamber in his brother's new establishment, leaving the control of the privy purse to Sir Robert Carey. But Carey knew the importance of the Bedchamber post so close to the Prince's person, and in securing it for himself was more than a match even for Prince Henry. There is no reason to believe that Charles ever resented this kindly but self-centred busybody, and he continued to treat him with favour. Among new friends who entered his service at this time was Sir James Fullerton, a Presbyterian Scot who had come to England with James. He had quickly made his way at the English Court and, despite an eye for his own advancement, proved a reliable member of the Prince's Household, serving him faithfully for many years.

Shortly after these important developments Charles was affected by an event of a quite different kind when the body of Mary, Queen of Scots, was brought from Peterborough to a magnificent tomb at Westminster. A public ceremony was considered inadvisable and the hearse was transported through London after dark. But the dead Queen's 'translucent passage in the night', with the light shining from multitudes of torches, with the tapers by her tomb smoking 'like an offertory' were more impressive, more moving, than any traditional memorial service. Her burial in Westminster Abbey brought his grandmother and her execution closer to Charles than ever before; she was released from the aura of legend and took her place within his family.

3

Heir Apparent

Charles's father, although he did not achieve the full union with Scotland which he desired, was nevertheless King of England as well as of Scotland. As such, he had a wider responsbility than before and his relations with Europe assumed a correspondingly greater significance. It was no easy role that James was called upon to play. France and Spain were poised in continued rivalry. The states of central Europe were held loosely together in a federation termed the Holy Roman Empire of the Germanic Peoples. The role of Emperor, which in theory was elective, had since 1437 fallen upon a member of the House of Hapsburg, a family which, by marriage and by conquest, constituted a further power grouping in Europe. Spain, Portugal, the Netherlands, Lombardy and the Kingdom of Naples, as well as the Empire itself and vast overseas territories in the New World all fell within the ambit of the Hapsburg, who were fervently Catholic themselves and expected religious conformity within the territories they controlled. The Reformation had complicated the situation as Lutheranism was followed by Calvinism and the forces of the counter-Reformation were marshalled by the Jesuits. Within the Empire a Protestant Union had been formed in 1608, followed by a Catholic League in the following year. Outside the Empire, Holland, Sweden, Norway, Denmark and a powerful minority in France were for the reformed religion, though not always for the same reforms; Spain and the rest of France were Catholic. It was a Spanish king, Philip II, whom a generation of Englishmen had fought under Elizabeth for the glory of God and the Queen, and whose Armada they had defeated in 1588.

James inherited this war from Elizabeth, though its momentum had been lost and in the new generation that was growing up the spirit of the Sea Dogs was dormant. He himself was not of the temperament to awaken patriotic fervour. He preferred to see himself as a peacemaker and one of his immediate aims was to come to terms with Spain. At the same time he was attracted to the role of leader of a Protestant Europe, and his chief problem in foreign affairs was how to combine the two roles. His natural allies were the Dutch, who were still fighting doggedly for their independence from Spain. James had to achieve peace with Spain without appearing to desert these fellow Protestants. It was a situation he felt he could deal with by holding a balance as he had done between warring families in Scotland. The peace with Spain, which he concluded in 1604, and a twelve-year truce between Spain and the Northern Provinces of Holland were good beginnings. Judicious marriages for his children would, James felt, confirm his position as arbiter of Europe.

On the Catholic side the daughters of Tuscany, Savoy, France and Spain were all considered for Prince Henry. The dowry from Tuscany would be large. Savoy was geographically important in commanding the Alpine passes from France to Italy, and the Princess was beautiful. A French Princess would bring a good dowry and politically the union was commendable. The prospect of a Spanish match, delayed for years on religious grounds, petered out in one of the policy shifts of the European kaleidoscope when the Infanta married the young French King Louis XIII whose sister, in turn, married the heir to the Spanish throne. The poor Prince Henry could only murmur: 'My part, which is to be in love with any of them, is not yet at hand.'

Elizabeth was being no less urgently considered for marriage. The son of the Duke of Savoy, brother-in-law to Philip of Spain, was suggested from the English side. Even Philip III of Spain, a widower, put himself forward. Anne was delighted at the glittering prospect of the Spanish throne for her daughter but James's mind was at this time fixed upon a Protestant match. The Elector Palatine of the Rhine, frequently known as the Palsgrave, leader of the Protestant Union and first secular Prince in Germany, was the suitor he had in mind. The Palatinate, with its capital at Heidelberg on the Neckar, was wealthy, so Elizabeth's dowry need not be large. Though the Upper Palatinate was comparatively poor the Lower Palatinate was a beautiful land of wooded hills and fertile valleys, watered by the Rhine and the Neckar, enriched by the wine-growing district between the Moselle, the Saar and the Rhine. The Palatine Electorate was hereditary in the German family of Wittelsbach, while the mother of Elizabeth's proposed bridegroom was the daughter of William the Silent of the Dutch

House of Orange. So, although Anne might mock her daughter as Goody Palsgrave, it was, in reality, marriage into a not undistinguished family and life at a Court both wealthy and cultivated, which were proposed for Elizabeth.

Nor was the marriage merely one of expediency. The Palsgrave was Elizabeth's own age, handsome, athletic, of a winning personality, and generous, his chief defect being a gentleness of character which led to indecision and bouts of depression. He could not fail to love Elizabeth. For her part she loved him on sight and they remained devoted to each other through the years of stress and tragedy that lay ahead. Prince Henry favoured the match, not only because of its Protestant basis but because he was happy to see his sister married to one so personable. But when Frederick arrived in England in October 1612 Prince Henry was unwell. He was met at Gravesend by the Duke of Lennox and other courtiers and at the watergate at Whitehall it was the Duke of York, now nearly twelve years old, who greeted him and conducted him to the Great Chamber where the King awaited him.

Henry attempted to throw himself into the betrothal celebrations but his face grew thinner and he became more melancholy. He seemed to believe that by strenuous exercise he could avert his illness. He swam in the river, he played violent tennis with Frederick, he walked by night. But the sickness and the pains in his head grew more severe and he took to his bed. He ate fruit and vomited. The doctors were puzzled, prescribed various treatments to no avail. On 1 November his parents, his brother and sister and the Elector were admitted one at a time to his bedside. It was the last time Charles saw his brother. Delirium set it, the doctors spoke of infection and would allow no one to come near him. Sir Walter Raleigh from the Tower sent a potion which, after testing, was given to the Prince but there was no improvement. Elizabeth, disguised as a country girl, tried several times to gain admittance to Henry but was recognized and turned back. He died on 6 November 1612 in the nineteenth year of his age, calling his sister's name. As wedding plans gave way to funeral preparations James himself became ill and Charles was called upon to take responsibility. Over-exercise, swimming by night or when over-heated, a surfeit of fruit, were among the reasons for Henry's death suggested by his stunned and stricken friends and family. Even poisoning was not ruled out. An heir to the throne as forthright, uncompromising, and staunchly Protestant as Henry was bound to make enemies, and the names of Rochester, King's favourite, and the

Roman Catholic Northampton were whispered. Incredibly the King himself, because of some known resentment to Henry, featured in some of the darker stories that were circulating. Later, typhoid fever was suspected to have been the cause of Henry's death. More recently it has been thought that he died of porphyria, a rare disease from which his grandmother, Mary, and his father might also have suffered.

As mourning for Henry spread over the country and into Europe, Charles, not yet twelve years old, had to stifle his incredulous grief and for a whole month devote himself to the funeral preparations. The King himself was too distraught to take charge. Tradition and protocol had to be followed and the harrowing procedure of royal burial could spare no one. Long after the doctors had opened the body and head and reported upon the condition of the organs, Henry's coffin remained in his black-draped bedchamber at St James's Palace. There it was watched by relays of ten servants, day and night, for four weeks while, according to custom, his effigy was made and placed on top of the coffin apparelled as he had been at his inauguration as Prince of Wales, with a crown on his head, his George, the insignia of the Garter, round his neck, and his golden staff in his right hand.

It took four hours to marshall the procession which set out at ten o'clock in the morning of December 7 for Westminster Abbey. The funeral chariot was drawn by eight black horses, there were 2000 mourners in black, while a multitude of all sorts of ages and degrees followed the hearse and lined the streets. Prince Charles was on foot as chief mourner, supported by the Lord Privy Seal and the Duke of Lennox and followed by the Elector Palatine and members of his suite. At the Abbey the funeral sermon was preached by the Archbishop of Canterbury to the text 'But ye shall die as a Man, and ye Princes shall fall like others.'[1]

With these words still in his ears Charles had now to shoulder the duties attendant upon his sister's wedding, as well as the wider responsibilities of heir to the throne. The betrothal ceremony had been held in November, before the funeral, the Princess in black for her brother, but the wedding had been postponed for three months. Longer delay was hardly possible. There was, indeed, already complaint at the cost of keeping the Palsgrave and his retinue in England. So, on Valentine's Day, 14 February 1613, Elizabeth and Frederick, both sixteen years old, were married amid considerable pomp and entertainment, though 'the sad countenance of many did sufficiently show that her invaluable brother's death could not yet be forgotten'. Fireworks figured prominently in the entertainments. On the 10th the representation of a dragon with St George on horseback, and other set-pieces, were 'reasonably well performed'. On the 11th the more ambitious attempt to show a fight on the river between Turkish and English ships was said by a spectator to 'come short of expectations,' but it was sufficiently realistic for several terrible injuries to eyes and limbs to be suffered by the operators.

Charles did all that his brother would have done, showing how completely he had conquered his physical weakness as he rode, hunted, and played tennis with Frederick in the weeks before the wedding. On the wedding day itself he, as a 'young bachelor', escorted his sister on her right hand while the Earl of Northampton, as an 'old bachelor', took her left. Elizabeth was in white, her golden hair loosely stranded over her shoulders and interlaced with gold, pearls and diamonds. On her head was a matchless golden crown adorned with diamonds and other precious stones 'so thicke beset, that they stood like shining pinnacles, upon her amber coloured hair'. The twelve attendants who held her train were also in white and so adorned with jewels 'that her passage looked like a milky way'. The handsome bridegroom in a white satin suit, richly set with pearls and gold, was a fitting counterpart. The King was in black, with a priceless diamond in his hat, the Queen in white satin, embroidered and jewelled. The inevitable masque that evening was written by Thomas Campion and produced by Inigo Jones. One spectator, at least, found it long and tedious, commendable only for its extravagance. The wasting Arabella in the Tower had brought four new gowns and begged that she might attend the wedding of the girl she had known since her childhood. But James, who had once been all kindness, could also be very cruel, and she was denied. Two years later she was dead.

The next day was passed in sports in the tiltyard in all of which Charles excelled: in running at the ring the Palsgrave took the ring twice upon his sword, James thrice, and Charles succeeded four times. That night further masquing was intended, this time provided by Sir Francis Bacon and members of the Inner Temple. The masquers came up from the City by river prepared to depict the marriage of Thames and Rhine but they got no further than the privy stairs. The hall was crammed full, ladies in their monstrous farthingales blocked the passage of all who wanted to get in or out, the King was sleepy and bad-tempered and told Bacon 'he had no edge' for further entertainment. Bacon entreated him to consider the disgrace to the masquers if they were sent away. 'It will bury them quick', he said. 'It will bury me quick if I go on', was the terse reply, 'for I can last no longer.' The masquers were sent away but James asked them to come again the following Saturday. Meanwhile an Order was hurriedly made that no lady should be admitted to any festivity in a farthingale.

The cost to the public and private purse of death and marriage was considerable, and the Exchequer was debited in 1613 with £76,738 for Henry's funeral and Elizabeth's wedding. This did not include her marriage portion of £40,000. Only one item for the year was larger – and that was the £120,000 spent on the interest on and repayment of loans. At the same time a private citizen like Lord Montague spent £1500 on his daughters' clothes for the wedding. The Palsgrave, not to be outdone, gave munificent presents all round, Charles receiving a rapier and a pair of spurs set with diamonds.[2]

The King, Queen and Prince Charles escorted Elizabeth and Frederick to Rochester, where James and Anne turned back to the capital. Charles intended to see his sister embarked at Margate in the *Prince Royal*, the ship so closely associated with Henry. But at Canterbury he was recalled by the King, who wanted his presence at St George's feast, the annual celebration of the Knights of the Garter. It was the last time he saw his sister. In spite of plans often made for journeys home, a growing family and political uncertainties never allowed the Princess to return until long after her parents were dead and the bleakness of events had killed both her husband and her brother.

James had allied himself to the European Protestants through his daughter's marriage and his own treaty of mutual agreement with the Protestant Union which he signed shortly before the wedding. Just after the marriage Frederick, at James's instigation, signed a similar treaty with the States General of the Dutch Republic, and James also engineered a peace between Denmark and Norway, thus removing a source of tension in the anti-Hapsburg forces. As the next step he could see himself lining up with a great Catholic power and cementing in his own person a powerful alliance between Protestant and Catholic. His thoughts at first turned to France and a marriage between Prince Charles and the Princess Christina, sister to the young King Louis XIII. But his versatile and impressionable mind was soon off on another tack. In May 1613 there arrived in England as Spanish

Ambassador Diego Sarmiento de Acuna, later Count of Gondomar, a man who was hampered by no sentiments of toleration or dreams of alliance between rival religions but was governed by the single-minded purpose of winning England to the Catholic faith. He knew, as the whole country knew, that there had always been a core of powerful Catholic families in England, as well as many others who put a face upon conformity while practising their religion in secret. But Gondomar grossly over-estimated their numbers, while the ease with which he thought England could be converted to the Catholic faith was out of touch with reality.

Yet in personal relations Gondomar was astute. When he arrived in England the situation was not favourable to him, yet against all the odds he not only managed to relieve the tension between Spain and England but was soon on intimate terms with the King of England himself. Gondomar patiently and painstakingly familiarized himself with the English scene – 'None knoweth so well the length of our foot', it was said – and was not above the distribution of largesse in the right quarter nor the exercise of his dignified Spanish charm where appropriate. Above all, he had just that blend of sophistry and learning which delighted James, and he could add a touch of humour in the King's own vein to their increasingly frequent and lengthening discourses. To James, the Spanish Ambassador was a decided asset, particularly since their thoughts were running in the same direction: but whereas for James a Spanish marriage for Prince Charles would strengthen the balance in Europe between Catholic and Protestant, Gondomar's intention was the conversion of the Prince and the nurturing of his children in the Catholic faith as a preliminary to the conversion of the whole country. Though Gondomar made his aspirations crystal-clear in secret despatches to the Spanish Court, James, as they talked, knew nothing of them. Still less did the subject of their discussions, Prince Charles himself.[3]

Charles was now more alone than at any time since coming to London. After Elizabeth's departure he fell ill. Believing the stories that Henry had been poisoned, he refused all medicines and his attendants feared his death. Not so his mother, who exclaimed in exasperation that he would not die but would live to plague three kingdoms by his wilfulness! Charles continued to believe to the end of his life that his brother had been poisoned.[4] Reports of his appearance at this time indicate depression and debility. The Duke of Saxe-Weimar, who was visiting England, noted him as being 'not of a strong constitution'. Gondomar wrote of him as 'a sweet and gentle child', a description hardly indicating robust good health. Sir Symonds D'Ewes, a notable observer of Court and Parliament, remarked that he was 'so young and sickly, as the thought of their enjoying him did nothing at all alienate or mollify the people's mourning' at the death of Henry. A portrait of Charles in his thirteenth year has all the delicacy of ill-health which these accounts indicate. It shows a child's face still, unsure and unassertive, at variance with the roles of chief mourner and bridesman he had so recently played with adult dignity.[5] The protective respite of illness was, indeed, necessary. Since Henry's death Charles had been swept along by events in which he had a leading part to play. Only now was there leisure to consider the longer and more exacting role he must undertake. He had overcome physical disability to the extent that in athletics he was more than adequate and continued to improve. In intellectual attainments he was above average. He understood Greek and Latin, his familiarity with French, Spanish and Italian later gave him fluency in all three languages. He was well read in history and divinity, he had a knowledge of mathematics and was not unskilled in drawing and painting, in dancing and music. Like Henry, he enjoyed the society and conversation of travellers and scholars, being naturally a good listener. But he was slow, and his stammer hampered him. Because he took a long time to reach a conclusion he was all the more tenacious in holding it when reached, and the taint of obstinacy was the result.

Like his brother, Charles was part Puritan, part Renaissance Prince. He took his devotions seriously, he led a life which, in contrast to that of his parents and of the Court, was orderly. The pleasure he took in assembling and enlarging the collection of coins, medals, paintings and *objets d'art* which Henry had bequeathed him fitted well with this side of his character. At the same time, like the Renaissance Prince, he had a wider interest in works of art in general, and the collections of his later life were based upon the interest which began at this time. Among those who had been in the service of Henry and who now came to serve Charles was Abraham van der Doort, one of a family of Dutch craftsmen with a specialized knowledge of coins and medals. When van der Doort later described and catalogued Charles's collections he included sixteen little Florentine statues in bronze which Henry had bequeathed to his brother. The largest, 'Diana with a greyhound', measured 1'9"; the smallest, 'a little Flora in her draperies', was no more than 3½" high.[6] With such small pieces Charles's art collections began.

Again like a Renaissance Prince and like his brother, Charles was intensely interested in military affairs. He read and possessed the *Civil and Military Aphorisms of Guicciardini*, and allowed his own portrait of 1613 to appear as frontispiece to the English translation published by Robert Dallington in that year. His own leather-bound copy of this edition was elaborately ornamented in gold and stamped with his initials and the royal arms.[7] Dallington, of Geddington in Northamptonshire, a man 'exact in his observations' and 'of excellent wit and judgment', had been a schoolmaster in Norfolk until he saved enough to support himself on the Continent, after which he published books on his travels – the *Survey of Tuscany* in 1605, the *View of France* in the following year. Both books were eminently readable and typical of the time in their mixture of geography, history and travel. It was characteristic of Prince Henry's interest in foreign lands and traveller's conversation that he took Dallington into his own household, and characteristic of Charles that, after Henry's death, he welcomed Dallington, as he did van der Doort, into his own service.

Guicciardini's *Aphorisms* had been much discussed by Henry and his circle. Indeed, the very translation was for the Prince's benefit and the dedication of the published work would undoubtedly have been his. In the event it was dedicated to the 'High and Mightie Charles, Prince of Great Britain'. 'All eyes are upon you . . . men looke upon your worthy Brother in your princely selfe; holding you the true inheritor of his vertues as of his fortunes. . . . So shall you like a great and high Steward . . . perfect the account you are to make, to your King and to your countrey.' In the boy of thirteen, whose diffident portrait adorned the book, pride mingled with apprehension. Nor were the civil maxims of Guicciardini likely to give him confidence. Guicciardini was a friend of Machiavelli and his work shows the same insistence upon the good of the state, as interpreted by the ruler, and the same justification of means to achieve that end. The notion that there could be a line drawn between private and public conduct and that a Prince, like Janus, needed two faces, made a deep impression on Charles: for a prince 'to be overt in expressing his nature, or free in venting his purpose, is a thing of dangerous consequence'; he 'that weareth his heart in his fore-head, and is of an overt and transparent nature, through whose words, as through cristall, ye may see into every corner of his thoughtes: That man is fitter for a table of good-fellowship, then a Councell table'; 'upon the Theater of public imployment either in peace or warre, the actors must of necessity weare vizardes, and change them in evarie Scene'; the object must always be 'the generall good and safetie of a State', though to achieve it 'men cannot alwaies arrive by plaine pathes and beaten waies. Wherefore a Prince may pretend a desire of friendshippe with the weaker, when he meanes, and must, contract it with the stronger.' This was not good fare for an impressionable boy struggling to keep up with the exaggerated expectations of those around him.

Dallington remained in Charles's service for ten years, joining Murray and the group which served as counterweight to courtiers like Carey and Fullerton. Murray was at the centre of this group and his influence was considerable. His position about the Prince could easily have been used as a path to preferment for himself and others but, although he was 'much courted', he continued to keep outside the Court circle and even the gossips had to admit his integrity. It was probably through Murray that Charles made contacts with urbane intellectuals like Dudley Carleton and Kenelm Digby, who sent books to the young Prince and added to his art collections, and with soldiers serving in the Netherlands like Sir Edward Cecil and Sir Horace Vere, who encouraged his interest in military strategy.

Early in 1616 Cecil wrote to Murray that he had found a set of model engines of war and artillery, sufficient for a model army, which he recommended as fitting study for the Prince, 'showing by demonstration rather than theory the verie practice of everie thinge, either defensive or offensive'. They were valued at £1000. The Prince was very interested but the money was not easy to find and it was not until July that, with the help of the financier Philip Burlamachi, Murray made a first payment of £250 and the 'warlike' and 'curious wrought engines' were brought over by a Dutchman, who set them up in St James's Palace before a delighted Charles, who insisted on keeping the man to explain in detail the working of each of the models. Shortly afterwards he asked for, and was sent, a book explaining their use. In the following year more models and 'designs of the army and camp', in which the models could operate against a suitable background, arrived from Dudley Carleton. The Dutch were well versed in these 'war games' and the Prince of Orange, himself a well-known enthusiast, added to Charles's collection by sending some ordnance, whose operation had to be kept secret.[8] Operating his models was an abiding interest for Charles and in later life he would retire for hours to his 'model house'. Perhaps he learned more of military strategy there than from Guicciardini's *Aphorisms*.

A third grouping round Charles in these formative years consisted of his chaplain and others concerned in his religious upbringing. In 1613, on the Easter Monday following his sister's departure, he was confirmed in Whitehall Chapel by the Bishop of Bath and Wells, Dr James Montague. So worldly a bishop might have been considered a strange choice for the occasion. Yet Montague's advancement to the see of Bath and Wells had been in the nature of a reward for helping James to write a pamphlet against Rome and he was now engaged in editing James's collected works. Charles was prepared for confirmation by his chaplain, Dr George Hakewill, one of two 'sober divines' who were appointed immediately after Henry's death to protect the Prince from High Church doctrine. Anne was rumoured to be close to the Church of Rome and the Protestant interests at Court were determined that no risks should be taken with the heir to the throne. Hakewill was learned and zealous as well as showing considerable adroitness. In the pamphlet he wrote for Charles on *The Ancient Ecclesiastical Practice of Confirmation*, for example, he contrived both to support bishops as descended from the Apostles and to offer words of approbation to presbyters and deacons. He was less than dexterous, nevertheless, in attempting to instruct the twelve-year-old boy. He preached no fewer than twelve sermons before Charles on the 101st Psalm, all of which were long and dull, covering when printed some 335 pages. Again the dedication was to the Prince: 'we may by God's help one day promise to our selves another Charlemaine, or rather the perfections of all the Edwards and Henries and James your renowned projenitors united in one Charles'. The intimidating unction of the dedication was balanced by advice which, if trite, was yet more fitting to a Prince's chaplain: 'you will valew Soveraignetie, not by impunity of doing evil, but power of doing good'. Hakewill also brought to Charles's notice in a practical way a current intellectual controversy. Godfrey Goodman, who would become Bishop of Gloucester in 1624, had propounded in his *Fall of Man* the widely held view that man, and indeed the world itself, were slowly decaying. Hakewill opposed this belief and the preparation of his reply, which was published in 1627, took place within the Prince's circle.

The other 'sober divine' placed near Charles after the death of Henry was Dr Richard Senhouse, formerly chaplain to the Earl of Bedford and now Rector of Cheam in Surrey. Senhouse was used to 'wakening men's consciences' with his quill, but it was as a 'master preacher', possessing 'royaltie of speech' that he was best known. Of friends of his own age, it was little Will Murray who was closest at this time to the Prince. He resembled Charles in remaining short of stature; like Charles he was receptive to the artistic influences of the Court; like Charles he had come from Scotland, though somewhat later, and his Scottish accent influenced Charles's own way of speaking as, with growing confidence, the words began to come more freely.

4

The Heritage

Charles was created Duke of Cornwall immediately after the death of Henry so that he might receive the royalties and rents pertaining to the Duchy. His investiture as Prince of Wales was delayed, partly for reasons of expense, partly out of sorrow for Henry, and partly, so some said, because James had chafed at Henry's independence and would not have the reins loose so early on his brother.[1] But whatever his own inclinations, and however tight the control, the heir to the throne could not stand outside Court life. There he was sure to encounter the King's favourites, foremost amongst whom was still Robert Carr, Viscount Rochester. Carr was handsome – 'straight-limbed, well-favoured, strong-shouldered, and smooth-faced', not over-tall but 'well compacted' with flaxen hair and, like James and many others, retaining still his Scottish accent. The King, it was noted, leaned on his arm, pinched his cheek, smoothed his ruffled garment. But Rochester had an eye on wider influence and his opportunity came with the death of Salisbury in 1612, for although the King kept the Treasureship vacant and Rochester did not, even then, attain to actual office, the threads of power, and the gifts that attached to them, now ran through his hands.

Rochester was rash enough, or unfortunate enough, to become at this stage a leading actor in the notorious affair of Frances Howard, Countess of Essex. James had always enjoyed a wedding, and on coming to England had fancied himself as a matchmaker who would unite the rival houses of his new kingdom by the marriage bond. It was a policy which had brought some success in Scotland and he had great hopes from the marriage of Frances Howard to the Earl of Essex in 1606. But Frances was then only thirteen and the Earl fourteen years old. Seven years later Frances was suing for divorce on the grounds of non-consummation of marriage. She was now a great beauty, impetous, used to having her own way in everything but this marriage, unprincipled in ridding herself of its ties. Her husband, although he was the son of Elizabeth I's dazzling, buccaneering favourite, had turned out to be stiff and awkward with few of the courtier's graces, though there is no reason to believe the Countess's charge of impotence. Rumour maintained, indeed, that the Countess herself prevented consummation with the help of drugs. Charles could not fail to know of his father's pressure on the Commission which granted the divorce, of the adverse comments of reputable men, or that the object of the divorce was the marriage of Frances with Viscount Rochester. Shortly after the divorce Rochester was created Earl of Somerset and at Christmas time 1613 the two were married, the King bearing the cost of the wedding and presenting the bride with jewels worth £10,000 paid for from the sale of Crown lands. James himself, with the Queen and Prince Charles, led the courtiers who attended the wedding, Thomas Campion provided the masque on the wedding day, Jonson followed with the *Challenge at Tilt* the next day and his *Irish Masque* on December 29. Inigo Jones produced and designed them all. John Donne wrote an *Eclogue* to Somerset and on January 6 the students of Gray's Inn, at the expense of Sir Francis Bacon, performed the charming *Masque of Flowers* which ushered in a fresh round of festivities for the marriage of Lady Jane Drummond, the Queen's favourite, to Robert Ker, Earl of Roxburgh. Thus literature and art combined to honour those upon whom the King smiled. Yet the King could ill afford the cost.[2]

James had a constant struggle to make ends meet, partly because of his exaggerated ideas of the wealth of England, partly because of an irresponsible and seemingly incurable extravagance that had been restrained in Scotland by the poverty of that country. He had been particularly lavish to his Scottish friends and his presents to the Spanish Ambassadors in 1604 were said to include more plate than Queen Elizabeth gave away in her whole reign. He had a passion for jewels, one diamond he wore in his hat being valued at £50,000, while the scale of his entertainment accorded both with the growing luxury of European Courts and with his own ideas of the exaltation of his state. Anne shared to the full her husband's predilections. Her childbed expenses amounted to £60,000 for the Princesses Mary and Sophia, the cost of her revels, masques, clothes, horses and carriages reached a prodigious total and by 1605 her debts were already over £40,000. When she was short of money she sulked, and to restore her good humour, for James liked a tranquil life, he would toss her some further source of income, as he did the sugar duties in 1603.

The royal couple's personal expenses were merely the centre of a vast network of Court and State expenditure which was rising faster than receipts. In James's defence it could be said that Elizabeth I died in debt, that James had a family, that everywhere in Europe display and ostentation were rising, and that the country was in the grip of a baffling inflation. But there was no regular income to foot the bill. Crown lands and feudal dues helped a little, the dowry of a son's wife added an extra dimension to the marriage contract. James was adept at the sale of honours, even creating the order of baronet half-way between a baron and a knight, which sold at £1095; but there were many cases of noble lords or baronets whose titles rested upon hire-purchase or who, in the world of business, would have been found in a debtors' prison, having received the goods without money to pay.

Such taxes as there were depended upon Parliament, the most important and regular being those known as tonnage and poundage, taxes levied at the ports upon outgoing and incoming goods and normally granted to each new monarch for life. The taxes known as subsidies, tenths and fifteenths were usually voted for a particular purpose, such as war. Generally speaking, tenths and fifteenths were levied outside towns upon the cattle and crops of landowners, and in towns upon the capital value of a man's stock-in-trade and chattels. In 1334 a composition was arrived at which was still in force in James's reign, when a fifteenth and a tenth together yielded about £30,000. A subsidy was a personal tax charged upon persons possessed of move-ables at the rate of 2/8d in the pound value, and upon persons possessed of land at the rate of 4/- in the pound of its annual value; no one could be double-charged. A subsidy yielded to James some £70 – £80,000, but the yield of all taxes was falling. An extra tax, known as an imposition, was a payment over and above the normal schedule of rates already authorized, but this was generally strongly opposed. When all else failed recourse was had to borrowing. Loans came from professional money-lenders like Philip Burlamachi, the man who helped Charles to buy his 'warlike engines', from corporations like the City of London, and from farmers of the customs. Sometimes they were made in return for favours given or in hope of favours to come.

James inherited a situation which was already difficult and which he had not the temperament to control. The men whom he saw before him in his first House of Commons were for the most part substantial landowners many of whom had close commercial ties, most of whom were wealthy. They were no fools and they placed their own interests high on the list of reasons for being there at all. Yet to this collectively experienced, determined, and hard-headed body James presented not only an emptying Exchequer but a preconceived notion of his own power. The obsequious flattery which he had met on his arrival in England had blinded him to the powerful self-interest of the men who sat before him. So he was surprised and affronted when his first Parliament of 1604 granted him tonnage and poundage for life but then, instead of proceeding to vote further supplies, turned to grievances, complaining of the pressure of various feudal incidents, voicing its fears concerning religion, and maintaining that it held its privileges as of right. Only in the expansive session following the Gunpowder Plot did it grant him a substantial supply.

By the time James's second Parliament met Henry was dead and Charles was heir to the throne. The Parliament which was summoned in 1614 to deal with the financial situation was opened on Tuesday April 5 with as much pomp as the bad weather allowed; Charles, in his robes of state, joined the procession to Westminster and for the first time watched his father open a Parliament. Nothing was achieved, neither in the redress of grievances by the King nor the grant of supplies by the Commons. Within two months James had dissolved his second – the 'Addled' – Parliament and had returned to his hunting. He was absent when, in July, King Christian of Denmark made a surprise visit to his sister, arriving unexpectedly at Denmark House as Anne was taking dinner. It is possible that the visit was prompted by rumours that Anne was unhappy, estranged from the King, and depressed by the death of Henry. At all events she was delighted to see her brother, tearing off her best jewel to give to the servant whom she at first would not believe when he said that Christian was at her window. Charles was not less pleased to see his favourite uncle and he entertained him nobly until his father's return. The usual bout of fireworks, provided by Christian, and of drinking, sponsored by James, then ensued, Christian again proving more than a match for anyone at the English Court and being even less inhibited at finishing the entertainment under the table or on the floor. On August 1 they all visited Phineas Pett at Woolwich and inspected his new ship, the *Mer Honneur*. When Christian departed, a few days later, apart from the customary lavish gifts made on such occasions, he presented his nephew with one of the three warships that had escorted him to

England – a gift beside which Charles's collection of model artillery looked very small.

Charles had now a baby nephew, Prince Frederick Henry, born to Elizabeth on 2 January 1614: it was sad that there was no money available for him to make the journey to Heidelberg in the only way considered appropriate to his rank. He was quite unaware that the gossips were still shaking their heads and asserting that he was unlikely to live to manhood and that this baby would be his father's heir. He was more interested in a situation of a different kind which was developing before 1614 was out. Although Somerset was still in the ascendant another name was cropping up: 'a youth named Villiers begins to be in favour with his majesty', it was said. George Villiers was the second son of a small Leicestershire landowner. His widowed mother did all she could to capitalize his physical attractions; he learned music, dancing, fencing, and at the age of eighteen went to France in the company of his friend, Sir John Eliot. Three years later he returned with little money but with all the accomplishments of the courtier. Shortly afterwards he came to London and in August 1614 was introduced to the King at Sir Anthony Mildmay's house at Apethorpe, whither James had rushed for refreshment after Christian's visit. Before long Villiers became James's cupbearer. His rise now seemed a foregone conclusion and it was helped by developments outside his control.

Since James made peace with Spain English Catholics had enjoyed a position of comparative security in which leading families of the Northampton-Suffolk-Howard connection were known and accepted as being Catholics or Catholic supporters. But, while Catholicism had to this extent been condoned, its reinforcement by alliance with the King's powerful favourite was going too far; Lady Frances Howard's marriage to Somerset was condemned as much because she was a Catholic as because of the moral issues involved. Since the Howard-Somerset marriage had not been prevented, powerful interests, foremost amongst whom was George Abbot, Archbishop of Canterbury, sought to counterpoise the alliance by the substitution of a new favourite. It is, indeed, not impossible that the meeting at Apethorpe had been deliberately arranged. 'We could have no way so good to effectuate that which was the common desire', wrote Abbot, 'as to bring in another in his [Somerset's] room; one Nail (as the Proverb is) being to be driven out by another.' The time was opportune. James was tiring of Somerset and he was instantly attracted to Villiers.

Nevertheless there were conventions to be observed. One was James's habit of winning Anne's approval before advancing a new figure at Court – in order, so it was said, that she might not later bother him with recriminations. In this case the issue was complicated by Anne's Catholic leanings and by the fact that 'having been bitten with Favourites both in England and Scotland' she 'was very shie to advanture upon' another. At the same time she had little sympathy for Frances, even if she had no quarrel with Somerset. The Archbishop worked hard upon the Queen. Villiers himself, with his courtesy and charm, was a powerful ally in his own cause and in the end there was staged a curious little ceremony in the Queen's bedchamber in which Anne called upon Prince Charles for his sword and presented it to the King who thereupon knighted Villiers and advanced him to the office of Gentleman of the Bedchamber, while Somerset at the door of the closet vainly called for restraint. Thus, involuntarily, was Charles brought in to play his part in the rise of George Villiers.[3]

Somerset had even greater troubles to contend with than the rise of a new favourite. There had been nothing essentially reprehensible in Frances refusing to consummate a marriage arranged by others for purely dynastic purposes when she and the bridegroom were children. But the undercurrent of gossip was fanned into flame by the death in the Tower of Sir Thomas Overbury, a literary dilettante who had remained close to Somerset throughout the favourite's rise to power. In the autumn of 1615 it began to be rumoured that the Somersets had contrived the imprisonment of Overbury and had subsequently poisoned him because he had knowledge that would have invalidated the Countess's case for divorce. Soon James had no alternative but to let the two come to trial. In an atmosphere infected by stories of potions and witchcraft the Countess admitted her guilt. Somerset pleaded his innocence long and desperately. Both were found guilty and sentenced to death but were remanded to the Tower. There was then nothing to impede the advance of George Villiers.

About this time a parallel move was made to counteract any Catholic influence within Prince Charles's own household. Possibly Fullerton was a little alarmed at Carey's friendship with the Catholic Earl of Suffolk, father of Frances Howard. At all events, Fullerton now brought in to serve the Prince Dr George Carleton, who since 1589 had been vicar of Mayfield in Sussex. Carleton was possessed either of wide tolerance or an ability to trim his sails. He was anti-papist yet maintained the Apostolic succession; Calvinist yet believed in episcopal divine right; not an Arminian yet questioned the doctrine of predestination. He had already written that he disapproved of the endless contentions in the Church and thought the true Church was that which served the same God, and held the same rule of faith, wherever it was placed. When he arrived at Court to take up service with Charles on 10 February 1615 he professed himself appalled at the conditions he found there, particularly with the 'shameless avidity' for preferment. But with Charles himself he was delighted. 'I would be silent about the Prince', he wrote, but 'I must praise his accomplishments, his skill in riding, running at the ring, etc. He has far more understanding than the late Prince at his age, and is in behaviour sober, grave, swete; in speache, very advised, without any evil inclinations and willing to take advice.'[4] Again – 'grave', 'swete', are the adjectives used of the young Charles.

Charles was now frequently with his father. In the March of 1615, braving the hard weather and 'extreme fowle wayes', they travelled to Cambridge where they met a considerable concourse of gallants and great men; in August they were at Gravesend, where Charles inspected the fleet on his own. They hunted together at Royston and made progress to Newmarket and Huntingdon. Charles sat with his father to receive the Venetian Ambassador in November and was reported to be 'quite robust'.

With his father Charles was feasted in the City on 14 June 1616 by Alderman William Cockayne and the new Company of Merchant Adventurers who gave £500 to him and £1000 to his father. He also met many of the dyers, dressers, finishers, and other cloth workers who were presented to the King. The occasion marked the official launching of Cockayne's project for dressing cloth in England, instead of exporting it undyed and undressed to be finished overseas. James had listened to the plausible talk of Cockayne. He had been dazzled by promises of high export duties on the finished cloth, of customs duty on dyestuffs imported, of duty on the alum used in dyeing, and by the handsome payment which Cockayne would make for monopoly rights. He himself would receive a continuing £300,000 a year, he was assured. That the breaking of the Merchant Adventurers' monopoly of the cloth export trade was an important part of the scheme could hardly have occurred to him. Nor, indeed, would it have mattered. For, superficially, the project had much in its favour. There would be work for dyers and finishers, dyed and finished cloth would command higher prices than undressed, the foreigner would be outdone, and a blow struck for national self-sufficiency. Cockayne had a reputation for plausibility and had not neglected to win over members of the Council. So the export of unfinished cloth was banned in 1614, the charter of the Merchant Adventurers was revoked, and the new company with Cockayne at its head was launched in 1616.

It was only a year after the celebration at Cockayne's house that the project collapsed. The Dutch, who normally took undressed cloth and finished it, had a great industry geared to this process. They not only refused to handle the English dressed cloth but started to manufacture their own. Other customers complained that English finishing was inferior to Dutch. Stocks of cloth accumulated in England and work-people were put off work. A reduction in exports meant a loss of imports, trade declined, and a scheme with apparently so much to commend it ground to a halt. James, complaining that he had been 'much abused', dissolved the new company and reinstated the old while taking refuge in an aphorism. 'Time', he remarked sadly, 'discovereth many inabilities which cannot at first be seen.'[5]

This was Charles's practical introduction to the woollen cloth industry upon which, more than any other single thing, the prosperity of his country depended. Woollen cloth comprised over eighty per cent of the country's exports, its production being based upon the sheep which, since the Middle Ages, had produced the best wool in the world. From the wide-spreading sheep farms of the Cistercian Houses in Yorkshire to the slopes of the Cotswold hills, from the Welsh border country to the plains of East Anglia, from rough pasture land in Devonshire to sweet grass on the Wiltshire Downs and a variety of grazing throughout Surrey, Sussex and Kent, there was scarce a farm with any grass that did not keep sheep. From the flocks of many thousands managed on business lines to the few sheep of a small farmer they all made their contribution. The sheep produced long hair or short hair according to their breed and their feed, but for the most part the quality was high and wool had been England's chief export until the paramount advantage of turning it into cloth at home had been realized. The change from the export of raw wool, to the export of woollen cloth, which had been going on right through the reigns of the Tudors, was completed by James when, after pronouncing in characteristic style that we should 'not be killed with arrows from our own quiver', he not only repeated the injunction that wool should not be exported, but abolished the European wool staple through which, for centuries, had passed the fleece of the English sheep. The policy of conserving wool in the interests of cloth-making was not entirely non-controversial. The great landowners whom Charles could see at the Council Table and at the Court were chary of any restrictions upon the sale of their wool. But the home demand remained high and their links with the clothiers who produced the cloth and with the Merchant Adventurers who exported it were strong. The wool embargo remained. But it would still be the sheep, grazing quietly in countless pastures, fields and wayside plots, which would be the greatest source of wealth in Charles's England.

5

Prince of Wales

Not until Monday 4 November, 1616, was Charles formally created Prince of Wales. It was a simple ceremony without show, for several reasons: it was very cold, Charles had been unwell, the Queen could not bear the memories evoked of Henry, the King did not wish to make too much of his successor, and money was short. But Charles came down river from Richmond on the previous Thursday, as Henry had done before him, and was 'most joyfully met' at Chelsea by the Lord Mayor of London and the City Companies in their various barges, with banners flying, music playing, and drum and trumpet sounding. Thomas Middleton composed a water masque for the occasion in which, braving the cold, London was seen sitting on a sea unicorn flanked by Neptune and the rivers Thames and Dee, with six tritons before her. Spectators thronged the banks of the river to see, if not to hear, Charles addressed as 'Treasure of hope' and 'jewell of mankind/Adorn'd in titles, but much more in minde'. After this they all proceeded down river, the tritons sounding their horns, and were met at Whitehall by the two deities, Hope and Peace, likewise defying the weather. Peace, sitting on a dolphin, concluded the river festivities with a song of welcome to the Prince:

> Welcome, oh welcome, Spring of Joy and Peace!
> Borne to be honour'd, and to give encrease
> Welcome, oh welcome, all faire joyes attend thee,
> Glorie of life, to safety we commend thee!

The Prince then landed at Whitehall stairs preceded by nobles and officers of the Court. As he made his way through the palace he was received by various dignitaries until he reached the door of the Presence Chamber where the festivities ended for the day.

On the following Monday, 4 November, the actual investiture took place. Preceded by heralds and trumpeters, by the Earl Marshal, the Lord Chamberlain, twenty-six Knights of the Bath newly created to mark the occasion and various dignitaries carrying his robes and symbols of office, came Charles, bareheaded, supported by the Earls of Suffolk and Nottingham and followed by the Gentlemen of his household. So he entered the Presence Chamber where the King was seated on his throne with his barons and bishops on one side, the Lord Mayor and Alderman of London with the Judges and members of his Council on the other. It was now Charles's turn to have the words of investiture addressed to him, to receive the ring and the sword from the hands of his father, to be robed and crowned as Prince of Wales. After the patent was read it was handed to him by the King, who kissed him twice. At this moment the trumpets and drums sounded, after which the King rose and departed.

Charles remained to dine in the Hall, and was served with great state and magnificence. The meal was formal, the Prince at the head of the table, the nobles seated according to their degree, none nearer than four yards to the Prince. The Earl of Southampton and the Earl of Dorset, bareheaded, acted as cupbearer and carver, Dr Senhouse, the Prince's chaplain of the golden voice, said grace. The newly-created Knights of the Bath sat at a separate table on the Prince's right and he courteously drank their health. At a decent distance were the members of the Court privileged to be onlookers, among them Sir Symonds D'Ewes, destined to report other things than the Prince's inaugura-tion, who remarked with satisfaction that he was standing very near the Prince's chair all the time. The King and Villiers watched from a balcony. If by Court standards the entertainment had not been lavish they had, as the Venetian Ambassador predicted, 'spent money by handfuls'.[1]

The Careys had again been observing the formation of Charles's household with more than ordinary interest. Would Sir Robert become Chamberlain to the new Prince of Wales? If he were so advanced, what of the influential bedchamber post? James, still deter-mined not to loosen the reins round Charles, gave orders that no one be enrolled into the Prince's household without his knowledge. This complicated matters. But Carey was equal to the occasion. He sought out the Queen, won her support – for had not he and his family served the Prince exceedingly well from his infancy? – and so managed affairs that he secured both offices. 'Thus', he remarked complacently in his *Memoirs* after telling the story in detail, 'did God raise up the Queen to take my part.' Carey had already married his daughter to Lord Whar-

48

ton's heir; his eldest son was made Knight of the Bath at the time of the Prince's creation, and in 1620 married Martha, eldest daughter of the wealthy City financier, Lionel Cranfield. Cranfield was then rising rapidly to the height of his power and influence; he had been knighted in 1613 and became Privy Councillor in the year of the marriage. In the following year he would become Lord Treasurer and in 1622 Earl of Middlesex, his rise being due to the simple fact that he was the only one to make some success of clearing out the Augean stables of the royal finances. His career was typical of the combination of business and politics, private interest and public advantage which were characteristic of the time. In giving good service while turning the occasion to his own profit, Lionel Cranfield was doing in one sphere what Robert Carey was doing in another.[2]

Charles, Prince of Wales, was, at sixteen, well accustomed to such men. He perceived, however, that in George Villiers, who was rapidly taking the place of both Salisbury and Somerset, James had an adviser of a different stamp. The rise of Villiers was unimpeded. Between January and August 1616 he had become Master of the Horse, Knight of the Garter, Viscount Villiers and Baron Whaddon. On 5 January 1617 he was created Earl of Buckingham. As he grew in power he grew in strength and beauty. He had, like Prince Henry, an indefinable charm. Like Henry he excelled in all things physical. Impetuosity and quick temper rather added to his charm until power and influence burned them to arrogance and impatience. The impact which his physical presence made on contemporaries is astounding. 'He was one of the handsomest men in the whole world', wrote Sir John Oglander. 'From the nails of his fingers – nay from the sole of his foot to the crown of his head, there was no blemish in him. The setting of his looks, every motion, every bending of his body was admirable,' wrote Bishop Hacket. Bishop Goodman wrote in greater detail:

> All that sat in the Council looking steadfastly on him, saw his face as if it had been the face of an angel. . . . He was the handsomest bodied man in England; his limbs so well compacted, and his conversation so pleasing, and of so sweet a disposition. . . . I have heard it from two men, and very great men . . . that he was as inwardly beautiful as he was outwardly.

Sir Symonds D'Ewes, not perhaps easily influenced, 'saw everything in him full of delicacy and handsome features'.[3] His wife repeatedly asserted that she regarded it as the greatest privilege to be married to him. King James was captivated and went so far as to acclaim his infatuation out loud to his Privy Council in the autumn of 1617: 'You may be sure that I love the Earl of Buckingham more than anyone else, and more than you who are here assembled. I wish to speak in my own behalf, and not to have it thought to be a defect, for Jesus Christ did the same, and therefore I cannot be blamed. Christ had his John, and I have my George.'[4]

But if Buckingham resembled Prince Henry in some ways, he was at the same time less earnest than Henry and intellectually less able. Charles was bound to compare the two. Moreover Buckingham, who was only eight years older than Charles, was usurping the place close to his father which Charles might well have expected to be his. That the Prince's own sword should have been used for Buckingham's first step up the ladder was bitter. The relationship between the two young men was strained. When Charles accompanied his father Buckingham was there too – quick of speech, sensing the appropriate remark, guiding the humour of the King. If Charles compared the new favourite with Henry he perhaps compared both with himself. Although he was now fit to take his place as Prince of Wales, not only without embarrassment but with dignity and a certain charm of his own, it was a strange irony that three of the people of his own generation to whom he was close early in his life were outstanding – his brother, his sister, and now his father's favourite. In spite of Charles's development some feeling of inadequacy, some failure, in his own mind, to measure up to what was expected of him, the awkwardness of his continuing stammer, even some resolutely suppressed resentment, show in the diffident stance of his portraits and the nervous fixity of his eyes. Nothing could express the difference between George Villiers and Charles Stuart more tellingly than two portraits painted by Daniel Mytens about this time.

Yet at fifteen Charles retained some of the boy's curiosity, some of the impish humour apparent in the letters to Henry and his mother. In 1616 he was attracted to a ring the favourite was wearing and tried it on. He absent-mindedly kept it. When, some time later, the ring was required it could not be found. James scolded Charles who was reduced to tears but ultimately the ring was discovered in the pocket of one of his suits. On another occasion, when the trio were walking in the gardens of Greenwich Palace, Charles turned the fountain of an ornamental pond full on Buckingham and drenched his suit. James boxed Charles's ears. Charles played tennis with Buckingham but they quarrelled. Buckingham's temper induced some physical action whereupon Charles responded every inch the Prince: 'What, Sir, you intend to strike me!' James was alarmed. He commanded the young men to love one another. Buckingham staged a great feast of reconciliation, which he termed the friends' feast, at his newly purchased house at Wanstead in Essex. It was held out of doors with hangings draped from the trees to form an imaginary palace. Many of the favourite's family were present and James drank to them all in turn, vowing to advance their race above all other and confident, so he said, that his posterity would do likewise. Charles entered into the spirit of the reconciliation and James wrote to him shortly afterwards: 'I must confess to my comfort without flattery that in making your affections to follow and second thus your father's, you show what reverent love you carry towards me in your heart.'[5]

Charles, indeed, needed a friend. He was genuinely fond of his father but such was James's regard for his favourite that he could not have one without the other. Subtly the relationship changed. Charles used for Buckingham the nickname James adopted, Steenie, because of a fancied resemblance to St Stephen. Buckingham called him, as his father did, Baby Charles. Charles's letters to Buckingham became intimate and he used him as intermediary with his father. There was, for example, a misunderstanding concerning his mother's will. Charles believed that the King wished him to persuade her to make one, leaving her jewels to Charles. James thereupon became extremely angry. Charles wrote a letter of apology and explanation. Buckingham then told Charles of his father's continuing anger, possibly exaggerating it, and Charles begged Steenie to intervene with his father, writing with a mixture of dignity and abjection: 'I sent to have the King's aprobation of that which I thought he had desyred . . . my meaning was never to clame anie thing as of right . . . I pray you . . . tell him . . . that I will be content to have anie pennance inflicted upon me so he may forgive me.' He signs himself 'Your treu constant loving frend Charles P.'[6]

In 1617 James paid his first, and what was to be his only, visit to Scotland since his accession to the English throne. He was absent from the capital for seven months, of which part of May and the whole of June and July were spent in his native land. Buckingham went with him but Charles, to his deep disapointment, was left behind. 'I am sorie for nothing', he wrote to his father after he had left 'but that I cannot be with your Majestie at this tyme both because I would be glad to wait upon you, and also to see the Cuntrie whair I was borne and the customes of it.'[7] The Prince, however, who had been made a member of the Privy Council the previous year, was one of a Council of six, which included his mother and the Archbishop of Canterbury, who would be responsible for governing the country while his father was away. Although the Venetian Ambassador remarked that he thought the Queen and the Prince would not play a great part in the decisions of the Council, Charles was becoming familiar with affairs of state. He received ambassadors, he was getting used to talking to them, he asked pertinent questions, and always took a written account of the proceedings to read to the King afterwards. He was described as 'very grave and polite' and he dressed for the occasion. When he received the Venetian Ambassador at the end of 1617, for example, he was in scarlet and gold with a gilt sword at his side and white boots with gold spurs on his feet.

The Venetian Ambassador noted that Charles was 'very dear' to his parents. But it was undoubtedly his father whose influence at this time was the most profound. Whatever the ultimate judgment on James, he was not a man to be ignored. The figure he cut at Court in his younger days was not unimpressive. The eyes were shrewd. Although not tall, he was above middle height and well built, while the hunting he delighted in gave him an air of physical fitness and a ruddy complexion: several of his early portraits depict a handsome man. His speech was 'swift and cursory, and in the full dialect of his country'. The remarks he made were terse and apposite though often astonishingly crude, metaphor, simile and allusion coming naturally to him. In serious discourse he could hold his own with anyone. If his undoubted learning did not sit lightly upon him he at least knew how to use it with effect; if his writings and his speeches were sometimes over-long they were packed with matter and were rarely dull.

Charles learned from his father the love of God and the supremacy of kings: 'first of all things, learne to know and love that God, whom-to ye have a double obligation; first for that he made you a man; and next, for that he made you a little God to sit on his Throne, and rule over other men.' He learned of the Divine Right of Kings and the importance of the royal prerogative; if in practice James stretched it too far yet he could warn that 'prerogative is a secret that ryves (tears) in the stretching'. He was warned against Puritans – 'very pests in the church and commonweal' not to be suffered 'except ye would keep them for trying your patience, as Socrates did an evil wife' – and against the 'horrible crime of witchcraft' which Charles was 'bound in conscience never to forgive'. He was told to embrace knowledge and learning, which is 'a light burden, the weight whereof will never presse your shoulders' and, particularly, to study his own craft, which was to rule his people: 'And when I say this, I bid you know all crafts: For except ye know everyone, how can yee controll every one, which is your proper office?'

As a guide to language, on which James was competent to speak, he advises 'be plaine, honest, naturall, comely, cleane, short, and sententious'. Indeed, in the apt phrase, the pointed aphorism, James had few equals, even in that age of fine language and word play. Whatever the occasion James could redeem it by a phrase. When he wished country gentlemen to leave the Court and return to their seats in the country he told them that a 'country gentleman in town is like a ship at sea, which looks very small; a country gentleman in the country is like a ship in a river, which looks very big.' His diatribes against tobacco were famous. It was probably his love of the hunting field with its good, clean air that gave him such a detestation of tobacco smoke that 'maketh a kitchen of the insides of men'. He cut down the *Preface* to the *Trew Law of Free Monarchies* 'least the whole Pamphlet runne out at the gaping mouth' thereof. He had decided opinions on most things. Football was 'meter for laming then making able the users thereof'; idleness was 'the mother of all vice'. If the royal pronouncements to Parliament were often far from tactful they contained many phrases upon which an heir to the throne could ponder.

In biblical matters James' thoughts ranged widely and his works included *A Meditation upon the Lord's Prayer*, dedicated to Buckingham in 1619, *A Meditation upon St. Matthew's Gospel*, written in 1620, and a translation of the Psalms, whose printing was authorized by Charles in 1631. 'Your inheritance', the Bishop of Winchester told Charles in editing James's collected works in 1616, 'consists as much in the workes of your Father's Royall Vertues, as in the wealth of his mighty Kingdom.'

Some of his precepts James most abjectly failed to live up to. The man who could advise his son: 'impaire not by your Liberalitie the ordinarie rents of your crowne' was doing exactly that. The man who could advise that kings in their persons should be 'as bright lamps of godlinesse and vertue' grew more dependent upon handsome young men, would be seen lolling upon their necks, caressing them in public. As he grew older James became, also, more careless of his appearance and would slobber his wine, of which he drank increasing quantities both with and between meals. He was also inclined to dribble his food. Possibly he gave little heed to his eating, for his custom was to have learned men near him with whom he could converse at meal times. In his dress in his younger days he was quite dapper, but he had a morbid fear of assassination, quite natural after the experiences of his youth, and took to wearing padded and quilted garments which gave him a somewhat grotesque rotundity. His legs, which had never been strong, were afflicted with arthritis and he tended to walk one-sided. His propensity for the ridiculous was constantly landing him in ludicrous situations, as when he was thrown from his horse into a stream in winter, going in through the ice head first and up to his waist so that only his legs were visible kicking the air. On another occasion he leaped from bed crying 'treason!' when some sporting guns were let off nearby. He slept in the middle of a mass of empty beds so that no assailant might come near him.

In his prime he was able to combine hunting and absence from Court with a steady hand upon affairs of state and he could get through more work in a couple of hours than most men in a day; that the hand was less steady and more often withdrawn in his later years was the effect as much of illness as of age or inability. Taking him all in all, James was no mean king and not one to be ignored. Nor, as a father, was he to be underestimated. And Charles neither ignored nor underestimated. The doctrine of the Divine Right of Kings he carried with him to his dying day, so implicitly that he never felt the need to enunciate it in so many words. It was his tragedy that, whereas James was not called upon in the final count to vindicate the theory, Charles gave his life for it, or for something very like it.[8]

The object of the Scottish visit was largely James's concern to bring the Scottish Church into a nearer conformity with English worship. His intention to end faction in the English Church had been demonstrated by the conference at Hampton Court over which he presided in the first year of his reign. That conference, if it did nothing else, authorized a new translation of the Bible and emphasized James's abhorrence of Presbyterianism in the words 'no bishop, no King'. Bishops had been re-established by the Scottish Parliament in 1612 but had been given scant approval by the Scottish people as a whole. James nevertheless now wanted to introduce other customs such as kneeling whilst taking communion. That he had his way, albeit with difficulty, was partly because the fervour of religious controversy in Scotland was at the time somewhat cooled. But there was nevertheless astonishment and protest at the installation of an organ in the chapel of Holyrood House and the arrival by sea of carved wooden figures of patriarchs and apostles. The carvings had to be removed as 'popish images' although, as James remarked, there would have been no objection if he had set up dragons and devils.

Nearly £22,000 had been assigned from the Exchequer for the Scottish journey, a sum not particularly large but sufficient to emphasize the shortage of money generally and so to add to the gloom of the autumn and winter of 1617/18 after the King's return. Charles agreed to act as sponsor to Elizabeth's second son, born on Christmas Eve, but there was still no money to attend the christening. James was plagued with arthritis and gout, Anne was ill, Christmas was dull, the Twelfth Night masque, Jonson's *Pleasure Reconciled to Virtue*, was undistinguished, although Charles's dancing was praised. But the February valentining went forward in the usual way. Each man and woman drew from one of two boxes and, thus paired, danced together, ate together, exchanged presents, and kissed whenever and wherever they met. Charles joined in with the rest. The royal family was further cheered in February by the Muscovite Ambassador, who paid his first visit to the King in great state. It was a considerable tonic to James that the presents he brought exceeded in value those he had given to Queen Elizabeth. They included skins of martens, of ermine and black foxes, silks and cloth-of-gold, heavily jewelled Turkish bows, scimitars with precious scabbards, knife cases powdered with turquoise and other fine jewels, and twelve large Icelandic falcons, their hoods embroidered with pearls. Sixty Muscovites, wearing their long native robes and fur caps, with gorgets of great price around their necks, marched through the streets of London before the gaping populace. The Ambassador himself, a 'bulky monster', dined with the King and threw himself on the floor, touching the ground with his head, when the King drank his health.[9]

Some of the great figures of Charles's boyhood were meanwhile making their final bow. Before the year 1618 was out the tragedy of Raleigh had drawn to its conclusion. Raleigh was released from the Tower in order to equip an expedition to search for the gold he still believed existed in the region of the river Orinoco near Spanish territory in Guiana, but on condition that he provoked no quarrel with Spain. Charles and his mother looked approvingly on Raleigh and watched his preparations with interest, while Gondomar spoke darkly to the King of upsetting Spain and jeopardizing the Spanish match. The inevitable clash with Spanish settlers occurred and Raleigh returned without gold and without his son, a young man of great promise who had been killed on the Orinoco. His trial and condemnation – he was still under the death penalty from his conviction at the beginning of the reign – followed inevitably though Anne interceded earnestly for his reprieve. Raleigh was beheaded on 29 October 1618 and one the last links with Elizabethan life was cut.

Bacon remained, shrewdly observing the scene. He could see Charles, as well as his father, being brought increasingly under the influence of Buckingham and as early as 1616 he had taken the bold step of writing to the favourite reminding him of his responsibilities to the Prince: 'it would be an irreparable stain and dishonour upon you . . . if you should mislead him, or suffer him to be misled by any loose or flattering Parasites'.[10] Charles, for his part, recognized the quality of the man and when Bacon became Chancellor in 1617 Anne and Charles showed their respect by sending, in the King's absence in Scotland, their own representatives to do him honour.

In Chief Justice Sir Edward Coke, Charles saw a man of different stamp, a lawyer whose name he would become accustomed to see widely in print and whose views would play a big part in the constitutional controversies of his reign. Coke's physical courage sometimes quailed before the wrath of James, but he never abandoned his position. When James assured Coke that he, as King, would defend the common law, Coke replied that, on the contrary, the common law defended the king. But when James turned on him in fury, shouting that the king was protected by none but God, that the king protected the law not the law the king, Coke fell on his knees in terror. Coke's insistence that the common law was supreme over any other jurisdiction, that it could be expounded only by the judges, and could be halted for no one, not even the king, hit at the heart of the prerogative as James understood it. He told Coke he was a knave who argued in sophistries and threw the ultimate jibe at the great lawyer – that he should go and study the common law. He proceeded to punish Coke by sequestering him from the Council; he forbade him to ride the summer circuit, insulted him by ordering him to revise his law reports, and dismissed him from the bench. Charles and his mother were very concerned for the Chief Justice, and Anne intervened with the King 'to have him used less insolently', but to no avail.

While his father and Buckingham increasingly supplied the impetus to his life, other influences round Charles were subtly changing. In 1617 Sir Henry Vane had joined his Household as cofferer. Vane's appointment, indeed his whole career up to this time, was typical of Court preferment in its mixture of patronage and purchase. According to Clarendon, who did not like him, Vane was a man 'of very ordinary parts by nature, and he had not cultivated them at all by art, for he was very illiterate. But being of a stirring and boisterous disposition, very industrious and very bold, he still wrought himself into some employment.' He was a very different type from the Murrays and Dallingtons, and even from the Careys of Charles's young days.

In the tittle-tattle of Court life, meantime, the old gossip flared up ʻfrom time to time. There were snide references to Jimmy Davidson. Occasionally the even uglier rumour was revived in great secrecy by Bedy the Dane, that *he* was the natural father of Prince Charles. Charles shut his ears to such talk. He blushed, indeed, 'like a modest maiden' at any loose conversation or lewd word and this, in itself, was sufficient to fan gossip. When the Venetian Ambassador wrote in 1616 that Charles's constitution was still sufficiently delicate for him to wait two or three years before taking a wife, the Courts of half-a-dozen Princes took note. Warming to his theme the omniscient Ambassador announced that Charles either did not feel, or instantly subdued, the passions normal to a young man. It was, indeed, still being rumoured widely in Germany in 1621 that the Prince was physically incapable of becoming a father. 'So far as one knows', wrote the Venetian Ambassador as late as 1622, 'he has not tasted certain youthful pleasures and apparently has not felt love except by some show of poetry.' But for once the Venetian was wrong. Charles had, in a stiff and decorous way, sown a very few wild oats. In 1615 he was involved in an affair for which, as he wrote to Buckingham, his father gave him 'a good sharp potion'. But, he continued, 'you took away the working of it by the well-relished comfits ye sent after it.' Charles had met a lady with whom he was enamoured and was going to meet her again – possibly the arrangements for the meeting were the 'well-relished comfits' which Buckingham sent.[11]

A few years later the verses, which are possibly those to which the Venetian Ambassador referred, were penned. In the summer progress of 1618 the King, Buckingham and Charles stayed at the house of Sir Nicholas Bacon where Anne Gawdy, his granddaughter, was also living. The girl was beautiful and was made much of by the King and the two young men. The Prince, in particular, was 'so far in liking' that he wrote some adolescent lines to her, whose merit depended solely upon the fact that they contained an anagram of her name:

> Heaven's wonder late, but now earth's glorious ray,
> With wonder shines; that's gone, this new and gay
> Still gazed on: in this is more than heaven's light –
> Day obscured that; this makes the day more bright.

It is likely that in this respect, as in other physical matters, Charles was late in developing – was 'slow enough to begin to be eager after the feminine prey', as Buckingham put it. Indeed, Buckingham did not regard him as ready and ripe for these affairs until he was twenty-one or two years old.[12]

But, quite apart from his own feelings or his own capabilities, the Prince of Wales could not be ignored in the European marriage market. Gondomar, in particular, had been sitting quietly at the centre of his own web of intrigue, close by the King's person, since 1613, and since time was on his side in the sense that the Prince must certainly marry someone, he was prepared to wait, weaving his web with patience, to ensure that the marriage would be between Charles and the Infanta Maria. James, for his part, was not sorry when the French match cooled in 1616 and he was able to turn his attention exclusively to Spain. But there were difficulties. His Privy Council would be against a Spanish match, his Archbishop of Canterbury would be against, Buckingham was against, a Parliament would certainly be against. Charles himself – conscientious, hard-working, dutiful, decorous Charles – was hardly considered.

6

The Palatinate

In 1617 attention began to be focused upon the Central European state of Bohemia, whose king was one of the Electors to the Holy Roman Empire and who was at that time the aged Hapsburg, Matthias, the Holy Roman Emperor himself. Matthias was childless. Wishing to perpetuate in the Hapsburg family the succession of both Bohemia and the Empire, he resigned the crown of Bohemia as a first step and nominated his cousin, Ferdinand of Styria, in his place. Ferdinand was accepted by a majority in the Bohemian Council of State and crowned in July 1617. But Bohemia was a country sharply divided by religious belief and economic interest, while Ferdinand was Jesuit-trained, sincerely if fanatically Catholic. The Protestants on the Council of State rose in protest and in May 1618 denounced the rule of Ferdinand and established an alternative government.

The effect on the rest of Europe was profound. No one was more closely concerned than the young Elector Palatine, son-in-law to James and leader of the Protestant bloc, and none was more ready for action. Outside the Empire no one was more closely concerned than the King of England, both through his treaty with the Protestant Union and his family connections with the Palatine, yet no one was less anxious to come to the issue. James was in the midst of his marriage negotiations with Gondomar, and was about to improve his financial position through the good offices of Lionel Cranfield: to spend money on war was the last thing he wanted. As Frederick prepared to fight and the English people demonstrated their support for the Protestant cause and the Princess Elizabeth, James was torn between conflicting desires to support his son-in-law, keep the friendship of Spain, and refrain from spending money. The first tentative moves came from Savoy. Count Mansfeld, a soldier of fortune with a personal vendetta against the Hapsburgs, had been in the service of the

59

Duke of Savoy and still had some 2000 troups under his command.
The Duke offered them to the Protestant Union and Mansfeld agreed
to lead them for what he might get out of the conflict.

James meanwhile seized upon a proposal reputedly made by the
King of Spain that he should use his prestige to mediate. This appealed
to James's vanity as well as to his desire to postpone action and might,
indeed, have offered a solution. But the mediator he chose to represent
him was the most unsuitable James Hay, Viscount Doncaster, a
courtier of wealth, good nature and personal charm whose talents lay
elsewhere than in the tough and intricate diplomacy required on this
occasion. As Doncaster made unhurried preparations for departure,
troops began to move in Europe and Frederick, in January 1619, sent
Baron Christopher Dohna to England to call upon his father-in-law
for aid and to renew the treaty with the Protestant Union which was
drawing to a close. It might have been taken as an augury that on the
12th of that month the Banqueting House in Whitehall, where
Elizabeth and Frederick were married, was destroyed by fire. James
renewed the treaty but nothing more. Charles made much of Dohna,
who was a link with his sister. He was impatient to do something
physical, something dramatic, for her cause. Instead of this he was
caught up in close domestic trouble with the illness first of his mother
and then of his father.

Early in 1619 Anne was taken ill. She had been in poor health for
some time, she saw little of the King, and her personal following had
dwindled. To Charles and to her brother she remained passionately
attached. At Hampton Court in February Anne seemed to recover
something of her old spirit, and the King went to Newmarket. But she
relapsed, had her favourite bed set up and sent for Charles on March 1.
He found her physicians in attendance, with the Archbishop of Canterbury and the Bishop of London already at her bedside anxious to
ensure that she died professing the faith of the Church of England. She
spoke a word to Charles in the old bantering manner, asking how he
did? 'At your service', he replied in the same spirit. She then begged
Charles to go home. 'No, I will stay to wait upon your Majesty.' 'I am
a pretty piece to wait upon', she replied wryly, once more commanding him to bed. He went unwillingly. After supper he returned and
spoke a few words to her. She would not believe her end was near and
very few of the courtiers who had thronged to Hampton Court on
hearing that her condition had worsened were admitted. She became
worse in the night, the Prince was sent for and she gave him her

blessing, her hand being guided and placed upon his head. She was just able to sign her will in which she left her property to Charles. Her power of speech was gone but the Bishop of London, Charles and her personal staff prayed with her. She called for James and made a sign to indicate that she died in the faith of the Church of England. 'She was in her great condition a good Woman', affirmed a near contemporary. Archbishop Abbot, many years after her death, perhaps wishing to scotch any rumour of Charles's illegitimacy, spoke of her as one of whose virtue he had not the least doubt.

For thirteen weeks Anne lay unburied while her effigy was made, money was with difficulty raised for the funeral, and the ladies of the Court quarrelled over precedence in the funeral cortège. Again the burden fell on Charles, for his father was ill at Newmarket. On the day of the funeral, 13 May 1619, Charles rode before the hearse and led the crowd of mourners, all in the black garments provided, as was customary, by the Court. It was, said an observer, 'a drawling, tedious sight', everyone being dressed alike and appearing 'tired with the length of the way or the weight of their clothes, each lady having twelve, and each countess sixteen yards of broadcloth in her dress.'[1] It was not what the high-spirited Anne would have wished. Charles was harrowed still further when James summoned him to his bedside and advised him on suitable counsellors for the succession.

The death of Matthias, the Holy Roman Emperor, on March 20 lost some of its impact in England in the midst of these domestic affairs, but Doncaster, delayed by the death of the Queen and the illness of the King, at last got off on May 12, while James recovered and entered London on June 1 to an enthusiastic welcome. There was room now for the feelings of expectation and urgency which Charles shared with the rest. Eagerly he perused Doncaster's despatches from Europe and wrote somewhat stiffly but full of boyish enthusiasm:

> I am verrie glad to heer that my brother is of so rype a judgement and of so forward an inclination to the good of Christendume as I fynd by you he is. You may assure your selfe I will be glade not onlie to assiste him with my countenance, but also with my person, if the King my father will give me leave.[2]

But while Doncaster was making his leisurely way across Europe, receiving lavish entertainment at Heidelberg and other capitals, events marched rapidly forward. Ferdinand, the deposed King of Bohemia, was elected Holy Roman Emperor in succession to Matthias and was crowned on August 18. Two days before that the Bohemian Council of State offered the throne of Bohemia to Frederick, Elector Palatine, James's son-in-law.

Frederick hesitated. Christopher Dohna was despatched again to England to seek James's advice. Elizabeth reputedly said she would rather eat sauerkraut as a Queen than eat off gold plate as an Elector's wife. James was thrown into an even wilder agony of indecision than before, for now a throne for his daughter was in the balance. He worried over the constitutional issue, evading Dohna, keeping him dangling between Bagshot, Windsor and Wanstead, but asking basic questions when they met: Could the Bohemian nobles of right choose their own king? What was Ferdinand's constitutional position? Not until a week after Dohna's arrival did he allow the matter to come before the Privy Council. This was already September 10 and a month had passed since Bohemia's invitation. It was not unreasonable that Frederick should act on his own initiative. He accepted the throne of Bohemia on September 28. He and Elizabeth entered Prague on October 31 and were crowned in November. The third of their children, Prince Rupert, was born there a month later on 7 December 1619.

The Catholic League could not accept such a situation. While rumours flew around of a flank attack by Spain upon Frederick's own Palatinate, feeling in England and in the Privy Council itself was running strongly against Spain and the Spanish match was discredited. Doncaster returned eager for war against the Catholic League. Achatius Dohna, brother of the unfortunate Christopher, was despatched as Ambassador from Frederick, King of Bohemia, to ask for his father-in-law's assistance in raising a loan of £100,000 in the City of London. Sir Andrew Gray, a Scottish officer in the Bohemian service, returned to England to beg leave to levy a regiment for his master to be paid out of the City loan. He brought with him a letter from James's little grandson, Prince Frederick Henry, which pleaded for help.

James was alone in seeing the other side of the picture. It was not his daughter's patrimony that was at stake, but a throne her husband had accepted rashly without waiting for his father-in-law's advice. At the same time Frederick's action had precipitated the Protestant-Catholic clash that James had laboured so long and so hard to avert. But, since the clash appeared imminent, should he not now throw his weight on the side of religion, his daughter, and the little grandson whose letter had so strongly affected him? A practical reason against doing so was a shortage of money. More importantly he would forfeit his ambition to be Europe's arbiter for the far less satisfactory possibility of being Europe's Protestant leader. He saw something of the terrible catastrophe of a war-torn Europe; he was distressed that it was his own son-in-law who had taken the step which was likely to reduce his peace policy to ashes. So strong was James's belief that he should remain uncommitted that it was not until March that he gave his consent to the raising of volunteers and permitted the City loan to go forward. He worried incessantly and gave vent to his feelings against Frederick: 'It is only by force that he will ever be brought to reason!', he exclaimed. 'If my son-in-law wishes to save the Palatine', he said on another occasion, 'he had better at once consent to a suspension of arms in Bohemia!'. He would not allow prayers to be said for Frederick as King of Bohemia. 'James is a strange father', the Prince of Orange reputedly remarked, 'he will neither fight for his children nor pray for them.' No wonder it was reported that the King 'seemed utterly weary'. 'I am not God Almighty', he was heard to mutter, a remark so out of character that in itself it demonstrated his depression. He busied himself with writing a meditation upon St Matthew's Gospel, which he called *The Crown of Thorns*.[3]

It was a different situation in August 1620 when, while the Emperor moved against Prague, Spain from the Netherlands invaded Frederick's hereditary territory in the Palatinate. James immediately announced to his Council that he would defend the Palatinate. Charles headed a subscription list for its defence with £5000. Buckingham gave £1000, the rest of the Council and the City of London brought the total to £28,000. But the rest of England could raise no more than a paltry £6000. Meanwhile on September 4 the Spanish General, Spinola, entered Oppenheim on the Rhine, well within the Palatine territory. James had no alternative but to call a Parliament, for which Proclamation was made on November 6. A fortnight later news reached London that on 29 October 1620 at the battle of the White Hill just outside Prague Frederick had suffered utter defeat at the hands of the Emperor and that he and his family were in flight.

Charles was at Royston with his father when he heard the news. For two days he remained shut in his room, speaking to no one. Inadequacy and insufficiency tormented him. Henry would have been in Prague or Heidelberg long before, fighting for his faith and his sister. Yet Charles's more statesmanlike feelings assured him that this could have given no more than an instant lifting of the spirit and the consolation of mutual support. It might have brought in more volunteers, more money, but would have been unlikely, in the end, to affect the outcome. If in part he regretted that his nature permitted no such spontaneous reaction, he had also to grapple with the consciousness that he loved neither his sister nor Frederick's Calvinism with the intensity that Henry had shown. Deep down an even darker consideration stirred – the unspoken fear that also haunted his father – fears of the popularity of the Protestant Princess whose resemblance to her brother Henry was still commented upon, fears of the succession of Elizabeth and her children if Charles left no heir: 'it hangs on a single thread', it was said, 'whether she and her children may not reign one day in these realms.' The desire of Elizabeth and Frederick to send one of their sons to England to be educated might be merely a device to depose James, by-pass Charles, and proclaim the boy king. James's refusal to allow his grandson to come had indicated some such train of thought. The King was reluctant, even now, when his daughter was in flight, to offer her a home in England. When it was rumoured that he had invited her and Frederick to come to England his comment was 'God forbid!' and he wrote to Carleton, Ambassador at The Hague, for 'the stay of his daughter . . . from coming into England'. Elizabeth was informed confidentially by the Dutch Ambassador and mentioned the matter no more. But she had her own personal reasons for wishing to remain with her husband near the scene of action, and whatever were James's motives, and they were probably mixed, Elizabeth herself felt strongly that to leave Continental Europe at this time would be both strategically and politically a false move.

The Parliament of 1621 was the first in which Charles played a full part, and he rode with his father to open it at Westminster on January 30. The King was suffering from arthritis and had to be carried in a chair into Westminster Abbey for the sermon and then into the House of Lords where Lord Chancellor Bacon presided. As the Commons crowded to the bar of the House James commended his son to them and they to him. The position in Europe was grim. Earlier in the month Frederick had been put under the ban of the Empire with all his lands and dignities confiscate. James told his hearers that he had borrowed from the King of Denmark and given from his own privy purse and now was reduced to begging 'as a man would beg an alms' for the recovery of the Palatinate. 'I declare unto you', he announced, 'that if I cannot get it with peace, my crown and my blood and the blood of my son shall not be spared for it.' A Council of War declared on February 12 that an army of 30,000 men was required at an initial cost of £250,000 and a subsequent charge of £900,000 annually. The Commons granted two subsidies, amounting to some £160,000 – but not for war, upon which they remained uncommitted, but for the King's general expenses. James was delighted to receive a promise of money so early in the session but it soon became apparent that before considering further supplies the House had affairs of its own to discuss.

Charles could now be seen regularly walking through King Street and Westminster Hall with his guard and retinue on his way from St James's to the Parliament House. He heard the Members discuss the economic situation. Trade had been declining, largely because of the loss of markets resulting from the European war; in the clothing areas, particularly, there was much unemployment and considerable distress. Members were concerned for the industry which was the very backbone of English prosperity and with which many of them were closely connected, and they were worried at the threat of insurrection as starving cloth workers began to take food from the market place and from the homes of richer people. Some employers were helping their workpeople by giving them food or keeping them on in work in spite of the fact that unsold cloth was accumulating in their barns. The House was sympathetic. Sir Edwin Sandys, who represented Ipswich in the clothing area of East Anglia, made an impassioned speech for 'the poor man's labour, his inheritance' and a few months later the first Commission on Unemployment was appointed.

Charles heard the Commons marshall their grievances and denounce monopolies, particularly the monopolies of inns and ale-houses and of gold and silver thread. He knew that Buckingham's family was concerned in these and he watched as Sir Giles Mompesson was made the scapegoat and was banished the kingdom. He enjoyed many of the debates, particularly the contributions of Sir Edward Coke. 'I am never weary of hearing you', he told the Chief Justice, 'you do so well mix pleasant things with these sad and serious matters.' He was able to calm the more excitable spirits in the House when James sent a tactless message. He intervened in the case of the aged Roman Catholic Floyd, a barrister who had been imprisoned in the Fleet by the Council for openly rejoicing at Frederick's defeat outside Prague. Though he denied the words attributed to him, the House of

Commons, which was doing nothing to assist the Palsgrave and his family, turned on Floyd in fury. 'Let a hole be burnt in his tongue', 'Let his tongue be cut out', 'Let his nose and ears be cropped off!' they cried one after another. The nauseating scene became merged in questions as to who could claim jurisdiction over the unfortunate old man. When it fell to the House of Lords they fined him £5000, imprisoned him for life, and ordered him to be whipped at the cart's tail from London Bridge to Westminster Hall. It was at the instance of Charles that the whipping was remitted.

This was also the Parliament of Bacon's disgrace. He had made enemies; and in his own conduct, in the sphere where his public duties impinged upon his private life, he was careless and gifts exchanged hands while suits were pending. There is no evidence that Bacon's judgment was affected and in an age where the line between bribery, gift, and legitimate payment was finely drawn it is unlikely that anything would have been heard to Bacon's discredit had it not been for jealousy and personal rancour. As it was, even with the support of the Prince and of Buckingham, Bacon could not stand up to the charges brought against him in the House of Lords. Charles himself carried to the House Bacon's letter of submission. On 3 May 1621 after the Great Seal had been taken from him and his further punishment was being debated, both Charles and the Earl spoke in his favour. The sentence, nevertheless, was severe and Bacon never returned to public life. James, for all his erudition, had never recognized the qualities of Bacon's scientific mind. Bacon's plea for a science based upon observation and experiment, and co-ordinated by an official body, could have blossomed into a national institution which would have redounded to James's credit. But James preferred an aphorism. The *Novum Organum* of 1620, which embodied Bacon's plan, 'resembled the peace of God', said James, 'for it passed all understanding'. Charles, on the other hand, kept Bacon's *Advancement of Learning* with him throughout the troubles of his later life and annotated the book in his captivity.

Charles delivered the speech of thanks from the Lords to the King on the adjournment on 4 June 1621. As the Members dispersed to their homes it became apparent that the bad summer was delaying the ripening of the crops. In the continuing cold of autumn the harvest was disastrous and the price of corn rose steeply. The Court augmented its supplies by progresses and cheered itself by entertainments. Ben Jonson's masque *The Gypsies Metamorphos'd* was played three times, Buckingham appearing as a gypsy in the performance at Windsor early in September. A feature of the play was the fortune-telling of the gypsies in which the first gypsy, taking the King's hand, asked

> Could any doubt, that sawe this hand,
> Or who you are, or what commaund
>   You have upon the fate of things,
> Or would not say you were let downe
> From heaven, on earthe to be the Crowne
>   And top of all your neighbour kings?

When a gypsy took the hand of Charles it was to offer a singularly apt and charmingly turned fortune, predicting a Spanish bride and

> . . . the promise before day
> of a little James to play
>   Hereafter
> 'Twixt his Grandsires knees, and move
> All the prettie waies of Love,
>   And laughter

It was enough to move the old King to tears!

Shortly afterwards James went to Newmarket, where he was confined by the cold weather and a slight indisposition. It was therefore Charles who, on his twenty-first birthday, rode in through the early morning chill from Newmarket, dining at Epping and reaching St James's by two o'clock in the afternoon, in order that the following day he might open the new session of Parliament.

The question of concrete help for the Palatinate was once again the main issue. Lord Digby, English Ambassador at Madrid, who also knew Central Europe and was more able than most to grasp the essentials of the situation, hammered home the points: the necessity of holding the Lower Palatinate during the winter, which meant supplies for the 20,000 men already there under Vere and Mansfeld; the need in the spring for an additional army for which some £900,000 a year would be required. But there was no enthusiasm for a land war which would have swallowed much money and still further disrupted trade and commerce. Members spoke instead of diversionary action at sea to cut off Spanish supplies – in other words a good old naval war in the old style for the glory of God, the winning of treasure and, they hoped, the discomfiture of Spain and the rescue of the Palatinate at little expense to themselves. They did, however, grant a subsidy for the maintenance of the troops already in the Palatinate (for which recusants were to be assessed at double rates), they asked for the enforcement of the anti-Catholic laws, and they begged that their Prince be married to one of the Protestant faith. Charles, bitterly complaining that 'his marriage was being continually prostituted in the House', sent to his father at Newmarket a copy of the petition in which the Commons had expressed their views. James exclaimed in wrath that 'some fiery and popular spirits' had been 'emboldened . . . to argue and debate publicly of matters far above their reach and capacity' and commanded Parliament not to 'presume henceforth to meddle with anything concerning our government or deep matters of state, and namely not to deal with our dearest son's match with the daughter of Spain'. The response of the Commons was first a further petition and then the Protestation of December 18 in which they maintained that 'affairs concerning the King, State and defence of the realm and of the Church of England, and the maintenance and making of laws, and redress of mischiefs and grievances' were 'proper subjects for debate in Parliament' and that in all these matters Members of Parliament had the right of free speech. This was too much for the harrassed King. He first adjourned and then dissolved Parliament on 6 January 1622; he imprisoned Coke and Sir Robert Phelips, confined John Pym to his house, and solemnly, in the presence of Charles and the members of his Council, tore the offending Protestation from the Journal of the House of Commons.

As the bitterly cold weather continued John Chamberlain took to wearing gloves as he wrote to his friend, Dudley Carleton, at The Hague. Among other events he reported a series of fires in the capital: the Fortune theatre was burnt down in two hours, destroying the players' costumes and their play books, there was a serious fire in the clerk's office in Chancery Lane. Though fire was not unusual in the close-packed streets of the capital with its many wooden or half-timbered buildings, Chamberlain thought the present outbreak was because 'some firie planet raigned'. More likely people were trying to keep warm with bigger fires than normally. On Twelfth Night 1622, the day James tore the Commons' Protestation from their Journal, Jonson's *Masque of Augurs* opened Inigo Jones's new Banqueting Hall, which replaced the one destroyed by fire three years earlier. Although the work was not complete and seats had to be improvised, the scale and balance of the building was unmistakeable. The bad weather continued into the spring when the anniversary celebrations of the King's coronation, including tilting and a masque devised by the Prince, were several times postponed, to Charles's extreme annoyance, not only because he had worked hard on the preparation of the entertainment but because he wanted to wear at the tilting a feather which had been sent him from the Infanta.

Charles had matured considerably during the Parliament of 1621. Not only had he made the acquaintance of some of the great orators and parliamentarians of the day but he had experienced personally the clash of his father's outlook and theirs. He was himself popular with the Members who liked his modest manner, his obvious desire to please, and his voice which was 'lowe' but 'good'. His popularity increased his poise and self-confidence, he was much less reserved than formerly, and spoke with greater firmness. He needed all the strength of character he could muster as, after the dissolution, his father became the laughing-stock of Europe. Why should James assume to himself the title of Defender of the Faith, it was asked, when he suffered the Protestants of Germany to be extirpated? When he was called at Court a second Solomon someone was heard to hope he was not, after all, the fiddler's son! In Brussels they depicted him with his pockets hanging out and never a penny in them, nor in his purse, turned upside down. At Antwerp they pictured the Queen of Bohemia as a poor peasant woman with her hair hanging about her face, and her child on her back, while the King, her father, carried the cradle after her. Comedies showed the Palatine being presented with 100,000 pickled herrings by the King of Denmark, 100,000 butter boxes by the Dutch, and 100,000 ambassadors by the English. In England the pamphlets *Vox Populi* and *Tom Tell-Troath* were repeating such gibes and many more. It was said that for one health drunk to the King, ten were drunk to the Palatine and to the Lady Elizabeth.[4]

Charles tried to assert his new-won confidence – 'showing his teeth' the Venetian Ambassador called it – though James still kept him tightly reined. But he would question others closely, using the knowledgeable Venetian, for example, to tell him about Count Mansfeld. Otherwise he kept his own council, still saying and doing what he was expected to say and do. Observers were puzzled. 'He moves like a planet in its sphere', wrote the Venetian Ambassador in 1622, 'so naturally and quietly that one does not remark it. In speech he shows good sense, his replies are prudent, he grasps things with quick judgment and leans to the better opinion. But if he hears his father or

the favourite say anything to the contrary, he immediately changes.'
Perhaps it was intended dissimulation, learned from James himself
('that falst Scotch Urchin' as Queen Elizabeth called him) or from
Guicciardini.

It was observed that he would retire for hours to his model house
working upon out-of-the-way mathematics and methods of campaigning and encamping, and that he was dressing 'absolutely without
jewels, more modestly than any gentleman soever', no doubt out of
sympathy for Elizabeth and her family. The year following the dissolution of Parliament was full of strange undercurrents. At Christmas-
time 1622 four of Charles's musicians performed in Gondomar's
Roman Catholic chapel; Charles dismissed them. But when Gondomar complained to the King, Charles was compelled to reinstate
them. About the same time the Lieutenant of the Middle Temple and
some thirty others drank the health of the distressed Lady Elizabeth,
kissed their drawn swords, and swore to live and die in her service.
James was displeased. Charles's reaction was touched with bitterness,
the more so that it was not he but their cousin, Duke Christian of
Brunswick, who was most vociferous and most active in helping
Elizabeth. Not only did he declare himself, 'Your most humblest,
most constant, most faithful, most affectionate, and most obedient
slave, who loves you, and will love you, infinitely and incessantly to
death', but he was actually fighting in her armies.[5]

Perhaps as a reaction to the enforced inactivity of his own life
Charles at this time entered into a freer, more light-hearted social
round than he had known hitherto. It is possible that his father had
encouraged Buckingham to lead him. At all events in Court entertainment Buckingham, his wife and Charles were now frequently
joined by the Duchess of Lennox, a thrice-married beauty, still young,
who was said 'to be much courted and respected by the Prince' and
even to have 'cast her cap' at the widower King himself. The quartet
were frequently observed going round from one place of entertainment to another, turning up unexpectedly with a minimum of
etiquette and an abandon of high spirits. When the Marquise of
Buckingham had smallpox the Duchess of Lennox attended her
assiduously. There was considerable gossip shortly afterwards when a
chain of diamonds, valued at over £3000, was put round the Duchess's
neck by Charles himself – 'which was taken by all for an extraordinary
and unusual honour done unto her'. But the chain carried the picture
of James, not Charles, and was said by some to be a tribute to her care

of the Marquise, of whom James was extraordinarily fond. Not long afterwards Charles gave another 'faire jewell' to another fair lady, the attractive Mlle St Luc, when she departed for home with her aunt, the wife of the French Ambassador. It was clear that Charles had thrown off much of his reserve and was enjoying the courtier's life in which hitherto he had shown little interest.[6] If there is any truth in the story that Joanna Bridges, who was living in Mandinam in Carmarthen- shire in 1648 and who married Jeremy Taylor as his second wife, was a natural daughter of Charles she would have been conceived at this time. Her mother could have been the Duchess of Lennox.

Charles was, indeed, thinking of marriage. His own inclinations were leading him in that direction and he was beginning to believe with his father that a Spanish match could, strange though it might seem, help the Palatinate. As he discussed the matter with Bucking- ham their friendship deepened. When the Venetian Ambassador found Charles in 1622 caressing Buckingham like a brother and 'behaving as if the favourite were prince and himself less than a favourite', he thought it was to please the King, but it was, on the contrary, the outcome of his developing affection for Buckingham and an indication of the interests they now held in common.

7

The Spanish Match

By 1622 the amazing Spanish marriage negotiations had continued, on and off, for eight years and opposition was found on both sides. James was well aware of the difficulties of a Spanish match. A majority of his Privy Council and his Archbishop of Canterbury would oppose it; so would Buckingham; and a Parliament would certainly be most vocally and distressingly in opposition. On the Spanish side Gondomar's enthusiasm had to be balanced against the doubts of the Spanish monarch, the caution of the Spanish Court, the reluctance of the Infanta, and the hostility of the Pope and the theologians. Two kings of Spain, three Popes, and innumerable theological junta addressed themselves to the question with no more eagerness than that shown by the English Parliament. That Spain entered into discussions at all was the result partly of fear and partly of hope. The fear was that an unfriendly Britain would cement a powerful anti-Hapsburg bloc in Europe and that the English fleet, united with the Dutch, would sweep the Spaniard off the seas; the hope was no less than the mirage produced by Gondomar of a Catholic Britain. These reasons for negotiation were clearly expressed in many communications by the Spaniards to each other, and never changed over the years. At the same time it is doubtful if, without Gondomar's determination, they would have continued after Spanish troops had invaded the Palatinate. As it was, Gondomar audaciously used the action to demonstrate that a marriage alliance was necessary to nullify the action and restore the Palatinate to Frederick. The terms of the marriage treaty, which continued to be discussed, amended, and haggled over, stipulated a large dowry of some £500,000 or £600,000 but did not mention the Palatinate. The English were expected to grant freedom of worship to the Infanta in her own chapels and to recognize her own Roman Catholic priests and her own Household, which would be nominated by the King of Spain. Though the English won the point that children of the marriage need not be baptized into the Roman Catholic Church, their education was to remain with their mother until an age which was still the subject of negotiation. Most importantly, the Spanish insisted upon the repeal of the recusancy laws in England and the consequent grant of freedom of worship to English Catholics as essential to the marriage treaty.

The Infanta was then seventeen years old, a gentle withdrawn girl, devoted to her religion, terrified at the consequences of marrying an infidel; she had announced that she would go into a nunnery rather than do so and had changed her mind only at the prospect of her mission of conversion. Charles knew much of this from the English Ambassador's letters to himself and to the King. The Infanta's portrait had not particularly excited him, though the round, girlish face with its blue eyes, pink and white complexion, full mouth and slightly protruding Hapsburg lip, framed by the pale hair of her Flemish forbears, showed promise of considerable beauty; nor was he much impressed by stories of the exquisite delicacy of her fine, white hands. It would be well, he remarked, if a Prince could have one wife for reasons of state and another to please himself. But Charles had no strong feelings against a Spanish marriage in itself. As a political alliance it appealed to him and he believed, like his father, that the large dowry, and the very fact of a marriage bond with a Hapsburg, would help his sister. And, as he assured Gondomar, he had no desire to persecute Catholics.

The fact that Charles could entertain a Catholic marriage at all gave something of a jolt to those who had been assiduous in supplying him with a Puritan entourage. They never understood that their handling had been too heavy, nor that his mother's influence had been against them. Throughout her married life rumours had persisted that Anne was about to embrace the Catholic faith and that she did, in fact, hear mass in private. It was she who had originally forwarded the idea of a Spanish match for Prince Henry, who had welcomed a possible alliance between Elizabeth and the Spanish king, and she would certainly not have neglected to talk to Charles of the advantages of a Spanish marriage for himself.

In such a situation Charles's Puritan chaplains should clearly do their duty. In 1621 Hakewill left with the Prince, on the understanding that it would not reach the King, a memorandum against a Catholic match. Two hours later the paper was with James and Hakewill was

thrown into prison. Though subsequently released, he never regained
his office about the Prince. There may have been misunderstanding,
though this is unlikely, and it seems that even Murray suspected some
breach of trust by Charles.[1] But the incident served to encourage the
Puritans to make a further effort to increase their influence with the
Prince, and their choice fell upon John Preston, a Cambridge tutor
and, like Senhouse, a 'golden voiced preacher', skilled in debate and
the lighter sophistry, who had delighted James at Cambridge by
successfully opposing the motion that dogs cannot reason in syllog-
isms. He was appointed chaplain to the Prince at the end of 1621.
Preston himself had worked hard to acquire this position of influence.
He had declined other appointments, cultivated favour with
Buckingham when the favourite was of a Puritan turn of mind, and
used his influence as a Cambridge tutor with the sons of wealthy and
powerful Puritan families who were his pupils. He was helped by the
general sympathy to Puritanism of Archbishop Abbot.[2]

It is a pity that there was removed from Charles at this time the
direct influence of Thomas Murray. It may have been a move to take
away one so influential with the Prince and so fundamentally opposed
to the Spanish match. But Murray had served the Prince well for
fifteen years and his retiring disposition gave him little zest to continue
Court life now that his charge had moved out into the world. It says
much for the regard in which he was still held that James offered him
the Provostship of Eton College, a post for which there was always
competition among men of the highest calibre. There is little to be said
for the unsavoury manoeuvring in which these men indulged, except
that it was normal at the time. As early as April 1614 Sir Dudley
Carleton, who was then Ambassador at Venice, was writing to his
friend, John Chamberlain, reminding him of 'a good morsel' which
would be given for the appointment. Three years later Carleton's
agent, Edward Sherburn, was asking how much he should offer for it.
Sir Henry Wotton was also asking after the post. Sir Henry Saville, the
sitting Provost, had remained in remarkably good health for an old
man, but when he became ill in the spring of 1619 the manoeuvring
started all over again. But Saville recovered. Two-and-half years later
he was again ill. Should Carleton try once more? Murray had taken no
steps to press his suit and it was assumed that without doing so no
office was obtainable. But James was extraordinarily loyal to the man
who had been his son's mentor for so long. Against the manoeuvring
of Court interests, against the even more powerful opposition of the

bishops, against the wishes of the Vice Provost and the Fellows of Eton College, he insisted on the election of Thomas Murray. Nor was he helped by that dour Scot who not only scorned to manoeuvre but steadfastly refused to take holy orders to placate the bishops. The Governors of Eton had, instead, to grant a dispensation for the acceptance of a Provost who was not in holy orders and whose appointment did not, therefore, accord with their statutes. There followed a few halcyon weeks in the summer of 1622 when Charles and Buckingham, forgetful of the Palatinate and the Spanish marriage, swam each evening in the Thames near Eton and Murray entertained them and their friends at the College.[3]

Francis Cottington, who succeeded Murray as Secretary to the Prince, was a man of different stamp. His family background was land on the borders of Wiltshire and Somerset, sheep, and the making of broadcloth – a conventional background which was combined with service in Spain. When the Ambassador was recalled in 1609 Cottington acted as English agent for a couple of years, he spent a year as Consul at Seville, and was again in Spain in 1616. His familiarity with the country at a time when the Spanish marriage negotiations were in full swing undoubtedly influenced his appointment, and his Catholic leanings did him little harm at that point; on the contrary, he was a good tool in the hands of the pro-Spanish party. He was in his middle forties when he took up his post. He was portrayed by Clarendon, who did not like him, as a great dissembler. But he was patient, tenacious, and his dry humour appealed to Charles: 'under a grave countenance', as Clarendon put it, 'he covered the most of mirth'. More importantly, Cottington proved a loyal servant and companion to Charles.

Endymion Porter, who was some ten years younger than Cottington, now became Groom of the Bedchamber to the Prince. He came of a Gloucestershire gentry family but had a Spanish grandmother and had been brought up in the same household as the Condé d'Olivarez, who was now chief minister to the King of Spain. Back in England he had served in the Villiers family, more recently in that of Buckingham himself, and he married one of Buckingham's nieces, who was a zealous Catholic. Like Cottington, he became a close and loyal friend to Charles.[4]

Meanwhile Buckingham, whose career had begun as a counterweight to Catholic influences at Court, now, like James and Charles, began to see the general advantages of a Spanish alliance. His support of the Palatinate and of Protestantism in general had been shaken by a personal dislike of Frederick and of the Dutch and he had been offended when his candidate, Sir Edward Cecil, had been passed over and the command of British troops in Europe given to Sir Horace Vere. At the same time family connections caused him to look more favourably upon the Catholic religion than he had done before. In May 1620 he had married Lady Catherine Manners, daughter of the Catholic Earl of Rutland. The Earl had objected to the marriage and it was, in a sense, a runaway match, which accounts for the fact that the wedding of the favourite had not been celebrated with the wealth and display that had accompanied lesser nuptials. Although his wife had been ostensibly converted through the good offices of Bishop Williams to the Protestant faith, it is likely that she remained basically Catholic. More recently, at the end of 1622, his mother had become a Catholic and it was rumoured that Buckingham himself was veering in that direction. So, in spite of the appointment of Preston as his chaplain, the influences round Charles had become basically pro-Spanish and far less Puritan.

The year 1621 had been inconclusive. The Infanta was said to have been offered in marriage to the Archduke Ferdinand and it was rumoured that her father on his deathbed in March commended this choice to her brother, his successor as Philip IV. In 1622 the Spaniards were asking for the Prince's conversion as an alternative to freedom of worship for Catholics in England, while the English were standing firm on the size of the dowry and the support of Spain in recovering the Palatinate for Frederick. John Digby, who was negotiating for terms in Madrid as Ambassador Extraordinary and whom James had created Earl of Bristol earlier in the year, prepared to throw in his hand, writing to the Spanish King that the marriage negotiations had not progressed a step further than the general terms in which they had been expressed seven years before. The reply was typically courteous but firm: the marriage depended upon liberty of conscience for Catholics, the Palatinate depended upon the Emperor.

James then instructed Bristol to get an answer from the King of Spain within ten days as to whether he would mediate for the restitution of the Palatinate or give James's forces free and friendly passage through his territories. James's messenger was Endymion Porter, who knew the contents of the despatch. The ten days passed and Bristol was still playing the diplomatic game with the Spaniards but Porter, impatiently, went to his old friend, Olivarez, asking bluntly for an answer. 'What!', exclaimed the Condé, 'my Master to assist with Arms against His Uncle, against the Catholic League, against the Head of His House! He would never do it!' Porter reported the affair to Charles and, according to Buckingham, it finally determined him to put the matter to the test himself.

In February 1623, in spite of the gout and arthritis that wracked him, James was feeling happy. Christmas and New Year had been particularly bright and pleasant. He was at his favourite hunting lodge at Royston and Steenie and Baby Charles were with him. For the moment the vexed question of the Palatinate could be laid aside. Perhaps he would send Steenie to Spain to conclude the marriage treaty; perhaps, even, Steenie would stand proxy at the wedding in Madrid. And after that, who knows, perhaps Baby Charles himself would sail to Spain to bring home his bride, as he himself had gone to Denmark and his father before him had gone to France. Pleasantly his thoughts wandered on, oblivious for the time that the treaty was still heavy on his hands, that he had no firm guarantee that it would restore the Palatinate to his son-in-law, that meanwhile his daughter and his grandchildren were largely dependent upon the charity of the House of Orange. While he was in this state of euphoria his two boys entered in high spirits. Baby Charles, particularly, was very excited. They wanted his permission for an enterprise they had in mind. It was very secret but their plans were well laid. They wished to ride to Spain to conclude the marriage treaty, which surely could not be delayed if the Prince himself were there. They would be accompanied merely by Francis Cottington and Endymion Porter and possibly a groom. They would then bring the Infanta home, help would be forthcoming for the Palatinate and the gordian knot which had resisted untying for years would be cut at one deft, bold stroke. In the mood James was in the plan chimed sweetly with his thoughts. Only later did its imprudence strike him in all its crudity. For the Prince to go in person before the treaty was signed was not only improper but tantamount to capitulation; his son was offering himself as a hostage to Spain and the anti-Spanish groups in Court and country would rise in protest. At the same time Charles would be exposing himself to the dangers of the long journey across Europe where it was easy to lose the way, where bandits fell upon unwary travellers, where falls and broken limbs, to say nothing of hunger and sickness, would be the least of his tribulations. What kind of king and father was he to risk his only son, the heir to the throne, on such an enterprise?

When Charles and Buckingham came next morning to arrange details they found James in a desperate state after a night of self-recrimination. He fell into a great passion of tears and told them that he was undone and that it would break his heart if they went. Charles reminded his father of the promise made the previous day and, like a petulant child, declared that if he were forbidden to go to Spain he would never marry at all. Buckingham more roughly told the King that if he broke his word no one would ever believe him again. Changing his tack James then exclaimed to Buckingham that if any evil befell the Prince it would be laid at his door and his ruin would be unavoidable. Finally Cottington was sent for. 'Cottington', said James, 'here are Baby Charles and Steenie, who have a great mind to go by post into Spain to fetch home the Infanta. . . . What think you of the journey?' The question had to be repeated to the incredulous Secretary who finally answered in a trembling voice that it would render fruitless all that had been done, that as soon as the Spaniards had the Prince in their hands they would propose new articles, particularly concerning religion. James in anguish threw himself upon his bed. 'I told you this before,' he cried passionately, 'I am undone! I shall lose Baby Charles!' In the near pandemonium that followed, the Prince and the Duke stood firm and James at last gave his consent to the journey.

There is no doubt that a visit to Spain by the Prince had been quietly talked about earlier, but that it meant no more than a journey to fetch home his bride after a marriage treaty, and possibly a proxy wedding, had been concluded. The more romantic episode could have been born in the fertile brain of the Duke. But Charles himself was now ready enough for action and later maintained that 'the heroic thought started out of his own brain to visit the Court of Madrid'. As a contemporary wrote, he was 'very apt to try conclusions', he was active, an excellent horseman, 'never perfectly well but when he was in action' and the physical challenge of the ride across Europe appealed to him. Intellectually he felt able to enter into any treaty himself and he believed the whole affair would redound to his credit. Sir Henry Wotton, saying that James cast the greatest trust upon Buckingham when he made him the companion of his son's journey into Spain, implies that the initiative was neither the Duke's nor the Prince's but the King's. This is unlikely and not in character. But it matters little where the first whisper came from; the escapade as it was carried out and the incredible naïvety which accompanied it were typical of the romantic adolescent that Charles had become, and it was his spirit, as much as anybody's, that carried it through to the end and beyond what should have been the end.

Cottington was created a baronet on February 16 and, taking Endymion Porter with him, he went to Dover to hire a vessel for France. On Monday February 17 Charles quietly took leave of his father, making public arrangements to meet him again at Newmarket, but instead joining Buckingham at his house at New Hall. Very early the following morning John and Thomas Smith, bearded youths, ordinarily apparelled and wearing large hats, rode off with Buckingham's master of horse, Sir Richard Graham, in the direction of Gravesend. At the Gravesend ferry they demanded to be put ashore at the outskirts of the town instead of the usual landing stage and handed the ferryman a gold piece without waiting for the change. Assuming they were setting off for France to settle a quarrel in a duel, and thinking it a shame that either of such generous young men should be killed, the ferryman gave information to the magistrates at Gravesend who sent off a postboy to stop them at Rochester. But Buckingham's mounts had reached the town long before and had been exchanged for post horses when, from the brow of the hill beyond Rochester, the little party saw one of the royal carriages approaching on the Dover Road. They took to the fields to escape detection – 'teaching post-horses to jump hedges' as Charles afterwards said – but they had been seen and were stopped at Canterbury as they were taking fresh mounts. Only by making himself known and saying he was going to inspect the fleet did Buckingham elude the vigilance of the mayor.

With such delays and with inferior hired mounts, unlike the horses they were accustomed to, it was not until six o'clock that evening that they reached Dover. The night was tempestuous, and it was six o'clock the following morning when the party set sail. Charles was seasick with the rest but they were in Boulogne at two in the afternoon, pushing on to reach Montreuil by evening. Two days later they were in Paris, not without adventures on the way. There was a nasty moment when two young Germans, who had seen them at Newmarket, commented upon their likeness to the Prince and Buckingham, and Dick Graham, with poker face, had to enlarge upon the extreme improbability of two such famous people travelling alone, so meanly.

In Paris they bought periwigs to aid their disguises, pulling them well down over their foreheads. Charles was in the highest spirits, enjoying his first visit abroad, and with Buckingham as guide spent the day sightseeing in the French capital. They were fortunate enough to see the French King in the gallery of his palace, to join without apparent detection a knot of people who were watching the Queen Mother dine, and to see the rehearsal of a masque by the royal family. Charles gazed with delight upon the Queen of France, sister to the Infanta whom he was wooing. He paid scant attention to Henrietta-Maria, the somewhat sallow little princess, of no particular beauty, who was also performing. When the stories of these adventures reached London James related them with delight, but there was not wanting those who found the reception of the Prince and his party a little too warm for strangers. Chamberlain judged that they 'went not unknown at the Court of France' but that the French 'dissembled the knowledge'.

The following day, February 23, they were speeding across France at three o'clock in the morning. They took beds at simple inns or peasant houses and for the most part aroused little comment, except at Bordeaux, six days from Paris, where Cottington had great difficulty in keeping them from being entertained by the Duc d'Epernon, who suspected that the fare of country inns was not quite what they were used to. They amused themselves with buying local homespun coats fashioned, as they laughingly described them, 'in a kind of noble simplicity'; they spent hours chasing goats in the Pyrenean foothills, trying to catch one to supplement the Lenten fare which was all the local inns provided: it was Charles who finally shot one from his saddle straight through its head. A few miles further on they met an English messenger, Walsingham Gresley, carrying despatches from the Earl of Bristol to England. They were 'saucy enough', as they put it, in one of their letters to the King, to open the despatches but were unable to read the cypher; but they took Gresley back with them over the frontier so that he could take a message home actually written on Spanish soil. Gresley reported to James that Buckingham looked weary but that Charles had never been so merry and danced for joy to be actually in Spain.

In England, meanwhile, rumour gave way to incredulity followed by consternation when it was learned that the Prince and Buckingham had really gone. There were even cries that Buckingham was guilty of treason in thus taking the Prince out of the country. James himself was now inclined to put the best possible face on the escapade and derived pleasure from the thought of the dash and daring of his 'sweet Boys and dear ventrous Knights, worthy to be put in a new Romanso'. He sent after them their robes and Orders of the Garter to wear on St

George's Day 'for it will be a goodly sight for the Spaniards to see my two boys dine in them'; he sent horses for tilting, and jewels in profusion for themselves and for the Infanta. He even composed a long poem:

> What sudden change hath darked of late
> The glory of the Arcadian state?
> The fleecy flocks refuse to feed,
> The lambs to play, the ewes to breed;
> > The altars smoke, the offerings burn,
> > Till Jack and Tom do safe return.
>
> The Spring neglects her course to keep,
> The air with mighty storms doth weep;
> The pretty birds disdain to sing,
> The meads to swell, the woods to spring;
> > The mountains drop, the fountains mourn,
> > Till Jack and Tom do safe return.

Gresley had to give his story over and over again in the greatest detail, including the number of falls each member of the party had had – Cottington twelve, Buckingham seven, but the Prince none at all. As the first to bring news of their arrival in Spain he was rewarded with £1000 and a pension of £500 a year for life.

Four days after meeting Gresley the travellers were in Madrid. It was Friday March 7, sixteen days after they had ridden out from New Hall, an average rate of sixty miles a day. For the last two days Buckingham and Charles had ridden ahead and they went straight to Bristol's house, reaching it at about five o'clock in the evening. Thomas Smith knocked on the door while John Smith waited in the shadows opposite. The incredulous Ambassador rushed them up to his bedchamber to keep them hidden while he considered the situation. Spanish intelligence, meanwhile, was well informed and in a state of great excitement Gondomar hurried to the royal palace where the Condé d'Olivarez was at supper. 'What is it?' asked the minister, 'one would think that you had got the King of England in Madrid'. 'If I have not got the King', replied Gondomar, 'at least I have got the Prince!'. Late that night Bristol sat down to report to James the arrival of his 'sweete boys'. When the news reached London bonfires and the ringing of bells signalized the people's joy; but the celebrations were by command of the King and Chamberlain's remark, 'God send we may praise at parting', more accurately expressed the general feeling.

The following day Olivarez and Gondomar were admitted to the Prince's presence. Gondomar was said to have fallen on his face and cried out 'Nunc Dimittis' while Olivarez 'kneeled and kissed his hands and hugged his thighs and delivered . . . high compliments'. Only one reason, it seemed to them, could have brought the Prince on such a journey in such a manner, and that was his intention to announce his conversion to the Roman Catholic religion. Charles's remark that he came thither not for religion but for a wife could have put an end to all the misunderstandings that followed, but in the exuberance of the moment no one seemed to pay much attention to it. The same day Buckingham was taken in a closed coach by a private way to the King. Already crowds were thronging to Bristol's house and rumours of the English Prince and his conversion were spreading. But there were difficulties in the way of seeing the Infanta. It was Lent, she was much engaged with her confessors and with prayer and meditation. But the Spanish royal family was accustomed to take the air in the Prado in the afternoons and it was arranged that on the Sunday the Prince should be in a waiting coach when the royal carriages passed by. The Infanta would be wearing a blue ribbon. Although the coaches passed and re-passed each other several times Charles could see little of the lady he had come so far to marry. She, probably, saw more; at any rate her attendants would have reported the royal presence, the grave brow, the expressive eyes, the curling chestnut hair and graceful movements of the young man as he repeatedly removed his hat and bowed his head in salute. It was said that the colour rose in her cheeks as she passed. That evening Charles met the Spanish King. As each of the young men disputed the honour of giving way to the other, Charles saw a boy of barely eighteen, but he was soon to learn that this boy had an appreciation of art and letters far beyond his own and that the Spanish Court was already showing the artistic brilliance that would characterize the reign.

On March 16 Charles and Buckingham made their official entry into Madrid and were conducted to the royal palace, where apartments had been prepared for them. The streets were thronged with excited citizens who sang the song of Lope de Vega:

> Carlos Estuardo soy
> Que, siendo amor mi guia,
> Al cielo d'Espana voy
> Por ver mi estrella Maria

The English party hunted the wolf, the wild boar and the stag, picnicking in the hills with the King and his courtiers. Charles made his kill; he distinguished himself in the tiltyard, he won general admiration by his grace as he dined in public, dressed very simply at first but later in the subdued elegance which was his taste. He was able to compare Spanish masquing with English and to watch that typical Spanish entertainment, the bullfight. He met a Sevillian artist, a year older than himself, who was painting an equestrian portrait of the Spanish King, and was impressed when the finished picture was put on public display in the streets of Madrid. Charles himself sat for the young Velasquez and paid one hundred escudos for the sketch which was made, perhaps intending a finished portrait for the Infanta. Above all, he revelled in the collections of Philip in the Prado and elsewhere. He saw many of the great Titians for the first time and was particularly enthusiastic over *Jupiter and Antiope*, which the King promptly gave him. Charles also acquired *The Girl with the Fur Cloak* and *Charles V with the White Dog*. He frequently visited the collector Don Geronimo Fures y Muenoz, who possessed many Italian masterpieces, and who presented the Prince with paintings and a number of curiously shaped weapons for his collection. Charles brought all the paintings he could, hardly caring what he paid, including Corregio's *St John the Baptist* and an *Erasmus* by Holbein. He was unable to secure some Leonardo drawings he desired and bid unsuccessfully against the King of Spain for a little *Holy Family* of Corregio. When Philip realized what had happened he immediately offered Charles the picture.

In England, simultaneously, official goodwill towards Spain was demonstrated in the entertainment given to the Spanish Ambassador, Inojosa, who was amused with bull and bear baiting but himself provided the best sport by turning a white bear into the Thames where the dogs baited him. The King of Spain sent to the King of England four asses, five camels and one 'ellefant', which created a considerable stir when they arrived in London. Letters came frequently 'To the best of fathers and masters' or to 'Dear Dad and Gossip' in which the writers referred to themselves as 'your Baby', and 'your Dogge' and James replied with long letters to his 'sweet Boys'. Friends, courtiers, servants, news-writers, even Archie, James's fool, were meantime following the trail to Madrid by sea or land in such numbers that Charles had to send some of them home as being too great a burden upon the Spanish Court. There was too great a burden upon the English Exchequer, also, as ships were fitted out to take men and robes of state, horses, accoutrements, presents and ordinary apparel. Ten ships of the King's fleet which had been prepared to fetch the Infanta home were costing some £300 a day as they waited in harbour.

But in Spain things were not going well. Bristol was tactless in mentioning to Charles that the Spaniards expected him to turn Catholic. Charles was indignant: 'I wonder what you have ever found in me that you should conceive I would be so base and unworthy as for a wife to change my religion!' But he did not repeat his remark to the Spaniards and continued to prevaricate when they raised the question of his conversion. He did, however, accept a challenge to dispute with their theologians. He took Buckingham with him and sat down in his chair, the rest on benches before him. There was deep silence. Finally Charles was asked what he would like to hear discussed. He replied that he knew of nothing upon which they could speak that would influence him as he felt no scruple whatsoever. When one of the Fathers nevertheless proceeded to expound upon some words of Christ to Peter, Charles told him he was doing violence to the text and the meeting broke up in disorder.

The Infanta, for her part, found it impossible to contemplate marriage to a Protestant and announced once more that she would enter a nunnery rather than do so. She and Charles had still not met privately and it was not until Easter Day, April 7, that Charles was solemnly escorted by the King himself and a large retinue to the Queen's apartments, where the Infanta sat with her attendants. Even now Charles was expected to address her in the formal manner which Spanish etiquette required. When he flung to the winds his carefully prepared speech and spoke words of his own they came over, even in translation, so highly inappropriate to the Spanish Court that everyone rose and left the room. Undoubtedly the Infanta's attractions were enhanced by her inaccessibility and Charles found himself watching her, 'as a cat doth a mouse', said Olivarez, placing himself where she was likely to pass by but, of necessity, so far away that Buckingham's wife sent him some 'perspective glasses', adding sagely that she thought it a bad sign for the marriage that they let him get no nearer. One morning early Charles determined to break down the ban and made his way to the Casa da Campo, a royal pleasaunce by the river, where the Infanta was accustomed to gather maydew. He gained admittance to the garden but found that a high wall kept him from the orchard where Maria was gathering her flowers. Not to be deterred, he got a lift up from the man who was attending him and leaped from the top of the wall into the orchard almost at her feet. Her shriek as she fled was not what a lover would have wished, neither was his peremptory dismissal by her guardian, who begged him to leave immediately, ushering him out in prosaic fashion through a door in the wall.

In the absence of the Prince's conversion a Papal dispensation was necessary to the marriage. While Charles waited in Madrid the Spaniards became more demanding in their terms and a junta of theologians was in almost daily session considering the minutiae of the situation. Humiliating as his position was, Charles had come to the point where he dare not let go. To return home without the Infanta appeared to him the worst of the possible alternatives. He wrote to his father on April 29 for a free hand to promise what he thought fit, Buckingham supporting the request. The letters from the two young men are extraordinary enough, but still more extraordinary was the easy acquiescence of James which gave Charles full freedom of action. Charles was aware that he could not sign away concessions which required Parliamentary sanction, but he thought he saw his way over this obstacle and wrote again to his father to the effect that he considered a promise merely a promise to do his best: 'if you do your best, although it take not effect, you have not broken your word, for this promise is only a security that you will do your best.' With this comforting self-deception, and a willingness to deceive either the Spaniards or Parliament or both, and thinking to conclude the affair by capitulation, Charles agreed to all the Spanish terms while James, with equal self-deception, showed his exuberance by conferring a Dukedom upon Buckingham on May 18.

The treaties which were accordingly drawn up for James and his Privy Council to sign with the Spanish Commissioners in England, and for Charles and the Spaniards to sign in Madrid, consisted of twenty-three public articles and four private, the private ones guaranteeing the repeal of the penal laws against Catholics within three years, 'a perpetual toleration' of Catholics in England, and free religious discussions between the Prince and his wife. There was nothing in the whole treaty about the Palatinate, the dowry, or even the date of the wedding. But by this time the Spaniards had again hedged and the junta had again come to their assistance: the King of Spain was responsible to the Pope for observance of the treaty and must therefore see it implemented before his sister left Spain. This would require a full twelve months after marriage. Charles was with Buckingham when Olivarez brought this shattering news and the Duke lost his temper in a thoroughly justifiable way. 'There is nothing but trickery and deceit in the whole business!', he exlaimed. 'It had been better you had never meddled with it but left it in Bristol's hands', replied the Condé coldly. The utmost he would concede was that, if Charles agreed to remain in Spain for another year, it might be possible for the marriage to take place immediately.

When Cottington arrived in England with this latest news, preparations were in full swing for the reception of the Infanta as Princess of Wales. Denmark House and St James's Palace were being prepared for her use by Inigo Jones and her chapel was being hurriedly built – a 'temple to the devil', as James described it in one of his less sanguine moments. James was horrified at the latest despatches. 'Your letter', he wrote to Charles, 'hath strucken me dead; I fear it shall very much shorten my days.' The appalling thought of not seeing his 'boys' for another year, of the need to stop the fleet from sailing, of making excuses all round, was finally swamped in the great urge to have them home at all costs. If the Spaniards will not alter their decision, he wrote, you must come speedily away and give over all treaty, otherwise

> never look to see your old Dad again, whom I fear ye shall never see, if you see him not before Winter: Alas, I now repent me sore, that I ever suffered you to go away. I care for Match for nothing, so I may once have you in my arms again: God grant it, God grant it, God grant it, amen, amen, amen.

When the marriage articles arrived shortly afterwards he was sufficiently recovered to go into consultation with Cottington and Conway and he decided to accept them, recommending that Charles be married at once and leave immediately, with the Infanta following in due course. This even meant foregoing the marriage portion, for this would only be despatched with her. He tried to put a brave face upon affairs, hunting as usual, but was apt to break down. 'Do you think', he exclaimed one day to an attendant, bursting into tears, 'that I shall ever see the Prince again?'

Charles believed that his father's consent to the marriage articles would induce the Spaniards to let him take the Infanta with him, but after the ever-courteous exchanges – except where Buckingham and Olivarez were concerned, for they were now barely on speaking terms – the Condé informed Charles that the utmost that could be conceded was a marriage in September and the departure of the Infanta for England in the following March. Charles then replied that he would have to regard the treaty as at an end. They would be grieved, they said, but no obstacle would be placed in the way of the Prince's leaving. The following morning, July 7, Charles requested an audience of the King intending, it was assumed, to take his farewell. To the general astonishment he completely capitulated. He would accept the marriage articles as they stood and agree that the Infanta remain in Spain until March.

For a few days it seemed as though he had won what he desired, even though on the harshest terms. The Infanta was spoken of as the Princess of England, she took English lessons, Charles saw more of her, although they were never alone, and she was allowed to appear in public at the theatre with him. Charles was, however, somewhat affronted when the jewels he produced for his bride were merely shown to her by the King and then set aside. When James heard what Charles had done he was angry but resigned. 'Since it can be no better I must be contented; but this course is . . . a dishonour to me', he wrote. But with the prospect of seeing his two boys soon his mind took a practical turn. A fleet to bring his son home and another to fetch the Infanta meant double charges: 'if they will not send her till March; let them, in God's name, send her by their own fleet', he instructed Charles on July 21 with something of the old spirit. And, he added, with a good deal of common sense and a startling juxtaposition of possibilities, 'upon my blessing, lie not with her in Spain, except ye be sure to bring her with you, and forget not to make them to keep their former conditions anent the portion, otherwise both my Baby and I are bankrupts for ever.'

By July 25 the treaty had been signed in England, James and the Privy Council had sworn to observe its terms – even the Puritan Archbishop of Canterbury behaving, as James put it, remarkably well – and Charles and Philip had signed in Madrid. At this point the Pope fell ill. Although he had agreed to the marriage on the amended terms he had not yet conveyed the necessary dispensation and he died before he could do so. A new dispensation from another Pope and another period of waiting loomed ahead. In the heat of the Spanish summer tempers frayed, quarrels between Protestants and Catholics were becoming embarrassing to Charles as even his own close attendants became involved. In an atmosphere of increasing exasperation he decided to leave for home without waiting for the dispensation, depositing proxy for his marriage with the Earl of Bristol.

Charles had tried too hard, stayed too long. It appeared that even with the most extreme concessions that he could make, short of his own conversion, the Spaniards would find some reason for not allowing the marriage to go forward. But the charade was carried on to the end. On August 29 Charles took his final leave of the Infanta in the presence of the Queen, presents were exchanged and the following day he started for the Escurial accompanied by the King of Spain and his brothers. They spent two days hunting and picnicking in apparent amity, Charles pleaded once more for his sister and Philip spoke of returning the Palatinate as a wedding gift. They said farewell near the Escurial. On September 2 Charles proceeded by coach to the coast with a magnificent escort while Buckingham, after high words with Olivarez, galloped on ahead through the heat. Charles showed his feelings in only one courteous exchange. Asked if he would like his carriage to be open or shut he replied that he would not dare to give his opinion without sending first to Madrid to consult the junta of theologians.

There was still one thing to do. Into one of the most recent exchanges between the Prince, Buckingham and Olivarez, Charles had read the certainty that, even if the marriage were to take place, the Infanta would immediately nullify it, as she would be allowed to do, by retreating into a nunnery. As he rode on, the certainty was borne in upon him that the proxy marriage was simply another chimera. By the time he reached Segovia his mind was made up and he sent Edward Clarke, a confidential servant of Buckingham's, back to Bristol cancelling the proxy which the Ambassador held. That the cancellation was not to be produced until the Prince was clear of the shores of Spain was perhaps a reasonable precaution, though there is no reason to believe that they would have stayed him. Less easy to explain is Charles's instruction that his messenger should not even present his letter to Bristol until after the new Pope's dispensation had arrived. In this way it would be the greatest possible humiliation to the Spaniards. But Charles possibly had also in mind that if the dispensation never materialized the cancellation need never be shown and the onus for the break would rest firmly with the Spaniards.

Early on the morning of September 12 the welcome sight of English horsemen, who had ridden through the night from Santander, brought the news that the fleet had arrived to escort them home. Charles lost no time and, with the bells of Santander ringing in his ears, was on board *The Prince* before nightfall. The sight of a magnificently appointed cabin for the Infanta hardly moved him as he sat himself down in an English ship and conversed at ease with the Earl of Rutland, Buckingham's father-in-law, who was in command, on the familiar topics of home and family. They were held up for some days by bad weather but on September 18, exactly six months after leaving New Hall, they sailed for home.[5]

Much had happened to Charles. If he had ever been in love with Maria he had fallen out of it; but he was aware instead of a deep affection for Buckingham. For six months they had been thrown closely together and Charles now, like his father, was emotionally involved with Steenie. His third emotion was mixed, comprised of a desire to be revenged upon Spain and a desire to find a scapegoat for the whole sorry affair.

8

The Prince's Parliament

Charles reached Portsmouth on October 5 and, despite rough weather, disembarked immediately. He spent a short night at the house of Viscount Annand at Guildford and long before dawn was on his way. News of his arrival had reached the City at midnight and his first sight of London, after six months' absence, was a dull red glow in a northern sky from hundreds of bonfires lit in joy at his return. As he crossed the Thames by Lambeth Stairs at daybreak the fires were paling but the bells of London were pealing out their greeting. He partook of hurried refreshment at Buckingham's house in the Strand, briefly receiving members of the Privy Council meanwhile, and, refusing the inopportune request of the Spanish Ambassador for an audience, took carriage with Buckingham for Royston where his father waited. But such a concourse of people had collected during his brief stop that his carriage could barely proceed up the Strand. It appeared to be 'carried on men's shoulders, and, as he passed, acclamations and blessings resounded from every side'. In the general rejoicing shops remained shut and work was at a standstill, wine was dispensed freely and tables set up in the streets for general feasting. A cartload of condemned criminals who crossed his path on their unhappy way to Tyburn were reprieved at Charles's own command. As evening fell the bonfires were rekindled, anything that would burn serving as fuel. 'The very vintners burnt their bushes in Fleet Street and other places, and their wine was burnt all over London and Westminster into all colours of the rainbow', while the cross in St Paul's churchyard was festooned with as many burning links as the Prince had years. The dull, wet weather made little difference. One hundred and eight bonfires were counted that night between St Paul's and London Bridge alone, and as light departed every window had its candle to illuminate the scene. But Charles and Buckingham had pressed on, pausing only to change coaches at Ware.

90

At Royston James came down from his room to welcome them. As they met on the stairs the Prince and the Duke fell on their knees before the old King and they all wept. Nothing more was seen by the courtiers as the three passed into the privacy of James's room. Apart from Charles's boast, 'I am ready to conquer Spain, if you will allow me to do it!', no details of that first meeting were allowed to penetrate the outer world. Low voices, occasional more emphatic tones and frequent bursts of laughter were all that could be heard. When at last they emerged James was saying that he liked not to marry his son with a portion of his daughter's tears – a remark which, in varying form, would be heard frequently in the following weeks. Once more the emphasis had changed. Little had been heard of the Palatinate during the marriage negotiations. Now that these had failed the three men made a virtue of necessity, attributing the breakdown to Spain's attitude to the German war.

The staging of the reunion at Royston was sound, for the place was distant from London, the roads wretched and the accommodation limited. The weather also helped to keep people away, and for a couple of weeks the three men were able to preserve their privacy, Secretary Conway probably being the only person in their full confidence. Meanwhile nothing could stem the continued rejoicing at the Prince's arrival without the Infanta. At Cambridge every college had a speech and an extra dish for supper, while at St Paul's a solemn service gave thanks for his safe return.[1]

Charles himself had little inclination to celebrate. Letters from Bristol informed him that the Infanta had no intention of going into a convent and could not be forced because after marriage she would be 'her own woman'; she seemed, indeed, the Ambassador reported, more loving towards the Prince than she had been while he was in Spain, she continued her English lessons, was called the Princess of England still, and was weary of the junta and all its restrictions. The Pope's dispensation was expected daily. A misunderstanding had already put Bristol in possession of Charles's cancellation of his proxy but in the circumstances Bristol decided to ignore it until he had heard further from England. Charles now panicked at the thought of being married by proxy to the Princess who, a few weeks earlier, he had so ardently desired. James once more brought in the restoration of the Palatinate as a condition of the marriage while Charles rushed off a series of urgent notes to Bristol: 'Make what shifts or fair excuses you will, but I command you, as you answer it upon your peril, not to deliver my proxy'; 'Whatever answer ye get, ye must not deliver the proxy till ye make my father and me judge of it.' But the Pope's approval of the marriage was delivered to King Philip in Madrid on November 19 while the courtiers bringing these despatches were still pounding their way across Europe. Bristol had only his own reading of the situation to guide him. In accordance with the proxy agreement the date of the wedding was fixed for November 29 and he and Aston ordered clothes for themselves and thirty rich liveries for their attendants. The Spanish erected a tapestry-covered terrace between the royal palace and the church, and invitations were sent out both for the wedding and for the christening of a baby Spanish princess, which was to take place on the same day. Then with preparations at their height, there arrived on the 25th, four days before the ceremonies, the four emissaries from England countermanding the proxy. If Charles's object had been the humiliation of Spain, he could not have succeeded better. The decorations were taken down, the Infanta's English lessons ceased, she was once more the Infanta of Spain and ceased to be the Princess of England.[2]

When he instructed Bristol to withhold his proxy Charles may not have envisaged a situation which worked out with quite so much public humiliation to the Infanta and her family. He did write to her, but his letters were returned unopened. He was then convinced that the Spanish Court had been deceiving him from the beginning and that she was as guilty as anyone else. This was particularly humiliating to a Prince who had wooed as ardently, and as publicly, as Charles. It was, moreover, virtually his first love affair and in the bitterness of his own rejection he had little thought for the feelings of the lady. It was left for the English Ambassador Extraordinary to make the only human comment. The lapse of the proxy, wrote Bristol, would not only put 'great scorn' upon the Spanish King but would be a 'great dishonour' for the Infanta. And, he added, 'whosoever else may have deserved it, she certainly hath not deserved disrespect nor discomfort'. Though her attitude and her feelings remain as remote as those of her family and friends, she was, perhaps, the greatest sufferer in the whole unhappy episode. But her marriage in 1631 to her cousin Ferdinand, the Emperor's son, was more than ordinarily happy. In due course she became Queen of Bohemia and Empress of the Holy Roman Empire, in strange contrast to Charles's sister, the exiled Queen of Bohemia, whose cause had been the origin of Charles's wooing. Maria died in 1646 in childbed of her fourth child with knowledge of the deep strife that wracked the country which might have been her own: whether events would have moved differently if she had been Queen of England neither she nor Charles could conjecture.

The close conference of the three men at Royston and the posting of couriers to and from Spain had occasioned the utmost speculation, and by the middle of October loyalty and curiosity could no longer be restrained, even by the state of the roads and the execrable weather, and everyone was flocking out to Royston to pay their respects. James and his son moved another thirty miles to Hinchinbrook and enjoyed some hunting. They moved next to Newmarket. Then, at the end of the month, with James suffering from undefined pains which made movement difficult, Charles posted to London with Buckingham and at a brief meeting of the Privy Council gave a short account of the Spanish business. As always, physically tireless, rising early and travelling hard in bitter weather, he merely gave himself time to relax in his own palace of St James's on November 1 to see the King's Company perform *The Mayd of the Mill* by Beaumont and Fletcher, and then posted back to Newmarket.

He was in London again on the 5th where, as part of the anniversary observance of the Gunpowder Plot, he saw the Cockpit Company at Whitehall perform *The Gipseys* by Middleton and Rowley. On the 9th he received the Spanish Ambassadors, doing so 'with . . . no more capping nor courtesie then must needs, a lesson belike he learned in Spaine', as Chamberlain noted. In this, and in the way he disposed ostentatiously to his servants of presents he had received from the Spaniards, he set the general tone. Archie, the jester, fooled around in a suit given him by the Condé d'Olivarez, the tongues of courtiers who had been in Spain were loosed, and stories of ill-usage, scant food, discourtesies, bigotry, as well as of the general poverty of the country outside the capital, were soon circulating. There was even talk of the Spaniard's design on Charles – it was a marvel he got away so easily – he had only his sister to thank for that, her succession being infinitely more to be feared by the Spaniards than his own. To emphasize the difference between the two countries, as well as to celebrate their return, Buckingham gave a feast of 'superabundant plenty' on November 18 of which the centre piece consisted of twelve pheasants piled on one dish, forty dozen partridges, and forty dozen quail. James and Charles partook and the three of them attended a masque by John Maynard, the main theme of which was congratulation to the Prince on his return.

In the general obsession with Spanish affairs the burning of Alderman Cockayne's house in Cheapside on November 15 created but a passing diversion, even though he lost £10,000 in goods and merchandise. He was a hard man, who had retained his own wealth in spite of the ruin of thousands of poor cloth workers through his unhappy project of dyeing cloth, and there was little interest and no pity to spare for him. More serious were the smallpox and a contagious, spotted fever which were raging as the year drew to a close, claiming their victims by death and by the dreaded pock marks. In spite of so many unpropitious circumstances, attempts were made by the Court to enjoy Christmas and to rehearse the Twelfth Night masque as usual. *Neptune's Triumph for the Return of Albion* by Ben Jonson had to be postponed and finally abandoned on the excuse of the King's indisposition, but rumour had it that the French and Spanish Ambassadors would not attend together, and it was difficult to give precedence to either. Charles, continuing to evince his pleasure in the drama, attended all the Christmas plays, which included *The Bondman* by Massinger and Middleton's *The Changeling*.

James was still struggling to maintain his policy of friendship with Spain. Charles, on the other hand, could see no alternative but war to recover the Palatinate and bring Spain to her knees. Buckingham agreed with him. He was not only stung by the failure of what he expected to be his greatest triumph, he was humiliated by the knowledge that his charm had not succeeded against the *gravitas* of the Spanish nobility. His measure of pique and irritation overflowed when he learned that his name had not been inscribed upon the commemorative pillar erected at the Escurial. But one thing was certain. If there was to be war there must be money. And to obtain supplies it was necessary to call a Parliament.

James accepted the situation reluctantly and on December 28, sorely against his will, signed the warrant for the issue of writs for the new Parliament. The dilemma he was in possibly accounts for the fact that there is almost no evidence of James's direct intervention in the elections. Charles and Buckingham, on the other hand, exerted themselves to the utmost to obtain the return of pro-war and anti-Spanish members who would support them. It was Charles's first experience of attempting to 'manage' a Parliament and he made no bones about using his patronage and pressing his candidates wherever he could.

On his Cornish estates, for example, letters went out in his name recommending candidates for at least thirteen boroughs, though only five were returned, including Sir Richard Weston for Bossiney and Thomas Carey, son of Robert, for Helston. At Chichester in Sussex Sir Thomas Edmondes's success was probably due to the Prince's support; Sir Henry Vane, Charles's cofferer, was returned for Carlisle – without patronage though he was a known friend of the Prince. Francis Finch, Charles's nominee, was returned for Eye in Suffolk and Ralph Clare, of the Prince's Privy Chamber, for Bewdley – but he was also lord of the manor and was supported by local loyalty. On the Prince's Yorkshire estates another second generation Carey, Sir Henry, was returned on Charles's nomination for Beverley. But there were also distinct refusals. In Boroughbridge Sir Edmund Verney, supported by the Prince, was turned down in favour of Ferdinando Fairfax. In Plymouth and Coventry the Prince's nominees were passed over in favour of the City recorders, John Glanville and Sir Edward Coke, while Cottington was turned down three times, possibly because of his Catholic affiliations, before being returned for Camelford. Obviously, apart from direct intervention, there were friendships, connections, and general goodwill which secured the return of candidates favourable to Charles.

Buckingham had less territorial patronage to exercise, but his network of family connections and office dependencies was vast and he was able to ensure the return of members who would support his policy. So the Parliament of 1624, although by no means 'packed', was an assembly in which there was considerable support for Charles and Buckingham. But although it was likely to be anti-Spanish, it was not so certain that it would also be pro-war. Members came to Parliament with many interests to serve. On the whole they were hard-headed and kept their purse-strings tight. Charles begged his father to act with decision, to think of his sister and her children. Elizabeth herself was full of hope; 'my brother', she wrote to Sir Thomas Roe, 'doth show so much love to me in all things, as I cannot tell you how much I am glad of it.' She had particular hope from the Parliament for it began on their dear dead brother's birthday.

On that day, February 19, after two postponements because of plague, James opened what was to be his last Parliament with considerable pomp. He told the members how sadly he had been deceived by Spain, how he wanted peace but was forced to admit that the omens were otherwise. He asked their advice: 'I assure you ye may freely advise me, seeing of my princely fidelity you are invited thereto.' This was an innovation, indeed, the King delivering to them, unsolicited, the right to discuss both foreign policy and, by implication, his son's marriage. He dealt briefly with the Spanish visit, explaining that Charles had gone to find out in the quickest way what the Spaniards intended. This was a good resolution, James asserted, clinching the matter with an aphorism: 'I had general hopes before, but Particulars will resolve matters, Generals will not'. The details of the Spanish journey, he told them, would be communicated by Buckingham supported by Charles. The Speaker, Sir Thomas Crew, indicated at once the anti-Papist feeling of the House by desiring the strict execution of the recusancy laws. On the question of the Palatinate he was cool: 'God, in His due Time, will restore the distraught Princess.'

On February 24, in the great hall of Whitehall Palace, where it was usual for kings to preside, Buckingham in robes of state held the centre of the stage while he gave his account to the Lords of the Spanish adventure, supported and supplemented by Charles. Three days later Weston, the Chancellor of the Exchequer, repeated the tale to the Commons. The detailed story made bitter hearing. The Duke was now at the height of his power and, next to the Prince, the most popular man in England. When the Spanish Ambassador complained that he had slandered the Spanish king Parliament promptly retaliated by declaring that Buckingham deserved commendation as good patriot and loyal minister. Even his former enemies now joined the anti-Spanish and pro-war group which he led. No wonder it was said 'that never before did meet in one man . . . so much love of the King, Prince and People. He sways more than ever for whereas he was before a favourite to the King, he is now a favourite to the Parliament, people, and city, for breaking the match with Spain'.[3]

Observers noted at the same time Charles's assumption of power, 'entering into command of affairs by reason of the King's absence and sickness, and all men address themselves unto him'. The 'brave Prince' never missed a day at the Parliament, he was frequently in the Council Chamber, he organized affairs tirelessly and with care, riding backwards and forwards between Royston or Newmarket and London, rebuking any who opposed him, keeping the reins firmly in his hands. He had grown a beard while in Spain, he was 'somewhat stouter' and the Spanish experience had matured him. One observer was so impressed by his bearing that he thought 'he had concealed himself before'. To some he seemed a little too popular. 'The Prince his carriage at this Parliament', wrote the Earl of Kellie to the Earl of Mar in May, 'has been lytill too populare, and I dout his father was lytill of that mynd.' As a result there was 'not the harmonye betwyxt the Kings Majestie and the Prince' as could be wished.

A surprising development, considering his speech defect, was the frequency with which he spoke in Parliament; his slight stammer persisted, but it never deterred him, and he knew how to use his youth and his rank to the best advantage. On March 12, for example, he reported to the House of Lords on the findings of a committee which had met the previous day. In supplying money for war, he reported, 'it was fit to use Expedition, and so to provide, that we might not only shew our Teeth and do no more; but also be able to bite, when there should be Cause'. 'And', he added,

> Gentlemen, I pray you think seriously of this Business: take it to Heart, and consider in it, First, my Father's Honour, Secondly mine, and more particularly mine, because it is my new entering into the world: If in this ye shall fail me, ye shall not only dishonour and discourage me, but bring Dishonour upon yourselves. But, if ye go with Courage, and shew Alacrity and Readiness in this Business, ye shall so oblige me unto you now, that I will never forget it hereafter; and, when Time doth serve, ye shall find your Loves and your Labours well bestowed.

The peroration was, perhaps, hardly adroit. But Charles had judged his audience well, and the immature words from the young Prince were strangely disarming. 'This Conclusion did so take us', wrote one who was present, 'That we all prayed God to bless him, as we had just Cause to honour him.' He was now, indeed, 'the glorious prince' of Conway's letter to Carleton, and the session began to be called 'the Prince's Parliament'.[4]

It was the considered policy of Charles and Buckingham to keep James away from Westminster, for they feared the influence of his basically pacific policy upon the basically parsimonious members. Conversely they wanted to keep away from James anyone who would encourage his lingering desire for peace with Spain. The two men whose influence they had most cause to fear were Lionel Cranfield, Earl of Middlesex, James's Lord Treasurer, and John Digby, Earl of Bristol, James's Ambassador Extraordinary in Madrid. Bristol they endeavoured to keep out of the country for as long as possible, Middlesex they turned upon immediately. Middlesex, James's most successful Treasurer, who 'had built up a surplus out of a deficit', wanted the Spanish dowry as much as James himself did. He was shocked at the expenditure incurred by the Spanish journey and in Council he spoke against all warlike proposals from the point of view of one who has to find the money. On Charles's return from Madrid he was the only Privy Councillor to maintain that the Prince ought to continue with the Spanish marriage, whereupon Charles lost his temper and 'bade him judge of his merchandise, for he was no arbiter in points of honour'. But Middlesex could not be dismissed in this way. His success as Treasurer and his position close to James made him dangerous. Yet he was also vulnerable. In removing financial malpractices, in sweeping away graft and unnecessary expenditure, in his attitude to monopolies, Middlesex, like Bacon before him, had made enemies. Like Bacon, he had swum a little too near the edge in his own financial practices, and his own fortune was considerable. It was not difficult for his enemies to build up a case against him. It came to a head on 18 April 1624 in charges of bribery, extortion, oppression and 'other grievous misdemeanours', which were laid before the House of Lords by Sir Edward Coke and Sir Edwin Sandys, who used for the purpose the old practice of impeachment which had been used for Bacon's trial three years earlier.

James did what he could to save Middlesex but was hampered by the knowledge that Charles was deeply involved. It hardly needed Williams, his Lord Keeper, to write to him, 'your Son, the Prince, is the main Champion that encounters the Treasurer; whom, if you save, you foil your Son. For, though Matters are carried by the whole Vote of Parliament, and are driven on by the Duke, yet they that walk in Westminster Hall, call this the Prince's Undertaking.' In the absence of Buckingham through illness it was, indeed, Charles himself who led the attack upon Middlesex, disregarding his father's advice 'that he should not take part with a Faction in either House . . .' and should 'take heed, how he bandied to pluck down a Peer of the Realm by the Arm of the Lower House, for the Lords were the Hedge between himself and the People; and a Breach made in that Hedge, might in time perhaps lay himself open.'

James made a good speech in the defence of Middlesex. 'I were deceived, if he were not a good officer', he said. 'He was Instrument, under Buckingham, for the Reformation of the Household, the Navy, and the Exchequer.' 'All Treasurers', he asserted in one of his telling generalizations, 'if they do good service to their Master, must be generally hated.' He emphasized the point that, apart from Bacon's impeachment, there was no precedent for informers being in the Lower House while the Judges were in the Upper House.

> If the Accusations come in by the Parties wronged, then you have a fair Entrance for Justice; if by Men that search and hunt after other Men's Lives and Actions, beware of it; it is dangerous; it may be your own Case another Time. . . . Let no Man's particular ends bring forth a Precedent that may be prejudicial to you all, and your Heirs after you.

The question was not publicly asked – but was James thinking of any particular man's 'particular ends', and could that man have been Buckingham? In private he turned upon the Duke with the fury of a Hebrew prophet: 'By God, Steenie!', he exclaimed, 'you are a fool, and will shortly repent this folly!' while to Charles he burst out in anger that he would live to have his bellyfull of impeachments. 'When I am dead', he continued with even more prophetic insight, 'you will have too much cause to remember how much you have contributed to the weakening of the Crown by the two expedients you are now so fond of – war, and impeachment!'.

The sentence against Middlesex, delivered on May 13, was severe. He was to lose all his offices, to be incapable of holding any state office in future, to be fined £50,000, prohibited from taking his seat in Parliament or even coming within the verge of the Court, and to be imprisoned in the Tower during the King's pleasure. His prison sentence was remitted, his fine reduced, but he had been rendered powerless.[5]

On March 8 an Address of Both Houses had recommended that the treaty with Spain should be broken, and on March 20 the Commons voted three subsidies and three fifteenths (about £300,000) to be in the Exchequer within one year of the breaking of the treaty. The pill was sweetened and James had to swallow it. On March 22 he agreed to annul the Spanish treaty although it was not until April 6 that he permitted the departure of the courier carrying the information to Spain. Even then a separate letter to the English Ambassador at Madrid directed him to inform the Spanish King that, although James had listened to the advice of his Parliament, he was not bound to take it. But if James was slipping from his part of the bargain, Parliament put a bite in theirs by electing a Council of War, the first of its kind, to administer the taxes raised under Parliamentary supervision.

For the time being there was general agreement that the subsidy should be used for the repair of fortifications, for fitting out the fleet, reinforcing troops in Ireland (England's 'back door'), and helping the Dutch Repulic. Clashes with the Dutch in the East Indies, even the so-called massacre of Amboyna on February 11, seemed so little relevant to the European situation that in June England agreed to pay 2000 troops for two years to help the Dutch maintain their independence against Spain. Mansfeld came to London in April in an interval of the fighting. Charles made much of him; and the London populace, who fully approved his lodging in state in the apartments which had been prepared for the Infanta, gave him an enthusiastic welcome. On the 16th he went to Theobalds to see James who promised him 13,000 men and £20,000 a month if the French would do likewise. Charles was jubilant. Now, he declared, he had something worth writing to his sister about and she would hear tidings better and better every day!

Yet when Bristol arrived home on April 24 there was bound to be some anxiety. James had called him home on December 30, ostensibly as a reprimand, but it was possible that he hoped for the support of his pro-Spanish Ambassador against his Parliament. It took Bristol some time to assemble his own household goods, the possessions which Charles had left behind, and the jewels which the Spanish royal family had returned. He also had difficulty in raising funds for the journey, having lent profusely to Charles to pay for the Prince's farewell presents. In the end he pawned his plate, but it was not until March 17 that he left Madrid, the Spaniards expressing the utmost sorrow at his departure. He hardly realized the strength of the forces against him until he reached the French coast and found no vessel waiting to bear him home. Such delay was in keeping with the endeavours of Charles and Buckingham to keep him out of the country until Parliament had risen, for they feared nothing more than a fresh appraisal of the situation under Bristol's guidance. When he landed in England on April 24 he was put under house arrest and refused access to the King. Although Buckingham was ill, Charles pressed the case against the Ambassador with vindictiveness: 'I fear if you are not with us to helpe charge him', he wrote to the Duke, 'he may escape with too slight a charge.' Bristol was still under restraint when the Parliamentary session ended on May 29. The only reply to his reiterated demand for a hearing had been the appointment of a commission who presented him with a series of interrogatories which, in substance, were the charges made against him by Charles and Buckingham: that he had expected, even encouraged, the Prince to change his religion on his first coming to Spain; that he advised the Prince to stay longer in Spain than he should have done; that he had never insisted upon the restitution of the Palatinate to Frederick; that, overall, he was dilatory in getting a conclusion to the marriage treaty; and that, in the end, he did not obey the Prince's instructions concerning the proxy. In short, everything that had been misconceived, everything that had gone wrong, all the mistakes made by Charles himself, were laid on Bristol's shoulders.

The Earl's reply to the charges, which he reiterated in many letters to the King and to his friends, was always the same: on the matter of religion he had done no more than ask the Prince to make his position clear, he had been at one with James in hoping to receive from the match a worthy lady for Charles, a portion three times as large as had ever before been given, and the restitution of the Palatinate – for which, Bristol asserted, 'a daughter of Spain and two million had been no ill pawne'. He maintained that three months more would have decided the matter one way or another, yet he had been forced to see 'the whole state of affairs turned upside down' through no fault of his own. As for the proxy, he had acted as he thought proper, and in accordance with the Prince's honour, until he received a direct cancellation from England, when he withdrew it immediately.

The replies were straightforward, the Commission declared itself satisfied, the King was willing to see Bristol. Yet the Earl had hardly been tactful: he had questioned Charles's honour over the business of the proxy, he had implied that Charles had not been forthright in maintaining his religion, that Charles's decision to leave was taken at the wrong time and, overall, that it would have been better if the whole affair had been left in his hands. Yet such was Bristol's loyalty that he could hardly be touched. 'Whilst I thought the King desired the match I was for it against all the world', he wrote to Cottington. 'If his Majestye and the Prince will have a warr', he continued, 'I will spende my life and fortunes in it.' Buckingham and Charles suggested that if Bristol would retire to his country house all proceedings against him would be dropped. Bristol, with calm, exasperating integrity, continued to assert that if he had done anything wrong let his case be investigated, for he required only justification or death. House confinement continued, mainly on his manor of Sherborne, but he was not allowed at Court and he never saw James again.[6]

Parliament meantime coupled the Subsidy Act with a promise from James that no immunity for English Catholics would be included in any treaty for his son's marriage, and it called for an oath from Charles, which he swore in Parliament on 5 April 1624, that 'whensoever it should please God to bestow upon him any lady that were Popish, she should have no further liberty but for her own family, and no advantage to recusants at home'. In calling for these assurances the Houses were not unmindful of rumours that another marriage treaty with another Catholic Princess was already under consideration. Perhaps they did not realize how far the considerations had already gone.

9

A Daughter of France

Even before they left Spain, and while the question of the proxy was still outstanding, Charles and Buckingham had turned their thoughts to general strategy and, in particular, to the question of an alternative marriage alliance. The obvious Court for a new wooing was that of France where, although two Princesses had gone, to Spain and to Savoy respectively, there still remained little Henrietta-Maria, now entering her fifteenth year. France was generally held to be less obdurate on religious matters than Spain, and she still had powerful political reasons for lining up against the Hapsburg. Charles and Buckingham had talked in Madrid to an enigmatic friar named Grey, who had let fall the no doubt inspired belief that a French match was still open to Charles, and he had been despatched from Santander, with great secrecy, before Charles sailed for home, to sound the French Court further. The response, though guarded, was sufficiently encouraging for Henry Rich, Viscount Kensington, to be sent to Paris at the end of February 1624 to pursue the matter.

On the social side Kensington's embassy soon made headway. Handsome, polished, easy spoken, familiar with the language, fond of the French and a former lover of the Duchesse de Chevreuse, he had soon met not only the Queen Mother but Henrietta-Maria herself. She was 'the sweetest creature in France', he assured Charles, she danced well and sang most sweetly; and, commenting upon her known small stature, 'her growth is very little short of her age', he said, 'and her wisdom is infinitely beyond it. I heard her discourse with her mother, and the ladies about her, with extraordinary discretion and quickness.' Kensington also indicated a warmth in Madame, as she was known, which had been all too lacking in the Infanta, telling how anxious she had been to see a miniature of the Prince which he had been showing to some of the courtiers. She contrived to borrow it, blushing as she

103

opened it, and kept it for an hour, finally returning it with many praises. It was not difficult for Kensington to talk himself into a private interview with the Princess in which he dwelt upon Charles's virtues and his ardent desire for marriage. Henrietta-Maria knew well enough that this was a second wooing but, according to Kensington, she 'drank down his words with joy' and, with a low curtsey, added 'that she was extremely obliged to his Highness, and would think herself happy in the occasion that should be presented of meriting the place shee held in his good esteem'. From other remarks attributed to her it is likely, indeed, that she wanted to be a queen, that to be Queen of England appealed to her, and that, moreover, she had been genuinely attracted to the Prince she had seen at the French Court but who had no eyes for her at the time. 'The Prince', she is reputed to have said, 'need not have travelled so far to find a wife.' On hearing a rumour that Mlle de Montpensier was to be offered to the Prince in her stead she fell into such a passion that her mother had difficulty in calming her.

This distant and successful love-making was sweet to Charles after the frustrations of the Spanish wooing. Henrietta-Maria was the sixth and youngest child and third daughter of the Italian Marie de Medici and the Bourbon Henri IV of France. She was still in her cradle when her father was assassinated by the Catholic fanatic, François Ravaillac, as a protest against the King's toleration of the Huguenots. Her eldest brother became King as Louis XIII at the age of eight in May 1610, her mother acting as Regent until 1614, when Louis came into his majority. The younger children were brought up at St Germain-en-Laye, about two hours' coach ride from Paris, under the care of Madame de Montglat – the Mamangat of their early letters – to whom they were devoted. Henrietta herself formed an even stronger attachment to her governess's daughter, Madame de Saint-Georges, who was her constant companion. There was not much formal education at St Germain-en-Laye, but Henrietta inherited the quick wit of her father, a French aptness for the right phrase, and an obstinacy that was all her own. At fifteen she had barely learned to translate this obstinacy into determination.

While on the personal side the French marriage negotiations seemed to be going well, there were signs that the French were going to be hard bargainers, second only to the Spaniards, and in May the Earl of Carlisle (the former Viscount Doncaster) was sent to Paris to lend weight to the diplomatic manoeuvring. The French, like the

Spaniards, refused to include a military alliance in the marriage treaty but they expected, nevertheless, toleration for English Catholics. The steps by which agreement was reached were all too familiar, the English being beaten, stage by stage, into promising more than they could perform. The French would accept no verbal guarantee of toleration but demanded a written statement, signed and sealed. In view of the undertaking made to Parliament by James and by Charles this was impossible. James refused the French request, Carlisle was angry, Buckingham was for acquiescence, Charles, at first indignant, lost his indignation and wanted his father to agree. After two days of torment, egged on by the Duke and the Prince, James agreed on September 7, but on condition that his acceptance took the form of a letter. Kensington was rewarded with a peerage and became the Earl of Holland on September 15. Charles was delighted. 'The business', he wrote to Carlisle, 'is all brought to so good an issue that . . . I hope that the treaties will be shortly brought to a happy conclusion.' The Privy Council was informed and had little alternative but to accept the King's agreement and its corollary – the suspension of the laws against recusants. But Parliament was due to reassemble on November 2, and to face the House before the marriage was actually accomplished was to invite disaster. So it was prorogued until February on the pretext of plague. Yet the French were not satisfied, they refused to accept a letter, and repeated their demand for an official document signed and sealed by James; at the same time refusing to put into writing the minimal engagements of financial and military aid which them-selves were prepared to undertake.

But Charles was now as bent upon the French match, and as willing to accept any conditions to effect it, as he had been upon the Spanish match. A rumour that the Spaniards were despatching Gondomar again to England alarmed him. He spoke plainly to his father. He would never match with Spain. If not with France, who would his father find for him? James was startled, horrified and angry. But there was logic in Charles's reasoning; what other alliance was there? So James agreed to do what Charles wanted – which entailed breaking his own and his son's engagement to Parliament concerning Catholics.

The English Ambassadors in Paris signed the treaty on 10 November 1624. On December 12 it was ratified at Cambridge by James and Charles in the presence of Buckingham and Conway, the only members of the Privy Council allowed to attend. James's hands were so crippled with arthritis that he could barely sign. The public engagements provided freedom of worship for Henrietta; gave into her care the education of any children of the marriage until their thirteenth year; guaranteed a chapel, which should be open to English Catholics, at all places where she resided; allowed twenty-eight religious attendants for her worship who would be permitted to wear their habits in public, and a domestic establishment of French Catholics chosen by the King of France. The secret engagement, signed by James and Charles, promised that all English Catholics imprisoned for their religion should be freed, that no English Catholic should be persecuted because of his religion, and that any Catholic deprived of property since the previous July should have it restored. In return for this, the French gave the bride a dowry of £120,000, a vague verbal assurance of military assistance, an unwritten promise to pay Mansfeld and his troops for six months, to allow him to land at a French port and to proceed through part of France if he thought fit.

Before welcoming the bride it was necessary for the English to carry out their part of the agreement, which they did as quietly as possible. On December 24 the recusancy laws were suspended. On the 26th an order was issued to the Lord Keeper for the release of all Catholics imprisoned for offences connected with their religion. James salved his conscience by a verbal twist – his promise to Parliament spoke of a treaty, his undertaking to the French was in an accompanying document. Charles later explained his agreement to the secret terms on the grounds that, with the French King's knowledge, he had signed in order to satisfy the Pope and obtain his dispensation for the marriage; it was never intended, he claimed, that the agreement should be binding.

He now felt he could write to Henrietta himself, but he had great difficulty in composing his letters, altering the rough drafts several times.

> I have not dared to take the liberty of testifying to you, by a single line, the great impatience with which my spirit has been tormented, during my long waiting for the happy accomplishment of this treaty, until I received good tidings of it; begging you to be assured that, besides the renown of your virtues and perfections, which is everywhere spread abroad, my happiness has been completed by the honour which I have already had of seeing your person, although unknown to you; which sight has completely satisfied me that the exterior of your person in no degree belies the lustre of your virtues. But I cannot, by writing, express the passion of my soul to have the honour of being esteemed
>
> Yours etc.

He sent the letter, with his portrait, by Sir Thomas Carey, and there followed jewels of great price, which included a necklace of one hundred and twenty large pearls, a diamond of 'incomparable size and worth', and two diamond earrings in the shape of pearls.[1]

Much had been accomplished in the fifteen months since the return from Spain, but the difficult weather and the emotional strains were taking their toll. Charles stood up to both better than his father and Buckingham. James was repeatedly ailing, Buckingham was seriously ill in May and when he reappeared in June looked so pale and haggard that people spoke of attempts by the Spaniards to poison him. This was not so far-fetched as might appear, for the Spanish envoys were doing their best to discredit the Duke. Diplomatic relations had not been severed with Spain and there remained in England the Marquis of Inojosa, who had been sent as Ambassador Extraordinary in the spring of 1623 to deal with the marriage negotiations, and Don Carlos Coloma, who had succeeded Gondomar as Ambassador. This Rosencrantz and Guildenstern combination, with the aid of a handful of Spanish agents, supplied a continuing chorus and much of the off-stage action to the first half of 1624. As characters they were Jonsonian rather than Shakespearean and their antics could hardly have been surpassed in the mind of Jonson himself. Four paid informants (whose names were never revealed in spite of Buckingham's offer of £10,000) kept them appraised of events in Parliament at £100 a time. Complaining that James was isolated by the deliberate policy of Buckingham, they were reduced to slipping notes to the King when Charles and the Duke were off their guard; they made contact with James through Don Francisco de Carondelet, Archdeacon of Cambrai and chaplain to Coloma; they obtained back-door access to him through various servants. Another member of the network was on his way from Spain with fresh instructions when he was set upon in Flanders and robbed of his papers by assailants disguised with false beards, whose identity was never discovered but who were suspected to be in the pay of Buckingham.

The object of all this activity was to keep England from war and, as an immediate goal, to separate Buckingham from James. Their attack upon Buckingham's narration to Parliament as a libel upon the Spanish King was too flimsy to gain credence but they then built up a more elaborate plot in which Charles figured as well as the favourite. James, it was alleged by the Spaniards in one of their clandestine interviews with the King, was to be kept in the comfortable seclusion of one of his country houses while the Prince, with the support of the Duke, ruled in his place. Already James was, they declared, a prisoner and besieged, his very servants creatures of Buckingham, and people were saying it would be a great happiness if the Prince reigned instead. On another occasion they brought up a story which had, in fact, been circulating for some time, that Buckingham planned to marry his little daughter to Elizabeth's son, so joining his family to the royal line and perhaps even securing the succession.

James remained calm, merely muttering that Buckingham had he knew not how many devils in him since his return from Spain, and that Charles was strangely carried away with rash and youthful notions; yet, if what he heard of Buckingham were true, he would have his head cut off! He was sufficiently upset to greet the two young men with tears in his eyes as he proceeded by way of St James's to Windsor for the Garter ceremonies of April 1624 and Buckingham did not accompany the King and the Prince. Shortly afterwards, however, the Duke made his peace, categorically denying any desire or plan to marry his daughter to Elizabeth's son. Elizabeth made her own denial. The Spanish envoys could not substantiate any of their charges and Inojosa left the country on June 26 in a merchant ship, a mark of grave disrespect to an ambassador.[2]

After a backward spring the summer of 1624 had set in hot and dry and plague and spotted fever persisted. Charles found time to remember his old friend, Dallington, who was knighted and given the headmastership of Charterhouse in July; as with Murray at Eton Charles had to fight the bishops in insisting upon the appointment for his nominee. In the autumn a mellow and temperate season brought relief as well as an abundant harvest of grain and fruit. Charles took pleasure in hunting, but suffered a severe fall from which it took him some while to recover. They all tried to enjoy Christmas with some of the old gaiety: after all, the French treaty had been signed, Parliament was not sitting, 10,000 volunteers had joined the Dutch in the summer and the drums in the City were beating up more, while sufficient men had been impressed to provide Mansfeld with an army of sorts. It was these pressed men and their pay and maintenance that were the most pressing problems. The men who already were fighting in Europe were volunteers. They knew what they were fighting for and their condition, though often bad, was rarely absolutely desperate. The men now pressed for Mansfeld's army were different. At the end of the year they were still at Dover, there were insufficient vessels to carry them to France, insufficient food to feed them while they waited, insufficient authority to discipline them. Many who had homes to go to were running away, those to whom pillage was second nature were sacking shops and ravishing farms; hunger, cold, dirt and disease were reducing the most ordinary of men, swept up from their villages and their occupations by the press gang, to bands of marauders seeking food and shelter. Mansfeld had exhausted the October and November payments and, while the Privy Council spoke of martial law, he was demanding payment for December. Charles, with the incisive action of which he was sometimes capable, perceived the need and borrowed on his own personal security from Philip Burlamachi.

Though this merely relieved, and did not solve the problem, Charles made a great effort to entertain his cousin Christian who had briefly interrupted his fighting for Elizabeth to visit England. There was a show of dancing and the Twelfth Night masque, Jonson's *The Fortunate Isles*, was played on January 9. But James kept to his chamber, suffering from gout and depression. Not only had his control of foreign policy, so jealousy guarded throughout his reign, been wrenched from him but Charles was so bent on war that even his relationship with his son had changed. The dominant relationship which at one time had been the King and the Duke and had then become the King, the Duke and the Prince, was now the Prince and the Duke. Infirmity combined with inadequacy to produce depression. 'I am an old king', James had said to his Parliament – and there had been the suggestion not only that he was old in wisdom but that he was old in years.

It is difficult to say how far Charles and Buckingham were thinking in terms of the succession. Charles was no longer in awe of his father, and in proportion as he found he could guide Parliament his dependence upon James lessened. But his determination to purge himself of the Spanish humiliation was something of an obsession and he could still fear the pro-Spanish peace policy of the King. It had been difficult to keep James from listening to the Earl of Bristol and there would be cause for alarm if the threatened conjunction with Gondomar was allowed to take place. How far Charles wanted to be free, to act without recourse to the old man who now so often waited at Theobalds or Newmarket or Royston for the messages of his son, is mere conjecture.

As for Buckingham, he was now so firmly attached to Charles that he had no fear of the succession: he might, indeed, even welcome an end to the maudlin protestations of affection which James, though somewhat perfunctorily, continued to bestow upon him. Moreover, there were straws to indicate that his popularity in that quarter might be waning, and it is possible that, once the joy of reunion was over, Buckingham sensed that his relationship with the King was not the same as before. The Earl of Clarendon, writing long after the event, said that the delicate Spanish marriage negotiations were 'solely broken' by the journey to Spain and that James 'never forgave the Duke of Buckingham'. The Venetian Ambassador, although thinking at first that the Duke was high in favour with James on his return from Spain, reversed his opinion later. 'I am assured', he wrote, 'that the King is tired of Buckingham.'[3]

In the New Year of 1625 James roused himself, took an interest in affairs, and hunted from some of his favourite lodges. But on March 5, while at Theobalds, he was taken with a tertian ague. At first it did not seem serious, but an intermittent fever became so severe that he was driven to thrust his hands in cold water and to drink quantities of small beer to cool himself. By the 12th these fits were subsiding and he prepared to move to Hampton Court. A curious situation then developed. Buckingham was at Theobalds, and so was his mother, a lady of whom James had never been fond. Together they decided to by-pass James's physicians and apply some remedies of their own which allegedly had helped the Duke when he was ill. Accordingly some medicine and a plaster were obtained from Dr John Remington, who lived at Dunmow in Essex. James was given the medicine by the Duke, the plaster was applied by Buckingham's mother in the absence of James's doctors. When the next bout of fever ensued it was very bad and the physicians, realizing what had happened, protested strongly. But they were ordered from the room and the same treatment was repeated with the same adverse results. Dr Crappe, who protested particularly violently, was ordered not only out of the room but away from the Court by Buckingham.

Later, realizing that he was now very ill, James begged the Earl of Pembroke not to leave him and sent for his old friend, Launcelot Andrewes, Bishop of Winchester. But Andrewes himself was too sick to rise from his bed and John Williams, Bishop of Lincoln, set out for Theobalds from London. William Harvey, one of the physicians in attendance, informed him that death was near, and with Charles's permission Williams prepared the King for his end. On March 24

James made profession of his faith in the presence of Charles, Williams, Buckingham, and his chief ministers, receiving communion according to the rites of the Church of England. He had a long talk, quite alone, with Charles, everyone else being ordered two or three rooms away so that there was no possibility of being overheard. The secrets of the deathbed confidences were never disclosed. For three more days he lingered. In the early hours of the 27th he called for Charles who came hurrying to him in night attire. But when Charles arrived his father was beyond speech and died shortly afterwards. He was in his fifty-seventh year.

After he had spent two or three hours in retirement Charles was proclaimed at Theobalds gate by the Knight Marshall as King of England, Scotland, France and Ireland. He then took coach for St James's and that evening was similarly proclaimed in London at Whitehall Gate, at Cheapside, and in other parts of the capital. Buckingham rode with him, in the same coach, and lay that night in the same chamber. Also in the same coach was the new King's Puritan chaplain, John Preston, who had hurried to Theobalds on news of James's relapse. Spiritual consolation would have been looked for from a chaplain and in the anti-Spanish turn of events Preston was not unwelcome: the significance of the episode was hardly as great as the Puritans cared to think. A suite was prepared for Buckingham next to the new King's in St James's, where Charles elected to stay until after the funeral, and the Duke was sworn of the King's bedchamber. Elizabeth wrote of the loss 'of so loving a father'; she could hardly say more, for his practical help had been little. But she said her sorrow would have been much greater had not God left her 'so dear and loving a brother . . . in whom, next God', she now placed all her confidence.

Rumours of poison were common enough in the seventeenth century. But many strange and unexplained circumstances surround the death of James. Why should Buckingham bring his mother to the King's deathbed? Why, when James appeared to be well enough to travel to Hampton Court, did he introduce another form of treatment? Why were the King's own doctors ordered from the room? Suspicions were strong enough for Dr John Eglisham to retrieve a piece of the plaster which had been used and to take it to Dr Remington who had allegedly supplied it. Remington, in surprise, declared it was not his plaster. Eglisham was compelled to flee the country but the following year published his evidence in a pamphlet printed in Frankfurt. Meanwhile, the doctors who embalmed the King found his organs reasonably sound and no signs of poison, while Dr Harvey consistently dissociated himself from the charge. It is possible that James, like his son Henry and his mother Mary, was suffering from porphyria; he had been subject increasingly to vomiting, pain, and intermittent fever and these, as with Henry, caused people to think of poison. Besides, Buckingham's actions were performed too publicly for those of a would-be assassin – unless he was relying upon his position and the very openness of his actions to shield him. Motive, indeed, there may have been for on the very day that James was taken ill there came news that Gondomar was on his way and that he came neither unwelcome nor unsent for. The French match was still not beyond a breach and it was being whispered that there was no bulwark strong enough against Gondomar, but that he would 'mar all'. There was even talk of the Spanish match again, and that Gondomar's coming would again quicken that business. Buckingham had no need to be reminded of the effect of Gondomar on the convalescent and still weak King. More sinister was the faintest of murmurs, to be heard more loudly the following year, that Charles himself had not been unaware of the events in James's sick room. Charles's movements at the time, were indeed, unspecified. With his father about to move to Hampton Court it is likely that he was not at Theobalds when Buckingham was applying his quack remedies.

James's body was brought from Theobalds to London on April 4 in a hearse lined with black velvet and accompanied by guards and heralds, Charles heading the nobility who accompanied it in coaches. It was nine in the evening when, in foul weather, the hearse came to Holborn and made its way through Chancery Lane and the Strand to Denmark House where the coffin lay for nearly five weeks, flanked by six magnificent silver candlesticks which Charles had brought from Spain. The funeral on May 7 was one of the most magnificent ever staged. Inigo Jones designed the hearse, and mourning was distributed to over 9,000 people. It was in keeping with James's life that Chamberlain should describe the funeral as at the same time 'somewhat disorderly'. Charles was chief mourner and established a precedent by walking on foot from Denmark House to the interment in Westminster Abbey. Bishop Williams preached the sermon which took two hours. It was later published as *Great Britain's Solomon* and finished, predictably, with a double compliment: 'Though his father be dead, yet is he, as though hee were not dead, for he hath left one behind him most like himselfe, whom God prosper and preserve.'[4]

When Charles on March 27 made his first journey as King into London it was raining. The weather, wrote James Howell,

> was suitable to the Condition wherein he finds the Kingdom, which is cloudy; for he is left engaged in a war with a potent Prince, the People by long Desuetude unapt for Arms, the Fleet-Royal in quarter Repair, himself without a Queen, his Sister without a Country, the Crown pitifully laden with Debts, and the Purse of the State lightly balusted.[5]

The summary was apt.

Charles himself was well aware that he had succeeded at no easy time. Yet the situation was largely of his own making. Foreign policy, since his return from Spain, had been his rather than his father's; his father's last Parliament had been called The Prince's Parliament; his father's ministers of state had consulted him; his father's favourite was his favourite. Charles had long ago accepted his position as heir to the throne, and James's ill-health, his own driving obsession with Spain and the Palatinate, and the presence of Buckingham all contrived to lessen the break of death and succession so that the transition to kingship was not as emotional as it might otherwise have been. At twenty-four Charles was confident, optimistic, physically strong and not overwhelmed with grief. He was glad that power was now in his hands, glad that he had the support of Buckingham, determined to attend meticulously to the day-to-day requirements of kingship; it is doubtful whether, at this stage, he looked beyond his immediate purpose to the wider responsibilities of a ruler. He accepted a divine right of kings, as his father had done, he had the same belief in his prerogative (did he remember his father's warning that prerogative 'ryves in the stretching'?). He had sufficient confidence in himself to believe that he could rule a kingdom of some 5,000,000 persons, including those as diverse as the Scots and the Irish. But there was no problem to him so large, so pressing, so all-consuming as that of war. Yet war was not altogether in his nature. He had been driven to it as the only way to help his sister and wipe out the memory of the inglorious Spanish adventure. He now derived some pleasure in putting to practical use the tactics he had worked upon with his model armies and the precepts he had imbibed from Guicciardini; he was fascinated by Buckingham's grandiose schemes for power and influence on the Continent of Europe; and the stronger the opposition the more determined he was to carry the enterprise through.

113

First, he must secure his wife and Queen. The proxy marriage, which Buckingham was to have attended, was postponed when James's illness became serious, but it was celebrated on May Day outside the West door of Notre Dame in Paris with the Duc de Chevreuse, a distant cousin of Charles's, acting as proxy. The little Princess wore a crown of diamonds and was gorgeously attired in cloth of silver and gold with a train so heavy that, it was said, the three bearers could scarcely lift it and a man had to walk beneath carrying the weight on his head and shoulders. As soon as the ceremony was over the waiting courier galloped off for England to take the news that Charles was married while Elizabeth, in exile, contrived to give a feast to honour the occasion. A little later Buckingham went to Paris to conduct the Queen to her husband. He also intended to negotiate military help from France. With these two important assignments on his hands Buckingham yet allowed himself to play a most extraordinary additional role, no less than that of lover to the Queen of France, whom he had seen on his way through Paris in 1623. Now he approached her more boldly, and when the royal party escorting Henrietta to the coast had reached Amiens he found an opportunity of being alone with her one evening in a riverside garden. So far, perhaps, Anne had not been averse to the attentions of the gallant Englishman, which were in marked contrast to her boorish husband's neglect. But whatever Buckingham attempted in the garden could not be permitted, and her cries brought her attendants rushing to her side.

The Queen stayed with Henrietta's mother at Amiens while the wedding party proceeded to the coast. Buckingham's farewells to her were more loving than courtesy required and he soon found an excuse to post back, leaving Henrietta in the care of her younger brother, while he carried on a series of open flirtations which were widely commented upon. The whole affair did nothing to cement the alliance between France and England. If that alliance was not to be close it would be the more unfortunate for the little Queen who had been diverted from Calais because of the plague and who reached the French coast at Boulogne on June 8. The farewells with her mother had been tearful. She had already promised the Pope and her brother, the King, that she would bring up her children as Catholics, and she had been charged with the heavy responsibility of acting as champion of the faith in an alien country. Now she carried a letter from her mother to the same effect. At Boulogne she spent some time gazing out at the sea which she had never seen before and met many of the

English courtiers who had braved the English Channel to greet her, among them Buckingham's redoubtable mother, who was one of the first to be presented. Toby Mathew, who had been knighted for his services to Charles in Madrid, acted as interpreter. In the account of the meeting he wrote for Buckingham's wife he remarked that Henrietta-Maria was taller than he had thought. He was clearly enchanted with her combination of youth and maturity: 'believe me', he wrote, 'she sits already upon the very skirts of womanhood . . . upon my faith, she is a most sweet lovely Creature . . . full of wit, and hath a lovely manner in expressing it.' But he perceived more: 'I dare give my word for her, that she is not afraid of her own shadow.'

In England all was excitement for her arrival. Charles himself set out from London on May 31 going by way of Gravesend and Rochester to Canterbury, where many of the Court were gathering. Impatiently he went on to Dover, climbing the Castle keep to look towards France. But the French cortège was still on the other side, making its slow way to the coast. The most he could do was to dine with Phineas Pett on the *Prince Royal*, the ship detailed to bring his bride over. Pett was at Boulogne in ample time to greet the new Queen but storms delayed their departure, and it was not until Sunday June 12 that they set sail, making Dover in a little over eight hours. Charles, who had returned to Canterbury, was told the moment the *Prince Royal* was sighted, and, as Henrietta-Maria disembarked, Robert Tyrwhitt, making the journey from Dover to Canterbury in thirty-six minutes, brought Charles the news. She came ashore by means of an 'artificial moveable Bridge' and was then carried in a litter to the town, where she was welcomed by the mayor, before proceeding by coach to Dover Castle. Her French attendants found the Castle dismal and the furniture old. Perhaps Charles should have been there. But he had promised Henrietta's mother to give her daughter a night's rest to recover from her journey before visiting her.

He gave her little more. The next morning, as she was breakfasting, news was brought that the King had arrived. Throwing composure to the winds she dashed downstairs preparing to kneel and kiss the hand of the young man who stood there. But Charles caught her up in his arms and embraced her with many kisses. Overcome, she began the speech in French she had been taught – 'Sire, je suis venue en ce pais de vostre Majestie pour estre usée et commandée de vous . . .' but burst into tears. Then she thought that Charles was looking down to her feet and, conscious of her small stature, hastened, like a little girl, to show him her shoes, saying in French, 'Sir, I stand upon mine own feet. I have no helps by art. Thus high I am, and am neither higher nor lower'. She reached, indeed, to his shoulder, which was fitting, for he was not tall. She was a bony little creature, quick in her movements; in contrast to the King, black-haired and dark-skinned. If her nose was a little large, her teeth a little prominent, her big black eyes obscured these shortcomings as they responded to every changing mood. She was fifteen, he was twenty-four. The couple retired in private for an hour, after which Henrietta presented her attendants to her husband and they all went in to dinner. Her Confessor, who was keeping as close to her as he could, kept reminding her that it was the eve of St John Baptist, a fast day. But Henrietta was young and hungry after the abstention of a rough sea passage and an interrupted breakfast. Moreover, her husband was carving pheasant and venison for her, and she ate heartily of both.

They went on then to Canterbury, but as they made to enter the royal carriage Madame de Saint-Georges, who was reluctant to leave her charge's side, was politely told by Charles that her rank did not permit her to ride by the Queen. In spite of Henrietta's appeal Charles was firm and Buckingham's wife, his mother, and the Countess of Arundel took their places in the royal coach. The villagers along the route turned out to greet them with cheering and the ringing of church bells. On Barham Down the King and Queen alighted to walk along the ranks of simple country people drawn up to wish them well. The French attendants, an onlooker reported, looked disdainfully on this English custom. But Henrietta performed her role admirably. After supper at Canterbury she was taken to her room by the Duchesse de Chevreuse. Charles followed and, when he was undressed, dismissed his two attendants and with his own hands pushed fast the seven bolts to the doors of the chamber. The following morning he lay abed until seven o'clock, which was late for him, and was found to be very merry and cheerful.

They journeyed to London by the route Charles had followed on his outward journey, going by river from Gravesend. The weather was bad, the plague deaths had mounted in London to a hundred in the week of the Queen's arrival, but everyone put on a brave show. The King and Queen were in green and kept the big window of their barge open, in spite of the rain, waving and smiling to the onlookers on shore and in the craft of all kinds and sizes which jostled for a view of the royal couple. Guns roared from the Tower of London as they passed and from the ships of the fleet which accompanied them. A pleasure boat capsized but everyone was saved and the incident added to the merriment. And so they came to Denmark House, the much-loved home of Charles's mother, where his father had lain in state before his funeral and which Inigo Jones had restored for his wife. It was 16 June 1625 when Henrietta-Maria alighted there. At a ceremony in Whitehall Palace the following day her marriage was confirmed and declared to be lawfully and fully consummated and she was formally declared Queen.[6]

Part II
The King

10

Charles's First Parliament

It was not only marriage that claimed Charles's attention. He knew well enough that his life had now to be lived on several levels. Even while he was greeting his wife at Dover and they were coming up river to the cheers of the London crowd, plague deaths continued to rise and economic distress associated with rising prices and unemployment was spreading. The Privy Council dealt with the plague in such ways as it could, closing the theatres, stopping the fairs, halting bull and bear baiting, limiting travel in and out of affected areas, collecting money for the relief of victims. He himself renewed a Commission, headed by Viscount Mandeville, to enquire into the causes of the decay of trade. He had to consider the new coinage necessary to a new reign, the designs for which old Abraham van der Doort was preparing. Questions concerning his coronation and the style by which he would be known needed to be settled: like his father, he wished to be King of Great Britain, but the Judges ruled against him and he had to be King of England, Scotland, and Ireland. He made over Denmark House and its contents to Henrietta-Maria for life, and transferred his pictures, tapestries, statues, and the precious contents of his little cabinet room at St James's to grander premises at Whitehall.

He confirmed twenty-eight of James's thirty Privy Councillors in their offices, excluding only Bristol, still in disgrace, and Lord Baltimore (the former Sir George Calvert) who, now a professed Roman Catholic, felt he could not take the oath of allegiance. Charles merely remarked that it was better for a man to state his opinions than to retain office by equivocation. He remembered his personal friends. His cousin, James Stuart, Duke of Lennox, a man twelve years his junior, became Gentleman of his Bedchamber. Sir Henry Vane remained his cofferer and was still 'well rooted in the King's heart'. Robert Carey, who had taken him in as a weak and backward child,

121

and who already was Baron Hunsdon and Lord Leppington, now became the Earl of Monmouth, with £500 of land made over to him and his heirs in perpetuity. Carey, who had been Chamberlain to Charles since the death of Henry, felt a pang when James's Chamberlain, Pembroke, was continued in office by the new king. But Charles could not demote Pembroke, who was in any case a younger man, and Carey, after a wry aside made largely for form's sake, conceded that 'the King dealt very graciously' with him. He lived to publish his *Memoirs* later that year and died in 1639. Cottington was temporarily out of favour, partly because of his initial reaction to the Spanish journey, but mainly because his Catholic leaning led him to oppose a Spanish war. Cottington did not join the Privy Council until November 1628.

If Charles had any doubts as to what it meant to rule a kingdom they were resolved as the papers flowed in for his perusal. Three hundred and forty-six times before the year was out, seven hundred and thirty-three times before the end of 1626 he would sign a wide range of documents of varying importance which came to him from his Secretary of State alone. He was sufficiently conscientious to read them all, and many times amended them in his own fine, spidery hand; and sufficiently punctilious to dispense with a sign manual and actually to write his name on each of those he approved.[1]

One of the first to receive his signature was a warrant to Lord Treasurer Ley to continue collecting customs duties as in his father's time; he instituted commissions of marque, or reprisal, against subjects of the King of Spain in the Low Countries; he continued the drainage of Sedgemoor in Somerset which his father had begun; he instructed compensation to be paid to a woman whose husband had been killed in the King's ship *Speedwell*; he granted dwellings in the almshouses at Ewelme to deserving persons; he pardoned a convicted murderer whose father had interceded for him, paid considerable sums of money to his jeweller, earmarked £150 to help establish the new draperies, and ordered the payment of £120 to Daniel Mytens for a copy of Titian's great Venus (the Venere del Pardo).[2]

He instituted a stricter regime at Court which rid him of a few expensive parasites and suited the greater decorum he intended to introduce. His own day was planned so that no time was wasted. He rose very early and thereafter every activity – prayers, exercises, Council business, eating and sleeping – had its appointed time. One day a week was set aside for public audiences and neither then nor at any other time would he see anyone unless sent for. But he gave general satisfaction by mixing with his courtiers in the Privy Chamber each morning, giving a word here, a salutation there. In private he might be observed reading in a little book whose contents were divulged to no one but were thought to consist of maxims in manuscript. His spirit was high. The Spanish Ambassador was told to say to his master that the Queen of Bohemia had now a King for a brother! He could even be firm with the Buckingham family, refusing to attach Kit Villiers to his bedchamber because he would have no drunkenness there. The Venetian Ambassador was delighted with him. 'The King's reputation increases day by day', he wrote to the Doge and Senate. 'He professes constancy in religion, sincerity in action and that he will not have recourse to subterfuges in his dealings'. Amerigo Salvetti was similarly impressed. 'Wise government by the new King may be anticipated', he reported. 'He was well, active, and resolute', wrote Toby Mathew to Sir Dudley Carleton. In Council, it was said, he would listen attentively and weigh the arguments carefully before coming to a decision.[3]

The question that concerned him above all others was the future of his sister. The restitution of the Palatinate was no nearer than when he had ridden to Spain two and a half years earlier with his hopes high, and Elizabeth was still living at The Hague with an annual pension of £20,000 from England and was so poor that Charles had not only paid a debt of £10,000 on her behalf but sent her money for mourning after the death of James. She displayed, nevertheless, much of her old spirit, unlike her husband who, for all his charm, was indecisive and inclined to melancholy. 'I think', said Charles, who by this time had taken the measure of his brother-in-law, 'the grey mare is the best horse.'

The most important decisions he had to take concerned the war that, in one way or another, directly or indirectly, would lead the Palatine back to his inheritance. Charles appointed a committee of his Privy Council to advise him on foreign affairs and went to Gravesend to inspect the merchant ships that still, as in Tudor times, were the backbone of his naval force. The Parliament of 1624 had earmarked part of its supply for refurbishing that force, Buckingham had lent £30,000, and other navy commissioners had raised a loan of £50,000. On May 1, disregarding the difficulties of earlier impressments, Charles ordered the raising of a further 10,000 men to accompany the fleet as soldiers, and the enterprise against Spain began to take shape as twelve ships of the royal navy, twenty armed merchantmen and fifty colliers were commanded to rendezvous at Plymouth in June 1625. There was also the question of La Rochelle hanging in the balance. This Huguenot enclave in Catholic France had revolted at the end of 1624 and early the following year Richelieu had asked James for ships – not to be used against the Huguenots but, by their presence, to prevent further rebellion. James was rarely deaf to an appeal to support authority, and he could hardly afford to offend France at this time. The loan of a few ships barely worried him. It took Charles longer to accept Richelieu's assurance that only a show of force would be necessary against the Huguenots, but Pennington sailed for France on 9 June 1625 with eight English ships.

Mansfeld and his hotch-potch army had meanwhile left Dover on 11 January 1625. Contrary to agreement the French refused them landing at Calais or Boulogne and they proceeded along the coast looking for the promised French cavalry. But these were not ready to embark and the little fleet, already in poor condition, cast anchor off Flushing on February 1. Mansfeld had expected to march to the relief of the Palatinate, but without French help he was powerless against the Imperial forces that barred his way. The Dutch begged for his help in holding Breda against besieging Spanish forces. James refused to enlarge the area of the war. The condition of the little force worsened as it waited at Flushing. They were short of food and water, inadequately clothed, so close-packed in their ships that movement was difficult, they stifled below deck and froze above. When at last they disembarked the Dutch provided a modicum of food and of straw to cover them at night, but they were dying at the rate of forty or fifty a day. 'We look for victuals and bury our dead', was a laconic report. By the end of February 1625 barely 3,000 of the original 12,000 were capable of bearing arms. These few Charles ordered on his accession to help the besieged at Breda, arguing that the continued locking up of Spanish forces round the town was an indirect help to the Palatinate. Many of them deserted to the Spanish, the rest remained before Breda for two months, unable to avert the inevitable outcome. When the city surrendered on May 26 the Dutch, with indecent haste, hurried Mansfeld and the desperate and marauding remnant of his army over the border on what they hoped was the way to the Palatinate. It was a sorry beginning to Charles's intervention in Europe. But the broader strategy remained in the form of the fleet which was being prepared for action against Spain, and the subsidies he had agreed to pay to the Protestant armies in Europe.

It remained to be seen whether he could meet these obligations: £240,000 a year for Mansfeld and his men; £100,000 annually to help maintain troops in the Low Countries; £360,000 for the armies of his uncle the King of Denmark; £300,000 or more to equip and pay for the fleet and army being prepared against Spain; £25,000 to protect Ireland. He had to find something like £1,200,000 in the next twelve months apart from the normal expenses of running his Court and Household. And these had been swollen by new or exceptional obligations: £40 or £50,000 for the old King's personal debts, £30,000 for his funeral, the accompanying receptions and gifts to servants; £40,000 for Charles's marriage and for the presents and entertainment involved; £37,000 a year to his Queen, as well as an immediate payment of £5000 and unspecified further sums to her French attendants – a total of at least £162,000. He could economize on personal expenditure and reduce such standing items as pensions, but the degree to which he was willing to do so made little difference. He raised some income by disparking most of his more remote parks and chases, either selling or leasing the land thus disafforested or turning it to profitable agriculture. He anticipated some of his customs revenue. He borrowed £60,000 from the City of London upon the security of Crown lands. Yet nothing could make an appreciable difference to the financial situation: he needed something like the £400,000 which had been his father's income in 1624 together with £162,000 to cover exceptional expenses, *and* the £1,200,000 required by his war expenditure.[4]

He could see no way of raising it except through a Parliament. He would have preferred to meet his first Parliament under more favourable conditions; for he knew that besides asking for large sums of money he would have to deal with the suspicions surrounding his marriage treaty, the commitments he had made in Europe, the uncertainties of the war, the failure of Mansfeld's expedition, and the growing unpopularity of Buckingham. He had seen enough of Parliaments to appreciate their potential power, but his experience of the Parliament of 1624 gave him confidence. He even considered reconvening the postponed session of that assembly, but the constitution demanded a new Parliament for a new reign and the writs went out on April 17. No more than the usual patronage appeared to be exercised and there is no evidence of hotly contested elections to the Parliament of 1625, though there were rumours that those opposed to the Court were 'exciting tumults' in order to win seats for their candidates. In the event the House of Commons was little different from that of the previous year, with Coke and Sir Robert Phelips prominent among the leaders. Sir Thomas Wentworth, who had been returned for Yorkshire, was the only Member with a disputed election on his hands and was absent for most of the session. Sir Edwin Sandys, Sir Dudley Digges, Edward Alford were there and, among the younger men, John Pym, Sir John Eliot, and John Hampden. Once more Benjamin Rudyerd, the friend of Pembroke (with whom he composed verses) was expected to be the spokesman of the Court party. They were all concerned with the authority of Parliament and their own right to freedom of speech. They all intended to safeguard their own interests and those of their constituents. This would be no rubber-stamp assembly. Charles, indeed, made some effort to influence the House through the presence of Privy Councillors. When Sir John Suckling, Privy Councillor and Comptroller of the Household, failed to gain a seat for Middlesex, patronage found him one at Yarmouth, Isle of Wight; and Sir Albertus Morton was helped in Kent by Buckingham, as well as by Westmoreland and Dorset. They need not have troubled for Morton was also returned for Cambridge University. In other respects James had been negligent, raising Conway to the peerage in the spring of 1624, so depriving the Commons of a useful Court spokesman. In the Upper House generally there was little change, and Charles still refused to allow Bristol to take his seat.

Charles was reluctant to face the Parliament of 1625 until his marriage was consummated, and its opening was twice postponed – from May 17 to the 31st and again until June 18, two days after Henriette-Maria reached London. It was unfortunate that by then the fall of Breda and the condition of the English troops in Holland were common knowledge and that the impressment which Charles had ordered for the fleet was causing grave unrest. Meanwhile, with plague ravaging the capital, the meeting of Parliament elsewhere had been considered; but in the end the convenience of London prevailed. The show normally attendant upon a state opening was curtailed, but nothing could stem the enormous enthusiasm which greeted the new King as he came quietly by water to his first Parliament. When he appeared before the House of Lords Charles was not only robed but crowned, in spite of the fact that as yet there had been no coronation, but as prayers were said he knelt by the chair of state and put off the crown. The traditional sermon was given by William Laud, Bishop of St David's. Speaking with the words of James he expressed the sentiments of Charles: the law and the Parliament were agents of the King, they received their power from the King and their function was to support his authority. It was not a helpful speech and did nothing to encourage the unity which Laud extolled. Charles was wiser. Whether from necessity or from a just appreciation of what his audience wanted, he hit the right note with simplicity and brevity, which made a welcome change from his father's long and erudite speeches. In his favour, also, were his youth, the good impression he had made on earlier parliaments, and the earnestness with which he was reforming the disordered Court.

'I thank God', he began, 'that the Business that is to be treated of at this Time, is of such a Nature that it needs no Eloquence for to set it forth; for I am neither able to do it, nor doth it stand with My Nature to spend much Time in Words'. He emphasized, nevertheless, that Parliament had urged the breaking of the treaties with Spain, that this presupposed war, and that war required money. He asked for 'assistance for those in Germany' and spoke of 'the fleet that is ready for action'.

> My Lords and Gentlemen, I pray you to remember . . . what a great Dishonour it were, both to you and Me, if this Action, so begun, should fail for that Assistance you are able to give Me . . . I hope you . . . will expedite what you have now in Hand to do.

Yet, even as he spoke, there hung over Parliament the broken promises of the previous year, the unrevealed disasters of the Continental war, the ugly rumours of help being given to France against the Huguenots. Charles did not tell them that he stood there perjured, either to them or to his Queen, in respect of the treatment of Roman Catholics; nor did he explain that the promise to reconvene the 1624 Parliament in the autumn of that year had been broken for fear of jeopardizing the French marriage negotiations. He had no reason to advance for not keeping his father's undertaking to account for the money already granted by Parliament. Still less did he speak of the commitments in Europe which he and Buckingham had undertaken in spite of the strongly expressed opposition of the previous Parliament.

Charles's Lord Keeper was hardly more explicit. His statement that the breaking of the treaties with Spain, 'the succeeding treaties and alliances, the armies sent into the Low Countries, the repairing of

127

the forts, and the fortifying of Ireland, do all meet in one centre, the Palatinate', must have left his hearers decidedly puzzled since it was accompanied by no specific information nor by any statement of the sums of money involved. True, there was no constitutional necessity for an explanation from the King. But the degree to which the monarch had taken Parliament into his confidence had been growing, and James had certainly invited his last Parliament to advise him on foreign affairs. When two days later the Speaker, Sir Thomas Crew, was presented to Charles his speech was understandably cool. He 'trusted' the King would be able to recover the Palatinate and he then plunged into another matter, asking Charles 'really to execute the laws against the wicked generation of Jesuits, seminary priests, and incendiaries, every lying in wait to blow the coals of contention'. A few days later the House settled down to a full debate on the question of religion. Although nothing specific was known of the contents of the French marriage treaty rumour was hard at work and members were clearly not convinced of Charles's integrity. On the 23rd a committee of the whole House was voted to consider the working of the recusancy laws and on the 30th a petition drawn up by the experienced Sandys and the young Pym begging the King to execute the penal laws in all their strictness and to take measures to prevent the spread of papist doctrines, was sent up to the Lords. On the same day Sir Francis Seymour rose unexpectedly in a thin House. He had been vociferous in the previous Parliament in insisting that England should not entangle herself on the Continent but should fight a lucrative war on the Spanish Main. He now proposed a grant of one subsidy and one fifteenth, a mere £100,000, and clearly not enough to provide for any aspect of the war. Rudyerd was taken by surprise. He stumbled to his feet to remind the House of the great expenses of funeral, marriage, coronation, and the entertainment of foreign ambassadors. With the more vital commitments in Europe and the need to supply the navy, he dealt only in general terms. The Commons were not impressed. Phelips, whether by previous agreement or not, quickly rose to support Seymour. The supply given by the previous Parliament had been generous yet was still unaccounted for. 'What account is to be given', he asked, 'of 20,000 men, of many thousand pounds of treasure, which have been expended without any success of honour or profit?' The money had been voted for war, he cried, flinging Charles's unsubstantiated demands back in his face, but 'we know yet of no war, nor of any enemy'. The comparison he drew was intentionally hurtful and damaging and drew together the religious and financial issues: 'It was not wonte to be soe when God and wee held together; witness that glorious Queen, who with less supplyes defended herself, consumed Spayne, assisted the Low Countreys, relieved France, preserved Ireland.' He nevertheless proposed the granting of two subsidies, some £140,000, which the House supported, partly on the grounds that fifteenths were burdensome to poorer people, though the fact that fifteenths were an assessment upon property may have made them less acceptable on other grounds.

With the petition of religion and the proposed supply, inadequate though it was, going forward on the same day, the issue was squarely before Charles: he had either to break his promise to Parliament concerning religion, in which case there would be no supply, or break his secret agreement with France – which meant, in effect, with his wife. The latter was easier. The French alliance was proving worthless, Buckingham was out of favour in France after his flirtation with the French Queen, Henrietta-Maria's French attendants were tiresome in themselves, a drain upon his resources, and a cause of friction between himself and the Queen. But before taking action he made one effort to secure a larger supply in return for the concession on religion he was about to make. The pestilence was raging in London and Charles himself left for Hampton Court, leaving Buckingham to attempt to hammer out some compromise with the opposition. On July 8, when many Members had left for home because of the plague, Sir John Coke made a fuller statement of the King's requirements than had yet been offered: £240,000 for Mansfeld; the same for the King of Denmark; another £133,000 for the fleet above the two subsidies granted. But it was too late to throw such figures at the House. They needed to be more fully informed. Perhaps they were stunned at the large sums named. Certainly they needed time for full and open debate. But with plague in their midst that time was not now, and there was no response to Coke's statement.

Meanwhile there had been further humiliation to swallow. On July 5 tonnage and poundage was offered to the King for one year only instead of for life, as had been usual since the reign of Henry VI. It is unlikely that this was a deliberate withholding of permanent supply; to have cut Charles off from the monarch's customary revenue at this stage presages a far wider and clearer breach between King and Parliament than had yet occurred. The reason was more likely to be found in the review of the customs which was proceeding and a reluctance, meanwhile, to pledge any revenue indefinitely. But the effect was the same on the harrassed King. With plague deaths amounting to more than 500 a week in London alone Parliament ground to a halt. On July 11 Charles renewed his promise to enforce the recusancy laws, Lord Conway accepted on his behalf the paltry grant of two subsidies, and the Houses adjourned.

The pestilence broke out in the King's guardroom, in his bakery, and among the Queen's priests. The Court thankfully moved to Woodstock and the Fellows and students of the University of Oxford moved out to make room for the Parliament men who assembled on August 1 in Christ Church Hall for the second session of the 1625 Parliament. Again religion and supply were coupled and Charles was immediately asked to account for the money granted by the 1624 Parliament and to explain why he had pardoned a Jesuit on July 12, the day after he had promised to execute the penal laws. At the same time the Commons returned to a religious issue which had troubled them in the previous session.

This was a matter not so much of Papists and the Papacy as of dissension within the reformed, Protestant religion itself. It had come to a head with two books written by Richard Montague, rector of Stanford Rivers in Essex. Montague was a scholar and author of some distinction who had publicly disputed with the learned John Selden himself on the subject of tythes. In an argument with Catholic priests in his parish he had taken up the position that they had no need of Rome since much of their doctrine was integral to the true reformed Church of England, a notion which appealed to neither Puritans nor Catholics. The Catholics responded in 1622 with *The Gag for the new Gospel*. Montague's reply of 1624, *A New Gag for an Old Goose*, was a vigorous pamphlet which, while rejecting Roman Catholic doctrines, upset Calvinists by its clear assertion of the dogmas of free will and salvation by works. In other respects Montague pleased neither side. He denied that the clergy could compel their parishioners to confession, but claimed that in some cases advice and consolation, even an intimation of divine pardon, might be given by a priest to a repentant sinner. He rejected transubstantiation of the bread and wine but believed in the immanence of Christ at communion. He opposed image worship yet believed that pictures and statues could help to bring God and the nature of Christian worship into the hearts of a congregation.

Montague's book had come to the notice of James's last Parliament. James was delighted with it, exclaiming that if it offered Popish doctrine then he was Popish too! By the time Charles's first Parliament met, Montague had produced another book, written at James's request, in order to clarify his position. Since James had died before its publication, the dedication of the *Appello Caesarem* was to Charles and the book concluded with the unnecessarily provocative exclamation: 'defend thou me with the sword and I will defend thee with the pen!' Incensed at what appeared to be an anti-Puritan alliance by the Church and the Crown the Commons summoned Montague to the bar of the House at Westminster and bound him over in recognisances of £2000.

Montague was typical of a number of intellectuals who professed to find their inspiration in the Early Fathers and disowned both the mediaeval Papacy and all forms of Puritanism. The English Church settlement of Elizabeth, they believed, brought the Church as nearly as possible into accord with the teaching of the Fathers. They believed that worship could be enhanced by individual acts of piety and good works and that it was in the power of the individual to live a godly life. A Christian was therefore not predestined to either salvation or damnation but could achieve grace through acts of piety. A leading exponent of free-will, Jacobus Arminius, gave his name – Arminianism – to the doctrine.

On the second day of the Oxford session Parliament returned to the Arminian issue and the subject of Montague. But Charles had put him beyond the reach of Parliament by making him his chaplain. The action was typical. Coldly disapproving of the Commons' conduct, he showed his support of Montague warmly by bringing him within his own household and under his protection. The lawyer Edward Alford at once perceived the wider issue: could the King's ministers and other public officers similarly be protected by the King or were they responsible to Parliament who could call them to account if it thought fit? The Commons thus stumbled upon the vital question of ministerial responsibility and inevitably the name of Buckingham was in every mind.

The question of responsibility became, indeed, more urgent as the situation deteriorated both at home and abroad. The delivery of the ships to the French and the rioting following the latest impressment for the fleet were by this time common knowledge, clashes between English and French merchantmen were affecting commerce, the menace of pirates was daily growing more acute and reports were

131

pouring into the Oxford Parliament of pirate raids on English shores. Hysteria and reality combined to crystallize the feeling against the Duke. One observer coupled 'the neglect of guarding the seas' with 'mis-spending of the public treasure' as the chief grievances of the Commons and laid the responsibility upon the man who was both the Lord Admiral and the King's chief adviser. All the Commons knew about Buckingham, his accumulation of office, the advancement of his family, his hold upon preferment his monopolies, his wealth, was suspect. So was his religion. He was the patron of Laud, he had supported Montague; his wife, though apparently converted, was of a Catholic family; his mother had adopted the Catholic faith; he himself was known to have flirted with it; his conduct in Spain was condemned.

Charles did nothing to appease his Parliament. On the 4th he came in from Woodstock to Christ Church Hall and reminded them that the two subsidies they had voted were 'far too short and yet ungathered', he put up Secretary Conway to say that £30–40,000 was needed for the fleet and Sir John Coke to name £600,000 a year as the cost of European commitments. Next day when his Chancellor of the Exchequer moved for a further two subsidies and two fifteenths (about £170,000) the House plunged into a disorderd discussion which reflected its bewilderment at the varying sums named by the King's advisers. Two supply votes were impossible in one Parliament, they said, it was too late for the fleet to sail, was there perhaps no intention that it should sail? Who was the enemy against whom preparations were being made? One voice, indeed, was raised for Charles when it was suggested that some other form of tax might be found which would raise money immediately; but the Members had too great a care of their pockets to support such a proposition. Sir Nathaniel Rich thought that the King's revenue should be examined with a view to its increase, a suggestion that would hardly help immediately, but the sting in his speech was a request that 'when His Majesty doth make a war, it may be debated and advised by his grave council', a hit, surely, at Buckingham. Sir Robert Cotton aimed in the same direction when he begged the King 'not to be led with young and single counsel' but to be guided by his great officers of state.

Buckingham was well aware of the way the debates were tending. Though he had been endeavouring to reach a compromise outside the House he had not heard within it any terms he could accept. So on August 8, never one to shirk responsibility, he himself came before Parliament in Christ Church Hall. He spoke with confidence of his popularity when he returned from Spain, and of his efforts since then to build up an anti-Spanish party. He asserted that he had always taken advice, that nothing he had done had been without the approval of Council, and denied that it was too late in the year to send out a fleet. 'Make the Fleet ready to go out, and the King bids you name the Enemy', he cried. 'Put the Sword into His Majesty's hands, and he will improve it to your honour.'

But the House was in little mood for rhetoric. The statement of the King's finances which the Lord Treasurer now put before them fell flat: it was, after all, the fourth time the King had offered figures and they could not reconcile the varying sums involved. On the 10th Phelips went to the heart of the matter by asking Sir Robert Mansell, a member of the Council of War, if he accepted joint responsibility for the war strategy? Mansell, after some hesitation, said 'No'. Later the same day Buckingham was named in the House by Seymour: 'Let us lay the fault where it is', he cried, 'the Duke of Buckingham is trusted, and it must needs be either in him or his agents'. Phelips rubbed in the salt. 'It is not fit', he exclaimed, 'to repose the safety of the Kingdom upon those that have not parts answerable to their places.' Well might a broad Scots voice be heard again: 'Ye'll live to have your bellyfull of Parliamentary impeachments!'.[5]

Charles saw at once the implications and summoned his Council that afternoon. He wanted an immediate dissolution. Buckingham and Williams begged him to be patient, both for the sake of supply and, as Williams strongly urged, to avoid an ignominious end to his first Parliament. But, even with Buckingham on his knees before him, Charles would not be persuaded. On August 12 he dismissed his first Parliament in order to protect his friend. As the Venetian Ambassador pointed out, he put the safety of Buckingham above the needs of the state. He might have added that Charles put the safety of Buckingham above the needs of his sister, for Parliament had granted nothing but a paltry and as yet ungathered supply while the tonnage and poundage bill lay uncommitted. Parliament had demanded that the King's actions on religious affairs be brought into line with its own beliefs, it had refused to endorse his foreign policy, it had condemned the influence and what it considered the ineptitude of the King's favourite. But Charles gave Buckingham a circlet of diamonds and a beautifully moulded little bronze horse. When others found fault with his friend it was always Charles's instinct to reward. The hurt must be wiped away and the world must see how truly the Duke was loved.

133

11

'Reason of the Spaniards'

While Parliament men dispersed to their homes Charles held a Privy Council at Woodstock on August 14. The fault had not been entirely his. Constitutionally he was not obliged to consult the Commons on foreign policy, nor had he any reason to believe that the Members were as well equipped as he himself to take decisions. He had accepted at face value their anti-Spanish sentiments and he might well have felt that his immediate policy was in accord with their wishes.

Even so, he had told them very little. What they did learn had been dragged from him piecemeal and added up to no coherent whole. This fumbling approach to his first Parliament could be accounted for partly by supposing that Charles feared the Members' reaction if they knew the extent of his European commitments, partly in terms of his own natural reluctance to explain. Yet his attitude throughout was in such marked contrast to his approach to the 1624 Parliament that there would seem to be some deeper cause for the change. Then he had been debonair, industrious, willing to charm – and his success should have induced him to act in the same way in 1625. Instead he was taciturn, glum, imperious, as though, in place of the rosy promise of 1624, he was already obsessed by a sense of failure, or perhaps was oppressed by a sense of guilt stemming from his broken vows on religion.

He probably knew better than Buckingham the difficulties of the strategy upon which they had embarked and this in itself could have induced his lack of communication; it is possible that he had yielded to Buckingham's impetuosity against his own better judgment and was defending a tactic in which he had less than complete faith. Perhaps, deep in his unconscious mind, there might already have been gnawing an enervating doubt about his ability to help his sister. The restoration of the Palatinate, indeed, no longer seemed as simple as it had at first, and the European power politics in which he was becoming involved were outside his inclination or his ability. Nor had the change from Prince to monarch increased his confidence. On the contrary, given Charles's notions of kingship and the exaggerated unction with which he had been treated since boyhood, it was in itself intimidating. James, for all his peculiarities, was a buffer between ideal and real, and the removal of that earthy character, with his good common sense and homely touch, left Charles exposed to a world, dominated by Buckingham, in which ideals and fantasy played a large part. When he was faced by the reality of hard-headed, close-fisted Members of Parliament representing constituents equally unwilling to open their purses for him, the confident King, who had been observed shortly after his accession sending arrogant messages to Spain, became the aloof monarch, puzzled and disappointed. Parliament's attitude in no way corresponded with the precepts of political obligation he took for granted nor with the welcome they themselves had accorded him the previous year.

It was, indeed, a Parliament guided by a self-interest which was becoming increasingly coherent. The Members and their constituents were for the most part closely bound together by ties of economic interest that stretched from the land and its produce east and west across the oceans to the far shores of China and America, and the general depression of the 'twenties affected them all. They knew that bad harvests, interrupted trade and, above all, the decline of the cloth industry which, from the sheep to the shipper, remained England's most important source of profit, were matters of more immediate concern to their constitutents than equipping a fighting fleet or raising an army. The topics they raised in debate while Charles was waiting for supply showed where their interests lay: they were troubled by the interruption of trade caused by French hostility and pirate impunity; they were concerned with the fishing of the English settlers on the coast of New England and with their rights to wood and timber; they were anxious to limit the import of tobacco to that grown in the colonies; they discussed the Eastland merchants and their timber and shipbuilding supplies; voices were raised against the Merchant Adventurers, against the attempted monopoly of Newcastle coals; objections were raised to the Court of Wards, there were difficulties over the Apothecaries being registered as a separate Company, the Goldwire Drawers' patent was to be withdrawn, voices were raised against a tax for the lighthouse at Winterton Ness; clothworkers, the aulnage, rates of tax upon perpetuanas and serges were briefly discussed; objection was taken to the 'multitude of Popish and seditious books' which were printed. Religion, indeed, appeared to be a chief concern. Yet, in spite of eloquent speeches and petitions which expressed anxiety for the Protestant cause, Charles's first Parliament was not a high-principled body and in the end had done virtually nothing for the cause it professed to have at heart, not even offering a word of cheer to its fellow religionists in Europe nor to the Princess who so recently had been the Queen of Hearts.

How had such a body generated the will and achieved the power to thwart the King? Basically, perhaps, because he was asking, they were giving: only a strong common purpose could bring those two opposites together. Even in the time of Elizabeth I, when Parliament and monarch had been united in opposition to Spain, the alliance was wearing thin and Elizabeth's last Parliament had its own terms to juxtapose to the financial demands of the Queen. Elizabeth got part of what she wanted but a bargain had been struck. The development of Parliamentary power had been assisted by the growing feeling of representation – that Parliament men sat in Westminster with the support of their constituencies, their 'countries' – and the more frequently Parliament met the stronger was the continuity and the bond between elector and elected. In Charles's first Parliament, following closely upon James's last, were many of the same Members, already familiar with the situation, emboldened by familiarity and the contact with friends and colleagues. Sir Edwin Sandys, Edward Alford, Sir Dudley Digges, Sir Robert Phelips, Sir John Eliot, Sir Thomas Wentworth, Sir Walter Erle, Sir Edward Coke, Sir Francis Seymour, John Pym, John Hampden, were only a few of the colleagues of more than one previous Parliament; Denzil Holles and William Strode and many more were fresh from the experience of the Parliament of the previous year. That Charles so badly wanted their support after the Spanish Marriage episode and that James had invited them to discuss foreign policy and his son's marriage could only augment their sense of power.

Procedural forms evolved by Parliament also helped it to stand against the monarch. It worked increasingly through committees, which could be managed so that royal nominees were outnumbered; or through a committee of the whole House where Members were freed from the control of the Speaker, who was a Crown appointment. Charles was well aware of this development:

We are not ignorant how much the House hath of late years endeavoured to extend their Privileges, by setting up general Committees for Religion, for Courts of Justice, for Trade, and the like; a course never heard of until late: So as, where in former times the Knights and Burgesses were wont to communicate to the House, such business, as they brought from their Countries; now there are so many chairs erected, to make enquiry upon all sorts of men, where complaints of all sorts are entertained . . .

Disputed elections were not uncommon and the right which Parliament won in 1604 to determine the issue through a committee appointed by itself added to its power; similarly the creation of new Parliamentary boroughs in 1621 both increased the membership of the House and brought in men whose industrial and commercial interests made them highly independent and strongly opposed to taxation; as Thomas Hobbes remarked 'tradesmen, in the cities and boroughs . . . choose, as near as they can, such as are the most repugnant to the giving of subsidies'. Crown policy should obviously have been to secure the election of Privy Councillors to the House of Commons, but both James and Charles were careless of this contrivance: Charles inherited a Council of thirty members from his father, but only six of them sat in his first Parliament.

The more it felt itself 'representative' – a term it increasingly used – the bolder Parliament became. In the new-style government that began to emerge it worked more closely with the constituencies, making use of the rapid development of printing to keep them informed of events at Westminster and of the attitudes of individual Parliament men. Even in Elizabeth's time Sir Robert Cecil had complained 'that Parliament and its daily goings-on were matter for gossip on the streets and in alehouses' and his perturbation was attributed to the fact that he saw in publicity a threat to statecraft. Now Parliament made use of, and fostered, a conscious opposition of constituency or 'country' objectives to those of the Court. The country gentleman who lived outside the circle of Court office and Court perquisites and possibly suffered a feeling of exclusion assumed a growing importance. A multiplicity of local matters were of more immediate relevance to him than the European war which, in any case, was not so easy to relate to his own affairs as his father's war on the Spanish Main in the days of Drake and Hawkins. To these men cheers for the Princess Elizabeth were one thing; money and men to fight in Europe were quite another. The realization that they were the instruments

137

through whom taxes in the localities would be collected increased their confidence in opposition, as well as the confidence of the men who represented them in Parliament.[1]

As Charles and his Council examined the financial position afresh on August 14 they saw two areas of abysmal want but one of reasonable sufficiency. On the one hand the shortage of money for day-to-day expenses was acute; the King's servants were unpaid, ambassadors were held up and embassies delayed for want of funds, there was barely enough money for the customary royal victuals. Far less was it possible to meet the big continental requirements. On the other hand the re-equipment of the fleet was virtually complete and the August and September instalments of the Queen's dowry, the tonnage and poundage which Charles would continue to collect in spite of Parliament's failure to proceed to an Act, would provide current cash for soldiers' and sailors' pay. Charles supplemented this by borrowing a further £10,000 in August; and in September, with the approval of the Council, privy seals were issued against loans of from £10 to £30 to be required of persons named by the Lords Lieutenants of the counties as being able to lend. The money would be required in twelve days and would be repaid in eighteen months. Such a sum, Charles said, few would deny to a friend.

Meanwhile, with Buckingham, he was putting the finishing touches to the strategy which would govern the sailing of the fleet. He made a further treaty with the Dutch at Southampton on September 8. They had already promised twenty ships for the enterprise against Spain and now they agreed to blockade the Flemish coast while the main English fleet was absent in Spanish waters. Sir Edward Cecil, the nominee of Buckingham, was appointed to the command. Cecil was an experienced soldier with much campaigning in the Netherlands to his credit he had accompanied the Princess Elizabeth to Germany in 1613 as her treasurer, he had advised Charles on the purchase of his engines of war. But he had little knowledge of naval warfare and his appointment was resented by the more experienced seamen he would command. The Earl of Essex, in particular, who would serve as Cecil's Vice-Admiral, would, both on his own merit and as the son of Elizabeth's famous sea-captain, have lent 'much lustre to the action' had he been appointed to the command.

Though one object was the capture of Spanish treasure ships, the overall aim of the expedition was the 'protection and restitution' of the

Elector Palatine and his wife; and, since the King of Spain had entered the field against them, he was to be weakened and disabled in his sea-forces and trade 'by taking and destroying his ships, galleys, frigates and vessels of all sorts; by spoiling his provisions in his magazines and port towns; by depriving him of seamen, mariners and gunners . . . by intercepting his fleets either going out or returning; and by taking in and possessing some such place, or places, in the many of his dominions, as may support and countenance our successful fleets.' The Palatine was urging desperately that the 10,000 soldiers destined for Spain would be better employed on the Continent, but Charles and Buckingham may perhaps be given credit for their wider strategy. But it would have to be successful. Full of hope, Charles took up residence in Portsmouth in September, going on board many of the ships and reviewing the troops on Roxborough Down. 'By the grace of God,' said Charles, 'I will carry on war if I risk my crown. I will have reason of the Spaniards, and will set matters straight again. My brother-in-law shall be restored, and I only wish that all other potentates would do as I am doing.'[2]

He had assembled nearly a hundred sail, including thirty merchantmen and a number of Newcastle colliers; 5000 seamen, 10,000 land soldiers, ten pieces of large ordnance, many smaller field pieces, fifty horses to draw the guns, fifty more for the use of the land commanders, besides ammunition, and provisions for men and beasts. There was much excitement when the twenty sail from Holland hove in sight on 4 October 1625, of which fifteen would accompany the fleet and five remain to help guard the coasts. The following day they set off. Storms drove them to return two days later, they put to sea again on the 6th and, though bad weather dogged them, one ship floundering with its total crew of 175 and the Admiral's flagship barely surviving, they rounded Cape St Vincent on the 20th. By this time it had been discovered that supplies were so short that the usual allowance for four men had to be apportioned between five, that many of the muskets issued were useless, and that in many cases the bullets did not fit the muskets. The pressed men were seasick, homesick, frightened and resentful, the High Command took too long in deciding where the blow should fall.

Finally it was agreed that Cadiz Bay was the spot where they would attack and wait for the homecoming treasure ships. They did not know, as they entered the harbour on the flood tide, that they had missed the West India fleet by four days and that the Brazilian fleet, getting wind of their arrival, had been diverted to Malaga. A little knot of Spanish ships and galleys at anchor in the Bay escaped into the security of the inner harbour: if Cecil had gone in on the ebb not one of them could have got away in this manner. As it was, he gave the order to attack Fort Puntal, which guarded this inner harbour, as a preliminary to taking Cadiz itself. Five of the Dutch ships bore the brunt of the fighting. The colliers who had been ordered to assist cowered behind them, the only one of their shots to hit any kind of target going through the stern of the Vice-Admiral's ship. Though Fort Puntal was finally taken, the clumsy and lengthy fighting left no chance of surprising Cadiz. Moreover, the city was found to be well fortified, having been fully informed of the preparations that had been going on in English ports, and reinforcements of infantry and horse were being hurried to the area.

In these circumstances Cecil landed under cover of Fort Puntal, but he found no army to engage, for the Spaniards predictably withdrew into the cover of a well-known countryside. As the English pressed after them through a scorching sun, it was discovered that no provisions had been brought from the ships and that the men had not eaten or drunk for forty-eight hours. Cecil ordered a cask of wine to be brought from a village house. It was then realized that the whole area was a wine-store for the West India fleets and that nothing could stop the men from broaching cask after cask. The whole English army was drunk. There was nothing to be done but get as many men as possible back to the ships before their helplessness should be apparent to the Spaniards.

It seemed now that no purpose could be served in Cadiz Bay and the fleet reformed and put to sea still with the intention of intercepting some richly laden fleet. But again they were forestalled. Well-advised by rumour, the Mexican ships had chosen to come by way of the African coast and crept into Cadiz harbour from the south behind the backs of the English who were watching the westward horizons.

On November 16 Cecil gave up and the fleet sailed for home. It was a long and terrible journey. Four vessels went down on the way. In spite of months of preparation many of the ships were in part rotten, the sails of one had been in use against the Armada, the food was putrid, the drink bad, the wounded were dying through want of care, sickness spread from ship to ship. Winter storms battered them all the way and even their own shores proved so inhospitable that gales prevented them rounding the Lizard and Cecil, with most of what remained of his fleet, made his way to Ireland. Here he remained for some time licking his wounds and reluctant, possibly, to make his accounting in England. But before he crept back sufficient stragglers had arrived to tell their stories and rumour provided the rest.[3]

Charles's first large-scale effort to help his sister had failed. He could not blame Parliament entirely although he might have felt that a less niggardly outlook would have resulted in a better-equipped fleet. The terrible truth was that a criminal irresponsibility had failed to ensure the seaworthiness of the fleet or the condition of the armaments, to check the quality of the provisions, to provide adequate medical care, or to stop the dishonesty and peculation that was rife in the shipyards. For the strategy in Spanish waters, indeed, the Commanders had to bear the blame. Sir William St Leger, writing to Buckingham from the Bay of Cadiz on October 29, had professed himself to be 'so much ashamed that he wishes he might never live to see his Sovereign, which he thinks he shall not do, for his heart is broken'. Yet ill luck also played its part. But for the storms which delayed their departure they would not have missed the Spanish West India fleet; on the other hand, a little more expedition would have got them off before the storm broke. But overall, though blame might rest upon a dozen unscrupulous or inefficient contractors, responsibility could be shouldered by no one but the Lord Admiral.

Perhaps for this reason Charles attempted no more than a perfunctory enquiry into what went wrong, and all the little peculators, all the big profiteers, went unpunished in order to protect the Duke from the charge of criminal incompetence. Perhaps he wished also to protect himself from the knowledge that his models, his war games, his books, had resulted in no more skilful deployment of his resources than this. The French were scandalized and blamed the English commanders. The French Ambassador in Madrid brushed aside an enterprise into which so much effort had been put as the 'youthful and unconsidered escapade of the King of England'. The Venetian Ambassador to London found the reason for this humiliation in bad management, division between the leaders, shortness of provisions and a fear that if the winter gales were allowed to take their final toll none of them would return.

Charles remained strangely unperturbed. Taking adversity without apparent emotion was, indeed, becoming characteristic. It was also a kind of defiance. Circumstances had treated him badly and no enquiry, no attempt to apportion blame, could alter the situation. In

141

Charles's mind, so far as the rest of the world should know, the episode was closed. He never again attempted a direct naval or military confrontation with Spain. He spent the autumn and winter endeavouring to bring Denmark and the North German Princes into a closer alliance with himself and the States General, and he sought new ways of raising money, one of which entailed offering the Crown jewels as security for a loan from Dutch financiers, but nowhere did he find much support. Even from France, in spite of his marriage treaty, he received little comfort.

12

Charles Saves the Duke

Relations with France were indeed deteriorating and incidents were accumulating daily concerning the merchant ships of each nation; on one occasion the whole English-Scottish wine fleet sailing from Bordeaux with a year's supply was seized by the French, and merchants' complaints to the Privy Council could not be ignored. Charles was mortified that the French had failed to keep their treaty obligations and had done little to help the Palatinate. His personal relations with the French in general were bad in spite, even because of, his French wife, and he demanded the recall of the Sieur de Blainville, the French Ambassador, whom he accused of causing trouble between Henrietta-Maria and himself. The French aversion to Buckingham continued and they refused to allow him even to pass through their country for any kind of negotiation. The Duke was now as strongly anti-French as he had been anti-Spanish and he made no more effort than Charles to save the alliance. All these factors combined and received expression in Charles's strong reaction to the plight of the Huguenots in La Rochelle. No doubt he felt some pang of conscience over the English ships he had lent to France, but the practical issue took shape after 5 September 1625 when the French defeated a Huguenot fleet under the Duke of Soubise, one of Charles's godparents, and laid siege to the town. There then began to rise in Charles the conviction, which over the next few years became almost an obsession, that he was in honour bound to help the Huguenots. As the battered wrecks from Cadiz crept back to English harbours during the winter of 1625 he was glad to discover a new focus for his warlike intentions, wiping out the ignominy of Cadiz by the thought of the relief of La Rochelle. That it. entailed fighting the French seemed scarcely to occur to him; nor the fact that to be on unfriendly terms with both France and Spain at the same time was upsetting the basic tenets of centuries of English foreign policy. His main concern was to find the money to re-equip the fleet and reluctantly his mind turned once more to a Parliament.

He made more effort this time to manage elections by exercising his right of appointment to the shrievalty: since a sheriff was not eligible for election to Parliament the device should rid him of the more troublesome Members of 1625. When his second Parliament met on 6 February 1626 Sir Robert Phelips was not there, nor Sir Edward Coke, Sir Francis Seymour, Edward Alford nor Sir Thomas Wentworth. Further intervention in the elections was not very effective. Sir Edwin Sandys, after an initial defeat, was returned for Penryn; he was joined by Sir Dudley Digges and, of the younger men, by Sir John Eliot, John Pym and Clement Coke, son of the eminent lawyer.

In the Upper House manipulation was at once more direct and more difficult; it is surprising that Charles had not used the obvious device of creating peers who would support him. He tried instead to disarm those who stood in his way. He had already relieved the moderate Bishop Williams of the Great Seal, he now imprisoned the pro-Spanish Arundel on a flimsy pretext, he placated the choleric Pembroke, he attempted to keep Bristol from taking his seat. Bristol succeeded in appearing on May 1, Arundel was not back in his place in the House of Lords until June 8. Both were petty and ineptly-handled affairs which did nothing to improve the political atmosphere.

The opening ceremony was kept at a minimum. Once more Laud preached the sermon, his theme the unity of the state in the person of the King: the session, unfortunately, raised doubts. The King's speech was even more brief than to the previous Parliament though it was, as usual, dignified. He came to them, he said, 'in the midst of necessity to learn how he was to frame his course and councils' and he warned them that 'unseasonable slowness may produce as ill effect as denial'. Again the Houses were given no concrete statement, no specific request. Still less was there any reference to what had happened at Cadiz. But they knew enough to be both angry and uneasy. Sir John Eliot was well aware, as a Cornishman, of the effect of pirate raids upon the West country; as Vice-Admiral for Devon he had watched the return of the ships and the pitiful remnants of their crews from Cadiz. Four days after the opening of Parliament he was on his feet demanding an enquiry into that expedition and some indication of future plans before considering supply. 'Our honour is ruined, our ships are sunk, our men perished; not by the sword, not by the enemy, not by chance', he cried, 'but . . . by those we trust'. Tension was running through the House. Since constitutionally the King could do no wrong the blame must be taken by the man with most power under the King – the Duke of Buckingham – who was, besides, the Lord Admiral. Moved apparently by sudden anger, perhaps feeling that in his father's absence some responsibility devolved upon him, Clement Coke, a man not usually vocal, exclaimed on March 11 that it were better to die by an enemy than to suffer at home! This loosened the tongue of Dr Turner, another Member not generally to the forefront, and he made an impassioned attack upon Buckingham. Had the Duke guarded the seas against pirates? Had he not, by the appointment of unworthy officers, caused the failure of the expedition to Cadiz? Had he not engrossed a large part of the Crown lands to himself, his friends and his relations? Had he not sold places of judicature and titles of honour? Was he not dangerous to the state, his mother and his father-in-law being recusants? Was it fit that he should, in his own person, enjoy so many great offices? The cause of all their troubles, he cried, was 'that great man, the Duke of Buckingham!'. Perhaps the House was not quite ready for such an outburst. At any rate it hastened to assure the King that no monarch was ever dearer to his people and that it wished to make him 'safe at home and feared abroad'. Charles's answer was to demand justice upon Clement Coke and Turner and to summon the Houses to Whitehall.

There, four days later, he spoke incisively. He might claim his stammer on occasion, but he could speak well and to the point when he wished. He now told them to spend less time discussing grievances and more time in preventing and redressing them. Then he went on:

> But some there are . . . that do make inquiry into the proceedings, not of any ordinary servant, but of one that is most near unto me. It hath been said, 'What shall be done to the man whom the King delighteth to honour?' But now it is the labour of some to seek what may be done against the man whom the King thinks fit to be honoured.

He reminded the Members that when Buckingham was to the fore in breaking the treaties with Spain he was considered worthy of all the honour James conferred upon him. Since then, Charles maintained, he had done nothing but what arose out of that policy and had engaged himself and his estate in furtherance of it and in the service of the King.

Indeed, said Charles, some of the actions of which the House accused him were done at his express command. 'I would not have the House', he concluded, 'to question my servants, much less one that is so near me.' Though the language was more restrained, it might have been James who was standing there before them. Once more he had disclaimed, emphatically, any question of the responsibility of ministers to Parliament.

March 27 was the day fixed to consider supply and once again Rudyerd spoke for the Crown, asking for three subsidies and three fifteenths. Eliot's reply indicated that Charles's speech had fallen upon deaf ears. How could they give, he cried, when enterprise after enterprise, at home and abroad, met with disaster? And he did not hesitate to name the cause. They were all undertaken, if not planned and made, by that great lord, the Duke of Buckingham. He had exhausted and consumed the treasures, not only of the subjects but of the King. Without some reformation in these things, Eliot averred, he did not know what wills or what abilities men could have to give a new supply. He proposed, and the House agreed, that the supply asked for should be approved but not converted into a Bill until their grievances had been redressed. The inference was clear. As the Commons set to work to build up the case against Buckingham Charles addressed them once more in a fighting speech. He had begun the war upon their advice and now

> that I am so far engaged that you think there is no retreat, now you begin to set the dice, and make your own game; but I pray you to be not deceived; it is not a Parliamentary way, nor it is not a way to deal with a king. Mr. Coke told you it was better to be eaten up by a foreign enemy than to be destroyed at home. Indeed, I think it more honour for a king to be invaded and almost destroyed by a foreign enemy, than to be despised by his own subjects. Remember that Parliaments are altogether in my power for their calling, sitting, and dissolution; therefore, as I find the fruits of them good or evil, they are to continue or not to be.

They were his last words to them before the Easter recess. They had so little effect that when the Commons reassembled on April 13 they immediately appointed a committee to formulate charges against the Duke.[1]

In this situation Bristol was doubly to be feared. From his seat in the Lords he could both attack and sit in judgment upon Buckingham. To prevent that, Charles on May 1 brought Bristol to the bar of the House of Lords on a charge of high treason: he had got Charles to Spain under false pretences, attempted to change his religion there, and had been willing to accept marriage terms less advantageous to the country than they could have been.

When Bristol rose to reply it was apparent at once that Charles had given him the very opportunity he needed, for he launched into a series of counter-charges against Buckingham: 'My Lords, I am a freeman and a peer of the realm, unattainted', he began. 'Somewhat I have to say of high consequence for his majesty's service; and therefore I beseech your lordships give me leave to speak.' This being granted, 'my lords', he said, 'I accuse that man', pointing to the Duke of Buckingham, 'of high treason; and I will prove it.' So Buckingham was in the unprecedented position of facing simultaneously an impeachment charge by the House of Commons and a charge of High Treason in the House of Lords. Part of Bristol's case covered familiar ground, the Duke's conduct in Spain, his intimations of the Prince's conversion to Rome – here Bristol made the point that Charles could at any time have scotched those rumours by a straightforward statement to the contrary – and, above all, he offered what appeared to be proof that the Duke, unknown to James, had planned the visit with Gondomar a full year before it took place. Time and time again as Bristol made his case Charles attempted to intervene. First he sent to the House of Lords to say that Bristol's charges against Buckingham were merely recriminatory, and that he himself could witness against them; then he contested Bristol's right to be counsel in his own cause. In neither case was his point taken.[2]

On May 8, with Bristol's trial in full swing, the Commons had completed their Declaration and Impeachment against the Duke of Buckingham and at a conference between the two Houses the charge was laid. It covered his plurality of office, his purchase of place, procuring honours for his kin, compelling the purchase of honours, failure to guard the seas, giving English ships to the French, 'exhausting, intercepting, and mis-employing the King's revenue' and his 'transcendent Presumption in giving Physick' to King James on his death bed. The impeachment did not include any reference to the charges which Bristol was making concerning Buckingham's part in the Spanish escapade. So far as the Commons were concerned, Bristol might have been flogging a dead horse.

Their charge against the Duke took two days to complete. Dudley Digges opened the case. He laid the ills of the country at the Duke's

147

door: 'the laws of England have taught us that kings cannot command ill or unlawful things. And whatsoever ill events succeed, the executioners of such designs must answer for them', and he ran briefly over the heads of the charges made against the Duke, concluding with a somewhat obscure reference to his presence by James's death bed. Buckingham himself appeared to take the proceedings lightly. Contrary to precedent he was in the House of Lords when his accusers came to the bar and when at one point in his charge Dudley Digges, speaking of Buckingham as 'a comet, exhaled out of base and putrid matter', looked up it was full into the smiling face of the Duke – 'sitting there, outfacing his accusers, outbraving his accusations'. Yet earlier in the session Buckingham had been worried and, as so often when he was under stress, he fell ill: 'it may be *animo* as well as *corpore*' remarked Mead to Stuteville.

Edward Herbert, a future Attorney General, followed Digges and spoke of Buckingham's monopoly of office, of his purchase of the Admiralty from the Earl of Nottingham, of the Cinque Ports from Lord Zouch. John Selden spoke of Buckingham's failure to guard the narrow seas, of the disasters to English ships and naval enterprise; John Glanville, who had been secretary to the Cadiz expedition, spoke both of that disaster and of the ships that had been sent to La Rochelle. Sherland told how the Duke had compelled the purchase of honours and office for money; John Pym how he had accumulated honours and rewards both to himself and to his family and friends. Christopher Wandesford, a friend of Wentworth, spoke guardedly of the charges of administering medicine to James on his sick bed. Sir John Eliot then rose for the summing up of the Commons' case against the favourite and chief minister of two kings, a man who was unique in that his influence with the son was even greater than it had been with the father. With burning oratory he went over the points again, spoke of the 'immensity' of Buckingham's waste of the revenues of the Crown: what they had granted in subsidies Buckingham had spent on himself. 'No wonder, then, our King is now in want, this man abounding so!' Having said the worst he could, Eliot could think of nothing more but a comparison: in his pride, his high ambition, his solecisms, his neglect of counsels, his veneries, his venefices, above all in his pride, Buckingham was like Sejanus who was styled *laborum imperatoris socius*. 'My Lords', concluded Eliot, 'I have done. You see the man. What have been his actions, whom he is like, you know. I leave him to your judgments.'[3]

Eliot had made an oratorically and emotionally strong case against the Duke, but he had put the House of Commons in a paradoxical position. While accepting the doctrine that constitutionally the King could do no wrong, they were seeking to condemn the actions of a minister which the King had already accepted as his own. They were driven back, consequently, on a series of specious arguments. If a king contemplated a rash act it was the responsibility of the minister to advise him against it, to appeal to his Council and finally to appeal to Parliament. Unless he did this he, and not the king, must bear the blame. Once more the responsibility of ministers to Parliament had been raised and the Commons were reaching out to a principle that would be basic both to the political thought of Englishmen and to the practice of constitutional government. At the same time, though even more dimly perceived, they were thinking in terms of Parliamentary sovereignty.

It was insulting and appeared to be a prejudging of the issue that the House of Commons asked for Buckingham's restraint while the impeachment was proceeding. The House of Lords refused the request. Charles spoke bitterly to his friends. 'If the Duke is Sejanus', he said, 'I must be Tiberius.' On May 11, the day after Eliot's summing up, he went from Whitehall by barge to Westminster accompanied by the Duke and other peers, and before the House of Lords made a full refutation of every charge made against Buckingham, taking all the Duke was charged with upon himself. But while speaking soft words to the Lords, in the Commons Charles had acted, seizing Eliot and Digges at the door of the House and taking them by water to the Tower. When the news of their imprisonment broke, the indignation, confusion, and uproar in the House should have warned Charles of the dangerous path he was treading. 'Rise! Rise! Rise!' shouted the Members, and the House broke up in confusion. But before it met again the following day the words 'liberty of Parliament' were on every lip, and the Speaker was not allowed to proceed with ordinary business. 'Sit down!, sit down!' the Members cried as he made to rise in his seat to open proceedings for the day. They were hardly mollified by Sir Dudley Carleton, speaking undoubtedly on behalf of the King, who begged them not to trench upon the King's prerogative lest they brought him out of love with Parliaments.

At this moment, with the charge of High Treason against Bristol and the impeachment of Buckingham in full swing, Charles perpetrated an extraordinary act of defiance. The Earl of Suffolk,

Chancellor of Cambridge University, died on May 28 and Charles nominated Buckingham for the office. It was a triple defiance in adding one more office to the accumulation which formed part of the indictment against the Duke; in demonstrating once more the King's confidence in his friend; and in showing his own opposition to Puritan beliefs. For Suffolk had been a staunch Puritan and his followers were advancing his son, the Earl of Berkshire, as their nominee. Buckingham secured the election by 108 votes to 103, although what degree of pressure was brought to bear is difficult to assess.

But the election could not affect the broader issue and on June 8 Buckingham began his defence. He was probably helped by Nicholas Hyde, later to be knighted and to become Chief Justice of the King's Bench, by Laud, and by the Attorney General, Sir Robert Heath. He was in the position of knowing far more of the circumstances and events at issue than the Commons who had accused him. Some charges he was able to rebut, some actions he claimed were on the King's orders, others, like the purchase of office from a retiring officer, were according to custom. He answered the charges of accumulating riches at the state's expense by claiming how largely he had spent them for the King and the country. 'I never had any end of my own', he said, and he cited the eight ships he had kept on the coasts at his own charge.

> When you know the truth and when all shall appear, I hope I shall stand right in your opinions. It is no time to pick quarrels one with another . . . though I confess there may be some errors I will not justify, yet they are not gross defects as the world would make them appear. They are no errors of wilfulness, nor of corruption, nor oppressing of the people, nor injustice.[4]

But the Commons were disregarding the most elementary principle of justice in paying no attention to Buckingham's defence. While he was answering their charges in the Lords they were working on a new Remonstrance which announced that they had presented only part of their case against him. They now declared in so many words that he was an enemy both to Church and to State, and they begged the King to remove him. For, they said, 'until this great person be removed from intermeddling with the great affairs of State, we are out of hope of any good success'. In particular they feared that any supply they might grant would, through his mismanagement, be turned to the prejudice of the kingdom. It was clear that they would withhold supply until Buckingham was gone, and it was clear that they intended to remove Buckingham.

Perhaps they realized the legal weakness 'of their case and intended to bluster through; possibly they felt driven to extremities by the Cambridge Chancellorship; it is possible that Charles, by throwing the Chancellorship into the ring at this time, was deliberately provoking the Commons. He certainly professed to be outraged by the Remonstrance. He was possibly glad to use it as an excuse for an immediate dissolution, ready to be quit of a Parliament that had yet granted him no supply, because he feared the outcome of the impeachment. Sir Robert Heath had assured him that its result could only exonerate Buckingham. But there could have been other issues, less openly spoken of, which alarmed Charles.

One of the reasons for Digges's imprisonment had been the way he dealt with the last of the charges in the Commons' indictment of Buckingham, that of administering medicine to the late King. There was considerable disagreement as to what he said. One report spoke of him as saying that he forebore to speak further on the poisoning charge in regard of the King's honour; another that he said he was commanded by the Commons, in making the charge, 'to take Care of the Honour of the King our Sovereign that lives'. Charles referred to 'insolent speeches against myself'. Digges maintained that he had not wished to reflect upon the person either of the dead or of the present King. Since much turned upon Digges's actual words a committee met on May 8 to determine them. Nothing conclusive emerged but a majority of peers expressed their belief that Digges had said nothing that reflected upon the King's honour. This was the ruling Charles wanted, and he released Digges from prison on May 16.

Wandesford, who had spoken to the actual charge against Buckingham of administering medicine to James, had merely spoken, like the indictment, of an act 'of transcendent presumption'. He had not been imprisoned. Eliot, on the other hand, in his summing up, had been even more damning than Digges against Buckingham, although he made no reference to Charles. 'Not satisfied', he said, with the wrongs of honour, with the prejudice of religion, with the abuse of State, with the misappropriation of revenues, his attempts go higher, even to the person of his sovereign. 'You have before you his making practice on that, in such manner and with such effect as I fear to speak it, nay, I doubt and hesitate to think it.' Eliot's imprisonment lasted longer than Digges's and he was not released until the 19th. On May

20 the Commons formally cleared both Eliot and Digges of any charges against them.

Whatever his intentions, however brave a show he put on in public, in private Charles was much distressed. 'What can I do more?' he was heard saying to the Duke in his bedchamber. 'I have engaged mine honour to mine Uncle of Denmark, and other princes. I have, in a manner, lost the love of my subjects. What wouldst thou have me do?' One thing was certain. All reports agreed that there was no abatement, but rather an increase, in his affection for the Duke. Whether for Buckingham, or whether to protect himself from further charges, Charles went to the House of Lords once more on June 15 to dissolve another Parliament. He was doing so, he said, because it was 'abused by the violent and ill advised passions of a few Members . . . for private and personal ends', that it neglected public business, was intent upon the prosecution of a peer of the realm, and that it had forgotten its engagements to the King and to the country. The Lords begged for two days more to complete their business. 'Not a minute!' was Charles's reply and his second Parliament was then and there ended without a penny of subsidy being granted or any customs duties legalized.

.   A Proclamation ordered the destruction of all copies of the Remonstrance and on July 7 Charles published his own account of the 1626 Parliament. Since he was no longer protected by privilege of Parliament Bristol was sent to the Tower. Charles wished him to be condemned and Buckingham to be triumphantly vindicated by a trial in the Star Chamber. Buckingham's trial there broke down because the Parliament men who had charged the Duke insisted that they had done so in the name of the House of Commons and that body being no longer in existence they could not proceed. After a merely formal hearing, therefore, the Star Chamber gave judgment in Buckingham's favour. Bristol fell ill. The charges against him were quietly dropped and he was allowed to return to his home.

Charles's second Parliament was no more high-principled and, in spite of the central theme of Buckingham's impeachment, no more coherent than his first. Eliot had assumed the leadership and given it such direction as it had. But the Commons as a whole were too obsessed with the charges they were levelling against the Duke, and with their determination to withhold supply, to consider general questions of policy. They showed little interest in Europe, little sympathy for their co-religionists who were fighting for their faith, no

152

understanding of the magnitude of the problems that Charles was trying to handle. Yet the dissolution of two Parliaments in so short a time by so new a king had inevitably caused misgivings. Some people forecast there would never be another. 'Is it not time to pray?' asked Mead of Stuteville when dissolution was imminent. The meteor that appeared over the Thames, the storm that swept Westminster on June 12, were taken to augur disaster. But Charles made no concessions. He had shown his faith in the Duke. Five days after the dissolution he showed his support of William Laud by appointing him Bishop of Bath and Wells. It was not the see that Laud would have wished, but he had to wait for dead men's shoes and, as he wrote, he 'had to fasten upon any indifferent thing' to get out of Wales. Three months later, when Lancelot Andrewes died, Charles kept his see of Winchester vacant for a year in order to give it to Laud, meanwhile conveniently appropriating its revenues to the Crown. The Deanery of the Chapel Royal, which Andrewes also held, Charles gave to Laud immediately. He had expressed, in no uncertain terms, his support of the Laudian Church as well as his devotion to Buckingham.

13

Charles Saves his Marriage

Throughout her husband's preoccupation with Parliament and his favourite, Henrietta-Maria remained thoroughly French in sentiment and religion. Unlike the Infanta of Spain she had taken no English lessons and, although French was spoken by many at her husband's Court and others, like Bishop Williams, took pains to learn it, language was still a barrier. In some ways, indeed, she was older than her years and her upbringing close to the French Court had taught her that a king had duties that stretched beyond his wife. Yet she might have expected a little longer grace before her husband plunged into affairs of state. Parliament opened two days after her arrival in London. Because of the plague she was moved from London to Hampton Court to Richmond to Oatlands to Windsor to Nonesuch to Woodstock. If she imagined that her place was by the King she was frustrated because the Duke of Buckingham was always there. She felt excluded, as Charles himself had done as a young man when his father and Buckingham were always together. The Duke himself made no attempt to woo her. On the contrary, he joined with Charles in attempting to foist upon her, as ladies of her bedchamber, attendants of their own choosing, in particular the Duke's mother, his sister, and his niece. Henrietta-Maria refused to accept them. It was contrary to the conditions of her marriage, she told Charles; she would not have spies in her bedchamber. The French Ambassador threatened to throw any message from Buckingham out of the window, and there the matter rested for the moment. Nevertheless, by the end of July a compromise had been reached whereby Buckingham's mother, as a Catholic, was admitted to the Queen's bedchamber while the other two ladies were admitted 'by permission' only. As in so many of the wrangles between the King and Queen there was reason on both sides. The Queen's only security and sense of continuity lay in her French attendants, yet not only were their numbers excessive, they appeared to dominate the Queen, they showed contempt for all things English, and they were wildly extravagant in the demands they made upon the English Exchequer. Even the lying-in of the Duchesse de Chevreuse was paid for by Charles. Apart from Chevreuse – 'who painted her face foully' – Madame de Saint-Georges was particularly hated and was still not allowed in the royal coach.

But her religious advisers had more control over her than her attendants. In their presence she could never forget her mother's letter and her promise to the Pope. It was rumoured that at confession they asked her how many times she had allowed the King to kiss her in the night. They reminded her of every Saint Day and her appropriate conduct, even emphasizing the nights upon which she must not let her husband approach her. She worshipped in what was described as 'a small monastery in her house', where she performed 'spiritual exercises with her ladies', sometimes withdrawing there altogether and 'behaving like a nun'. Much of this was reaction. She had come to England under the assurance of freedom for her own worship and of a wide tolerance for Catholics, yet the English Parliament at Oxford spoke of her religion as 'this dangerous disease' and her husband had promised to expel her fellow believers as a 'wicked generation of Jesuits, seminary priests, and incendiaries'.

After the dissolution of his first Parliament on 12 August 1625 Charles's mind was only half on his marriage and probably less on his wife. He went, not to Henrietta, but with Buckingham to Beaulieu to hunt in the New Forest. Buckingham's wife was for the first time pregnant and was at Beaulieu, but Henrietta went from Woodstock to Tichfield on Southampton Water. Here, as was customary for houses in royal occupation, a room was established as a chapel for English services, in spite of the Queen's protest that, since she was in residence and not the King, it was unnecessary to provide for anything but her own worship. In sheer defiance she made her protest like a small child, playing practical jokes on the chaplain, passing through the English chapel at sermon time, laughing and chattering with her French attendants and her dogs. Charles visited her from time to time but there were always quarrels. Buckingham also went to see her at Tichfield and told her that, unless she changed her ways, she would not be treated like the Queen of England but like the silly little girl she was.

But she continued to be happy with her French friends, too often sulky with the English. A smile could change all too quickly to a frown when matters were not quite as she wished them – when there were, for example, too many people watching as she and the King dined in public, or when people pressed too closely to her. At grace at meal times her chaplain refused to give way to English customs. There was one occasion when he actually competed with the King's own chaplain who was saying grace and there was such confusion that Charles, in a great passion rose from the table, took the Queen by the hand, and retired into his bedchamber.

At the beginning of 1626 the plague was abating – some said in the week following the proclamation against Papists, some said after the seventh general fast – but it left a trail of distress in its wake. The rich had fled from the cities, trading was virtually at a standstill, unemployed men and women were begging in the streets. Appeals were made by magistrates and ministers for the relief of the poor and homeless, voluntary collections were made throughout the country, the poor rate was doubled. There was nevertheless a public thanksgiving in January for deliverance from the pestilence and the playhouses, which had been shut for eight months, re-opened. The return to London and the prospect of entertainment was a great stimulus to the Queen. Her first birthday in England (her sixteenth) had been celebrated at Hampton Court in December with some success and Charles was persuaded that, as he put it to Buckingham, his wife was 'mending her manners'. A new theatrical company was formed in her honour – Queen Henrietta's Men – which immediately started playing with two plays by James Shirley which were performed in the Cockpit at Whitehall. The Queen appeared happy enough and Charles had no misgivings as he made plans for his coronation.

To a man of Charles's temperament the coronation was a more than usually solemn service of dedication. Instead of the customary purple he chose to wear white as a symbol of the purity with which he came to his people, and he had no qualms concerning the presence of his wife on such an occasion. But to Henrietta-Maria and to her brother, King Louis, a daughter of France could not be crowned in a Protestant church in a ceremony performed by Protestant bishops. Louis wrote that, although he desired his sister to have this crown it must be without prejudice to her conscience and that if she had to choose, a heavenly crown was better. Even the small curtained box in which it was suggested she might sit, unseen, even if she would play no part, was refused. So, on 2 February 1626, Charles was crowned alone. The absence of his Queen gave a greater prominence to Buckingham and an incident occurred during the ceremony which appeared to cement their relationship. Charles stumbled in mounting the steps to the throne and Buckingham made to assist him but Charles removed the Duke's helping hand and instead put his own under Buckingham's arm, saying with a smile, 'I have as much need to help you as you to assist me.'

Williams, as Dean of Westminster, should have conducted the ceremony, but Charles chose instead William Laud, who was one of the prebendaries of the Abbey, and it was Laud who delivered into Charles's hand the staff of Edward the Confessor. The Earl of Pembroke bore the crown, his brother, the Earl of Montgomery, bore the spurs. When the King was crowned the Earl of Arundel, as senior Earl, presented him to the people. For a moment, probably because of some misunderstanding, there was silence. But when Arundel told them what to do, 'God save King Charles!' sounded on every side, amid great crying and shouting. The King was crowned. But the absence of his Queen revealed, perhaps, a flaw in his domestic life as well as a rift in his religious settlement. To what extent Charles perceived the implications, to what degree he cared, whether his stumbling on the steps of the throne or the people's brief silence after his proclamation or the absence of his Queen appeared to him as omens, he gave no sign but turned his attention to his second Parliament which was due to meet within the next few days.

Charles wished his wife to watch the opening procession to this Parliament. As usual, they were soon bickering. At first she was to watch from a window of the Banqueting House in Whitehall. But when she was already there with the French Ambassador and other French friends, Charles sent word that it would be better if she watched from the balcony of the house of Buckingham's mother in King Street. Henrietta-Maria excused herself on the grounds that it was raining and she did not wish to cross the street and get wet. Charles retorted that it was not raining. When Buckingham went to her on the King's behalf, the French Ambassador joined him in advising compliance, and the Queen allowed Buckingham to take her hand and lead her to his mother's house. It was an open manifestation of the Buckingham family's position in the royal household. But Charles was incensed against his wife, complaining that she took more notice of the French Ambassador than she did of him. For three days he would not speak to her. When she asked him in what she had offended he replied that he expected her to acknowledge her error. 'In what?', she asked. 'You said it rained when I told you it did not.' 'If you think that an offence', she replied, 'I will think so too.' And so the matter ended. Charles considered he had asserted his authority, kissed his wife, and turned back to Buckingham and to Parliament.[1]

After the Court's return to Whitehall at the beginning of 1626 there was the usual round of parties and diversions such as the visit of the Persian Ambassador, who proceeded in state to the Banqueting House from Bishopsgate on March 10 in a procession of thirty coaches. But, apart from her priests, Inigo Jones was the Queen's greatest solace, and she spent many hours with him planning her Shrove Day masque for 1626, which would be both her first and the first of the new reign. They chose to perform Racan's *Artenice*, of whose production at the French Court seven years earlier Henrietta had vivid memories. When the play was presented on February 21 at Somerset House on a specially constructed stage it was seen that Jones had introduced the proscenium arch and perspective scenery and that there was a succession of changing scenes after the French fashion. He had even simulated varying weather conditions, the play opening in moonlight, changing to storm, and returning to a peaceful moonlit night. The scenes themselves changed from deep forest glades to pastoral villages, to lakes and Italianate villas.

Early in the New Year the Queen began to rehearse her ladies, who were to act the entire production, and to train the dancers for the masque which would follow the play. Charles's mother had appeared in Court masques with little criticism (except when she blackened her face) but this would be the first time that a Queen of England had spoken a role or that her ladies had taken male parts. The performance was therefore kept strictly private, and Charles allowed no printing of the text. Those who were privileged to view the performance were delighted, and Charles was particularly pleased with his wife's acting. The King and Queen, indeed, were showing rather more affection to one another, yet the quarrels continued. Buckingham may have been sincere in trying to help; he certainly believed he knew all there was to know about love. But when he tried to talk to Henrietta-Maria on the subject she recoiled and repulsed him. He then went to Madame de Saint-Georges and begged her to try to improve the relations between the King and the Queen. She replied that she thought they were satisfactory. Buckingham said that they might be so during the day but that the Queen did not respond as she should at night. Madame de Saint-Georges was embarrassed and said she did not meddle in such affairs though, according to Buckingham, she promised to speak to the Queen. Charles believed his wife did become more affectionate towards him, but was deeply humiliated when he was told that he was indebted to Madame de Saint-Georges. The general worry was, in fact, making him more impatient than ever with Henrietta's French attendants. He had unburdened himself many times to Buckingham about the 'Monsieurs', threatening to send them all back to France. The deteriorating relations between France and England did not help, and the departure of Blainville, the French Ambassador, on April 19 increased Henrietta's sense of isolation.

Shortly afterwards there was a quarrel over her marriage jointure, the Queen demanding that it should be managed by at least some people of her own choosing. She spoke to the King one night in bed, sulkily asserting that she would accept no jointure at all if she could have no hand in managing it. As usual, they were soon in the middle of a regular quarrel in which Henrietta alleged her general unhappiness, refused to listen to her husband, and cried out that she was not of such base quality as to be used so ill. 'Then', wrote Charles later, 'I made her both hear me, and end that discourse.'

It was, however, religion that brought matters to a head. There was trouble about English Catholics frequenting the chapels established for the Queen and her attendants, trouble over the numerous saint and fast days she observed at the behest of her religious advisers, trouble over the number of her priests. One day, 6 July 1626, it happened that after a period of private worship she had come across St James's Park to Tyburn, where Catholic martyrs had suffered and died, and she was moved to kneel by the gibbet in devotion. When Charles heard this his unaccustomed anger flared. 'They would separate me from my wife!' he exclaimed, and after informing his Privy Council of his intentions he sent for the Queen on the 10th. She declined to come, as she so often did, this time alleging toothache. So Charles, with members of his Council, went to her apartment at St James's and shut himself in with her alone while in an outer room Secretary Conway told her French staff they must go. Their resistance was so strong and vocal that the yeomen of the guard had to be called to clear them out. As they gathered in the courtyard below, still shouting and protesting, the Queen, realizing what was happening, rushed to the window and beat at the glass, breaking the panes and cutting her hands so that they bled. Charles dragged her back into the room and kept her there forcibly while her attendants were taken to Somerset House. 'I command you', Charles wrote to Buckingham, 'send them all away tomorrow – by fair means if possible, but stick not long in disputing, use force if necessary and drive them away like so many wild beasts until ye have shipped them, and so the Devil go with them.' It needed the guard once more to get them to Dover where they were sent to France by the earliest possible boat. A knot of people jeered them on their way and someone threw a stone at Madame de Saint-Georges which knocked her hat off. But they had little reason to complain. They were given jewels and money amounting to about £23,000 and Charles ironically told them that if they were not satisfied they could take more from that part of the Queen's dowry which had not been paid. Of her original attendants Henrietta was allowed to keep her two English priests, her old French nurse, her dresser, and some dozen cooks, bakers and others employed on less personal tasks.

Although she had no alternative but to submit, she still reached out to assert herself in some way. One night in August she returned to the matter of her household, telling her husband that she desired no more for its regulation than his mother, Queen Anne, had enjoyed. The King replied that his mother was in a different category. To this the Queen retorted that there certainly was a great difference between a daughter of Denmark and a daughter of France and Bourbon. Charles then remarked that a daughter of France was nothing very great, as she brought no prerogative with her beyond her simple dowry, and, besides, she was the third and last and therefore of less account.

It was a blessing all round when Marshal Bassompierre arrived from France in September with the mission of settling disputes and of healing, so far as could be done on the personal side, the breach between France and England. He proved to be a man of soothing presence and great tact. He alone seemed to perceive that the rift between the King and Queen owed as much to one partner as to the other. He advised Charles, he spoke sharply to Henrietta-Maria. The Queen's household was made as agreeable as possible to her and, although it still included Buckingham's mother, wife and sister, she soon found herself on more friendly terms with them and even with the Duke himself. In short, she found that it was not only with her French ladies that she could enjoy herself. Buckingham, in defiance of the money shortage and all that was being said about his extravagance, mounted a wildly exuberant but most effective masque at York House in honour of the French Ambassador, with the theme of renewed amity between the two nations. So, while relations between Charles and Buckingham remained the same, those between Charles and Henrietta, and even between Henrietta and the Duke, improved, and there were the beginnings of a triad similar to that of his father's time – he, like James, drawing together the two people closest to him. Still, however, there was no sign of an heir. As the Venetian Ambassador said to Carleton, the 'King of Great Britain had married to have a successor, as was only reasonable, but children come from love and not from anger'. The anger was dying but there was still an impediment.[2]

14

La Rochelle

On the war front, while Charles and Buckingham were pinning their hopes upon a fleet to relieve La Rochelle, nearer the heart of the struggle the news was bad. Mansfeld was defeated by Wallenstein at the Bridge of Dessau in the summer of 1626, Christian of Denmark was defeated by Tilly at Lutter on August 27, a defeat on a scale which virtually meant abandoning the whole of North Germany. Christian was bitter, accusing Charles of bad faith in leaving him to struggle alone. Charles, hearing the news on September 12, showed a rare agitation. He rushed to London, called a Council meeting which lasted four hours, sent for the Danish Ambassador and, with tears in his eyes, protested that he would stake his crown and his life for his uncle, but reminded him of the dire financial straits he was in.

The situation was, indeed, desperate. Charles had hoped to show he was master in his own house by throwing out the Monsieurs and throwing out two Parliaments, but he was a master without resources and unless he could raise money he was helpless. He offered the Crown jewels once more – this time to the City of London – and although the citizens declined to lend upon so doubtful a security, a few people made gifts instead. There were three sales of royal plate in August and September 1626. A proposal, supported by Buckingham, to debase the coinage was turned down on arguments brought forward by Sir Robert Cotton. The raising of money by privy seals had not proved sufficiently successful to merit its repetition. The substitution of free gifts for the subsidies promised, but not passed into law, by the previous Parliament appeared a likely way. But the success of this enterprise depended upon the Justices of the Peace who would be expected to collect the gifts. Since it was apparent that such Justices as Eliot, Phelips, Seymour, Alford, Mansell, Digges and Wentworth would not co-operate, Charles removed them from the Commission of the Peace and attempted to make a reasoned claim for the money through specially appointed commissioners in each county who would assess the inhabitants in accordance with previous Parliamentary assessments. To make payment easier he abandoned the idea of a free gift and promised that the money would be repaid 'as soon as we shall be any ways enabled thereunto', at the same time pledging his royal word that not a penny would be spent upon anything but public service.

In Middlesex, Essex and the home counties the response was at first encouraging, but just as plans were being made to extend the collection the Judges stepped in with a veto, claiming that they could not be certain of its legality. Charles dismissed the Chief Justice, Sir Randal Crew, and replaced him by Sir Nicholas Hyde. But the news of the resistance of the Judges encouraged people to refuse to lend and some who had already consented revoked their promises. There was a suggestion that troops recruited for the new naval enterprise should be quartered upon the counties most reluctant to lend, but reflection indicated that since both the soldiers and the populace were equally disaffected the action would create rather than suppress disturbance. Instead, rich men were imprisoned by warrant from the Privy Council while poorer men were forced under martial law to serve as soldiers. The names of those who resisted what was now generally termed a forced loan sound like a preliminary roll-call for the struggle to come, including Essex, Holles, St John, Warwick, Saye and Sele, Hampden, Eliot, Wentworth, Darnell. Five of them appealed in November for cause of their imprisonment to be shown. But a majority of King's Bench ruled that the command of the King was in itself sufficient cause and the five knights were returned to prison. With tonnage and poundage Charles felt he was on firmer ground, for not only were customs duties an established form of royal revenue, but his Parliament had expressed its willingness to confirm them and had merely delayed because of an irregularity. So, in the face of growing opposition from merchants, he issued a commission to collect taxes at the ports. Naval foraging, that other source of revenue, met with little success until in March 1627 Pennington took three French prizes, the proceeds of which boosted the preparations in English ports.

Meanwhile, they had all been trying to keep up appearances. Buckingham joined with the Venetian envoy in baiting a lion at the Tower; in the Queen's masque in January Charles led the dancing with his wife and Buckingham, and the revels continued until four in the morning. But the kind of gossip that circulated did the Duke no good: he had been carried in a litter to tennis while the King walked at his side; when he arrived late at the Christmas play it was begun again for his benefit. More serious were the riots at the ports where sailors were crying for wages. Groups of them came up to London demanding satisfaction of the Lord Admiral, they forcibly stopped his coach and created disturbances outside his house so that he was compelled to barricade his gates. When they were threatened with hanging they said that there were plenty more of them to come, and they were, indeed, joined by soldiers similarly demanding wages. In the crescendo of antagonism against Buckingham all the ills of the state seemed to combine. He was held responsible for the Queen's sterility, and even the death of his baby son, aged sixteen months, in March 1627 brought him little sympathy. Only Charles continued his support in spite of the fact that there were rumours that he himself was being included in the general dissaffection by, for example, sinister groups of Scotsmen who went about demanding that they would know how James met his death!

Nevertheless, the Rochelle project went forward and when on June 11 the King was once again at Plymouth dining aboard his flagship there was an air of joviality about his visit. Mirth and music were contributed by Archie the Fool and by the Duke's musicians. Charles himself talked of nothing but his ships, he continually sent healths across the water to neighbouring vessels, and he ordered a five-gun salute to the Duke of Soubise, the Huguenot leader they were sailing to help. Buckingham himself was in command of the fleet of eighty-four ships, which, with some 10,000 men, left Stokes Bay on June 27. They carried battering rams, landing trains, lodging materials, scaling ladders, guns, cannons, and other materials of war. Besides victuals their cargo included cows, sheep and poultry for the benefit of the besieged, an assortment of musical instruments, bedding, much 'brave apparel' for the Duke (doubtless to wear when he appeared among the Rochellese as their liberator), his own rich coach and his litter, many jewels, horses for tilting, and what the Venetian Ambassador caustically described as 'other hindrances to warfare'. The fleet, he asserted, was 'so furnished as to arouse no fear'. But its intentions were grandiose, as the instructions Charles gave to Buckingham on June 19 made clear. The French were encroaching upon English rights on the seas and, in spite of the terms of the marriage treaty, were endeavouring 'to root out that religion whereof by just title we are the defender'. Buckingham, therefore, was to capture or destroy any French or Spanish ships that seemed likely to interfere with English shipping; he was to proceed to La Rochelle and, if his assistance was still needed, was to hand over his soldiers to Soubise, who would accompany the expedition. Buckingham would then free the English vessels still detained by the French at Bordeaux, establish mastery of the seas round the coast of France, and break up Spanish shipping, securing such French and Spanish prizes as he could.

Spanish and French shipping had retreated into the shelter of their ports, and apart from a futile chase after four Dunkirkers, the English fleet had an uneventful journey to Rochelle. The weather was particularly foul, and it was not until July 10 that they anchored off the Isle of Rhé which controlled the approach to the town. The capture of the island, besides breaking the blockade of the town on the seaward side, would be of great value to Britain. Its harbour would shelter her commerce, it would be a good base for striking at French and Spanish shipping, its command of the salt marshes round the French coast would contribute considerably to private income and the royal revenue. In the face of stiff opposition from the French and casualties on both sides a landing was made and the English settled down to besiege the fortress of St Martin, the chief town of the island, mounting a strong blockade and barricading the seaward approaches to the town. The enterprise seemed straightforward enough. But the fort was well held, the rocky ground upon which it stood was unsuited to siege warfare, and the French had the advantage of reinforcements on the mainland and ships in nearby French ports. The English, on the other hand, were at the end of a long and slow line of communication whose reliability depended upon the weather. The reinforcements which Buckingham sent for were held up first by lack of money but then by a great storm which so battered the ships in their English harbour that repairs were necessary, supplies were consumed, and they had to be revictualled before they could sail.

As summer gave way to autumn on the Isle of Rhé the situation of the besiegers was difficult. They held on through expectation of help from home and in the knowledge that the Fort was reaching starvation point. It seemed, indeed, on the point of surrender when, on September 28, a night of favourable winds, supply ships battered their way through the English vessels and past the barricades to drop supplies before the fort. A decision to abandon the siege was made, then reversed when news came that the English reinforcements were on their way. But by October there was still no sign of them. By this time French troops were landing on the island from the mainland, the weather was wet and cold, the condition of the besiegers deplorable. Buckingham decided on a desperate attempt to take the fortress, but the garrison was forewarned, the scaling ladders proved too short, the siege cannon, instead of being ready for use, had mistakenly been reshipped. The assault was a complete failure. Buckingham halted his retreat in order to collect his wounded and then began to move across a narrow causeway to his ships. As he did so the French inflicted merciless casualties in the confined passage: they had the killing, taking, and drowning of our men at their pleasure, as an eye witness said.

Buckingham's personal bravery was never in doubt, nor his devotion to his men, his care of the sick and wounded, his willingness to share hardship with them, even to risk his life for them. He had also shown an aptness in learning the art of war that deserved more co-operative commanders. The failure of the assault, the disastrous retreat, resulted from immature judgment, a shocking breakdown of support from home, a lack of co-ordination among the high command and a reluctance to fight among the rank and file. Yet Buckingham could have been successful. If the wind had not been in the right direction supplies would not have got through to Fort St Martin; if the wind had not been in the wrong direction reinforcements would have reached him from England in time to affect the issue; even in the tragic farce of siege ladders being too short the issue might have been turned if someone had not blundered.[1]

Charles had followed events from home as closely as the distance allowed and throughout July was urging the officers of his Treasury to raise money for Buckingham's relief. The 'forced loan' had produced something like £240,000, for most of those assessed, moved by exhortation or threat, had contributed. But this money had already been swallowed up. An extra £14,000 was urgently needed if Buckingham was to be supplied. Yet, even at this time of stress, Charles had other projects on his mind. The rumoured sale of the Mantuan collection of pictures, brought to his attention by the Countess of Arundel a few years earlier, had never been far from his thoughts. Nicolas Lanier, one of his musicians, whom he had sent to Italy shortly after his accession to seek out art treasures, had been staying in Venice with Daniel Nye, a shadowy figure purporting to deal in rare perfumes, furs, and other luxuries, under cover of which he had become a familiar figure in the half-light of international art dealing. He had acted as agent for Sir Henry Wotton, Dudley Carleton, and Buckingham himself, and he now threw himself with zest into the most exciting deal he had yet undertaken.

The Gonzalez, Dukes of Mantua, were not art lovers, and their stupendous collection had been formed for the aggrandisement of their Court and State rather than to gratify their artistic sense. The interests of the present Duke certainly lay elsewhere: it was said he would pay more for a dwarf than an Old Master and he was rumoured to have his eye on a particularly delectable female dwarf while the sale of his art treasures was being negotiated. A decline in the silk industry upon which much of Mantua's prosperity depended was a further factor inclining him to exchange his art collection for ready cash. By August 1627 the work of Nye and Lanier was bearing fruit and Charles was asked to provide £15,000 for the bulk of the Mantuan collection, including Titian's *Twelve Caesars*, Raphael's *Holy Family*, and canvases of Caravaggio, Andrea del Sarto and Correggio. This was a month after Buckingham had arrived before Rhé and when it had become evident that further supplies would be needed for his aid.[2]

Charles's anxiety was apparent in the letters he was despatching to his Treasury officials in July. There was desperation in his note to Marlborough and Weston from Woodstock on August 1:

> . . . if Buckingham should not now be supplied not in show, but substantially, having so bravely, and I thank God, successfully, begun his expedition, it were an irrevocable shame to me, and all this nation; and those that either hinder, or, according to their several places, further not this action, as much as they may, deserve to make their end at Tyburn.

Yet, whatever inward struggles Charles may have had, he clinched the art deal on August 10 and ten days after writing this letter instructed Burlamachi to pay £15,000 to Nye for the Duke of Mantua. Burlamachi appeared more conscious of the threat to Buckingham than Charles himself and wrote frantically to Charles's secretary: 'I pray you, let me know where money shall be found to pay this great sum. If it were for two or three thousand pounds, it could be borne, but for £15,000 besides the other engagements for His Majesty's service, it will utterly put me out of any possibility to do anything in those provisions which are necessary for my lord duke's relief.'

Charles did not change his mind though he suffered severe pangs of conscience. 'I have understood your necessities for fault of timely supplies', he wrote to Buckingham on October 13, and 'I still stand in fear that these may come too late.' By November 6 his fears were even greater and he dreaded that Buckingham might have abandoned the enterprise. If so, he took full responsibility upon himself because of the failure to send supplies in time. He sent a letter to await Buckingham's return: 'in case you should come from Rhé without perfecting your work, happily begun, but I must confess with grief, ill seconded.' 'I assure you', he said, 'that, with whatsoever success ye shall come to me, ye shall ever be welcome, one of my greatest griefs being that I have not been with you in this time of suffering, for I know we would have much eased each other's griefs.' Buckingham's mother saw clearly what was happening, and while the Mantuan deal was going through wrote curtly to her son before Rhé: 'at home . . . all is merry and well pleased, though the ships be not victualled as yet, nor mariners to go with them.'[3]

It is not certain that supplies would have arrived in time even if Charles had not put the Mantuan deal first, or that they would have made any difference to the little force before Rhé. What is certain is that the failure of the expedition destroyed both Buckingham's and Charles's credibility as commanders. 'The disorder and confusion', wrote Denzil Holles to his brother-in-law Wentworth, describing the retreat, 'was so great, the truth is no man can tell what was done. This only every man knows, that since England was England it received not so dishonourable a blow.' It was thought that 4000 of the 6000 men who sailed had been slain, four colonels lost, and at least thirty-two colours lost or in the enemy's hands. The expedition had failed 'with no little dishonour to our nation, excessive charge to our treasury, and great slaughter to our men'. The irony of the French King in restoring freely to his sister all English prisoners was probably lost upon Charles. Louis' remark that if he had known that his brother of England had longed so much for the Isle of Rhé he would have sold it him for half the money he had spent, probably hurt more.

The most charitable interpretation of Charles's action in buying the Mantuan collection at such a time is that he was not deliberately abandoning the Duke in favour of Mantua but that he was hoping, by prevarication, to get both relief for Buckingham and the art treasures he coveted. The pictures began to be shipped almost immediately but Nye protested that he had not been paid and that Burlamachi would not accept his bills because the money had not been provided by the King. Charles seemed to be solving his problems by paying over the money in driblets. Nye received nothing until 23 November 1629 when he got £11,500; on 15 December 1630 he received £3,000, on 25 July 1631 a further £2454.14.3d. In all, bills were paid to Nye which raised something over £18,000, which included the cost of shipping the collection. On a less charitable interpretation Charles was pre-pared to abandon Buckingham and La Rochelle, which he had repeatedly insisted was bound up with his sister's fortunes, in favour of the mouth-watering morsels which Nye dangled before him. He had chosen not Buckingham, not the Huguenots, not his sister, but a fabulous art collection. But upon the Duke's return his action was fully in character. He sent his own coach to Portsmouth to fetch Buckingham and rushed to meet him 'as if he were returned from some conquest'.[4] Within a year Charles was engaged in further negotiations with Mantua. The Mantuan Duke had reserved nine of his choicest canvases, including Mantegna's *Triumph of Julius Ceasar*, as well as many fine statues from the first sale, Nye wrote. Now his son had succeeded him and would sell them to raise money for war. Cardinal Richelieu and the Queen Mother of France were in the market for the treasures but if Nye acted promptly he could secure them for Charles for a further £10,000. Charles clinched the deal and in April 1628 bought the second part of the Mantuan collection.

15

The Assassination of the Duke

So far as the war was concerned Charles still did not know what it was to give up. 'Louis XIII is determined to destroy La Rochelle', he told the Venetian Ambassador after the return of Buckingham, 'and I am no less resolved to support it.' The Duke, apparently bearing Charles no rancour, was no less adamant; 'It is useless', he said, 'to think or speak of peace.'[1] So another fleet was prepared, more money sought. An excise upon bread and beer was considered but came to nothing. Charles pledged more of his jewels. He thought of asking for a general contribution to the fleet but opposition was fierce and the ship-money letters had to be withdrawn. Buckingham, arrogant and undaunted as ever, favoured another Parliament. At first the King was firm. He had no wish for a Parliament in itself, he said, and 'the occasion will not let me tarry so long'. But when the Council joined with Buckingham, and guaranteed there would be no revival of Buckingham's impeachment, Charles gave way. The writs went out early in 1628, less than six months after Buckingham's return. Sheriffs had just been chosen, so there could be no exclusion in this way. Charles considered banning lawyers, but this was hardly practicable. In the event there was little interference with elections and there was, indeed, some show of compromise: seventy-six of the men who had refused to make the forced loan had already been released, no objection was raised to Bristol taking his seat in the Lords, and there was even talk of reconciliation between him and the Duke.

Nevertheless, when Parliament opened on March 17 it was again Laud who preached. Charles, looking down at the Commons below the bar, seeing the familiar opposition faces, including some of the men he had imprisoned, offered no concessions in his opening speech. James would have scolded and lectured the House with warmth. Charles was cold, so unconciliatory that he seemed intent on marking the gulf between them. But he was brisk. 'These Times are for Action', he said, 'wherefore, for Example Sake, I mean not to spend much Time in Words; expecting accordingly, that your . . . good Resolutions will be speedy, not spending Time unnecessarily or (that I may better say) dangerously; for tedious Consultations at this Conjecture of Time is as hurtful as ill Resolutions.' 'I think there is none here', he continued, 'but knows what common Danger is the Cause of this Parliament, and that Supply at this Time is the chief End of it.' If the situation was not clear, he said, 'no Eloquence of Men or Angels will prevail'. If they did not do their duty in this he would use other means. And, he said in conclusion, 'Take not this as Threatening for I scorn to threaten any but my equals.'

It was not an auspicious beginning and it was soon clear that the pattern of this Parliament would be not unlike that of previous Parliaments. Rudyerd asked for supply without specifying the amount. He emphasized that dangers to the kingdom were great, and that there were dangers to themselves if they offended the King. It was, he said, 'the crisis of Parliaments'. If Members took the point they interpreted it in another way. As they rose to make their comments it was clear that forced loans and the five knights' case were uppermost in their minds. Eliot and Wentworth, in their different ways, stressed the danger to property if money was raised without Parliament's consent. If the ancient laws and constitutions were laid aside, said Eliot, all rights of property would also go and the old chaos and confusion, the will of the strongest, would prevail. Wentworth more realistically asserted that the prerogative of the King had been extended 'beyond its just symmetry' and had been 'tearing up the roots of all property'.

Speaker after speaker emphasized that there could be no taxation without parliamentary authority, and Sir Edward Coke reminded the House that no imprisonment was legal unless cause was shown. Phelips widened the issue to one of political obligation: 'It is well known the people of this state are under no other subjection than what they did voluntarily assent unto by their original contract between King and people', he said. The collective will of the House coalesced into a stand upon the old principle of redress of grievances before the grant of supply. Sir Nathaniel Rich urged a petition rather than a bill to embody their demands for, he said, an immediate answer was required to a petition, whereas a bill could be rejected by the King after the end of the session when subsidies had already been granted. Accordingly, when Selden emerged from committee on May 8 he

171

held in his hand the document whose name alone became a household word – the Petition of Right.

The Petition of Right was a straightforward document, containing four simple demands that went to the heart of the Commons' grievances. There should be no taxation without consent of Parliament and no imprisonment without cause shown; no billeting of soldiers or sailors upon householders against their will, and no martial law to punish ordinary offences by sailors or soldiers. These 'rights' and 'liberties', as they called them, were claimed by the Commons under the laws and statutes of the realm already in existence and they cited Magna Carta and laws of Edward I, Edward III and Richard III. The third and fourth demands, indeed, seemed more immediate, less fundamental than the others, reflecting the disastrous impact of Charles's foreign policy upon everyday life. Yet they, too, were grievances basic to a society which levied troops without barracks or other accommodation to house them. No less a document than Magna Carta had expressly forbidden the billeting of soldiers and sailors except at inns or with the householder's approval.

Charles and Buckingham realized fully that here was no Remonstrance, damaging as that could be, but an attempt at a statutory limitation of royal authority such as no monarch had suffered for a century and a half. Charles's first reaction was to dissolve Parliament, but he thought better of it. He created five new peers who would support him in the House of Lords and questioned the Petition closely point by point. He tried in particular to reserve to himself the sovereign power that would give him discretionary action in emergency, and Arundel proposed and the House of Lords accepted a clause to this effect. But the Commons would hear nothing of 'sovereign power'. 'Let us give that to the King that the law gives him, and no more', said Alford. Pym professed not to know what sovereign power was. 'All our petition', he said, 'is for the laws of England, and this power seems to be another distinct power from the law. I know how to add sovereign to his person, but not to his power.' Coke clinched the matter with his great authority. 'I know that prerogative is part of the law', he said, 'but sovereign power is no parliamentary word. In my opinion it weakens Magna Carta and all our statutes, for they are absolute, without any saving of "sovereign power" . . . Take heed what we yield unto: Magna Carta is such a fellow that he will have no "sovereign"'. Perhaps thinking that Coke was offering a straw to clutch at, Buckingham and other friends of the

King then pressed that the Petition should expressly preserve the prerogative and advised the Lords that they could accept it with this proviso. But the Commons forced the Lords to give way and on May 26 the Petition went forward as it stood.

Charles had one more card to play. On June 2 he gave an answer to the Petition which was regarded as no answer at all.

> The King willeth that Right be done, according to the Laws and Customs of the Realm. And that the Statutes be put in due Execution, that His Subjects may have no Cause to complain of . . . Wrongs and Oppressions contrary to their just Rights and Liberties; to the Preservation whereof he holds Himself in Conscience as well obliged as of His Prerogative.

He could hardly have expected the Commons to be satisfied. They were, indeed, bitterly angry and Coke struck again at the man they still considered at the root of their troubles: 'let us palliate no longer. . . . I think the Duke of Buckingham is the cause of all our miseries . . . That man is the grievance of grievances . . . Let us set down the causes of all our disorders, and they will all reflect upon him.'[2]

While Parliament was talking another fleet had sailed for Rochelle, financed and equipped in the same haphazard manner without even the advantage of a commander who believed in his cause and with sailors so disinclined for the battle that they had barricaded themselves in Plymouth town hall in an attempt to resist enlistment. When the Earl of Denbigh reached Rochelle on May 1 he found it under siege from French troops. Moles had been built on either side of the narrow entrance to the harbour and approach in the face of French opposition was virtually impossible. Before he could receive Charles's order of May 17 to hold on for as long as he could he was on his way home with the usual problems of sickness, rotting food, and unwilling men. For once Charles was furiously angry. 'If the ships had been lost', he cried, 'I had timber to build more!' He did not say whether he had more lives to spare. When Denbigh arrived off the Isle of Wight he was told to go back to Rochelle and await reinforcements. But continued sickness, the need for repairs, and the capture by Dunkirk pirates of three vessels laden with corn for Rochelle, marked the end of the expedition.

On the continent of Europe, while resources were being squandered off Rochelle and Parliament men were beginning to consider the principles of political obligation, the death knell had sounded to Elizabeth's hope that her brother might be of help in recovering the Palatinate. This had, indeed, been apparent long before, but the end came when the little knot of English volunteers holding out in the town of Stadt at the mouth of the Elbe were forced into surrender on April 27. The details began to come in during May: a garrison of 4000 men, with practically no assistance in money or supplies from England, reduced by sickness and starvation to 1600, yet receiving more honour from the enemy General Tilly than from their own people, marched out of Stadt with arms in their hands and flags flying. For Charles, who had staked so much upon Rochelle, so little upon Stadt, the poignancy was less than the humiliation of knowing that in Europe he had reached the end of the road. It was too much that, while shaken by the surrender of Stadt, the failure at Rochelle, the hammering on his prerogative, he should be faced with a renewed attack upon Buckingham. Two days after Coke's outburst Charles, from his throne in the House of Lords, assented to the Petition of Right in the time-honoured way applicable to a private bill: *Soit droit fait come est desiré*. The Lords immediately ordered that the text of the Petition with Charles's second answer be printed like a Statute and enrolled in the Parliament rolls. On the 16th the Commons passed the Subsidy Bill.

There were bonfires in the streets of London that night and the church bells rang from City steeples; some said the rejoicing was due to the mistaken belief that Buckingham had been apprehended and some City youths burnt the scaffold on Tower Hill saying there would be a new one for the Duke. His unpopularity had by this time reached fever heat. Remaining covered in the King's presence was the least of the crimes attributed to him. He had not only poisoned James but half a dozen peers as well; he used love potions to inflame the women he could not otherwise win; he kept safely out of the way of danger on the Isle of Rhé. What might happen to the Duke was demonstrated when Dr Lambe, a quack doctor and astrologer, believed to be associated with Buckingham, was beaten to death in the streets of the City in a particularly brutal fashion, and it was allegedly said that if the Duke had been there he would have been treated worse. 'Who rules the kingdom?' asked a broadsheet found nailed to a post in Coleman Street. 'The King.' 'Who rules the King?' 'The Duke.' 'Who rules the Duke?' 'The devil.' 'Let the Duke look at it!.' This was but one of many ballads and verses chanted in City streets or passed from hand to hand.[3] As the Commons proceeded to prepare a Remonstrance that put the blame for all the disasters of the reign upon the Duke, Buckingham begged the King on his knees to be allowed to answer the charges. Charles refused permission and held out his hand for the Duke to kiss. Once more he had demonstrated his faith in his friend. But he was alarmed, and when the Commons returned to tonnage and poundage, maintaining that his acceptance of the Petition of Right had acknowledged it to be illegal without Parliamentary sanction, Charles hastened to end the session, before they could proceed further against the Duke or present him with a new Remonstrance.

Charles made it absolutely clear in his prorogation speech of June 26 that he had never intended to surrender his right to levy customs duties. He also made it clear that he never intended, and did not believe that Parliament had intended, to harm his prerogative, which he considered to remain intact, regardless of the Petition of Right. He told the House of Commons that they had no power to make or declare a law without his consent, and he reminded them that the Judges, under the King, were the sole interpreters of law. Besides the question of interpretation, there was also the question as to whether, and in what sense, Charles had given his approval to the Petition itself. Parliament had ordered its printing with Charles's second answer attached. But on the day Parliament rose Charles ordered the destruction of the 1500 copies so printed and the substitution of the Petition with his first answer and his prorogation speech. In this form the Petition of Right, with Charles's own explanation attached, was circulated in the country. The Parliament, Charles said, had put a false construction upon what he had granted, and the country must not be allowed to reach erroneous conclusions. Both sides were already appealing beyond the walls of Parliament to the people. The war of words had begun. But for the time being Charles's mind was chiefly on Rochelle, and with the expectation that some £275,000 would be coming into his treasury from the subsidies voted after his acceptance of the Petition of Right, he was fitting out yet another fleet, impressing yet more men. Charles went to Southwick, near Portsmouth, to help with his presence, while the Duke busied himself between London and the port. Buckingham's family was worried for his safety, a friend begged him to wear a suit of mail beneath his clothes, but Buckingham took little notice. His wife and sister were with him at Portsmouth on 23 August 1628. After breakfast that day he rose to enter an adjoining room where officers and friends, members of his

175

staff and others were jostling to talk to him. As he stepped into the crowd and leaned forward to answer a question a man struck him in the left breast with a knife śaying, 'God have mercy upon thy soul!' Buckingham drew the knife from his breast, but could do no more than cry, 'Villain!' before collapsing with blood pouring from his wound and from his mouth. He died instantly. A simple act, that could easily have been averted, had struck down at the height of his power one of the most remarkable men of his age. The favourite of two Kings, adored head of a large family, loved, feared, hated, admired, envied, bestriding his world, if ever any did, like a colossus, was struck down, not by an enemy who had watched and waited, not by the mob who had murdered Dr Lambe, not by anyone close to him, but by a half-crazy lieutenant named John Felton who had served at Rhé and whose motives were never quite clear. Felton had been refused promotion, was poorly paid, had read various declarations of Parliament and had come to believe that Buckingham was the cause both of the country's ills and his own. At a cutler's shop on Tower Hill in London he had bought a cheap knife and then made his way to Portsmouth. He mingled with the crowds around Buckingham's lodging and, since he had no fear for himself, the rest was easy and he stepped boldly forward to acknowledge himself as the assassin.[4]

The news was brought to Charles at morning prayers at Southwick. Great shock is like a sudden blow. He gave no sign except for a spasm that crossed his face but knelt where he was and stayed in chapel until the service was done. Only then, flinging himself upon his bed, he gave way to bitter sobs. Buckingham had been as much part of Charles as one person can be of another; he was the only friend Charles ever had; Charles never assumed a kingly authority with Buckingham. As he wrote when he feared the disaster on the Isle of Rhé, if they had been together, they would much have eased each other's grief. Now Buckingham was gone and there was at once the overwhelming grief and no such consolation.

He kept his room for two days without admitting anyone, but he sent for the Duchess to be brought from Portsmouth to a village nearby. He ordered Court mourning for two days. He had Buckingham's body taken to London in his own coach. It was difficult to avoid the general rejoicing and the lighting of bonfires as the news of the Duke's death spread. Felton had to be executed, but he died amid general sympathy and well-wishing. Buckingham had to be buried, but his funeral was quiet and unobtrusive. His body, it was said, was taken to the Abbey the day before the interment, in the night of September 10, to avoid abuse by the crowd. So even the consolation of burying his friend with pomp and honour was denied to Charles. All he could do was to bury him and reserve a place for his tomb in Westminster Abbey, among the kings of England. He could not even erect that tomb himself for he could hardly erect a monument to his friend before he had built one to his father.

He did all he could for Buckingham's family, paying his debts, preventing the sale of some of the Duke's jewels, confirming grants to his family, and maintaining his servants until they could be suitably discharged. Buckingham's wife he visited constantly, joining his sorrow to hers. Buckingham's children would be brought up in his own household. The world, he said, 'was greatly mistaken' in the Duke 'for it was thought that the favourite had ruled his Majesty; but it was far otherwise, for that the Duke had been to him a faithful and obedient servant.' He intended, he said, to manage all affairs of state himself, and there was no more than a brief hiatus before he flung himself into work, presiding always at the Council, familiarizing himself with its activities, going through all documents, amending and annotating with his own hand, getting through more work in fourteen days than Buckingham had done in three months. On September 7, four days before Buckingham's funeral, the fleet the Duke would have commanded sailed for Rochelle under the Earl of Lindsey, the former Lord Willoughby. The story of previous expeditions was repeated and while Lindsey was vainly encouraging his half-mutinous men the inhabitants of La Rochelle were literally starving to death. On October 18 they cut the knot and, in full view of the English fleet which had done nothing to help them, surrendered to Richelieu. The peace was not vindictive. If the Rochellese lost their privilege of a fortified enclave in a Catholic country they gained, with all Huguenots, a recognition, unpersecuted, within a united France.

For England and for Charles the surrender of Rochelle was the greatest blessing as well as the greatest humiliation. La Rochelle, more than anything else, had caused 'the crisis of Parliaments'. It was not the Palatinate which had reduced Charles to extremities. He had not asked for money for the Spanish war, to which the Commons had some commitment, nor for a European war such as his sister desired. Instead he had become bogged down in relieving La Rochelle because, so he thought, his honour was involved. It might be felt that his greater obligation was to his sister's cause. Perhaps he shied away

177

from the wider European strategy. Perhaps his intellect was too narrow for the wider theatre of war. Perhaps the details of a siege, the relief of a town rather than the broad movement of troops on the map of Europe were what he had learned from his models and his books. After the surrender of Rochelle Charles worked to extricate himself from direct involvement in war, though his financial commitments to the European Protestants remained. Already, in Buckingham's time, peace feelers had gone out to Spain and commissions of investigation sent to central Europe. Would his father's peace policy prevail after all? The journey to Madrid and the resentful aftermath were now as though they had never been. His efforts to help the French Huguenots were relegated to some part of his mind that could register defeat without being worried by it. A trail of wasted lives, treasure, time and talent marked the intense activity his foreign policy had generated. George Villiers, the uniquely beautiful Duke of Buckingham, was dead. Charles was left, not with the Spanish wife of his father's diplomatic choice and his own early passion, but with a *faut-de-mieux* French Queen who so far had brought him nothing but trouble. But she was now all he had.

Henrietta–Maria, now eighteen years old, realized the situation better than Charles himself. When the news of Buckingham's assassination reached her, she set out at once to join Charles at Southwick.[5] His loss and her sense that he needed her dispelled the petty misunderstandings of the past three years, and they were back to the day of their first meeting when he took a nervous little girl into his arms and kissed her. Now it was her turn to comfort him.

16

The Last Parliament

Those who said the Duke swayed all looked in vain for a drastic change of policy now that Charles stood alone. Certainly there were modifications in government – but nothing immediately significant; efforts at retrenchment – but that was not new; attempts to raise money – but the methods had been drawn up at a Council meeting even before Buckingham's death. Moves towards peace with both Spain and France had begun in the Duke's time and the same influences continued to sway men's loyalties and actions. Charles showed the same attitude to the Palatinate, he made the same speeches, he kept up his reassuring correspondence with Elizabeth. There was, indeed, nothing to suggest that the guiding hand had been Buckingham's, no indication that Charles would now have either a different policy or no policy at all, no evidence that the Duke led the King. Policy, it seemed, had been based upon complete understanding and mutual trust between the King and his chief minister. This would not happen again. Laud would share his confidence to some extent; he would look to Weston for supplies; in the crisis of his reign he would turn to Wentworth. But never again would there be so close a relationship, so full an understanding, personal and political, with any other man. He found, indeed, now that he was alone, that he enjoyed it, and was at his best when acting singly – he 'now at last feels himself master, and perhaps begins to enjoy it', as the Venetian Ambassador put it. A month later Contarini was a little more doubtful. 'Since the Duke's death the King remains in suspense . . . He shows himself more confused than resolute', he wrote to the Doge and Senate. But the opinion was probably influenced by Charles's refusal to embrace the French–Venetian alliance that the Ambassador was pushing.[1]

In considering his team of ministers anew, Charles's greatest emotional difficulty concerned the offices which Buckingham had held himself. The Admiralty, which the Duke had made particularly his own, Charles put in commission, the money saved being used to pay the Duke's debts. The Earl of Holland became Charles's Master of Horse. He was a Buckingham supporter, which was one reason for the appointment; another may have been Henrietta's affection for the courtier who, as Henry Rich, Lord Kensington, had wooed her in Paris on his master's behalf. Holland also succeeded Buckingham as Chancellor of Cambridge University and in December 1629 he became High Steward to the Queen. In spite of these marks of favour Holland nursed a resentment at not being given the Admiralty. Changes in government which Charles and Buckingham had made in the summer of 1628 gave Charles Sir Richard Weston, whom he had raised to the peerage as Baron Weston in April 1628, as his Lord Treasurer and Henry Montague, Earl of Manchester, as Lord Privy Seal. Towards the end of 1628 Charles made further appointments. Secretary Conway was growing old. Charles made him President of the Council, bringing in Lord Dorchester, formerly Sir Dudley Carleton, to serve in his place. The other Secretary was Sir John Coke. Neither was particularly outstanding. Coke was slow, though careful, and his long association with the Admiralty was a decided asset. Dorchester was an upright and agreeable man but with the qualities of the dilettante rather than of the administrator: yet no one, Charles once said, could draw up a document more in accord with his own intentions than Dorchester. Already a strong influence on Charles, though not yet of his Privy Council, was William Laud, Bishop of London.

In the more intimate posts of Gentleman and Groom of the Bedchamber Charles kept his two friends, Will Murray and Endymion Porter. Both appreciated the paintings which were his passion and were themselves avid collectors. Murray, the little boy who had shared his early lessons, was his oldest friend; Porter was a lavish spender who wrote verses, bought pictures, and acted as an art agent for Charles. Both men could be trusted with a delicate commission and Porter had, indeed, served Charles well in this respect during the Spanish adventure. Two of the Carey sons Charles also kept close to him, and Tom and Will filled many roles as messengers and agents.

James Hay, Viscount Doncaster, Earl of Carlisle since 1622, was a great favourite with Charles. He held no office but was well versed in affairs of state and his influence was considerable. Believing that the French had broken the terms of the marriage treaty he had helped to negotiate, he also had turned towards Spain. He was an inveterate spendthrift, willing to celebrate any occasion of note in an appropriately expensive manner. His wife, Lucy Percy, daughter of the Earl of Northumberland, served the Queen as a Lady of the Bedchamber. She was a great beauty and became one of Henrietta's closest friends. The boisterous Sir Henry Vane retained, perhaps surprisingly, the King's confidence. Though he was not yet a Privy Councillor his influence would increase over the years.

It soon became apparent, however, that Charles's most influential adviser after Buckingham's death was Lord Treasurer Weston. Weston understood well the twin needs of saving money and of raising money and his nature fitted him to do both, while his early training as Justice of the Peace, customs official, committee man, and Chancellor of the Exchequer gave him an insight into the niceties of administration. His equable, unheroic nature provided the prop that Charles needed, while his single-mindedness enabled him quite effortlessly to move from Charles's premise that because of his wars he needed money, to the more realistic assertion that he could not wage war because he could not afford to.

Weston had served in Parliament almost continuously since 1604 and, as Privy Councillor since 1621, had played an important role in the Lower House. He had served on the Royal Commission to reduce expenditure in 1617 and on the Navy Commission in 1618; he had reported on English trade in the Far East, on the tapestry industry, and the dyeing of silk. After the fall of Middlesex he had acted as Treasurer for seven months until the appointment of Sir James Ley, doubling meanwhile with his office of Chancellor of the Exchequer. Friendship with Middlesex may have helped to delay his rise to the highest office; a close relationship with Sir Arthur Ingram, the financier, and consequent contacts with other City magnates were useful. He was something of a scholar, and enjoyed the patronage of Arundel. While not a connoisseur in the best sense of the word, he had a lively appreciation of paintings and antiquities. Charles had been aware of Weston, in one way or another, nearly all his life. But the first time he really made his mark with Charles was when, with Secretary Conway, he headed a small embassy to Europe at the beginning of the Thirty Years War. He was with Elizabeth at Prague at the time of the battle of the White Mountain and fled with her and Frederick the following day. Diplomatic immunity speeded his way over the disturbed continent and he arrived in England with the first personal news of the Elector and his family. Weston had been sufficiently pliant to support the Spanish

181

policy of Charles and Buckingham and in the 1624 Parliament sat for Bossiney in Cornwall on the nomination of Charles. He had relayed Buckingham's narration in the Lords to the House of Commons; in later Parliaments he had supported subsidy bills, he had approved the forced loan and he played no part in the impeachment of the Duke.

Weston was in many ways typical of his age. The cloth industry, the City of London, the law, an estate built up in two generations, such was his family history. He himself was at Trinity College, Cambridge and the Middle Temple. He held stock in the great customs farm, his mercantile interests included stockholding and membership of the East India Company. His second wife was a Catholic and he had many Catholic friends, including Cottington. Weston required the services of the shrewd, pro–Spanish courtier and partly through his influence, partly because the situation called for his services, Cottington was restored to favour and admitted to the Privy Council in November 1628. Less than a year later he became Chancellor of the Exchequer. Charles knew of Weston's Catholic sympathies but now, when peace with Spain was again being considered, that was no handicap. In any case, it was not in Charles's nature to judge a man for his religious beliefs, and he was confident that Weston's main virtue, retrenchment, would not be affected by his religion. Weston, for his part, while he was fathering five sons and six daughters, finding husbands and dowries for the daughters, rich heiresses for the sons, had watched the shy, withdrawn little Prince develop into the sovereign under whom he would achieve eminence. Though twenty-five years older than Charles he had been content, under Buckingham's patronage, to wait upon events and his patience had been justified.[2]

Of the other possible ministers Charles, even before the death of Buckingham, had begun to single out Sir Thomas Wentworth, 'Black Tom of the North' who, like Weston, begrudged the money spent on war. He was six years older than Charles, his elder brother, too, had died young and, like Charles, he was left with the responsibility not, indeed, of a kingdom, but of an estate and a family of ten brothers and sisters. Land, sheep, wool and aristocratic descent had combined to help his family rise to wealth and influence in Yorkshire. His education was conventional – St John's, Cambridge, the Inner Temple, travel in Europe. He came to Court at eighteen, was knighted by James and in the same year married a daughter of the Earl of Cumberland. Wentworth drew attention to himself in 1626 by his refusal to

. contribute to the forced loan. Like Sir John Eliot he was imbued with a strong sense of property and went to prison, not because he could not afford to pay, but because he saw a threat in extra-Parliamentary taxation. Wentworth was released with others in December 1627 and in Charles's third Parliament of 1628 he sat for his native shire. In attempting to bring together King and Commons, supply and redress of grievances, Wentworth was a leading figure in this assembly. The framing of the Petition of Right owed much to him but he lost his ascendancy in the dilatory proceedings which followed and took no part in the renewed hostility against the Duke. He was not a Buckingham man yet had never joined the hue and cry after him, giving the impression that he was less concerned with personalities than with constitutional issues.

Wentworth was a tall, spare, dark man who rarely smiled. He had no part to play in the artistic world of Charles and he was no scholar in the narrower sense. Yet he had a great feeling for words and had studied the classical orators. He could deliver a speech as elaborate and more cogent than most, but he could also be blunt and forceful. Charles realized something of the power and stability of the man. In 1628 he became Baron Wentworth, and by the end of the year was Viscount Wentworth and Lord President of the Council of the North. His first speech as President appeared to justify Charles's confidence. 'The Authority of a King', he said, 'is the keystone which closeth up the arch of order and government.' The metaphor was not original, being part of the common coin of seventeenth-century political discussion, but coming from a powerful minister it emphasized the joint interest of sovereign and subject. It told against Wentworth that Christopher Wandesworth, who had joined the impeachment against Buckingham, was his close friend, and that Denzil Holles, who was prominent in opposition in the 1629 Parliament, was his brother-in-law by his second marriage; but on the whole Charles's favour appeared to be justified and on 10 November 1629 Wentworth became Privy Councillor.[3]

On 23 January 1629, meanwhile, after a seven-month recess Charles met his first Parliament without Buckingham. He had continued to levy tonnage and poundage but many merchants, encouraged by Parliament's Remonstrance, had refused to pay. Some had been brought before the Privy Council and were now imprisoned in the Fleet or the Marshalsea while their wine, currants and other merchandise were seized at the ports to the accompaniment of considerable tumult in the customs houses. Prominent in organizing this resistance were the merchants John Rolle, who was a Parliament man, and Richard Chambers, who had told the Council to its face that merchants in no part of the world were so screwed and wrung as in England and that even in Turkey they had more encouragement. Chambers was referred to the Star Chamber for daring to imply that Charles's 'happy government' could be compared to a 'Turkish tyranny'. He refused to submit, coupling his refusal with many biblical texts, was fined £2000 and committed to the Fleet where he remained for six years. Parliament was on dangerous ground in encouraging disobedience but covered itself by insisting that it was acting in accordance with the Petition of Right. Charles continued to deny their interpretation of that document and claimed that if there was any question it was the Judges and not the House of Commons who should decide the issue.

In spite of this inauspicious background to the second session of his third Parliament, the Commons were mollified by Charles's first words. He had not, he said, taken tonnage and poundage as a right, pertaining to his prerogative, but as a necessity, and merely until Parliament had granted it to him, being assured, he asserted, that in the previous session they 'wanted Time, not Wills', to give it him. He spoke with the charm and slight diffidence he knew how to assume, cleverly taking the initiative in disclaiming any intention of arbitrary power. Now that Buckingham had gone the odds were in his favour, the speech was received with a murmur of applause, and men remarked on 'the King's fine speaking'. But, as Charles bitterly remarked later, 'his speech which was with good applause accepted, had not that good effect which he expected', for the Commons proceeded to make a further Protestation on March 2 in which they not only encouraged merchants to refuse to pay customs duties but branded those who did so as capital enemies to the kingdom and betrayers of the liberties of England.

This was not all. Even while tonnage and poundage appeared uppermost in their minds they had not let go of the religious issue. They were particularly incensed at the pre-empting of important church offices by Arminians. The years 1627 and 1628 saw the advancement of Richard Neile to Winchester, Joseph Hall to Exeter, John Buckeridge to Ely, John Howson to Durham, Richard Corbet to Oxford, Laud to London, and Samuel Harsnet to the Archbishopric of York, while the particularly controversial Richard Montague went to

Chichester in 1628. Charles offered compromise by suppressing the sermons of Roger Mainwaring to which the Commons had taken particular objection – 'No subject may, without hazard of his own damnation in rebelling against God, question or disobey the will and pleasure of his sovereign' – and the *Apello Caesarem* of Montague. At the same time he threatened that if controversial preaching and printing continued he would take action that would make the perpetrators wish 'they had never thought upon these needless controversies'. There was little doubt that Charles was thinking more of the proliferation of sectarian writing and printing than of the works of Mainwaring and Montague.

As the Commons turned to consider such questions they ordered a fast to prepare themselves for the transition. Charles sent word tartly that 'fighting would do them more good than fasting', that religion was not in such danger as they feared, and that he wished for a conclusion to the customs debate 'not so much out of the greediness of the thing' as to get it settled. But Oliver Cromwell, the Member for Huntingdon, making one of his earliest contributions to the debates of the House, proposed that the business of the King of Earth should give place to the business of the King of Heaven, and his motion was carried.

The business of the King of Heaven, it became clear, was the suppression of Papists and Arminians – 'An Arminian is the spawn of a Papist' – and the encouragement of 'godly' ministers. They believed, contrary to the King's assertion, that 'God's religion' was 'in great peril now to be lost', that popery was on the increase in England, that there was a frequent and public resort to mass, particularly in the Queen's household. Everything they objected to as 'Popery', 'superstitious ceremony' or 'innovation' was condemned and was to be removed. Charles lost patience. They had left tonnage and poundage high and dry for a formless and biased discussion on religion and on February 25 he adjourned the House for a week while his supporters tried to secure an understanding with the opposition. When a further adjournment was proposed on March 2 the House of Commons was angry and disorderly. 'No! No! No!' came from every side. Eliot half rose but the Speaker said he had an absolute command from His Majesty to leave the chair instantly if anyone attempted to speak. As he made to rise two young men, Denzil Holles and Benjamin Valentine, strode forward and held him down. Privy Councillors who were present helped him to break away, others stopped him, and he was pushed back into his chair. 'God's wounds! you shall sit till we please to rise!' cried Holles. All was confused. Some Members tried to leave the Chamber but were restrained by others, orders were shouted to the Sergeant at Arms to close the door. When he hesitated Sir Miles Hobart turned the key in the lock and put the key in his pocket. Many Members tried to speak and called for a vote to express their views. Soon Black Rod, sent by the King to dissolve the House, was knocking at the door. Holles then, while the knocking continued, briefly recapitulated what he knew was in their minds: no innovation in religion, no tonnage and poundage unless sanctioned by Parliament; innovators in religion, any who counselled, gave or took tonnage or poundage to be proclaimed an enemy of the state. Holles himself put the question. 'Aye, Aye!' came from all sides of the House. The Commons then voted their own adjournment, the doors were thrown open, and the Members streamed from the House. It would be eleven years before the doors opened upon another Parliament. Charles immediately afterwards drew up a Proclamation for the dissolution and on the 10th went to the House of Lords himself. As he put it,

> I never came upon so unpleasant an occasion. The reason is to declare to you, and all the World, that it was merely the undutiful and seditious Carriage in the Lower House that hath caus'd the Dissolution of this Parliament . . . yet . . . let Me tell you . . . that I know that there are many there as dutiful Subjects as any in the World; it being but some few Vipers amongst them that did cast this Mist of Undutifulness over most of their Eyes . . . To conclude, as these Vipers must look for their Punishment; so you, My Lords, must justly expect from me that Favour and Protection, that a good King oweth to his loving and faithful Nobility.

Once again he made the sharp division, consciously or unconsciously employing the old tactic of divide and rule.

As he disrobed after the dissolution Charles looked pleased and declared that he would never put on those robes again. This was not to be quite true, though there were many people, including the Venetian Ambassador, who shared this view. Meantime the chief 'vipers' Eliot and eight others including Holles, Selden, Valentine and Strode – were sent to the Tower or other prisons.[4]

But Charles's mind was only half upon such affairs. His wife was five months pregnant. When he returned from the disorder of his Parliament to the tranquility of his home he was in high spirits as if, remarked an onlooker, he had freed himself from a yoke.

17

Peace

The toils from which Charles expected to free himself included war as well as Parliament. He had realized at last the limitations imposed by his finances and without Buckingham his grandiose conceptions of foreign policy shrank to practical size. Already he was considering both French and Spanish peace proposals.

It had long been apparent that the French war was of no help to the Palatinate and that England could be of no assistance to the Huguenots. At the same time France under Cardinal Richelieu was preparing to stand against both Spain and the Holy Roman Empire and sought the neutrality, or better still the assistance, of the English fleet. The Venetian Republic had its own reasons for requiring peace between France, who could protect it against the Empire on land, and England, who could protect it against Spain at sea. The merchant classes of all three countries, who were losing money heavily in the disruption of trade which accompanied hostilities, were strong advocates of peace, while Charles himself would benefit from the increased customs revenue that would accrue from the free flow of merchandise. The efforts of the French and Venetian Ambassadors were backed by courtiers like the Earl of Holland who were pro-French in their sympathies, by ministers who knew the financial necessity of peace, and by the Queen herself, who ardently wished her husband and her brother to be reconciled.

Henrietta-Maria was, indeed, truly happy for the first time since she came to England. In spite of the war Charles sent to France for wine and fruit for her[1] and he now talked to her of public affairs as well as of the trivia of everyday life – not that she enjoyed affairs of state but she no longer felt excluded. It was noted that the King was always with her, that he loved her dearly, and that his satisfaction over her pregnancy defied exaggeration. Their master and mistress, wrote one of the Carey sons to Carlisle, were 'at such a degree of kindness as he would imagine him a wooer again, and her gladder to receive his caresses than he to make them'. Charles celebrated her birthday by riding at the ring in truly chivalrous fashion, instituting himself her champion and taking the ring upon his sword in her honour. The Venetian Ambassador decided that the Queen's influence would grow and that he should ingratiate himself with her.[2] Their happiness was clouded by the tragic news from The Hague early in 1629 of the fatal accident to Elizabeth's eldest son, the young Prince Frederick Henry. He had been with his father on the Haarlem Mere off Amsterdam when the weather suddenly deteriorated and their boat was rammed by a larger vessel in thick fog. The Elector was saved but the boy, who had just passed his fifteenth birthday, was found the next day, frozen to the mast to which he had been clinging in the icy weather. Charles put his Court into mourning for the nephew he had never seen, he sent Sir Robert Carey to the stricken parents, and tried to cheer Elizabeth by letter.[3]

When a peace treaty between France and England was signed at Suza on 14 April 1629 the French made no claim for special treatment for Catholics in England, while the English were silent on the question of the Huguenots. Henrietta-Maria took part of the credit to herself and on May 10 came by river from Greenwich to Somerset House where a *Te Deum* was to be sung to mark the end of hostilities. As she eagerly rose to disembark the impact of the barge on the landing stage made her stumble backwards. She was tired on her return to Greenwich and was startled by two dogs fighting near her. Whatever the reason she fell into premature labour two days later and became critically ill. Madame Peronne, the famous French *accoucheuse* who was to have come from France, had not arrived; nor had Dr Mayerne, the royal physician. A local midwife was hurriedly summoned but the responsibility was too great and she swooned away in the royal bedchamber. The doctor in charge was left to do his best with a difficult breach delivery. Charles was distraught. He remained by his wife's bedside begging the doctor to save her life regardless of the child. On the morning of the 13th Henrietta-Maria gave birth to a son, who lived for only a few hours. She herself rallied, fortified by her husband's devotion and her own buoyant spirit. It was unfortunate that Charles had to fight off her religious advisers in an anti-room to ensure the child's baptism by William Laud in the Anglican faith. The baby was buried that night in Westminster Abbey, close to his grandfather, the funeral service being spoken by Laud.[4]

It was hard that after four years of marriage an heir should be born only to die immediately. But premature birth and death were too common to be regarded as a tragedy, even by the parents. Henrietta Maria's condition was the more alarming. As Charles had said when he begged the doctor to save her life, he would rather save the mould than the cast. But this was not the chief reason for his anxiety. The possibility of losing the wife he had treated so perfunctorily, and only recently learned to love, made him aware of the depth of his feeling for her, and as they resumed their normal life together Charles's affection appeared even greater than before. He kissed his wife repeatedly in public. 'You do not see that in Turin . . . Nor in Paris either!' he exclaimed, referring to the marriages of her sister and her brother. So difficult did he find it to tear himself away from her that some of his Councillors complained of his inaccessibility and he laughingly told her he wished she could accompany him to the Council Table! She went to Tunbridge Wells to complete her recovery, but so dependent had they become upon one another that she cut short her stay and rushed back towards London to be met half-way by a husband who, similarly, could not bear the separation.

So little was religion now a bar between them that, as her second pregnancy advanced, she would sometimes lie late in bed and Charles would scold her for not hearing mass before noon. So little did she care for public affairs at this time that even the efforts of the Marquis de Chateauneuf, the new French Ambassador, could not move her into the world of intrigue and, instead of drawing England into an alliance against Spain, as he had hoped, he was obliged to watch her amorous exchanges with a husband who thought she could do no wrong. Even her extravagances Charles treated lightly: after all, his mother had been extravagant. 'She is a bad housekeeper' was all that he would say, complacently. Henrietta's mother, fearing that badly-sprung English coaches had caused the miscarriage, sent her a wheelchair, in which she might make short excursions, and a little locket and chain for good luck. 'God be thanked', Charles wrote to his mother-in-law in acknowledging the gift, 'she is so careful of herself that I need exert no other authority than that of love.' Madame Peronne was again booked for a confinement.[5]

The Court was already reflecting the King's tastes. Pictures from the Mantuan collection were still arriving, carefully packed and shipped by his agents and Ambassadors. All over Europe and the Near East ambassadors, friends, and agents were seeking out pictures and other art treasures for his collections and those of his courtiers. Artists and art-lovers were beginning to flock to Whitehall. In 1626 Buckingham had invited the Pisan, Orazio Gentileschi, to England; he painted ceilings at York House and Greenwich Palace as well as many canvases. Not least of his attractions was his daughter, Artemisia, who accompanied him and herself painted several pictures. Charles made much of the Gentileschis. He also enjoyed the work of Gerard Honthorst, who arrived in England in 1628 and painted a large portrait group of Buckingham and his family shortly before the Duke's death. The poets, dramatists and men of letters were so numerous they were almost taken for granted by a Court where Sir Henry Wotton, John Suckling, Edmund Waller and a dozen more were normal contacts, while in the City the old master, Ben Jonson, continued to regail the younger poets at his London tavern until his death in 1638. Robert Herrick visiting the capital from his west-country vicarage, Richard Lovelace turning charming verses with his friends at Oxford, the young John Milton beginning to use his talent for words and imagery at Cambridge – all were part of the cultured and pleasant world in which Charles had moved all his life. That they clustered more thickly now was a tribute to himself and his Court. Among much that was ephemeral Charles recognized the enduring worth of some of their work and he acquired the 1635 edition of Donne's collected poems. But he enjoyed the playwrights most of all and particularly, perhaps, Beaumont and Fletcher. He had seen *The Knight of the Burning Pestle* as a young man; it exactly matched his sense of humour and the two dramatists were much in demand at his Court. He possessed a collected edition of their plays and, as he loved to do, made a list of the titles with his own hand.

It was particularly pleasant when Peter Paul Rubens came to the English Court as the accredited representative of Spain. It was not unusual to use an artist as diplomat and, indeed, diplomats were frequently amateur artists and art collectors. Charles and Buckingham had frequently employed Balthazar Gerbier – artist, architect, inventor, collector, dealer, and curator of Buckingham's art collection at York House – on their diplomatic missions. Sir Dudley Carleton who, before he became Secretary of State, was Ambassador first at Venice and later at The Hague, was painstaking agent for Charles and others, using his position at Venice to search out antiquities and works of art. He himself was an enthusiastic collector, particularly of Venetian paintings, and he did much to bring their vogue into England. Sir Henry Wotton, sometime Ambassador at Venice, was equally assiduous as diplomat and art collector.

Rubens was in a class apart and was well known to Charles as a painter of the first rank. He was a Flemish Catholic, owing political allegiance directly to the Hapsburg Regents of Flanders and through them to Spain. Early in his career he had been used by the Duke of Mantua to take costly presents to Philip III of Spain and while in Madrid had painted the equestrian portrait of the Duke of Lerma which Charles had seen during his visit. His studio in Antwerp was famous for his own paintings and for the pupils he gathered round him. One of these, Anthony van Dyck, had already visited England briefly, but was now travelling in Italy. Rubens continued to mix art with diplomacy and business with both, and in 1621 had negotiated with Sir Dudley Carleton for the sale of a large canvas depicting a lion hunt for Charles's gallery. Charles possessed at that time only one painting by Rubens, an early work depicting Judith and Holofernes which he felt did little credit to the master's skill, and he was anxious for a more mature canvas. But the first picture sent was basically by a pupil of Rubens and, although allegedly gone over carefully by the master himself, was not acceptable to Charles, who found in it little evidence of the artist's own hand. As Rubens was at the same time executing a life-sized canvas of a lion hunt for Lord Digby on behalf of the Marquis of Hamilton he was probably pressed for time, but the real reason for the scant respect shown to the Prince's perception seems to have been money. He would have charged twice as much, Rubens told Carleton, for a picture entirely by his own hand. He nevertheless agreed to paint one for Charles.

Carleton himself was more fortunate. He had himself made an impressive collection of antiquities, including statues, torsoes, heads, urns and bas-reliefs and these he exchanged with Rubens, who wanted them for the large villa he had built outside Antwerp, in return for several of the artists' own canvases. About the same time Marie de Medici, the Queen Mother of France, asked Rubens to design and paint the panels for her new palace at the Luxembourg outside Paris and in 1625 the artist's twenty-five pictures depicting her early life were unveiled at a wedding feast to celebrate the proxy marriage of her daughter to Charles. While Rubens was in Paris to instal the canvases he met Buckingham and Gerbier, who were there to conduct Henrietta-Maria to England. He had time to draw the Duke's likeness

191

in preparation for an equestrian portrait which was commissioned, and there was also a certain amount of diplomatic exchange in which Rubens stressed the advantages of peace with Spain.

Rubens and Gerbier continued these exchanges over the next few years and there was a superficial friendship between Rubens and the Duke. But the artist–diplomat had not formed a high opinion of Buckingham, thinking he was 'heading for the precipice' and that when he considered his 'caprice' and 'arrogance' he 'pitied the young king who, through false counsel, was needlessly throwing himself and his kingdom into war'. Nevertheless Rubens, who had possibly tired of his antiquities and whose style of life required a great deal of money, was quite prepared to sell them to Buckingham together with paintings by Italian and North European masters. It was an imposing acquisition for the Duke but Rubens prided himself on the fact that he kept back the gem of his collection, 'a divine cameo', a head of Octavius Augustus in white on a background of sardonyx with a garland of laurel in high relief. It was, wrote Rubens, 'of workmanship so exquisite that I do not recall ever having seen the like'.

But art and diplomacy were still hand in glove and the sale covered increased diplomatic activity between Rubens and Gerbier. An attempt of the two agents to meet at Calais without arousing suspicion did not succeed and Rubens kicked his heels vainly for three weeks. But early in January 1628 the two men met in Paris and late in February Gerbier was able to put Rubens in direct touch with Buckingham under cover of the art sale. Throughout the year the agents met in various cities of the United Provinces and by the spring of 1629 Charles was indicating that he would be pleased to deal with Rubens as plenipotentiary without waiting for the exchange of regular envoys with Spain. Charles had, indeed, every reason for wishing to meet Rubens and Cottington's statement, 'The King is well satisfied, not only because of Rubens's mission, but also because he wishes to know a person of such merit', was no doubt inspired. The despatch of Cottington himself to Madrid as Ambassador in August further indicated Charles's willingness to treat.

These diplomatic exchanges were as well known to Christian of Denmark as the actual treaty of peace with France and, angrily, he himself made peace with the Emperor at Lubeck on 12 May 1629. What else could he do? He had been fed with promises too long. Whatever his feelings towards his favourite sister's daughter, he received back his hereditary possessions that had been lost in the fighting and retired from the war. This was a help to the Anglo–Spanish peace negotiations. The gallant Gustavus of Sweden continued his course. Charles did all he could, allowing Gustavus to levy one regiment of volunteers in England, another in Scotland. He permitted the Dutch – who had no alternative but to continue the war, for to cease fighting meant to cease to exist – to take English soldiers into their service.

Rubens arrived in London on 3 June 1629, and stayed with Balthazar Gerbier. It was less than three months after the dissolution of Parliament, less than two months after the treaty with France. He found, on the one hand, a peace party which was partly Hispanophile, to some extent Catholic, and wholly devoted to retrenchment. On the other hand, there was an anti-Spanish group, activated by the French and Venetian Ambassadors, who wished the English alliance with France to be cemented into an alliance against Spain. This was a Puritan and opposition group, but was in no sense a war party. However much religion cut across Englishmen's allegiance at this time, very few people wanted war, and Charles could count on support for his peace policy.

The day after his arrival Rubens was summoned to Greenwich where he talked a long time with the King. Charles emphasized, as he had always done, that neither his faith, conscience, nor honour would permit him to enter into any agreement with Spain without the restitution of the Palatinate. He added, however, that since he knew it was not in Spain's power to hand over the entire Palatinate, he would be content if the King of Spain would give up his garrison towns. Rubens, though not a trained diplomat, pointed out that such a gesture did not rest with Spain alone, since she held only some of the Palatine garrisons and that if she vacated these the Emperor and the Catholic League would immediately take possession. Charles brushed the argument aside with such impatience that Rubens feared the breaking off of negotiations; yet when he said as much to Weston and Cottington they told him the King had been too hasty and that the Privy Council would not endorse such a stand. Rubens remarked that 'Whereas in other courts negotiations begin with the ministers and finish with the royal word and signature, here they begin with the king and end with the ministers.' He felt that he was negotiating on two levels and remarked sadly that he was 'very apprehensive as to the stability of the English temperament'.

He did not understand, as Charles's ministers now did, that it was

193

necessary for Charles to say and to believe that he was acting in the interests of the Palatinate. Thus he told the Venetian Ambassador in August, when Rubens had been two months at Court, that his interests in Germany could not be exaggerated, that he kept his attention fixed there and was determined to do all in his power for the relief of his sister.[6] Though his European commitments had fallen to pieces, and while he was actually negotiating for peace with Spain, Charles was making the same speech he had made at intervals over the years. Rubens, not at first realizing this, was understandably puzzled at the seeming difference between the King's heroic sentiments and the terms of the treaty his ministers seemed about to conclude. Later he jumped to the opposite conclusion, assuming that Charles in his heart desired a simple treaty with Spain and 'cursed the day when the Palatinate was forced upon his attention'. This may have been true at one level of Charles's consciousness, yet his affection for his sister and his determination not to relinquish his efforts on her behalf were real at another level, and resulted in the series of great self-deceptions that started in Spain at the time of the Spanish marriage negotiations. A Spanish marriage, a war against Spain, the relief of Rochelle, and now, once again, friendship with Spain, would somehow, by some alchemy, re-form the Palatinate out of the melting pot of European war so that he could restore it to his sister. His subconscious might have added: to restore it as Henry would have done.

His practical French wife knew better than he did that he was play-acting and, though she herself was traditionally opposed to a Spanish alliance, she accepted the inevitable. She would express her opinion now and then, but on the whole she was too taken up with her private life and her second pregnancy to make much of a stand. One morning, indeed, when Charles indicated the extent of his worry by sending her a white hair he had discovered on his head, she could not resist sending back word that Spain would give him many more before they consented to restore the Palatinate![7]

While his diplomatic negotiations continued Rubens also had the opportunity to see at first hand the art collection of which he had heard. With Rudolph II's great collection at the Hradschin Palace in Prague broken up and plundered during the course of the war, and the Mantuan collection largely in Charles's own hands, this was, indeed, apart from the Spanish, perhaps the most impressive collection in Europe, and Charles himself was probably the best informed of princes, as well as the best judge of a canvas. As Rubens examined the

Tintorettos, the Caravaggios, the Raphaels, he had never, he exclaimed, seen in one place so many fine pictures! He remarked, particularly, on 'the marvels of the cabinet of his Majesty' where Charles kept some of his choicest pieces. He told Charles of the Raphael cartoons – *The Acts of the Apostles* – which Pope Leo X had sent to Flanders as models for the tapestries he required for the Vatican. They had been retained by the weavers as pledge for payment and were stored at Brussels. Rubens advised their purchase, but it was not until 1630, with his help, that Charles acquired them and sent them to his own tapestry works at Mortlake.

Rubens was impressed, also, by the collections, particularly the statues, of the Earl of Arundel, by the Greek and Latin inscriptions published with commentaries by John Selden, by the fine antiquarian library of Sir Robert Cotton, and by the superb collection of works of art made by Buckingham, which his widow kept intact at York House. He was hardly less enthusiastic about the hospitality he received and by the state in which some of the King's ministers lived. Cottington, for example, entertained Rubens at his country house at Hanwell in Middlesex where, wrote the artist, he lived 'the life of a prince, with every imaginable luxury'. Rubens enjoyed London. He portrayed Charles and Henrietta-Maria as St George and the Princess in a big landscape he painted showing the Thames as he saw it from his window in Gerbier's house. He depicted Gerbier's children in the great canvas *The Blessings of Peace* which symbolized his mission. He gave both pictures to Charles – indubitably by his hand and perhaps to make up for that first endeavour of the King to secure a mature Rubens. He also gave a self-portrait to Charles – the only monarch he had so honoured; and he agreed to design and execute a series of paintings in commemoration of James I for the ceiling of Inigo Jones's Banqueting Hall in Whitehall. He found Charles himself no mean draughtsman and went over some of his sketches with help and advice. Charles, for his part, knighted the painter with his own hand at Whitehall on 3 March 1630 afterwards presenting him with the jewelled sword which had been used for the ceremony, a diamond-studded hat-band, and a ring from the royal finger.[8]

They were happy days for Henrietta. She wore always her mother's locket and her pregnancy proceeded normally, her only anxiety being the fate of her midwife and her dwarf, who were captured by pirates in the Channel when coming to England. An appropriate ransom, and perhaps some element of gallantry, secured their release. The anxiety of Elizabeth and Frederick waiting in Holland was less easily assuaged, and they could scarcely believe the news of the negotiations in England. Frederick broke into sobs in front of Sir Henry Vane; Elizabeth, with tears in her eyes, declared her faith in Charles's old promise, and refused to believe that he would ever consider a treaty that did not include the full restitution of the Palatinate. She, like her sister-in-law, was pregnant. Henrietta's child was born on May 29, a large, healthy, very dark, and not at all beautiful boy who was christened Charles. A little girl, who was to be Elizabeth's last child, was born on October 13 and christened Sophie; she was a lively and pretty baby whose line was destined to take over the throne of England from her Stuart cousins. The christening of the two infants could not have been more dissimilar.

Charles was christened in the public chapel at St James's Palace on 27 June 1630. Turkish carpets covered the floors, there was rich damask on the altar and on the stairways, crimson taffeta curtains hung on the walls. Mary, Marchioness of Hamilton, carried the baby, wrapped in ermine, from the nursery to the chapel, preceded by the Aldermen of London in scarlet gowns, the peers, heralds, pursuivants, Gentlemen ushers and the deputy godparents. Laud read the prayers, a choir with two organs sang the Lord's Prayer. As the onlookers in the two galleries along each wall watched, Laud baptized the baby according to the Book of Common Prayer, the heralds recited the infant's titles, Laud preached the sermon, and led prayers for the King, the Queen, and baby Prince. The godparents had not been a difficult choice. Religion apart, Charles wanted his sister and her husband to share in his happiness and their consent gave general satisfaction. But politically, as well as for his wife's sake, he had to ask her brother, the King of France, and her mother, the dowager Queen, to sponsor the baby. He hoped, indeed, that none of them would be present at the christening, partly because he preferred a quiet ceremony, partly on grounds of expense: a French contingent, particularly, would cost more than he could afford. In the event Louis, on religious grounds, declined to sponsor the child, the Queen Mother felt it impolitic to come, and the Duchess of Richmond stood proxy for the Palatines, giving the baby a jewel worth £7000. Charles gave £1000 to Madame Peronne and appropriate presents all round. Henrietta-Maria was enormously proud of her big, ugly baby. 'He is so ugly that I am ashamed of him', she wrote to Madame de Saint-Georges, 'but his size and fatness supply the want of beauty. He is so fat and so tall, that he is taken for a year old, and he is only 4 months: his teeth are already beginning to come: I will send you his portrait as soon as he is a little fairer.'⁹

Meantime the diplomatic activity heralded by Rubens's visit ran its course and the Treaty of Madrid between Spain and England was signed by Cottington in Madrid on 5 November 1630. The King of Spain promised to do his best for the recovery of the Palatinate, Charles promised to mediate with the Dutch with a view to ending their resistance to Spain. French hopes of a union with England against Spain were dashed and England stood as uncommitted in Europe as she had done after James's treaty with Spain in 1604 – which, indeed, the new treaty much resembled. The Spain that thus held out the hand of friendship was less belligerent and weaker than the Spain that Charles had known in the previous decade, the fears of earlier years had died down and there was little open opposition to the treaty in England even if there was not much general enthusiasm – except, perhaps from the mercantile classes. Charles wrote affectionately to Elizabeth, assuring her he would always remain a good brother. Elizabeth was now able to take the news of the treaty calmly while her husband remarked that he supposed the King of England could not make war upon everybody. The wheel had come full circle. James's peace policy had prevailed. But his dream of heading a Protestant League in Europe lay in ashes, while his daughter and her family remained the visible sign of that failure. For Charles the spectre was always there. Not so much for the sake of religion; to lead a Protestant crusade was never his ambition. But the failure of his relationship with Elizabeth was ineradicable. The extent of his concern, and the lengths to which he was prepared to go, are indicated by the secret treaty he allowed Cottington to sign on 2 January 1631, by which he agreed to make war upon the Dutch and to partition the Netherlands with Spain in return for a nebulous offer of support in recovering the Palatinate. The terms were obviously unacceptable and Charles never ratified the engagement; but neither was Cottington reprimanded. On the contrary, he brought home £80,000 worth of Spanish silver bullion to be converted into Bills of Exchange payable in Brussels for the maintenance of the Spanish troops who were holding down the Dutch. Silver in hand in return for promises to pay so delighted Charles that he immediately raised Cottington to the peerage as Baron Cottington of Hanworth in Middlesex on 10 July 1631.

But there were other things for Charles to think about. He now had a son who was the first male heir born to a reigning English monarch since the time of Henry VIII. The baby, moreover, whereas Charles himself was by birth a Scot, had been born on English soil: in the third generation the Stuart line had established itself in unimpeachable legitimacy and 'Englishness'. Henrietta-Maria's nationality did not affect this aspect of the situation. But her religion did; there was considerable unconcealed dismay at a half-Popish heir who would take precedence over the offspring of the Protestant Elizabeth, and the bonfires celebrating the birth of Prince Charles owed as much to obligation as to spontaneous joy. It was all the more necessary for Charles to show that the Prince would be brought up in the Protestant faith. He made one mistake in putting the baby in charge of the Countess of Roxburgh, a Scottish Catholic who, as Jane Drummond, had been one of his mother's closest friends and whose appointment would have pleased his wife. But he soon placated Protestant opinion by replacing her with the Countess of Dorset, the wife of the Queen's Lord Chamberlain, of unquestionable Protestant family.

He was, according to his lights, practising conciliation both at home and abroad and he had few misgivings for the future as family life opened up before him.

Part III

Personal Rule

18

The King in Council

As he turned his back on war and embraced a domestic happiness Charles could, with some justification, envisage a rosy future for himself and for his country. Economic conditions were on the whole favourable with the rate of inflation slowing down and prices rising less steeply than he could remember, while a general well-being among his more wealthy subjects was expressed in their willingness to invest in a wide variety of projects. The woollen industry, in particular, was responding to the marked improvement in trade which followed the end of hostilities with France and Spain and even the Mediterranean was receiving English cloth, sending back, in English ships, a plentiful supply of wine and oil, olives, dried fruit and raw silk. Moreover, as France and Spain drifted into a more open antagonism with each other and trade between them dwindled, England took advantage of the situation and reaped what Charles's sister termed an 'incredible profit' from the commerce that now flowed into English ports. Besides her own Mediterranean trade English ships took Spanish wool to Italy, Sicilian corn to North Italy and to Spain. Sugar from the West Indies was conveyed on the final stages of its journey from Portuguese and Spanish ports to the Mediterranean and to Northern Italy in English ships. English ships were hired by the Portuguese to bring sugar from Brazil to Europe. Even Venice was hiring English vessels. Charles had only to look down from his wife's palace at Greenwich onto the veritable forest of masts in the river below, or take one of his frequent journeys by barge down river past the bustling wharves that lined the Thames, to feel the beat of a commercial nation. Increased trade induced merchants, including the Merchant Adventurers, to put profit before principle and concede tonnage and poundage. Now was the time to make better bargains with the customs farmers. In 1634, guided by Weston, Charles increased the rent of the

Great Farm by £10,000 to £150,000 a year, and amalgamated three of the petty farms at an enhancement of £16,000 a year so that they brought him in £60,000 annually. At the same time, again with Weston at his elbow, he revised to his advantage the Book of Rates. In the same year, in return for a loan of £10,000, he confirmed the 'ancient privileges' of the Merchant Adventurers, which had been under attack from several parliaments.

His relations with the East India Company were less fortunate, which was a pity because, in spite of Dutch rivalry in the East Indies and antagonism at home, the Company continued to expand, and its import trade and re-export trade in pepper and spices, silks and calicoes, was very profitable. Its great galleys – 'like moving sea fortresses' – served the double purpose of war and trade. But neither Charles nor his father had felt it politic to take a firm line with the Dutch and to demand compensation for the massacre at Amboyna in 1623, and the loan of £10,000 for which he asked the Company in 1628 was refused. It was a form of retaliation when in 1635 Charles sold licences to Endymion Porter, Sir William Courteen and others to trade to Goa and parts of the East Indies, himself taking shares in the enterprise. He was careful to avoid an open breach with the East India Company by directing the new licences to areas where the Company's writ did not run and was therefore extremely angry when he thought that a petition presented to him the following spring concerned Courteen's ships. He snatched the document from the unfortunate envoy's hand and was appeased only when he realized it again related to Amboyna. He had, he told the man petulantly, always resolved to be righted concerning Amboyna. Charles's impatience when thwarted was becoming more noticeable. In this case it could have stemmed from his knowledge that his East Indian enterprise was ending in failure.

Other old-established Companies like the Greenland Company and the Russian Company also benefited from the peace, and Charles sold a charter to a new African Company in 1630, while taking his share of the profits of them all at his customs houses. From the West he was garnering a harvest of trade from the English settlers who were establishing themselves on the Eastern seaboards of America and in the West Indian islands, and from the traders who were bringing home tobacco and sugar from the Southern states, timber and ships' supplies from the Northern. England had been among the first to settle the New World. Virginia on the American mainland, Bermuda and other West Indian islands had been colonised by Englishmen. In

1620 the *Mayflower* had reached New England, and now the route to the West was being travelled not only by Puritans for conscience sake but increasingly by merchants and business men with money to invest, by adventurers who had no money but hoped to make some, and by English vagrants, bound apprentice by some local JP to learn such skills as the new lands might require. Carolina, named after Charles, Maryland, named after Henrietta-Maria, Monserrat, Antigua, were settled in one way or another in the expansive 'thirties. To earlier trading companies Charles added the Massachusetts Bay Company in 1629, and the Providence Island Company in 1636. The New World also met some of what he considered his obligations to his friends and servants, and lands he had never seen, and of which he had scant knowledge, were lightly given away to courtiers and adventurers, sometimes twice over.

Charles was fully aware of the profit he could reap from these distant lands. Tobacco, in particular, promised to be particularly rewarding. Charles disliked 'the weed' with an intensity no less than his father's, describing it as 'a vain and needless' commodity 'which ought to be used as a drug only and not so vainly and wantonly as an evil habit of late times has brought it to'. It was nevertheless reasonable, if only for the sake of the planters, that he should allow a limited import into England and that he himself should reap the maximum benefit from doing so. His actions showed an effort to combine all three points of view. In 1627 he appointed Commissioners to buy Virginia tobacco and sell it in England on his behalf; he limited its import, under licence, to the Port of London; he forbade both the import of foreign tobacco and the planting of tobacco in England. The legislation was confused but it brought Charles £9000 a year in licence fees, while the tobacco colonies gained from a virtual monopoly and took no notice of Charles's hints that they should turn to more worthy production: he was, he told them, 'much troubled that this plantation is wholly built upon smoke'.

There were other ways in which the Plantations were in a unique position to help the mother country. When Charles had asked his Commissioners for Trade in 1626 to advise him as to what 'maie best advaunce the Trade of Merchandize and not hinder us in our just profits', it was partly the Plantations he had in mind. James had already ordered that their tobacco should be landed in England before proceeding to other countries and that it should be carried only in English ships or those of the Plantations. Charles in 1633 underlined the policy by forbidding aliens to engage in any direct trade with Virginia, the chief tobacco colony. The lucrative carrying trade would in this way be kept in English hands, English ships and English men would be trained and ready for war, and the customs returns would gain. In his attitude to the Plantations, particularly in navigation policy, Charles was in line with the most advanced economic thought of his time: he was following a policy begun by his father, which would be built up into a system under the rule of his son, and which later generations would know as Mercantilism.

Commercially, Charles could see himself ruler of an expanding, enterprising and wealthy nation reaching eastwards and westwards to new trade and fresh settlement. When he turned to industrial development he perceived a restless, innovating society already breaking the bonds of the old craft economy, using machinery and employing capital on a growing scale. As the demand for coal grew at home and abroad, increasing quantities of capital were being injected into the mining industry and from Newcastle alone some 400,000 tons of coal a year were being shipped – a twelvefold growth in a century. Iron, tin, and lead mines were becoming deeper, and their output increased, as capital provided new techniques suitable to larger-scale production; the great blast-furnaces for smelting ore in the iron districts were in themselves visual manifestations of the expansion that was taking place in the heavy industries.

There were factories with water-driven mills for making paper and hemp; the Mines Royal and the Society of the Mineral and Battery works, which Elizabeth I had established in an endeavour to produce brass and copper, were receiving fresh infusions of capital. There were large alum houses at Whitby, of which his father had been particularly proud, where many thousands of pounds were sunk in smelting machinery and many hundreds of workmen were employed. Round his capital city little factories were springing up and expanding as machine production began to oust the domestic worker in numerous enterprises such as brewing, soap-making, tanning, and the production of saltpetre. Above all, the woollen cloth industry, a highly organized, capitalist enterprise, still accounting for eighty per cent of the country's exports, remained its greatest asset, making all Europe, it was said, England's servant since it wore her livery.

In agriculture the disturbances caused by turning arable land and common grazing land into sheep runs were dying down and a new equilibrium between arable farming and sheep farming was being achieved. The unenclosed strip-farming of the open-field villages found fewer advocates as a new scientific approach to agriculture, depending upon single ownership and enclosure, and stimulated by a growing demand, began to make headway. The yeoman was still the backbone of English farming. He was the owner-occupier, hard-working, good-living, unostentatiously prosperous – but perhaps he was a little less self-contained, a little more conscious that he was 'a gentleman in ore', a little more inclined to think of his coach on Sunday rather than his plough on Monday. Above him in the social hierarchy many gentry families were likewise thinking of the Great Estate, and if they sometimes were reduced to yeoman status there were others who, by judicious marriages and preferment at Court or in office, joined the aristocracy within a generation or two. The repetition, both in James's and Charles's reigns, of Proclamations commanding gentlemen to return to their homes in the country, indicates that a considerable number of them spent their time in and around the Court seeking, if not office itself, then some of the less lucrative spoils of office.

But there were many landowners of all ranks who remained in the country and concentrated upon improving their estates. Agricultural writers found a ready market for their books and there were many translations of Dutch and Flemish authors. The sowing of seed in regular rows instead of broadcast, and the use of fertilisers and manures were actively discussed. There were experiments with new crops such as rape for cattle feed and oil, saffron, woad and madder for dyeing. Potatoes and clover were being introduced as field crops, and both turnips and clover were being used experimentally as part of a three-year rotation that would replace the customary third fallow year. Advice was published on the raising of cattle and sheep, on the care of horses, on bee-keeping. The perennial question of the conservation of woodland was being widely discussed. Methods of drainage and water supply were assuming a new importance.

Behind the experimentation, the new techniques, the popularization, was a rising, vigorous population demanding food. Since the accession of James the population of England had risen from about 3,750,000 to some 5,500,000, nearly twice as fast as in the previous century, a growth particularly marked in the ports, the towns, and – above all – in London. Capital city, port, financial centre, seat of government, home of the courts of law, of art, and of fashion, the normal abode of the Court, London was the magnet that drew trade and production, money and population into its orbit. Charles's London had reached a total population of some 600,000 people. Bristol was thriving on the opening of the Atlantic trade, and her rising population was somewhere around 25,000; Norwich and Exeter prospered on their textile manufacture; Newcastle as a port and the chief coal town was growing rapidly; but none could touch London for its bustling, overflowing exuberance. There was inevitably criticism but the rest of the country, by and large, saw where its advantage lay and did what was necessary to supply so opulent a market.

To keep London warm Newcastle colliers plied a constant coastal trade. To feed it corn came not only from Kent but from as far afield as East Anglia and Norfolk. Cattle on the hoof made their way from breeding grounds in the south-west to be fattened on nearer meadows before proceeding to the butchers of London. Poultry farms, pig farms, dairy farms, orchards and market gardens flourished round the capital city, stretching along the Thames and down into the fertile fields of Kent. There were apples in great variety, pears, cherries, plums, greengages, quinces, and mulberries from the trees which James, shortly after his accession, had caused to be planted near the capital and in each county town. Sir Walter Aston, who had been Ambassador to Spain in Charles's courtship days, was now Keeper of the Mulberry Gardens at St James's (and of the silk worms which were the reason for planting mulberries) at a stipend of £60 a year.[1] Henrietta-Maria added to the abundance by sending to France for fruit trees to enrich the English orchards. Well-off Londoners prized particularly the delicate asparagus provided by nearby market gardens. The Thames itself, besides watering the gardens and orchards on its banks, provided its own delicacy in the form of salmon. Herrings – salted, smoked, or packed in salt – might come from Yarmouth, and were enjoyed by rich and poor alike; but the wealthy valued above all the salmon from London's river, the more so, perhaps, since of all the City's food the salmon alone failed to keep up with demand and in the 1630s its price was soaring.

On the whole economic conditions were so favourable that Charles failed to see why he could not wipe the slate clean and, free from wars and foreign commitments, start afresh. In ruling without a Parliament he would not be doing anything unusual. Henry VII held only seven Parliaments in a reign of twenty-four years. Elizabeth I had ruled without a Parliament for periods of three-and-a-half, four, and four-and-a-half years, and had stretched intervals between sessions of a single Parliament to nearly five years. James had governed for as long as six-and-a-half years without a Parliament. History taught Charles that the summoning of Parliament had for the most part coincided with the monarch's financial needs – the warring Edward III had called forty-eight Parliaments in the fifty years of his reign – and this reinforced his determination to pay his debts and avoid war. He recognized the strength of Wentworth by making him Deputy Lieutenant of Ireland in January 1632, while not depriving him of the Council of the North. At home he would be advised by the great officers of state – the Lord Chancellor, the Lord Privy Seal, the two Secretaries of State, the Chancellor of the Exchequer and, above all, by the Lord Treasurer. They all had seats on his Privy Council which, besides its advisory function, was also his chief instrument of government and would promulgate the Orders in Council which would take the place of Acts of Parliament. He was accustomed to the workings of the Council, which he had attended assiduously in times of stress both as Prince and in the early years of his reign: in the crisis months of 1627 and 1629 he had attended practically weekly. Among other things he had learned the disadvantages of size and in the first five years of his personal rule Charles reduced the number of his Privy Council from 42 to 32. But even thirty people form an unwieldly vehicle for discussion, some Councillors naturally proved more useful or more congenial than others, and there developed an inner committee of the Privy Council, sometimes referred to as a 'junta' or 'cabinet council', where Charles and his closest associates could determine policy before putting it to the Council as a whole.

The Privy Council met normally on Wednesday and Friday afternoons, generally in the Council Chamber in Whitehall, but sometimes in Wallingford House, the seat of the Treasury and the residence of Weston.[2] There were various standing Committees of the Council which Charles had appointed, or which he had continued from his father's reign. The standing Committee for Trade was important and Charles attended frequently, enlarging it to become the Committee for Trade and Plantations, and the importance of the colonies was further recognized in 1632 by the appointment of a Committee of Council on the New England Plantations, which became the Commission for Foreign Plantations in 1634. Reports came to Charles not only from these standing Committees but from various Departments of State – from the Admiralty, in particular, at whose meetings he was, again, a frequent participant and whose reports he read carefully and annotated repeatedly. He extended his care to the Provinces of the Church, reading and making marginal comments on the Reports that came in from the Bishops. He kept his hand on foreign affairs to such a degree that Sir Thomas Roe was able to write to Wentworth in December 1634 that it was only the 'great temper, justice, and wisdom of his Majesty' that corrected and dispersed ill humours. He insisted on personal consultation in all matters. Edward Nicholas, the secretary to the Council, listed the points on which Charles was to be consulted and afterwards noted the results of the consultation: 'The King approves of this'; 'The King likes it well but . . .' His ministers knew they could consult him at almost any time on important issues, as when Henry Vane arrived at Hampton Court after six o'clock one evening on Palatine business. Weston was early instructed by Charles 'to believe nothing of importance until he speaks with his Majesty'.

The machinery of the law remained the same whether Parliament was sitting or not. Chancery, King's Bench, Common Pleas, Requests, continued their normal work; Justices of Assize made their circuits; the courts of Star Chamber and of High Commission, the Councils of the North and of the Marches of Wales maintained their authority. The Departments of State were no more efficient, no more corrupt, without a Parliament than with one, their staffs still remained dependent upon some form of perquisite or bribe to augment their salaries. In the localities, at the operative end of most laws or directives, it was still the JPs upon whom Charles would have to rely. They were men of diverse character, interest, and determination, most of them were of gentry or aristo–gentry stock, and they included many of the most influential members of Charles's last Parliament some of whom, including Sir John Eliot, were still in prison for the part they played in the dissolution. It was a disturbing thought that his government might be only as effective as these men made it. But, though Charles instituted several enquiries into central administration he left local government untouched.

Charles was prepared to thrust such thoughts into the background as he turned to the immediately pressing problem of his debts. The question was not quite so straightforward as at first appeared, partly because of the size of his commitments, which included some of his father's debts as well as his own heavy war expenditure, partly because of the complicated system of borrowing and credit in which he was enmeshed. It was difficult to establish the full extent of his indebtedness, but it could have been of the order of £1,500,000, of which the faithful Burlamachi was claiming £500,000. Most of Charles's foreign transactions had gone through Philip Burlamachi, whose credit stood pledged all over Europe to meet Charles's needs. Burlamachi supported Mansfeld's expedition in this way, he paid Charles's subsidies to Christian of Denmark and other Princes, he transmitted to Germany sums of money voluntarily collected in England for the cause of the Princess Elizabeth, he paid for the Mantuan collection of pictures, he provided funds for foreign embassies, gave security to agents of the Crown abroad, paid pensions to the Palatine family as well as advancing money for men and equipment at home. Charles was fortunate in having in his service one of the great international financiers of the age whose word and whose credit were unquestioned from the time he advanced money for the little Duke's engines of war until he himself crashed in 1633.[3]

On domestic loans Charles normally paid the current rate of interest, which was eight per cent after 1624. Borrowing was generally secured upon the receipts of the Exchequer in general or upon specific branches of the revenue, collectors being instructed to honour debts out of the proceeds of their collections before the money reached the Exchequer. In either case over-assignment was not unusual, nor were the persons who received money in this way necessarily those who made the loan in the first place. The tallies which represented debts often became a kind of currency in themselves, passing from hand to hand at a decreasing price until they reached a person who knew how to get them cashed at a favourable rate. It was difficult for Charles to know how many tallies were circulating against him. At the same time, with interest accumulating, the more he struggled the more securely he was enmeshed. By August 1630 future revenue stood mortgaged to the extent of nearly £278,000, with some revenues anticipated to 1637.[4]

Charles and Weston faced the question squarely: Crown lands were given or sold on reasonable terms to recoup debtors, the City of London alone receiving nearly £350,000 worth in settlement of debts incurred by James. Holland, the King's friend, was promised a pension of £2000 a year for twenty-one years, possibly in respect of some £23,000 still due to him for his expenses in France when he was wooing Henrietta-Maria on the King's behalf. Royal jewels passed to other creditors. Two men were satisfied with the imposition of a new duty of 4/- a chaldron on seacoal which they were allowed to manage until their debts had been met; others were promised the reversion of fines imposed in certain courts. In addition, about £100,000 was paid out in cash during 1630 and 1631, a great deal of which came from the customs' duties which, enhanced by Weston's new Book of Rates, were now Charles's most important source of revenue. They remained, also, a continued means of anticipating income and were Charles's chief source of borrowing in the 1630s. Burlamachi, in spite of some slightly questionable accounting, received his £500,000 in various forms, but it was not enough to save him from the effects of twenty years of financial juggling. When everything blew up in his face in 1633 Charles showed his customary concern for a man who had been faithful to him for more than a decade. He helped Burlamachi with money and gave him the administration of the alum farm. A few years later he appointed him Postmaster. But Burlamachi was too deeply enmeshed to pull himself clear and he died in penury some ten years later.

But, debts apart, how could Charles make ends meet without the subsidies which only a Parliament could sanction? He totted up his responsibilities: payments to staff and servants of various kinds, including those who served him in high office; he felt keenly his obligations both to their standards of life and to their pensions. He honoured his father's intentions (which were also his own) towards Buckingham by providing for Buckingham's wife and children. He helped Weston who, on accepting the Treasurer's white staff made it clear that he could not support the dignity of the office out of his own means. Charles gave him £10,000 in cash and made over to him such perquisites as the lease of the sugar farm, amounting to approximately £9000 a year, and a third part of the imposition upon coals, some £4000 annually. The Queen, with an extravagance and way of life dictated by her upbringing and her temperament, required well over £30,000 a year. Charles had already added lands in the Duchy of Lancaster to her jointure and in 1629 he included various parks nearer home at Greenwich, Oatlands, Isleworth, Edmonton and Twickenham, as well as the manor of Holdenby in Northamptonshire.

There was also a pleasant need for additional expenditure on the royal nursery, where Buckingham's children were now established with his own. He felt his obligations to his nephews and nieces and in

1629 extended to Rupert and Elizabeth the pensions already paid to their mother and elder brother. The giving of presents was a part of life and in 1630 Charles presented the Savoy Ambassador with a gold tablet set with diamonds bearing a picture of himself and the Queen, valued at £500; in 1636 he and Henrietta-Maria gave horses worth £500 to her brother, the King of France, and made a similar present to his sister, Elizabeth. He himself, though he economized in dress, bought for £300 a ring set with a large, square diamond, and in 1634 he was fondling a 'great round rope of pearls' which had been imported duty free for his inspection. He paid £110 to Michael Crosse for copying pictures in Spain; early in 1631 he employed Inigo Jones to catalogue his Greek and Roman coins and medals; he counted himself fortunate in getting the French engraver, Nicholas Briot, to provide engravings for the English coinage and to produce such beautiful pieces as the medals which marked his Coronation and his claim to Dominion of the Seas.

In 1629 Charles sent the Gentileschis to Italy with a view to buying the picture collection of Signor Philip San Micheli, subject to the approval of Nicholas Lanier. Fortunately for his Exchequer Lanier advised against the purchase. Eight years later, however, Charles purchased the Italian collection of the German artist, Daniel Fröschl, who had been painter-in-ordinary to Rudolph II, thus adding twenty-three pictures to his collection, including six grisailles attributed to Caravaggio, and canvases by Titian and Guido Reni. He bought, as Rubens had recommended, the magnificent Raphael cartoons and sent them to his tapestry workers at Mortlake. True, what he bought or what he commissioned was not always a guide to what he paid. In 1638 payments were still being made to Rubens in respect of £3000 due to him for pictures sold to Charles 'long since'; the chain of gold which Charles sent him in March 1639 may have been in part recompense, but it may have been in acknowledgment of the Banqueting House paintings which were delivered in 1637. Charles welcomed, even urged, Anthony Van Dyck to reside in London as Court painter but Van Dyck's payments also lagged both in respect of his retainer and for the portraits he painted of the royal family. Gentileschi was still installed in York House in 1631 refusing to move until he had received what was owing to him, while the Duchess of Buckingham entreated the King to pay him so that she might have York House to herself again. Charles paid £200 to the artist who, in due course, moved on.

Other expenses were more difficult to justify. Even though

Weston was serving him well and the memory of Buckingham was green, was it necessary to give £3000 to Weston's daughter on her marriage to Lord Fielding, the Duke's nephew? Or £3000 to Lady Anne Fielding, the Duke's niece, on her marriage to Baptist Noel, Viscount Camden's heir, who, in gambling, lost in one day a nearly equivalent sum?[5]

It was difficult to know where retrenchment should begin. Charles had nineteen palaces, castles and residences to keep up which required renovation, repairs and replacements, as well as a permanent nucleus of staff. Hunting at Newmarket, in the New Forest and elsewhere cost money even when entertainment was provided, as at Wilton, by the King's friends. But Charles's passion for the chase now equalled that of his father, and it kept him in health. Nor could the Queen's visits to the spas at Bath or Matlock be curtailed. He not only needed money for his pictures and works of art but, with Laud and Inigo Jones, he had schemes for beautifying his capital, including the rebuilding of St Paul's, which his father had begun. London's cathedral was in a ruinous state, its steeple had been destroyed by fire at the beginning of Elizabeth's reign, ramshackle shops and houses leaned against its outer walls damaging the fabric and destroying the proportions of the nave. Inside it was given over to strollers and gossip-mongers and 'Paul's Walk' was the commonly accepted resort of anyone anxious to purvey or to receive news. The case of Francis Litton illustrates its condition. Litton came up from a remote village three miles from Bedford to London to be married and was apprehended by the High Commission for 'pissing against a pillar' in St Paul's. The bewildered countryman explained 'he knew not where he was' as he had never been in London before, and 'knew it not to be a church'; also he suffered from the stone and was unable to make water when needful yet at other times 'he could not hould but must needs ease himself'. The pillar of the church appeared to him nothing but the most convenient place for doing so. When he fell down on his knees and wept before the Commission, pleading that he was far from his friends, the court granted him bail and presumably released him.[6]

When Laud, as Bishop of London, asked Charles in 1631 to continue the work his father had begun, Charles was only too ready to do so. He visited the Cathedral himself, appointed Commissioners to collect money for repairs, put Inigo Jones in charge of the overall plans. In spite of exhortation and Charles's own example of pledging £500 a year for three years, not much more then £5000 was collected over the next two years, but Charles had already instructed the work to proceed and most of the houses built against the walls of the church had been demolished. There had been objections, but compensation had been paid, and the splendid proportions of the long nave were revealed. Jones's plans now included a classical portico at the west end of the church, and when Charles visited it in the summer of 1634 he was so pleased with the progress of the work that he undertook the whole of the western end at his own expense.

In other directions expenditure was more questionable: improvements to his manor of York; the conversion of a tennis court at Somerset House into a chapel for Henrietta-Maria; above all, the making of a new deer park between Richmond and Hampton Court. Much of the land involved was Charles's own, and a great deal of it was waste and rough woodland which would benefit from his plans. But many poor people held common rights in these areas and more substantial men held good, working farms interspersed with the waste. Charles's intention was to buy out these landlords and to put a brick wall round the whole of the area he acquired. Some landlords agreed to his terms, some held out, reluctant to abandon their homes and their estates, the poor were upset at losing their common rights. Most of Charles's ministers, including Laud and Cottington, disapproved of a scheme which would cost a lot of money and alienate many people. In the high-handed way in which he was now conducting all his affairs, Charles disregarded them. Cottington, however, was very outspoken and Charles's anger flared: he had caused brick to be burned for making the wall, he said, and was resolved to go on with the scheme. Laud assumed he had an ally in Cottington and when the application for money came before the Treasury Board stoutly opposed it. But Cottington, either because he wished to keep the King's favour, or because of his antipathy to Laud, spoke in favour of the grant: 'since the place was so convenient for the King's winter exercise, it would minimise his journeys', he said, 'and nobody ought to dissuade him from it'. Laud flew into a passion, telling Cottington that such men as he would ruin the King and cause him to lose the affections of his subjects. Cottington taunted him: 'Those who did not wish the King's health could not love him; and they who went about to hinder his taking recreation which preserved his health might be thought . . . guilty of the highest crimes.' He was not sure that it might not be high treason. Laud rushed to the King, but Charles merely laughed, at once perceiving Cottington's intent both to curry favour with him and to tantalize Laud. 'My Lord', he said, 'you are deceived: Cottington is too hard on you,' and he told him of Cottington's opposition to his plans. Charles's New Park at Richmond was begun in 1636 and completed in 1638. But Charles forgave Laud more easily than he forgave Cottington for opposing him.[7]

19

Modern Prince and Feudal Lord

Economies like cutting pensions and reducing Court expenditure, extravagance like the making of Richmond Park, create enemies, but on the whole the raising of money makes more. Weston was more aware of the difficulties than Charles himself. He was already stepping up the receipts from the customs houses in what was likely to be the biggest contribution to the King's finances, but his natural caution enabled him to foresee danger in some of the other money-making devices that Charles was contemplating. A Treasurer whose influence was on the side of caution was bound to have some effect upon the King, yet Charles was never deflected from any purpose he had in mind: he simply used other instruments if one failed him. The influence of Laud was less direct. His natural austerity acted as a break upon expenditure, his urge to improve the King's finances caused him to press economy and pursue money-raising devices with a ruthless integrity. Unlike Weston, he seemed utterly impervious to the dangers of arousing vested interests.

In the raising of money by the sale of monopoly rights in various forms Weston was particularly cautious, while Charles was at his most expansive, carrying his Council with him into an amazing series of projects. The granting of monopoly rights of production, sale, or management in return for a fee or rent had become a scandal even in Elizabeth's time and James had agreed to the abolition of the practice. The Monopolies Act of 1624, however, allowed two exceptions which were in accord with public sentiment. The first was in respect of new inventions or infant industries where it was considered reasonable to allow a period of monopoly protection. The second was in respect of corporations. Seventeenth-century opinion was still widely influenced by the medieval concept of the corporate society in which trades and trading bodies, towns, religious organizations and fraternities were organized on a corporate basis and acted as monopoly bodies. To have pronounced these illegal would have been to remove the underpin from society itself. So, in spite of abuses, corporations remained, with new inventions, outside the scope of the Monopolies Act. That Act, however, had not intended, and could not have envisaged, the mushroom growth of patents and monopolies which came into being under cover of these exceptions.

A Crown monopoly of playing cards and dice gave the King a fifty per cent profit on sales. Monopoly rights to individuals included the transport of lamperns, the making of spectacles, combs, hatbands, tobacco-pipes, bricks; there were monopolies for the gathering of rags, for sealing linen cloth and bone lace, for gauging butter casks, for transporting sheepskins and lambskins. Sir William Alexander was given a patent for printing the Psalms of King David translated into English metre by King James. The rights were all paid for in one way or another. John Pearson and Benjamin Monger of London 'set forth the inconveniences and mischiefs which arise from dishonest servants, and the impositions practised by charewomen and dry nurses'. They proposed a Register of Masters and Servants, the fee being 2d from the master and 1d from the servant, and they offered the King a payment of £10 a year for the privilege of the sole running of the registry.[1] Charles liked the idea and the project was approved. Somewhat different was a scheme proposed by Sir John Coke, which never saw the light of day, for the formation of a Loyal Association, whose members, besides paying an entrance fee, would pledge themselves to serve the King in person, goods, and might. They would be distinguished by a badge or ribbon in the King's colour and would be entitled to precedence at public gatherings.[2]

Frivolous or lightweight as most of these projects appeared, others were in line with an economic self-sufficiency that for hundreds of years had been the goal of the King's ancestors. Elizabethan statesmen, as well as his father, had pursued this end and many of his own most influential subjects were urging its necessity. Mansell's glass patent, which Charles renewed, might be considered in this category; the alum works whose monopoly Charles continued, certainly could be; when Sir Thomas Russell was licensed to use a process of his own invention in the production of saltpetre, Charles was following the lead of Elizabeth and of James; a crown monopoly of the sale of gunpowder followed naturally and, besides being profitable, could be justified on grounds of national security. The saltpetre monopoly ran quickly into difficulties when the Admiralty learned that some saltpetre men were being over-zealous, abusing their rights of search for the raw material by digging in barns and churches, houses and sick-rooms regardless of the old, the sick, and women in childbed, undermining walls and making great holes which they failed to fill up. But the Government needed saltpetre and Charles caused a Proclamation to be made in 1634 empowering any three or more JPs to 'enter, break open, and work for it in the lands and possessions' of himself or of any of his subjects in England and Wales.

In incorporating William Shipman and others as the Society of Planters of Madder of the City of Westminster, he was again following the lead of his father, who had already attempted to restrict the import of this important dye in order to render the cloth industry more self-sufficient. In turning his attention to salt, seeking to substitute a native product for the imported article, Charles was pursuing the same well-trodden path towards self-sufficiency. In 1636 he prohibited the import of salt from Biscay and issued licenses for its manufacture and sale in England, hoping to receive ten shillings a wey for his support and protection. Unfortunately the contradictions inherent in the policy of self-sufficiency were glaringly obvious in this case: the price of salt rose and affected the fishing industry, particularly the important herring fishery, which depended upon salting its catches; Trinity House complained that ships which had formerly brought back salt from Biscay now returned unladen from the south of France and might be compelled to abandon their voyages altogether; while the benefit Charles received from the granting of licenses was partly offset by his loss of duty on the imported product.

The patent for soap demonstrated the same mixture of motives as well as providing one of the most colourful episodes of the time. Again the project had been aired in James's reign and was an attempt to raise Crown revenue while promoting self-sufficiency. Foreign soap was excluded and the home-produced article was to contain nothing but native materials. To this end a group of soapboilers was incorporated in 1631 as the Society of Soapmakers of Westminster, and was instructed to use vegetable oil in place of imported whale oil. This obligation extended to all soapboilers and its enforcement was put in the hands of the new company. To make control easier the production of soap was confined to London, Westminster, and Bristol. The new Society thus held a virtual monopoly of soap manufacture, and in order to protect the consumer the price was fixed. The King was to receive a payment first of £4, later of £6 a ton of soap marketed. But the public did not like the new soap, and the old was soon selling at higher prices as independent soap boilers continued to produce clandestinely. They were called before the Star Chamber but neither their punishment nor testimony from selected witnesses, including the Queen's laundress, could convince consumers that the new product was as good as the old; rumour, indeed, had it that the Queen's laundress continued to use Castille soap. Public laundry trials organized in the City of London gave conflicting views on the efficiency and 'sweetness' of the new soap; as a final throw the independent soap-makers offered the King an annual payment of more than the new society was paying and the monopoly was bought out. But these operations enhanced the price of the product and, although Charles continued to reap as much as £18,000 in 1636, the best year, his subjects were the losers.[3]

Charles made no attempt to control any basic industry. A government monopoly of coal was considered but the Committee for Trade advised against this on the grounds that it would raise the price and arouse the 'clamour of the people'. It would also have meant confronting the powerful monopolists who already controlled the industry and who doubtless had influenced the verdict of the Committee. If it could have been managed, control of a basic industry would not only have been financially advantageous to Charles but would also have bolstered the aim of economic self-sufficiency which, as it was, appeared to be pursued in somewhat piecemeal and haphazard fashion.

Trading monopolies had, on the whole, even less to say for them. The Company of Vintners, for example, paid to the King a duty of 40/- a tun of wine sold in return for monopoly rights of sale and an increase in price of one penny a quart on French wines and twopence a quart on Spanish wines. Charles farmed the tax to a group of vintners for £30,000 a year, but it is doubtful whether he ever received as much as this.

The group of projects which covered inventions was mixed. In agriculture there were many schemes for drainage, several inventions for mechanical sowing and for improved ploughs. A patent for the much-needed cleansing of the Thames did more harm than good in scooping up gravel from the river bed 'and making great holes'. In view of the feared shortage of timber it was, however, timely to give a fourteen-year patent to Dud Dudley and his partners for smelting iron

218

with coal, or with peat or turf, in return for an annual rent; it was reasonable to license Edward Ball to prepare peat by reducing it to a coal that would 'serve for melting iron, boiling salt, and burning brick'. The many new patents for the drainage of mines, like that granted to Daniel Ramsay and his associates 'for raising water out of pits by fire' showed, possibly, a too-credulous belief in experiment. Sir Henry Clare, searching for the philosopher's stone, strained that credulity too far and Charles turned down his request for financial aid. There was, however, a lively interest in hidden treasure. In April 1630 Francis Tucker and his associates were given licence to conduct such a search on the understanding that Charles received one-quarter of anything they found. Two years later Charles listened to Richard Norwood who had 'found out a special means to dive into the sea or other deep Water, there to discover, and thence by an Engine to raise or bring up such Goods as are lost or cast away by Shipwracke or otherwise' and he licensed search in the water as on the land.[4]

Charles was present to hear the case made by Thomas Russell for the use of human urine in the manufacture of saltpetre. Russell estimated that if 10,000 villages, each with forty houses occupied by four persons who all cast their urine upon a load of earth for three months, and then let it rest for three months longer, ripe saltpetre would result. Feeling, perhaps, that this was a viable alternative to the ravages of the saltpetre men, Charles ordered all cities, towns, villages and other habitations to use their urine in this way, guaranteeing that the earth would be taken from them without trouble or charge,[5]

Charles and his Council were certainly attracted by anything out of the ordinary, and the exuberance and inventiveness of the time was encouraged by their support. Charles himself was genuinely interested in projects, and his eclectic mind enjoyed ranging over the schemes brought before him. He was eager, assiduous, hard-working, even if, together with his Council, a trifle over-sanguine and too ready to attempt to fill the royal purse at the expense of credulity. An Order in Council later lamented the various licenses which had been procured 'upon untrue suggestions' or which in execution had been found to be 'far from those grounds and reasons wherefore they were founded' and which proved 'very burdensome and grievous to the King's subjects'. Using the expression that James had used when things went wrong, they complained that they had been 'notoriously abused'.

Charles received a valuable income from his monopolies and patents: £30,000 from the wine licences: rather more from the soap monopoly: a useful £13,000 or so annually from tobacco licenses: a small but helpful £750 annually from his monopoly of playing cards and dice: rents from the alum and glass works: small sums from the various patents he sanctioned.[6] Several contemporaries asserted that he was being defrauded and received but a fraction of what was intended. More serious was the criticism that since there was nothing to prevent the fees which were paid to the King from being passed on, it was the consumer who paid the King's commission in the form of higher prices. A discriminatory excise on luxury goods could have brought in as much and caused less hardship to the poor though possibly more protest from the rich. Charles excused himself by remembering that England was still the least taxed country in Europe, with no official excise and no regular direct taxation. Certainly projects and monopolies were not the most efficient nor the most equitable way of raising money, but in the absence of any other form of taxation it was possibly more appropriate to criticise the nature of the project itself than the fact that it imposed a tax upon the community. A tax arising from the monopoly of an essential article like glass or soap was different from a tax imposed in order to foster a new technique in industry or agriculture. Taxes on playing cards and dice were annoying rather than burdensome to the public. The real abuses were taxes that affected industry and reacted on workers as well as their employers, the monopolies that rebounded against themselves by causing shortages and dislocation elsewhere. On the credit side were benefits like the infusions of capital which followed the new leases issued to the Mines Royal and the Mineral and Battery Works, the encouragement of the home production of the important wool cards by a prohibition of import; and there were other grants, restrictions, and prohibitions whose value depended upon the point of view, such as the prohibition of the use of brass buckles as being not so serviceable as iron. Obviously, in considering methods of raising money a line had to be drawn somewhere. Charles drew it by not debasing the coinage, by not taxing food, and, while allowing the price of wine to be enhanced, by not taxing the people's beer.

In a somewhat different category were schemes bequeathed to Charles by his father which concerned water supply and land drainage, both matters of concern to a growing population which required both water and food, and both possible means of channelling money into the Exchequer.

220

Sir Hugh Myddelton, a Welshman with a lively interest in affairs and with financial and other connections in the City where he practised his craft as jeweller, goldsmith, banker and clothier, was among those who had been considering the idea of a continuous supply of sweet water to London. He was a great friend of Sir Walter Raleigh with whom he would sit outside his goldsmith's shop, smoking tobacco and talking endlessly of projects and exploration while the London populace looked on. It was possibly then that the idea was born of channelling springs of fresh water from Chadwell and Amswell, near Ware in Hertfordshire, by means of an artificial waterway or New River to Islington on the outskirts of London, where it would flow into a reservoir to be called the New River Head. James already had dealings with Myddelton as a jeweller, and his curious mind was attracted when he saw engineers making investigations near Theobalds on Myddelton's behalf. In 1612 James agreed to pay half the cost of the works, past and future, in return for half the profit. The first stretch of New River was completed by 1617 when it was opened with considerable festivity and enthusiasm. James had by that time contributed over £9000 to the enterprise but profits were not high and in 1631 Charles commuted his inherited half-share to £500 a year.

But there were still many families in and near London without sweet and wholesome water or, indeed, without access to water for cleansing or for fire-fighting, and when in 1631 projectors claimed to have discovered new springs, hitherto unused, that could be channelled to London and Westminster along a stone or brick aqueduct there seemed no reason not to licence the undertaking. That Charles did so with care was an answer to those critics who blamed him for sanctioning 'rival' projects. The scheme commissioned in 1631 was supplementary to Myddelton's and its provisions were carefully laid down. In spite of Sir Hugh Myddelton's work, ran the caption to the grant, 'Wee are credibly informed that there are very many families, both within the Citty of London, and the suburbs thereof and Streets adjoining in the County of Middlesex, which want sweet and wholesome water to Bake and Brew, Dress their Meat and for other necessary uses, and cannot fitly be served or supplied with any the Water works which are now in use.' The licence was to bring water to London by an aqueduct of brick or stone from any spring or springs, pool or pools, current or currents, place or places within one-and-a-half miles of Hoddesden and to disperse it through several pipes, provided that hitherto untapped sources only were employed and that their use did not 'diminish any of the Springs, or take away any of the Water' already brought to London or Westminster by Sir Hugh Myddelton. Charles's share of the profit was to be £4000 a year and he authorized the holding of a lottery or lotteries in any town or city of England to help raise money for the project. Lotteries were popular among his subjects – the more so since none had been organized for some time – and the tickets were soon taken up.[7]

Under the influence of the Dutch the reclamation of swamp and fenland by drainage had also been considered. Henry VIII had drained marshland at Wapping, Plumstead and Greenwich and there had been similar small-scale enterprises for an immediate purpose. But little as yet had been done to reclaim large areas of land where long-term planning and a great deal of capital would be required. An obvious target was the Great Level of the Fens which stretched inland from the Wash to cover an area of nearly 700,000 acres. It was watered by six rivers which overflowed their banks constantly in winter and frequently in summer so that throughout the year the area was a flat, watery plain where the inhabitants walked on stilts or travelled by boat. Fishing and fowling dominated their lives, yet when the waters retreated the soft earth was covered with lush grass for cattle and sheep, and there was always turf and sedge in abundance for firing, reed and alder for thatching and furniture-making.

The fiercely independent people who lived there were content with the life they knew and, with fish and fowl in abundance as well as cattle and sheep, a modicum of crops and the normal fare of the farmyard, they were probably better-off than many small farmers living more conventional lives. Even the less well-off among them were better placed than they would have been in a more organized society where they would be classed as sturdy beggars under the Poor Law. The basic wealth of the area was shown, indeed, by the churches, cathedrals and monasteries which had been raised over the centuries in stone brought from outside the fenland by barge down the many rivers. Naturally enough the possibility of drainage had been considered. But although the area was potentially rich and the prospects of profit were high, drainage was expensive, most of the inhabitants were content as they were and, apart from the bigger landowners, there was little interest in land reclamation. Particularly bad periods of flooding were dealt with by ad hoc Commissions of Sewers until the area reverted to its old life.

A growing population made the prospect of a larger farming area more attractive, and James, dramatizing the situation after his own fashion, had announced that 'for the honour of his kingdom' he 'would not longer suffer these countries to be abandoned to the will of the waters'. Accordingly, he engaged the Dutch engineer, Cornelius Vermuyden, and sponsored the work of reclamation in return for 120,000 acres of the reclaimed land. James died before the work was begun but Charles carried on, at first content for local landowners to act as undertakers, putting up the money, shouldering the risk, and claiming their proportion of reclaimed land. But nothing came of this and in a welter of conflicting opinion, which included opposition to drainage itself and opposition to Vermuyden as contractor, the rivers got completely out of hand and several smaller owners of permanently flooded land approached Francis, fourth Earl of Bedford, who owned 20,000 acres near Thorney and Whittlesay, to help. In 1630 the Earl contracted to improve all the southern Fenland within six years so that it would be free of summer flooding. Thirteen others joined him in putting up the capital, Vermuyden was put under contract, and in 1634 Charles granted a charter of incorporation for the drainage of the Great Fen. Charles's fee for the charter was to be 12,000 acres of the drained land out of the 95,000 which would fall to Bedford.

By the autumn of 1637 the undertaking appeared to have succeeded and Charles received his 12,000 acres of land. But the work had been done against a background of opposition and rioting by the local population, not only because they feared to change their ways, not only because, in the reapportionment of land, many commoners lost their rights of pasturage and of fishing, but, more fundamentally, because the Great Level was an area which could not be stereotyped or subjected to any basic rule of thumb. Levels of flooding were different; some flooding was gainful; the prevention of flooding in some places merely inundated others which had previously been dry.[8] Charles saw nothing of this and he was obviously not familiar with the detailed geography of the Fens. Even Vermuyden, who planned and carried out the bulk of the work, lacked adequate topographical knowledge: both men could have relied more heavily upon local advice. Even so, Charles and his Council acquired a considerable understanding of the problems involved. Charles, for example, instructed the Commissioners of Sewers on the north-east side of the river Witham that, although their lands had been drained, it was necessary, in order to keep them dry, to maintain the river banks in repair between specified points. He showed care for the poor in instructing the Commissioners in charge of apportioning land after drainage to convoy 2000 acres to the use of poor cottagers and others, and he was sufficiently astute to order a proportion of reclaimed land to be tied to the perpetual maintenance of the work.[9]

But when a way of life is disturbed, when outsiders make foolish mistakes, such concessions are unimpressive. All over the Fenland men and women came out with pitchforks and scythes to fend off the innovators. Sometimes a landowner of greater sophistication would offer a more durable form of defence as in 1637 when Mr Oliver Cromwell of Ely, in return for a groat for every cow upon the common, offered to hold the drainage commissioners of Ely Fen in suit of law for five years. But Charles himself intervened shortly afterwards. He was not satisfied with the way the drainage had been carried out for, although the Fens were now free of flooding in summer, they were still subject to winter flooding. After many complaints had been received by the Privy Council he stepped in personally, declared himself 'undertaker' and promised to make the Fens 'winter as well as summer lands'. Meantime he gave the inhabitants full rights over their lands and commons until the work was completed and the final apportionments made. Before that was accomplished both he and Mr Oliver Cromwell had been swept along by events even more important than the drainage of the Great Fen; when they came face to face it was upon other issues.[10]

Charles liked to see himself as an 'advanced' monarch, patronizing inventors and giving scope to innovation and improvement. But he was also aware of his position as feudal overlord and was as willing to raise money from the one role as from the other.

Already in 1626 he had appointed a Commission to consider means of augmenting his revenue and reducing his charges. Among the matters under review were his forests and chases and now, with the help of Weston, Charles considered them anew. These large, dispersed areas were not necessarily wooded but were technically land reserved for royal hunting. Their native inhabitants were few and largely itinerant with a way of life that was simple and not necessarily meagre. Though they were subject to forest law instead of common law, which entailed severe penalties for interference with the forest or its wild life, royal connivance had left them for the most part in peace to a life freer and more fruitful than that of many peasants elsewhere. The royal forests contained also a few settlers whose existence was connived at. Even enthusiastic huntsmen like James had not used all forest land for hunting, and as forest laws had fallen into disuse many peasants had, in fact, used the forest amenities as they would those of ordinary woodland or waste and had even brought some of the forest area under cultivation. Forest verges, in particular, had frequently come under the plough. In this way the extent of forest land had been reduced and dwellings, in some cases entire villages, had grown up within the bounds of what were technically 'forests'. Here and there richer men, some already big landlords, were deliberately farming large stretches.

The suggestion now was that royal forests should be restored to their ancient boundaries and that transgressors should be fined for encroachment or for infringing forest law within that enlarged area. In this way practices that had come to be considered normal would be penalized, whole villages – there were seventeen of them in the Forest of Dean alone – would be subject to penalty for breaking forest law, and even those who farmed the verges would be fined. Though much of this would be small-scale penalization, and not intended to be carried out, the amount of discontent which the very idea would generate was bound to be considerable. It was, however, the big encroaching landlords who were the real target.

The ancient office of Justice in Eyre, which administered forest law, was revived for the purpose and in 1630 the Earl of Holland was appointed Chief Justice with the assistance of Lord Keeper Finch, the Speaker who had been held in the chair in Charles's last Parliament. Neither man was popular. It fell to Finch in the Forest of Dean, where Holland took up his Justice Seat in July 1634, to make the important pronouncement as to what were legally considered the ancient bounds of the forests and to what extent, consequently, infringement had occurred: the King's claim was to the boundaries as enacted by Edward I before subsequent amendment and he was, therefore, laying claim to the maximum area of forest land, despite the changes of three centuries.

As expected, the fines imposed upon forest dwellers or little nibblers were small or were allowed to lapse, and the main penalties were reserved for the big and wealthy landowners. In Dean, where the Lord Treasurer himself was implicated, one of the largest fines, of £35,000, fell upon Gibbons, his agent, who was commonly thought to be the scapegoat. Sir Basil Brooke and his partner, who were said to have used trees set aside for the navy for their iron works in the Forest, were fined £98,000 jointly, which two years later was commuted to £12,000. Enormous fines in the New Forest, in Rockingham and other forests were similarly reduced but in all brought about £37,000 into Charles's Exchequer between 1636 and 1640. Frustration, indignity, and a sense of injustice festered. It might have been legally defensible to reassert a boundary three hundred years old, it might have been equitable that untaxed landlords should make some contribution to the royal Exchequer in respect of lands and profits which they had acquired by no right but custom. But to impose a fine which was so large that it was certain to generate the maximum resentment and then to remit or substantially reduce it, was a policy of ill-advised, deliberate confrontation to no purpose. Not that this always happened. There were cases when the project worked more smoothly and Charles was paid all, or nearly all, he expected.[11]

Besides dealing with the ancient bounds of his forests and chases Charles had asked the Commission of 1626 to recommend how he could restore parts of them to a 'profitable cultivation'. In carrying out their recommendations he ran into agrarian troubles already rampant in three of his Western forests – Gillingham in Dorset, Braydon in Wiltshire, and the Forest of Dean in Gloucestershire.

In Gillingham lands had been granted to Sir James Fullerton and George Kirk, two of Charles's Scottish friends and Gentlemen of his Bedchamber. They were given licence to depark and proceeded to enclose and farm. But the forest dwellers, on the grounds that their ancient rights of common were being violated, pulled down the fences as fast as they went up. Messengers from the Privy Council were whipped and their orders burnt while soldiers in the neighbourhood rescued the few rioters who had been apprehended. In November 1638 the High Sheriff of Dorset brought in more troops but found 'a great and well armed number' of rioters holding their position under the slogan 'here we were born and here we stay'. Some eighty of them were fined by the Star Chamber, but a couple of years later the struggle was still continuing under a leader styled 'the Colonel'.

In the Forest of Braydon Charles was more closely concerned, for here he was attempting to enclose and farm himself. Commissioners whom he sent down to smooth the way were told that enclosure would spell the 'utter undoinge' of many thousands of poor people by depriving them of rights of common and other perquisites. Fences were no sooner up than they were torn down. The local people were very much at one, even the larger landlords sharing the claim to what

226

were looked upon as customary rights. Privy Council messengers were beaten up and were powerless to stem the destruction of fences and ditches or to silence the 'jeering and unbecoming speeches of the rioters'. Only by means of informers were some of the leaders apprehended. But Charles had no taste for this kind of struggle, and he granted large areas of the Forest of Braydon to freeholders and other tenants, while continuing merely a modicum of farming himself.[12]

The Forest of Dean presented an even more complicated picture, for here was a way of life that for three hundred years had suffered no external interference. The forest proper was in poor condition through lack of care, indiscriminate felling and failure to replace; in rough forest clearings, which often stretched for miles, small-scale agriculture and common land were interspersed with coal and iron-mining, with charcoal burning, with tanning and other small enterprises that depended upon bark or other forest products. Monarchs had long since abandoned the Dean as a hunting ground and its inhabitants responded to little law but their own. If Charles were to farm or to use the timber resources of the Forest systematically he would be stirring up dozens of vested interests. Under a leader called Captain Skimmington the inhabitants of Dean made it clear that they would tolerate no interference. They were in touch with the protesters in Gillingham and Braydon and, again, Charles was not prepared to force an issue. He got even less from his attempts to farm his forest lands than he did out of his forest fines.

More rewarding were the Crown lands proper. Sir Julius Caesar had judged them 'the surest and best livelihood of the Crown', in spite of the heavy sales of Elizabeth and of James which had much reduced their annual value, from around £111,000 in 1608 to less than £84,000 in 1619. Although he himself had been compelled to part with Crown lands to settle some of his debts, Charles succeeded, by careful management, in reversing the trend. Entry fines on new leases were raised; rents were increased, though they were still mostly lower than elsewhere; in cases where entry fines were fixed the tenants were sometimes persuaded to buy their freeholds at from twenty to fifty years purchase. His woods and coppices were surveyed, the timber trees numbered and valued and, where appropriate, were sold; new plantings were made and, where possible, enclosure protected the young growth. Charles noted the consumption of wood by iron works, and to reform 'the great waste of timber' appointed a Surveyor of Iron Works to exact fees in proportion to timber consumption. Judges of

Assize were instructed to implement existing laws governing the preservation of forests. But the Crown lands were scattered, frequently uneconomic in themselves, their administration was too often weak, costly and venal. Although Charles did succeed in raising his income from them, his careful work brought in not more than £10,000 a year from woodlands and £80,000 from the rest. A compact area of land, such as Salisbury's Great Contract had envisaged, would have served him better.

As a further result of the Report of the Commission on the raising of Money, John Borough, Keeper of the Records in the Tower of London, was instructed in January 1628 to search through his documents for precedents relating to another issue. His findings resulted in the appointment of a commission two years later 'to compound with persons who, being possessed of £40 per annum in lands or rents, had not taken upon them the order of knighthood'. And so knighthood fines came into being. It had been customary for every person of a certain standing to come forward at a king's coronation to receive the honour of knighthood but, as feudalism decayed, so had this practice, and for over a hundred years it had been in abeyance. Charles now declared that he would revive the practice and fine those who had not been knighted. The actual fine, assessed by local officials in accordance with a man's ability to pay, generally amounted to a sum between £10 and £100 and on average to about £17 ot £18 a person. Between 1630 and 1635 the 'business of no-knights' brought Charles about £180,000 in knighthood fines. There was little opposition, the levy was accepted as reasonable, and the individual sums were not large.

Forest fines and distraint of knighthood both arose from Charles's position as feudal overlord. A third form of revenue deriving from the same source was the most anachronistic of all. The rights of wardship depended upon the fact that many landowners still held their land, theoretically, on feudal tenure from the King by Knight service, and that he could exercise the feudal right of taking charge of their heirs who succeeded while under age. The Crown could administer the lands of these minors, supervise their upbringing and education and plan their marriages, through the Court of Wards. Idiots and lunatics of any age who inherited such lands came within the scope of the court; the re-marriage of widows who had been wards of court remained its concern. Though wardship originally comprised an element of protection to the minor, by the seventeenth century the Court of Wards had become a court of profit so brazen that wardships were openly sold, leases of wards' properties put up to the highest bidder, wards' marriages not only arranged but bargained for. Charles used his opportunities to the full. Whereas between 1617 and 1622 the net revenue from wardship had been just under £30,000 a year, between 1638 and 1641 it averaged close on £69,000 annually. As with other sources of revenue the mastership of the Court of Wards was not normally in royal hands but was leased for a fee: Salisbury had done very well as Master, Cranfield had held the post, Sir Robert Naunton held it from 1623 to 1635 when he was succeeded by Cottington.

Allied with wardship was livery, which derived from the King's feudal right to approve the succession of those who held lands direct from him and was now exercised in the form of a tax or fine of succession. Altogether sufficient vestigial feudal practices survived to make an appreciable contribution to the King's income. The reverse of the coin was that they also operated as a tax upon the King's landed subjects. Forest fines and Knighthood fees were once-for-all payments. Wardship and livery were the more pernicious in being continuous. Whatever Charles gained from any of them, it was not difficult to surmise that he would have to pay the price in some form of concerted opposition to his policy.

20

The King's Great Business

Charles's mind was meanwhile reaching out to other aspects of sovereignty: overlordship of the land would be matched by dominion of the seas. His passion for ships and for the sea had never flagged, and he was well aware of the contribution that fishing could make to the navy and to national prosperity. Fishing fleets were the nursery of sailors; fishing provided employment for thousands; the fish themselves enhanced his trade and fed his people; the herrings that swam in the seas round his shores seemed as native to Britain as the sheep that grazed her pastures. The fishing off the Newfoundland coasts, the deep-sea fishing and whaling in the Northern seas, were additional assets. But while English fishermen might have a virtual monopoly in more distant waters, the Dutch were pressing strongly in the North Sea and round the home shores, even in the Channel and off the coast of Yarmouth where the herring shoals were thickest.

The Dutch had been fishermen for centuries and even laid claim to the invention of herring curing, which they attributed to a thirteenth-century inhabitant of Vierveldt. Permission to fish in waters which the English claimed as their own had been conceded in return for the purchase of licences and the acknowledgment of England's claim to sovereignty of the seas. But in 1609 the Dutch made a counter-claim to freedom of the seas in the *Mare Liberum* of Hugo Grotius, on the strength of which Dutch fishermen became more audacious. They evaded payment of licence, their armed escorts became more obtrusive, at rendezvous in Shetland they could muster 26,000 herring busses and they brought armed ships with them for protection – ostensibly against pirates. They made free of English ports, spreading their nets upon the strand, victualling their ships from English towns. Yarmouth, it was reported, employed forty brewers in their service.

The reply to *Mare Liberum* was *Mare Clausum*, written by John Selden in 1619 on James's instructions. Selden admitted that the extent of British sovereignty had never been clearly defined, but he claimed roughly the whole of the North Sea, the English Channel, the Bay of Biscay as far south as the coast of Spain, and indefinite stretches of ocean north and westward. The situation had not materially changed when Sir Robert Heath in 1632 was jotting down his thoughts on the subject: 'our strength and safety lies in our walls, which is our shipping . . . we should maintain the King's prerogative of fishing round our coasts and secure his mastery of the Narrow Seas.' Charles had been thinking along similar lines. There seemed no reason why such a natural bounty as fish should not, if properly managed, be a pillar of national prosperity, a nursery for the navy, and a source of revenue to the Crown.

For the protection of the fish themselves repeated proclamation prohibited the use of the trawls that were destroying the small fry. To encourage demand Fish Days and Fast Days were enforced. Charles himself was much concerned in the deliberations of a Commission he appointed in 1630 to study the matter, and he amended extensively in his own hand the draft proposals which Secretary Coke drew up. These resulted in 1632 in the incorporation of the Society of the Fishery of Great Britain and Ireland whose purpose was to encourage and maintain fishing fleets round the English, Irish and Scottish coasts. A large curing and packing station for herrings was established on the Isle of Lewis and Charles insisted upon including into the scheme any 'poor fishermen' whose normal livelihood would be jeopardised. He expected to make an annual profit of £200,000 from the enterprise. But, although the Lord Treasurer himself took shares in the Society, and powerful Privy Counsellors like Arundel and Pembroke were among its members, it lasted no more than two years. The herrings, it was said, 'failed to come'. In fact this was not the full story. Herrings, like salmon, travel a well-defined path and the lochs of the Isle of Lewis were an occasional rather than a regular haunt. Land had been bought without due consideration, the curing sheds, the storage huts, the houses for workpeople had been built too soon on too large a scale, supplies had been ordered prematurely in excess of what could be required. Money and labour had been expended unskilfully and wastefully, if not fraudulently. Employees of the Society were deliberately misled by uncooperative natives whose chief object was to see them depart, they were harrassed by Dunkirk pirates.

Above all, they built boats unsuitable to the herring fishing and failed to learn either from the efficient Dutch herring busses or from their own more experienced fishermen. It was one more example of good intention warped by faulty execution.[1]

Charles had been deeply involved, and the failure of the Fishery Society was a great disappointment, particularly since England's position as mistress of the seas was becoming more precarious. There were clashes with the Dutch in the East Indies, where the Dutch East India Company was challenging the British, the Dutch were becoming troublesome in the New World, where their fishing vessels were competing with the English and where they were attempting settlement on the mainland. Nearer home Jerome Weston was returning from an embassy in France in the spring of 1633 on the *Bonaventure* when he fell in with eight Dutch merchantmen in the Channel. The English captain required the Dutch to lower their topsails as the normal mark of respect. When they refused, his answer was to fire a couple of shots at them, upon which they responded with their own guns. The English, outnumbered by eight to one, left the honours to the Dutch. As such incidents multiplied neither the Dutch nor even the Spanish paid much respect to English sovereignty, chasing each other with impunity into English harbours, abusing to excess Charles's patience, as the Venetian Ambassador put it. Charles was particularly annoyed when a Dutch ship seized an English barque carrying a courier with letters for the Venetian. He was angry when in March 1635 Dunkirkers captured and retained as prize a ship carrying tobacco to Holland. He never forgot that when his wife was pregnant in 1630 her midwife had been captured by Dunkirkers in the Channel. He read with bitterness Secretary Coke's report in June 1634 telling of the 'scant respect' shown to the English in various parts of the world: 'Our ancient reputation is not only cried down, but we submit to wrongs in all places which are not to be endured'.[2]

Charles had already asked for a restatement of the doctrine of Sovereignty of the Seas and Borough's work, based largely on precedent, was finished in 1633 and dedicated to Charles. Two years later Selden's *Mare Clausum* was printed and again the dedication was to Charles. Supported by his Council, and on the authority of an eminent lawyer and an eminent antiquarian, Charles took his stand on the principle of *mare clausum* and reiterated his country's claim to sovereignty of the seas. 'We hold it a principle not to be denied', he told the Dutch in 1636, 'that the King of Great Britain is a monarch at land and sea to the full extent of his dominions, and that it concerneth him as much to maintain his sovereignty in all the British Seas as within his three kingdoms.' It would be maintained, he said, 'not so much by discourses as by the louder language of a powerful navy, to be better understood when overstrained patience seeth no hope of preserving her right by other means'. He added that he intended to keep a naval force at sea to enforce British Sovereignty.[3]

Charles's heart was still in the sea. He was constantly at the Admiralty discussing in detail the condition of his ships, deciding which should be refitted, considering docking arrangements and other facilities at Portsmouth and elsewhere. One of his greatest pleasures was dining with his wife aboard one of his ships with a supporting vessel of kitchen staff drawn up alongside. In spite of the disasters of Cadiz and La Rochelle, in spite of his inability to control piracy round his own shores, in spite of the successful competition of the Dutch as carriers and as fishermen, he had nevertheless built up a navy of 22,000 effective tonnage, which was larger than that of the Tudor Queen who was so often held up to him as a model. He had rebuilt the *Vanguard* in 1630, he revived a decree of 1618 to build at least two new warships a year, and time after time he attended their launchings from his shipyards, living again the thrill of earlier days when he was carried along by the enthusiasm of his brother, dreading a disaster like that when the *Prince* stuck on the slips.

At the end of January 1633 he saw the *Charles*, a ship of 810 tons and 44 guns slip gracefully without incident from her launching bay at Deptford and raced in his barge in her wake as she proceeded down river. A few days later he watched with his wife as the *Henrietta-Maria*, of 793 tons and 42 guns, was successfully launched at Woolwich. But she was a poor ship according to Admiral Pennington. Even worse was the *Unicorn* built by Edward Boate a little later in the year. She was dangerous and unserviceable and had obtained a certificate of seaworthiness from Trinity House only because the authorities hesitated to disgrace her builder. There was certainly a need for a general overhaul of British shipbuilding. A good English ship was solid and 'full of timber' and could last for seventy years. But the Dutch could run circles round her and she would never catch a privateer. Moreover English ships were not given the constant care and attention necessary to keep them in good condition. As Pennington wrote to the Admiralty in 1634, the Dutch kept their ships 'all tallowed and clean from the ground . . . every two months, or three at the most' while English ships were cleaned two or three months before they came into use, and never tallowed, so that they were foul almost before they sailed. They were given no regular care after sailing and if kept out for eight or ten months were 'so overgrown with barnacles and weeds under water' that it was 'impossible that they should either go well or work yarely'. All men of war, he concluded bitterly, 'of what nation soever, whether Turk or Christian, keep this course of cleansing their ships once in two or three months but us.'[4]

The best ships were still being built by a Pett, and for greater speed they were being made longer in proportion to their breadth. It was Peter, son of Phineas, who built the *James* at Deptford in 1633; and to Phineas himself fell the task of reviving the glories of his youth in another *Sovereign* – a *non-pareil* with three decks, over a hundred guns, and a gross tonnage of more than 1500 tons. She was to be 127 feet long, 46.6 feet wide, and 19.4 feet in depth and would be the largest ship afloat. The Masters of Trinity House thought a three-decker of such a size to be 'beyond the art or wit of man to construct' and that even if built there would be no port in which she could ride, no tackle that would hold her. But in January 1635 Charles personally called for an estimate for building such a vessel, insisting upon 102 guns against a first costing for a ninety-gun ship. In March Phineas was ordered to prepare a model and told he was appointed by His Majesty as builder, with his fifth son, Peter, associated with him in the actual construction. Charles himself earmarked the forests which would supply the ship's timbers – Sherwood, Dean and Chopwell – while Phineas selected the actual trees most suitable to his purpose. The keel of the *Sovereign* was laid at Woolwich on 16 January 1636 in the presence of Charles and Henrietta-Maria. Charles was impatient to see her afloat and insisted upon the autumn of 1637 for her launching against Pett's strong recommendation that the following spring was a better time since she would grow foul lying in the river during the winter. But Charles would not listen. 'I am not of your opinion', he brusquely scribbled on Pett's note.[5]

The *Sovereign* was launched in October 1637 having cost, exclusive of her guns, nearly £41,000 compared with about £6,000 for a forty-gun ship. But the expense was not all because of her guns. She was a beautiful vessel with graceful lines, perfectly executed joinery and exquisite carving. She proved somewhat top-heavy at sea, possibly because of the number of her guns, but Charles proudly caused to be inscribed upon each one of them: *Carolus Edgari sceptrum stabilivit aquarum.*[6]

Ships, however, absorbed money: £60,000 a year for the upkeep of the fleet, £60,000 for the Admiralty, apart from new building. How was the money to be found? Although Charles knew the answer the Tower records were once more searched, this time by William Noy, who had become Attorney General in 1631. Noy confirmed that from at least the time of the Plantagenets the ports had been called upon in times of danger to provide ships for general defence, and he reminded Charles of half-hearted and unsuccessful attempts made in his father's reign and early in his own to revive the tax. Charles realized the need for caution. 'Danger' was difficult to specify and precedent was irregular and tentative. But the goal was worth while; for if ship money worked it could raise more money than a couple of subsidies. Charles held the reins firmly in his own hands. An inner circle which included Noy, Weston (now Lord Portland) and Secretary Windebank assessed the situation. Charles was convinced that both by law and by precedent he could go ahead and by June 1634 he was ready to take his whole Council into his confidence. Windebank was for further delay until the details of assessment and collection had been worked out, urging that the good or ill success of 'the King's Great Business' would depend upon the manner of its execution. Portland was cautious throughout. But Charles was convinced he was right and would brook neither delay nor opposition, removing from their posts without compunction Sir Robert Heath, Chief Justice of the Common Pleas, and Richard Shilton, the Solicitor General, who were likely to prove difficult.[7]

The Council agreed with Noy that the tax should be levied upon maritime counties as well as port towns, that the money raised should be kept apart from royal navy receipts, and that the ship-money fleet should be administered direct by the King and Council. The most difficult question was that of assessment. Charles knew he was treading upon dangerous ground and was almost fanatically anxious to forestall opposition. After long discussion he acted on the advice of Lord Keeper Coventry, whose long letter reached him while he was on progress at Belvoir, and adopted a compromise which involved borough officials as well as sheriffs and assumed that the subsidy rolls already in existence would be the basis of assessment. The first writs of ship money went out on 20 October 1634. Noy had died two months earlier, but it was so much Noy's business that as he lay dying the

Privy Council, it was said, came to his bedside for suggestions and advice. The writs were directed to the cities, port towns, and maritime counties of England, and their demands were in the form of ships, which were to be fully manned and provided with arms, ammunition, and victuals for twenty-six weeks from 1 March 1635. The reasons given for the demand were protection from pirates, the defence of the kingdom, the safeguard of the seas, the security of the subjects, safe conduct of ships and merchandise, and the maintenance of the sovereignty of the seas hitherto pertaining to kings of England. Commutation into money was expected, the total being estimated at a little over £104,000.

The careful approach had its reward. The first collection of ship money came in reasonably well. London protested, largely on the grounds that tonnage and poundage was intended to provide protection on the seas, but nevertheless paid – in ships. The Venetian Ambassador thought the good response was because the people were 'eagerly jealous' to secure the sovereignty of the sea. But it is likely that the smallness of the tax had something to do with the lack of protest.

The immediate object of the first ship-money fleet, consisting of 25 or 26 ships which went to sea the following year, was to show that Britain was still a force to be reckoned with. It had a limited success in the Channel, causing Dutch vessels for a time to lower their flags and to purchase fishing licences. But the fleet was capable of nothing very ambitious, there was no patriotic upsurge to match the grandiose doctrine of sovereignty of the seas, and no evidence in Europe that the fleet had caused more than the slightest tremor. This was partly because the care taken with victualling and recruitment had in no way matched the care taken in raising the money. The Earl of Lindsey, Commander of the first ship-money fleet, had to tell the Lords Commissioners of the Navy in 1635 that the beef supplied to his ships was so tainted that when it was moved the stench alone was sufficient to breed contagion. Crews were still a hotch-potch, including Thames watermen and reluctant landmen pressed into the service. They still ran away. They were still sick. The majority had no knowledge of seamanship. Lindsey reported that out of 260 men in the *James* not more than twenty could steer, that in the *Unicorn* there was hardly a seaman besides the officers, that one-third of the crew of the *Entrance* had never been to sea, and that of the rest only twelve could take the helm.[8]

Nevertheless the actual raising of money on the first ship-money writ was sufficiently successful for the second writ of August 1635 to be extended to the whole country, inland counties as well as maritime. It was arguable that defence concerned everyone and should be paid for by everyone, wherever they lived, but the extension both enlarged the area of protest and increased its bitterness. At the same time, as the levy was repeated in 1636, 1637 and 1638, alarm grew that what had appeared to be an emergency tax was becoming regular and permanent. Evasion became more determined and widespread. It was obvious that considerable latitude must be allowed to the sheriff, but it was not expected that he would be evading payment himself, shifting the highest assessment on to the parishes most likely to pay without fuss, or giving preferential treatment to parishes where he had friends or relations. The unpaid constables who, in the absence of any paid officials, were responsible for the actual collection of ship money found themselves in an intolerable position when local magnates refused to pay or proferred only part of the sum at which they were assessed. A constable, faced with the man he knew as master in normal situations, found himself utterly unable to enforce payment. Complaints soon came in to the Council of richer men assessed at 2d or 2½d an acre while smallholders were paying as much as 2/4d an acre. Soldiers and even paupers were being told to contribute.

The Council insisted that no one in receipt of alms, no cottager unless he had resources over and above his daily earnings, and no soldier who was dependent entirely on his pay, should be assessed. Charles personally ordered that the poor should be spared. On the other hand there were, as the Council said, people able to pay by means of their wealth in trade or personal estate who remained untaxed while the subsidy rating was in respect of land only; they would remove the anomaly of a small landowner being liable even though he was 'weak of estate' while a wealthy tradesman was untouched. But assessment was more difficult and resistance was stronger from the wealthy tradesman than from the 'weak' landowner, and rather than face a struggle with the commercial interest the Council quietly dropped the idea of assessing wealth other than land. They had struggle enough upon their hands as a concerted opposition to ship money began to build up, based not only upon evasion, but upon a refusal to pay the tax as a matter of principle.

But in spite of refusals and evasion, ship money was bringing in more than the original estimate and for the first three years averaged about £188,000 a year. The money raised was all spent on the fleet. It was tragic that gross incompetence, a venal administration, inadequate recruitment, and a criminal disregard for the well-being of the crews should have prevented the putting to sea of a navy which was worthy of the effort spent on it.[9]

When Portland died in 1635 after a painful illness that perhaps impaired his service at the end, his memorial stood in the condition of the King's finances. By 1636 Charles could estimate that he had raised his income from some £700,000 in 1630 to over £1,000,000 a year. There was still not much margin, not enough to allow him to think in terms of the Palatinate, except by way of diplomacy, but there was sufficient to give him some confidence in his personal affairs. His Lord Treasurer had served him well. Weston came somewhat reluctantly into ship money but worked loyally for it. He was not much loved – but what Lord Treasurer was? He was much devoted to family interests – but no more than most men of his generation. He was accused of improper practices in connection with disafforestation – but few public men escaped such charges. If he had enemies that was common enough in public life. Charles, as he normally did with his friends and servants, stood by Portland throughout his career. On the news of his last illness Charles hastened to his bedside and was much upset by his suffering. He stayed but 'a very little while in his chamber; he breathed with so much pain and difficulty that the King could not endure it'.[10] After his death Charles spent a little time mourning the man who stood as close to him as any since the death of Buckingham: it was hard that within a year he should have lost, with Noy, two financial advisers. Much would depend upon Portland's successor. There was a great deal of lobbying but it was generally expected that the succession would go to Cottington, already Chancellor of the Exchequer and said to be high in the King's favour. But a certain astuteness in Charles, a realization that perhaps for all his virtues Cottington was not of the calibre for highest office, that one who practised such high living himself would hardly economize in affairs of state, perhaps some rancour over the affair of Richmond Park, caused Charles to hold the Treasurer's office in commission and to appoint, instead, Cottington, Laud, Coke and Windebank as Treasury Commissioners. Of these Sir Francis Windebank was newest to office, having been a surprise appointment as Secretary of State on the death of Dorchester in 1632. Sir Thomas Roe, traveller, diplomat, loyal and knowledgeable, a man of wide sympathy and large understanding, who would have liked the post, was inexplicably passed over – perhaps because of his very closeness to Charles's sister – and it was Windebank, a hitherto obscure clerk in the signet, but a protégé of Laud and of Catholic leanings, who was advanced.

The four Commissioners made little departure from Portland's policy and under Laud's relentless eye there was an even keener attention to detail. When a new Lord Treasurer took office in March 1636 it was William Juxon, Laud's successor as Bishop of London, who took the post. The appointment entailed again passing over Cottington and was a further mark of Laud's influence, which was emphasised when he became chairman of Charles's Foreign Affairs committee.

Charles knew there were other things to do besides paying debts and raising money, important though these were. Social policy was, indeed, the 'King's great business' in a more fundamental sense than the raising of ship money and Charles met the problem with all the means at his disposal, through the standing committee on trade, through the Privy Council and through the JPs. The problem was brought sharply to his attention by the bad harvests of 1629 and 1630 and the visitation of plague in the spring of 1630. The cloth industry, always sensitive to calamity, slumped badly with resultant unemployment and distress and there was rioting in many parts of the country as corn supplies dwindled and prices rose. The Privy Council was inundated with letters from the local magistrates and with petitions for relief from workers and their employers. 'In this time of dearth', wrote the JPs of Nottinghamshire in a typical letter, we have 'little rest at home or abroad, and find many difficulties to content poor people . . . All men's barns are now empty.' The Council acted promptly. The export of corn was forbidden and its price fixed; better stocked districts were instructed to send supplies to help others, strict measures were put in operation against regraters who held corn back in hope of a price rise, the strict observance of fast days was enjoined, the quantity of grain used by malsters and starchmakers was strictly regulated. Employers were ordered to keep their people on work and the Council charged those who in former times had gained by their industry 'not now in this time of dearth to leave off trade whereby the poor may be set on work'. Many offenders were dealt with locally or at the Assizes but some of the more important cases came before the

Star Chamber. When a certain Archer was charged before this Court with hoarding corn and thereby enhancing its price, the Attorney General declared the crime to be 'of high nature and evill consequence to the undoeing of the poor'. Laud rounded on Archer and told him he was 'grinding the faces of the poor' and the court agreed that he should be made an example. He was fined 100 marks to the King, £10 to the poor, and condemned to stand in the pillory in Newgate, in Leadenhall market, and in his native Chelmsford with a paper in his hat giving the cause of his punishment. On the whole the response to the Privy Council's emergency measures was good, local constables were energetic in searching for hoarded corn, and fines were as high as £100.

Enclosure was a problem which stood by itself. When Charles came to the throne the movement of depopulating enclosure had almost run its course but it was still necessary to tread cautiously and there were still enclosing landlords whose activities could not be ignored. Investigatory Commissions went out from the Council in 1632, 1635 and 1636 while the reports it called for came in by the dozen, evidence of its ability to inject its own sense of urgency into the localities. Offenders were again brought before the Star Chamber where, again, Laud was severe. He turned upon Thomas Lord Brudenell telling him he had 'devoured the people with a shepherd and a dog', imposed a fine of £1000 and ordered him to restore eight farms. The sentence was not untypical. The prosecutions brought what a contemporary termed a 'terror' to depopulating landlords and from the Midland Commission alone the Exchequer reaped £30,000 or more, large fines being normally accompanied by detailed instructions for reconversion to pasture and the rebuilding of decayed farms. There was criticism that the fine was more important to Charles than the restoration of tillage, and patents issued by the Privy Council in 1635 and 1637 empowering commissioners to compound with offenders at their discretion appeared to support this view. On the other hand it is hard to believe that the Orders, the Commissions, the Justices' Reports, the proceedings in Star Chamber, Laud's attitude to the men brought before him, the carefully worked-out estimates of the number of houses to be replaced, the amount of pasture to be restored, were all part of an elaborate device for bringing into the Exchequer, not the fine itself, but part of the fine. It is more likely that the Council was making a genuine attempt at reassessment and the rectification of mistakes. To think otherwise accords neither with the

240

brusqueness, even brutality, with which Laud confronted depopulating enclosures in Star Chamber, nor with Charles's general attitude
towards the poor, which was consistently one of compassion.

Apart from particular social problems Charles, like all English
monarchs before him, had to face the overall question of destitution.
The problem had been tackled piecemeal until the comprehensive
Poor Law legislation of 1585, codified in the Elizabethan Act of 1601.
But Charles's Privy Council believed that the Poor Laws were for the
most part 'little regarded'. They accused JPs of neglecting their duties,
they maintained that money bequeathed for charitable purposes was
being misappropriated, and alleged that people dared not complain for
fear of the great landowners. They concluded that not more laws, but
better execution was needed.

It was a mark of the seriousness with which Charles regarded the
matter that the Commission he appointed on 5 January 1631 included
Laud and Wentworth and a majority of the Privy Council. It was
instructed simply to see that the laws were effectively put into execution. The country was divided into six circuits to each of which groups
of Commissioners were appointed, while Orders in Council required
the JPs and other local officials to assess the situation in their districts,
to take appropriate action, and, as with enclosure and depopulation, to
send reports to the Commissioners. To make quite clear what was
expected of them a series of Directions was also issued by the Council
which more or less repeated the terms of the Elizabethan code. At the
end of January over 300 printed books containing these Orders and
Directions, each accompanied by a letter from the Council, went out
to all the sheriffs of all the counties of England and Wales to be
distributed by them throughout the counties and boroughs under
their jurisdiction.

The JPs responded with a readiness that made it seem that only
strong directive had been lacking. Their Reports positively poured in
to the Council. Some simply stated that they put in operation the
Book of Orders. At the other end of the scale some JPs sent very
detailed accounts of their activity, which covered far more than the
Poor Law itself. They suppressed alehouses, controlled the price of
corn, punished 'wandering rogues', apprenticed children, restrained
malsters from taking corn, repaired a House of Correction, put the
poor on work repairing bridges. Some magistrates instituted a comprehensive search for grain of any kind that might have been withheld
from the market. The City of London, in a detailed report, told of 773

poor children maintained by Christ's Hospital, forty apprenticed to trades in England, seventy working as apprentices in Bridewell, and fifty who had been bound apprentice to merchants in Barbados and Virginia. The returns form a running commentary on conditions in England.

The Book of Orders was effective throughout the decade. There was nothing unfamiliar in the policy it attempted to enforce, nor was it a novelty for the Privy Council to believe that it could operate for the general good. What was new was the comprehensive nature of Charles's social policy and the energy and determination which was put into its execution, both centrally and in the localities. That Charles had a genuine care for the poor and unfortunate was evident over and over again. He was careful to ensure that poorer people kept land after the drainage of the Fens; he wished to incorporate poor fishermen into his fishing enterprises; when Galtes forest was disafforested he awarded every landless cottager four to seven acres of good land 'in pity and commiseration of the estate of the poorer sort of inhabitants'; when in 1635 a custom of sea coal was abated for the poor of London Charles wanted proof that the poor really benefited and ordered the City to provide a certificate to this effect; he supported the unemployed cloth workers against the clothiers, the hungry poor against the great cornmasters, the dispossessed against enclosing landlords. In so doing he made enemies. Landlords and industrialists, parishes who paid higher rates to implement his poor law directives, as well as those subject to forest fines or assessed for ship money, resented the imposition, and Charles himself bore the main responsibility. 'Everyone walks within the circle of his charge, his majesty's hand is the chief, and in effect the sole directory', Dorchester wrote, and this continued to be true. The annotation on document after document, the fact that he still refused a sign manual but appended his own signature to every document of which he approved is one mark of this continued conscientiousness in public affairs.[11]

After the death of Portland the man who was constantly at Charles's elbow was William Laud, who became Archbishop of Canterbury in 1633, Treasury Commissioner between the death of Portland in March 1635 and the appointment of Juxon a year later, and chairman of his Foreign Affairs Committee. Charles was not conscious of his partnership with Laud as he had been of his relationship with Buckingham. He was not personally attracted to Laud but their co-operation was in many ways more effective. For Laud had a single, driving purpose in place of the disparate energy of the Duke and, above all, there was nothing in worldly pomp or riches to attract him personally and he had no dependents or partisans who could hope for favour on personal issues alone. His sole ambition was to establish a clean-cut Church and State, each free of the excrescences of rival forms of worship or of rule, from which graft, dishonesty, slackness and inefficiency should be rooted out. In each case organization and government should be known, expressed, and rigidly adhered to. As the Church should observe the forms of worship laid down by the Fathers, so the State should enforce the laws and issue fresh directives where necessary to preserve that social hierarchy which so completely expressed Laud's notion of society, with the monarch at the apex supported by his people in their degrees, and reaching down to the merest beggar. The edifice of the State, as of the Church, would be swept clean, and kept clean, by a policy which Laud expressed in the one word, 'thorough'. If the meticulous little man scarcely considered the vested interests that would rise around him, this was partly because he lived his life in blinkers which cut him off from understanding anything but his rigid purpose, partly because he had the kind of courage that saw nothing but what it was necessary to do. It was unfortunate, though natural, that this kind of dedication to duty should be accompanied by a lack of warmth that cut him off from real friendship. James had never responded to him. Charles did so because of their joint purpose, but not with warmth. Besides, Charles had something of Laud in him that denied the easy contact of friendship. The person who came closest to Laud was the man who became Lord Deputy of Ireland at the beginning of 1632 – and Wentworth, like Charles and Laud, was a man of few close contacts and fewer warm friendships.

21

The King and his Court

There was a definitive regularity about the Privy Council. Its numbers could be adjusted, it was subject to control. The Court, on the other hand, was amorphous both territorially and numerically. It was undefined, unwieldy, difficult to control and even more difficult to evade, being normally in existence wherever Charles himself happened to be. He could absent himself from Privy Council meetings without arousing much comment; he could escape the Court only by deliberate withdrawal into privacy and the risk of anxious speculation.

The Court was a world in itself. It even embraced part of the government, for business was carried on in private meetings, by personal soundings, by a word here, a glance there, while the very aspect of the King, or of one of the great officers of state, was sufficient foundation for rumour or surmise.

The London home of Charles and his family, where the Court was most enveloping, was Whitehall. Whitehall was a palace, the main seat of government and of many state departments, the home of Court officials, officers of state, friends of the King and Queen. Its untidy, almost ramshackle, redbrick buildings covered about twenty-three acres and contained some 2000 rooms. Wolsey had begun some of the buildings, Henry VIII had taken up residence there after Wolsey's fall from power and added considerably to its extent as well as changing its name to Whitehall. Since then it had suffered fire and decay. James had commissioned Inigo Jones to replan and rebuild the whole but because of shortage of money he had got no further than the splendid Banqueting Hall. Whitehall had its own stables, a sports area which included indoor and outdoor tennis courts, and a tilt yard; it had its own playhouse, banqueting hall and chapel. Its eastern side straggled along the Thames with various privy stairs leading down to landing stages and the barges that conveyed the denizens of Whitehall

1 Charles shortly after coming to England, aged about four, by Robert Peake. The haunted look of the sick child is in pathetic contrast to the richly embroidered robes.

Charles   Duke of York.

2 Charles, Duke of York, aged probably eight or nine, showing the bright
little face of a happy and well-balanced child in good health. Artist
unknown.

3 Charles at the age of ten or eleven proudly wearing the ribbon of the Garter. The fair hair and skin are apparent in all these early portraits. From the miniature by Isaac Oliver.

4, 5 Charles and his brother, shortly before Henry's death in 1612. Charles still wears his fair hair brushed up from his forehead in contrast to Henry's smoother, dark hair. Artist unknown.

6 James I by an unknown artist, probably shortly after his accession to the English throne.

7 Queen Anne, by William Larkin, 1612. The Queen is in mourning still after the death of Henry.

8 Charles's sister, Elizabeth, as he knew her, from a miniature painted about 1610 by Isaac Oliver.

9 Charles, as painted by Daniel Mytens, after his return from Spain, probably in 1623. There is diffidence still in his stance though his legs are undoubtedly straight and do not look noticeably short.

10 The Duke of Buckingham, also painted by Mytens at about the same time. In contrast to Charles his whole bearing portrays confidence and command.

Je n'ay osé prendre la hardiesse de vous
tesmoigner par un mot de lettre l'impatience
dont mon ame a esté ~~pour~~ gehenne durant
ma long attente pour l'accorde des ces tret=
té, jusques atant que j'en eus ~~ne~~ receu les
bonnes nouvelles, je vous priant de vous asseurer
qu'outre la renomme de vos vertus et per-
fectionns qui s'eclatte par tout, je le tien
pour comble de mon bonheur, que je ~~eu~~
l'honneur d'avoyr deja veu vostre per=
sonne, bien qu'incognu de vous qui m'a
rendu infinement satisfait que l'exterieur
de vostre personne ne dementi rien au lus=
tre de vos vertus; mais ne puisse exepi
mer par escrit la passion de mon ame pour
avoir l'eur de parvenir a la complicement
lettre estimé vostre

11 A page from a draft of Charles's earliest love letter to Henrietta-Maria,
whom he has not yet seen. His indecision and diffidence is still apparent in
the many erasions and, indeed, in the fact that he made a draft at all.

12 At the end of the 1620s, Charles passed into the happiest period of his life. This portrait by Gerrit van Honthorst, painted informally from life towards the end of 1628 as a study for the great canvas of *Apollo and Diana*, shows Charles as a relaxed and happy man.

13 This unusual and informal representation of Charles at cards, at about the same time, by an unknown artist of the studio of Rubens, is undoubtedly based on descriptions by the master of the life he experienced at the English Court. Charles's enthusiasm for card games is well attested.

14 Charles as Van Dyck saw him at the height of his personal happiness and seeming prosperity – serene, elegant, fastidious, slightly ethereal, the great star of the Garter blazing on his blue cloak.

15 Charles, the proud and happy monarch and husband, being presented with a laurel wreath by his Queen; a portrait symbolic of victory over strife and discord. Similar pictures were painted by both Mytens and Van Dyck. This one is by Van Dyck.

16 Charles dining with his Queen in Whitehall Palace, talking to his friends, waited on by his great lords and courtiers, privileged onlookers at a discreet distance. Painted by Gerard Honckgeest.

17 Charles during the civil wars, after the original miniature of John Hoskins. Probably painted during his imprisonment at Hampton Court. There is a marked difference from the serene monarch of the previous portrait.

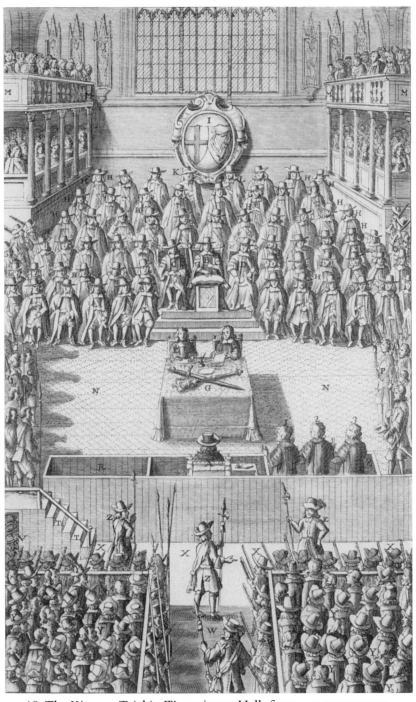

18 The King on Trial in Westminster Hall, from a contemporary
engraving. Charles sits in the dock, facing his accusers.

19 The three children whom Charles saw in his captivity at Hampton Court, where this miniature was painted by Hoskins. James, Duke of York, shortly afterwards escaped but Elizabeth and Henry visited him on the day before his execution.

20 The execution of Charles I as seen by a French contemporary. None of the extant drawings is accurate, but this one gives a realistic general impression of the scene.

21 Charles the Martyr as portrayed, in slightly varying form, in thousands of copies of the *Eikon Basilike* published immediately after his death and reprinted dozens of times.

upstream the short distance to Westminster or beyond, downstream to the City and Greenwich. On the west side was St James's Park, whose grass and pleasant walks lay around the redbrick Tudor palace which was the London home of the children of both Charles and Buckingham. Within Whitehall itself was a large privy garden and orchard and a series of small courts and gardens, including an open preaching area complete with pulpit. The small Council Chamber lay near the King's own apartments which consisted of a series of rooms of increasing privacy. In the Presence Chamber he would mix with his courtiers, exchange words with his intimates, be seen by many who had won no more than the privilege of being there. The Queen was sometimes present and audiences might be granted: more likely Charles would give audience in greater privacy in the Audience Chamber, and then only by appointment, for he would rarely countenance the casual boon or receive the impulsive courtier. Charles's withdrawing room, his privy chamber, his study or cabinet room, his oratory, his bedroom, were kept as private as possible, served only by courtiers in the more intimate positions of Gentlemen of the Bed-chamber. The Queen's apartments, on a smaller scale, matched those of the King.

A public road, spanned by two bridges, ran through the middle of Whitehall connecting Westminster with Charing Cross at which point the Strand, which was in the real sense a strand, its gardens running down to the river, followed the bend of the Thames and connected Whitehall with the City. York House, where Buckingham's widow still lived, was at the Whitehall end of the Strand. At the City end was Somerset House which, as Denmark House, had belonged to Queen Anne and was now Henrietta-Maria's dower house. Between the two were the town residences of the great and wealthy. The opposite side of the Strand was mainly open to the fields, with only an occasional building to break the view to the heights of Highgate and Hampstead. Much of this land belonged to the Duke of Bedford and he was using Inigo Jones to design a church and a piazza after the Italian style in the old convent garden that lay north of the Strand.

Downriver at Greenwich was the partly finished house which Inigo Jones had designed on the site of the old palace of Placentia. It had been termed the Queen's House in the time of Charles's mother and he now wished it to be completed for his wife – partly because he enjoyed Greenwich with its smells of tar and timber and its closeness to the ships he loved. A few miles south and east was the Palace of

Eltham, which he never used, upriver there was the Palace of Sheen at Richmond, closely associated with his brother, and a little higher up Hampton Court, his mother's favourite residence. Windsor, the great fourteenth-century castle with its chapel built by Henry VII, was not popular with Charles or his family, but Oatlands near Weybridge, and Nonesuch at Ewell, both south of the river, were favourites of Henrietta-Maria. Charles himself enjoyed Theobalds in Hertfordshire for its hunting, as well as Royston, where his father had built a little hunting lodge as a place of retreat, and Newmarket, further afield. Other royal palaces and houses served more for occasional than regular visiting.[1]

The Court itself, in spite of efforts Charles had made when he came to the throne, remained an enormous, clumsy device consisting of thousands of people where, as Rubens had written, splendour and liberality were of primary consideration, and which was, as the Venetian Ambassador put it, 'extravagant with superfluity'. Officers of State had their 'households', each 'household' had its 'table', and the board and lodging costs alone were alarming. High-living courtiers like Carlisle, Holland and Cottington entertained lavishly at Court as well as at home and set a standard beside which Charles's own economies in, for example, apparel and the use of perfume, were a drop in the ocean. Court expenditure had actually risen since his accession. A Court masque alone could cost well over a thousand pounds and there were often half a dozen and more different masques in a year. Nor was it only the expense of the masque itself that had to be reckoned. Seating had to be provided, the close stools moved in, and food and drink on a lavish scale were expected.

Charles insisted upon order in the cumbersome Court of which his life was part and early in 1631 he felt compelled to reinforce the reforms made on his accession by laying down strict rules for its conduct. Boots and spurs were banned in the royal presence; none under the rank of baron was allowed to enter the inner closet; no one under royal rank might sit in Her Majesty's presence, and the distances that various ranks should keep from the King and Queen were carefully prescribed. Noblemen and their ladies in general were to 'use great distance and respect to the royal persons, as also civility to one another', and ladies about the Queen were 'to keep their places as orderly as the lords'. The *Orders for Conduct at Court*[2] are a commentary in themselves, but although they produced some outward improvement the civility to each other which Charles required of his

246

courtiers was not always there. In the overcrowded, hothouse atmosphere of Whitehall jealousies smouldered and quarrels flared. Young
pages at Court, like young apprentices in the City, were apt to relieve
boredom by pert or unbecoming conduct which easily developed into
squabbles and fights. The Cockpit, in particular, became notorious
for brawling and Charles was obliged to enforce stringent regulations.
Quarrelling among his older courtiers could be more serious. In the
spring of 1633 trouble broke out close to the King and Queen themselves when Holland challenged Jerome Weston to a duel and Henry
Jermyn carried the challenge. Lord Fielding, Buckingham's nephew,
who was about to marry Weston's sister, then intervened and challenged George Coring who had become involved on Holland's side.
Partisanship ran high and Charles had twice to impose his authority to
stop the duels and restore some sort of amity.

There were other respects, too, in which Charles's Court was
perhaps not so decorous as he could have wished. When Dr John Dee
preached before the King at the end of 1633 to the text 'Blessed is the
womb that bare thee and the paps that gave thee suck' and took the
occasion not only to extol womankind but to praise virginity in
unmarried women he aroused caustic comment – 'Sure the doctor
made no good choice of the court to commend virginity in.' There
was certainly censure if a lady-in-waiting became pregnant by a
courtier, but not necessarily moral condemnation. Even Henry Jermyn,
close as he was to the Queen, dared to get one of her ladies, of the Villiers
family, with child. From every point of view Charles's anger was justified but Jermyn was banished from the Court only briefly. Incest,
which was not altogether uncommon, was generally condemned and
punished by fine, though the moral stigma did not prevent the
money going into the royal purse; the Queen, for example, took
the fine imposed upon Sir Giles Arlington for this offence.

Charles could see well enough the effect of propinquity upon the
tempers and morals of his courtiers, and whenever plague reappeared
the physical dangers were equally apparent. He was also aware of the
wasted lives of those who were not employed at Court but who hung
around in the hope of reaping some crumbs from what appeared as an
overflowing cornucopia. Like his father he issued repeated injunctions
to such people to return to the country. His contempt for their wasted
lives, for the way they and their families spent their time, were
stringently expressed and did nothing to endear him to those he sent
packing.

He himself tried to observe the same carefully-planned day he had instituted when he came to the throne. He still found that periods of quiet and contemplation were essential to him and would spend hours in his little study reading and copying out anything that appealed to him, like a long prayer in Scottish spelling. His scholarship was sufficiently precise, and his religious susceptibilities sufficiently sensitive, for him to be considerably affronted when the royal printers made serious misprints in an edition of the Bible. The unfortunate men were fined £300 by the Star Chamber. But about the same time Patrick Young, the classical scholar who was Keeper of the King's Library, published a Latin translation of a Greek manuscript which had been given to Charles by Sir Thomas Roe. This so delighted the King that he conceived the idea of printing Greek as well as Latin manuscripts and promised to pardon his printers if they would procure Greek type and publish one Greek manuscript a year. Shortly afterwards he wrote to the Turkey Company requiring that every ship of their fleet should on each voyage bring home one Arabic or Persian manuscript for, he said, there was 'a great deal of learning fit to be known written in Arabic, and great scarcity of Arabic and Persian books in this country'. His mind also ran a great deal upon English history and antiquity. He thought it 'not the least care in our Government to preserve the Antiquities of former Ages' and 'knowing how great a worke . . . the composing of our English story will be', he commissioned Sir Henry Wotton at a salary of £500 a year to write it.[3] Sir Henry wrote verses, collected works of art, in 1624 dedicated a book on architecture to Charles, and wrote a short biography of Buckingham, yet his history of England never saw the light of day. Charles's patronage of the tapestry works at Mortlake was more productive. As Prince he had procured the painter, Cleynes, to live in England and make designs for which he was provided with gold and silver thread, he had procured the Raphael cartoons and sent them to Mortlake, and the tapestries woven there, still under the direction of Sir Francis Crane, whom James had appointed, continued throughout the 1630s to vie with the great French works of the Gobelin looms.

Any mechanical device appealed to Charles. In Gresham College, founded by Sir Thomas Gresham in the reign of Elizabeth, there was considerable experimentation inspired by the Gresham Professor, Henry Briggs, and his team. Many practical artisans came to learn from these men, among them Richard Delamain, who turned his skill to the production of certain 'mathematical instruments', as he called them. One was a form of quadrant design, said its inventor, to take mathematical measurements at sea. Delamain presented to Charles a small version of this quadrant, made of solid silver, which the King kept always in his bedchamber and he turned his mind to inventing a similar device himself. Delamain also invented a 'mathematical ring' which, by the moving of concentric circles in a prescribed manner, worked 'arithmetical and mathematical questions only by the eye with . . . facility and expedition', as its inventor claimed. *Grammelogia*, the book in which this device was described, was dedicated to Charles. Shortly afterwards Charles actually acquired one of these mathematical rings, which so fascinated him that it never left him and he bequeathed it to his son. Delamain was a humble man, describing himself in the frontispiece of one of his books as a 'student and teacher of the mathematics'. Charles liked him and appointed him both tutor to the King in mathematics and quartermaster general.[4] It was consistent with this attitude that William Harvey should be appointed personal physician to Charles, as he had been to James, and that Charles should allow him to experiment upon deer in the royal parks. Harvey's great work on the motion of the heart and blood in animals was published in 1628 and dedicated to Charles. The King in his kingdom, said Harvey, is like the heart in the body.

Charles spent less time now in his model room but his picture galleries and the Cabinet room where he kept his choicest pieces remained his greatest delight. His collection continued to grow. Buckingham had presented him with two Holbeins – *Frobenius* and *Erasmus* – before he went to the Isle of Rhé, as well as with two delightful miniatures of the children of the Duke of Brandon. Though Charles's Holbeins could not match in number and quality the superb collection of the Earl of Arundel, he had an early self-portrait of Rembrandt and the sixteenth-century northern artists were well represented in his cabinet: he had several Breughels and three portraits by Dürer – a self-portrait, a picture of the artist's father, and the portrait of a young man – all presented to him by the City of Nuremberg through Arundel.

When Arundel was in Prague on embassy in 1634 he met Wenceslaus Hollar, who had been travelling in Europe and drawing views of the principal cities he visited. His *Prospect of the City of Prague* so impressed Arundel that he persuaded Hollar to accompany him and delineate further cities. In 1637 they arrived in London and before the year was out Hollar had produced a *Prospect and View of Greenwich* on the strength of which Charles engaged him as drawing master to Prince Charles.

Van Dyck meanwhile had returned to London and Charles had persuaded him to stay in the role of Court painter. He was fully justifying Charles's confidence with portraits of the royal family and their courtiers which would give posterity that idealized picture of the Stuart Court which was in the King's mind. Charles was now enjoying what a contemporary termed 'the full flower of robust vigour natural to his time of life'. 'He is well proportioned and strong', continued the description, but below the average height. 'Although more disposed to melancholy than joviality, yet his aspect, with his comeliness, is no less pleasing than grave. His actions disclose no predominance of immoderate appetites or unruly affections, indeed, he is a prince full of goodness and justice.' He was rarely ill. On one occasion, though, he gave cause for alarm. He became hot at tennis, red spots showed on his body and memories of Henry's death were revived. But the doctors diagnosed smallpox. Henrietta would not leave her husband, night or day, in spite of the danger of infection. Fortunately Charles had only a light attack. He even seemed to enjoy his enforced inactivity, sitting up in a chair in a furred robe, playing games, chatting, and eating and drinking heartily. The illness was soon over and left no afternath.[5]

Henrietta-Maria appeared to be an admirable partner. She was now dressing beautifully in the subdued shades of gold and blue, sometimes set off with a touch of red, which were so admirably suited to Van Dyck's brush. She had borne Charles a daughter, Mary, on 4 November 1631 when she was twenty-two years old, and James, Duke of York, on 14 October 1633. Elizabeth followed at the end of December 1635, and Anne on 17 March 1637. By now Henrietta-Maria's bony little frame had filled out, a full lower lip attractively masked the slightly protruding teeth, and in the more rounded contours of her face the nose no longer looked too large. Her vivacity was undimmed, her countenance was alive to every mood and passing thought, her large black eyes as bright and expressive as when Charles had first seen them, full of apprehension, at Dover. She wore her hair in the new fashion, drawn back from her face with flat ringlets on her forehead and a curl or love-lock at her neck. She had grown very little in height and was still barely past her husband's shoulder. Charles could esteem his wife both fashionable and a beauty. Although she was not robust, and her pregnancies frequently caused anxiety, she, like her husband, was rarely ill.

At Court the Queen was constantly at her husband's side and she accompanied him on progress. She was, indeed, excluded from the Council, but never lacked information concerning its deliberations. Hunting, alone, was the activity she did not share. Unlike Charles's mother she was no huntress, while Charles's enthusiasm for the chase was becoming so consuming that he would spend as long as three weeks away from her on hunting expeditions. She had, however, her own interests, apart from the masque, exercising her French taste on the internal decorations of her house at Greenwich and at Somerset House. She now had many French friends and visitors without disturbing her relations with the King. Her illegitimate brother, the Duc de Vendôme, visited the English Court, and a Monsieur de Jars, who had all the social graces, including a witty tongue, played tennis with Charles, but was suspected of being a French agent. Of English courtiers the handsome Holland, Henry Jermyn who became her Vice Chamberlain in 1628, and George Goring, Lord Goring's son, were high in her favour. That religion was no barrier between her and her husband was demonstated when in September 1632 Charles accompanied her to Somerset House to help her lay the foundation stone of her new chapel on the old tennis court. He appeared more aware of his wife's pleasure than of the criticism of his Protestant subjects.

They saw a great deal of their children, who would join them for walks in one of the royal parks or gardens or spend amusing evenings in one of the great drawing rooms, where Archie Armstrong, the Court jester, or Jeffrey Hudson, the Queen's favourite dwarf, would entertain the courtiers while the King played at cards and the Queen fondled her pet monkeys or her dogs. Sometimes the children were present on more formal occasions. In 1635 Charles took the Prince of Wales to the Garter ceremony at Windsor. When the Venetian Ambassador was received at Richmond in 1637 all the children were there. Correr remarked appropriately that he rejoiced to find His Majesty in the midst of his greatest felicity, while Charles reproved the Prince of Wales for having received the Ambassador too stolidly when his hand was being kissed.[6] A little later in the same year Prince Charles and Princess Elizabeth acted as proxies at the christening of their sister, Anne.

The King and Queen liked to feel in control of the lives and fortunes of the men and women who composed their world, and the marriages of their friends' children, remained with Charles, as with James, a matter of deep concern. In 1635 Mary Villiers, aged thirteen, was married to Pembroke's son and heir, only a few years older. It was a match that would have pleased her father but the young bridegroom died of smallpox in Florence before the year was out. A few years later Mary married Charles's cousin James Stuart, Duke of Lennox. In the meantime Buckingham's widow had forfeited her place in the royal favour by a marriage with Viscount Dunluce, an Irishman several years her junior, of great charm but little fortune.

So there unfolded the day-to-day happenings of a Court that was a microcosm of the world. Charles liked to think of it as an ordered society from which strife had been banished. If he could not reach this stage of perfection in reality he could attain it in the contrived performances of the masque with which Inigo Jones continued to delight the Court. Jones's quarrel with Ben Jonson had not been healed but for Jones, to whom the form of the masque was all-important, this mattered little and he continued to co-ordinate every visual detail of his invention, from scenic fancy to the style and colour of a garment. As it happened there was sufficient talent at Charles's Court to supply fairly adequately the gap left by Jonson, but it was, by and large, the continuing fantasies of the ever-fertile Inigo Jones that held the Court not only entranced but assured that in this world of contrived balance and form, where virtue triumphed and the Gods were on the side of the King and his Court, they could see mirrored their own existence.

The King's masque, *Albion's Triumph*, performed on 8 January 1632 was, as its name implied, a glorification of the King and his state; *Tempe Restored*, written by Aurelian Townsend for the Queen's masque, was postponed because she had a sty in her eye, but when it was performed on Shrove Tuesday it proved to be one of Jones's most elaborate fancies. Fourteen children including, naturally, Villiers and Feildings, danced delightfully, Nicholas Lanier, who composed the music, and his musicians were airborne on a great cloud that hung above the stage, heavenly stars descended to earth in a blaze of light and the Queen herself, with supreme confidence, allowed herself to appear in the heavens as Divine Beauty in a golden chariot and to be lowered from aloft in full view of the audience. *Tempe Restored* highlighted the beauty of the Queen, which pleased Charles, and the ingenuity of the mechanical devices highly delighted him. *The Triumph of Peace* was the fitly-entitled masque by James Shirley and Inigo Jones performed at Candlemas (February) 1633, to which the public were admitted. The lesson was learned, for turnstiles were installed at the King's masque by Thomas Carew, *Coelum Britannicum*, which followed shortly after. To add to the general harmony the four Inns of Court combined in the autumn of 1633 to prepare a masque to offer to the Court. The names of the great and the learned appeared as sponsors: Edward Hyde and William Whitelocke of the Middle Temple; John Selden of the Inner Temple; William Noy of Lincolns Inn; Sir John Finch of Gray's Inn. It was presented on Candlemas Night, 1634, at the end of the Christmas festivities, in the presence of the King and Queen, who were so pleased that they asked for it to be repeated for the benefit of the London citizens. The learned sponsors obviously enjoyed it too. Whitelocke turned aside from his diary of more serious events to record the details of the preparations and performance, concluding with an audible sigh when it was all over and he returned to more mundane affairs: 'Thus these Dreams past, and these Pomps vanished . . .'

The masques continued – ten, twelve, sixteen in a single season from September to February – but there were plays as well. The season of 1633/34 was particularly full. On Charles's birthday, November 19, *The Young Admiral* by James Shirley was played and the King and Queen were said to have liked it. A week later came *The Taming of the Shrew*, also noted as 'liked' and the following day Fletcher's *The Tamer Tam'd*, which was said to have been 'very well lik't'. On December 10 another Beaumont and Fletcher, *The Loyal Subject*, won much approval from the King. *Cymbeline* was performed on New Year's Day 1634 and was highly praised by Charles, and six days later Beaumont and Fletcher were again chosen with *The Faithful Shepherdess* (for which clothes from the Queen's masque were used). It was 'lik't'; so was another Shakespeare, *The Winter's Tale*, given on January 16. But Ben Jonson's *Tale of the Tub*, which burlesqued Inigo Jones, was definitely 'not lik't'. Charles had not reached saturation point even after all this fare and on February 6 was able to exclaim with enthusiasm that *The Gamester*, by Shirley, which was given on that day, was the best play he had seen for seven years.[7]

22

The Yearly Round

Charles gave much thought and time to restoring the significance and enhancing the ceremonies associated with the Order of the Garter and the cult of St George. James had been overwhelmed with the splendour of the ceremonies and the regalia of the Order, particularly with the Great George, the massive collar of gold worn by each Knight on ceremonial occasions with the jewelled likeness of St George slaying the dragon suspended from it. These were the Orders which he had sent out to Spain for his 'boys' to wear on St George's Day in order to impress the Spanish Court, and it was for St George's Feast that he had cut short Charles's attendance on Elizabeth after her marriage.

To Charles the religious ceremonies associated with the inauguration of new Knights and the annual feasts themselves offered a highly emotive form of dedication and worship. St George himself shed any vestige of the pagan knight and became the Christian hero whose pictures and images would adorn the chapel of the Knights of the Order. James had appointed a Commission in 1611 which led to minor changes, and in 1630 Charles appointed a standing commission of Knights to consider the restoration of the Order to its ancient purity. He restored the Grand Feast permanently to Windsor where Matthew Wren, the Dean, was only too anxious to associate High Church practices with the ritual of the Order. Ceremonies became more elaborate, tapestries showing the Virgin and St George covered the altar in St George's Chapel, his image appeared on the walls, the feasts of St George became more of a dedication, less of a public spectacle.

Shortly after he came to the throne Charles had added to the regalia by embroidering on the cloak of every Knight a large cross within a garter with a 'glory' of silver rays emanating from the cross. In 1629 he struck a special commemorative medal with the legend *Prisci Decus*

254

Ordinis Auctum, and in that year the inauguration ceremonies of the Duke of Northumberland reached a new height of elaborate ritual. Rubens, wishing to compliment the King and Queen, had portrayed St George with his foot on the dragon's neck in a typically English landscape with a suggestion of Charles and Henrietta-Maria about St George and the Princess. Pembroke not only possessed Raphael's *St George* but had engravings made which were the basis of little bronzes of George and the Dragon which were made for Charles and members of his Court, where devotion to St George became a fashionable and essential cult. Nevertheless, when Charles attempted to revive a decree of 1618 that each Knight should contribute at least £20 towards a new set of plate for the Chapel, he found that even those most intimately connected with the Order were as reluctant to pay for its embellishment as they were to contribute to ship money or other tax, and he was still endeavouring to collect their contributions at the end of the 1630s.

The mystique surrounding the Order of the Garter, its regalia and ritual, and in particular the use of images in which the Virgin could be associated with St George, were at one with Charles's attitude towards his Church. In being religious, the Order and its ceremony were of more significance to Charles than the Court masques which were mainly classical in theme and allusion. George, for example, in one of his rare appearances in a masque, was the folk hero and not the saint. But it was the Saint to whom Charles gave special veneration not only in the Great George but more particularly in the Lesser George. The Great George, the massive gold collar with its pendant image of St George slaying the dragon, was worn on ceremonial occasions, but the Lesser George, which was a picture of the Saint often contained in or engraved upon a locket, could be suspended from a blue ribbon round the neck or pinned upon the breast. Charles wore his Lesser George constantly. It contained a portrait of his wife, as well as of the Saint, and it was with him on his dying day.[1]

Charles was also interested in the occult, though on the whole he was inclined to discount prophecy or 'revelation'. He had, indeed, been extremely angry when his wife consulted Lady Eleanor Davies about an heir to the throne and in 1633 he countenanced the imprisonment of the same 'prophetess' by the High Commission for printing a 'revelation' concerning the fate of himself and his Archbishop. In demonology Charles had a more personal interest, for his father had been morbidly attracted to the subject and had written a book on witches. The public as a whole shared this concern. In an age of sudden and sharp calamity, where unexpected storms caused shipwreck and harvest failure, where draught dried up the seeds in the earth, where plague and death were swift and unexplained, it was all too easy to see intentional malevolence at work, and only a step further to single out particular persons as responsible. The old, the bad-tempered, the physically deformed, the eccentric, often those who were merely wiser than their neighbours, could be categorized as 'witches'. Sometimes malevolence would deliberately build up a case on false evidence which the unfortunate victim of the charge was unable to refute. There had been witch trials and executions in Charles's own lifetime but the series of trials in 1634 in Lancashire concerned him personally. It was then asserted that seven Lancashire witches had raised the storm that caused the King's boat to capsize the previous summer in the Firth of Forth, and the women were condemned on this and other charges. Four of them died before the matter could be taken further, another confessed but pleaded penitence, and two completely denied the charges. The three surviving women were brought before Charles. The charge against the self-confessed witch, a widow of sixty years old, was now admitted to have been fabricated by the boy who was her accuser. Of the other two, Mary Spencer was a milkmaid aged twenty who enlivened her days by rolling her milk pail downhill, running after it and calling it to follow her if she outstripped it. She was accused of calling on the devil, and in the crowded Lancashire court where she was charged she was unable to hear what was said against her and quite incapable of explaining what she was accustomed to do. Charles spoke kindly to her and to the others, but though he promised the women their lives they were not released. Two years later Mary Spencer, and eight others, were still confined as witches in Lancaster gaol.[2]

Many who believed in the evil power of witches believed also in a beneficent power in kings to exorcise the evil disease of scrofula, or allied diseases, by means of the royal touch. To cure by the laying on of hands was a direct injunction of Christ to the Apostles and it accorded with Charles's views of kingship to use 'the touch' as English kings had done for centuries. The custom had been observed more meticulously in France than in England, and Charles, subject to French influence as well as his own conviction, built up the practice which his father had somewhat let decay. The ritual involved was quite elaborate, starting with the washing of the patients, with the

King drawing his hands gently over the afflicted places at the reading of the Gospel: 'they shall lay their hands on the sick and they shall recover'. The King would sometimes touch again and would put round the neck of each suppliant a 'healing angel' – a gold piece with a hole bored in it for a ribbon. After 1634 Charles had to abandon gold in the interests of economy and he used a silver coin instead, but a sufficient number of cures were attested, and enthusiasm was sufficiently high, for Charles to find it necessary to issue repeated Proclamations to limit the times when sufferers could come to be touched and to ensure that none came twice. In times of plague, particularly, access to Court to be touched for the King's Evil was forbidden. Some people would attempt to get private treatment. In December 1629 Sir William Russell used Endymion Porter to exert his influence with Charles to 'touch' Russell's nephew; when Charles was staying at Hatfield a little girl of ten was brought to him in the garden to be 'touched' for blindness – with, apparently, most encouraging results.[3]

Much as he enjoyed his life at Whitehall with access to his pictures and the possibility of contemplation in his study, there was also a growing restlessness about Charles that demanded physical action. The progresses that were part of the yearly round were all the more welcome for this reason. Basically, indeed, they were necessary as well as pleasant. They saved the King money, for he was entertained at his subjects' charge; they gave time for cleaning his main residences; they were an escape in times of plague; they enabled him to be seen and himself to see a variety of people and of landscape, giving him a greater familiarity with the country he ruled over; they gave him fresh hunting and they gave Henrietta-Maria the variety and movement she loved.

When the King went on progress a large part of his Court went too and a sufficient number of officers and messengers to carry on state business. The strain on the roads was considerable and the question of passage for all the vehicles and horses involved was a perpetual worry to the JPs, who were constantly importuning the Council to make regulations to preserve and improve such roads as existed. The strain on the great houses that were expected to accommodate the influx was even greater.

Nearly every year they went to Wilton, the home of the Earl of Pembroke, Charles's Lord Chamberlain and good friend, where

Charles found the hunting particularly exhilarating and where he enjoyed watching the progress of the re-building with which Nicholas de Claus had been entrusted. He had recommended Inigo for the work but Jones was too busy to give more than a general approval to the plans. Wherever they went Charles and Henrietta-Maria were interested in anything out of the ordinary. Charles went to great pains to protect from damage a strange rock and water formation at Enstone in Oxfordshire which he termed – erroneously, for it was artificially contrived – 'that rarity of nature'.[4] He turned aside in 1631 to see the well-known household of the Ferrars at Little Gidding in Huntingdonshire. Nicholas Ferrar was the son of a wealthy merchant, he had himself been employed by the Virginia Company and had sat in the Parliament of 1624. But his thoughts were already turning in other directions and he settled with his family on the manor of Little Gidding, a typical 'deserted village' where pasture farming had replaced a busy open-field community and the inhabitants had drifted away. The family restored the house and church and began a simple and orderly life based upon scripture readings, for which they gathered three or four times a day. They wrote school books for the neighbouring children whom they taught to read; they gave food to local people once a week at their own board; they practised certain simple crafts and the women, in particular, became skilled at bookbinding, producing several beautifully bound volumes of the Psalms and passages from scripture embellished with elaborate illustrations which Nicholas Ferrar collected on his journeys. The household of the Ferrars, with its quiet orderliness, appealed to Charles in itself and his interest in bookbinding had been aroused by accounts of the stamped work upon velvet which they had brought to a high degee of perfection. One particular volume produced at Little Gidding had won particular acclaim and Charles asked if he might borrow it. Nicholas Ferrar was in London and the rest of the household, taken by surprise, declared that the book, which had been made for younger members of the family, was not fit to be lent to the King. But Charles persisted, promising to return it before he left the district. Though he possessed many volumes bound in leather or rich velvet, this one surpassed them all and he was as delighted with its contents as with its appearance, reading it daily while on progress. Three months later he still had the book and returned it only on a promise that an exact copy would be made for him.[5]

About the same time Lucius Carey was settling in at the manor house of Great Tew in Oxfordshire, which he inherited from his father, Lord Falkland. Like Ferrar, the new Lord Falkland recoiled from religious strife, but whereas Ferrar was content to lead his own life without clothing his actions in words, to Falkland continued debate was the basis of belief, and he opened his house to any who cared to contribute to the discussions of the circle he gathered round him. Although his palace of Woodstock was neaby, Charles never visited Great Tew, neither in the earlier days when it was a centre for men of letters like Ben Jonson and Sir John Suckling, nor later when religion and philosophy took over. Yet the outlook of the men who met there was in some respects not unlike his own: when William Chillingworth, for example, wished that all men 'instead of being zealous papists, earnest Calvinists, rigid Lutherans . . . would become themselves, and be content that others should be, plain and honest Christians' he was expressing a point of view which Charles himself frequently maintained in not dissimilar language.

The tranquillity of the King and Queen had been temporarily shattered by news of the death of Frederick of the Palatinate at Mainz of a fever on 19 November 1632. Elizabeth's grief was so intense that for three days she was unable to speak. 'I never felt frighted before', she afterwards said. Charles put his Court into mourning and invited his sister home. Apartments were prepared for her in her old lodging in the Cockpit at Whitehall, and Eltham Palace was made ready for her children. The *Victory* would bring her home, Arundel would accompany her, and the fleet would escort her. Henrietta-Maria made no protest, though it would have been an embarrassment to have living in England the popular Princess who would be bound to assume a leading position among English Puritans. Charles was well aware of the difficulties but there was nothing lukewarm in his offer to provide for his sister. Elizabeth herself was equally firm in declining. Now, more than ever, she must remain in charge of her family and their fortunes to which Continental Europe had more relevance than England. Besides, she wrote, she would rather meet her brother, after all those years, without any tinge of sorrow.

The death of Frederick had overshadowed for his family what was, for the Protestant cause, a severer blow. Thirteen days before, though he had won the battle, Gustavus Adolphus had been killed at Lutzen. Since his victory over Tilly at Breitenfeldt in September 1631 he had swept on through Nuremberg, Augsburg and Munich, but it seemed now that the tide would be reversed. Charles had nothing to offer but diplomacy. He had sent Roe to Gustavus Adolphus in 1629/30, Vane on a special mission to the Prince of Orange and the Palatinate in the spring of 1629, Sir Robert Anstruther to Vienna in 1630, Vane again to the Netherlands in March 1631 and Weston's son to France and Italy in July 1632.

After the signing of the treaty of Madrid in 1630, his chief ambition was to preserve the balance of power. He told the Dutch Ambassador in October 1634 that he was resolved to live at peace with everyone and to keep himself a general friend. He did not want the House of Austria to advance to excessive power, but neither was the too-evident aggrandisement of France under Richelieu to be desired. He would rather employ himself upon a universal adjustment than in fomenting a war which had already been carried on too long. Most of the Court were throught to agree, 'grown drowsy', as the Venetian Ambassador commented, 'in the delights and commodities of the country and in the charms of peace'. But Charles's policy was realistic. After the death of Gustavus the whole of Central Europe lay under the dominion of the Hapsburg Empire and the Roman Catholic Church. The only effective counterweight was the France of Richelieu which, in spite of religious differences, was looking for co-operation with the Dutch. Charles's aim of holding the balance between these two powerful blocs was not unrealistic. But he would need the help of Spain. He still also believed that Spain had it in her power to deliver to him the Palatinate and to this end he was negotiating with her in 1634. It was said he showed more consideration to them in the Channel than he did to the Dutch; he allowed some of the gunpowder of which he had a monopoly to be sold to Spain (though at double the usual price). At one time his ships escorted Spanish troops across the Channel to Flanders. Elizabeth refused to believe that he was again toying with a Spanish alliance. She was 'inflexible . . . to the blows of time', thinking of nothing but her set purpose, to which she trained her children, taking up every contact that would help her cause, tirelessly writing letter after letter to the Courts and statesmen of Europe as well as to her friends. The Peace of Prague of 20 May 1635 was a blow both to her and to Charles. It showed how little either of them counted in the affairs of the Empire and, indeed, how little Charles's friendship with Spain had done for his nephew's cause. For the Peace expressly stated that the Palatinate would not be restored to the late Elector's family.

Still undaunted, Elizabeth launched her eldest son, Charles Louis,

Elector Palatine since his father's death, into his uncle's Court. He arrived in England on 1 December 1635 to an inauspicious welcome when gunners, firing a salute from the shore, hit the Prince's ship by mistake, killing five people, two of whom were standing close to him. Charles Louis was a shy, reserved boy who, because of the plague then rampant in England, had brought with him few attendants. The Venetian Ambassador found him looking 'careworn and sad'. He was welcomed into the life of the Court, he joined his uncle on progress, but he came at a difficult time.

The year 1636 was a restless one for Charles's followers. He was hunting in one area after another, sometimes escaping with only a few attendants, rarely staying more than a night or two in the same place. Repeated outbreaks of plague added to the uncertainty. The King abandoned a visit to Theobalds in July because of the pestilence, going to Bagshot instead. When the Court was at Salisbury in August plague broke out in a merchant's house where followers of the Palatine were staying and the whole Court left in some confusion at daybreak. Charles himself went to the village of Bradford where he took over a gentleman's small house and decided to wait for Henrietta-Maria, who was at Oatlands. Tagging along as usual with other foreign diplomats was the Venetian Ambassador. Correr was never a man to miss an opportunity and he seized his moment one evening when Charles was walking practically alone in his host's garden. But Charles was more than equal to the wily Venetian. When the Ambassador tried to draw him on the question of the Palatinate he merely expressed his desire to see his nephew's cause 'properly adjusted' and Correr had to admit that Charles 'fenced cleverly' with all his leading questions.

Charles intended to proceed to Oxford with Henrietta-Maria, where Laud was to entertain them on behalf of his College and of the University, but first one of the Palatine's men, then one of the King's own guards, died of plague, the Court panicked, abandoned most of its baggage, and made off in various directions. The Venetian miserably pursued his duty and kept close to the King. 'I will follow him', he wrote home, 'as I have already done for 2½ months, but I ask the state to consider the burden thus thrown upon me.' The King and Queen reached Oxford on August 29 together with the Elector Palatine and his younger brother, Rupert, who had arrived during the early summer. In contrast to Charles Louis, Rupert was bright and extrovert, delighting in Court life, amusing himself particularly, it was said, with the ladies. Charles received him, as he had done Charles Louis, with the warmest affection; but the Venetian Ambassador remarked cynically that he was not in reality so welcome because they feared that by degrees the whole family would come and take root.[6]

When they reached Oxford they found that there had been a great deal of tidying up in the city, some taverns had been closed, and regulations governing students had been tightened. The guests were lodged in Christ Church, there was a service in the Cathedral, a play (an extremely bad one) in Christ Church Hall. Charles Louis and Rupert were suitably honoured, the Elector receiving a copy of Hooker's *Ecclesiastical Polity* and Rupert a copy of Caesar's *Commentaries*. Charles particularly enjoyed the Bodleian Library, though his own bust by Le Sueur, which Laud had recently presented to the library, was not yet in its niche looking down upon the readers. At St John's he noted with interest the new building undertaken by Laud with the pillars of grey marble which had been brought from a quarry near the royal palace at Woodstock. The magnificent banquet that followed supplied every servant of the Court and of the College in attendance. The play that evening was Cartwright's *Royal Slave*, which pleased Henrietta-Maria so much that she had it repeated later at Hampton Court.

Charles had intended to proceed to Windsor, but the plague had broken out there so he made for Southampton, reaching the Earl's house in early September. It was here that he met with what might have been a serious accident when his horse was submerged in a bog in the New Forest. Charles disengaged himself, clambered out, changed clothes with the first person he met, procured another mount, and continued the chase.[7] He was back at Oatlands at the beginning of October where, with the Queen, he received the Spanish Ambassador. The envoy brought with him an English Jesuit as interpreter. This was straining too far the patience with which Charles normally met matters concerning the Catholic church and he was furiously angry: that the Ambassador should bring to his face to such a public function one who by the laws of the realm was a rebel against the Crown was insupportable, he said, and the Jesuit was sent packing. A week later Charles was off to Theobalds and Newmarket for fresh hunting.

By this time the Elector and Prince Rupert were back in Europe fighting against the Hapsburg. Charles had declined to commit himself to an alliance with France and Holland. He still talked about the

Palatinate, going through the motions of support, writing affectionately and, sometimes, with determination, to Elizabeth. But there was
less evidence of the urge to right a wrong, of the chivalrous defence
of his sister's honour. Perhaps he knew that without a Parliament,
even though he had the ship money fleets, he was not strong enough to
give effective help. Perhaps he really believed in the help of Spain;
perhaps he was right in avoiding an entanglement that would have
consumed him. Perhaps he also realized how small a part the restitution of the Palatinate played on the wider European scene and knew it
was only in his sister's inextinguishable spirit that it stayed alive. At all
events, as the wheel turned, as home events played a greater part in his
life and he began to look away from Europe, the inner hurt was less
than it had been.

One slight worry on the home front was the continued captivity of the
men Charles had imprisoned after the dismissal of the 1629 Parliament. Eliot was suspected of plotting with his visitors and at the end of
1631 had been placed in close confinement, with no light but a candle
and no fire, even in that freezing winter. As consumption weakened
him, Eliot petitioned for temporary release to recover his health, but
Charles would neither forget his opposition in Parliament nor his
antagonism to Buckingham and refused his request. Eliot died on 27
November 1632. His family petitioned for leave to take his body
home for burial. Again Charles refused. 'Let Sir John Eliot be buried
in the parish where he died' was the brutal remark he wrote on the
paper. Valentine and Stroud also remained in prison, and though their
confinement was probably less stringent it remains true that throughout the years of his greatest happiness Charles kept the men who had
opposed him shut off from the normal intercourse of daily life. He
was, indeed, not only showing that he could be vindictive, but was
growing more imperious with the years. He could not bear to be
crossed and in his relations with his courtiers there was often little of
the diffident young Prince. When the Earl of Suffolk, for example,
was ordered to give up his post of Captain of the Pensioners, he came
to Charles saying that the mere rumour of his discharge had drawn all
his creditors upon him, for he was much in debt. 'What care I for your
debts!' cried Charles, shaking with anger. Later, however, he agreed
to let Suffolk keep the post until the 'noise of losing it was over'.

But on the whole Charles's Court was a place of laughter, not
much troubled by tragedy or misadventure outside itself, moved to

mirth by little things as when Ambassador Joachimi, on taking leave of the Queen, paid his respects to her dwarf, thinking he was the young Prince. The King of Persia'a Ambassador was also very amusing since he spoke no English and brought no interpreter. But to Charles one of the most exciting events was the arrival in 1632 of the beautifully bound and written concordance of the Four Evangelists promised him by Little Gidding. The richly gilded velvet of the cover was worked in the characteristic fashion of Little Gidding and Charles asked many questions about the book and those who made it. 'Truly my lords', he exclaimed to those standing round him,

> I prize this as a rare and rich jewel, and worth a King's acceptance . . . for the skill, care, cost, used in it, there is no defect, but a superlative dilligence in all about it . . . it shall be my *Vade mecum*. How happy a King were I, if I had many more such workmen and women in my kingdom! God's blessing on their hearts and painful hands!

His courtiers declared it to be a precious gem, and worthy of his cabinet. Charles then remarked that he had often read the Books of Kings and Chronicles but had found in them many contradictions. He wished very much he could have one book in which the stories of Kings and Chronicles were so interwoven 'as if one pen had written the whole book, making a complete history, but so that he could read them separately if he wished'. He had often spoken to his chaplains about this but they had always excused themselves. At Little Gidding, however, they promised to put the work in hand immediately. It was ready within a year and sent through the Archbishop of Canterbury. Charles, seeing him one day with a great book in his arms, realized immediately what it was and rose from his chair in delight. 'What!', he said, 'shall I now enjoy that rich jewel I have thus long desired! Give it me! Give it me!' he cried, seizing the book and taking it to a table. First he gazed upon the outside. 'My lords', he cried, 'the outside thus glorious, what think you will be the inside and matter of it?' He then turned the pages leaf by leaf, examining them all with the greatest care. 'Truly', he said, 'it passeth what I could have wished . . . this is a jewel in all respects', and he showed his friends the contrivance of the two books united together in one history, as if written by one man's pen. 'I will not part with this', he said, gathering the book up in his arms, 'for all the jewels in my jewel house.'[8]

Prince Charles was by this time begging his father to let him have the first book sent from Little Gidding, but the King would not part with it for, he said, he daily made use of it. The Prince, then, with his father's permission, sent to Little Gidding for one like it. Old Nicholas Ferrar was by this time dead but his nephew and the ladies of the house undertook to make a concordance for the Prince in four languages as well as some additional pieces for the King.

Thus the yearly round unfolded, the physical movement Charles required supplied by his Progresses and his hunting, the intellectual stimulus he welcomed provided in a dozen different ways. One such stimulus was provided by his religion.

23

The King and his Church

Religious issues could never for long remain in the background. The peoples of Charles's kingdoms were for the most part religious people, the majority of whom shared a spiritual zeal that for a couple of generations had been channelled into opposition to Spain and the Papacy. Since the defeat of the Spanish Armada the dread of popery and the Roman Catholic Church had gradually subsided, but a majority of Englishmen were still anti-papist under the skin. An irrational fear of 'popery' and 'papists', whatever the terms might mean, ran in many Englishmen who had nevertheless accepted a Catholic Queen and two peace treaties with Spain, and who had done little to help the Protestant Princess Elizabeth in her opposition to the Catholic bloc in Europe: Parliament had failed her, volunteers to fight for her numbered no more than a few thousands, money to support her arms amounted to only a trickle from the public at large. From time to time murmurs of a purely Protestant succession disturbed the English Court, but as Mary followed Charles, and James followed Mary, and Elizabeth followed James the rumours accorded less and less with reality. When the Prayer Book of 1636 was found to have omitted the customary prayer for the Queen of Bohemia and her family, the initial consternation was assuaged by the practical realization that there were now four English royal children to pray for.

Charles was never likely to make an issue of religion. So long, he always said, as a person accepted the fundamental belief of Christianity he had no quarrel with him. That he was basically tolerant his relations with his wife and his mother bore out. He had Catholic friends and advisers, he accepted the Puritan sympathies of Pembroke, he took as given the Calvinism of his brother-in-law Frederick and the staunch Protestantism of his sister; he had accepted, indeed loved, his Presbyterian tutor Thomas Murray and his Lutheran Uncle of

Denmark; he had understood and never quarrelled with Buckingham's religious vicissitudes. Theological disputation learned at his father's knee remained an enjoyable but superficial titillation of the intellect unaccompanied by any expectation of conversion. But the rules of the game had to be kept; when, as in Spain, he felt his opponents were not dealing fairly with him, he would break off the discussion immediately. From more earnest efforts at conversion he shied away, and he disliked his father's theological college at Chelsea for the very reason that it trained men to combat Romanism; it would be better, he considered, if instead of studying controversy it worked for union.[1]

A man's religion is a reflection of his character and the very fastidiousness with which Charles shrank from any controversy that might sully his worship was basic to his nature. His need for order, without any adventurous intellectual probings, was reflected in his religion. In this respect his reliance upon Laud was of the same kind as his reliance upon van der Doort. As the one catalogued and cared for his pictures, leaving to Charles the aesthetic pleasure of viewing them, so the other ordered and arranged his Church, leaving to Charles the beauty of untroubled worship. Charles came increasingly close to Laud in an unemotional way, not only choosing him to preach on public occasions, but to baptize and bury the royal children, and he supported the efforts which Laud made, as Bishop of London, to bring the London churches into a condition not only of order but of conformity: for order must apply to the whole as well as to the parts, and order implied regularity. The *extempore* preaching of Puritan ministers, still less of the itinerant 'lecturers' who were accustomed to address Puritan congregations, had no place in this intended order, and Laud was zealous in securing their dismissal. He also took every opportunity of removing the communion table to the position of an altar, of embellishing the City churches with images, and doing reverence to them and to the crucifix. The repair of church fabric, essential in itself, too often became an issue between Puritans and the Bishop of London. Particularly notorious was the case of the reconsecration of St Mary Cray in the City when Laud's 'unseemly' kneeling and bowing was exaggerated and remembered to his cost. It was unfortunate, though natural, that the kind of uniformity Charles and his Bishop were insisting upon should raise afresh the spectre of an all-devouring Papacy. Puritans who had been watchful under Elizabeth, suspicious under James, became increasingly militant under Charles. They were encouraged by the Bible, the pulpit, and the press.

Translations of the Bible had begun with Wycliffe's work at the end of the fourteenth century, but none had made a stronger mark than the new translation whose publication James authorized in 1611. This was made in the full flowering of an English language which was magnificent to listen to and splendid to roll on the tongue, and it caught the imagination of a generation accustomed to be moved by the power of words in the theatre of Shakespeare and Marlowe. Moreover, the people had their own theatre in the pulpit, their own actors in the preachers who told with shattering rhetoric of the power of the Lord, the terrors of hell, the wickedness of the devil, and of his representatives on earth, the Pope and the bishops. To the Bible and the pulpit were added a growing number of printed pamphlets and books. Since 1557 a monopoly of printing had rested with a Company of 97 London stationers and a few years later the right to license was vested in the Archbishop of Canterbury or the Bishop of London. It was then necessary for a book or pamphlet first to be licensed and then to be registered with the Stationers for publication. The regulations could not prevent the appearance of clandestine publications, and in opposition to Laud's policy printed sermons and tracts of all kinds proliferated.

Charles had ample warning of what was happening. There was, for example, the case of Alexander Leighton, a Scot by birth and early education. After practising as a preacher in Durham, Leighton finished his education in Leyden, allegedly in medicine but no doubt under the influence of the many secretarians in that city. The London College of Physicians failed to recognize his degree and back in London Leighton took again to preaching, which became increasingly, and popularly, anti-episcopal. In 1628 he had ready *Sion's Plea Against Prelacy*, a petition calling for the extirpation of bishops, to which he claimed 500 signatures. To evade censorship the petition, now swollen into a considerable treatise, was printed in Holland. A copy reached Laud, Leighton was arrested and the Star Chamber sentenced him to whipping, to stand in the pillory at New Palace Yard there to have one of his ears lopped off, his nose split, and his face branded with the letters S.S. for sower of sedition. He was later again to be whipped and pilloried at Cheapside where his other ear would be cut off. The fine of £10,000, which he had no means of paying, was an example of the exemplary fines imposed by the Star Chamber and

High Commission with the possible hope that a small sum might accrue to the Exchequer.

On 26 November 1630, when Leighton's punishment was carried out, the scene set the pattern for dozens that would follow: the procession of friends supporting him to Westminster; his wife glorifying his punishment; his own ecstacy. 'This is Christ's yoke!', he cried, as the pillory was clamped upon him. 'Blessed be God, if I had a hundred, I would lose them all for the cause!', he exclaimed as the executioner lopped off his ear. On Charles's orders further suffering at Cheapside was remitted; but the procedure had been established from beginning to end: the petition, the signatures, the printing in Holland, the inevitable discovery, the Star Champer conviction (which was not unduly harsh for the time), the procession to the pillory, the speech to the people. Even the mixture of personal rancour and religious zeal shown by Leighton was to be present in later martyrs of the Puritan cause.[2]

Another foretaste of the future was given in the same year when an unnamed oatmeal maker was brought before the High Commission for taking upon himself to preach. He refused to take off his hat and when asked why, said he would never doff it to bishops. 'But you will to privy counsellors?' he was asked. 'As you are privy counsellors', he responded, suiting the action to the words, 'I put off my hat, but as ye are rags of the beast, lo! I put it on again!' Towards the end of his interrogation the Bishop of Winchester arrived and took a vacant seat at the bottom of the table. 'Let us dismiss this frantic, foolish fellow', he advised, 'we do but lose our time.' 'Hold thy peace!', roared the oatmeal maker, 'thou tail of the beast that sittest at the lower end of the table!'.[3]

All this was highly repugnant to Charles. Sectarianism polluted his religion, he believed with his father that it threatened the political stability of his kingdom, its very fervency appeared to him as raucous and ranting; its intolerance would breed its opposite: 'The neglect of punishing Puritans breeds Papists' as he would write on the margin of a Report from Archbishop Neile of York in January 1634. No disturbances among his courtiers upset the equilibrium of his life so much as this unseemly conduct of the Puritans. He was content that Laud should deal with them, intervening only, as he had done with Leighton, to let his natural compassion prevent too harsh a punishment.

Like other rulers of diverse territories Charles wished for greater unity between the various parts of his kingdom and he shared the feeling which was growing on both sides of the border for a Coronation in Scotland and for a Scottish Parliament. Meantime the Scottish bishops who had been appointed by James to prepare a Prayer Book for their country had finished their work, though no attempt had been made to bring the book into public use. Though in form not unlike the English Book of Common Prayer the Scottish Book had a definitely Puritan slant. Many sections showed the influence of John Knox, it omitted certain rituals such as the sign of the cross in baptism, and it laid down that the altar might be placed as the minster found convenient. Laud advised that it could not be accepted and that 'it were best to take the English liturgy without any variation'. Charles agreed in spite of Scottish warnings that not only religion but national feeling was involved. And so the ill-fated decision was taken, and when Charles set out on 13 May 1633 he had resolved that the unity between the two countries should be religious as well as political. Henrietta-Maria could no more be crowned in Edinburgh than in London so he necessarily went alone, in some slight anxiety since she was again pregnant, though his spirits were high at the prospect of seeing at last the country where he was born.

It was no mean enterprise to convey the paraphernalia of a king's suite over the long route from London to Edinburgh, and Justices of the Peace were ordered well in advance to attend to the condition of the roads, an injunction which many of them took badly: it was too early in the year for road repairs, the weather was not seasonable, the highways were in deep clay, bridges were not completed, though fords, they grudgingly conceded, were passable. Many of the articles intended for use in the Chapel Royal, including musical instruments, were sent by sea from Tilbury to Leith in the *Dreadnought*, which was taken off her duty of guarding the narrow seas. Laud, as Dean of the Chapel Royal, was to accompany the King, orders for provisions and lodgings had been sent on ahead.

Charles hunted and enjoyed magnificent hospitality on his way.[4] He called again at Little Gidding and stopped at Worksop, Stamford, Grantham and York, where he rode to see Lord President Wentworth's new park. He noted the condition of York Minster and of Durham Cathedral, later writing to their Deans to suggest improvements. He reached Edinburgh on June 15 when one of his first acts was to make Laud a Privy Councillor of Scotland, which was a severe affront to the Scots in seeming to emphasize the importance of an English bishop in Scottish affairs. The Coronation itself on June 18 was a splendid affair in which, again, Laud's prominent role offended the Scots. A question of precedence also marred the proceedings, Charles wishing the Church in the person of the Archbishop of St Andrews to take precedence of Lord Chancellor Hay, Earl of Kinnoul. He was very annoyed at having to give way, 'I will not meddle further with that old cankered goutish man!', he exclaimed angrily,[5] showing a characteristic impatience at being crossed together with an unaccustomed lapse from courtesy. But mutual oaths were taken in the Cathedral, first by the King, who swore to observe the fundamental laws of the realm, then by the Scottish Lords who swore obedience and fealty to the Crown. Immediately the ceremony was over Charles despatched letters to the Queen that were delivered to her only forty hours after they were written. Charles was delighted with the affection shown him which, he wrote, surpassed all belief. At the royal table he was served by all the leading Earls, and he created twelve new knights, a Viscount, two Earls and a Marquis. There was nevertheless much disquiet at the form of the service in Holyrood chapel on the day of the Coronation. The Scots were quite unused to the sight of bishops in their robes and of clergy in white surplices genuflexing to the crucifix on an altar at the East end of the chapel. They were still more perturbed when similar practices were brought to the people's church at St Giles.

Two days after his coronation Charles opened the Scottish Parliament. He followed its business day by day in person, anxious, indeed, to get two particular Bills through, one confirming the church legislation passed in his father's reign, the other confirming his own right to settle the apparel of judges, magistrates and clergy – which meant, in effect, to insist upon the wearing of robes and surplices. The Bills passed, but only just. Charles anxiously noted the votes and there was even rumour of manipulation in order to achieve the desired result. He refused even to look at a supplication against the legislation. His other business in Scotland concerned the Prayer Book. Having quietly dropped the version prepared by the Scottish Bishops he allowed Laud to propose the introduction of the English Prayer Book instead. But the majority of Scottish Bishops were so insistent that such an action would be unwise that it was agreed to attempt a compromise, with the instruction that the new liturgy should be 'as near that of England as might be'.

Charles continued to show his usual good health and tirelessness. On July 1 he set out on a sentimental journey to Dunfermline, where he was born, and to Stirling, Linlithgow and Falkland so closely associated with his family. He was greeted everywhere with the greatest enthusiasm. The only misadventure occurred when he was crossing the Firth of Forth from Burntisland to Edinburgh, where a sudden storm blew up and his boat capsized. Charles escaped unhurt but the incident was afterwards attributed to the malevolent influence of the witches Charles spoke to in 1634. On the 14th he set off for home. Outstripping his suite, he rode post from Berwick to London in four days, crossed to Greenwich from Blackwall to avoid the City, and was with Henrietta on the 20th. She was said to have been 'a perfect mourning turtle' in his absence, but she had nevertheless gone up river to visit the Duchess of Buckingham and had enjoyed racing her boat with George Goring.[6] Three months after Charles's return she gave birth at St James's Palace to James, Duke of York.

On August 6, on his first visit to Charles after their return from Scotland, Laud received a new greeting: 'My Lord's Grace of Canterbury', said the King who had just received news of the death of Abbot on August 4, 'you are very welcome'. Although the appointment hardly changed the relationship of the two men it gave Laud greater authority, and one of his first actions was to send Sir Nathaniel Brent as his Vicar-General over the whole of England south of the Trent to report upon the state of the churches.

Brent found that church fabric was often decayed, that churchyards were overgrown and sometimes used as mustering grounds for the trained bands, that pictures and images were neglected. Irreverence in church took many forms. There was often a general tramping about and talking during service, even an exchange of remarks with the preacher; the altar was used as a hat-stand, as a table upon which people scribbled notes, or simply as a seat. It is hardly surprising that there was also a failure to bow at the name of Mary or Jesus. Indeed, one minister was so anxious to avoid this practice that he contrived to omit the names from his service. Many preachers were cheerfully conversational and breezily abusive. Reports of stipends received and duties neglected were common. For sheer desecration perhaps nothing exceeded the actions at Saxby of Lord Castleton's bailiff who stripped the lead from the church roof, melted it in the middle aisle of the church and, when some of the liquid lead ran through the floor on to a coffin beneath, took up the floor and recovered the lead by burning the coffin with the corpse in it.[7]

The abuses were so diverse and so widespread, ranging from trifling to fundamental, that any attempt to impose uniformity and decency was an augean task. In clearing up obvious desecration, in insisting upon the repair of fabric, restoring impropriations, and calling abusive clergy to order, Laud was on safe enough ground. The question of ceremonies was far more difficult and nowhere was this more apparent than in the altar controversy. Permanently fixed at the East end of the church and railed, it would be safe from desecration but implied a form of worship remote and mystical, requiring priestly mediation in the act of worship rather than the direct relationship with God that the Puritan expected. The widespread use of *extempore* prayer was similarly difficult to deal with, insistence upon the use of the Prayer Book seeming to imply that the individual was incapable of direct communion. Besides, as Samual Ward of Ipswich said, it was impossible for anyone to carry about with him a manual of prayer suitable for all occasions. He declared further that a parrot might be instructed to use set forms and an ape might be taught to bow and gesticulate. Ward was brought before the High Commission and imprisoned.

Another matter on which Charles was opposed by his Puritan subjects was Sunday sport. James had found that many people were debarred by Puritan opinion from Sunday recreation and in his *Declaration of Sports* declared it his wish that, so long as they had attended church on the Sabbath, they should not be hindered from partaking of any lawful form of sport or dancing. Charles's notice was brought to the matter in connection with the church feasts called wakes, and in particular to the Somersetshire Ales which a Puritan magistrate had forbidden on the ground that they led to drunkenness and brawling. Charles intervened personally, brought the offending magistrate before the Council, commanded him to rescind his ban, and ordered the republication of *The Book of Sports* in October 1633. As a normal means of spreading information it was to be read from all the pulpits in the land. Refusals to read it were widespread and contributed further to the sources of conflict between Charles and the Puritans.[8]

There was more behind the controversy than the issue as to whether or not the Sabbath should be reserved solely as a day of worship. Puritans would gather together after church service for further preaching and discussion, and their leaders had come to rely heavily upon these meetings for building up their organization. To them such an attractive alternative as Sunday sports was dangerous.

But they hardly realized the extent to which discussion was splitting their own ranks. Already Puritanism had taken two main forms – the Presbyterian based upon Calvin's Church-state at Geneva, in which authority was vested in groups of ruling elders and ministers known as Presbyteries and whose organization was as rigid as Laud's; and the Independents who had little use for organization but based their Church upon the instructions of Robert Browne that any group of believers constituted a Church 'without tarrying for any'. They recognized no separate priesthood, ministers and officers were elected from the whole congregation, their only requirement being the covenant they took with each other and with God to form a Church. Such people were open to the continual reception of new ideas. The parting words of Henry Robinson to the *Mayflower* – 'If God reveal anything to you by other instruments of His, be as ready to receive it as ever you were to receive truth through me' – was the essence of a toleration even wider than that which the Independent Church claimed for itself. Access to the Bible in English; emphasis upon the sermon rather than the set pieces of the Prayer Book; a growing literature of unorthodoxy; increasing numbers of people from all walks of life who stood up on their own doorsteps to expound the word of God as they understood it; above all, the belief that 'form' was inessential and that only 'spirit' mattered gave vitality to the words of Browne and Robinson.

The Privy Council indicated its perception, as well as its dismay, when it complained that

> there remain in divers parts of the Kingdom sundry sorts of separatists, novelists, and sectaries, as namely – Brownists, Anabaptists, Arians, Traskites, Familists, and some other sorts, who, upon Sundays and other festival days, under pretence of repetition of sermons, ordinarily use to meet together in great numbers in private houses and other obscure places, and there keep private conventicles and exercise of religion by law prohibited, to the corruption of sundry his Majesty's good subjects.

They ordered JPs to enter any suspicious house and to search every room for people and unlicensed books.

The heady wine of sectarianism was particularly strong in London, in whose narrow streets and alleys conventicles would form and secret printing presses be established. All over London, indeed, Puritanism in its widest sense was gathering large audiences to listen to preachers who denounced Laud and the bishops in the most lurid terms and whose sermons were associated largely with vengeance and hell fire and to a lesser degree with forgiveness and the love of God. All had in common a belief in a predestination that marked them as God's Elect, certain of salvation, while those who failed to respond were certain of hell fire and everlasting damnation.

Puritanism needed its martyrs and was bound to have them. In June 1637 William Prynne, Henry Burton, and John Bastwick marched in procession to the pillory at Westminster as Leighton had done. Prynne was a lawyer who already had turned his amazing verbosity and violence of language against the practice of drinking healths (*Health's Sickness*), and the fashion of wearing a lock of hair over one shoulder (*The Unloveliness of Love-Locks*). In 1633 he published *Histriomastix* which fulminated against dancing and acting, the use of boys in women's roles, and the appearance of women upon the stage. Prynne's style was emphatic. In spite of the fact that his pamphlets ran to inordinate length and were embellished with a wealth of marginal notes, being, indeed, essentially boring, they were sparked into life by an excessive use of vituperation. He used his learning to draw on the classics and declared Nero's murder to be justified because of his fondness for the theatre. Those who enjoyed plays were 'devils incarnate', women actors were 'notorious whores'. Not surprisingly a reference to the Queen was assumed, and Prynne's punishment was severe. In May 1634 the Star Chamber fined him £5000, he was expelled from Lincoln's Inn, deprived of his Oxford degree, and shorn of both his ears while he stood in the pillory first at Westminster and then at Cheapside. He was to be imprisoned for life.

It was evidence of his Puritan connections that, in spite of his imprisonment, he contrived not only to continue to write but to publish unlicensed pamphlets. One of them, *News from Ipswich*, was a violent attack upon bishops and it was for this that in 1637 Prynne was once again standing in the pillory with his two friends. Henry Burton was vicar of the church at Friday Street in the City of London and had been in the households of both Prince Henry and Charles. He had preached and printed from a secret press two sermons fiercely attacking the Laudian injunctions to bow towards the East, to set up crucifixes, and to turn tables into altars. John Bastwick, the third of the trio, was a doctor of medicine from Essex, nurtured in the Puritan Emmanuel College at Cambridge and with fighting service in the Dutch armies to his credit. He had published several pamphlets in Latin attacking bishops before he put out the fiercely vituperative and hard-hitting *Letany* in English: the prelates were the enemies of God and the King; they were the tail of the beast; the Church was as full of ceremonies as a dog is full of fleas. 'From plague, pestilence and famine, from bishops, priests and deacons, Good Lord deliver us!'

The punishment of the three men was a repetition of Leighton's seven years earlier. The wives of Burton and Bastwick accompanied their husbands to Westminster, the way was strewn with flowers and sweet herbs by well-wishers who offered words of sympathy and cheer. The victims were allowed to speak to the assembled crowds in Palace Yard, who followed every word of the argument and, afterwards, every action of the executioner and his victims. Prynne's stumps of ears were hacked a second time, the burning iron pressed into his cheek once, twice, then a third time because one of the letters had been incised upside down. The journeys to their remote and far-separated prisons were triumphant progresses.

Far away, to the north, in the county of Durham, in a small manor house in a little town called Thickley Punchardon, a boy had meanwhile been growing up in the Puritan tradition inculcated by his father, a modest landowner, and his uncles, business men in Newcastle. Like many younger sons, John Lilburne came to London and was apprenticed to a cloth merchant in the City where he soon came under the influence of the Puritan preachers. He joined the crowds who thronged to see Bastwick at the Gatehouse prison before his sentence, and was honoured to be charged with the task of taking the manuscript of the *Letany* to Holland to be printed. The exercise was by now routine, so much so that the authorities found no difficulty in arresting Lilburne on his return and confiscating the offending pamphlets. He, in his turn, stood in Palace Yard in the spring of 1639, his flamboyant nature finding no difficulty in following, and even surpassing, the showmanship of the earlier Puritan martyrs. Like them he was thrust in prison; but he had a gift of words even greater than theirs and, since he was kept in the Fleet prison in London, the growing Puritan organization had the opportunity to supply him with pen and ink, to smuggle his manuscripts out of prison, and to get them printed, not only in Holland, but by various secret presses in the City of London itself.[9] Thus there began the career of one of the most prolific, hard-hitting and influential of all the Puritan pamphleteers.

While Laud was holding his position against Puritanism with one hand, he was also aware of what appeared to be Charles's flirtation with the Church of Rome. Charles never intended to go to Rome, he expected his Catholic officers to take the oath of allegiance, and he maintained the recusancy laws, albeit with a certain slackness. He also allowed his wife's Catholic chapels, and the chapels attached to foreign Catholic Embassies, to become more crowded, while he himself passed many hours in pleasant conversation with her Capuchin monks, finding with them a satisfaction he never found with his Puritan contacts. In the same way the example of Henrietta-Maria, observing the Church calendar, at mass with her friends and servants, making manifest the beauty of form and order, was in pleasing contrast to the strident improvisations of the Puritan worshippers of the conventicles. It was natural that he should think in terms of mutual understanding between the Church of England and the Holy See, and to that end a Scottish Roman Catholic, Sir Robert Douglas, arrived in Rome in October 1633.

The Papacy was well aware of the importance of this visit. Ever since Charles went to Spain it had watched him hopefully and the Papal Intelligence office, considering its reports on the state of England, noted both the harrying of Puritans and the growing number of Catholics, or near-Catholics, close to the King – Portland, Cottington, Porter, Windebank – as well as several important recent conversions which included the Dean of Lincoln. But, as it set to work to assess the situation, it had to take into account the King's sister and the Palatinate: for Charles to change his religion would seem like deserting her; possibly he was merely angling for Papal aid on her behalf. 'Charles's motives', wrote the aged Cardinal Bagna, to whom the matter was referred, 'as all who know him at all will admit, are beyond guessing.' Nevertheless, it would be unwise to let an opportunity slip, and throughout the 1630s there arrived at Charles' Court from the See of Rome a series of Papal envoys and a succession of valuable art treasures.

The Italianate influence which had come to Charles through his mother and her friends, enriched by the knowledge he had acquired of Italian art, made this contact with polished Italian intellectuals the greatest delight. They understood his relationship to art and to religion in a way that even Rubens, the Northerner, could not do, that certainly Laud could not achieve, and, indeed, that none of his friends, with the exception of Buckingham, ever did. First to arrive was Gregorio Panzani, who reached England in 1634. His first interview with the King was arranged quietly and privately by the Queen, and

Charles greeted him cordially, taking off his hat while Panzani kissed his hand, assuring him that no Catholic blood would be spilled in his reign and that Panzani himself would not be molested. When Puritan representatives tried to warn the King against the arrival of a Papal agent Charles merely smiled his tantalizing smile and said he was no stranger to Panzani's arrival.

Panzani found Charles 'a person of strict virtue and of great benevolence' and the nation as a whole 'not so bitter and scurrilous against the Pope' as formerly. He noted with great satisfaction that Cottington was a particular friend of the Jesuits and rejoiced at several recent conversions. Charles continued to maintain that there was much in the Roman Catholic religion with which he agreed, and that nothing would please him more than a healing of the breach between the Roman and the Anglican Church. He expressed himself strongly one day early in 1635, saying he would rather have parted with one of his hands than have had such a breach occur. One of his courtiers venturing to say that such sentiments were dangerous Charles instantly averred: 'I say it again: I wish I had rather lost one of my hands!' All this encouraged Panzani to such an extent that he was warned from Rome against optimism: 'The English are a mysterious people . . . The sea which you passed to visit them is an emblem of their temper.'

The Papal See nonetheless continued to woo Charles with the gifts most likely to influence him and there arrived a large picture of Bacchus by Guido and many presents for the Queen, including an exquisitely-worked relic case of gilt and crystal which particularly surprised and delighted him.[10] When he heard some time later that further pictures were on the way from Italy his impatience knew no bounds. They arrived while the Queen was lying in of her sixth pregnancy, and she immediately ordered them to be taken to her bedchamber, whither Charles made all haste, and together they exclaimed at the amazing bounty of canvasses by Corregio, Veronese, Leonardo, Andrea del Sarto and many more. The Papacy also paid Charles the special honour of allowing Bernini to make a bust of him in the winter of 1636/37 from the triple portrait painted by Van Dyck. When it arrived in England in July 1638 Charles and Henrietta were both delighted. It was practically the only bust made by Bernini of a Prince not of the Roman Catholic church.[11]

Meanwhile the talk went on and Panzani was succeeded by George Con, who had recently been made a Cardinal. It was fortunate, remarked Panzani before he left England, that Charles had taken to Con, for 'it is well known that His Majesty is altogether immoveable in his affection and aversion'. The handsome and urbane Con was no less an Italianate Papist through being born a Scot, and his presence served to confirm Charles in his conviction that so long as a man became intellectually civilized his place of birth, or whether he went to mass or took communion, made little difference. Nothing was more typical of Charles's relations with the Papal envoys at this time than when he kept a Garter ceremony waiting in April 1637 while he completed a tour of his picture gallery with Con.

In the theological discussions of his private circle his mother-in-law as well as his wife would sometimes join. For the influence of Marie de Medici was at an end in France and she had been forced to leave her country in 1631, largely through the intrigues of Richelieu. After seven years in the Spanish Netherlands she decided to move to her daughter in England – much against the will of Charles, who knew too well the effect of a strong-minded, intriguing Roman Catholic Queen Mother upon his subjects and upon his relationship with France, as well as the drain of a dowager Queen and her Court upon his treasury. But when he learned she was on her way he accepted the inevitable gracefully, sent to welcome her at Harwich where she arrived on 19 October 1638, and himself rode to meet her at Chelmsford to bring her to St James's Palace through a London suitably, if not spontaneously, decked for the occasion. He made her an allowance far in excess of what he could afford for herself and an entourage far larger than he had expected.

Henrietta was in a whirl of excitement at the thought of seeing again the mother whom she had left thirteen years earlier in Amiens. She was again pregnant and it was arranged that she should be seated at the foot of the grand stairway of St James's Palace to welcome her parent. She had stationed herself at an upstairs window, however, where she could watch for the arrival, and when she saw the royal carriage approaching previous plans and discretion were thrown to the winds as she tore downstairs, her children after her, into the hall, out into the courtyard where, with trembling hands, she tried to open the carriage door. As her mother alighted Henrietta-Maria knelt on the ground with her children round her to receive the blessing she had foregone for thirteen years.[12] The comfort of her mother's presence was marred three months later, on 29 January 1639, when Catherine was born and died on the same day.

The family was sitting together one day when Con again expressed his hope of Charles's conversion. Charles burst out laughing: 'My dear friend, I *am* a Catholic!' 'None could wish it more than I', responded Con, while the Queen Mother added, 'One must be an Apostolic Roman Catholic', to which Charles replied, 'You ladies will not understand me but he will: *Est implicanties in adjecto.*' Charles, indeed, used the term 'Catholic' in the sense of all-embracing or universal and meant by the Catholic Church the whole body of practising Christians. In no sense would he agree that a member of the Church of England was a schismatic. 'With your kind permission', he smilingly taunted Con, 'I too belong to the Catholic Church.'

Charles's position was precisely what it had been when he supported the Arminian, Montague, against the House of Commons. He did not believe in Papal supremacy, he would never admit the right of the Pope to interfere with a temporal ruler, but he found that the English Prayer Book had much in common with the mass book (as he had attempted to point out to his wife) and he found many of the tenets of Roman Catholicism thoroughly acceptable. He continued to believe in confession which was, indeed, a favourite topic with him. He would discuss it at dinner and it frequently formed the subject of sermons before him. Confession to him was moral discipline and he himself made use of the confessional. He went so far as to advocate, apparently in all seriousness, that celibacy in the clergy was necessary because a married man would not easily keep the seal of the confessional.[13] Even to the thorny question of indulgences he turned a favourable eye, pointing out that the indulgence was not to condone the sin but to remit the penalty imposed for the sin, and there might be reason for doing this. For the Inquisition itself he could even find a good word: it was useful, he would say, for checking men's tongues and pens. It was in accord with his aesthetic appreciation that he should also welcome the use of images and ritual in his worship. He sent away to Spain for a crucifix and venerated a piece of what purported to be the holy cross found in the Thames. He refused to give it to his wife, but assured her it would be venerated and protected. He objected to an excessive cult of the Virgin, remembering how shocked he was in Spain to see people kneeling to the Madonna while only bowing to the Crucifix. Of fasting he approved – it was customary for his own Parliament to fast after its first meeting and in times of stress – but suggested that the food saved should be given to the poor, a sentiment in line with his general feeling for the under-privileged.

Between the Thirty-nine Articles of Faith of the English Church and the Roman Catholic Creed he could feel little essential difference. This, again, was a subject frequently disputed before him.

Small wonder that Charles felt that union with the Roman Catholic Church was not impossible. But it remained essential that the Pope should give up his claim to depose heretic Princes. 'You must induce the Pope to meet me half-way', he expostulated to Con. The astute envoy was equal to the situation. 'His Holiness will even come to London to receive you into the Catholic Church', he countered. And there, more or less, is how the matter ended. Charles was all along considering nothing more than a union between two Churches. The Papacy was interested in the conversion of Charles and, ultimately, of his whole kingdom. The second attempt to convert Charles to the Roman Catholic faith, like the first, had failed.

Part IV
Conflict

24

The King and the Scots

Charles's coronation in Scotland, though accompanied by a certain amount of outward enthusiasm, had not really endeared him to the Scots while the Church ritual which accompanied his visit and the rumours of a new Prayer Book based upon the English aroused the deepest suspicion. But it was not only on religious matters that he had failed to satisfy his Scottish subjects. Having left Scotland at the age of three, he had not set foot on Scottish soil until thirty years later when his stay was short, even cursory. He had made no attempt to call a Scottish Parliament until 1628, three years after his accession, and this had been repeatedly prorogued until he went to Scotland in 1633. Then, and thereafter, there was little to appease the Scots in this cold, alien king who showed little evidence of his Scottish birth except for his accent – and this, evident enough to English ears, was nothing like the broad dialect of his father and his Scottish subjects.

James had not achieved the union of England and Scotland that he desired, but he had not been altogether unsuccessful in ruling Scotland from England. He was a Scot through and through, he had been King of Scotland for almost as long as he could remember and his reign had been remarkably successful. So, if he governed from a distance, he knew what he was doing, he had many Scots of his own generation and upbringing about him, and, above all, he had his own good sense and homely touch to guide him.

Even so, there were difficulties exacerbated by the constitutional position. The Scottish Parliament consisted of a single House dependent upon the King for its calling which meant, after 1603, that its very existence was dependent upon the summons of a king who normally lived in England. It had, moreover, very little power, initiative normally resting with the Privy Council, which consisted of officeholders and others appointed, as in England, by the King – which meant, again, after 1603, by the King of England. When Charles became King this Privy Council consisted of 47 members, nearly half of whom were officers of state and of whom so few normally attended that it was difficult to form a quorum. Day-to-day government was carried on otherwise by a number of committees. This lack of firm government in Scotland did not appear important to Charles for, without his father's knowledge of Scotland or feel for its people, he determined to keep Scottish affairs in his own hands, relying increasingly, as he liked to do, upon one or two people. But he was without the benefit of the older generation of Scottish advisers and the man most frequently in his counsel was the Duke of Hamilton, whose ability was questioned by his contemporaries and whose ambition was thought to be too high and too much influenced by his dynastic closeness to the royal line. Sounder advice could have saved Charles from several gross errors of judgment.

As a result of numerous royal minorities in Scotland it was recognized that a monarch might, by an Act of Revocation, recall all grants of royal property made during his minority, provided this was done between his 21st and his 25th year. Since Charles was nearly twenty-six when he ascended the throne he had to act quickly and, characteristically, he acted with secrecy. The result was the Act of Revocation of October 1625 which not only took the Scots by surprise but was very sweeping. It revoked all gifts of royal or church land made to subjects in Scotland not, indeed, during his minority, for there had been no such period, nor even during his lifetime, but since 1540. Since the very existence of the Scottish nobility depended upon the vast amount of church lands they had acquired the intention was staggering. Although it was soon apparent that Charles would not proceed to confiscation, continued ownership was made conditional upon the payment of an annual rent so that the whole exercise became a way of instituting an annual land tax. Some land, indeed, was appropriated to the Scottish Church, which Charles considered to be lamentably ill-endowed, and for this he paid compensation from his English revenue. At the same time he instituted a much needed reform of tythe payment, which had often been taken by the landowner rather than the Church, and in many cases was able to substitute a regular money payment for the cumbersome and wasteful payment in kind. But what Charles thought of as reform was a further tightening of the screw on the Scottish nobility. The Act of Revocation and the accompanying decrees meant to them a loss of prestige, a diminution of power, a reduction of income in respect of tythes foregone and annual rents to be paid. It was, said Sir James Balfour, 'the ground stone of all the mischief that followed after'. Charles was raising a hornet's nest in Scotland.

Seemingly oblivious of trouble he aimed a further blow by a decree intended, as he put it, to draw back into his care all the heritable offices of Scotland. This meant that many powerful nobles had to resign prestigious and profitable offices in the localties and receive them back, if at all, by favour instead of hereditary right. At the same time expenditure and taxation were mounting in Scotland. James had revised the Book of Rates so that merchants were liable to higher port duties. His visit in 1617 had to be paid for and it included repairs to several royal buildings that had fallen into disrepair since 1603; one reason for the delay of Charles's coronation in Scotland had been shortage of money to pay for the necessary further repair to royal residences. It was extraordinarily unperceptive, though typical, of Charles to have insisted nevertheless upon building a new Parliament House in Edinburgh before his coronation that would accommodate not only Parliament but the Court of Session and other courts. The building was planned on a steeply sloping site, it entailed the removal of three ministers' houses, and was correspondingly expensive. Then, after the creation of the new Archbishop of Edinburgh, he desired St Giles's church to become a cathedral. The partition walls that had divided the building into three churches were to come down and new churches built for the worshippers so deprived. At the same time Charles planned to increase ministers' stipends by a new assessment on house rentals. All this was a tremendous burden on Scottish people unused to such demands. It was small recompense that Charles made Edinburgh a City and formally designated it the capital of Scotland: its expenditure before 1625 had been under £51,000 a year; ten years later it was nearly £150,000.

Other, more subtle, causes of discontent were less easily perceived. Influence which, in a dozen different ways, might be acquired at Court, was difficult to achieve when the focal point was hundreds of miles away. From patronage and perquisites, from the profitable gossip of backstairs and chamber, the Scottish courtier was estranged, and he was acquainted only at second hand and after the lapse of time with those intangible developments at Court which led to favour here or disgrace there. A sense of estrangement persisted which, together with the very real threats to property, political influence and religious worship, coalesced into open opposition.

In 1636 Charles published a Code of Canons which announced as obligatory the acceptance of the Service Book upon which the Scottish bishops had been working since his Coronation. When they published their work a year later it was seen to be basically the English Prayer Book in spite of a few substitutions such as 'Presbyter' for 'Priest'. It was to be introduced without the approval of either the Scottish Parliament or the Scottish Church Assembly. Instead, it was prefaced by a Proclamation enjoining its use by royal prerogative and it was handsomely bound and embellished with red lettering as well as the customary black type. Charles no doubt thought he was doing honour to the new Prayer Book, but to the Scots the substitution of such finery for their homely and familiar book was further evidence of the worship which Viscount Kenmure had described as 'idolatrous and anti-Christian'.

The new Prayer Book was first used on 23 July 1637 in St Giles's church in Edinburgh. The riot that ensued was probably prearranged, the women who created an uproar in the church, crying 'the mass is come amongst us!', were most likely there by design and could even have been apprentices in women's attire. The one who hurled a stool at the minister's head as he attempted to read from the Book was remarkably strong and rumour had it that if not an apprentice in disguise she had been specially brought in from the streets for the purpose. But part at least of the religious opposition that swept the country was sincere and the Scottish Council itself appeared to be surprised by its strength. Letters and petitions poured into them from all parts and from all kinds of people: 'the like hath not been heard in this kingdom', it was said. Charles's response was typical. 'I mean to be obeyed', he said. The years of personal rule, with his Privy Council a willing instrument and his Court only too ready to follow his lead, had accustomed him to getting his own way and strengthened that determination, or obstinacy as his mother had called it, that he frequently showed when crossed. It was the more evident now since he appreciated the fact that to give way in Scotland would weaken his position in England. He consequently ordered that no magistrate should hold office in Scotland unless he accepted the new Prayer Book.

Such orders had no effect upon what was virtually a united Scotland, and the people prepared to express that unity in a way they knew and had used before – by a covenant one with another. The document was signed by ministers, gentry, and nobility in Grey Friars church in Edinburgh on the two days 28 February and 1 March 1638. On the following day the people of Edinburgh flocked to the churchyard where the long Covenant was laid out on a tombstone for their signatures. They could hardly have read it before they signed but they were told that basically they were covenanting to preserve the true reformed religion against all innovation and that, in the words of the final paragraph, they were promising to 'defend the same and resist all those contrary errors and corruptions' to the utmost of their power.[1]

For Charles it was deep humiliation. Compromise began to mix with obstinacy in the worst of all solutions. He maintained that he had no intention to innovate, he promised to introduce the Prayer Book in a fair and legal manner, but he insisted that the Covenant be withdrawn. Otherwise, as he said to Hamilton, he had no more power than a Doge of Venice. The Scots had no intention of abandoning the Covenant and Charles sent Hamilton to Scotland to negotiate. His frustration and anxiety began to show. If he had thought of war it was war in Europe or at sea for the recovery of the Palatinate, not a war against his Scottish subjects in order to secure religious conformity in his own kingdom. He lost his habitual interest in tennis, even hunting gave him little pleasure, he shortened the summer progress and it was noted that his face was drawn with worry.[2]

On July 1 he at last took his Council into his confidence. The Catholic councillors were for firmness, even to the extent of war; others were hesitant. Northumberland wrote to Wentworth in Ireland that many of the people who were resisting ship money were as likely to support the Scots as the King. Charles sought legal opinion as to whether landowners in the North of England could be asked to arm at their own expense for the defence of the country. He had an affirmative answer and the nobility and gentry were charged with the number of horse they should bring in. He awaited Hamilton's report on the possibility of blockading the Scottish coast and he appointed a Council of Eight to advise him on Scottish affairs. On the advice of Hamilton he authorized the meeting of a Scottish Parliament and a Scottish Church Assembly. In September he offered a 'King's Covenant' in place of the National Covenant. It was turned down. He offered to limit the authority of the Scottish bishops. It was beyond his competence to do so, said the Scots. Instead the Scottish Assembly abolished the Service Book, the Canons and Episcopacy itself, re-establishing full Presbyterianism while ordaining that the Covenant be taken by all Scotsmen.

Ten years of prudent finance had left the King with enough money to fight a Scottish war. Yet did he want to? It seemed he would have little choice. Early in 1639 the Scots chose Alexander Leslie, a soldier who had seen distinguished service in the German wars, as their General. He was 'an old, little, crooked soldier' whose deformity in no way detracted from a personality that could inspire his soldiers with respect and devotion, and an ability that could turn them into an organized fighting force. 'We are busy preaching, praying, drilling' wrote the army chaplain Alexander Baillie, who was as completely under Leslie's spell as any soldier.[3] War appeared inevitable. Charles published a Proclamation in which he said that the very safety of England was at stake. 'The question is not now whether a Service Book is to be received or not, nor whether episcopal government shall be continued or presbyterial admitted, but whether we are their King or not.' Newcastle and Hull were put in a state of defence, Charles instructed the Lords Lieutenant to call out the trained bands, he made special provision for Henrietta-Maria in case of his death, instructed his Privy Council to keep her informed, and started for York. When he entered the city on 30 March 1639 the Covenanting Scots had already taken control of most of the cities in Scotland where any support for him lay: Edinburgh, Dumbarton, Dalkeith, even Aberdeen had been abandoned by his friends.

The nobility of the borders had not been so ready to answer the call to arms as Charles had hoped, but he nevertheless found himself in command of a force of some 18,000 foot and 3000 horse – whose fighting potential, however, appeared less than their numbers would indicate. The trained bands were virtually untrained; the pressed men followed the usual pattern. 'Our men are very raw, our arms of all sorts naught, our victual scarce, and provision for horses worse', wrote Sir Edmund Verney, the Knight Marshall, to his son on May 9.[4] Money was scarce. The ship-money response had been abysmally small in the current year, possibly because of the general uncertainty, and of the £70,000 asked for only some £17,000 had come in. But in any case, Charles would not touch this. Henrietta-Maria had herself raised more from her Catholic friends – a sum of £20,000. In contrast Leslie's army of some 22,000 foot and 500 horse, hardly larger than the

English, had all the advantages of conviction, popular support, and the training which many of them had received in the continental wars.

Henrietta-Maria was unwell and nervous, lonely without the King, frightened at the possibility of battle, deriving little help from the presence of her mother and her French friend, Madame de Chevreuse. Only the previous January, with much pain, she had given birth to the baby girl, Catherine, who had lived but an hour or two. Charles had been all solicitude and her only comfort. Yet, even then, she had had thoughts for one of her favourites, the Earl of Holland, and begged the cavalry for him in the army command her husband was drawing up. Charles may have been surprised, even affronted, possibly aware of the foolishness of the choice, but it was not in his nature to refuse his wife's entreaty at such a time, and he gave Holland the command. It was unwise. Holland was militarily unknown, he had no experience of battle, and his appointment received little support. No less unwise was the appointment of Arundel as Commander-in-Chief. Again, he had no experience of war and had even less stomach than Holland for a fight. But he was Charles's senior Earl and his opposition to the Covenant was unquestioned. Hamilton had been put in command of a small fleet which it was hoped would be strong enough to interrupt Scottish commerce and to cause a diversion.

Charles advanced to Berwick. It was his first experience of war, his first taste of life under canvas.[5] He enjoyed it. He rode from four in the morning till five in the evening at the head of his men, wearing out two horses as he rode from place to place to view their quarters. It was unfortunate that the somewhat amateurish campaign was accompanied by constant friction between the Protestant and Catholic elements in his central administration in Whitehall so that what might have been a healthy stiffening was lacking. On June 3 the Scots were at Kelso on the border; Holland, with 3000 foot and 300 horse, was ordered to drive them back. He found himself opposed by a vastly superior force of possibly as many as 10,000 men and he feared that more were waiting in ambush. Perhaps wisely, though with ignominy, Holland retreated without fighting. Two days later Leslie himself appeared at Dunse, some eleven or twelve miles on the Scottish side of the border and in sight of the English camp. Charles appeared more interested in the strategical possibilities than in the reality. He trained his telescope upon the enemy camp and stood viewing it for a long while. 'Come, let us go to supper', he remarked at last in copybook style, 'the number is not considerable.'[6]

Charles had hoped that Wentworth might be able to send a small force from Ireland to threaten the Scots from the West. The Deputy found this impossible but was ready to pretend such a diversion by massing men at Carrickfergus as though ready for the crossing. He advised Charles to procrastinate for as long as possible while he assembled a larger force. The Scots had their own reasons for attempting negotiation. War, they feared, particularly if it were war fought on English soil, might well raise against them an English force that had more stomach for fighting than the army which now lay so near them. Charles was undoubtedly pleased when peace feelers reached him from Leslie's camp, and on June 6 six Scottish Commissioners and six English were sitting down together in Arundel's tent. Charles himself unexpectedly joined them, apparently enjoying the opportunity of demonstrating his dialectical skill.[7] His wife, still a prey to nervous anxiety and egged on by Chevreuse, was thinking of hurrying to her husband's side to beg him not to expose himself to danger. But the evident lack of resources did more than her presence could have done to speed an agreement with the Scots and on June 18 the Treaty of Berwick was signed by which both sides agreed to disband their armies and Charles to call another Scottish Parliament and another Scottish Church Assembly.

Henrietta's joy was unbounded. But Charles did not immediately return home. Ten days after signing the Treaty he wrote to Wentworth from Berwick saying that he intended to be present at the new Scottish Assembly and Parliament: 'nothing but my Presence at this Time in that Country can save it from irreparable confusion', he wrote.[8] But matters went differently. The Scots were slow in dissolving their Committees. They maintained that Charles had agreed to the abolition of episcopacy, which he resolutely denied. English royalists were attacked in Edinburgh and elsewhere. Charles sent for the Scottish leaders to meet him again at Berwick; only six turned up. Charles lost his temper with the Earl of Rothes, calling him an equivocator and a liar.[9] Rothes retorted that if bishops remained in Scotland the Scots would enlarge their attack to include all bishops, in England and Ireland as well as in Scotland. Hamilton was instructed to act the spy and to gain the confidence of the Scottish Covenanters by any means. When Charles at last reached London, on August 3, he had far less confidence in his own ability to save the Scots than he had had when he wrote to Wentworth.

When the Scottish Assembly opened on August 12, without his

presence, it immediately abolished episcopacy and called upon every Scot to sign the Covenant. The Scottish Parliament, meeting on August 31, confirmed the abolition, remodelled its Committees in order to keep power in its own hands, instituted taxation to cover the cost of the war, took under its own nomination the governorship of the important castles of Edinburgh, Stirling and Dumbarton, and showed without a shadow of doubt its ability to rule in the absence of the King of England. It was prepared, nevertheless, to observe the form of obtaining the King's subsequent approval, and on November 7 the Earls of Loudon and Dunfermline reached London as Commissioners from Scotland directed to this end. Charles and his Council of Eight declined to treat and prorogued the Scottish Parliament until the following June.

Wentworth came to London on 22 September 1639. Charles had called him as early as June in a letter from Berwick desiring his 'Counsel and Attendance'. But, said Charles, do not come openly at my summons but pretend some other occasion of business. Rest assured, he said, that 'come when you will, ye shall be welcome to your assured friend Charles R.' Wentworth had not yet left when Henrietta-Maria's prettily worded request in French for his help and attendance reached him. He did not need a double summons. The utter scorn in which he held the Scots is apparent in every word he wrote: 'such insolency . . . is not to be borne by any rule of monarchy'. 'This is not a war of piety, for Christ's sake, but a war of liberty for their own unbridled, inordinate lusts and ambitions'.[10]

Charles's friendship with Wentworth had developed in a formal way through many letters in which Charles signed himself affectionately. He had refused Wentworth the Earldom for which the Deputy asked at the end of 1634 but in such a way that it implied a promise of future reward. 'I acknowledge that noble minds are always accompanied by lawful ambitions', he wrote, 'and be confident that your services have moved me more than it is possible for any eloquence or importunity to do. So that your letter was not the first proposer of putting marks of favour on you.'[11] But, he said, he would do things in his own time. Wentworth had to wait for five years, but when he arrived in England in the autumn of 1639 his presence was immediately felt and his reward came. He was created Earl of Strafford and promoted from Deputy to Lord Lieutenant of Ireland.

The money saved during ten years of peace had been dissipated on one short, ignominious campaign, and the overriding question was whether enough could be raised to support another army. The ship-money returns from some parts of the country were not discouraging: 'there is no grudging', wrote a correspondent to Cottington from Devon and reports from Hampshire were not dissimilar. But Charles still would not divert ship money from its purpose, though the imposition of a similar tax for the raising of land forces was considered; an excise was also suggested. But Strafford was firm in his advice that there was only one possible course of action – the calling of a Parliament. Charles was strongly and bitterly opposed. Laud and Hamilton sided with Strafford. With his success in Ireland a witness to his authority and ability Strafford's advice could hardly be ignored, and on 5 December 1639 Charles informed his Privy Council of his intention. The writs, summoning Parliament for 13 April 1640, went out in February. Before signing them Charles had obtained the assurance of his Council that if the Commons proved refractory the Lords would support him: as the Venetian Ambassador noted, he appeared to have little faith in the Parliament he was calling. He derived greater pleasure from drawing up the names of his Council of War which included, naturally, the Lord Lieutenant of Ireland.[12]

Strafford showed his appreciation of the honours conferred upon him by heading a list of loans to the King with the princely sum of £20,000, secured upon the Northern recusancy fines which, as Lord President of the North, he collected. Members of the Privy Council and others followed with lesser sums to the total of £300,000 and Charles later asked his lower officials to contribute loans of £2000 apiece. In the spring Strafford was able to announce that the Parliament at Dublin had voted no less than thirteen subsidies to the King, which covered the contributions of the clergy and a backlog of uncollected tax. At the end of 1639 Charles was naming his commanders. Arundel was relieved of his post of Commander-in-Chief with little formality and Northumberland was put in his place with the double command of the navy and the land forces. Nor was Holland given longer shrift. His command of the cavalry went to Lord Conway, the son of James's Secretary of State, who had seen service in Europe. Strafford was named as Lieutenant General under Northumberland.

For the royal family the year 1640 dawned far happier than the previous one. Henrietta-Maria had recovered her health and gaiety. Charles was with her. He played long at cards in the evening, keeping his secretaries waiting as they attended with papers for him to sign.[13] He consented to perform in the new masque by Inigo Jones and Sir William Davenant – the *Salmacida Spolia* – in which he appeared splendidly dressed on a throne of honour surrounded by his courtiers, having rescued his kingdom from Discord. He was rewarded by the Queen and her ladies, dressed as Amazons, who descended from heaven in a cloud. The performance on January 21 was so successful that it was repeated in February.

Early in April there was a most welcome diversion. Charles was one day standing before the fire in one of his drawing rooms at Whitehall, as he loved to do, with his courtiers round him, when the Archbishop of Canterbury entered followed by a nervous young man carrying a large box. It was young Nicholas Ferrar, the nephew of old Nicholas, and he brought with him the promised concordance for the Prince of Wales. The book was of green velvet, richly gilt and edged with gold lace. 'Here is a fine book for Charles indeed!', exclaimed the King, remarking that the Prince would reap a double benefit from its beauty and from the four languages in which it was written. He was even more amazed when young Nicholas presented him with a New Testament in twenty-six languages bound and written in the unmistakeable Little Gidding style. How could he possibly be familiar with so many tongues, the King wanted to know. Nicholas Ferrar was sent next day to deliver his book to the Prince personally. 'What a gallant outside!', exclaimed the young man and, dutifully turning over the leaves, 'Better and better', he remarked. The little Duke of York was not going to be left out. 'Will you not make me also such another fine book?' he asked, insistently demanding how long it would take. The courtiers laughed at the little boy's earnestness and Nicholas Ferrar promised to put the work in hand.

Charles meanwhile was talking with his courtiers about him, his own experience having led him to note the painful efforts of the young man to avoid stammering. 'What a pity it is', he remarked to the Archbishop, 'that the youth hath not his speech altogether so ready as his pen and great understanding is.' Laud remarked that it was that very impediment that had led him to turn to other things and make such a success of learning foreign languages. Holland said that he would do well to carry always some small pebbles in his mouth. 'Nay, nay', said the King, 'I have tried that, but it helps not. I will tell him that the best and surest way is to take good deliberation at first, and not to be too sudden in speech. And let him also learn to sing, that will do well.' Charles arranged to send Nicholas to Oxford at his own charge and promised also to help with books and anything else he required, but the poor young man, who was not robust, sickened and died before he could take advantage of the opportunity.[14]

The apparent contentment of the Court was cemented by the fact that the Queen was once more with child, and she was at her best when pregnant, in spite of the difficult births she had to endure. She and Charles even began to think in terms of marriage for their children. Chevreuse had made the daring proposition, to which Charles listened in all seriousness, that there should be a double wedding with Spain, their eldest son and daughter marrying the eldest daughter and son of the Spanish King. At the same time the Prince of Orange made a more formal proposal in January for the marriage of Elizabeth, their second daughter, to his only son. Either alliance would be profitable in terms of money, but as he pondered his children's usefulness in this respect and joined happily in his wife's diversions, Charles was also garrisoning the border fortresses, arranging an exchange with Holland of one hundred expert veteran soldiers for 200 raw recruits, and preparing for Parliament.

25

The King and the Opposition

With a Court of some culture, with his art collections well-known and respected throughout Europe, with his own understanding of the arts recognized, his own physical prowess manifest, if not so much now in the tourney as in the hunting field, with his growing family evidence that the early rumours of physical inadequacy had been scotched, the shy, physically handicapped little boy had achieved something of the eminence of the Renaissance Prince he had always aspired to be. He had governed for ten years without a Parliament, his country prospered economically, his capital was being beautified, all over the country churches were being repaired, his social policy, he felt, benefited the poor. The only blot upon his achievement so far had been the Palatinate. But now his Scottish subjects threatened his stability and, if it had been in his nature to read the signs, he could have been warned also of a growing, coherent opposition to him from a wider section of his people.

Ten years without a Parliament had not reconciled the opposition that had so nearly toppled Buckingham, and the grievances of those years were not only not forgotten but many of them appeared to be perpetuated in a continuingly inept foreign policy, extravagance and inefficiency at the centre, patronage, spoils of office, and a Court still 'extravagant with superfluity'. More importantly, a dichotomy between Court and Country in which success, power and wealth resided at Court while the country gentleman was left deprived, even if not more marked than it had been in Buckingham's time, was being felt more acutely. At the same time a form of religion that was not generally acceptable was being prescribed with authoritarian certainty by a King and an Archbishop who appeared to have leanings towards the Catholic faith, influenced, so it was thought, by a Catholic Queen. These basic grievances were exacerbated by Charles's methods of raising money in the absence of Parliament and by his social policy which interfered with vested interests.

Opposition to be effective requires a focal point, and in the absence of Parliament some other had to be found. To a large extent it was the Puritan movement itself that provided the focus: it gave unity a belief, of organization, and of location as its members assembled in church or conventicle; of its nature it encouraged a 'seeking after truth' which implied talk, discussion, and a dependence upon the sermon and *extempore* prayer that enlarged the context of worship to embrace a broad area of discontent. Puritan ideas were spread beyond the preacher and the conventicle by the Bible in English, and by printing presses that evaded the censorship, and it had enough 'martyrs' to provide its own hagiography. The independent thinking that Puritanism encouraged embraced other activities, and in his business affairs the Puritan was as likely to oppose interference as in his religion.

The wide social and intellectual spread of the movement was initially one of its strengths. It comprised the poor and lowly, men of high estate, and people from all walks of life; Prynne, Lilburne, John Pym, John Hampden, Oliver Cromwell, Lord Saye and Sele, the Earl of Essex, the Duke of Bedford, were all opposition men on religious grounds alone. The desire for liberty had taken many of them to the New World whence their letters continued to encourage their friends at home and to point out the business opportunities, as well as the liberty of worship, that waited overseas. The increasing importance of colonial affairs, canalizing their religious and their economic interests, providing a focal point in the various committees and chartered companies which were formed, gave the opposition an opportunity.

In December 1630 Charles granted a charter of incorporation to the Governors and Company of Adventurers for the Plantation of the Islands of Providence, Henrietta, and the adjacent Islands. Henry, Earl of Holland was the first Governor of the Company, John Dilke, a merchant, was Deputy Governor, John Pym was Treasurer. Its members included Saye and Sele, Warwick, Robert, Lord Brooke, Richard Knightley, Oliver St John, John Hampden; a month later Sir Thomas Barrington was admitted and in May 1638 John Pym became Deputy Governor. Did it occur to Charles that he was incorporating a close group of Puritans? Did he connect their enterprise with the fact that it was founded less than two months after the dissolution of his third Parliament?

Holland's Court connections partly obscured the fact that he was the brother of that 'curious Puritan' the Earl of Warwick, who combined a great deal of piracy on the high seas with his Puritanism and whose tenants in Essex were likely to follow his lead in any enterprise. Lord Saye and Sele was the largest landowner and a leading Puritan in the county of Oxfordshire, being particularly influential in the Banbury area; he had long since made his position clear in the statement that 'he knew no law besides Parliament to persuade men to give away their own goods'. Lord Brooke was a leading spirit with Lord Saye in the foundation of Saybrook, a Puritan colony on the Connecticut shore of Long Island Sound, which was incorporated in 1632. Their associates included Sir Nathaniel Rich, Henry Darley, Henry Lawrence, Arthur Haselrig, as well as members of the Providence Island Company. Richard Knightley, of Fawsley in Northampton, the son of a prominent Puritan, married John Hampden's eldest daughter. His home, where his father had set up a printing press, was the centre of many meetings. Sir Thomas Barrington was close to the Earl of Warwick, served as his Deputy Lieutenant in Essex, was related to Saye and Sele, and his family connections covered most of the Eastern counties. John Hampden, one of the wealthiest commoners in England, had family connections all over Buckinghamshire and Oxfordshire and as far away as Huntingdon, the home of his kinsman, Oliver Cromwell. Oliver St John was connected by family and marriage to the Cromwell and Barrington families of East Anglia as well as being lawyer to the Earl of Bedford. John Pym also, who had sat in Charles's Parliaments since 1621, was under the patronage of Bedford. Bedford himself – not a member of the Providence Island group – was a man of immense wealth founded on Abbey lands; he was an austere Protestant, he had voted for the Petition of Right in 1628, he had done practical work in draining his lands in the Fens, looking for a sound return on what he regarded as an investment, and had spent lavishly in rebuilding his property at Covent Garden in London with a view to increasing his rents.

Of other opposition peers the most significant name was that of the Earl of Essex. Since the early years of his life, embittered by the humiliation of the Howard-Somerset intrigue, Essex had served in the Palatinate, contracted a second unfortunate marriage, and suffered the death in infancy of his only child. He had thrown in his lot with the peers who had remained outside Court patronage but had nevertheless consented to serve under Buckingham at Cadiz, the mortification of that experience driving him further away from the Court. He was

299

overlooked by Charles for any subsequent appointment of note. His patronage was immense and at least fifteen Members of Charles's earlier Parliaments had owed their election to him. He was not a vindictive man, but he was not a good man to have in opposition; he was a person whom Charles might have cultivated. Charles chose, instead, to pile on further humiliation both for Essex and other peers whom he removed from the JPs' bench in 1629 when they refused to make the loan he demanded.

In its offices in Grays Inn Lane the Providence Island Company had ample opportunity for organization other than that which concerned its trading activities. Here, and at Saye's home at Broughton Castle near Banbury, at Fawsley where it had its printing press, and at other private houses, the opposition met and planned throughout the 1630s. Its common bond, besides religion, was wealth and a determination that its property would not be interfered with. Its members were aristocratic as well as gentry; the Parliament which was their immediate aim would contain a core of opposition Peers as well as a House of Commons which they expected to control.[1]

In other respects Puritanism was developing in a more emotional, more spectacular way. The outdoor preachers continued to gather large crowds, in the conventicles discussion ranged over subjects not necessarily connected with religion, and an organization of protest emerged. It was not quite the same protest as that which was being made by the men who were meeting in Grays Inn Lane or in the seats of the aristocracy. Knighthood fines, the extension of forest bounds, the court of wards, aristocratic privilege, meant very little to the men and women of the conventicles. When they spoke of the King's 'arbitrary government', as they increasingly did, they referred to interference with their worship, the censorship laws, punishment by the 'prerogative' courts of Star Chamber and High Commission. The ship-money tax hit some of them, increased prices through higher port dues and monopolies were felt by most; but on the whole they were using the words 'arbitrary government' to cover a great deal that they did not really understand and which they could not make explicit. It was material which the more coherent opposition might use at first but which would be dangerously independent later on.

It was on Charles's carefully prepared ship-money writs that the opposition had taken its first stand. Its case rested largely on three charges: that Charles intended it to become a regular annual tax; that

300

he was not spending the money raised exclusively on the navy; and that he was levying it without the authority of Parliament. Collections were on the whole going well, the Council was following their progress daily and meeting each Sunday afternoon to hear the reports of Edward Nicholas, who had been assigned to the Committee of the Navy to coordinate the 'King's Great Business'. It came as something of a shock, therefore, that when the second ship-money writs reached Buckinghamshire in August 1635, a ship of 450 tons or the sum of £4500 having been apportioned to the county, there should have been a lengthy list of refusals. Buckinghamshire was a county of wealthy landowners, many of whom had commercial and business interests as well, and there seemed no reason why they should not contribute the small sums asked for. Heading the list of refusals was the name of John Hampden, who refused payment on all his manors in the county but chose to take his stand in denying the 20/- for which he was assessed on his Stoke Mandeville estate; it seemed to have been the intention of those who drew up the list of refusals that Hampden's case should be the one on which they would fight.

Hampden had been elected for Wendover in Charles's first Parliament and had been imprisoned in the Gatehouse for refusing to subscribe to the loan of 1627. He was a close friend of Sir John Eliot and after his death became guardian to his children. He was a founder member of the Providence Island Company. By friendship and marriage he was connected with Lord Saye, who already had done everything possible to hamper the collection of ship money round Banbury. Charles was not particularly perturbed, and it was all the greater shock, therefore, when Henry Danvers, Earl of Danby, an old soldier of Elizabeth's reign, who had long been a familiar figure in the royal household, presented him out of the blue with a letter in December 1636. Danby was visibly embarrassed and acted only from a sense of urgency, but he chose an inopportune time to produce his letter, when Charles was chatting informally to a few friends in his room. As Charles read it, he changed colour, his face hardened, and without saying a word he broke off his conversation, rose, and paced angrily about the room. The gist of Danby's letter was that it was not so much ship money, as the method of raising it, of which people were complaining, and that only by summoning a Parliament could Charles reconcile his subjects to payment. In making his case Danvers spoke in terms of common law and of 'fundamental law'. A month later another term, also to become only too familiar, was heard from the

301

Earl of Warwick, whose tenants in Essex were being particluarly lax in paying ship money. They could not consent, he said, to such a prejudice to the 'liberties of the kingdom'. He spoke to Charles to his face and the King schooled himself to maintain a smiling countenance.[2]

In spite of such ominous rumblings, Charles persisted with Hampden's case but took the precaution of going once more to his judges, and early in 1637 he obtained the ruling that the King was judge as to whether a state of danger existed and how it should be dealt with, and that he was, therefore, justified in imposing a ship-money tax if he thought fit. Such preliminary skirmishing over Hampden's trial began on 6 October 1637 before the Court of Exchequer. Immediately, as the opposition intended, it focused attention. Hampden's counsel were Robert Holborn and Oliver St John, both lawyers of Puritan belief with professional ties with the Duke of Bedford and the Providence Island Company. Their defence was clever in not attempting to deny the King's right to be judge of danger or to initiate defence, but it denied his right to levy any tax which he considered necessary to that defence except through Parliament. The trial lasted until December 18. When the verdicts of the twelve judges were gathered in on 12 June 1638 there were seven for the Crown, three for Hampden, and two for Hampden on technical grounds.[3] The King had won, but at the cost of giving his opponents a platform and a great deal of publicity while raising sharply constitutional questions which concerned the relationship of an anointed King with an elected Parliament. That relationship was about to be tested.

Charles was under fewer illusions than most of his advisers. Parliament was to him 'that Hydra . . . as well canny as malicious'. If he had to have one, let it be short, for Parliaments were 'of the nature of cats, they ever grow cursed with age'. So he had written to Wentworth.[4] Yet now he made some concessions. He withdrew a few monopolies in the autumn of 1639; he released Valentine and Strode from the custody in which they had been held, even if not with the full harshness of the law, throughout his personal rule. But when the Lord Keeper Coventry died on 14 January 1640 Charles replaced him by Finch, the Speaker who had been held in the chair in Charles's last Parliament, the Judge who had announced the extension of forest bounds, who had upheld ship money in several judgments, who had shown particular vindictiveness in the Star Chamber against Puritans.

No more unwise appointment could have been made. He made a further misjudgment in overlooking the Earl of Leicester as successor to the aged Secretary, Sir John Coke. Leicester was connected by marriage to the Northumberland family and, like them, was strongly Protestant although not Puritan. His candidature was supported by Strafford, by Hamilton, and by the Queen, whose friend, Lucy Carlisle, was Northumberland's sister. Yet Charles passed him over, some said because of Laud's influence: 'To think well of the reformed religion', Northumberland wrote to Leicester, 'is enough to make the Archbishop one's enemy.'[5] So Charles missed an opportunity to win support from the moderates and chose instead Sir Henry Vane, a man of less ability, who was conducting a personal vendetta against Strafford, who had nothing very positive to recommend him save a bustling self-assertiveness, but who was Henrietta-Maria's second choice.

The fact that eleven years had elapsed without a Parliament made it no easier to meet one now. Nor did the reason for the summons arouse any confidence that a Parliament would be helpful to the King, for there was likely to be little enthusiasm for a Scottish war among a generation which had accepted Scotland as part of Great Britain: 'For my part . . . I shall be glad to live to do my master service in the wars out of Great Britain; I care not much for fighting in this island', wrote Sir Richard Cave to Roe, and his sentiment was echoed in all ranks of society.[6] Moreover, religion formed a bond between many English and the Scots which was stronger than the bond which bound them to each other. In the borders, where the King would most particularly look for support, Puritanism was strong, as witnessed by the Lilburne family and their connections. In London, which would exert considerable influence on a Parliament sitting at Westminster, the Puritan congregations had for years been working up political opposition as well as religious dissidence.

In the country generally delight was tinged with disbelief that a Parliament was really to be called. No man would believe it, wrote a correspondent to Cottington from Devonshire. Of the King's friends Vane was guarded: there were many difficulties yet great hope that so happy a meeting might be followed by a like conclusion. Nicholas shook his head sadly: 'I think they will be happiest who are not of the House', he wrote to Pennington.[7] In the event, on the rumour that he was a 'rank Papist' he was not returned for Sandwich. As elections got under way a pamphlet was hurriedly issued instructing the procedure

303

in so unaccustomed an assembly as a Parliament.[8] There was considerable competition at the polls and the influence of the Court party was by no means always successful. In Gloucestershire Sir Robert Tracy brought 800 of his tenants to the polls, but 'received not twenty back'. Candidates made personal election speeches in a new way, offering themselves as servants of the electors, dwelling on the power of the electorate, modestly placing themselves in the background as mere instruments of the will of the people.

There were disturbances in Northamptonshire, in Cheshire and at Lewes. In Essex it was said that the Puritan Earl of Warwick was intimidating voters by the threat of calling them to the levy if they opposed him. There were complaints of bribery by the Court party, one of them, for example, offering to give to the poor of Hastings £20 down and £10 a year during life, besides two barrels of powder yearly to the town for exercising its young men, if the burgesses would vote for him. Petitions began to appear, mostly sponsored by opposition candidates and all strangely alike – perhaps because the petitioners were suffering from the same grievances, but there was more than a hint of central organization. Very comprehensive was one that appeared on April 4. 'Of late', said the petitioners,

> we have been unusually and insupportably charged, troubled and grieved in our consciences, persons and estates by innovations in religion, exactions in spiritual courts, molestations of our most Godly and learned ministers, ship-money, monopolies, undue impositions, army-money, wagon-money, horse-money, conduct-money, and enlarging the forest beyond the ancient bounds, and the like; for not yielding to which things, or some of them, divers of us have, been molested, distrained, and imprisoned.

Almost as an afterthought, it seemed, the petitioners asked for annual Parliaments. Mr Nevill of Cressing Temple found it all too much and was for raising the qualification for voting from 40/- to £20 which, he correctly maintained, was the equivalent value of 40/- at the time the Enfranchisement Statute was made. But Sir Thomas Barrington, Sir Harbottle Grimston and the Earl of Warwick, all leading Puritans, were content with things as they stood and remained closeted in Warwick's lodgings as the election results came in.[9] Charles was less content as it became apparent that the electors had, for the most part, chosen not only Puritans but any who had been in opposition to him and that they had emphatically excluded Catholics and all who had served against the Scots. He was disappointed and uneasy. He passionately wanted to return to the life he had enjoyed in the previous decade, yet the Scots were continuing their warlike motions and this Parliament seemed unlikely to give him the means of quieting them unless accompanied by concessions he felt he could not make. As the Venetian Ambassador expressed it, they would not give satisfaction before receiving it. By summoning Parliament had he not given substance to his worst fears and created the vehicle which would give voice and unity to the opposition?

As the 15th approached the newly-elected Members from the shires and boroughs rode in to Westminster from all over the country, many of them bearing in their hands the petitions of the freeholders and citizens they represented and which they themselves had helped to draw up. To many it was their first Parliament, it would be, perhaps, their first sight of the King and possibly the capital. If they were not all rich men, most of them were comfortably off, they took their religion seriously and they valued their worldly goods with a greater intensity, possibly, than their religion would justify. They were summoned to a Parliament for the age-old purpose of providing a king with money. But they knew enough of the Parliaments of the 1620s to understand that what had been an instrument in the hands of the King had now developed an identity of its own.

Parliament was opened about noon on 13 April 1640. The King rode in state from Whitehall to Westminster Abbey for the service of dedication accompanied by his nobles, the principal officers of state and, for the first time, by his son, the Prince of Wales, who was nearly ten years old. In the House of Lords the Prince, in his robes of state, sat on his father's left hand and listened gravely as Charles briefly opened his fourth Parliament: 'There was never a King that had a more great and weighty Cause to call His People together than Myself', he said, and he desired attention for the Lord Keeper.

Finch's speech was long and flowery, full of obligatory classical allusion but too tedious for his hearers. Its substance lay in its request for supply and for a Bill that would grant the King tonnage and poundage retrospectively from the beginning of his reign. Its conclusion, 'let us ever remember that, though the King sometimes lays by the Beams and Rays of Majesty, He never lays by Majesty itself', was inappropriate to the occasion.

Back in their own House the Commons chose John Glanville, a lawyer of Puritan leaning, as their Speaker. Then, business over, they sat and looked at each other, uncertain how to begin on such a momentous task as they had set themselves. They showed little interest in what was to have been Charles's trump card – an apparent appeal from the Scots for French aid, in which the French King was addressed as their sovereign. Far more emotional was the scene as one after another they rose to present their petitions or to speak to the grievances of their constituents, the hard-headed Harbottle Grimston, Member for Colchester, being the first to throw off the nervous tension that hung over the House. The roll-call of grievances that followed was the indictment of Charles's rule – not, indeed, from all his subjects, for there were many he had helped, such as cloth workers, fishermen and peasants, whose voices were not heard and whose hands had not touched the petitions because they were not qualified to vote – but from the men whose constantly expressed concern was for their property and who, in its defence, were gathering the will and seeking the power, though they would not yet have expressed it so, to break the King. They were well prepared by their leaders. They ordered a committee of the whole House to consider religion, of which, significantly, Pym was in charge, and another to consider grievances. They called for records of the proceedings against Eliot, Strode, Selden, Valentine, Holles and others; they ordered all records concerning ship money, including Hampden's case, to be brought before them; they appointed a committee for establishing whether or not there had been a violation of the privileges of Parliament on the last day of the previous session. Nothing had been forgotten in eleven years.

When Pym spoke on April 17 in a two-hour speech, which was long for the House, with little classical allusion and little rhetoric, his new-style oratory found immediate acceptance. 'A good oration!' cried Members as he sat down. He had summed up the grievances which 'lay heavy upon the Commonwealth' under three heads – liberties and privileges of Parliament, innovations in religion, and 'the proprieties of our goods', bluntly announcing that these were the grievances which had disabled them from granting supply, and would still disable them, until they were redressed.

Charles continued to assert that he had no intention, and never had, of depriving them of their property or their freedom. 'God is my witness', he said of ship money, 'I never converted any of it to my own profit, but to the end of preserving my dominion of the seas.' As to their private property: 'I never designed to molest: it is my desire to be a King of a free and rich people; if no Property in Goods, no rich people.' He offered to give up ship money for twelve subsidies. The offer was not unreasonable, though most of his Council, including Strafford, thought he might have asked for fewer subsidies. But Vane, who put the offer to the Commons, bungled the matter 'either as a knave or foole' and 'play'd the King's cards so ill, that there was noe right understanding betweene the King and the House of Commons in that matter', as one Member wrote.

By April 22 Charles was exasperated. On impulse he went to the House of Lords, not troubling to robe himself. It seemed to Giustinian he was about to use force 'to bridle the insolent demands of Parliament and make them do their duty'. But he merely spoke to them once more. They were putting the cart before the horse, he said. There could be no delay over supply; let them but grant this and he would attend to their grievances. The Lords agreed. But the Commons were listening to the report of the committee for grievances and there was no mistaking their drift. In vain Charles urged that delay was as desperate as denial. After a further fortnight of fruitless talking he gave up. To a Privy Council meeting summoned at 6 am on May 5 he announced his intention of dissolution. Strafford still urged patience. Laud, who had been misinformed of the time of the meeting, arrived too late to influence the issue but it is doubtful whether he would have supported his friend. In the end Strafford gave way. When he went to the Lords later that day Charles bitterly expressed the dilemma: 'The fear of doing that which I am to do to-day, made me not long ago to come into this House where I expressed My Fear, and the Remedies which I thought necessary for the eschewing of it', he said. Once more he separated the Lords from the Commons. 'My Lords of the Higher House, did give Me so willing an Ear, and such an Affection . . . if there had been any Means to have given a happy end to this Parliament, it was not your Lordships fault that it was not so.'

As to grievances, he said, certainly there were some, yet 'not so many as the Public Voice would make them'. He assured them that out of Parliament he would be as ready, if not more so, to remedy them as in Parliament. Finally he reminded them that he had said that delay constituted a greater danger than refusal. He would not put the fault for this on the whole House, he said – 'I will not judge so uncharitably; but it hath been some few cunning and some ill-affectioned Men, that have been the Cause of this Misunderstanding.' No King in the world, he concluded, 'shall be more careful to

307

maintain the Propriety of their Goods, the Liberties of their Persons, and True Religion, then I shall be. And now, My Lord Keeper, do as I have commanded you.'[10]

It remains questionable whether Charles, with a little more patience, a little more adroitness in his policy of dividing the Lords from the Commons, might not have won a favourable response from this Parliament. But finesse was never his strong point; which was the greater pity for not only Strafford but several Members of the Commons believed that if Parliament had continued longer it would have complied with the King in some measure. If it had done so, it would have been a shrewd blow at the opposition. But if Charles made a mistake in dismissing this Parliament so soon it arose as much out of his general distrust of Parliaments as out of the immediate situation. He feared the machinations of those he had called 'vipers' in 1629 and now termed 'cunning and ill-affectioned men'. If his fears caused him to make a mistake, it was a costly error. It not only left him without supply but the dismissal supplied fuel to the opposition in giving a credibility to their account of the dismissal of the 1629 Parliament, of which some Members had no first-hand knowledge, and revealing the King as the tyrant they liked to depict. At the same time it left them with a programme and an organization which had been strengthened by the experience gained. They could be sure that, when another Parliament was called, as they were now certain it would be, they would be starting with an advantage they did not have in April 1640.

When Charles published a Declaration of the Causes which moved him to dissolution, he was justifying himself to the world at large as he had done after previous dissolutions and was treating his statement rather like a royal Proclamation. It was more significant that abridgements of Pym's speech in the Commons had been immediately printed and despatched throughout the kingdom where they were 'with great greediness taken by Gentlemen and others'. Members were accustomed to writing letters to their families or their constituents and, apart from the official record of proceedings in the House which was usually fairly perfunctory, speeches had sometimes been printed subsequently in abridged and often garbled form. But never before had the machinery of abridgement, printing and distribution been waiting and ready to serve the propaganda purposes of a party in Parliament. For the first time opposition was conscious and concerted. It was no longer a case of Members rising in their places on impulse. They got to their feet to say what they had planned to say, they held in their hands the petitions they had engineered, and their words were intended for a wider audience than Parliament. Charles only partly understood what was happening. He did not realize the size or the efficiency of the opposition or the extent of their organization. Nor did he realize that over against monarchy there had been raised a rival power – that of the electorate. The feeling of representation was growing – a consciousness of the people behind the Parliament man – the idea of 'trust' in the sense of delegation of authority: 'nor shall we ever discharge the trust of those that sent us hither . . . unless His Majesty be pleased first to restore them to the Property of their Goods and lawful liberties', as Edmund Waller said on April 22. They were unconsciously preparing the way for the greatest of all forms of sovereignty that would stand against the King – sovereignty of the people.

26

The King and Parliament

The Council for Scottish Affairs met in the afternoon of the day on which the Short Parliament was dismissed. Its members were sombre, even gloomy: an English Parliament dissolved, a Scottish Parliament prorogued; the issues of religion, of government, and of the authority of the monarch himself at issue between the two countries; a Scottish army still in being, an English army hardly formed; the Scottish Parliament taxing the Scots, including the minority who supported the King, to pay for their victorious arms; Charles, having emptied his treasury for unsuccessful war, unable to raise by tax or loan anything like sufficient money to provide another army; Scottish soldiers disciplined and willing, English (such as there were) undisciplined and unwilling; a Scottish nation virtually at one behind its army, an English nation deeply disturbed with barely suppressed antagonisms – all the Council could hope for was a defensive war, a holding operation, that might bring in the trained bands of the border shires and hold the Scots back from England. Only Strafford was still undaunted. He spoke rapidly, urgently. Sir Henry Vane, the secretary to the committee, scribbled with difficulty trying to keep up with the flow of words. 'Go vigorously on', Strafford was saying. 'You have an army in Ireland you may employ there (or here) to reduce this (or that) Kingdom . . . Confident as anything under heaven, Scotland shall not hold out five months . . . One summer well employed will do it . . .'[1]

Strafford was supported by Laud and this was the only positive advice Charles received. He himself still believed that it was a question of money and that if he could pay his soldiers he could raise an army that would deal with the Scots. Whether he was temperamentally capable of the stern offensive that Strafford was calling for was another matter. For the time being he had exercised his initiative by keeping Convocation in being, contrary to precedent, after the dismissal of Parliament. It was not for nothing that he had done so, for it voted him an annual subsidy of £20,000 for six years. At the same time it promulgated seventeen new Canons which enjoined the practice of High Church Arminianism in extreme form. It was an unnecessary, though typical, defiance which confirmed the resolution of the Scots, alienated his own people, while only marginally helping his finances. On the contrary, it encouraged resistance to further demands. London citizens refused to lend the £300,000 which Charles asked for and four leading Aldermen were imprisoned; sheriffs and other collectors of taxes, even Lords Lieutenant, were subjected to pressure with little result save the impression that Charles was prepared to resort to force to gain his ends.

Strafford took up again the question of a Spanish marriage for the King's children, promising the Spaniards support against the Dutch when the Scottish was ended. Henrietta-Maria, through the medium of Windebank and the Papal agent, Rossetti, who had succeeded Con at the English Court, applied for aid to the Pope. Charles himself approached France and Spain. Ship money was pressed; coat and conduct money was demanded in spite of repeated warning that it was even more objectionable to the people than ship money. Two of the Northern Parliament men, Sir John Hotham and Henry Bellasys, who had told the Short Parliament that their constituents would rather pay three subsidies than ship money, and that coat and conduct money was more objectionable than either, were questioned after the dissolution and imprisoned for failing to remember what they had said. Their statements provided evidence that Charles might, indeed, have obtained subsidies in exchange for ship money if the affair had been well handled.

At St George's Fields in London a great meeting named Strafford, Hamilton and Laud as enemies of the Commonwealth and six days after the dissolution a crowd of some 2000 people proceeded by night to Lambeth Palace, beating drums, brandishing weapons, and crying for the death of William the Fox. Laud had fled across the river to Whitehall leaving his Palace well defended. Thomas Bensted, who was wounded in the affray, was betrayed by his surgeon and was hanged, drawn and quartered on June 2. Posters appeared urging people to preserve their ancient liberty and eject the bishops; they threatened the Queen's mother and the Queen's priests. Another advertised the King's palace as To Let. On a window in Whitehall

311

someone scratched the words: 'God save the King, confound the Queen and her children, and give us the Palsgrave to reign in this kingdom.' Charles shattered the pane with his hand and a strong guard was called out to protect the Queen and the children. When rioters broke open the prisons Charles summoned the trained bands from the home counties to protect the capital. He also made concessions and Bellasys, Hotham, and the four City Aldermen were released on the 15th, the day after the attack on the prisons.

But disturbances in various parts of the country continued as pressed men refused to move outside their counties. There was news of soldiers tearing up altar rails for bonfires and throwing down images, of murdering Roman Catholic officers and committing such atrocities that commissions for holding courts martial were hurriedly issued. When Sir Jacob Astley wrote to Conway on July 18 and ended his letter with 'God help us!' he was thinking, not of the Scots, but of his own men. Rumours that Charles was thinking of bringing in Danish cavalry to quell the disturbances increased the tension, the courts martial were questioned as being without authority in the absence of Parliament, while a petition from Yorkshire complaining of the violence of the soldiery asserted at the same time that billeting was contrary to the Petition of Right. Worst of all were the words reported from Scotland that a king who sold his country to a stranger, who deserted it for a foreign land, or who attacked it with an invading force, might lawfully be deposed.

The usual rumours meanwhile circulated: that the King and Queen went to mass together, that the King loved a Papist better than a Puritan; that he would say in defence 'my wife is a Papist, shall I not love them?' A new story was told at the Three Cranes Wharf in Thames Street concerning the Prince of Wales who was said to have been troubled at night with dreams and seen during the day weeping bitterly. When his father asked him what ailed him he, after some persuasion, replied: 'My grandfather left you with four kingdoms and I am afraid your Majesty will leave me never a one!'

With the Pope predictably offering help only if Charles became a Catholic, with the City still refusing a loan, and the taxes promised by the Irish Parliament bringing in much less than was expected, Charles gave orders for debasing the coinage, but was compelled to rescind the command in face of reasoned argument from his friends and outcry from his opponents. In July, as a last resort, he seized a considerable portion of the silver bullion which was lying in the Tower ready to be minted, promising the merchants and the Spanish government, to whom much of it belonged, an interest rate of eight per cent. This did little to ease the considerable shock or silence the loud outcry that followed. 'Great heart-burning this hath made in the City', wrote a Court correspondent on July 10. 'It is thought this will overthrow the Mint, mar all trading, undo the best customers, and so turn at length to His Majesty's extreme prejudice'.[2] The atmosphere was such that it was even rumoured that Charles had taken £60,000 of the money contributed to the repair of St Paul's.

On July 12 Charles joined Henrietta-Maria at Oatlands. Most of his ministers attended him and there was no cessation of public business when she gave birth, with comparative ease, to another son, Henry – 'of Oatlands', as he came to be known. The Queen was never better nor so well of any of her children, it was reported. The child was christened there on July 21, his brothers and elder sister holding him at the font. His grandmother would not attend because of the difference in religion and the time was not opportune for any kind of public ceremony.

Strafford continued to insist upon resistance to the Scots and the suppression of any opposition. The Scots published an appeal to the English nation, negotiations with Spain for financial assistance began to wear thin and even Strafford could not raise money from Puritans who were so united in resistance that in the county of Buckinghamshire of £2600 demanded in coat and conduct money only £8 came in; nor, in the time available, could he produce soldiers where there were none, or turn what could be scraped together from the trained bands and the pressed men into a fighting force. Moreover, Strafford was a sick man, wracked with the pain of gout, weakened with dysentery. But such was his iron will and strength of purpose that his very presence shored up Charles's resolution. The King ordered the Lords Lieutenant of the Midland and Northern counties to call out the trained bands for military service; he directed all persons holding land by knight service to follow him to the field or commute by payment; he made the greatest efforts to keep the Yorshire gentry firm and the northern army mobilized; he commanded the instant collection of all outstanding taxes; and when Northumberland became ill he named Strafford to the supreme land command while Northumberland kept the fleet.

When the Scots, demanding an extension of the Covenant to England and justice on Laud and Strafford, prepared to cross the

Tweed, Charles accepted the inevitable. He left London for York, on August 20, the day the Scots crossed the border at Coldstream and entered England, 25,000 strong. Strafford was full of admiration for Charles; 'in my life', he wrote, 'I have not seen a man begin with more life and courage.' There was less enthusiasm among other members of Charles's Council. The Scots, Windebank had written to Conway, 'understand too well our slowness and defects, and what a powerful party they are likely to find here that will rather join with them than oppose them'. Charles left Cottington in London as Constable of the Tower, a position from which he would be able to protect the Queen and her children, and three days after leaving London he was again at York. The previous day Cottington had secured him some £60,000 from the East India Company by an elaborate deal in which he appropriated and sold cheaply a large cargo of pepper and spices on promise to repay the Company later with interest. This was useful but could not prevent the Scots fording the Tyne at Newburn on the 28th with little effective resistance. The English cavalry broke, rallied briefly, and then gave up. In the little burst of resistance Endymion Porter's second son, Charles, aged eighteen, was killed.[3] The Scots pressed straight on to Newcastle, which they entered on August 30. They were well-disciplined and well-mannered and at first provisioned themselves or paid for all they took.

With Scots on English soil and Charles powerless at York, a group of Peers, which included six members of the opposition, prepared a petition which reached the King on August 28. It enumerated once more the country's grievances, asked for a Parliament and, ominously, demanded the punishment of the King's advisers. Charles, as he had done before when Buckingham was alive, expressed his defiance of fate and his confidence in his chief minister by summoning a special chapter of the Garter to York, and on September 13 he invested Strafford with the blue ribbon of his most exalted honour.

But there were reports of a London petition similar to that of the peers, signed by four Aldermen and with 10,000 further signatures; there was news of more rioting in the capital directed particularly against the High Commission and the Star Chamber, in which St Paul's itself was raided in an attempt to locate the records of those courts. Charles had to make some decision. He agreed to the summoning of a Great Council of Peers at York such, it was said, as had been used in the past and could be used again to authorize the raising of money. But when it met on September 24 there was little time. His army was disintegrating as men slipped away, Cottington's pepper money was mostly spent, and there was nothing to tide him over while he waited for more. So, once more Charles yielded and, for the second time in twelve months, set the machinery in motion for the meeting of an English Parliament. The date was to be November 3, which gave just less than the forty days enjoined by law between the writs and the poll.

Charles's old enemy, Bristol, was the leading spirit and spokesman of the Peers. But there was no mistaking his loyalty nor his integrity as he led the negotiations with the Scots which ended with the Treaty of Ripon on October 14. By this treaty the Scots were to remain on English soil and would receive £850 a day for their keep while they awaited the meeting of the English Parliament with which, it was implied, the final agreement would be made. This in itself was humiliating for Charles. Again, he might have done better with a little more patience at this point and if he had played his cards differently. It was ironic, for example, that, with the Scots becoming an increasing menace as they began to live off the country, the spirit of the border was reviving in the English who now showed more enthusiasm for fighting than they had done before; Charles might have re-organized his army and rallied support even at this late stage. He might also have kept back a little longer his strongest card, the calling of a Parliament, and refused to use it while the Scots were in England. He not only failed to do so but played directly into the hands of the Scots by allowing their Commissioners to come to London to conclude the treaty there, so giving them and the opposition the benefit of mutual support.

The writs for the new Parliament were slow in going out so there was even less time than expected for campaigning. There was nevertheless more excitement than for the previous Parliament. There was much competition – a 'great shuffling for burgesses for the Parliament', as John Nicholas put it to his son, the Secretary. Both sides did their best to secure support. On September 17 and again on October 1 Vane wrote to Windebank on the King's instructions that, in order 'to sweeten' proceedings in the election he should release all prisoners committed for matters that might cause dissidence, such as coat and conduct money, and he named certain people whom the King would like to be provided with safe seats, including some judges, law officers, and officials of the Council of the Marches.[4] Royal patronage was exercised to the full in the Queen's dower lands, the Prince's Duchy of Cornwall, the Cinque Ports (where Charles's cousin, Lennox, was Warden) and the Crown lands generally. Ministers and courtiers were more than ordinarily careful of the constituencies in their patronage and contacts were pursued personally or by letter. The opposition was no less mindful of its influence. The Herbert and Pembroke families in Wiltshire, Saye and Sele in Oxfordshire, Bedford in East Anglia and Devon, pressed patronage and family loyalty in their own interests; pocket boroughs were generally controlled by the opposition. Four of Strafford's friends were unsuccessful in the city and county of York, including Sir Edward Osborne, Vice-President of the Council of the North, and Sir Thomas Witherington, the Recorder of York. King's Lynn refused Arundel's nomination and Cottington's attempts to control the counties of which he was Lord Lieutenant were no more successful. Edward Nicholas, one of the clerks to the Council, was not returned, probably because of suspected Catholic affinities; nor was Windebank's nephew, in spite of his uncle's influence. On the whole the King's party did badly.

The opposition did better not only through patronage but because its plans were more carefully laid. Hampden had even before the Short Parliament ridden to Scotland to contact the Covenanters and did so again; with Pym he rode round England conferring at the 'Puritanical' houses in England, particularly at Fawsley and at Broughton Castle. Sir John Clotworthy, an Irish Presbyterian landowner who had frequently opposed Strafford was offered the choice of two safe seats under the patronage of the Earl of Warwick. In general, the opposition found it easy to win support and any who had opposed the government during the personal rule or in the Short Parliament were returned. Once it had assembled, the majority party found it easy to rid itself of yet more of its opponents by the customary scrutiny of election returns and the rejection of members who were held to have adopted unfair tactics. The committee of Privileges who decided such matters was dominated by Pym and all the members disqualified were Royalists or likely Royalists.

As he awaited the meeting of Parliament Charles was worried and irresolute but still buoyed up with the hope that all would turn out well. He was nevertheless considerably dashed by a personal defeat at the very outset. He had intended Sir Thomas Gardiner, the Recorder of London, to be the Speaker of the new House of Commons. London had rarely rejected its Recorder, yet in this election not one of its four places had been found for him. Efforts to find him another seat were frustrated, often by doubtful means, and on the morning of the 3rd Charles was informed that Gardiner was not in the House. He postponed the opening from morning till afternoon while he considered alternative names and his choice fell upon William Lenthall, a bencher of Lincoln's Inn of no outstanding talents, who was with difficulty persuaded to accept the office. It was understandable that Charles made less of the opening ceremonial than usual, going by barge to Parliament stairs and so to the Abbey as though to open an adjourned or prorogued Parliament. He nevertheless took his son with him to sit on his left hand as he formally opened proceedings.

He probably knew already that there were 493 Members in the new House of Commons, of whom over sixty per cent had sat in the previous Parliament and forty per cent in earlier Parliaments of his reign. It was a young House. About a third of the newcomers were under thirty years old and among them were 23 mere striplings, not yet of age. But on the whole it was a not inexperienced House and the majority had held office of some kind in their counties if not in some central department. There were 79 lawyers among them, 55 were associated with trade or commerce; 49 were central or local officials; there were a physician and a naval officer and nine professional soldiers, 13 agents or secretaries of various kinds and three members who were associated with the Church. About three-fifths of them had been to Oxford or Cambridge Universities – a rather higher number to Cambridge than to Oxford – and sixty per cent had attended one of the Inns of Court. Most of them, whatever their occupation or social background, held land, even if they were not big landowners. The majority were wealthy, all were comfortably off. Trade and commerce, industry and finance, the professions and landowning interlocked in a bewildering but unmistakable manner through family and business association. Even the lawyers, though not as a class so wealthy as the big landowners or men of commerce, had their interests outside their profession, as well as ties of marriage and family, which frequently lifted them into the ranks of the wealthy. Speaker Lenthall, for example, was a man of quite considerable wealth. In total it was a House of greater wealth than the House of Lords. A newswriter in 1628 had reckoned that the Commons could buy out the Lords three times over; and if there was any difference in wealth by 1640 it was on the side of the Commons.

The Members whom Charles would regard as most dangerous

317

were in the middle age group, between about forty and sixty years old. Here were Pym and Haselrig, Hampden and Barrington, Denzil Holles, Valentine and Strode, the merchant Rolle and his brother; Alderman Soame, the rebellious citizen of London; the East Anglian squire, Oliver Cromwell. Charles had sufficient knowledge of the family connections of his subjects to be aware of the manifold ties of birth and marriage that bound these people together and that also connected them with the House of Lords. Even more grounds for apprehension lay in the considerable number of them who themselves, or whose friends or family connections, had resisted the King's demand for loans, opposed ship money or coat and conduct money, resisted royal authority as clothiers, enclosing landlords or encroachers upon the forests, and been fined, imprisoned, or penalized in one way or another by the King's Prerogative courts. Hampden was still the hero of the ship-money opposition, Strode and Valentine were remembered for their long imprisonment, Holles for his role in the last hours of the 1629 Parliament; many more were equally the heroes of resistance in their own counties: there were few in this group who had not in some way contributed to the political and economic opposition to the King.

It was also clear, as Charles scrutinized the list of Parliament men, that few of them would support the religious system that he and Laud had laboured so hard to build up. The Puritan Members from East Anglia, many of them nurtured in the Puritan colleges of Cambridge University and typified by Oliver Cromwell, one of the Members for Cambridge; the Puritan Members for Buckinghamshire and Oxfordshire, typified by Hampden and bound together by family ties, would offer no compromise on religious issues. He might have afforded a wry smile as he considered the influence upon these men of John Preston, who had once been his chaplain.

Geographically the only areas of the country favourable to him, judging by their returns, were Wales, Rutland and Somerset, Westmoreland and Cumberland. Cornwall, Hereford and Shropshire, Lancashire and Yorkshire, appeared to be evenly divided. He was bound to notice that the richest and most populous part of the country, with the exception of Somerset, had declared against him. The only comfort Charles could take was from the presence of 22 courtiers and five Privy Counsellors in the House – Jermyn, Roe (appointed to the Council at last in the summer), Sir William Uvedale (recently appointed as secretary to the army), Vane and Windebank – and of

good old Benjamin Rudyerd who had so valiantly spoken for supply
in previous Parliaments. If he totted up the numbers he would have
found something like 182 Members of the Commons likely to support
him; 354 for the opposition; and about eleven uncommitted. It was
difficult to estimate the coherence of either grouping or to judge how
easily individuals could be swayed from one side to the other.

There were 124 peers in Charles's House of Lords in 1640 against
only 59 when his father ascended the English throne; they could
probably boast fewer representatives of ancient lineage than the
Commons, though family connections ran strongly between the two
Houses and it was not always easy to draw the line. Nor was it easy to
estimate their allegiance. Bedford, Warwick, Brooke, Saye and Sele,
Fiennes were all closely linked to the opposition in the House of
Commons. Yet behind this energetic and vocal fringe lay the 24
bishops and two Archbishops and a phalanx of uncommitted lordship
where Charles's chief hope lay.

Observers were on the whole not hopeful. The Venetian Ambassador reported to his Doge and Senate that there was great fear that
reforms and changes of great moment would ensue, not without a
very considerable diminution in His Majesty's authority. 'And now',
remarked an English commentator, 'the Kinge was in the trap or snare
which he had so longe laboured to avoide'.

Charles had subjected himself to considerable soul-searching
while the elections were pending, and the election results themselves
could but reinforce the conclusion that something had been wrong
with his personal government. He could not, indeed, take the responsibility upon himself, but admitted the 'odium and offences which
some men's rigour in Church and State' had contracted upon his
government. 'I resolved', he afterwards wrote, 'to have such offences
expiated by such laws and regulations for the future as might not only
rectify what was amiss in practice, but supply what was defective in
the constitution.' He would approach Parliament with a determination to reform – even to lessen the area and the application of his
prerogative – if only Members would meet him with 'modest and
sober sense'. Unfortunately his opening speech hardly bore out his
intentions and the Venetian Ambassador was of the opinion that he
did not really want a Parliament.

He was, as usual, short and to the point. He had called his previous
Parliament because of the knowledge he had of the design of his
Scottish subjects: 'had I been believed, I sincerely think that things had

not fallen out as now we see'. It was not a gibe, merely a statement of fact as Charles saw it. He proceeded to name the two areas where action was needed: 'the chasing out of the rebels' and 'satisfying your just grievances'. The first must be done as quickly as possible, but not at the expense of the English armies who also needed pay. 'I leave it to your consideration', he said, 'what dishonour and mischief it might be if, for want of money, my army be disbanded before the rebels be put out of this kingdom.' He had shown tact and good sense in himself coupling grievances with supply, before Parliament could itself bring them together, but to speak of the Scots as 'rebels' and of chasing them out of the kingdom was hardly tactful before an Assembly which had considerable sympathy with Scotland. Nevertheless, the points he made were valid; it was necessary to raise money in order to pay the Scots according to the Treaty of Ripon and to pay the English armies before they were disbanded, all previous loans and donations having been spent. He did not tell them that while the election was proceeding he had offered to sell himself to his shirt as security for a further city loan but had been turned down.

'One thing more I desire of you', he said, 'as one of the greatest means to make this a happy parliament, that you, on your parts, as I, on mine, lay aside all suspicions one of another . . . it shall not be my fault', he concluded, 'if this be not a happy and good Parliament.' But the Members were not prepared to take the King at his word and the speech of Lord Keeper Finch, which was again long, fulsome and tiresome, did not help. Moreover, the reference to the Scots as 'rebels' so rankled that Charles came again to Parliament to apologise for his words in a speech which, in contrast to his opening words, struck the Venetian Ambassador as so effusive and showing so much submission, that his words came ill from the mouth of a great Prince.

If he was being realistic the most that Charles could hope for from this Parliament was a sufficient number of subsidies to enable him to pay the Scots and get them off his back. The Commons, however, had come together with far wider plans in mind. In the interval between the two Parliaments the opposition had consolidated; they accepted the need to pay the Scots and, indeed, the prospect gave them a certain amount of pleasure. But, in the leadership at least, there was the further resolve to sweep away what they termed the 'arbitrary' rule of the previous twelve years and replace it by the framework of 'constitutional' government. The terms they used to justify their intent were ill-defined but the substance was clear: most of the means by which the

King had raised money in the absence of Parliament were illegal and must be stopped; the courts which were his instrument must be curbed; and Parliament must be given a clearly defined existence of its own, independent of the will of the monarch. Religious requirements were less clear-cut, but there was a general feeling in favour of a Protestant religion free from excessive ritual and image worship that could be related to the English Church of the Reformation. A petition received from Londoners to extirpate bishops 'root and branch' was received coolly on December 11 and laid aside. There was no anti-monarchical feeling in their sentiments and Parliament clung closely to the belief that the King could do no wrong; aberrations were the fault of his evil counsellors. The belief was founded upon centuries of theory and, even if they had considered questioning it, it would have taken men stronger than they felt themselves to be at present to do so. But the fiction, if such it were, served them well for it would enable them to get rid of the man they most feared – the Earl of Strafford, the strongest and most influential of the King's advisers.[5]

27

The King and Strafford

Preliminaries over, Parliament turned to establish its normal procedural machinery and Friday 6 November, 1640, was spent in appointing committees for religion, grievances, trade, privileges. On the following day the petitions began to be read and Member after Member rose to enumerate with compelling eloquence the evils to which his constituents had been subjected – monopolies and taxation, innovations in religion, religious persecution, arbitrary courts, ship money, coat and conduct money, fine, imprisonment. Some of the speakers fumbled towards the cause – 'arbitrary government', 'evil counsellors', 'intermission of Parliaments'; or towards the remedy, mostly expressed in terms of Parliament, for Parliament was 'the great physician of the Commonwealth', as Sir Francis Seymour put it. Even Benjamin Rudyerd gave Charles no comfort, for he spoke against the Declaration of Sports. Many of the speeches were immediately printed and distributed round the country; for the statement of grievances, as well as being an indication of the Members' reforming intent, was now an established propaganda exercise and a method of justifying themselves to their constituents. On November 8 motions for the release of Prynne, Bastwick, Burton and Leighton were approved; on the 9th Cromwell spoke similarly for John Lilburne, thus beginning a love–hate relationship between them which would last for well over a decade. On the same day monopolists were excluded from the House and twelve more Court votes were conveniently lost. There was a fire running through the House of Commons which was being fed by the ardour of the Members themselves. Pym knew well enough that the flame would in time burn less brightly and that he must act quickly. Charles also perceived that he was facing a situation different in intensity from anything he had known before. Both men turned to Strafford.

Strafford, as Commander-in-Chief, had remained with the army in the North, and both he and Charles were aware that there was danger for him at Westminster. Nevertheless Charles sent for him. Possibly they planned some joint action, like the impeachment of the opposition leaders. More likely it was simply Charles's need for someone stronger than himself to lean upon. He assured Strafford that he need fear for neither life nor fortune. Strafford needed no such assurance and he did not hesitate: he was too 'great hearted', as Hamilton put it after he had warned Strafford of the danger he was running into.

For Pym had moved as quickly as Charles. He knew both that speed was the essence of the situation and that the opposition must plan more carefully than it had done with Buckingham, who had slipped through the net. A preliminary meeting of the opposition leaders had named Strafford, Laud, Finch, and Cottington as the 'evil counsellors' to be impeached and when Pym moved in the House of Commons for a committee to consider Irish affairs, with an invitation to the Irish to bring their grievances before it, Strafford's friends knew that he was to be the first target. He reached London on November 10, less than a week after the opening of Parliament, and fully aware of the situation. His prompt arrival indicated that no time could be lost and two days later, before a detailed charge could be drawn up, Pym charged Strafford with High Treason before the House of Commons. In vain the judicial Falkland urged that they should examine evidence and digest the charges made before converting them into treason. The opposition made much of alleged troop movements round the Tower with the suggestion that Strafford intended to subdue the City, Pym raised the bogey of a Catholic plot and Clotworthy 'revealed' the intended use of the Irish army against England. Tension was heightened by Pym calling for doors to be locked, and in a conspiratorial atmosphere, tense, as yet unused to their position, capable of being led, the Commons listened to the charge of High Treason against the Earl of Strafford. There was no one critical, detached or fearless enough to support Falkland. The committee appointed to draw up the charge was ready to go to the Lords that same evening, evidence enough of the deliberate plan and the detailed preliminary work that had preceded the opening of Parliament.

Strafford was with Charles and other friends at Whitehall when a sympathetic peer came hurrying over from Westminster with the news. Strafford's instinct was to be in his place in the Lords when the charge was brought against him. But he was too late. Pym had already made the short journey from the Commons House to the Lords and as Strafford made to take his seat he was met with cries of 'Withdraw!, Withdraw!' and was compelled to wait outside the Chamber while the Peers considered their attitude to the charge which Pym had brought against him in the name of the Commons of England. When, after about ten minutes, Strafford was called in he was made to kneel while the brief, formal charge of treason was read. He was forbidden to speak, deprived of his sword, and taken away in custody. Outside the House the crowd that grew as rumour spread had no more sympathy than his colleagues within: so Strafford learned how bitterly he had alienated both his peers and the populace.

In contrast the following days were filled with rejoicing as the Puritan martyrs were released. Lilburne, being imprisoned in London, was the first to be welcomed; Prynne and Burton reached the capital from their remote prisons on November 28, Bastwick on December 4. A hundred coaches, 2000 horsemen and a great crowd on foot wearing twigs of bay and rosemary in their hats as signs of triumph and remembrance, escorted them. It was not until the middle of November that Parliament approached the City for a loan and were promised £21,000 while Members pledged themselves to bring the sum up to £90,000 so that interim payment could be made to the Scots. On December 7 ship money was declared illegal by the Commons, and only then, with this tax out of the way, did they consider subsidies. On December 10 two, on the 23rd two more, were voted. This was satisfactory except that Parliament gave no indication that the King would control any of the money. He received a further snub in November when Parliament appointed Commissioners to meet the Scottish delegation at Westminster. Charles assumed he would be present, as he had been at Berwick, and perhaps looked forward to demonstrating once more his dialectical skill. But it was the last thing that either side wanted, and Charles was firmly repulsed.

Though it laid aside the Root and Branch petition received on December 11, Parliament was occupying itself with excluding Catholics from positions of influence, and instructions were sent to the Northern armies to eject Catholic officers. It was established that few priests and Jesuits had felt the weight of the recusancy laws during the personal rule and that their immunity had generally been authorized by Windebank. The Commons were far too excited to ask, perhaps they did not want to know, on whose authority Windebank had acted, but the Secretary had his own reasons for alarm, for it was he who had acted for Henrietta-Maria in forwarding a request for Papal aid. Windebank took no chances and, with Charles's permission, he fled the country on December 10, the first of the King's supporters to do so. Did he know that even as he was fleeing from the results of his indiscretion the Queen was preparing to appeal again to Rome for aid?

On the day of Windebank's flight Charles announced to his Privy Council that his second daughter would marry Prince William of Orange. It had been natural to consider their eldest daughter as a future Queen of Spain: whatever past relations had been, or however much Spain's position in the world had declined, it was still a high-ranking position. But those negotiations had fallen through and they were now seeking an alliance where money lay. Europe was well aware of their desperate position and when the Prince of Orange again offered his son in marriage, with considerable financial backing and a suggestion of mediation between Charles and his Parliament, or even of troops to help the English King, he stepped up his demand to take the elder, rather than the second daughter. Charles and Henrietta-Maria, though it was not a match they had envisaged in their happier days, had no alternative but to agree. Mary was nine, her intended bridegroom was nearly fifteen years old and was a bright and attractive boy. Like the marriage of Charles's sister to the Palatine, it was not a marriage of great prestige, but Mary would go to a comfortable and wealthy Court and her future husband had in person, and so far as was known in character, a great deal to commend him.

Eight days after the wedding announcement it was the turn of Laud, twin pillar with Strafford of all that the Commons detested. Laud was impeached of High Treason on December 18, sequestered from his place in the House of Lords and committed to custody. Harbottle Grimston had pronounced him to be 'the root and ground of all our miseries'. But the specific charges would have to wait. Now they turned on Lord Keeper Finch and his impeachment followed inevitably. Finch made a strong and not ignoble speech in his own defence but the virtually unanimous vote of the Commons to proceed with the charge was a foregone conclusion. Two days later, on December 21, Finch, again with Charles's permission, fled to The Hague in a ship belonging to the royal navy.

Two of the King's 'evil counsellors' had slipped away within six weeks of the meeting of Parliament, two more were confined and the charge against one of them was being prepared as hurriedly as the lawyers would permit. Meanwhile it was essential to keep control of Parliament. Charles might dissolve it as he had done before, helped by the money already voted and by the prospective dowry of his daughter. But Pym was too quick for him. A Bill for triennial Parliaments laid down that the monarch was obliged to call a new Parliament within three months of ending the old. The Bill passed the Commons on January 20, the Lords on 5 February 1641. While Charles was considering how to avoid parting with so large a part of his prerogative, Strafford's trial was proceeding.

He was brought before the House of Lords to hear the details of the charge against him on January 30 – gaunt and ill after two months' confinement in the Tower. He had misappropriated the revenue, encouraged Papists, fomented war with Scotland, subverted the government of Ireland, acted with tyrannical despotism as President of the Council of the North, betrayed the army, broken the Short Parliament, prevented the calling of another, and finally agreed to its meeting only in order to discredit it. His vehemence against London Aldermen who had refused to lend the King money was not forgotten, he was accused of advising the King to seize the bullion in the Tower and to debase the coinage. Finally – and this was estimated to be the most telling charge against him – he was accused of offering to bring over the Irish army to subdue the kingdom of England. The charge was an undigested mixture of the general and the specific.

While Strafford was preparing his defence, Charles was considering the Triennial Bill. He had declared he would never part with so large a part of his prerogative as the Bill implied but when it came before him on February 15 he found that the old subterfuge had been employed and it was coupled with a subsidy bill. There were rumours of Parliament ceasing all business until it was passed and, between threats and inducement, Charles gave way on the 16th. He was, he said, 'yielding up one of the fairest flowers of his garland' by abandoning his right to call Parliament when he wished, but since he had, in any case, determined to govern in future through Parliament, it made little difference. Three days later Charles made what appeared to be a half-hearted attempt to gain support from the House of Lords by appointing as Privy Counsellors seven of their Members who had been opposing him – Bristol, Bedford, Essex, Hertford, Saye, Mandeville, and Saville. He may have read the situation correctly in assuming that their opposition arose partly from their exclusion from office, but it was a little naive to offer such a sop at this late stage to men of such calibre.

Eight days after Charles had given way on the Triennial Bill Strafford was at the bar of the House of Lords to answer to the charges against him. He had had only three weeks in which to prepare his preliminary answer but appeared to be cheerful and composed. He and Charles reached the Lords at about the same time and Charles called Strafford to him in an inner room. For about an hour they spoke privately while the House waited. When Charles took his seat upon the throne and Strafford was brought to the bar the King publicly greeted his minister across the floor of the House with an affectionate gesture and a smile. In a long answer which took three hours to read and covered over 200 sheets of paper Strafford rebutted all the charges against him. The next stage was the open trial which was fixed for March 22.

While Strafford worked upon his detailed defence Pym and his friends, with a grim determination that no part of their quarry should escape, adopted in practice, though they would not have expressed it in so many words, the concept that the end justifies the means. Public feeling against Laud was not allowed to sleep and on the day on which Strafford was making his defence in the Lords the impeachment charge was made in the Commons against Laud. It was voted unanimously that the Archbishop was guilty of treason in attempting to alter religion and the fundamental laws of the realm. Without an opportunity of making a defence he was committed to the Tower on March 1, angry crowds attempting to drag him from his carriage as he passed by under the protection of the guard. Meanwhile, with a total disregard of the principle of justice or fair play, and without consulting the Lords, the House of Commons caused to be printed and published the articles of the charges against Strafford. To the people who read them the printed words were the truth, and Strafford was condemned by an angry populace before one word had been spoken at the actual trial. He came to Westminster Hall on 22 March 1641 guarded by soldiers. The royal family sat in a screened box where they might see without being seen, but Charles tore down the lattice. Henrietta-Maria stayed for only a couple of hours, but Charles stayed throughout with the Prince who occasionally came forward to take his seat by the throne, which remained unoccupied.

Pym brought forward his most telling evidence, which was the note of Strafford's speech in Council taken down by Sir Henry Vane on May 5 in the previous year. Vane's son, an enthusiastic supporter of Pym, had found the paper in his father's study and had made a copy which he took to Pym. Now the alleged substance of the notes was brought forward in evidence against Strafford to prove that he had urged the bringing over of Irish troops to subvert England. Had Strafford used the words 'this country', meaning England, or 'that country', meaning Scotland? Had he not said that, being reduced to extreme necessity, the King was absolved from all laws of government? Vane senior was troubled and inconclusive in his answers. Northumberland, Hamilton, Juxon, Goring and Cottington failed to remember words that could have had any such interpretation. On April 10 the trial was adjourned in some confusion with nothing proved against Strafford. As the court broke up Charles and Strafford looked at each other across the Hall. The King laughed.

In other respects Charles had less reason for satisfaction and little room for manoeuvre, and his thoughts turned to the army in the North, still not disbanded and still only partly paid. When on March 6 £10,000, previously assigned to the English army, was handed over to the Scots, discontent was ready to take positive form. Edmund Verney, with the army, writing to his brother Ralph, with the Parliament, two days later, depicted a dangerous situation: 'The horse . . . will not muster till they are paid. If the foot do the like . . . believe me, it can tend to no less than a general mutiny.' Two groups of people were preparing to take advantage of this situation. In the army Henry Percy, the brother of Northumberland, was the leader of a group of officers who prepared a letter embodying their grievances which was presented first to Northumberland and then to the King. In London two courtiers, the Queen's favourite, Henry Jermyn, and the poet Sir John Suckling, were in touch with George Goring, another friend of the Queen, who had recently been appointed Governor of Plymouth. Their wild scheme involved bringing the army to London and securing the Tower while Goring used Plymouth to receive the aid the Queen expected from the Continent.

Charles and his wife were both aware of what was going on, and Charles engineered a meeting between the two groups. But they were completely incompatible and Charles's worst fears were realized. 'All these ways are vain and foolish!', he exclaimed, 'and I will think of them no more.' Goring, in frustration, disclosed the so-called 'army plot' to Members of the House of Lords on April 1, but it is likely that rumour had already been at work. With fears of an army plot spreading and their case against Strafford halting, the opposition once more took stock of its position. The words were spoken by Essex but they were Pym's too, and those of his associates: 'Stone dead hath no fellow.' Since the charge of treason looked like faltering they would obtain the death penalty against Strafford by the savage procedure of a Bill of Attainder, which required no more formality than the passage of an Act of Parliament. It was Haselrig who drew the Bill from his pocket, ready prepared, on the evening of the 10th – the opposition's reply to the King's laughter. To obtain votes for this procedure Pym produced his own copy of young Vane's copy of his father's scribbled notes taken in the agitated meeting of the Scottish Committee ten months earlier. Confusion surrounded the whereabouts of the original copy and the original document itself, though the elder Vane maintained it had been burnt on the King's command. What was certain was that in the copy which Pym now produced the impression was conveyed that Strafford was reported as saying that the Irish army could be used *here* – in England – to subdue *this country*. No one could remember exactly how the minute had read before.

While this document of Pym's was being used as evidence first in the House of Commons and then in the House of Lords, in the main trial itself the final defence had yet to be heard. When on April 13 Strafford came again to Westminster Hall to make his last speech the Bill of Attainder had already been presented to the Commons by Haselrig. It made little difference that Strafford's defence was clear and eloquent and that for two hours he tore down article after article of the charge made against him; that he was able to show that so far from committing any treason he had always acted in accordance with the laws and traditions of his country. He warned his hearers: 'These gentlemen tell me they speak in defence of the commonweal against my arbitrary laws; give me leave to say that I speak in defence of the commonweal against their arbitrary treason.' The power was now with the opposition and when the Bill of Attainder was put to the vote in the Commons on April 20 it passed by 204 votes to 59.

It needed courage to be one of the 59. Outside the House as well as within, the opposition had worked up a furious dislike of Strafford, and all who supported him. The apprentices, always ready for a riot, were streaming day after day from the City to Westminster and were joined by older and more sober citizens all crying for the blood of Strafford. Notable among those who dared to confront the Commons and its allies was young George Digby, son of the Earl of Bristol. With his father's insight, but with more than his father's passion, he risked his life in telling Pym openly in the House that the piece of paper he had copied from young Vane's copy of his father's garbled notes was no evidence against Strafford: no one, he pointed out, not even old Sir Henry himself, would say categorically that the Earl had offered to bring over an Irish army to subdue England. Digby was supported by the Member for Windsor who was courageous enough to warn the Commons that if they passed the Bill they would 'commit murder with the sword of justice'. Evidence of the deliberate policy of intimidation practised by the House was the posting up in London and Westminster of a list of the names of those who voted against the Bill with the superscription: 'These are the Straffordians, enemies of justice, betrayers of their country.' Digby survived the attack upon him but the Member for Windsor was expelled the House.

Charles remained confident, even after this vote, and on the following day wrote to Strafford. 'I cannot satisfy myself in honour or conscience', he said, 'without assuring you now, in the midst of your troubles, that, upon the word of a king, you shall not suffer in life, honour, or fortune.' But the opposition would not be deflected now, and in order to make sure of the Lords a gigantic petition was engineered said to bear 20,000 signatures, which on April 24 was brought to Westminster by the customary noisy crowd calling for vengeance upon Strafford. Two days later the House of Lords gave the Bill its first reading and the following day, the 27th, passed it a second time. At this eleventh hour there appeared signs that Charles was taking action. Cottington resigned as Chancellor of the Exchequer, it was rumoured that the post was being offered to Pym, and that the Earl of Bedford would become Lord Treasurer and lead a group of moderate men acceptable both to Charles and to Parliament. Charles had two interviews with Pym of which nothing leaked out. But this revival of an earlier scheme came to nothing. Pym refused the proferred post, Bedford was taken ill and died shortly afterwards, leaving the moderates with no strong leader. In view of all he had said and done Pym was bound to refuse office at this point. Bedford, but for his death, might well have accepted and brought into the ambit of government the peers recently appointed to the Privy Council. For exclusion from office and influence had been one of their chief grievances and, even at this late stage, Charles might have made amends. He lost heavily by Bedford's death and might have pondered whether earlier conciliatory action might not have altered the sequence of events.

At the same time Charles was engaged in yet another plot, this time to engineer Strafford's flight. The Earl himself seems to have agreed to the plan and offered £20,000 to Sir William Balfour, the Lieutenant of the Tower, to connive at his escape while his faithful secretary, Guildford Slingsby, waited at Tilbury with a ship ready to sail. The plan was frustrated by Balfour's loyalty to Parliament, and by the 28th news of the attempted escape was flying round Westminster and the City. Charles chose the same day to make an extraordinary announcement in person to the House of Lords, telling them that he intended to keep the Irish army in being until the English and Scottish forces were disbanded. It was inevitable that the announcement should bring with it some of the overtones of Strafford's alleged assertion of the previous year: was it bravado on the King's part? Was it a threat? The House looked askance at the King. Charles sat for some time looking around him as though expecting some support 'but there was not one man gave him the least hum or colour of plaudit to his speech', wrote one who was there, and the King left the House. If it did anything Charles's statement reinforced the case against Strafford. On the following day Oliver St John, speaking in favour of the Bill of Attainder, argued that 'it was never accounted either cruelty or foul play to knock foxes and wolves on the head . . . because they be beasts of prey'.

Charles now employed two contradictory tactics. He was persuaded by his supporters and by Strafford himself that he might be able to put in the right plea to Parliament for the Earl's life. It was a delicate situation that needed careful handling. There was already a core of 'Straffordians' in the Houses and in spite of the army plot and other rumours that Pym was assiduously nursing there was a middle group that might be won if Strafford were shorn of all power. Charles went to Parliament on May 1 and, as he had so often done, he misjudged the situation. He promised, indeed, that he would never employ Strafford again in any capacity. He assured his hearers that no one had ever advised him to bring the Irish army to England or to change even the least of the laws of England. But he made no attempt to speak against the Attainder Bill, to question the constitutional issues it raised, to point out the dangers of such a Bill being used as a precedent. Nor did he refer to Strafford's defence or to the extent to which the case against him had failed or succeeded. Instead Charles made a personal appeal concerning his own conscience, which, he said in effect, would not allow him to sign Strafford's death warrant, and

331

he begged his hearers to relieve him of the dilemma he was in: he was not asking for Strafford's release from the death penalty, but for his own release from a matter of conscience.

Strafford heard of the speech with resignation and no hope. Laud was saddened. The speech, he later wrote, 'displeased mightily and I verily think hastened the Earl's death'. On the same day Charles attempted to infiltrate the Tower guard with his own men, but again the Lieutenant frustrated his intentions and immediately informed the Parliamentary leaders. The state of uncertainty and alarm was not only for Parliament itself – was it to be dissolved? Would Charles use force against it? – but was felt in a deep uncertainty over the City as a whole, where business and trade had virtually stopped in the general confusion, men hardly knowing who was their leader and what was the position of the King. Charles himself was distraught. His mind was partly on other things. For if the life of Strafford was important so also was the fortune of his eldest daughter who was due to be married the following day to Prince William of Orange.

The Prince had arrived on March 13 with 400 gentlemen attendants and was staying at Arundel House. He had been officially welcomed by the Earl of Lindsey at Gravesend and had been brought to Whitehall where he was met by the Prince of Wales and the Duke of York who conducted him to their parents and other members of the family; it was noted that the Queen and Princesses would not let him kiss them, presumably because he was not of sufficiently high rank. But he and Mary were immediately attracted to each other – like another young couple 27 years before – and Mary very soon allowed herself to be kissed. She and her mother took some interest in her clothes. The wedding could not be so grand as her aunt's had been, even though that was held under the shadow of her uncle's death, but her dress was of silver, round her auburn hair and her throat were ropes of pendant pearls, her long train was carried by attendants dressed in white. Her bridegroom was bright and gallant in a suit of rich pink velvet and satin. From a curtained recess in the chapel at Whitehall Henrietta-Maria watched the simple Protestant ceremony and saw Charles give his daughter away. The marriage was popular with the people, yet nothing demonstrates more clearly the desperate straits to which Charles had been reduced than this marriage of his eldest daughter whose terms, and the very person of the bride herself, had been dictated by the Dutch. To add to the incongruity of the occasion the Elector Palatine had arrived unexpectedly on the same day as the Prince, to the dismay of the King and Queen, claiming that the Princess had been promised to him. He sulked in his room during the wedding ceremony.

Henrietta-Maria walked with her children in the park that afternoon as a substitute for the celebrations that would normally have followed. In the evening she went through the accepted ritual of undressing the little girl and putting her to bed in the presence of her father, her brothers and sisters and members of the Court. The bridegroom was then brought in by the Prince of Wales and Charles led him to the bed to kiss the bride. He was allowed to lie with her for half an hour with the drapes of the bed open and in the presence of the courtiers. The marriage was then pronounced consummated and William spent the rest of the night in Charles's room where, it was said, the King made much of him.[1]

Henrietta's delight in pageantry and the masque should have had ample scope in the marriage of her eldest daughter. The intrigue in which she was indulging was possibly something of a substitute for here she could combine the drama of play-acting with what she believed was positive assistance to her husband. While Strafford's trial and her daughter's wedding preparations were proceeding she was making clandestine appointments with various members of the opposition, hoping to influence them, descending by back stairs and the light of a single candle to her rendezvous. Not surprisingly the news of such meetings soon got about and did no good to Strafford, to her husband, nor to her own reputation. The crowds were continuing to flock day after day to Westminster and Whitehall and after two big demonstrations on the 3rd and 4th demanding the life of Strafford the Earl himself wrote to the King absolving him from any promise he had made to save him. On the 5th Pym opportunely disclosed, officially, the details of the army plot, intimating that the Queen intended to go to Portsmouth to await French forces while the King went North to take command of his troops. On the 6th Jermyn, Suckling and others concerned fled the country. On the 8th the Lords gave the Bill of Attainder its third reading by 26 votes to 19 – an appallingly thin House and a shockingly small majority and evidence of considerable support for Strafford. But how could Charles make use of it?

The Bill of Attainder now came before Charles for the most momentous decision of his life. Many of his supporters had fled; the London populace was seething not only in the streets and in

Westminster but round the Queen's apartments in Whitehall; rumours of her backstairs intrigues had now swollen to include charges of infidelity with Henry Jermyn. Again it was being said that Parliament would impeach the Queen if Strafford was not surrendered. Charles called his bishops to him. They were divided. His Council advised him to yield. The opposition let it be known that, even if he refused his consent to the Bill, Strafford would still die. The Judges, when questioned, alleged they held Strafford guilty of treason. Henrietta-Maria lost some of her defiance and was reduced to tears of frustration and fear. Through the night of the 8th there was panic in the City and in the King's household. Charles, after all, had Strafford's letter of release. Should he use it? On the evening of the 9th he gave way and signed with tears in his eyes. The news was carried to Strafford. In spite of his letter he was incredulous and the statement had to be repeated. 'Put not your trust in princes nor in the sons of men for in them there is no salvation', he cried out in his anguish. The news was carried to Laud in his room in the same fortress.

Charles took the one remaining action that was possible and sent the Prince of Wales with a letter to the House of Lords begging mercy for Strafford: not, indeed, pardon but the commutation of the death penalty to life imprisonment. The boy, who was still outside factional strife, would be a better instrument than his father. But it was a strangely abject letter, not seeming to expect compliance. The post-script: 'If he must die, it were charity to reprieve him till Saturday' was an abandonment of hope and was disregarded. The Earl of Strafford was beheaded on Tower Hill on the morning of 12 May 1641 in front of a concourse of some 100,000 people very few of whom expressed anything but satisfaction at the sight. One of the few was John Evelyn who recorded in his diary that he saw 'the fatal stroke which sever'd the wisest head in England from the shoulders of the Earle of Strafford; whose crimes coming under the cognizance of no human law, a new one was made'.[2]

28

The Last of London

Throughout the spring and summer of 1641 the Commons continued their work of tearing down the edifice of personal government. It was important to deprive the King of extra-Parliamentary sources of income, and in the Tonnage and Poundage Bill to which he was ironically compelled to acquiese on June 22 he agreed to forego forever the right to levy customs duties without consent of Parliament, that consent being given in the first place for a period of two months. The machinery through which he had governed without Parliament was demolished with frenetic speed, the courts of Star Chamber of High Commission and the Councils of the North and of Wales being abolished on a single day, July 5. The taxation he had imposed through these bodies was declared illegal a month later; on August 7 all ship-money proceedings were annulled, the verdict against Hampden was declared null and void, the boundaries of forests were restored to their limits at the end of James's reign; three days later knighthood fines were declared illegal. Charles had no weapons with which to resist, no machinery of government or administration to set his will in motion, no money to give him independence, no army except those troublesome units that still stood under arms in the North and were as likely to support Parliament as himself. Moreover, together with Strafford's Attainder, there had come before him for signature a Bill which precluded the dissolution of Parliament without its own consent: a Bill for perpetual Parliaments. Now, indeed, he was truly in the snare he had laboured so long to avoid.

Religion the Commons had barely touched, apart from releasing the Puritan martyrs, and the Root and Branch petition still lay undiscussed. Even the impeachment of Laud, and he lay half-forgotten in the Tower, was as much for his civil as for his religious offences. But Parliament had acted against the Queen's Catholic priests and forced

335

Charles on June 25 to dismiss Rossetti, the last of the line of Papal envoys to reside at Court. On the following day Rossetti had a long interview with the Queen, during part of which Charles was present. The King, Rossetti reported to Rome, talked more like a Catholic than a Protestant, promising, if ever he was again in control of his kingdom, to treat the Catholics with all possible leniency. When they were alone Henrietta-Maria repeated to Rossetti, as she had done before, that Charles was not disinclined to the Catholic faith, but was 'timid', 'slow', and 'irresolute in action'. She assured the envoy that whatever promises a King of England made to his Parliament under compulsion he was not bound to keep.[1] Parliament may have suspected something of this attitude, though Charles himself would not have put the matter so bluntly, even to himself. To guard against such a possibility it was necessary to prevent the King from getting control of any armed force, and on the day that he consented to dismiss Rossetti he was also obliged to consent to the disbandment of those Northern armies whose existence, poor as they were, had been his only comfort.

Charles had already made up his mind to go to Scotland and now it was necessary to go as quickly as possible before disbandment took place. Parliament was suspicious but could find no good reason, or no good way, of preventing the King from journeying to his northern kingdom when he had agreed with the Scottish Commissioners in London, in his one outstandingly good move, to be present in the Scottish Parliament to pass the Act of Pacification which would formally end the war between the two kingdoms. Undoubtedly Charles had more subtle reasons for undertaking the journey; he could make contact with his own army in the North, he probably hoped for some support among the Scots, he was anxious to get away from the English Parliament and possibly thought that from a distance he might see matters in perspective. Basically the need for physical activity was important. It was still true that he was at his best when active and less prone to the uncertainties of intellectual decision. This was one reason why hunting was so good, why he had flourished and blossomed during the Spanish adventure, in spite of its bitterness. Let him but get away from the endless talk of Parliament, the religious controversy of Roman Catholic and Sectarian, let him feel a good horse under him, putting mile after mile between himself and the suffocating capital, and all might yet be well.

The proposed visit took on more the nature of a plot since his wife was at the same time talking of a journey. Henrietta had had her own experience of intrigue and although it had come to nothing it had given her the taste for what was basic to her nation and to her own character. Now she had plans for proceeding to the Continent with the Crown jewels and raising support for Charles in Holland or France. Parliament was suspicious when it heard she thought of going to Spa for her health and asked for the views of Doctor Mayerne. The doctor was a good professional man, besides being the royal physician, and could only give his opinion that her physical health did not justify the journey, though mentally she was much troubled: it would have been more in keeping with his profession if he had declined to discuss his patient's health at all. With Parliament about to prohibit her journey the Queen abandoned her immediate plans with a certain grace and tact though she was far from giving up the idea of seeking help abroad.

By the end of July, though Parliament had had its way with the Queen, it had not been able to do more than delay the King's departure for Scotland. This was, indeed, one of the few occasions when he stood firm and he left on Tuesday afternoon, August 10, after approving a Bill embodying the treaty with the Scots and a final payment to the Scottish armies of £220,000. A somewhat discomfited House of Commons appointed Parliamentary Commissioners to follow him, presumably to keep an eye on his activities. His nephew, the Palatine, accompanied him, as well as Lennox, Hamilton, Vane, and Endymion Porter who, besides being Groom of the Bedchamber, now sat in Parliament for Droitwich. His wife was to see her mother embarked for Holland, the situation having at last proved too much for the old Queen. Her departure was a source of satisfaction to Charles who sent her off under the escort of Arundel with all honours. With her departure and the legislation of the summer he had little fear of mob violence against his family during his absence, though he arranged that Henrietta-Maria should reside at Oatlands, well away from any likely source of trouble, with the children either with her or at nearby Richmond.

His journey was quite a success. Not only the English army but the Scots round Newcastle greeted him with enthusiasm and he reciprocated by promising an earldom to Leslie. The Scottish army crossed back into Scotland on the agreed day, Charles ratified such Bills as the Scottish Parliament required, and attended their Presbyterian services with a show of devotion, listening to their sermons and singing psalms after the Scottish fashion. He believed he had won their support and wrote to Henrietta that 5000 foot and 1000 horse were to remain at his disposal from Leslie's army. But Porter was not so sure; 'his majesties businesses', he wrote to Edward Nicholas, 'runn in the wonted channell, suttle designes of gaineing the popular opinion and weake executions for the uphowlding of monarkie! The King is yet perswaded to howld owte, but within twoo or three dayes must yeld to all; and here are legislators that knowe howe to handle him . . .'[2] Endymion Porter, the dilettante, the art collector, lover of gardens, trusted emissary, Groom of the Bedchamber, who never aspired to, and never held, political office, had learned to know his friend and master. The 'subtle design', the 'weak execution', the ultimate yielding were all too typical of a King who was never able, in time of crisis, to match intent, which was often over-subtle, with action, which was too often untimely or unrealistic. These faults of character, which had not shown during the personal rule when he was unopposed, were now relentlessly exposed.

The second strategem Charles was setting in motion was in Ireland, where he had hopes of winning the as yet undisbanded Irish army to his cause on the promise of religious liberty. Parliament was nervously listening, a prey to rumours that their leaders were to be seized. They were having difficulty in holding their forces together, for Members were not used to long absences from their homes. The initial enthusiasm for a Parliament died away with the expense of living in London, the discomfort of the hot summer, and the mounting plague deaths. At home, on the other hand, the harvest was ready to be gathered, and a multitude of domestic affairs cried out for attention. By the end of August only some dozen Peers and eighty Parliament men remained in their places. Parliament accepted the situation and adjourned from September 8 until October 20. Its leaders continued to watch the Queen closely, and it was said that she and her children were hostages for the King's good behaviour. Part of her time she spent profitably and blamelessly enough in writing to her husband's supporters to be sure to be in their places when Parliament reassembled, part less discreetly with the French Ambassador and her Catholic friends, indulging in talk of 10,000 men who would rise in her husband's support.

Charles was writing to her at least three times a week from Scotland, mainly through Edward Nicholas. Nicholas had been secretary to the Lord Warden of the Cinque Ports and so came under the notice of Buckingham who advanced him to the secretaryship of the Admiralty. After the Duke's death the Commissioners of the Admiralty kept Nicholas in office until Northumberland took over the Admiralty in 1636 when Nicholas became clerk of the Privy Council and so more directly under Charles's notice than before. The King obviously liked him, he had been efficient and painstaking in dealing with the ship-money correspondence, and he had Catholic leanings. He wrote careful, full, and regular despatches to Charles while the King was in Scotland and when plague in London became menacing he moved to his country house, near Oatlands, where he was close to the Queen. He was the chief medium of communication between Charles and his wife while the King was away and Charles's marginal notes and instructions on Nicholas's letters make clear how much he was coming to rely upon his wife for advice and information. He instructed Nicholas to write to those Parliament men sympathetic to him to be in their places when the Houses reassembled – 'my wife', he wrote, 'will give you the names'. He wished to sell or to renew the pawn upon a 'great collar of rubies' and instructed Nicholas to go to his wife for details.

Charles continued to honour the Scots, Argyle becoming a Marquis, Hamilton receiving a dukedom, and he made no move to return to London. He could not come so soon as he wished, he wrote to Nicholas, but there was 'necessity' in it. 'I hope that many will miss of their ends', he added gleefully; 'all their desynes hit not', he scribbled in the margin of another letter, 'and I hope before all be done that they shall miss of more'. Nicholas reported meantime that the opposition was hard at work. Their meeting place was Lord Mandeville's house in Chelsea and here they prepared for the next Parliamentary session and devised schemes for maintaining public opinion on their side. The Parliamentary committees that remained in session during the recess were under their control. Charles's written comment in the margin of the letter ran: 'It were not amiss that some of my servants met lykewais to countermynd ther Plots, to which end speake with my Wyfe and receave her directions.' His spirits were clearly high, and he was obviously immersed in some scheme which was giving him satisfaction. When at last he was ready to leave his return was as carefully planned as any opposition manoeuvre.[3] The gentry and freeholders of Hertfordshire came to meet him at Ware, Charles stopped in the town for 'the better sort' to kiss his hand, while he talked to the rest. They then accompanied him to Theobalds where

339

he was met by his wife and children. But more important than this show of support was the genuine swing of feeling in Charles's favour. In the City a Royalist mayor and Common Council had replaced the outgoing opposition members; the people as a whole were thankful that the Scots had gone home, they were weary of the taxation which Parliament had necessarily to impose, they were disturbed by the interruption to business and trade caused by the uncertain situation. Most of the King's 'evil counsellors' were dead, imprisoned, or fled; the money-raising devices of the personal government were ended; those who thought about such matters were satisfied with the constitutional government which had come into being. Now, it seemed, the King would be welcomed back – still monarch, but in such a position that even the most evil influence could not effect the people's liberties. The fiction that the King himself could do no wrong made it easier and the enthusiastic welcome accorded to Charles as he rode into London with his family on November 24 was not entirely due to careful planning. They all attended a banquet at Guildhall and proceeded to Whitehall by torchlight amid cheering crowds. Charles thanked the citizens in a short speech and promised to govern 'according to the laws of this kingdom, and in maintaining and protecting the true Protestant religion'. He would care for the prosperity of the City and, in particular, would 'study to re-establish that flourishing trade which now is in some disorder amongst you'. The day after his return he knighted Edward Nicholas at Whitehall and on the 27th appointed him Secretary of State.

Charles's mysterious activities in Scotland, the swing of public opinion in London, upset the opposition. It was a measure of Pym's uncertainty that, instead of advancing to a new position, he found it necessary to go back over old ground and, shortly after Parliament reassembled, to bring forward for discussion a document which had been lying on the table since the previous November. The Grand Remonstrance on the state of the kingdom consisted, broadly, of three parts: a statement of grievances; an enumeration of the measures which had dealt with them; and a series of further demands. It was a clever document in many ways. To draw attention to achievements is always a good preparation for further action, and its content was sufficiently mixed to make opposition to the document as a whole difficult, even in respect of the new measures proposed. These concerned two of the thorniest questions left for solution: the settlement of religion which had barely been touched upon; and the control of the armed forces, including the milita, which had been considered but without a decision being reached. To bring both issues forward in this way at the end of a long document which could hardly be controversial was bound to raise suspicions of trying to rush Parliament. In general, the impression left by the Grand Remonstrance was not one of strength but of weakness, and this was confirmed by the debates themselves and by the voting. The Grand Remonstrance received a majority in the Commons of only eleven votes, being carried on November 22, two days before Charles's return to London, by 159 votes to 148. But not until 3 o'clock in the morning was the small majority achieved, and then it passed so tumultuously, wrote a Member, 'I thought we had all sat in the valley of the shadow of death, ready to catch each other's locks and sheath our swords in each other's bowels.'[4]

As Pym had expected it was the religious clauses of the Grand Remonstrance which aroused most opposition, and a neutral clause proposing that church matters should be settled by a Synod of Divines drawn from England and other Protestant communities in Europe fell flat. Charles's reply on December 10 that religion should be observed as it was established by Elizabeth I and his father found a far more ready acceptance. But more immediately vital to the opposition was the control of the militia and the trained bands. They had no real hold upon the machinery of government unless they controlled the armed force which, in the last resort, lies behind government. Religion might be shelved, but, whatever the voting on the Grand Remonstrance, the control of the armed forces must be secured. To this end the support of the House of Lords was necessary and here the Bishops' votes had become of crucial importance. A Bishops' Exclusion Bill had been laid aside in October but was now revived. Charles swore he would never deprive the Bishops of the votes to which they were entitled under the ancient constitution of the realm.

The opposition was fumbling and Charles was beginning to assume the initiative when events in Ireland took a hand. When news broke on November 1 that the Irish were in revolt, Parliament immediately seized the opportunity to give out that the rebellion was fomented by the Roman Catholics, the Pope, and the Queen. Fear of the papacy reached panic proportions in England as stories of atrocities, true and untrue, came out of Ireland. An alleged Catholic plot to massacre English Protestants and establish the Pope in England

341

was uncovered. Parliament voted that the Popish religion should no longer be tolerated in any part of the King's dominions. The Irish rebellion did irreparable harm to Charles's cause. It 'made a wonderful impression upon the minds of men, and proved of infinite disadvantage to the King's affairs, which were then recovering new life', as a contemporary wrote.

Meanwhile elections in the City of London unseated the royalist mayor and Council and Pym was driving home his advantage by working up demonstrations against the Bishops and the Queen. Predictably, Charles reacted strongly, as he always did when Henrietta-Maria was concerned, and on December 23 he sought once more to get control of the Tower of London by replacing the opposition Lieutenant with his own man, Colonel Lunsford. His position would have been stronger if he had selected someone else. Lunsford's reputation as a bully and bravado gave him little credence as a man of goodwill, even among Charles's own supporters, and three days later Charles was compelled to climb down and dismiss him.

Agitation for the dismissal of Lunsford coincided with well worked-up demonstrations before the House of Lords against the Bishops, who were manhandled to such good purpose that on December 28 all but two stayed away. George Digby, who had been raised to the peerage as Lord Digby, moved that the House was acting under duress and should remove to a place of greater safety. Though the argument was superficially reasonable the Lords realized that this was a two-edged weapon. Could not 'duress' invalidate much of the legislation already passed? They refused passage to Digby's motion, but by four votes only. When the Bishops returned to their places it was with a Protestation maintaining that measures passed in their absence were invalid, which implied that Digby's motion still stood. The implied threat to Parliament's legislation alarmed moderate as well as more extreme opinion; perhaps rumours of the Queen's rash statement to Rossetti, that the King was not bound to honour commitments made under duress, had reached Westminster. Pym, as usual, dramatized the situation when the Bishops' Protest was sent to the Commons from the Lords on December 30. He called for doors to be locked and the City trained bands to be sent for while he castigated the documents as of 'high and dangerous consequence' and called for the impeachment of the Bishops. The Lords sequestered them and sent all but the two oldest and most infirm to the Tower.

The year 1642 began in the utmost confusion. The general uncertainty was reflected in sparsely attended Parliamentary sittings. Charles, intent on subduing the Irish rebellion by his own means, was recruiting into his service officers disbanded from the northern armies. In an effort to restrain riotous citizens he commanded gentlemen of the Court to wear swords and he set a guard at Whitehall Gate. The Lords asked for protection against the citizens, Pym refused to do anything to stop the people expressing their 'just desires' in any way they chose, and there were fresh rumours of the impeachment of the Queen for communicating with the Irish rebels. In such an atmosphere Charles's constitutional moves in appointing two 'moderates' to office made no impact. Falkland as Secretary of State and Culpepper as Chancellor of the Exchequer could now do little good. Impelled by fears for the safety of the Queen he put into motion the plan he had been hatching in Scotland.

He sincerely believed in the evidence he had gathered there against leading members of the opposition. He thought they had conspired to bring the Scottish armies into England to serve their own ends and that the long train of events that followed had been deliberately planned. He also believed that he could substantiate the case against them, that it would be upheld by the Judges, and that their fall would topple their party and leave him with a Parliament he could control. Such, at least, is the kind of reasoning that drove him to the action he now took. First he declared through the Attorney General that five Members of the House of Commons and one Member of the House of Lords were guilty of treason and he sent a herald to the House of Commons to demand that the five be handed over to his custody. The House of Commons naturally refused to comply with the King's command as being an interference with Parliamentary privilege. It is strange that Charles had not considered such a possibility. After a night of vaccillation he was still doubtful what to do when Henrietta-Maria's words stung him to action. 'Go, you coward!', she cried, 'and pull these rogues out by the ears, or never see my face more.' Charles hurried to his guardroom, calling in a loud voice for his loyal subjects and soldiers to follow him. They needed no second bidding, and with 500 armed men behind him and the young Elector Palatine at his side, he flung himself down the stairs of his palace and into a private coach which happened to be at the gate, commanding it to take him to Westminster, while his soldiers and others, swollen to a great crowd, followed on foot. 'In an hour', he threw over his shoulder to his wife, the deed would be done. Striding through Westminster

Hall he bade his followers wait there while he proceeded to the Commons' Chamber with only the Elector at his side. The Members were standing bareheaded as the King, restraining his anger, stepped over the threshold of the Assembly that no monarch had looked upon before. Charles walked slowly to the Speaker's chair, looking to right and to left. He soon perceived that the accused were not in their places. 'Gentlemen', he said, seeking for certainty, 'you must know that in cases of treason no person hath a privilege; and therefore I am come to know if any of those persons that were accused are here.' Then, turning to Speaker Lenthall, 'Are any of these persons in the House?', he asked again. The Speaker, Charles's own choice for the office, fell on his knees and humbly begged the King's pardon, but he had no comfort to offer. 'I have', he said, 'neither eyes to see, nor tongue to speak in this place but as this House is pleased to direct me, whose servant I am here.' The privilege of Parliament could not have been more succinctly expressed. Though humbly spoken it was spoken to the King's face and left him nonplussed. Charles looked round again, 'I see the birds are flown', he said, and left the chamber with the cry of 'Privilege, Privilege!' sounding behind him. Charles's carefully planned counter-attack had failed. Clearly the Commons had been warned in time for the five Members to slip away from Westminster by river to the City and it was useless to speculate how the betrayal, for such it seemed, had occurred. Henrietta-Maria later took the blame upon herself. She was watching the clock, she said, mindful of her husband's last words and at the end of an hour sprang up on impulse crying out that the deed was now done! Lady Carlyle, who was sitting with her, realized the import of the words. Besides her family connections with the opposition, she had an association with Pym, closer, it was rumoured, than friendship, and she sent a messenger with all speed to the Commons to warn them of the King's coming. Charles had been delayed on his way by the crowds who thronged round his coach, he took some time to walk through Westminster Hall with his followers around him and arrived just too late. His wife's impulsive words, as she believed, had 'ruined' him. But 'never', she said years later, 'did he treat me for a moment with less kindness than before it happened'.[5]

The following day Charles went to Guildhall to demand from the City the persons of five Members, but his unprecedented entry into the House of Commons had put him in the wrong and the cries of 'Liberty of Parliament' which greeted him had more than usual justification. As he came away someone threw into his coach a paper containing the words: 'To thy tents, O, Israel!' His heralds proclaimed the six impeached Members to be traitors while his armed soldiers and courtiers at Whitehall became more aggressive. The City trained bands stood ready to defend the privileges of Parliament and Philip Skippon, an experienced soldier, was appointed their Sergeant-major General. Arms were distributed to the people, the shops remained shut, the Thames watermen offered to defend Parliament, John Hampden announced that thousands of his Buckinghamshire men were on their way to Westminster with a petition. The House of Lords stood with the Commons and the name of Henrietta-Maria was once more bandied about. The Irish revolt was spoken of as 'the Queen's rebellion'. Whatever else he feared, whatever else he had in mind, it was anxiety for his wife that impelled Charles to action. He feared they would take her from him, he told the Dutch representative at Court. It was merely a minor irritant that he knew the six impeached men were to return to Westminster in triumph on January 11, but it perhaps determined him to leave the day before. After much discussion he had persuaded his Council and most of his influential courtiers to support this move though Holland, Essex and Lady Carlyle sought desperately to change his mind. On 10 January 1642 Charles left London with his family for Hampton Court. So great had been the confusion of rumour, so swift the current of events, that nothing had been prepared for them and they spent the night in one room. When they awoke next morning it was to the knowledge that this was Parliament's day of triumph, signalized as only London knew how with flags flying, bands playing, watermen plying their gaily decked boats, apprentices, trained bands, citizens and Parliament men all celebrating the return to Parliament of the men the King had attempted to impeach. Among the friends who accompanied the King was Endymion Porter. A few days later he wrote to his wife. 'Whither we go, and what we are able to do, I know not, for I am none of the Council. My duty and loyalty have taught me to follow my King and master, and by the grace of God nothing shall divert me from it . . . I wish sweet Tom with me, for the King and Queen are forced to lie with their children now, and I envy their happiness.'[6]

It was resolved between the King and Queen that she should leave the country, her excuse being the need to take Princess Mary to her husband in Holland. On February 23 Henrietta-Maria and her daughter sailed from Dover, taking the Crown jewels with them. This time

345

Parliament made no objection. Mary was pleased enough to be joining her husband, but to the rest of the family the parting was deep sorrow. The children wept at losing their mother and their sister, Charles and Henrietta-Maria could hardly tear themselves apart. Not only they but most of their following were in tears. Charles galloped along the cliffs to see the last of his wife's vessel, as he had ridden to see her incoming sails fifteen years before. When he turned at last he was marked with sorrow: 'They have left the King to his loneliness and deeply moved.'[7]

Part V

Civil War

29

The King's Standard Unfurled

When Charles turned at last from the coast he made his way to his wife's palace at Greenwich and sent for his eldest son. Parliament wanted to separate them but Charles was firm, not only through affection but because he knew the political value of the Prince of Wales. Two issues were on his mind: the Bishops' Exclusion Bill and the Militia Bill. He had agreed on February 13, as a matter of policy, to the exclusion of bishops from the House of Lords but took his stand on the immediately vital question of the militia. His wife was safe and, as he said to Hyde, 'now that I have gotten Charles, I care not what answer I send them', and he refused to surrender his power of granting commissions for the raising of troops. At the same time there was a necessity, if help was to be received from the Continent, of securing a seaport. Hull, Newcastle, Berwick appealed to him since in the North he was more likely to win support than nearer London, but he also had his eye on Portsmouth. Before he left Greenwich he commanded that his bust by Bernini should be brought in from the garden where it stood. As it was being carried towards the house, face upward, a bird dunged upon it and the stain, according to the servants, turned the colour of blood and could not be erased.

Charles's refusal to pass the Militia Bill and his journey northward, which he began on March 3, alarmed Parliament. On the same day, using the procedure they had learned while Charles was in Scotland, they converted the Militia Bill into an Ordinance, enforceable by contempt proceedings, which put the militia into the hands of Lords Lieutenants, whom they appointed themselves. Four days later Charles was at Newmarket where a Parliamentary deputation reached him seeking for a compromise. They carried with them a Declaration of Both Houses which expressed their fears and asked for the King's return to London. Alterations in religion had been schemed by those in greatest authority about him, the document claimed, the wars with Scotland as well as the Irish rebellion having been fomented to this end. The document hardly breathed the spirit of compromise and Charles was aghast at what he termed the 'strange and unexpected' nature of the charges against him. 'God in his good time,' he exclaimed with passion, would 'discover the secrets and Bottoms of all Plots and Treasons: and then I shall stand right in the Eyes of my People.'

'What would you have?', he demanded, as he had done so many times before. 'Have I violated your laws? Have I denied to pass any Bill for the Ease and Security of my Subjects?'

When Holland murmured 'the militia' Charles retorted 'That was no Bill!' and when Pembroke begged him to grant the militia for a limited period, Charles exclaimed, 'My God!, Not for an hour!'. 'You have asked that of me', he added, 'was never asked of any King.'

When Pembroke pressed the point, saying that the King's intention was unclear, Charles rounded upon him in anger. 'I would whip a boy in Westminster school', he exclaimed, 'who could not tell that by my answers!'[1]

Two days later he gave practical shape to his intentions by the issue of Commissions of Array which directed the trained bands to place themselves at his disposal. Henceforth Militia Ordinance and Commission of Array stood in opposition, calling upon people to take their choice between Parliament and King.

On March 15 another step was taken on the road to war when Parliament instructed Northumberland to yield the command of the fleet to the Puritan Earl of Warwick. Northumberland was a weak, possibly a sick man; he had Puritan leanings and Charles had not taken sufficient care to support the interests of his family in matters of Court promotion. He made no protest. Parliament predictably took no notice of Charles's order that Pennington should succeed to the command, Pennington himself was not strong enough to make a stand. Charles was reaping the reward, perhaps, of the little care which, inexplicably, he had expended upon the men who manned his ships. The rotting food, the unpaid wages, the lack of medical care, the squandered lives at Cadiz and Rhé rose up against him, and his carefully nurtured navy, his lovingly launched ships, passed to Parliament without a blow at the beginning of the conflict.

Charles continued his journey northward without haste and with little visible emotion. He stopped at Cambridge, where he visited

Trinity College and St John's, and he called once more at Little Gidding whose tranquil atmosphere broke through his defences: 'Pray, pray for my speedy and safe return', he begged on parting. When he reached York on March 19 one of his first actions was to send for his second son, James, Duke of York, who had been left at Richmond under the care of the Marquis of Hertford. Parliament made no attempt to hinder the boy's journey and in his delight at the reunion Charles created him a Knight of the Garter, as well as providing him with a guard of honour and setting off a blaze of welcoming fireworks.

Shortly afterwards James was called to duty. Hull had become Charles's immediate objective, for in this city were stored the arms left from the Scottish wars. Yet the attitude of the Governor, Sir John Hotham, who had been imprisoned by Charles in 1627 for refusing to collect a forced loan, was uncertain. Charles therefore sent the boy with his cousin, the Elector Palatine, on an ostensibly social visit to Hull which was intended to sound the feelings of the inhabitants. The young men reported on the loyalty of the city and next day, April 23, Charles advanced to request admission. To his dismay Hotham, who had been appointed by Parliament as a good Commons man, refused him entry. Charles proclaimed him a traitor and withdrew, though it is likely enough that the citizens would have followed the King against their Governor if they had been given a chance. More satisfactory was the ease with which the Yorkshire gentry provided him with a personal bodyguard, which he entrusted to the leadership of the Prince of Wales.

He was being joined now by many of the big northern landowners and their followers, including the Earl of Newcastle, Governor to the Prince of Wales, the Stanleys of Lancashire, and Lord Lindsey, the robust veteran of the Spanish Main and the Low Countries. Friends were also coming in from London and from Parliament itself. Edward Hyde, who had already shown himself a valuable counsellor, now felt he could serve the King at Westminster no longer and turned his back irrevocably upon the Parliament, bringing with him his friends Lord Falkland and Sir John Culpepper, both of whom had been appointed to the Privy Council at the beginning of 1642 in one of Charles's attempts at compromise. Falkland, in particular, was deeply distressed and undecided, yet was forced to the King's side on the religious issue.

At the beginning of June, Lord Keeper Littleton, somewhat timidly, fled to York bringing with him the Great Seal; by the middle of the month the King's companions included Secretary Nicholas, Lord Chief Justice Bankes, and some thirty-five Peers including Salisbury, Bristol, Richmond, Bath, and Dorset, and he was holding court in York in a manner which would have delighted his wife. That he was able to do so was due to the magnificent generosity of the Earl of Worcester and his son, Lord Herbert. Charles had left Greenwich with virtually no money and no means of raising any but, as he made his way northward, Herbert contrived to secure £22,000 of the family assets which he presented to the amazed and grateful King. By July no less than a further £100,000 had been raised for their sovereign by this practical and loyal family. It was through their generosity that Charles was enabled to start recruiting as well as to live in a manner not too far removed from his normal style.

For a few months after he left London Charles was prepared to be conciliatory – at first until he knew his wife was safe and his sons were with him – and later under the moderating influence of Hyde, Falkland and Culpepper. He even agreed in early March to speak fair words concerning the five Members: 'if the breach of Privilege had been greater than hath beene ever before offered', he was persuaded to say, 'our acknowledgement and retraction hath beene greater than ever King hath given'. The King's studied moderation and Parliament's mistakes had their reward in the steady building up of a King's party. On April 29 a great concourse of people met at Blackheath to support a petition drawn up by the men of Kent and to select 280 of their number to carry it to Westminster. It was mainly concerned with religion, asking for the execution of laws against Catholics, the retention of Episcopacy, the protection of the liturgy against profanation by sectaries, and an end to the 'scandal of schismatical and seditious sermons and pamphlets'. It exactly conformed with the King's own position and Parliament's reaction was foolishly, if predictably, harsh. It sent for four of the signatories as 'offenders', imprisoned two of them and voted the petition 'scandalous'.

At the same time Charles was receiving many reasoned petitions, to which he gave reasoned replies, taking the opportunity of stating his case against Parliament. It is not unlikely that his advisers were taking a leaf out of Pym's book in engineering such an advantageous exchange of views and, just as the Kentish petition and its treatment by Parliament did great harm to his opponents, so this exercise undoubtedly also helped his cause. So did his reasoned answer to the Nineteen Propositions.

Parliament's Nineteen Propositions, the second document sent after
Charles since his departure from London, reached him at York at the
beginning of June. It was so patently unacceptable as to be little more
than a propaganda exercise: it denied the right of the King to choose his
own ministers, obliged him to accept the Militia Ordinance, to reform
the Church according to the findings of a Church synod, and to place
the education and marriage of his children in the hands of Parliament.
Charles's first instinct was to ignore so extreme a document as being
sufficiently damaging in itself to his opponents. But his advisers
persuaded him otherwise and on June 8 his reply, drafted by Falkland
and Culpepper, put his case with remarkable prescience.

In reaffirming his acceptance of the Triennial Act and the Act
preventing the dissolution of Parliament, it confirmed his moderation; in recording his personal reactions to the Propositions it revealed
the extent of Parliament's designs: if their proposals were accepted, he
said,

> we may be waited on bareheaded, we may have our hand kissed, the
> style of majesty continued to us, and the King's authority declared by
> both Houses of Parliament may be still the style of your commands;
> we may have swords and maces carried before us, and please ourself
> with the sight of a crown and sceptre . . . but as to true and real
> power, we should remain but the outside, but the picture, but the sign
> of a king.

The real force of the reply, however, lay in its counter-proposals.
Charles did not claim a Divine Right of Kings, nor did he speak of the
Prerogative. He asserted instead that the laws of the country were
'jointly made by a King, a House of Peers, and by a House of
Commons chosen by the people'. In this 'regulated monarchy'
government was entrusted to the King who had, consequently, the
powers of choosing his advisers, of making war, and of preventing
insurrection, and in whom must reside the power necessary 'to con-
serve the laws in their force and the subjects in their liberties and
properties'. Parliament would act as a bulwark to prevent any abuse of
this power, the Commons through the weapon of impeachment and
the raising of supply, the Lords through their judicatory function.

By contrast, the role assigned to the monarch by the Nineteen
Propositions, Charles claimed, would leave him with nothing 'but to
look on', he would be unable to discharge the trust which is the end of
monarchy, and there would follow a 'total subversion of the
fundamental laws'. This situation would beget 'eternal factions and

dissensions', Parliament would be the recipient of such propositions as the King now had before him, until

> at last the common people . . . discover . . . that all this was done by them, but not for them, and grow weary of journeywork, and set up for themselves, call parity and independence liberty, devour that estate which had devoured the rest, destroy all rights and properties, all distinctions of families and merit, and by this means this splendid and excellently distinguished form of government end in a dark, equal chaos of confusion.[2]

In this enunciation of constitutional monarchy, this accurate forecast of future developments, it is difficult not to discern the fruits of discussions at Great Tew where Falkland and Hyde, Chillingworth and Hobbes had pursued just such questions of political obligation. It did Charles's cause a great deal of good, yet in offering a concept of constitutional government far beyond anything yet envisaged as practical, it was, in a sense, offering hostages to fortune.

The Nineteen Propositions and the King's *Answer* were part of a war of words that had been rapidly gaining momentum since the opening of Parliament. In November 1640 Henry Parker outlined from Parliament's point of view *The Case of Shipmoney*, in June 1641 Parliament published a collection of *Speeches and Passages in Parliament*, a fat book whose perusal John Lilburne gave as one of his reasons for joining Parliament at the outbreak of war. When the King published his *Answer to the Nineteen Propositions*, Parker replied with *Observations* upon the King's *Answer*. Various replies then came from the King's side to Parker by such men as Dudley Digges, Thomas Morton, and Sir John Spelman. Robert Greville, Lord Brooke, whose wide humanity matched that of Falkland but who believed his path lay with Parliament, wrote his splendid plea for toleration – *A Discourse opening the Nature of that Episcopacie which is exercised in England* – at the end of 1641, about the same time that Parker published the case against bishops in the *Divine Right of Episcopacie truly Stated*.

The statement of its case by either side implied justification. Parliament had greater need of justification than the King, for it was in the more unusual position of fighting an anointed monarch whose hereditary succession to the throne was unimpeachable. It was no Bosworth Field for which they were heading, they were not advancing a rival dynasty, but they were seeking to establish, or to reestablish, a constitution. In doing this they could either regard themselves as rebels, in which case they had to prove that their rebellion was justified; or, if they chose not to regard themselves as rebels, they had to prove that they, that Parliament, was constitutionally and legislatively supreme. At the beginning of the struggle they sought to avoid the issue by such tortuous reasoning as that they were fighting not the King but his evil counsellors. But soon they were seeking justification in precedent no less diligently than Charles had done, relying upon the common law as expounded by Coke, upon statute law (but not recent statute law for this was too closely associated with the regime they were opposing), upon the ancient constitution, upon real or imagined history, and upon the very principles of political obligation. They selected for approval certain landmarks, particularly Magna Carta and their own Petition of Right: the former, being the more remote, was particularly useful and its clauses concerning free men and imprisonment were particularly apt. They spoke of a golden age where all men were free. They explained the need for such charters as Magna Carta by adopting the fiction of a free Anglo-Saxon society upon whom the Norman yoke had been riveted by William the Conqueror. Events subsequent to the Norman Conquest then became the winning back of lost freedoms by the people of England and the present struggle could be seen as one event – supposedly the last – in such a chain.

There still remained difficulties in deciding what was a good law and what a bad law. Pym had said, and his words were widely echoed throughout the conflict, that the law is that which puts a difference between good and evil, between right and wrong. But people could ask: whose law? and attention was turned to the 94th Psalm with its profound assertion of possible evil in the law-giver – 'he who frameth mischief by a law'. By what yard-stick should a law be judged? There were many answers, but the terms 'natural law' and 'fundamental law' began to take their places in the pamphlet literature. But what was 'natural' or 'fundamental' law? Was it always beneficial? And, if beneficial, to whom? The protagonists looked even further back than Anglo-Saxon society to a 'state of nature' whose inhabitants voluntarily abrogated their authority in favour of one or some who would act for them. Generally they thought in terms of a monarch who made a compact with his people which was repeated in the Coronation oath of subsequent kings. This brought the opposition on to surer ground. If an anointed monarch broke his coronation oath might he not be replaced, as having broken the original compact made between ruler and ruled?

355

At this point they had a wide literature to call upon. In the French wars of religion the question of deposing an unsatisfactory king had been widely canvassed, and though the context had been for the most part religious, the issue was much the same. The author of the *Vindiciae contra tyrannos*, published in 1574, asked squarely whether subjects ought to obey Princes who commanded that which was against the law of God, or whether they should resist a Prince whose actions were oppressive or ruinous to the state? It was the easier for Parliament to supply the answer since so much of their Puritan tradition was concerned with resistance first to the Pope and then to a persecuting monarch. 'Think you that subjects, having power, may resist their princes?' was the first question that Charles's grandmother, Mary, Queen of Scots, put to John Knox on their first meeting.

Behind the question of obedience lay a second, and even more profound, question: in whom does sovereign power reside? Parliament answered emphatically that it itself was sovereign and, not surprisingly, its old champion, William Prynne, weighed in heavily with a long, tortuous, and margin-ridden treatise on *The Sovereign Power of Parliaments*. Behind the verbiage he and others were claiming that Parliament was supreme because it was representative, but since the right to vote was vested in property owners, a considerable sleight of hand was necessary to carry through the assertion that Parliament was representative in the full sense of representing all the people.

For Charles the questions were more easily formulated and simpler to answer. He was defending his position as monarch by divine right, heredity, and anointment, holding his prerogative, 'the fairest jewel in his crown', to use in case of necessity and claiming to rest his government upon the law and his people assembled in Parliament. His contribution to the paper war was consequently smaller in volume than that of his opponents. Generally speaking, the Royalist writers agreed with the King but got into difficulties in trying to combine a semi-mystical approach to sovereignty with the recognition that the King was subject to law and that law could be made only with and through the Parliament. Nevertheless they were unequivocal in refusing to recognize a right of resistance to the sovereign by Parliament or anyone else. In any case, wrote John Bramhall in 1643, the kingdom had suffered more from resistance in one year than under all the kings and queens of England since the union of the two roses. As for the liberty which Parliamentarian supporters were claiming, this could be expressed only through the law, and then very inadequately. 'The true debate among men', wrote Dudley Digges in *The Unlawfulness of Subjects taking up arms*, published in 1643, 'is not whether they shall admit of bonds, but who shall impose them. Though we naturally delight in a full and absolute liberty', he continued, 'yet the love of it is over-balanced with fears . . . that all others should enjoy the same freedom.'

The principles under discussion were of basic importance yet they brought no nearer a solution of the differences between Charles and his Parliament. But, although the drift to war was unmistakeable, no one would yet admit of such a bleak development. The pamphlet war that for a few brief months took the place of physical conflict was partly a desire for justification, but partly also an effort to avert the inevitable catastrophe. Certainty existed in the minds of only a few – and these, perhaps, were the lucky ones. Some simply wished to remain neutral in a quarrel which barely touched their lives. For others the doubts and questioning were intense and resulted in rifts that ran through Parliament, through counties, through towns, through families. Possibly half the peers had by now come into the King and about a quarter were uncommitted, leaving a quarter who were still with the opposition. Of the Commons only a minority had so far decided for him. Towns were divided, as Charles had seen at Hull. Families were divided, his Knight Marshall, Sir Edmund Verney, remaining with him while of the Verney sons one was with Parliament, the other with his father. Yet it was impossible for the two sides to remain locked in words and movement of some kind was inevitable. Predictably the incidents piled up. Militia Ordinance and Commission of Array were the most obvious points of conflict, openly juxtaposing the two sides. Lord Paget, originally a Parliament man, was driven by the Militia Ordnance to change sides:

> my ends were the common good, and whilst that was prosecuted, I was ready to lay down both my life and fortune; but when I found a preparation of arms against the King under the shadow of loyalty, I rather resolved to obey a good conscience than particular ends, and am now on my way to his Majesty, where I will throw myself down at his feet, and die a loyal subject.

Religious differences, which perhaps had been tolerated amongst friends and neighbours, became more irritating; personal feuds took on a wider significance. The Earl of Warwick used the ships under his command to remove the arms stored at Hull and convey them to the

Tower of London. Charles made a further vain attempt to win over Hotham and take the town on July 17. He began to move southwards and westwards from York, assessing allegience, gathering support, collecting money and plate to convert into coin. On July 9 he appointed the Earl of Lindsey Commander-in-Chief of the forces he believed he could raise. Robert Bertie, Lord Willoughby de Eresby, had been created Earl of Lindsey for services under Buckingham at La Rochelle. He had seen energetic campaigning in Europe and adventures on the Spanish Main that smacked of successful piracy. He had made an advantageous marriage, improved his estates at Grimsthorpe Castle near Stamford, and did well out of Fen drainage. He was physically tough, outspoken, and almost boisterous in his manner. He was a good all-rounder to have as Commander-in-Chief.

Three days after Charles had made his choice Parliament named the Earl of Essex Captain General of the Parliamentarian army which, they oddly claimed, had been levied 'for the safety of the King's person, the defence of both Houses of Parliament, and of those who have obeyed their orders and commands, and for the preservation of the true religion, laws, liberties and peace of the kingdom'. Essex was brave, but lethargic. His coffin, his winding-sheet and his scutcheon accompanied him on his campaigns and he took no notice when Charles declared him a traitor.

It was now a question of a definitive act that would be a declaration of war and Charles decided to raise his standard. But where? The Lancashire tenantry were following their hereditary leaders, the Stanleys, and it was in Manchester, in opposition to Parliament's Militia Ordinance, that there occurred on July 15 one of the first skirmishes of the war. In Northumberland and Durham the Earl of Newcastle was marshalling his tenants for the King and was in possession of Newcastle, Shields and Tynemouth Castle. Herefordshire, Worcestershire, parts of Warwickshire, were friendly, and in Wales he could count upon strong support. Finally, against a strong case for Lancashire, Charles decided in favour of Nottingham, a compromise position between the North and Wales, well placed by river communication with the Eastern seaports where, in place of Hull, his wife's arms might land, and conveniently near to London. For, insofar as he already had an objective, it was the capital with its prestige, its wealth, its possible Royalism once the influence of Parliament was broken, its access by sea northwards and to the Continent, its radius of communications over the country, and its appeal as his home and the seat of his government throughout his reign: he might well be regretting the night of panic that caused him to leave his capital city.

The raising of his standard at Nottingham on August 22 was not the dramatic affair that Charles could have wished. He had been refused entry to Coventry two days before and a Proclamation calling for support had not attracted the numbers he expected. For various reasons – uncertainty, bad weather, the requirements of harvest – there was no vast or enthusiastic concourse at Nottingham and it was not until six in the evening of a bleak and stormy day that Charles, his two sons, his nephews Rupert and Maurice who had lately joined him, Dr Harvey, a few courtiers, the heralds, and Sir Edmund Verney with the standard, rode to the top of Castle Hill. As the pennant was unfurled and a herald, with a flourish of trumpets, made to read a proclamation, Charles snatched the paper from him and hurriedly scribbled some amendments as best he might in the blustery wind, with the consequence that the herald, stumbling over the spidery handwriting, failed to make the dramatic summons that was called for. Later in the week the standard was blown down.

On that fateful day Charles had no more than 800 horse and 3000 foot that he could call an army. He commissioned Prince Rupert, who already had won a considerable reputation as a cavalry officer in Europe, as General of Horse, confirming the appointment made by Henrietta-Maria in his name. Although his wife had sent a warning that the Prince was still young and headstrong and needed watching, Charles granted Rupert's request that his command should be independent of the Commander-in-Chief and that he should be accountable to the King alone. His mother had tried hard to keep him in Europe, away from the maelstrom she saw developing in England and closer to the scene of his hereditary struggle, but Rupert equalled her in force of character; he not only came himself but brought his younger brother, Maurice, Bernard de Gomme, a skilled draughtsman and engineer with experience in siege warfare, and Bartholomew La Roche, a 'fireworker', who would be useful in the artillery train.

Perhaps because of the paucity of his following, perhaps through fear of the irreversible step, Charles's advisers called for one more approach to Parliament. For once Charles opposed this advice. In his slow fashion he had at last accepted war and he would not be thrown back into an agony of indecision. When he at last yielded, it was with bitter tears of frustration. But he had been right. Parliament scornfully rejected his overtures. Only if he furled his standard and recalled his declaration of treason against their commanders would they treat.

Charles's frustration had been caused partly because he knew that further attempts at negotiation would be fruitless, partly because he wanted to vindicate himself in his wife's eyes and to free himself from the terrible scorn she was pouring upon his diffidence and uncertainties.

Henrietta-Maria was by this time firmly established at The Hague, where she and the Princess Mary had arrived on February 25 to a welcome which was warm if not enthusiastic. In the welcoming party was her sister-in-law, Elizabeth, with her youngest daughter, Sophie, who was about the same age as Mary. The anxieties of the past year had left their mark on the Queen and a rough Channel crossing in which one of the baggage ships sunk within sight of land had not improved her looks. Little Sophie, who had been deeply impressed by the Van Dyck portraits of her aunt, was sadly disappointed at the sight of what she later described as a little, lop-sided lady with big teeth but who nevertheless possessed beautiful big eyes and a good complexion. Sophie was far more impressed with her elegant cousin and was highly flattered when Henrietta-Maria commented upon a likeness between the two children.[3] It was the first meeting between the two mothers – Charles's sister and Charles's wife – and they rode in the same carriage with William and Mary, talking earnestly.

Henrietta-Maria was comfortably lodged in the new palace of the Prince of Orange, but she soon made it clear that her object was solely that of supplying her husband with money and arms. There were difficulties in selling or pawning the jewels she had brought with her, for dealers were reluctant to touch anything that might belong to the Crown; security for a loan was similarly difficult to obtain. In long letters in cypher to Charles she related her experiences and told him what he must do. It was evident that she felt the need to bolster his resolution and was afraid of the mistakes he might make without her presence. Nothing so much indicates the hold she had over Charles as her letters from Holland. When she heard he had been denied at Hull she was first incredulous, then scathing. She had left England, she wrote, so that he would not be hampered by feelings of responsibility towards her. Now she perceived it was not thoughts for her but his own weakness which impeded him. She herself had long ago accepted the necessity for war and urged her husband over and over again not to delay his preparations. 'Delays have always ruined you', she wrote, no doubt thinking of the Five Members. She accused him of being up to his 'old game of yielding everything'. She, who knew him so well, and who had made light of his faults when they appeared to be of little significance, now, in time of stress, remembered them all, and Charles accepted her strictures. He did nothing without his wife's approbation, wrote Elizabeth to Roe about this time.

Henrietta-Maria drove herself to extremities of fatigue by poring over Charles's cypher letters. She was terrified lest he should lose the code. She had noted his habit of thrusting things into pockets and saw that he had done the same with the precious cypher: 'take care of your pocket', she admonishes, 'and do not let our cypher be stolen.' Her endeavours were reflected in her health. Not only were her eyes troubling her, her head ached, she had pains in her legs and was becoming lame, she was distracted by toothache and had a severe cold. The difficulties of communication alone were sufficient to deter a less resolute woman. Little Will Murray, as Henrietta-Maria always called him – was he shorter even than Charles or herself? – the two brothers Slingsby, Sir Lewis Dyve, Walter Montague her chaplain, were among their go-betweens. But the weather delayed vessels, Parliament's shipping was strong in the Channel, one vessel carrying letters was driven back to Brill after four days at sea, on another occasion a bag of letters was jettisoned through fear of capture and it was some time before it could safely be fished up again. They supplemented the letters with agents of various kinds – a 'poor woman' at Portsmouth, a man who came to Holland ostensibly as a bird-catcher and who reached the Queen a fortnight after he left Charles. But it was inevitable there should be gaps filled on the Queen's side, at least, with conflicting rumours. On one occasion she was so tormented by stories of defeat and death that she made her way in disguise to a bookshop which stocked *corrantos* or news-sheets, but fled on being recognized. Some of Charles's letters giving details of his requirements nevertheless reached her and she was having some success in raising money and in buying arms. Some things she merely pawned, hoping to acquire them again in better days – her 'great chain' and the cross from her mother. But she sold her 'little chain' and dismembered Charles's pearl buttons: 'You cannot imagine how handsome the buttons were, when they were out of the gold, and strung into a chain . . . I assure you, that I gave them up with no small regret.'

While his wife's activities gave him hope of assistance and stiffened his resolution, Charles still had to bear the anguish of separation, the worry of her ill-health, the difficulties of communication, and at the same time prepare for war. Her letters, indeed, aroused mixed feelings and her forceful comments on his character could be painful in the extreme. Yet her letters were also the most poignant love letters. 'If I do not turn mad', she wrote, 'I shall be a great miracle; but, provided it be in your service, I shall be content – only if it be when I am with you, for I can no longer live as I am without you.'[4]

30

Commander-in-Chief

After his standard had been somewhat ignominiously floated at Nottingham Charles moved westward to gather the support he believed to be awaiting him in Shropshire and in Wales. He left Nottingham on the 13th for Derby, where the miners came into him in considerable strength, mostly joining the Lifeguard commanded by Lord Willoughby d'Eresby; he was welcomed at Shrewsbury on the 20th where he was joined by Patrick Ruthven with twenty or so experienced officers. Baron Ruthven of Ettrick was a hard-drinking, experienced solder, already some seventy years of age, who had seen much service in the European wars and been Charles's Muster-Master in Scotland and Governor of Edinburgh Castle. In his pleasure at seeing him Charles now created him Earl of Forth. At Chester on the 23rd recruits began to flock in, not only from the immediate neighbourhood but, as expected, from North and South Wales and from Staffordshire, and also from Lincolnshire, Bedfordshire, and further afield.

The Parliamentarian forces under Essex had hoped to surprise the King at Nottingham, but, learning of his departure, had stopped at Northampton and on the 19th began a westward march towards Worcester parallel to the King's own. Worcester had opened its gates to Royalist troops but Rupert, probably correctly, judged the city untenable against Essex's advancing army and was covering the Royalist evacuation of the town when, quite accidentally, he fell in with a small group of Parliamentarian horse at Powicke Bridge. Rupert had the advantage of seeing the enemy before they saw him and in a brief little encounter on 23 September 1642 the first real engagement of the war occurred, in which the Parliamentarian horse broke and fled, not drawing rein until they had joined their main army, many miles away. The news of Powicke Bridge was brought to

Charles at Chester by Richard Crane, Commander of Rupert's Lifeguard, who was knighted on the spot by the delighted King. Though only about 2000 men in all had been involved Charles had, indeed, cause for satisfaction as he gleefully examined the six or seven captured cornets of horse who were brought in. First blood of the war had gone to him and casualties were few, though among the wounded were his nephew, Maurice, and his friend, Sir Lewis Dyve.

In common with the majority of the men who were joining up on either side, Charles had to learn the strategy of war in a country like England. Some of the recruits had had experience in Germany or the Low Countries, some had fought under Gustavus Adolphus and were familiar with the Swedish form of fighting, others favoured the simpler Dutch formations. Some, like the King himself, had experimented for hours with model soldiers and artillery. None of them had fought before on English soil with its own particular problems. Where fields had been enclosed, for example, there was little opportunity for deploying an army – certainly not the cavalry – and the weather played its part. Roads were execrable, bad enough for individual horsemen, almost impassable for the numbers who were now beginning to turn even the best of them into mud and quagmire as the ruts and holes common to most surfaces were filled to overflowing by the heavy rains of September 1642. For men to be knee-deep in mud and water was not uncommon, while horses, carts, waggons and coaches had to be pushed and hauled time and time again through the enveloping slime. The drill books and manuals of war that were brought out might in some respects put a captain ahead of his men, but they gave no real insight into the situation. Neither side, for example, had envisaged the number of horses that were needed – not for the cavalry since volunteers brought their own mounts – but cart horses for drawing gun-carriages and other heavy vehicles. It took six or eight cart horses, harnessed in tandem, to pull a field gun; the heaviest cannon required twelve or fourteen. Charles, whose study of warfare had familiarized him with the problem, had encouraged James Wemyss, his Master Gunner, to produce a lighter and more mobile piece of artillery. Wemyss had actually constructed a gun consisting of a copper tube strengthened with iron bands and covered by a leather skin, but this had not yet come into general production, and markets and farms for miles around Charles's army were being scoured for horses and, failing horses for oxen, to draw his heavy guns. Carts and wagons were in similar demand for conveyance, and denuded farms were paid by the day for their use, with a bonus if the driver came too.

Food, fodder, the paraphernalia of cooking and eating, cooks, provisioners, traders anxious to provide anything that was required for man or beast; shovels, spades, pickaxes, wheelbarrows; ropes, spare harness, materials to repair the constant breakages which the conditions of travel entailed, came along with the army. In particular a contingent of smiths and wheelrights were there, for the roads played havoc with horses' hooves and with the wheels of vehicles, and in hostile country the inability to secure the services of these craftsmen could be very serious.

Normally the Royalist army on the march consisted of two brigades of cavalry in the van, followed by a brigade of foot. Charles followed on horseback supported by his Lifeguard with his banner and flanked by his Council of War, with secretaries and messengers to hand. There followed another infantry brigade and then the enormous and unwieldy artillery train protected by musketeers, the horses pulling desperately at the heavy guns and at the carts and wagons loaded with arms and ammunition. Courtiers and courtiers-turned-soldier frequently brought their wives who travelled in carriages. They all brought much personal baggage. Even the lower-ranking soldiers came with their wives, their wardrobes and their household goods, while the secretariat had its own wagon of writing materials, documents, letters, duplicates, the King had his personal wardrobe and his more private correspondence, prostitutes cheerfully tagged along, and in the rear a further brigade of cavalry, sometimes in front of, sometimes behind the baggage trains, completed the tale of an army marching to war. The untidy, heterogeneous procession covered some five miles or more from van to rear of the muddy and difficult roads of the Midlands, moving so slowly that it took Charles ten days to cover less than a hundred miles between Shrewsbury and Banbury, which was not considered bad going and which was better than Essex did on his nearly parallel journey from Worcester to Kineton when he averaged only eight or so miles a day, and then left part of his army far in the rear.

The army carried few tents and little camping equipment, so the surrounding countryside was scoured to find billets for the 12,000 or so troops on the move. Charles and the High Command generally lodged in some nobleman's house while the men slept in scattered villages as far as ten miles away. The total area occupied by an army, simply to move from one place to another, was very considerable. Though provisions were at first paid for and often eaten in camp, it is understandable that the advent of an army came to be dreaded and that its passage was likened to the passing of a horde of locusts. It would seem difficult to conceal its whereabouts. Yet, in spite of the strategy learned on the Continent and the frequent recourse to drill books and military manuals, the art of reconniassance was so lacking, or so extremely elementary, that commanders frequently seemed unaware of the presence of the enemy until they were on top of them.[1]

After Powicke Bridge there had been some discussion of strategy among Charles's High Command: should they engage Essex then and there and endeavour to take Worcester? Or should they march on London? The former was ruled out partly because the enclosed nature of the countryside made cavalry deployment difficult, and partly because Charles's growing resources made the bolder plan viable. His armies were increasing daily and he now had no scruples in accepting Catholic money or plate or, indeed, Catholic services: 'this rebellion is grown to that height', he wrote to Newcastle, 'that I must not look what opinion men are who at this time are willing and able to serve me'.[2] He left Shrewsbury on October 12, making for London in a south-easterly course with some idea of taking Banbury on the way. Passing between hostile Warwick and Coventry he stopped at Southam and reached Edgcott, four miles from Banbury, on the evening of October 22, where he lodged at Sir William Chancie's house with Rupert nine miles away at Wormleighton, Lindsey at Culworth, and his men dispersed to such scattered quarters as they could find. The weather was atrocious and bitterly cold. About midnight Rupert sent word that Essex, who had been on the shorter march from Worcester, was at Kineton, some seven miles west of the main Royalist position. The two armies, though they marched the same way and had been only twenty miles apart when they started, and for the last two days had been on a parallel course only ten miles apart, had until then no knowledge of the whereabouts of each other.

There was danger to Charles in continuing his march with Essex in his rear, so when Rupert reported in favour of battle Charles readily accepted his advice. 'Nephew', he hurriedly scribbled, 'I have given order as you have desyred; so I dout not but all the foot and canon will bee at Edgehill betymes this morning, where you will also find Your loving oncle and faithful frend.' Discussions concerning tactics soon reached deadlock; Lindsey favoured the Dutch order of battle, Rupert the Swedish in which pikemen and musketeers were interspersed in the battle line-up, and Charles supported his nephew. The fatal flaw in the command which allowed Rupert to be independent of the Commander-in-Chief had already led to difficulties and now the volatile and haughty Prince appeared to be taking over the whole strategy of the battle, foot as well as horse. When Lindsey cast his baton on the ground declaring: 'Since your Majesty thinks me not fit to perform the office of Commander-in-Chief I would serve you as colonel only', Charles cut the Gordian knot by instructing Lord Forth to draw up the army in battle order while he himself assumed the overall command.

The ridge of Edgehill, where the Royalists would take up their position, was some five miles west of Edgcott and only two miles from Kineton. By early morning Rupert's horse were drawn up on the ridge and Charles was gazing through his perspective glass at the awakening Parliamentarian armies below. It was afternoon by the time the Royalist foot had been brought in from the scattered villages where they lay, and by that time Essex had collected the main body of his army and had deployed it in one of the open fields of that still largely unenclosed countryside. He was perturbed at the numbers he saw massing against him, which far exceeded any reports he had received, particularly since two of his regiments of foot and one of horse were a day's march behind him. He did the only thing that was open to him. He stayed where he was and waited for the enemy to attack. Charles meantime, having sent his sons firmly away to comparative safety in the charge of the faithful Dr Harvey, was riding up and down amongst his men with a black cloak over his armour encouraging everyone. By three o'clock they were ready. 'Go in the name of God', he said to Lindsey, 'and I'll lay my bones by yours.' He had under his command some 2800 horse, 10,500 foot, 1000 dragoons, and some twenty guns drawn up, in customary fashion, with the foot in the centre and the cavalry on each flank. Many prayers went up that day. Sir Edmund Verney, bearing the royal standard in a conflict he could not believe in; Lord Lindsey, no less determined to fight in the King's forces although he was no longer their leader; Lord Falkland, no fighter by inclination and hoping to end the strife in one swift blow; cavaliers who had followed Rupert from Europe; courtiers, excited and scornful of the enemy; country gentlemen and their sons whose only experience of war was in the tales of their fathers and the dusty textbooks they had routed out; raw recruits, frightened and uncertain, whose instinct was to break and run for home; Charles himself whose baptism in battle was about to begin; seasoned veterans like Sir Jacob Astley whose spoken prayer served for them all: 'O Lord!, Thou knowest how busy I must be this day. If I forget Thee, do not Thou forget me'.

Rupert, on the right of the King's army, was the first to charge using the full weight of his horsemen, in his accustomed style, to break the enemy, reserving his fire for the pursuit. The Parliamentarian left wing was shattered by the impact. Rupert and his cavaliers pursued the fleeing horsemen to Kineton and beyond, only drawing rein when two of Hampden's regiments were seen advancing towards them. The Royalist left wing had acted similarly, if not so dramatically, and the brunt of the fighting in the field had been left to the two blocs of infantry where Charles remained, urging on his men, commanding mercy to the enemy, in the midst of terrible slaughter. His commanders begged him to retire to the top of the hill, which he did for a while, but he was soon down amongst his men again. As evening fell Rupert's horsemen returned to the battle which might have been decisively won but for their long absence. Falkland urged one more charge, possibly thinking to end the war then and there, but it was too late; men and horses were spent and darkness was falling. Charles refused to leave the field lest the enemy attempt another attack or construe his withdrawal into an admission of defeat. He slept fitfully in the uncertain light and scant warmth of a small fire made from such wood and brush as could be found, the dead and wounded of both armies lying near him on the battlefield. Before he slept he rewarded one act of heroism, while mourning its necessity. Verney had fallen in the battle and the royal standard had been seized, but Captain Smith, slipping through the enemy lines after dark with a few comrades, recaptured it and brought it to the King, who knighted him on the spot. He had no news of Lindsey, or of Lindsey's son, who had last been seen standing over his wounded father in an attempt to save him.

By first light the wounded were being brought in and the dead identified. They had lost some 1500 men in all. Lindsey's son was a prisoner, Lindsey himself had been carried to a barn where he lay without medical attention, bleeding to death; others who remained in the cold of the battlefield all night fared better, as Harvey recorded, for the frost congealed the blood on their wounds. It was soon apparent that Essex was moving off to Warwick, and the way to London was open to Charles. If the battle itself had been indecisive the result of the battle was a victory for the King, for it had achieved his objective.[3] Rupert proposed to the Council of War that a flying column of 3000 horse and foot should immediately march on Westminster and take the capital by surprise. Charles could not bring himself to entertain so immediate a confrontation. But neither, it seems, could he envisage a more sober approach to the city. Instead he marched to Banbury, where he secured supplies of food and clothing for his men, and he captured Broughton Castle, doubtless deriving satisfaction from the knowledge that he was master in the Puritan territory of Lord Saye and Sele. He and his army then moved forward unmolested to Oxford, whose loyalty to the King was unquestioned in spite of some difference of opinion between the town and the University. But in doing this he allowed Essex to make a leisurely return to the capital. Neither side hurried. The initial impact of civil war had been sobering and the armies were not yet willing to risk a fresh encounter. But Charles, by the delay, lost more than his opponents, for he never again had the opportunity of occupying London. Perhaps, thereby, he lost the war.

Charles entered Oxford on October 29 at full march accompanied by the four Princes and with the sixty or seventy colours captured at Edgehill borne before him. The welcome was warm and the mayor presented him with a bag of money. The deputy orator welcomed him more effusively for the University and, with his sons, he took up residence in Christ Church, while Rupert went to St John's where, in Laud's time, he had been accepted as a commoner. The foot-soldiers were billeted in the villages round Oxford, the cavalry headquarters were at Abingdon, many important officials remained near the King – Culpepper and his family in Oriel College, other members of the Privy Council in Postmaster's Hall opposite Merton College where the Warden's lodgings were being prepared for Henrietta-Maria.

The arms and ammunition they brought with them joined the stores already in the cloisters and tower of New College, twenty-seven pieces of heavy ordnance were driven into Magdalen Grove. Grain was stored in the Law and Logic Schools, fodder in New College, animals were penned in Christ Church quadrangle. In the Music and Astronomy Schools cloth was cut into coats for soldiers and carried out by packhorse to be stitched by seamstresses in nearby villages. The mill at Osney became a gunpowder factory, a mint was erected at New Inn Hall to turn the plate that had been brought in to the King into negotiable money. Nicholas Briot's assistant, Thomas Rawlins, who was with Charles, had much of his master's skill and, apart from utilitarian pieces needed for soldiers' pay, the mint produced a beautiful golden crown piece to his design and a medal to mark the victory at Edgehill – for so the Royalists termed it, though Charles was well aware of the greater victory it might have been, as he told the Venetian Ambassador who visited him at Christ Church; if the cavalry had not overcharged and returned to the field too late to do further battle, he said, it would have been a great victory indeed.

Charles made one not very convincing attempt to march on London when Rupert, on November 11, took and briefly held, a Parliamentary outpost at Brentford. But the London trained bands streamed out to protect their city, and faced with a force of 24,000 men, outnumbering him by two to one, Charles withdrew. He might have crossed into Kent at Kingston and drawn upon the support for him there, but the campaigning season was over and he preferred to settle down in Oxford for the winter. The fortifications of the city, begun before Charles's arrival, were continued. The High Street was blocked at East Bridge by logs and a timber gate, while a bulwark between it and the Physic Garden wall supported two pieces of ordnance, and loads of stone were carried up Magdalen Tower to fling down upon the enemy. The digging of trenches was ordered at vulnerable points between St John's College and the New Park, and in Christ Church Meadow, but the response was poor and when Charles reviewed the work he spoke to the citizens personally, afterwards issuing an Order that everyone over the age of sixteen and under sixty should work on fortifications for one day a week or pay twelve pence for each default. Plans were made to use the waters of the Thames and Cherwell, which surrounded the city on all sides except the North, as an additional defence, the vulnerable North being protected by regiments at Enstone, Woodstock, and Islip. Communications with Reading, which the Royalists held, were kept open by garrisons at Wallingford and Abingdon. Strong garrisons at Banbury, Brill, Faringdon and Burford completed an outer ring of defences behind which Charles at last had a little time for contemplation as he and his army settled in for the winter.

But first he attended to the pleasant task of honouring his children by conferring the degrees of MA upon them; for Dr Harvey, Cambridge and Padua, there was the distinction of an Oxford MD. So popular among his followers were these awards that Charles found himself sponsoring 18 Doctors and 48 Bachelors of Divinity; 34 Doctors and 14 Bachelors of Civil Law; five Doctors and eight Bachelors of Physics; 76 MAs and 12 BAs. As the day of inauguration wore on the Chancellor's actions became more mechanical, his attention lapsed, and many men who had not been named thrust themselves forward after candlelight to receive the coveted honour. The granting of degrees was an easy way for Charles to reward his followers, and by the following February the University was tired out with one Convocation after another and Charles, without ill-will, agreed to curtail his academic awards.[4]

Meanwhile printing presses, many of them clandestine, were proliferating, especially in London, giving vent to every kind of opinion, religious, social, political; reporting battles, conferences, proceedings in Parliament or in Oxford. They came from both sides and neither side and voiced complaints that could be laid at the door of either party or no party, they proposed solutions that were practical or Utopian, they expressed new antagonisms, new alignments as the struggle proceeded and they reflected every shade of opinion and belief that the violent opening of society generated. A London bookseller, George Thomason, set out to collect a copy of every pamphlet and news-sheet that came his way from the beginning of the Long Parliament. For the year 1642, the peak year, he had well over 2000 and the numbers were always well over a thousand. They included the news-sheets which were the successors of the *corrantos* brought to England from Holland during the earlier stages of the Thirty Years War and which now began to appear as regular weekly newspapers. Charles had been as quick as anyone to appreciate the value of print and of regular reporting. He took a printing press with him when he left London and one of the first things he did in Oxford was to inaugurate a weekly newssheet. Its first appearance as *Mercurius Aulicus* in January 1643 was preceded by a few days by Parliament's *Kingdomes Weekly Intelligencer*. *Aulicus* was published from Oriel College under the editorship of Dr Peter Heylin, the Laudian divine, but its leader-writer and subsequent editor was Sir John Berkenhead, a brilliant protégé of William Laud, a Fellow of All Souls College, Oxford, who had worked for some time with the Archbishop at Lambeth Palace. *Aulicus* seems to have had two printing presses at Oxford and, remarkably, it was also printed in London. The opening paragraph of the first number referred to its rival – 'a weekly cheat' put out to nourish falsehood amongst the people and 'make them pay for their seducement'. *Aulicus* would make them see 'that the Court is neither so barren of intelligence . . . nor the affaires thereof in so unprosperous a condition, as these Pamphlets make them'. In its 118 numbers, ending with the issue of 31 August – 7 September, 1645, *Aulicus* maintained a high standard of informed and witty reporting, receiving its news items and effecting a system of distribution and sale in and out of Oxford and even in London under the very eyes of Parliament.[5] It competed with some 170 different news-sheets which appeared for longer or shorter periods and hundreds of pamphlets, many of which made their way to Oxford. Charles was enormously interested in all the pamphlet litera-ture. Early in January 1643, for example, *The Complaint of London, Westminster, and the parts adjoyning* was being read to him while he was taking supper and he did not rise until it was finished.

Insofar as it was possible to make any calculation at this stage, it seemed that a majority of the House of Lords were following Charles and some forty per cent of the Commons, which was considerably more than the attitude of either House had indicated in the early days of the Long Parliament. Of the Commons possibly 236 Members were Royalists, most of whom had joined him, while 302 remained at Westminster. The tenants of the great landowners were for the most part following their lords – if they did not stay away from battle in an effort at neutrality; industrial towns, particularly the clothing towns of Lancashire, were for Puritanism and Parliament, while the sur-rounding areas, which contained many Catholics, were for the King. Similarly Bradford and Halifax contributed much support for Parlia-ment, while round them rural areas followed the Royalist allegiance of their landlords. On the whole Charles had great hopes of the North, where he had appointed the Duke of Newcastle Commander of the four northern counties; in March 1643 he stiffened the inexperienced lord by giving him James King, Lord Eythin, a Scot who had seen active service on the Continent, as his Lieutenant-General. By the middle of December Newcastle was virtually in control of Yorkshire, and Lord Fairfax, the Parliamenterian Commander, had fallen back to Selby. In Cornwall the Marquess of Hertford, William Seymour – at one time the husband of the unhappy Arabella Stuart – who was Lieutenant General of the Western Counties, was in virtually com-plete control, with Ralph, Lord Hopton, his second-in-command and such men as Bevil Grenville, grandson of the hero of the *Revenge*, fighting with him.

Charles's opponents had the advantage of London, of most of the wealthy towns and important ports, but south of the capital he could count on support in Kent. Roughly speaking, Charles might call the North and the South-West, including Wales and Cornwall, his country, the East and South-East Parliamenterian country, with the Midlands somewhat unevenly divided in favour of Parliament. But everywhere there were pockets of individual allegiance, and all over the country great houses were standing out in hostile territory. Charles saw among his own supporters large and small landowners, old landed families and new, merchants, industrialists, lawyers, rising gentry and falling gentry – but he saw them on the other side, too. Even past favours had not guaranteed support. He wryly watched the Earl of Holland with his friends of the Providence Island Company, and he wondered why Wemyss, his master gunner, with whom he had appeared to be on good terms, had taken up arms on the other side.

Why, indeed, were they fighting at all? Edward Hyde had often told him that the number of those who desired to sit still was greater than those who desired to engage on either side, and the philosopher Thomas Hobbes was saying that there were few of the common people who cared much for either of the causes, but that most would have taken either side for pay or plunder. There certainly had been reasons for the antagonism of the Long Parliament. But that was past history. The abuses of which they complained had been removed, the constitutional government they demanded had been secured by the summer of 1641. Was it purely rancour that made people fight against him? Were they remembering the past – the forced loans, the monopolies in which they did not share, the tonnage and poundage, so necessary a tax in an untaxed country like England, lack of preferment at Court or in office, the enclosure prohibitions and the accompanying fines at which Laud had been so adept, his own knighthood fees, forest fines and the ship money he had used for the ships which now were in Parliament's hands? If Charles had given way on the militia could he have averted war? Was it over the control of the armed forces that they were fighting? If he had abandoned Episcopacy would he have averted war? But they had not wished him to do that, as the debates on the Grand Remonstrance and the opposition to the Root and Branch Bill made abundantly clear. Did they really believe that he

373

was so lukewarm in his religion, or so much under the influence of his wife, as to consider joining the Roman Church? Did they consider for a moment that his relations with Spain were anything but opportunist or that he had in any way encouraged the Irish rising in 1641? He remembered angrily that the people who now accused him of betraying the Protestant religion were the very ones who had refused aid to his sister. He still could not see why a compromise had not been reached. Had Bedford served him ill by his death at the moment when a middle group might have negotiated a settlement? But, whatever the answers, it takes two to make a quarrel and it takes two armies to wage war, and unless there had been a significant reaction against Parliament the formation of a King's party would have been unlikely and the outbreak of war impossible.

Possibly the split had occurred between those who believed in his promises and those who did not believe that he had abandoned forever the right to supply without the sanction of Parliament. But a tax would be a tax, money would be required, whether for King or Parliament, and Charles could watch, even with amusement, the response accorded to his opponents' efforts to raise money. When Pym had met with a poor response from the City earlier in 1642 and spoke of 'compelling' the Londoners to lend, their defences had gone up immediately. Certainly, said D'Ewes, 'if the least fear of this should grow, that men should be compelled to lend, all men will conceal their ready money, and lend nothing to us voluntarily'. There was a similar reaction at the end of December when the City refused to lend unless the Upper House set an example. Some noble lords refused absolutely, others took time to consider, Lord Saye subscribed a mere £100, the Earl of Manchester £300.

Many people undoubtedly believed that to continue the quarrel with the King would be to unleash anarchy, and in this respect the petitions and rioting at the end of 1641, which Parliament itself had encouraged, did them harm. The Venetian Ambassador noted the apprehension lest an attenuation of royal authority 'might not augment licence among the people with manifest danger that after shaking off the yoke of monarchy they might afterwards apply themselves to abase the nobility also and reduce the government of this realm to a complete democracy'. Sir John Hotham, a little too late for Charles's satisfaction, came over to the King's side after the fighting had started, giving as one of his reasons that he feared 'the necessitous people' of the whole kingdom would rise 'in mighty numbers, and whatsoever they pretend for att first, within a while they will sett up for themselves to the utter ruine of all the Nobility and Gentry of the kingdome'. This danger of anarchy was one of the reasons for preserving episcopacy. As his father had said, no Bishop, no King; and Sir Edmund Waller had pointed out the relationship in greater detail. Episcopacy, he said, was 'a counterscarp, or outwork; which, if it be taken by this assault of the people . . . we may, in the next place, have as hard a task to defend our property as we have lately had to defend it from the Prerogative. If . . . they prevail for an equality in things ecclesiastical, the next demand perhaps may be lex agraria, the like equality in things temporal.' Or, as Sir John Strangeways put it in the course of the debate on the Root and Branch petition, 'If we make a parity in the Church we must come to a parity in the Commonwealth.'

As far as Charles could see the choice of sides rested almost entirely on the answer to the question whether property, and the civil and ecclesiastical order which upheld it, would be safer under King or Parliament. Those who supported Parliament might have had some doubts when in October 1642 a lawyer named Fountain appealed to the Petition of Right when refusing a 'gift' to Parliament and was told bluntly by Henry Marten that the Petition was intended to restrain kings, not parliaments. Fountain was sent to prison.

But while for richer people the issue had come to be very largely one of property, there were many who were now supporting Parliament under the wider banner which Charles's opponents had appropriated to themselves – that of 'Liberty' or, in the plural, 'Freedoms'. Charles could now see his mistakes in censoring the press, in allowing the 'Puritan martyrs' their platforms; he could see that 'little men', defeated by poverty, left behind by economic developments, were unafraid of anarchy but simply hoped for a new deal under Parliament; he knew well enough the power over these people of such fanatics as John Lilburne, who turned up as prisoner in Oxford after the taking of Brentford, having lost nothing of his old fire. In court he objected to being charged as a 'yeoman', being of gentry stock; he argued with the Earl of Northampton, and challenged Prince Rupert to combat, an unexpected invitation which caused the Prince to leave the room saying 'the fellow is mad!' In his captivity in Oxford Castle Lilburne kept up such a furore that the Royalists were only too happy to exchange him in May 1643 for Sir John Smith, whom Charles had knighted on Edgehill field.

The new Earl of Lindsey, who had remained a prisoner in Warwick Castle since Edgehill, was also exchanged in 1643 and joined the
King. From such friends and supporters who came into him at Oxford
Charles reaped great satisfaction. On the anniversary of Edgehill he
called Edward Lake to him. Lake was a lawyer who, despite his
inexperience, had shown remarkable bravery. When his left hand was
shot he placed his horse's bridle in his teeth and fought with his sword
in his right hand until the end of the day, when he was captured and
imprisoned. Seven weeks later he escaped and made his way to
Oxford. Charles was deeply impressed; 'you lost a great deal of blood
for me that day', he said, 'and I shall not forget it.' Then, turning to the
bystanders, 'for a lawyer', he said, 'a professed lawyer, to throw off
his gown and fight so heartily for me, I must need think very well of
it'. Charles not only created him a baronet but showed his habitual
care over detail by taking a personal interest in Lake's proposed coat of
arms, himself augmenting it by the addition of one of the lions of
England.[6]

As winter set in at Oxford the Court of Whitehall reproduced itself as
best it might. The city was now full of soldiers and courtiers, Privy
Councillors, secretaries, officials and supporters of many kinds,
mostly accompanied by their families, all crowding in on the limited
accommodation, generally content to exchange their normal state for
a couple of rooms in an overful lodging just for the sake of being there
at all. Fashionably dressed ladies walked in college gardens or watched
the recruits, mostly scholar-turned-soldier, marching down the High
Street and out to the New Parks for martial exercise, or drilling in the
meadows by the Cherwell under the walls of Merton College.
Domestic troubles began to assert themselves: Prince Charles had the
measles; Prince Maurice, more seriously, had an attack of the stone
which worried his mother more than the war itself; Charles had to
send to Whitehall for stockings and other small necessaries. The
House of Commons debated whether a servant should be allowed to
take them to Oxford and decided by a vote of 26 to 18 that Charles
might have them. He did not know which was worse – the lack of
interest in his needs or the fact that the matter should have been
discussed at all. More serious was the news in March 1643 that
Henrietta-Maria's chapel in Somerset House had been ransacked and
that Parliament had sequestered the lands of bishops, deans and chapters, appropriating the income to their own use.

Meanwhile Charles played tennis with Rupert, he hunted as far away as Woodstock, he received Ambassadors, including the Venetian and the Frenchman, who was a constant visitor; he even did his best to celebrate a wedding when a Groom of his Bedchamber married the reigning beauty of the exiled Court. But all this was accompanied not only by the drilling of recruits and the construction of fortifications but by the clatter of cavalry as horsemen moved in and out of the city. The most advanced post of the Parliamenterian armies was at Windsor, where Essex was covering the western approaches to London, and while the armies of both sides lay in their wide-spreading winter quarters there was a constant movement of patrols, reconnaissance parties, and probing detachments of horse. The spring offensive was heralded when Parliamentarian forces took Reading, only twenty miles from Oxford. At the beginning of June they were in Thame and ventured into Wheatley but were beaten off by a Royalist garrison on Shotover Hill. Rupert disliked this forward probing and hoped to retaliate by securing a convoy of money which he had heard was on its way from London to Thame. He missed the convoy but on his way back to Oxford on June 18 he dispersed a small enemy force at Chalgrove Field, ten miles south-east of Oxford. In this little skirmish John Hampden was mortally wounded and died in Thame six days later. The removal of his moderating influence was a serious loss to Parliament.

The time was now approaching when Henrietta-Maria herself would be joining her husband with the arms and money she had collected. As they made plans for their reunion the couple set about deliberate deception. 'All the letters which I write by the post, in which there is no cipher, do not you believe', she instructed, 'for they are written for the Parliament.' So it was given out that she would land at Yarmouth or Boston, whereas she intended Newcastle or Scarborough. But as the time for her departure drew near communications failed completely. As Powicke Bridge and Edgehill were fought the couple were out of touch and only the most dramatic rumours reached the isolated Queen. At last, with communications restored, she set sail in January 1643. First her little flotilla was becalmed off the Dutch coast. When they finally got away they were struck by storms of unprecedented ferocity and for nine days were beaten to and fro off the Dutch shore with no opportunity of making land. The Queen sustained her terrified ladies by assuring them that Queens of England were never drowned, acting at the same time as father-confessor to those who were convinced their end was near. When at last they were able to make land, it was Holland and not England to which they had come. The third effort was successful and Henrietta-Maria landed at Bridlington on February 22. She was given Royalist cover from the land and a troop of cavaliers rode in to greet her a few hours after her arrival. Charles was overwhelmed with relief and admiration: 'when I shall have done my part', he wrote from Oxford, 'I confess that I shall come short of what thou deservest of me.' Her trials were not yet over for the small house in which she prepared to spend the night became the target of bombardment from Parliamentarian ships and she was compelled to take the shelter of fields and hedges while cannon shot burst round her. Even when she was ready to ride south there were difficulties, for Fairfax with his army lay between her and Oxford. It took her nearly five months to reach Stratford where she was met by Rupert on July 11. But by that time her journey had become a triumphant march. Volunteers flocked in to her and with the arms and ammunition she had brought from Holland she was accompanied by 2000 foot, well armed, 1000 horse, six pieces of cannon, two mortars, and 100 well filled wagons. Newcastle was her escort, Jermyn her Commander-in-Chief, and she herself, as she wrote exultantly to Charles, was her 'she majesty, generalissima' over all. Two days after leaving Stratford she met her husband and her two eldest sons at the foot of Edgehill. They slept that night at Sir Thomas Pope's house at Wroxton and the next day proceeded to Woodstock and thence to Oxford.

The welcome to Oxford was dubbed 'triumphant' and 'magnificent' with soldiers lining the streets, houses packed with spectators, trumpets sounding, heralds riding before her. At Carfax the town clerk read a speech and presented her with a purse of gold, at Christ Church the Vice Chancellor and the Heads of Houses in scarlet gowns welcomed her, students read verses in Latin and English, and she received the traditional University present of a pair of gloves. Charles then conducted her, by a private way through Merton Grove, to the Warden's Lodgings in Merton College which would be her home.[7]

With the Queen's arrival Oxford resembled even more the Court at Whitehall, with courtiers flitting between Christ Church and Merton, ladies dressing elegantly in spite of the cramped rooms in which they were compelled to make their toilets. Practical jokes were played on academics who were a natural butt, it was even possible to produce a masque. But more serious was the renewal of the gossip and rivalry her presence brought. Digby, now one of her favourites, was at odds with Rupert; Holland, who had begun the war on the other side, came to Oxford to make his peace with her and spent far too long in her elegant drawing room at Merton, frequently in the afternoons when Charles himself was visiting his wife. Charles would not receive him back into favour and Holland departed for London and the Parliament. As he prepared for the coming campaign, Charles could have done without such distractions.

31

The Second Campaign

By this time Charles and his Council of War had decided upon their general strategy and were preparing their main offensive for 1643. Newcastle would march south from Yorkshire, Sir Ralph Hopton would gain control in the south-west, while Charles himself would command in the centre. The task was not altogether easy. While Hull was in Parliament's hands, threatening their homes in the rear, Newcastle's progress was limited by the disinclination of his men to progress further south than Lincoln, and Cornishmen were similarly troubled at leaving Portsmouth in enemy occupation while they marched through Devon. Charles in the centre had suffered a reverse when the Parliamentarians captured Reading on April 27. But victories at Landsdown and Roundway Down near Bristol on the 5th and 13th of July strengthened his position, while Rupert's capture of Bristol on July 26, two days after the Queen's arrival in Oxford, was of outstanding importance.

The direction of Charles's central thrust occasioned long deliberation in the Council of War. At last it was decided that he should take Gloucester in order to open up the Severn valley and ensure communication with Royalist support in South Wales. This meant abandoning an immediate push to London up the Thames valley, which might have been supported by a parallel drive by Prince Maurice through Hampshire and Sussex. But the western army was still occupied and Newcastle was still no further south than Lincoln. Moreover, it was felt that a threat to Gloucester would lure Essex away from the capital.

For the first time since his arrival in the city Charles left Oxford for a major campaign on Wednesday 10 August 1643. Gloucester did not immediately capitulate, though Essex, as predicted, began his march westward. Charles therefore, fearing to be cut off from his base and hoping to turn the tables by preventing Essex's retreat to London, abandoned the siege. On September 20 the two armies came face to face at Newbury, with Charles barring Essex's route to the capital. The King was in command and he had been joined by Rupert. As at Edgehill the battle was indecisive but, unlike Edgehill, Charles drew off in the night leaving the way to London open to Essex, while he himself went north to Oxford. There were rumours that he had run out of ammunition, but if he had remained on the field it is likely that Essex would have retreated leaving the Royalists still barring his way to London. It was perhaps another lost opportunity to the King: he had neither taken Gloucester nor opened up a route to the capital nor prevented Essex from returning there. He had lost also his Secretary of State, one of the noblest of his subjects: for Falkland, who had never come to terms with civil war, had been seen to ride deliberately to his death in the battle. In appointing Lord Digby in Falkland's place Charles brought even closer to him than before a man who was deeply attached to his cause but who was impulsive and unreliable and, moreover, still hostile to Rupert, the most able of the King's commanders. Charles's first sally from Oxford, while not disastrous, had done him little good.

In the autumn of 1643 the King's armies retook Reading and some regiments from Ireland joined him. But on October 11 a new sharpness was apparent in the Parliamentarian attack in a small cavalry engagement at Winceby in Lincolnshire when Oliver Cromwell, with a detachment of the hand-picked troopers he had been recruiting in East Anglia, decisively defeated a Royalist force. The year ended in stalemate. Charles was still in Oxford, firmly entrenched behind a ring of well-fortified garrisons, but no nearer to an occupation of London. Parliament had been sufficiently dissatisfied with its military achievements to seek the assistance of the Scots. In return for military aid they agreed to support the Scottish Presbyterian form of worship and to reform the English 'according to the word of God', which was assumed by the Scots and the English Presbyterians to be the same thing. The Solemn League and Covenant which signalized the agreement was taken by the English on September 25 and every officer of the Parliamentarian army was expected to subscribe to it.

Partly as a counter-measure and much as he disliked Parliaments, Charles determined to demonstrate his own strength by rallying to his side all those who had left, or were prepared to leave, Westminster for Oxford. The Parliament which met in Christ Church Hall on 22

January 1644 consisted of some 44 Lords, including the Prince of Wales and Prince Rupert, and 118 Members of the Lower House. But for their war duties and other pressing commitments Charles would have had about 82 Peers and 175 Commoners in his Oxford Parliament – which was a majority of Peers and about one-third of the Commons. There was not much, however, they could do. The Oxford Parliament was prorogued in April 1644 and adjourned in March 1645. It continued to meet from time to time but its records were destroyed during the seige of Oxford. Charles, indeed, lost any faith he may have had in 'this mongrel Parliament', as he ungraciously termed it in a letter to his wife, as action of another kind became necessary.

The fruits of the Covenant appeared at the opening of 1644 when a Scottish army entered England, commanded by Alexander Leslie, the little, old crooked soldier who had crossed the border in 1639 and whom Charles had created Earl of Leven in 1640. By the spring Parliamentarian troops were once more manoeuvring in the South and South-west and Oxford began to look like a beleaguered city. Charles's trials as a Commander were matched by his anguish over Henrietta-Maria. She had not taken kindly to Oxford, she was pregnant and unwell, once more wracked with pain and rendered by her pregnancy anxious and alarmed as the war approached the city and she feared that any escape route would be cut off. Charles could not guarantee her safety if she remained with him; her presence might interfere with military strategy; she herself was anxious to bear her child away from the clangour of war. So once more they prepared to part after less than a year together. Charles with their two eldest sons escorted her to Abingdon on April 17 and left her in the care of Jermyn, her destination still undecided. He received such alarming accounts of her condition that he sent an anguished note to their physician, who remained in London: 'Mayerne, if you love me, go to my wife!', and then, of necessity, turned his attention to his Council of War.

Rupert advocated the holding of Oxford firmly in the centre within its outer garrisons while he went north to aid Newcastle, who had fallen back on York, and Maurice completed the conquest of the West. No sooner had he departed for the North, however, than Charles saw the disadvantages of his own position. He had little freedom of movement while the armies of Essex and Waller were probing and manoeuvring close to Oxford, the city was ill-supplied with provisions, and if he allowed himself to be besieged he would be starved out in a fortnight. He decided to abandon Reading in order to acquire its men and arms and the city changed hands for the third time on May 18 when the garrison was dismantled and Essex and Waller were free to move in. A week later Charles abandoned Abingdon, so leaving open the entire southern approach to Oxford. To the East, Essex was now approaching Islip and probing as far forward as Cowley and Headington, while Waller began an encircling movement from the West. The situation was sufficiently delicate for someone to talk of surrender on terms. 'What!', exclaimed Charles, 'I may be found in the hands of the Earl of Essex, but I shall be dead first!'

So, after taking a day's hunting in Woodstock, where he shot two bucks, he proceeded to action. Leaving part of his army in the city, and after feigning an attack on Abingdon which drew Waller southwards, he rode out northwards as soon as it was dark on the summer evening of June 3, with 3000 horse and 2500 foot. He rode through Port Meadow by the wide-spreading Thames to Wolvercote and Yarnton, the spires of Oxford fading behind him in the darkness. He crossed the little Evenlode at Hanborough Bridge while his friends left lighted matchcord in the hedges at Islip to deceive the enemy. He proceeded to Witney and reached Burford the next evening, the following night he was at Bourton-on-the-Water and so proceeded to Evesham and Worcester.

But once the exhilaration of action was over he began to doubt his own wisdom: he had left his base both short of food and, with the abandonment of Reading and Abingdon, ill-defended. At the same time, as he might have predicted, Essex and Waller appeared to be joining forces for a combined attack upon him while Rupert was miles away in the North and Oxford could give him little help. Hurriedly he wrote from Worcester to Rupert on the 7th: 'I confess the best had been to have followed your advice . . . yet we doubt not but to defend ourselves until you may have time to beat the Scots, but if you be too long in doing it, I apprehend some great inconvenience.' Fears for the northern project now began to fill his mind also, and a week later he wrote again, unexpectedly, and confusedly:

> If York be lost I shall esteem my crown little less. But if York be relieved and you beat the rebels' army of both Kingdoms which are before it, then . . . I may possibly make a shift . . . to spin out time until you come to assist me. Wherefore I command you and conjure you by the duty and affection which I know you bear me that, all new enterprises laid aside, you immediately march according to your first

intention with all your force to the relief of York. But if that be either lost, or have freed themselves from the besiegers, or that, for want of powder you cannot undertake that work, that you immediately march with your whole strength directly to Worcester to assist me and my army.

Charles was clearly torn between his desires for the relief of York and his need to be relieved at Worcester. But, against the odds, the wheel of fortune now began to turn in his favour as the armies of Essex and Waller, far from planning a concerted attack, appeared about to separate, with Essex marching into Devon and Waller alone pursuing the King. With a certain arrogance Charles now doubled back over the Cotswolds, through Broadway and back to Woodstock, collecting men and arms as he went. On June 22 he even pushed over to Buckingham, in enemy country. A Council of War here debated three possibilities, each of which demonstrated their changed fortunes: marching northwards to assist Rupert; falling alternately on the two enemy armies; or making a sudden attack on London. So meagre did London's defences appear at that time that the last plan seemed feasible.

But before Charles could act Waller's army had caught up with him on June 24 by Cropredy Bridge on the banks of the little river Cherwell between Banbury and Daventry. Charles, with the Prince of Wales, was in the main body of the army throughout the engagement that followed, within pistol shot of the enemy. It was said by captured soldiers that the King's person had been deliberately aimed at and that they had focused upon him with their perspective glasses to make sure where he was and what he looked like; it was a different story from the initial one of protecting the King's sacred person and punishing only his evil counsellors. Patrick Ruthven, Earl of Forth, recently created Earl of Brentford, led the Royalist vanguard, a cavalry brigade brought up their rear, while Waller continued on a parallel course on the opposite side of the Cherwell. Each army had about 5000 horse, Charles some 3500 foot, Waller rather more. As they neared Cropredy Bridge Charles sent forward a small detachment to hold the bridge and protect his flank. On the news that a Parliamentarian force was approaching from the North, which might be cut off, this detachment hastened its pace to such effect that a gap appeared between van and rear of the Royalist army. Waller was quick to seize the opportunity and threw a considerable force across a ford at Slat Mill, half a mile to the south of the bridge. Charles, however, regrouped his men in time to repulse Waller with considerable loss of men and material. By evening the two armies were once more eyeing each other across the Cherwell. Charles sent a message of grace and pardon to Waller who replied that he had no power to treat and the next morning Charles decided to draw off without further engagement, his army being short of victuals and news coming in of a further Parliamentarian detachment marching to the relief of Waller. With little loss to himself, Charles had captured the whole of the enemy artillery train and inflicted considerable casualties. It was a resounding victory, an engagement that Charles liked to remember, and when his secretary, Sir Edward Walker, wrote a detailed account of the battle, Charles annotated the work himself.[1]

Charles was now free to engage Essex and he turned southwestward, making for Exeter. He had learned while he was on the march that Henrietta-Maria had given birth to a daughter in the city on June 6, and at Buckingham on the 25th he began a letter to her that the requirements of battle left unfinished. After Cropredy Bridge, in the humble house at Williamscote where he slept, he completed the letter, but she never saw his loving words, for the letter was intercepted.

Dr Mayerne had come to her and Madame Peronne had been sent by her sister-in-law from France, but she remained ill and depressed in spite of the healthy, pretty little girl she had borne and called Henrietta after herself. She feared to be taken by the Parliamentarian forces now marching into the West, and her one obsession was escape. So, leaving her baby with Lady Dalkeith, she fled from Exeter with a handful of companions, including her faithful dwarf, Geoffrey Hudson. The dangers and privations of her journey were terrible, but at Falmouth a Dutch vessel, hired by Jermyn, was waiting and on July 14 she sailed for France. She still had to face bombardment by Parliament's ships and the storms that always dogged her, but she reached Brest two days later, only a year after her reunion with her husband at Edgehill. When Charles reached Exeter on July 26 his wife was on the road to Paris waiting to hear whether the waters of Amboise would help her to regain her health; but he fondled his baby daughter – the prettiest, so it had been reported to him, of all his children – and made arrangements for her christening in Exeter Cathedral.

Not only had he missed seeing Henrietta-Maria but, as he hastened westwards, the news from the North was bad. Rupert's approach to York had been sufficient to cause the besieging Parliamentarian armies to retire, fearing to be caught between the oncoming Rupert and Newcastle's men in the town. By a quick feint and a rapid march

Rupert bypassed them as he approached the city, putting the river Swale between his forces and theirs and triumphantly calling upon Newcastle to join him. He then wheeled round to meet the Parliamentarian forces with the intention of crushing them before they had time to group. Thus he would be carrying out Charles's instructions to the letter: to relieve York and beat the rebels' army. Speed was the more necessary as he had not yet heard of Charles's victory at Cropredy Bridge and now pictured him sore beset and awaiting his nephew's return. The characters of Rupert and Newcastle, and an old rivalry dating from the war in Europe between Rupert and Lord Eythin, Newcastle's second, dashed Rupert's plans. Rupert did not stop for the courtesies of the occasion; he spoke to Newcastle, who was twice his age even if less than half as good as a soldier, as though he were the junior officer. Newcastle courteously hid his resentment but he was slow in following Rupert; Eythin encouraged his men to demand their pay before engaging further. Rupert was left on Marston Moor far below the strength he needed and, as he waited for Newcastle and Eythin, the enemy had time enough for their own dispositions. It was four in the afternoon of July 2 before Eythin followed Newcastle to the field, bringing up his foot. He was then dissatisfied with Rupert's dispositions and, though it was too late to alter the plan, it was six or seven in the evening before all was in place. Meanwhile Rupert could hear across the moor the psalms which Cromwell's troopers were accustomed to sing, prompting his question to a captured Parliamentarian soldier: 'Is Cromwell there?'

He was not expecting battle that night, and with other Royalist commanders was preparing to eat his supper when the enemy attacked, their combined forces numbering some 26–27,000 to Rupert's 17–18,000. Moreover, the surprise caused Rupert to lose the initial impact of his cavalry, upon which he relied. Though his men fought hard and bravely the Parliamentarian victory was complete by the end of the day when 4000 Royalist dead lay on the battlefield. Rupert had interpreted Charles's letter to mean the relief of York and the defeat of the Parliamentarian armies. Victory in the field had gone to 'old Ironsides', as Rupert now termed Cromwell in reference to the impenetrable strength of his troops. York surrendered on July 16. Newcastle 'in shame', as he said, at the magnitude of the defeat, left the country together with Eythin and other officers, Rupert collected what men he could and made his way south through Lancashire, too short of ammunition for any engagement.[2]

Charles, meantime, in spite of his wife's departure and the bad news from the North, had been conscious since the end of June of a feeling resembling satisfaction, almost of fulfilment, as though the earlier events of his life were falling into place: the war-games of his youth; the hours he spent in his cabinet room as a young man seeking escape from the difficulties outside which were too personal to be resolved; the fling for independence when he rode off to seek the Infanta's hand. He was fighting now in a cause he had been brought up to believe was right and he was in full command – unlike the years at Whitehall when Parliaments and Privy Council, ministers and courtiers had bullied him beyond belief and talked incessantly, driving him to the solace of his pictures. Even at Oxford they were doing the same; and at Oxford there were too many military commanders. Now he was on his own, now was the time for action, with one simple task before him. He was, as Roe had perceptively remarked years before, at his best when alone, acting in the awareness of his own responsibility. He did the things he wanted to do. He took the Prince of Wales to a great concourse of people on Dartmoor. 'Your cheerfulness in this service I shall requite if it be in my power', he said to them; 'if I live not to do it, I hope this young man, my son, your fellow soldier, to whom I shall particularly give it in charge, will do so.' When he made contact with the enemy he was in no hurry to strike but awaited the right moment. He knew the game was in his hands.

When Charles entered Exeter, Essex was at Tavistock, having had an easy march and being satisfied that Plymouth was safe, though he was well aware of the danger in his rear and sent urgently to Parliament for reinforcements. Yet, in spite of the difficulties of his situation, or because he hoped for Cornish support, or because he had designs on the profitable tin mines whose proceeds were helping to support Charles, or merely because some of his followers held land in Cornwall and were anxious to inspect it, Essex pushed further on into the peninsular and crossed the Tamar on July 27. Charles could have predicted the welcome he got, for Cornwall was Royalist to a man, and, in steady pursuit, he rode into Liskeard on August 2 while Essex moved to Bodmin and Sir Richard Grenville occupied Grampound, hoping to catch Essex between the two Royalist forces. Essex struck due south towards the sea, where the chance of being cut off was less, and reached Lostwithiel on August 3. Skilfully and without haste Charles set to work to contain him. On the 4th he occupied Boconnock, Lord Mohun's house, lying to the East; on the 12th Grenville seized Lord Robart's house at Lanhydrock and secured the Respryn Bridge over the Fowey river, which effectively shut Essex in on his landward side. Charles then turned his attention to the seaward side of Essex's position. Essex had control of the western arm of Fowey harbour but Royalist forces took possession of key positions on the opposite side, nearer the mouth of the harbour, so that Essex was effectively blocked for exit or entrance. Charles was still in no hurry, and when Essex's cavalry rode out of Lostwithiel in the early hours of August 31 towards Plymouth he made no attempt to stop them.

It was different with the foot, and later that day battle was joined. Making a reconnaissance before the fighting started, Charles came under fire and a fisherman standing by him was killed. The King remained unmoved. Once more he fought in the midst of his army, he supped that night with his men on the field, and slept under a hedge during the wet, stormy night. By morning Essex had escaped to Plymouth leaving Skippon to accept Charles's terms, which were magnanimous enough, merely requiring the complete surrender of all their arms and equipment while the men were left free to make their way as best they might. What would he have done with prisoners? They would have required guards, food, lodging, and the difficulties of transporting them would have been considerable. Charles was probably pleased to see Essex go and he had no wish to take Skippon. The war had not yet reached the stage when the execution of a commander was considered just or helpful. But Charles had dispersed his opponents in the West, he had once more opened up the western thrust to London, and he had acquired 42 guns, a mortar, 100 barrels of powder, and 5000 small arms. It was perhaps not much to place against Marston Moor, and only about 16,000 Royalist horse and foot and 10,000 Parliamentarian had been involved in all, but it had revealed the inability of the Parliamentarian command to support its officers in the field and, in spite of the intervention of the Scots, in spite of Cromwell and his Ironsides, the autumn of 1644 was full of doubts for Parliament.[3]

Charles, on the other hand, after a season of successful campaigning, had never felt better. As he turned towards home his object was to relieve Banbury and to raise the sieges of Basing House and Donnington Castle – all garrisons useful to Oxford – before going into winter quarters. Marching slowly he reached Newbury on October 22. But the Parliamentarian generals had read his intentions correctly and were massed on Clay Hill, north of the river Kennet, to offer battle.

The second battle of Newbury was indecisive and about 500 men were killed on each side. Charles had no wish to risk further losses when he was outnumbered and victory was uncertain, so he drew off in the night to Wallingford and entered Oxford on the 28th. Scarcely pausing, he immediately, with an escort of 500 horse, made for Bath to consult with Rupert. The two left Bath together on the 30th with some 3000 horse and foot and came by way of Cirencester and Burford (where they left a detachment) to Oxford again, which they reached on November 1. Five days later Charles reviewed his army – 15,000 strong – on Bullingdon Green and announced the replacement of old Patrick Ruthven, Earl of Brentford, by Prince Rupert as Lieutenant General, with the Prince of Wales as titular Commander-in-Chief. He made one more foray to secure Donnington Castle and was riding at the head of his men, as usual, when, in a sharp little affray, his horse was wounded in the foot, but there was no serious resistance and he secured the Castle and took over the artillery which was stored there.

He returned to Oxford for the winter on November 23 1644 when the leaves had fallen from the trees and the mists were rising from the meadows. The old city looked dank and cheerless. The Court had shrunk, the courtiers' gossip was less shrill, the students had departed. Merton College was quiet once more and no one trod the private way between his room and Henrietta's. She was now in Paris, the guest of her sister-in-law who was Queen Regent during the minority of the little Louis XIV, somewhat better in health and beginning once more to seek aid for her husband. The letters had started coming through again but, because of headaches and eye-strain, she more often gave them to Jermyn to render into code; Jermyn also, Charles assumed, would decypher his letters to his wife. The knowledge was not pleasing to Charles. There had been various stories of the Queen's unfaithfulness: even when she was coming to meet him at Edgehill the gossips had spoken of too close a friendship with Lord Charles Cavendish, for whom she was rumoured to have delayed her journey. The Earl of Holland had figured largely in earlier days and Charles could not forget how assiduously Holland had courted her in her rooms at Merton. Impudent and scandalous remarks concerning the Queen and Henry Jermyn had recently come to his ears. Jermyn he knew as a faithful friend and servant to the Queen but he remembered how her first request on their meeting at Edgehill had been for a peerage for Jermyn. He was distressed but he was quite unbelieving of any scandal. The actions of his nephew, the Elector Palatine, were in a different category. That young man had left England after the disastrous summoning of Hull, in which he considered he had played an undignified part, but had returned at the end of August, taken the Covenant, and attempted to ingratiate himself with the Parliament, letting the rumour gain ground that he would be willing to accept his uncle's throne. Even more sinister talk hung in the air, forgotten as soon as whispered, though it had reached Charles's ears, of an intention to depose him in favour of his son, the Prince of Wales.

More concretely his thoughts turned to his old friend, Archbishop Laud, whom he had not seen since the day he was placed under arrest. Laud had remained in prison, half forgotten, it seemed, during the early stages of the war. But Prynne had not forgiven and in the early spring of 1644 the old man was brought to the bar of the House of Lords to answer to a charge of treason brought forward by a Committee of the House of Commons based upon a case made out by Prynne in his usual style of verbose hatred, whose substance was that Laud had attempted to subvert the established religion and the very law itself. The trial resembled that of Strafford except that his accusers found it less interesting, wandering in and out of the chamber at will, rarely caring to devote their afternoons to listening to the prisoner's case which, week after week, for ten whole months, he laboured to put before them. It was difficult to make a charge of treason stick, and the procedure familiar in the trial of Strafford was carried through: first, the petitioning and the angry crowds at Westminster demanding the life of the Archbishop, then the Bill of Attainder. Strode spoke of the need for 'expedition' in the business and claimed that 'multitudes' were 'demanding justice'. 'Is this', cried Essex, who had borne the brunt of their fighting, 'the liberty which we promised to maintain with our blood? Shall posterity say that to save them from the yoke of the King we have placed them under the yoke of the populace?' The speaker carried no more weight than the argument. They were remodelling their armies and in the new command Essex would have no place.

Laud was executed on 10 January 1645, maintaining to the end that he lived and died in the Protestant religion as established in England and that he had laboured to keep a uniformity in the external worship of God according to the doctrine and discipline of that Church.[4]

To Charles the news brought a strange justification of all he had done, an expiation, through Laud, for the death of Strafford. In a letter to Henrietta-Maria a few days after the Archbishop's death he wrote:

> Nothing can be more evident than that Strafford's innocent blood hath been one of the great causes of God's just judgment upon this nation by a furious civil war, both sides hitherto being almost equally guilty, but now this last crying blood being totally theirs, I believe it is no presumption hereafter to hope that the hand of justice must be heavier upon them and lighter upon us, looking now upon our cause, having passed through our faults.

The conduct of the trial, as well as the execution itself, confirmed his belief in the necessity to continue the war, and his interest was focused upon the strategy of the coming campaign rather than the tortuous or insulting peace proposals that were put to him from time to time.

Parliamentary Commissioners were in Oxford when he returned from the relief of Donnington Castle and he received them the following day – his old enemy Denzil Holles, and the lawyer, Bulstrode Whitelocke, for whom he had some respect. The basis of their proposals was ludicrous enough, entailing the setting up of Presbyterianism as the national religion and he himself taking the Covenant; and when they read the list of Royalists to be excluded from pardon the names included his nephews Rupert and Maurice. Charles was glad to hear the contemptuous laughter of his courtiers. He went that evening with Rupert to the Commissioners' lodgings. The talk was amiable enough but Charles treated them with a certain disdain. 'You told me twice', he said, 'that you had no power to treat . . . that you were only to deliver the propositions. A postillion might have done as much as you.' He therefore declined to give his answer in any form but in a sealed envelope which they were to deliver to Parliament. When they were reluctant to accept it he spoke sharply: 'You must take it', he said, 'were it a ballad or a song of Robin Hood.' When the packet was opened by Parliament it was found to contain nothing but a request for a safe conduct for two of the King's advisers to bring his formal answer to Westminster. The humiliation of the two Commissioners was probably in bad taste, but it was his way of replying to their insult to his nephews. The substance of his reply, when it was sent for discussion at Uxbridge in January 1645, was in the remark he made when taking formal leave of the Commissioners: 'There are three things I will not part with – the Church, my crown, and my friends; and you will have much ado to get them from me.'[5]

32

'My marching Army'

The peace proposals indicated by the Commissioners at Oxford in the autumn of 1644 were repeated more formally at Uxbridge in the early months of 1645 and lost nothing of their sting. Charles smothered his indignation and infinitely improved his constitutional image among those who had time to think about such matters by his counter-proposals which, in substance, proposed the adoption of the constitution as it stood in the summer of 1641, the preservation of the Common Prayer Book from 'scorn and violence', and the framing of a Bill for 'tender consciences'. He even suggested that both armies should be disbanded and he himself come to Westminster – though what he meant by the proposal was not clear. He assured Henrietta-Maria that it did not mean surrender: 'As for trusting the rebels, either by going to London or disbanding my army before a peace, do no ways fear my hazarding so cheaply or foolishly.' I 'pretend to have a little more wit', he said, 'than to put myself in the reverence of perfidious rebels.'

Both sides, indeed, knew that the position was not yet amenable to peace propositions. Parliament continued its plans for remodelling its army, the fruits of which appeared in the New Model Ordinance of January 1645. Charles strained every nerve to build up his fighting force. He had never despaired of foreign aid, but one by one his contacts were failing. His Uncle of Denmark remained unmoved, the French made no response to his wife's importuning. In an effort to make available further resources from the family of Orange, the Prince of Wales was offered as husband to the daughter of Dutch William, but the match no longer sounded worth the expense to that practical sovereign; he was said to have informed Jermyn that the best course for the King of England would be to make peace at any price with his subjects. But Charles had said to Newcastle years before that he saw no reason why his Catholic subjects should not fight for him, and he saw no reason why he should persecute them for their religion. Now his thoughts turned to Ireland. If he could satisfy the Catholic Irish he could bring them to fight for him and at the same time release the English soldiers who were holding them and thus, in one operation, acquire two armies. By the beginning of 1645 he was deep in plans with the Catholic Earl of Glamorgan, the son of the Marquis of Worcester who at the beginning of the war had so unstintingly poured money into his cause. Glamorgan was to offer the Irish a mitigation of the recusancy laws with their total repeal later in return for 10,000 Irish who would land in North Wales to help the King and a further 10,000 in South Wales, where they would be joined by loyal Welshmen. At the same time French troops, encouraged by France and by the Pope, would land in the eastern counties to assist a monarch whose attitude to Catholics was so sympathetic.

One of the many difficulties of the situation was that the Marquis of Ormonde, who became Lord Lieutenant of Ireland in 1644, had himself arranged a 'Cessation' with the Irish, although not upon such favourable terms, and had already sent Irish troops both to England and to Scotland. He knew nothing of Glamorgan's commission, while Glamorgan, in his enthusiasm, exceeded the terms of Charles's authority and disregarded his injunction not to proceed to action without consulting the Lord Lieutenant. Charles, holding many irons in the fire, was sorely missing his wife and his dependence upon her grew in her absence as they communicated about the troops who would come to his assistance and where they would land. Some might march through France, thought Charles – but, he hastily adds, 'this is an opinion, not a direction'. On even the smallest matter he waits for her consent – even a bedchamber post in the Prince's household. He begs Jermyn to give him an account of her health. It was altogether a different man from the one who had commanded in the Lostwithiel campaign.

But with willows whitening along the rivers and the meadow grasses springing underfoot the King's mind turned once more to the new season's campaigning, and his spirits rose at the prospect of action. The victories of Montrose in Scotland indicated a northward march to join forces with him but Charles's freedom of movement was inhibited by the activities of Cromwell who was harrying the country round Oxford, keeping the garrisons on the alert, scooping up all the available draught horses. Before he could leave the city Charles needed more than 400 of these animals and they had to be found in an area already heavily drawn upon. It was not until May 11 that his needs were supplied and he managed to elude Cromwell, marching out with 11,000 men to join a Council of War at Stow.

The divided counsels that were so common among the Royalists led to the decision to separate, Charles and Rupert heading north, Goring marching westward to confront Fairfax. Neither deployment was initially successful. Goring failed to hold Parliament's forces in the West with the result that Fairfax was able to join Cromwell at Marston, a couple of miles from the centre of Oxford, on May 22. Oxford was poorly supplied and its ability to withstand a siege was sufficiently uncertain to keep the main Royalist army within striking distance of the city. Within these limits, however, it was moving fairly freely and on May 31 it captured Leicester and made towards Daventry.

Its pace was on the whole leisurely, though on one occasion it marched from 4 am to 6 pm without rest, and there was ample scope for young Richard Symonds, a trooper in Charles's Lifeguard – one of a divided family, for his brother was with Parliament – to satisfy his passion for topography and to fill his notebook with interesting details of their marches: the black earth which people cut into turf above Uttoxeter, curiously wrought statues in alabaster in a church, 'a flowery cross', 'a private sweet village'.[1] But a free-moving Royalist army jotting down its impressions of the countryside was not what the Parliamentarian army command had envisaged, and on June 7, at Daventry, Charles learned that his opponents had changed their tactics and lifted the siege at Oxford. The welcome news, however, was mitigated not only by the necessity of revictualling the city before he moved on, but by the knowledge that Fairfax and Cromwell were now free to harrass him more directly.

The first move of the Parliamentarian commanders was to the Eastern Association, which they thought was Charles's objective and which, indeed, his Privy Council at Oxford had urged him to attack instead of persisting on his northwards march. When Charles replied to this advice he was at his most dignified and unrealistic. 'You know', he wrote to them from Daventry on June 11, 'that the Council was never wont to debate upon any matter not propounded to them by me, and certainly it were a strange thing if my marching army – especially I being at the head of them – should be governed by my sitting Council at Oxford.' The following day forces even less acceptable were dictating his strategy.

Charles was in the grip of that lethargic belief that all was well, or would become so, which in times of stress sometimes overcame him. His attitude was also bound up with the luxury of dependence, in this case upon Rupert, which was so much part of his character. When he was in sole charge, as in the Loswithiel campaign, he planned every move with the greatest care. Now he was so little heeding the New Model Army, which could not be so very far off, that on the 12th he went hunting in Fawsley Park, three miles south of Daventry on the Banbury Road, the property of that Knightley family who had been prominent among his opponents. As at the taking of Broughton Castle there may have been some feeling of retribution in the action. The exhilaration of the sport was rudely disturbed towards evening, however, by Rupert's urgent summons: enemy horse were in the neighbourhood.

The first instinct of the Royalists was to put ground between themselves and their opponents. Neither Goring nor Gerard had joined them from the West and they would be heavily outnumbered. So throughout the night of the 12th the scattered Royalist troops and equipment were called in from the villages round Daventry, and by the morning of the 13th the King's army was making its way towards Harborough. Meanwhile Fairfax had reached Kislingbury, about eight miles from Daventry, and on the 13th he was joined there by Cromwell. That same evening a party of Parliamentarian horse under Henry Ireton, probing forward, found a group of Rupert's cavalry playing quoits and another eating supper at Naseby, apparently unaware of, or unheeding, the proximity of the enemy. Charles himself spent the night at the village of Lubenham near Harborough and before turning in he wrote to Nicholas, perhaps intending to mitigate the sharpness of his earlier letter. 'I assure you', he said, 'I shall look before I leap further north.' But he had little time for looking. He was aroused in the middle of the night by the news that the Parliamentarian army was upon them.

When manoeuvring for position was complete the two armies were facing one another from serrated ridges of higher ground separated by broken land of furze and scrub, the Parliamentrians having the advantage of slightly higher ground as well as a superiority in numbers of two to one, their combined forces amounting to some 14,000 against 7500 Royalists. Both sides were drawn up in similar conventional array with cavalry on either flank, infantry in the centre and supporting musketeers lining the hedges at appropriate points.

Charles, his lethargy vanished in the need for action, reviewed his men. His army was a splendid sight, the regiments in the colours of their commanders, banners fluttering, horses groomed to a peak of perfection. Charles was filled with pride and drew his sword as he paraded before them in full armour, the very picture of a mighty sovereign leading his men to war. Then he took his place in front of the reserve of horse and foot which was stationed immediately behind Astley's infantry. When Cromwell, on that bright June morning, looked across the little valley and saw his enemies in full array involuntary words of admiration rose to his lips, but he merely felt the more elated that it was he who was the chosen instrument of the Lord to humble that mighty show.

At ten o'clock in the morning of June 14 Rupert on the Royalist right wing led the cavalry charge against Ireton's horse on the Parliamentarian left, his accustomed speed and force somewhat diminished by the nature of the ground between the two ridges and the subsequent uphill drive. But he broke through and was at Naseby attempting to secure the Parliamentarian baggage trains while Cromwell on their right was routing the Royalist left with cavalry to spare to help his foot in the centre. Charles immediately brought his reserves into action to help Astley's infantry: 'One charge more, gentlemen, one charge more', he was crying, 'and the day is ours!' In the midst of the mêlée the Earl of Carnwath seized his bridle. 'Will you go upon your death in an instant!' he cried, with several full-blooded Scottish oaths, and swung the horse's head to the right. The confusion was too great for Charles to repair the move instantly and to some of his men it appeared as though an order to right turn had been given; in obeying it they left Cromwell's cavalry unmolested and themselves galloped off some quarter of a mile to the rear, carrying the King with them. Rupert had not lingered at Naseby but when he returned the situation was already beyond repair. The remnants of the Royalist army made for Leicester, fourteen miles away, harassed by enemy troopers. The bodies of the slain covered an area of four square miles; they were thickest upon the little hill where the King had commanded.

Naseby was a complete military disaster for Charles. A thousand of his men were dead; 5000 were prisoners or wounded, including 500 officers; his foot, as a fighting force, had ceased to exist; the royal standard was taken, the Queen's colours, the Duke of York's, the banner of every infantry regiment on the field was with the enemy. Charles's artillery train, powder, arms, baggage and wagons, including his own coach where he kept copies of his correspondence and his private papers, including his wife's letters and copies of his letters to her, fell to the enemy. Thirty-five of the letters, going back to his letter to Buckingham about his wife's 'Monseiurs' and including many of personal endearment, were immediately published by Parliament. More important to them were the letters that revealed the plans for military assistance which Charles had been discussing with his wife: the landing of French troops on the English coast at Selsey or thereabouts; the intended rising in Wales to coincide with the landing of Irish troops; the parts played by Ormonde and Glamorgan; Charles's offer to suspend, and ultimately to repeal, the penal laws against Catholics.

Naseby was a victory of 14,000 over 7,000 and was defeat without dishonour, owing much to the fact that Cromwell had sufficient cavalry to turn on the Royalist centre after he had dealt with their left wing. Moreover, while it was a defeat that had scattered Charles's infantry and destroyed his arms it had left him with a considerable force of cavalry. Could he retrieve the remnants of the foot, add to them the armies that still existed in the West, and recruit more men to build another fighting force? With thoughts of support among the Welsh, of help from Ireland, and of Montrose's victories in Scotland, his only idea was to try.[2]

Charles spent the night of Naseby at Ashby-de-la-Zouche while the wounded were taken to Leicester, then, with his remaining cavalry, he marched westward through Lichfield to Hereford, which he reached on the 18th after a difficult march through hilly and woody country where, as young Symonds noted, the churches were very poor. At Hereford Charles learned that Fairfax had taken Leicester, and here Rupert left him to take command of the garrison at Bristol, which was sorely pressed. Charles pushed on and was at Abergavenny on July 1 and on the 3rd reached Raglan, the splendid and well-fortified home of the Earl of Worcester whose generosity had enabled him to begin his campaign in 1642. Here for a few days he was able to refresh his mind and body while remaining at the centre of what he hoped could be a revival of his cause. Glamorgan was still in Ireland and he had the brief and relaxing experience of viewing the waterworks, pumps, irrigation devices and hydraulic lifts which the busy mind of that young man had erected in his family home. But Charles's mind was more upon his own son, the Prince of Wales, whom he had sent, in the charge of two of his most trusted councillors, to Cornwall.

Within a week Charles's hopes were dashed. Goring was defeated at Langport on July 10, Bridgwater fell on the 23rd, support promised from Wales failed to materialize. All men, it was said, 'grew less affected or more frighted', many were compounding with Parliament, scattered pockets of Royalist resistance were giving up. There was talk of peace, in which even Rupert shared. Charles was at the bottom of the trough. 'Nephew', he wrote to Rupert on August 3 from Cardiff, having left Raglan on July 18,

> I confess that, speaking either as a mere soldier or statesman, I must say there is no probability but of my ruin; but as a Christian, I must tell you, that God will not suffer rebels to prosper, or this cause to be overthrown . . . I know my obligations to be neither to abandon God's cause, injure my successors, nor forsake my friends.

Charles was repeating his stand on his religion, his Crown, and his friends; and, like Cromwell, he believed that God was with him.

Two days later Charles wrote to his son. 'It is very fit for me now to prepare for the worse', he said, and he instructed the Prince: 'whensoever you find yourself in apparent danger of falling into the rebels' hands, that you convey yourself into France, and there to be under your mother's care; she is to have the absolute power of your education in all things, except religion, and in that not to meddle at all, but leave it entirely to the care of your tutor, the bishop of Salisbury.' On the same day, August 5, with some 2500 horse and foot he set off over the rough Welsh mountains to Brecknock, Radnor and Ludlow, with the general intention of proceeding north to join Montrose. With little rest he passed through Shropshire and on to Derbyshire until on August 15 he came to Welbeck in Nottinghamshire, one of the homes of the Duke of Newcastle, where he rested for two nights, leaving after Sunday service on August 17. The following day he was at Doncaster, where he was heartened by the appearance of some volunteers who came in to join him. But there was no rest, for enemy forces were gathering to the north under Colonel-General Poyntz while Leslie with 4000 Scottish horse was approaching from the west. So he made south-eastward, reaching Huntingdon on the 24th and Woburn on the 26th, where he slept in the house of the Duke of Bedford, and two days later, with his men and animals badly needing refreshment, he came once more to Oxford, reaching the city on August 28.

In two days he was off again. There was something of desperation in his ceaseless marching. Even the ebullient Digby began to despair:

there is such an universal weariness of the war, despair of a possibility for the King to recover, and so much of private interest grown from these upon everybody [he wrote to Jermyn], that I protest to God I do not know four persons living besides myself and you that have not already given clear demonstrations that they will purchase their own and – as they flatter themselves – the kingdom's quiet at any price.

But Charles's obsession now was the relief of Bristol, which even Rupert's presence in the city had not been able to free from the pressure of enemy troops. He instructed Goring to draw what force he could from the west and march to the Somerset side of the town, while he himself advanced with horse and foot across the Severn not far from Gloucester. To make final plans for this unrealistic scheme Charles went once more to Raglan and here, on September 11, he received the 'monstrous intelligence', as he termed it, of Rupert's surrender of Bristol the previous day.

It was a blow which in his weakened state he could hardly take, and for the first time Charles refused to support a subordinate or a friend who had failed him. The crime was deeper in that Rupert was the King's own nephew, that to Charles he had been almost another Buckingham. But whereas when things had gone wrong with Buckingham Charles had rewarded him and hidden the hurt that the revelation of a flaw in his idol had occasioned, now his reaction was violently opposite. The Prince had no one in Charles's immediate circle to speak for him, Digby was too likely to believe the worst, and Charles did not wait for details or explanation. Instead, all the anguish of the war, of defeat, the utter weariness of the marching backwards and forwards, came out in one harsh, savage letter:

Nephew,

Though the loss of Bristol be a great blow to me, yet your surrendering it as you did is of so much affliction to me, that it makes me forget not only the consideration of that place, but is likewise the greatest trial of my constancy that hath yet befallen me; for what is to be done? after one that is so near me as you are, both in blood and friendship, submits himself to so mean an action (I give it the easiest term) such – I have so much to say that I will say no more of it: only, lest rashness of judgment be laid to my charge, I must remember you of your letter of the 12 Aug., whereby you assured me, (that if no mutiny happened), you would keep Bristoll for four months. Did you keep it four days? Was there any thing like a mutiny? More questions might be asked, but now, I confess, to little purpose. My conclusion is, to desire you to seek your subsistence (until it shall please God to determine of my condition) somewhere beyond seas, to which end I send you herewith a pass; and I pray God to make you sensible of your present condition, and give you means to redeem what you have lost; for I shall have no greater joy in a victory, than a just occasion without blushing to assure you of my being Your loving uncle, and most faithful friend.

Rupert was required to deliver up his commission immediately and Charles sent to Nicholas at Oxford to arrest the Governor of the city, who was Rupert's friend, and who Charles felt might try to mitigate the Prince's punishment. 'Tell my son', he added in a post-script to Nicholas, 'that I shall less grieve to hear that he is knocked on the head than that he should do so mean an action as is the rendering of Bristol castle and fort upon the terms it was.'[3]

Charles had two more lines of hope. He still thought of joining Montrose, not yet knowing that three days after the surrender of Bristol Montrose had been decisively defeated by Leslie at Phil-liphaugh, but more immediately his mind was on the port of Chester where troops from Ireland might land but which was being threatened, though not yet invested, by Parliamentarian troops. Losing no time he left Raglan on September 18 and started marching again over the Welsh mountains, where ten miles felt like twenty and where for long stretches they 'saw never a house or church' as Trooper Symonds recorded. In an ill-provisioned countryside their fare was meagre and Charles shared even his cheese on one occasion with fellow-travellers at an inn. On Sunday September 21 they came to Chirk Castle, twenty miles south of Chester, whence Charles sent a message to the Governor to hold out for a further twenty-four hours. Chester was still open to the south and west and Charles hoped that his cavalry would be able to repulse the enemy horse while he himself entered the city with his Lifeguard of about a thousand men by the Dee bridge. But at Rowton Heath, two miles from Chester, his troopers suffered another defeat on September 24 and he himself watched from the city walls as the leader of his Lifeguard, young Bernard Stuart, whom he had recently created Lord Lichfield, sallied from the city to their assistance only to be slain himself amid fearful carnage outside the city walls as defenders and attackers became inextricably mixed. It was the end of the gallant troop of horse who had followed him since Naseby.

With no more than a small bodyguard Charles refreshed himself at Denbigh Castle for three days and then made for Newark, arriving there on October 4. Here Rupert sought him out, demanding to be judged by court martial, compelling Charles to assimilate the stark facts that Bristol was contained by sea and land, that it was bound to fall, and the only question was whether this would be with the minimum loss of life or with great slaughter. The court martial unanimously found Rupert 'not guilty of any the least want of courage or fidelity' but there was an ugly scene between the King and Rupert's friends, and both Charles and the Prince remained angry and bitter.

Parliament was mopping up fragments of Royalist resistance in the west and the Midlands and Charles decided to make for Oxford. To escape detection he left with a few friends at 10 o'clock in the evening of November 3; at 3 am on the 4th they were at Belvoir but pushed on until, towards evening, Charles was so weary that he was compelled to sleep for the space of four hours in the village of Codsbury, a few miles from Northampton. At ten in the evening they started again and before daybreak were past Daventry, reaching Banbury shortly before noon on the 5th whence a party of horse from Oxford escorted them to the city. It was nearly a year since the King's triumphant return to Oxford from the west. The city was now more grey, more sad, more still than before. Charles had taxed himself physically to the utmost, having been on the move, almost incessantly, for six months, either on horseback or on foot. He had covered more than 1200 miles of difficult country in long marches, sometimes from dawn until midnight, whose nature can be gathered from his men's descriptions: 'a cruel day', 'a long march over the mountains', 'no dinner', 'dinner in the field'. How could so brave an army as he had had have suffered such a sore defeat? Only on the stage of universal history could his own tragedy find its place. But even here he found no compliance. He sent to the Bodleian Library for a copy of D'Aubigné's *Histoire Universelle*. But John Rous, Bodley's Librarian, sent back a courteous denial and brought the statutes of the Library for the King to see. They forbade lending and could not be set aside, even for a reigning monarch. Charles readily accepted the situation. But in his exhausted condition it seemed like another repulse.[4]

But, even without D'Aubigné, there was enough to ponder on. Charles had many good commanders both old and young with war experience. Rupert was perhaps the most brilliant but he had faults of arrogance and impetuosity and his close kinship with the King led to difficulties which were exacerbated by the jealousies of others about the King, particularly by Digby – also young, brilliant, and arrogant.

401

It was possibly a mistake, as some of Charles's advisers thought, to raise Rupert to the supreme command under himself, yet there were many professional soldiers who welcomed the appointment.

In the early stages of the war Cromwell observed a 'spirit' among the cavaliers that he felt was lacking in Parliament's troops. The men who came into Charles were fired with an enthusiasm to defeat the 'rebels' and were inspired by their Cause, by their King, and by Rupert's charisma. But when Cromwell raised his 'men of a spirit' in East Anglia who knew what they wanted and were prepared to fight for what they knew, he was forging an army with a spirit that was even more pervasive and more durable than that of the cavaliers. His 'Ironsides' fought, it was said, with a sword in one hand and a Bible in the other, and when, with the new-modelling of their army, they were also subject to efficient control and direction they became virtually invincible. That Cromwell himself, besides being essentially professional, was also a brilliant soldier, was recognized by his opponents. When Rupert asked before Marston Moor, 'Is Cromwell there?', it was the respect of one brilliant, professional soldier for another.

There was, nevertheless, an amateurishness about a great deal of the Royalist fighting, typified by Charles hunting in Woodstock before leaving Oxford for a major campaign or hunting in Fawsley Park on the eve of Naseby. There were occasions when divided counsels harmed his prospects, particularly at Stow-on-the-Wold in May 1645 when Goring went into the west leaving Rupert and the King to go northward. Charles was probably wrong in sending his most experienced counsellors, including Hyde and Culpepper, into the west with the Prince of Wales, so depriving himself of strong advisers to counterbalance the volatile young men who remained with him. There were probably missed opportunities, like the failure to advance to London after Edgehill or after the first battle of Newbury. But basically Parliament had the more resources in its control of London and Westminster and its access to the City and most of the wealthy towns and ports. It had also a wider-based support than Charles had in the many ills and grievances which united for a time in opposition. The disparate nature of this support would prove to be a weakness, but it helped to win the war. Even so, Parliament had to call upon the assistance of the Scots and its victory was no foregone conclusion.

For Charles himself the war had opened up opportunities that he took with open hands. He was no cardboard commander but actively participated in general strategy and individual campaigns, rapidly turning theoretical knowledge to practical use. He was brave, he was tireless, he marched with his men, often on foot, rarely using his coach; he shared in camp life, took his place on the battlefield, matched his endurance with the strongest of his men. Yet now his friends were leaving the country or compounding with Parliament on such terms as they could and his last army perished at Stow-on-the-Wold shortly after Charles got back to Oxford, when Sir Jacob Astley was trying to get through to him. After his defeat the old man sat himself on an upturned drum and addressed his captors: 'You have done your work, boys', he said, 'and may go play, unless you will fall out among yourselves.' That they would do so was almost the last hope that Charles had left.

33

'Never Man So Alone'

The most simple division that Charles could see among his opponents was into Parliament, Army, and Scots. There was also a division into Presbyterians and Independents, but this was by no means straightforward, for while the English Parliament and the Scottish army were predominantly Presbyterian, the English army was for the most part strongly Independent in religion with an expanding periphery of sectarianism. Questions of soldiers' pay were also important as Parliament tried, by one means or another, to find money for their wages. Daily becoming more vocal was a wide discontent compounded of soldiers and civilians, Independents and sectaries, mostly of the poorer sections of society, who had been hurt by the fighting or who had not received the benefits from the war that they had expected. Three years of war had increased taxation, disrupted trade, laid waste parts of the country, and broken up homes. The poor who hoped for an end to poverty, those who expected lower taxation, were disillusioned. Many who had turned away from Charles's Anglicanism found in Parliament's Presbyterianism an equally rigid and intolerant worship and reached out to wider forms of nonconformity. As protest grew poverty and sectarianism joined hands and vented their grievances with fresh urgency in dozens of pamphlets and petitions, using the art which Parliament had taught them and turning their complaint against Parliament itself with the general refrain: 'What have we fought for all this while?' The comprehensive cry for Liberty or Freedom recoiled like a boomerang on the heads of the Parliament men who attempted to stem the spate of words by a revival of the printing Ordinances. The press was muzzled more effectively than it had been under the King, and punishment was meted out – not by the Star Chamber or the High Commission for they had been abolished – but by Parliament's own committees.

All through 1645 opposition to Parliament had been hardening and men and women were responding to the leadership of that same John Lilburne who had already crossed Charles's path in London and Oxford. In 1645 he wrote and published from a secret press *England's Birthright Justified*, which was virtually the manifesto of a party. Perhaps the Leveller party matured a little too late for Charles to take advantage of it; but, in spite of the general concern for the under-privileged that he had shown in the course of his government, it was not in his character to assume the leadership of a discontented populace, and it is unlikely that he, or any adviser who was now with him, would have been clever enough to turn the popular resentment against Parliament to the King's advantage. Charles also let pass another opportunity when some of the leading Independents indicated that, in return for the toleration of their religion, they would be prepared, with the support of the army, to yield a greater control of government to Charles than any terms had yet proposed.

The French were at the centre of a move that attracted Charles the most. After Naseby Cardinal Mazarin had cause to fear the power of the victors, and the Queen Regent was anxious to help her sister-in-law. The Scots had their own reasons for fearing a combination of army and Parliament and both French and Scots were ready to con-sider a solution in which they made use of the King as a bargaining factor. In the three-cornered negotiations that built up in the winter of 1645/46 the French Ambassador, Jean de Montreuil, who was young, enthusiastic but not very experienced, was the intermediary.

Charles was in an agony of indecision throughout the period, as his letters to Henrietta–Maria reveal. He was not only tossed this way and that by conflicting suggestions but the Irish affair threatened to blow up in his face as Glamorgan's activities were insistently questioned. If Charles was forced back on to the letter of his agreement with Glamorgan and Ormonde he would have to repudiate the lengths to which Glamorgan, in his enthusiasm, had gone and this would end his hopes of Irish assistance. The dilemma caused him to lean more heavily towards the Scots, and as it became clear that Oxford would not be able to hold out for much longer against the encircling enemy, he listened once more to Montreuil. The Scots had led him to believe that if he would recognize their Presbyterian establishment in Scot-land and would not interfere with the Presbyterian form of worship in England, they would see that he was restored to his just rights and privileges. So, to avoid the risk of capture, he laid his plans to join the

Scottish army at Southwell, outside Newark, which was one of the few places which had not fallen to the enemy.

On Sunday 26 April 1646 one of his chaplains, Dr Michael Hudson, brought the necessary disguise to Ashburnham's chamber. Jack Ashburnham was a lively courtier, a couple of years younger than Charles. He was related to Buckingham and had been under the Duke's patronage, moving easily in the royal circle. On Buckingham's death he became groom of the bedchamber to the King and was particularly friendly with secretary Nicholas and George Goring. He sat for Hastings in the Long Parliament but followed the King and became treasurer and paymaster to the royal army. Parliament had deprived him of his seat and sequestered his estates while Ashburnham, jaunty and somewhat feckless, faithfully followed Charles and now was ready to help his escape from Oxford. Charles, for his part, both loved and trusted the young courtier. Hudson was a versatile and enterprising man who had been first a servant and then a Fellow of Queen's College and had married into a local gentry family, so he knew the Oxfordshire countryside intimately. He had become chaplain to the King after Edgehill, Charles trusted him and had used him on several delicate missions. About midnight the King arrived with his cousin Richmond, Ashburnham cut his lock and trimmed his beard and Charles assumed the garb of a serving man. Then they sent for the Governor of the city and instructed him not to allow anyone in or out of Oxford for five days. The Governor accompanied them to the East Gate and locked it behind them. 'Farewell Harry!' were his last words to Charles. The clocks were striking 3 am as the three men passed over the East bridge and made their way through Marsh Baldon, Dorchester, Benson, Henley, and Nettlebed. When challenged on the road they displayed a pass with Fairfax's signature which had belonged to a soldier who had had leave to travel to London. At Slough they were joined for company by one of Ireton's men and continued through Maidenhead and Uxbridge to Hillingdon, which they reached at 10 o'clock the next morning.

Hudson had considered the curious route towards London a necessary feint, but it now became apparent that Charles was once more wavering and was again considering the possibility of presenting himself at Westminster. Possibly he expected some communication at Hillingdon. But a defeated king arriving in the capital at this stage of the struggle with no following could inspire little confidence. His contacts clearly met with no response and any communication he might have expected at Hillingdon failed to materialize. So, after waiting for three hours, he turned northwards through Harrow and St Albans to Wheathampstead, where he spent the night. The following morning, the 28th Hudson was sent off to make contact with Montreuil while Charles and Ashburnham journeyed to Downham, a few miles south of King's Lynn, doubtless having in mind the use of that seaport as an escape route if Hudson's report was unfavourable. Hudson had family connections in the area who protected Charles while he was waiting for news. He also went once more for comfort – secretly and in the night – to Little Gidding which he found untouched by war.

Hudson got nothing from the Scots in writing, but a verbal assent to a paper drawn up by Montreuil appeared to him to be satisfactory and he returned to Charles with the assurance that the Scots would ask him to do nothing contrary to his conscience and that, if Parliament refused to restore him to his rights and prerogatives, the Scots would declare for him. It was not as much as Charles had hoped but, as he weighed up the courses open to him, it still seemed that joining the Scots was the best alternative. But the decision hung on a knife's edge. If Hudson had failed to make contact with Montreuil, or if Montreuil had been less persuasive in that last interview, or, indeed, if Montreuil himself had assessed the situation correctly and reported less favourably, Charles would have turned back to London or would have taken Ashburnham's advice to go by sea to Newcastle where he might have had a little respite. As it was, continuing his circuitous way in order to avoid capture by Parliamentarian troops, he looped down to Huntingdon, crossed the Nen and the Welland to Melton Mowbray, doubled back to Stamford, and then made north-north-west, skirting Grantham, over the Trent to Southwell and to the house of the French Ambassador, where he arrived at 7 o'clock in the morning of May 5 after a journey of ten days. It was virtually his last taste of freedom.

Once with the Scots it was clear that both sides were at a loss. The Scots professed surprise at his coming and their immediate object, apart from the taking of Newark, was to get as far away from Parliament and its armies as possible while they considered the situation. Charles, knowing that Newark could not hold out, sadly ordered its surrender remembering the many times he had found refuge there. But in spite of this show of goodwill on the King's part the Scots made further demands which were entirely at variance with his own, or with Montreuil's understanding of the terms under which he had come among them. They pushed the question of religion 'so ungraciously that they could not have done differently had they wished to give him an aversion for the establishment of their Presbyterianism', as Montreuil wrote to Mazarin. They demanded that Charles sign the Covenant and that he establish Presbyterianism in England and Ireland; on his refusal they treated him like a prisoner, placing guards at his door.

When the first panic of the King's flight was over and Parliament realized where he was, they ordered the Scots to send him to Warwick Castle but the Scots were still not sure how great a prize had fallen into their hands and on May 7 they started for Newcastle, which they reached on the 13th. Parliament then, angry and suspicious, tried to get hold of the King's two friends but the Scots, unexpectedly magnanimous, turned a blind eye when Charles commanded them to escape. He sent by Ashburnham a brief note to Henrietta-Maria 'transferring at this time the freedom of my pen to his tongue'. He also sent to Secretary Nicholas at Oxford to treat for the city's surrender, adjuring him to take particular care of the University and to have the Duke of York sent to his father. Oxford surrendered on June 24. Though the University was not harmed the Duke of York was sent under restraint to St James's Palace. Wallingford, the last of the Royalist fortresses, surrendered on July 27.

At Newcastle formal disputations began at the end of May with Alexander Henderson the Scottish Divine, in an endeavour to convert Charles. He had no alternative but to join in the wearisome and fruitless exchanges; in any case there was little else to do except write letters and hope he could smuggle them out. Although he also played chess and golf it was the most wretched, the most deeply humiliating period of his life. James Harrington, a friend of his sister, was permitted to take Ashburnham's place as groom of the bedchamber, but he was a prisoner, unable to leave the Scottish army, treated with increasing disdain and subject to 'barbarous usage' as he put it to his wife. He could not even call upon a servant without getting leave, the Scots did the contrary to whatever he asked: each day, he said, was 'never wanting new vexations'. 'I have need of some comfort', he begged her, 'for I never knew what it was to be barbarously baited before . . . there was never man so alone as I . . . no living soul to help me . . . all the comfort I have is in thy love and a clear conscience.' 'I hope God hath sent me hither for the last punishment that he will inflict upon me', he wrote more lightly, 'for assuredly no honest man can prosper in these peoples company.' In spite of his anguish he retained an outward dignity that struck all who saw him. He supported it all, wrote Montreuil, 'with an equanimity that I cannot enough admire, having a kindly demeanour towards those who show him no respect, and who treat him with very little civility.' Charles knew how to take adversity; it was decision he found so difficult.

But decision he had to take when on July 13 Commissioners arrived at Newcastle from Parliament with Nineteen Propositions, which were not unlike those proposed at Uxbridge the previous year, demanding a Presbyterian settlement of religion, in which Charles took the Covenant, and Parliamentary control of the militia for twenty years. Charles's answer was evasive. As he wrote to Henrietta-Maria, 'all my endeavours must be the delaying my answer'. His wife and the advisers with whom he was in touch – Jermyn, Culpepper and Ashburnham – advised him to accept Presbyterianism, on the grounds that it would come anyway. Henrietta-Maria, however, was adamant on the necessity of retaining the militia. Charles saw matters differently. The point he made over and over again was that his opponents sought to control the state through religion: 'unless religion be preserved, the militia will not be much useful to the crown . . . if the pulpits teach not obedience . . . the king will have but small comfort of the militia'. Or, as he put it more explicitly, it ' is not the change of Church government which is chiefly aimed at . . but it is by that pretext to take away the dependency of the Church from the Crown, which . . . I hold to be of equal consequence to that of the Militia; for people are governed by the pulpit more than the sword in times of peace.'

Charles felt so strongly on the matter that he wrote a long letter to the Prince of Wales on August 26. Take it from me, he said,

> as an infallible maxim . . . that, as the Church can never flourish without the protection of the Crown, so the dependency of the Church upon the Crown is the chiefest support of regal authority. This is that which is so well understood by the English and Scots rebels, that no concessions will content them without the change of Church government . . . Therefore, my first direction to you is, to be constant in the maintenance of that Episcopacy, not only for the reasons above said, but likewise to hinder the growth of Presbyterian doctrine, which cannot but bring anarchy into any country, whenever it shall come for any time.

Charles's second obsession at this time was the preservation of the rights of his son. 'I conjure you, by your unspotted faithfulness, by all that you love, by all that is good', he wrote to his three counsellors on July 22,

> that no threatenings, no apprehensions of danger to my person, make you stir one jot from any foundation in relation to that authority which the Prince of Wales is born to. I have already cast up what I am like to suffer, which I shall meet (by the grace of God) with that constancy that befits me. Only I desire that consolation, that assurance from you, as I may justly hope that my cause shall not end with my misfortunes, by assuring me that misplaced pity to me do not prejudice my son's right.

What was the worst that he envisaged for himself at this time is not clear.

In sending his first formal reply to the Propositions on August 1 Charles made the point that the proposals had taken twice as many months to prepare as he had taken days for his answer, yet they imported such changes in both Church and State that he suggested a full debate for which he proposed to come to London, or any of his houses. The offer was not taken up, nor did a second evasive reply in December meet with any response. His only thought then was escape. But again Henrietta-Maria opposed his plans. 'Everyone here', she wrote from Paris, was startled at the idea. 'I . . . conjure you, that till the Scots shall declare that they will not protect you, you do not think of making any escape from England . . . you would destroy all our hopes, besides the danger of the attempt.' She may have been right. But there were rumours then and later that this vehement rejection of a plan which would bring them together and which there were good reasons for supporting at that time were due to her alarm lest his coming should disclose and interfere with her relationship with Jermyn; one near contemporary was very certain that she had a child by Jermyn. She had certainly become exasperated with Charles's refusal to compromise on religion and had threatened to take no further part in his affairs. His panic-stricken, abject replies could have alienated her still further: 'I assure thee, both I and all my children are ruined, if thou shouldst retire from my business: for God's sake leave off threatening me with thy desire to meddle no more with business . . . as thou lovest me give me so much comfort (and God knows I have but little, and that little must come from thee) as to assure me that thou wilt think no more of any such thing.' It is apparent that the Scots had worn down the spirit of the man whose physical endurance had appeared unbreakable.

Neither the Scots nor Parliament were getting anything out of the situation and when Parliament paid the Scots £100,000 as the first instalment of the money owing to them, the Scots left Newcastle for home, leaving Charles in the hands of Parliamentary Commissioners, who included his old friends Pembroke and Denbigh. After consulting Parliament they agreed to his suggestion that they all go to his wife's house at Holdenby – it was a convenient distance from London and well removed from the influence of the army – and, to his utter relief, they set off on 3 February 1647, more than nine months after he left Oxford. The journey of some 160 miles was a veritable progress in the old style through Durham, Leeds, Nottingham and Leicester, with people flocking to see him, pressing forward to be 'touched' for the 'Evil', and accompanying him on his journey with cries of joy and prayers for his preservation. At Holdenby the welcome was warm from the many country gentry and ordinary people who greeted him with affection. An officer of the Wardrobe had prepared the house for him, his chaplains were in attendance, his usual state was observed, and he 'touched' many more people who came to be cured. War had deprived them of the opportunity and he was gratified at their continuing belief in his powers. Apart from the Commissioners the only evidence that he was not quite his own master was the appointment of Parliament's nominee, Thomas Herbert, to share with Harrington the duties of groom of the bedchamber. Herbert was a quiet, unassuming man, who came to know the best side of the King's character, while Charles developed a complete trust that was almost affection for the man Parliament had chosen to be his constant companion. The two grooms were shortly joined by a third, James Maxwell, personally known to Charles through his experiments in the manufacture of iron, the patent for the manufacture of pipe clay which Charles had granted him, and, more particularly, for the generous loans he had made to the King on the security of the royal jewels. Maxwell had married the widow of James's surveyor of stables.

Charles now re-formed the ordered life he enjoyed. Private devotions on Sunday, two or three hours' reading each day, chess and walking for recreation when Pembroke would with difficulty keep pace with Charles's rapid pacing up and down the long gravel walk in the garden. He continued to be abstemious at meals, drank only a little beer and wine, and was never in better health. One of his pleasures was riding to Harrowden, nine miles away, or to Althorpe, which was nearer, for a game of bowls. As he crossed a bridge going to

Harrowden one day a labourer was detected thrusting a parcel into his hands which proved to be a packet of letters from the Queen. The 'rustic' was Major Bosvile, who was apprehended and sent away. A few weeks later a lady described as 'handsome' and 'bold' was seized and searched after visiting Charles at Holdenby. Nothing was found on her and she was released, but later a letter in cypher was found behind the hangings where she had stood in Charles's room. The woman was most likely Jane Whorwood who later made several more efforts to communicate with Charles and to help him escape. At Holdenby, at least, she would have been in touch with him through her stepfather, James Maxwell, for Jane Whorwood was the daughter by her first husband of the widow whom Maxwell married. After these episodes Charles's servants were restricted and more closely watched, but Maxwell remained with him.

While Charles's days at Holdenby passed pleasantly enough, in spite of the fact that he was in custody, the victorious army and Parliament, having dismissed the Scots, were falling out amongst themselves. The cleavage between Presbyterian and Independent was becoming more markedly one between Parliament and army with the Parliament, having established a Presbyterian religion in January 1645, continuing to refuse freedom for nonconformity. Added to this, Parliament's financial difficulties were becoming greater and army pay was falling so severely behind that the Horse and Dragoons were forty-three weeks, the Foot eighteen weeks in arrears by March 1647. Parliament was nevertheless proposing to disband part of the army and to send the rest of it to Ireland. Working on the soldiery was the ubiquitous firebrand, John Lilburne, who, besides forming a Leveller party among civilians, was engaged in forming one in the army. So successful were he and his friends that by April the soldiers were electing representatives or agitators to state their case and were forming a Council of the Army to take charge of their affairs. War between Parliament and Army was open when Fairfax announced on May 31 that he would not draw up his regiments for disbandment. On the same day Lilburne published from imprisonment in the Tower *Rash Oaths Unwarrantable*, in which he castigated Parliament men as dastardly renegades and announced that 'King Charles his seventeen years misgovernment before this Parliament . . . was but a flea-biting, or as a molehill to a mountain, in comparison of what this everlasting Parliament already is.'

For Cromwell and the High Command the position was delicate. Cromwell had several times begged Parliament to consider freedom of conscience; he was reluctant to see the men who had won the war deprived of their wages; while not anxious to become a political man he had no wish to see the army's victory thrown away by politicians at Westminster. Like Lilburne, and like the agitators, his thoughts turned to the King. The events of the next few days are shrouded in secrecy. But Charles was playing bowls at Althorpe with two of the Commissioners in the early afternoon of June 2 when he was informed of horsemen approaching Holdenby. The players returned to the house but it was not until midnight that a party of horse drew up before it and placed guards on all the entrances. When asked his name and business the officer in charge replied Joyce, a cornet in Colonel Whalley's regiment and his business was with the King. The statement was greeted with laughter, but it seemed less amusing when the soldiers guarding Holdenby fraternized with Joyce's men and put the Commissioners under guard. Joyce, having found his way about, then knocked at the King's door. Charles's attendants asked through the locked door who it was disturbing the King's rest at that time of night, and he replied again that his name was Joyce, an officer in the army, and he was sorry to disquiet the King but could not help it for speak to him he must, and that at once. Demands and resistance continued until Charles was awakened and rang his silver bell to enquire what the noise was about. When he sent word that he would not rise nor speak with Joyce until morning the officer was disgruntled but had no alternative but to wait.

Charles rose a little earlier than usual, performed his morning exercises and sent for Joyce, who approached him with no more deference than if he had been a superior officer. Charles immediately asked about the Commissioners.

'By your favour, Sir', he said, 'let them have their liberty and give me a sight of your Instructions.'

'That', said Joyce, 'you shall see', and taking the King to a window he showed him his troop of horse drawn up in the inner court. 'There, Sir, are my Instructions.'

The King took a long look at the troop, found them good men, well groomed, well mounted and armed. 'Your instructions', he told the Cornet, 'are in fair Character, legible without spelling.' He accordingly made ready to depart, insisting that the Commissioners went with him. The King was merry, almost certainly not unaware of the

413

dissensions in the South, and hoping that the new developments could not be to his disadvantage.

‹ Charles was escorted to Hinchinbrook, followed by 'the confident Cornet', where he received a hearty welcome from the people, and on to Childersly, four miles from Cambridge, where he stayed for three days while the Masters, Fellows, and students flocked in to kiss his hand or merely to see him. More importantly the Army Command came also and for the first time the King and Cromwell came face to face. When Fairfax and Cromwell disavowed Joyce's action in bringing him there Charles laughed: 'Unless you hang up Joyce I will not believe what you say!'

They moved on to Newmarket on the 8th, where Charles's hunting lodge had been made ready for him, and all the while crowds were gathering to see him and the Army officers were in close attendance, particularly Cromwell and Henry Ireton.

Charles resumed his routine, keeping his usual hours of private devotion, but he also dined frequently in public, basking in the prayers and acclaim of the byestanders. He was in custody, but it was pleasant. And he was now constitution-making with the Army which, for the time being, he infinitely preferred to constitution-making with the Scots or with Parliament.

On the surface the movement of events was to Charles's advantage. Cromwell and Ireton consulted him on the heads of a scheme which Ireton had drawn up, and Ashburton and Sir John Berkeley, who had recently arrived from France, joined the discussions. Berkeley was a cousin of Sir Thomas Roe, a kinsman of Jermyn, who had undertaken diplomatic missions for the King and given good service in the wars. He had been present at the baptism of Henrietta-Anne in Exeter Cathedral and had recently spent some time with the Queen and Jermyn in Paris. On this account alone he was welcome to Charles, but he was thought also to have some influence with the Parliamentarian army.

Ireton met the King's wishes on several points and the Heads of the Proposals, as finally submitted to the Council of the Army on August 1, were the most advantageous terms that Charles had been offered – and, indeed, the best that he was likely to get. Parliament was still to have control of the militia and the appointment of officers of state for ten years, but there would be no established Presbyterianism and no compulsion to take the Covenant, though neither would the use of the

Prayer Book or church attendance be obligatory; it was, in fact, a fairly comprehensive toleration which Ireton was offering. A Council of State would participate with the King in foreign affairs and in control of the army; the existing Parliament would end within a year and new Parliaments would meet every two years and sit for a limited time; Royalists would be treated leniently and a general amnesty be declared.

It is possible that Charles regarded his negotiations with the Army as mere preliminaries, believing that Parliament was certain to outbid the Army in the terms it offered him, and he probably had little faith in the Army's power to carry out its undertakings. There was certainly a clash of personality between him and Ireton. Charles was unused to the waspish tones of the Commissary General, who spoke in sharp sentences and would not wrap up a denial in the manner to which the King was accustomed. When Charles told the soldiers, frankly but lightly, at the beginning of their negotiations, 'You cannot do without me. You will fall to ruin if I do not sustain you', Ireton was emphatic and unsmiling: 'Sir', he said, 'you have an intention to be the arbitrator between the Parliament and us, and we mean to be it between your Majesty and Parliament.' When Charles later remarked 'I shall play my game as well as I can', Ireton answered, 'If your Majesty have a game to play, you must give us also the leave to play ours.' Neither man breathed the spirit of compromise. But there had been sufficient concession on the part of the Army Command to alarm the soldiers. Having fought the King for five years, they asked, why did their officers now make an idol of him? 'Why permit they so many of his deceiptfull Clergy to continue about him? Why doe themselves kneele, and kisse, and fawne upon him? . . . Oh shame of men! Oh sin against God! What!', they exclaimed using a new term for the first time, 'to doe thus to a man of blood; over head and eares in the blood of your dearest friends and fellow Commoners?'

The situation was a little more delicate than Charles understood. While he was travelling from Holdenby, and again on June 10, the soldiers had held massive meetings at which they threatened to march on London unless their demands were met. While he was talking to the King at Newmarket Cromwell had this on his mind and at last decided to take control of a movement that he had little chance, and little inclination, to stem. With the whole army behind him he marched to London, and on August 2 they drew up, 20,000 strong, on Hounslow Heath. Independent Members of both Houses rode out to

415

meet them and there was great shouting and acclaim, with men throwing their hats in the air and crying for 'Lords and Commons and a free Parliament!'. Six of the leading Presbyterians, including Charles's old enemy, Denzil Holles, left the House. But still the Presbyterian majority remained until, on the 20th, Cromwell himself, with other officers who were also Parliament men, went to Westminster, while a regiment of cavalry was drawn up in Hyde Park. The issue needed no underlining. The most prominent Presbyterians left the House, leaving control, for the time being, to the Independents.

While the army moved towards London, Charles went, too, on what was a leisurely progress, stopping at noblemen's houses on the way. He stopped for dinner and a joyous meeting with his three children at Sion House, and was joined there by his nephew, the Elector Palatine. He reached Lord Craven's house at Caversham on the south bank of the Thames on July 3, where Cromwell visited him several times and where he was allowed to have his children with him for two nights. Eagerly he rode to Maidenhead to meet them. Cromwell, an emotional man, was deeply moved at the reunion. Berkeley met him as he was coming from the King with tears in his eyes. He had just seen, said Cromwell, 'the tenderest sight that ever his eyes beheld, which was the interview between the King and his children'. He wept at the memory and declared that never man was so abused as the King, who was 'the most uprightest and most conscientious man of the three Kingdoms'. Yet still there was no agreement between them. Pompone de Bellievre, who was now Ambassador from France in Montreuil's place believed that Charles might have had the army with him if he had frankly accepted their proposals at this time. But Charles constantly hoped for more from someone else; he had so firmly grasped the fact that his opponents were divided that he could not believe that he would fail to retrieve all if he played his cards carefully. He was encouraged by a resurgence of Royalist pamphlets and the unaccustomed words of pity and sympathy provided a new support.[1]

34

Dum Spiro Spero

Charles's destination was his own palace of Hampton Court where Colonel Edward Whalley, a cousin of Cromwell's, was in charge. Captivity sat lightly upon the King and he had many visitors, including not only Cromwell but Cromwell's wife, his daughter, and her recently-married husband, Henry Ireton. His children also visited him and they all sat to John Hoskins, the miniaturist. Charles's chaplain, Jeremy Taylor, also came. He had been with the King during much of the fighting and had been one of those honoured in 1643, at Charles's request, by the University of Oxford, who conferred upon him the degree of Doctor of Divinity for his pamphlet, *Episcopacy Asserted*. Now he had published his *Liberty of Prophesying*, which interested Charles although he did not altogether agree with it, but there were probably other reasons for his visit. He lived ten miles from Mandinam in Carmarthenshire, the home of Joanna Bridges who was rumoured to be Charles's natural daughter. At all events Charles gave Taylor a ring with two diamonds and a ruby, a watch, and a few pearls and rubies which ornamented the ebony case in which he kept his bible. There was no reason why he should give these to Taylor unless they were to pass on to Joanna Bridges, whom the divine later married as his second wife. Charles hunted in his familiar parks, played bowls, walked the terraces and gravel ways of the gardens, watched the Thames, the familiar river associated with his happiest days. In the great house itself, of some 1500 rooms, he had virtual freedom, for he had given his word not to try to escape. He was, nevertheless, so carefully watched that he had little communication with Henrietta-Maria. Yet, despite this deprivation, he remained buoyant and was confident of the future. But he was slow in coming to an agreement with anybody. Berkeley urged him to make a decision. Was he letting slip another opportunity? It seemed likely, for Cromwell's position was once more endangered in the autumn of 1647 by Lilburne and the agitators who were increasingly restless at his failure to produce the expected results.

Charles was well aware of Lilburne's plot to capture the army. Sir Lewis Dyve, his own supporter, had been imprisoned in the Tower since the capture of Sherborne Castle in August 1645 and was in close touch with the voluble and excitable Leveller leader, who disclosed his plans to Dyve who passed them on to the King. But Lilburne was at the same time suggesting collaboration with Charles, whose reign he still maintained was 'but as a flea biting' to the enormities of Parliament. The King was also being approached by other sectaries, notably by William Kiffin, the Baptist, who reported to Lilburne that Charles had given him such assurances of liberty for the future that he was completely satisfied of the King's goodwill. On the strength of this Lilburne tried to arrange through Dyve a meeting between some of the leading agitators and the King. If the King would satisfy these men, Lilburne would pawn his life, so Dyve reported to Charles on October 5, 'that within a moneth or six weekes at the farthest the wholl army should be absolutely at your Majestie's devotion to dispose thereof as you pleased'. But Charles was of the opinion, with some justification, that Lilburne at this stage did not represent the true feelings of the Levellers and he heard enough of Cromwell's strength in the Army Council meetings of October and early November to discount the dreams of Dyve and Lilburne. Moreover, he found the reports of the army debates at Putney, which lasted from October 28 to November 11, particularly disturbing, for Levellers and agitators were there discussing a document called The Agreement of the People which claimed a Parliamentary vote for all men on the grounds that the 'poorest hee' in England had as much right as the greatest. Charles was left further away than ever from the possibility of any approach to such men. The violence of their language may, indeed, have contributed to the decision he was about to make.

He had received several round-about reports of plots on his life and the dismissal of Ashburnham, Berkeley and other attendants on November 1 increased his sense of isolation. He had been growing increasingly melancholy at his enforced captivity. Lady Fanshaw, who had made one of the war marriages at Oxford, saw him about this time and was much distressed at his sadness: 'when I took my leave', she wrote, 'I could not refrain from weeping: when he had saluted me, I prayed to God to preserve His Majesty with long life and happy years; he stroked me on the cheek, and said, "Child, if God pleaseth, it shall be so, but both you and I must submit to God's will, and you know in what hands I am".' A mysterious letter warning him directly of a plot by the agitators to kill him arrived on the 9th. But his plans were already laid. On the evening of November 11 he left his greyhound bitch whimpering in his room and walked out of Hampton Court. He was joined near the Palace by Colonel William Legge and himself led the familiar way to Thames Ditton where Ashburnham was waiting with Berkeley and horses from his own stables. The little party made for Bishop's Sutton in Hampshire, but the weather was foul and even with Charles as guide they lost their way in Windsor forest. It was dawn before they arrived at the inn where fresh horses were waiting and they were warned by an accomplice that a Parliamentary Committee meeting was already in progress there. So, changing mounts but without rest or refreshment, they pushed on. As when he left Oxford, Charles was undecided where to go. If a boat had been ready he might have gone to Jersey or to France. Perhaps he allowed himself to be influenced by Ashburnham, who was inclined to favour the Isle of Wight. It was still within his kingdom, it was reasonably remote from any assassination attempt, there were a number of good Royalists there, and it offered escape to the Continent if necessary. Moreover Charles seemed to think, without any very good reason, that the new Governor of the Island, Colonel Robert Hammond, would be in sympathy with him.

No contact had been made with Hammond but the Earl of Southampton, who had visited Charles at Hampton Court shortly before he left, welcomed the King at his old haunt of Tichfield on Southampton Water and here he waited with Legge while Ashburnham and Berkeley went over to the Island to feel their way with the Govenor. Their passage was delayed by bad weather and they handled the affair ineptly. They did not know Hammond nor he them, and Ashburnham was staggered by Berkeley's open and, as he termed it, 'verie unskilfull entrance into their business' when, immediately after the opening of formalities, he asked Hammond if he knew who was near him. Naturally enough Hammond replied in the negative and Berkeley rushed on: 'Even good King Charles, who is come from Hampton Court for feare of being murdered privately.' It is difficult to know who was more confused in the subsequent exchanges. Hammond recovered first and suggested that they all three of them go to the King.

Charles had found the waiting long and had put out feelers for a boat to France, but the ports had already been closed on news of his escape. When at last his friends returned Ashburnham went in to him and told him that Hammond was outside. 'Oh Jack! thou hast undone me!' cried Charles. His place of retreat was revealed, what he had intended to be exploratory had become obligatory and there was no going back. They crossed to Cowes the same day and went on to Carisbrooke Castle in the centre of the Island. The people greeted him with affection as he passed and a woman thrust a damask rose into his hand, plucked from her garden at that late date. The Army Command had found the note that Charles had left at Hampton Court saying he feared for his life, as well as the warning letter signed E.R., and the search parties were out; it was not long before Hammond was in communication with them and Charles's whereabouts were known.

Some of Charles's friends believed that the army were glad he had gone, on the grounds that he had proved no use to them and was encouraging the rift between the Command and the agitators. Whether Cromwell and his friends had planted the idea of murder in Charles's mind, whether he himself had manufactured the idea as an excuse to be gone, or whether the notes and his fears were genuine, some of his supporters nevertheless believed he had made a mistake both in leaving Hampton Court and in going to the Isle of Wight. But at first Charles had no reason to regret the change. People were friendly and supporters flocked to Carisbrook to see or speak with him. There was also some justification in his own belief that in dealing with the Army alone he was negotiating on too narrow a front, for, before the year was out, both Parliament and Scots had sent Commissioners to him on the Island. He deliberately played for time, came to the conclusion that the Scots were offering better terms, and made a secret agreement with them in which he promised Presbyterianism for three years and they agreed to raise another army for him. Their solemn agreement was buried in lead in the Castle grounds, at the end of December. Charles tried to postpone his reply to Parliament, but the Commissioners insisted he make known his response to their overtures before they left the Island, and he was forced to admit that he had rebuffed them.

Although he had not expected to declare himself so soon, he had been well aware of the hostility that would result and had again been thinking of escape. But where? To the Scots? To Jersey or France while the Scots raised their army? On the day the Parliamentary

Commissioners left he learned that the ship he had been expecting was at Southampton and that a small boat was in readiness to take him across from the Island. The wind was set fair. Hurriedly he prepared for the journey. Hammond was attending the departing Parliamentary Commissioners and there was no one to stop him. But a glance out of the window at the last moment revealed that the wind had changed and was blowing from the North, making it impossible to leave the Island.

His captivity had hitherto sat lightly on him. Many of his household had joined him, his carriage and a quantity of his books had been sent over, he had driven round the Island, seen the Needles, walked about Newport and other towns and villages. But on the strength of the King's refusal to Parliament's terms and the knowledge of his agreement with the Scots, tighter security at Carisbrooke was imposed, his Household was reduced, and Ashburnham, Berkeley and Legge were sent away. A sympathetic officer in Newport attempted to rescue him but his plan was discovered before it could be tried, and on 15 January 1648 Parliament passed a vote of No More Addresses to the King.

Escape was now more than ever on his mind and the number of people willing to help him indicated both the extent of royalism in the Isle of Wight and his own ability to command support. There were soldiers like Colonel William Hopkins and his son George, who lived at Newport; Captain Cooke, one of his guards, who had come over to his side; Captain Silus Titus, who had originally served Parliament but had been won over by Charles at Holdenby, had come south with him and remained near him at Carisbrooke; there was the sailor who unsuccessfully tried to get letters to the King from his wife and children. Among civilians were Abraham Dowcett, Edward Worsley, Boroughs, Cresset, Napier, who all had access to Carisbrooke; and more than one who, like John Newland of the Corporation of Newport, owned a boat which could be put at the King's disposal. In Charles's household at Carisbrooke were Henry Firebrace, now twenty-eight years old, his page of happier days; David Murray, his tailor; Uriah Babbington, his barber; and a Gentleman Usher named Osborn, who was appointed as a spy but defected. Osborn's duties entailed waiting upon Charles at table and taking care of the royal gloves during the meal; it was easy to convey and receive messages in the fingers of the gloves. There were also Mrs Wheeler, who was in charge of his laundry, and her assistant, Mary, as well as the old man

421

who brought up coals. Working between London and the Island was his old friend, Jane Whorwood, and Mrs Pitt, a contact of Titus at Southampton. The Earl of Alford, who had spoken so strongly for Parliament in the 1620s was ready to help at his home near Arundel, and Sir John Bowring, who had become a clerk to the Privy Council at Oxford and who had useful connections in the Isle of Wight, had for some time been a trusted confidant and go-between. There were in addition many who helped in carrying letters; Major Bosvile, who had turned up at Holdenby disguised as a rustic, was still active; Clavering of the Post Office was usefully placed; a sailor, a physician, well-dressed women, poor people, and apparently ordinary people were all at various times part of the line of communication that Charles succeeded in maintaining, albeit imperfectly, with his wife and his supporters.

The laundry woman, Mary, had access to Charles's rooms during the day when they were empty and unguarded, and it was simple for her to conceal letters under the carpet or behind the wall-hangings and to indicate to the King where she had hidden them. In this way, with the help of Abraham Dowcett, Napier of the town, and the tailor, David Murray, a plot was hatched in February for making a hole in the ceiling of Charles's room through which he could make his way to an upper storey and so to an unguarded part of the Castle. But Hammond's vigilance was too much for them and the plans were revealed. Mrs Wheeler and Mary, with other servants including (mistakenly at this time) the royal barber were dismissed. Charles would not allow a Parliament man nor a soldier to approach him with a razor and preferred to let his hair and beard grow.

It was about this time that Charles started communicating with Titus on odd scraps of paper, some no more than one inch across, disguising his handwriting and using a cypher for the most important parts of his messages. Parliament became suspicious enough to order Hammond to search his room. Charles surprised the Governor while he was doing so, there was a scuffle in which the King received some small injury, but he succeeded nevertheless in throwing his papers into the fire before Hammond could get them.

Charles's position certainly looked brighter in the spring. The Scots were ready to cross the border in his support, Irish troops had promised help, in South Wales Colonel Poyer declared for the King, all over the country discontent and royalism were joining hands. Cromwell sent Ashburnham and Berkeley to the Isle of Wight in one more attempt at compromise, but Charles gained far more from the welcome contact than he gave; for why should he compromise when events appeared to be going his way? The one essential was escape.

Henry Firebrace was the leading spirit in the fresh attempt, and he was confident enough to assure the Scots that the King would shortly be joining them. He communicated with Charles through a hole he made in the wall of Charles's bedroom, underneath the tapestry hangings, and Charles knew precisely how and where to surmount the two castle walls that stood between him and the two horsemen who would be waiting with three horses beyond the outer defences. He was convinced he could get out of his chamber window for he had tried the space with his head and refused Firebrace's urging to tamper with one of the bars. On the coast Newland would be ready with a boat to take him to the mainland, he would ride straight to Edward Alford's house at Arundel and thence be conducted to Queensborough in Suffolk where a ship would be waiting.

On the night of Monday March 20 all was ready; but the King failed to come: his body would not follow where his head had gone and after a desperate struggle in which he feared he would not be able to move either way he was thankful to get back into his room. In a note to Titus Charles begged that his friends should be given thanks for their part in the enterprise and almost immediately further plans were set on foot for weakening one of the bars on his window with *aqua fortis*, or nitric acid, after which it might be pulled from its socket. Jane Whorwood obtained the acid in London but it was spilt on its journey to the Isle of Wight. A further supply was procured which was later found in Charles's room, but an alternative means of removing the bar was also provided by the 'fat plain man' who brought a 'hacker' to Charles – an implement that could convert two plain knives, such as the King possessed, into a saw that would cut through the bars of his window. But too many people were involved in this plot and on June 2 Hammond was able to disclose it to Parliament, although not before a bar of Charles's window had been actually cut. 'He hath one or two about him who are false', reported Hammond, and he sent some of the faithful, including Titus, Boroughs and Cresset away from the Island. They thought of setting fire to the Castle before they left and rescuing the King in the confusion. More practically, Titus managed to stay behind.

While the King was vainly trying to escape, what was virtually a second civil war was flaring round the country. Reaction had set in fuelled by sequestration, taxation, intolerance, food shortages, censorship, repression. The reaction had not gone the way of the Levellers but the way of the Royalists. By the beginning of May the whole of South Wales was in revolt and Cromwell was hastening westwards. Berwick and Carlisle had been taken for the King, Surrey and Kent, even the Eastern counties were in arms. The Prince of Wales was at sea with a Dutch fleet, and reached the mouth of the Thames, the Duke of York escaped from St James's on April 21 disguised as a girl and reached Holland. In May there was mutiny in the navy. On July 8 a Scottish Royalist army at last crossed the border under the Duke of Hamilton. If Charles had been in any place but the Isle of Wight, separated by sea from his supporters, a Royalist force might have rescued him to lead his armies; if he had gone overseas he might, even now, have been landing with the Prince of Wales on English soil to fight once more for his Crown. Instead there was only expectation and hope, followed all too soon by despair. At the beginning of June Fairfax defeated the Royalists at Maidstone and turned to deal with those in Essex; early in July Cromwell completed the suppression of Charles's supporters in Wales and marched northwards to deal with the Scots, whom he defeated at Preston on August 17. Hamilton was captured shortly afterwards and the capitulation of Colchester on August 28 marked the end of the war in the Eastern counties. Charles was helpless.

Hammond meanwhile was doing what he could for his captive. Charles found the wine poor and the bed-linen not over-clean. But a golf course was made within the outer defences of the Castle, in one corner of which a little summer house was built where he could watch the sea and the shipping and the soft line of green hills which were not visible from his room. He spent nevertheless many hours indoors, praying, reading, and writing. One of his concerns was to record his own reactions to the condition in which he now found himself, another – as far as he could understand them – the reasons for the conflict between himself and his Parliament. As he wrote of the present he could forget his attempts to escape and the defeat of his followers in a resignation so complete that it seemed to embrace whatever the future might bring. His mood of resignation was fostered by the scant communication he had at this time with his family; he complained to Titus that his wife's letters seemed to miscarry, and there was a hint of bitterness in his remark that he received answers to other letters but not to those he sent to her.

When he wrote of the past he explained, and sometimes excused, his actions. If he had called Parliament to any place but London, he believed, the consequences would have been different; when he left Whitehall he was driven by shame rather than fear, in order not 'to prostitute the Majestie of My Place and Person, the safetie of My Wife and Children'; he passed the Triennial Act 'as gentle and seasonable Physick might, if well applied, prevent anie distempers from getting anie head'; when his wife left England it was not even her going that hurt most but the 'scandal of that necessity'. He was bitter at the publication of the private letters to his wife, which had been captured after Naseby. No man's malice, he wrote, could 'be gratified further by my letters than to see my constancy to my wife, the laws, and religion: bees will gather honey where the spider sucks poison . . . the confidence of privacy may admit greater freedom in writing such letters which may be liable to envious exceptions'.

He harked back to the death of Strafford, which was always on his mind, acknowledging his greatness, his abilities, which 'might make a Prince rather afraid, then ashamed to emploie him in the greatest affairs of state'. Charles had been persuaded to choose what appeared 'safe' rather than 'just' and the Act that resulted he described as a 'sinful frailtie'. To his son he wrote that the reflections he was putting down were mainly intended for him, in the hope that they would help to remedy the present distempers and prevent their repetition. The fact that the Prince of Wales had experienced troubles while young may help him 'as trees set in winter, then in warmth and serenitie of time' frequently benefit. He urged him to be Charles 'le bon' rather than Charles the Great, to take heed of abetting faction, to use his prerogative to remit rather than to exact and, above all, to begin and end with God.

Charles also made translations from Latin, which he had always enjoyed doing, he wrote favourite passages in the fly-leaves of some of his books, he read the Bible, Bishop Andrewes's sermons, Hooker's *Ecclesiastical Polity*, Herbert's *Divine Poems*, and many more religious works. For lighter reading he chose Spenser's *Faery Queen* and Tasso's *Godfrey of Bulloigne*. He kept Bacon's *Advancement of Learning* by him, carefully continuing his annotation. He could still get pleasure from books. Although, as he wrote, they had left him 'but little of life, and onely the husk and shell' yet 'I am not old, as to be wearie of life', he said, and he wrote over and over again in his books: *Dum spiro Spero*.

The second civil war ended the possibility of any agreement with Cromwell and the army. Charles was once more the Man of Blood and the renewed fighting was a punishment for not having dealt firmly with him before. Charles was all the more glad when Parliament sent Commissioners to Newport to treat in early September 1648. In the absence of the army, which was still in the field, it was a Commission dominated by Presbyterians and it contained several of Charles's old friends.

After a second military defeat Charles had little bargaining power, yet such was the aura of kingship that negotiations were planned and conducted almost as though he were a free monarch. On giving his word not to escape he was conducted to Newport on September 18 and settled in the best state the town could offer, which was at the house of his friend, Colonel Hopkins. Negotiations were conducted in the school house where Charles sat on a chair of state, he was allowed several chaplains, advisers and friends, who included Richmond, Hertford, Southampton, Lindsey and Ashburnham. Some came with their wives, so that evenings once more became social occasions, while during the day Charles again enjoyed the exhilaration of horse riding.

But, although he put on a show, Charles had little spirit for the negotiations. He was determined to give nothing away and obtained the agreement of the Commission that no section should be held binding until the whole proposed treaty had been discussed. Forty days had been allowed for discussion and week after week went by with no tangible result. Charles's friends believed that the Independent faction was playing for time until Cromwell and Fairfax had completed their military work: with the army once more in control there would be an end to negotiations and Charles's life would be in danger. But to all plans for escape he turned a deaf ear. If the Independents were playing for time, he was too, though to what end he was not quite sure. He made concession after concession, sometimes going further than he had done before, sometimes bitterly reproaching himself for doing so, sometimes assuaging his conscience by reminding himself that by his covering stipulation he need hold nothing binding until the conclusion of the whole treaty. When he did consider escape he was brought up against his parole. He was particularly evasive over Irish affairs but finally agreed to settle Ireland as Parliament should decide. In the general coming and going occasioned by the treaty negotiations his communications with France and Ireland had been easier and he knew that his wife and Ormonde were still planning a Royalist rising in Ireland. In a burst of hope he saw himself escaping and joining them in the field, and he wrote to Henrietta-Maria, telling her he was acting under duress and warning her not to be deceived. 'If the rumour of his concessions concerning Ireland', he wrote to her, 'should prejudice my affairs there, I send the enclosed letter to the Marquis of Ormonde, the sum of which is to obey your command, and to refuse mine till I certify him I am a free man.' He was acting just as, seven years earlier, she had told the Papal agent he would act.

But he had, on the whole, little confidence either that the concessions he had appeared to make would help him or that he was right to have made them. Night after night he went through the day's proceedings with his secretary, Sir Philip Warwick, meticulously, yet with a growing weariness, on one occasion turning away from Warwick and others in the room to hide his tears. Finally he yielded to his friends' importunities and agreed to escape. But scarcely had he done so when he reversed his decision. Signalling privately to Bowring one day to follow him into an inner room, he told him he had just received letters from overseas advising him not to leave the Island and assuring him that the army had no power to harm him. 'So now', said Charles,

> if I should go with you, now, as I thought to have done, and things fall out otherwise than well with me; and the rather because my treaty hath had so fair an end . . . and that my concessions are satisfactory, and especially since I have received this advice (you guess from whence it comes) I shall be always blamed here after . . . Therefore I am resolved to stay here, and God's will be done.

It was Charles at his most typical. The letter was obviously from Henrietta-Maria and he was once more tormented with anxiety that she might blame him for doing the wrong thing if he refused to follow her advice. She had also persuaded him to cover his negotiations with a rosy, but false, hue of optimism which he had not felt before. He did not appear to question the reason for her anxiety that he should remain on the Isle of Wight at this time – as once before she had urged him to stay in England.

By the middle of October Charles had agreed, as he had done before, to grant Presbyterianism for three years; he still refused to take the Covenant, but he allowed of 'counsel and assistance' by a Presbytery at the end of the three years. The militia he agreed to abandon first for ten years, but later he conceded twenty. He would on no account consider the death penalty for his supporters, but agreed to punishments of fine and the confiscation of part of their estates. But by this time his mood had again changed and the optimism had faded. On October 9 he wrote to Hopkins in despair: 'notwithstanding my too great concessions already made, I know that, unless I shall make yet others which will directly make me no King, I shall be at best but a perpetual prisoner . . . To deal fairly with you, the great concession I made this day – the Church, militia, and Ireland – was made merely in order to my escape, of which if I had not hope, I would not have done.' To return to prison now, he said, 'would break my heart, having done that which only an escape can justify'. My only hope, he concluded, 'is that now they believe I dare deny them nothing, and so be less careful of their guards'.

One thing Charles did continue to deny them and that was Episcopacy; he would not give it up as his personal religion and he would not suppress it so long as he had power. He had made concessions to Presbyterians and would foster a fairly wide toleration but from that position he would not budge. Partly on this rock, but partly because there never really was any hope of success, negotiations by the end of October had virtually ground to a halt. On November 12 Charles was enquiring urgently of Hopkins about tides and had decided to make for Gosport on the night of the 16th or 17th when Newland would once more have a boat ready. But it seemed that he no longer had any hand in ordering his own affairs. Hammond knew of his plans on the 13th and the enterprise was necessarily abandoned at the very time that Jane Whorwood reported from London through Sir John Bowring that a plot was actually in being to murder him, and that Sir Peter Killigrew came to warn him that the army intended to bring him to London for a public trial. In his bitterness Charles complained that his friends had failed him and his melancholy grew.

While negotiations had been proceeding at Newport the Army was once more facing its own problems. Internally it had to deal with the Levellers, who were still seeking their own form of constitutional settlement based on universal suffrage and a wide toleration, and particularly with Lilburne, who was still asserting that they could not in law bring the King to trial and that to do so would be to open the door to further arbitrary government. But the trial of the King was precisely what the majority of the soldiers now wanted and Ireton embodied their point of view in a Remonstrance which was published in the middle of October. But the army had to face the fact that Parliament was still negotiating with the King and that a conjunction between Parliament and King, or the King's escape, might at any moment jeopardize their military victory. At the end of November Ireton's Remonstrance was laid aside by Parliament and Fairfax, albeit reluctantly, once more began to move with his troops towards the capital. They were continuing their discussions with the Levellers, but while the most articulate soldiers were talking the majority could see only the black and white of the situation and by the beginning of December events had begun to move quickly.

On November 27 Hammond, on his refusal to take orders from anyone but Parliament, was removed from the Isle of Wight and the following day placed in custody by the Army, whose headquarters were now at Windsor. On the 30th Lieutenant-Colonel Cobbett and Captain Merryman arrived at Newport with a company of soldiers. On the night of December 1 his friends were urging Charles that now, if ever, was the time to escape. Captain Cooke assured him that he had horses and that a boat was ready. He had the password, and to demonstrate to Charles how easy escape would be he passed and repassed the guards with Richmond. But Charles was overcome with weariness and with inertia, his old fatal disease, and in spite of all he had said he now declared he would not break his word or his parole; he had made an agreement with Parliament and he would keep it. They argued desperately that it was the Army they were now dealing with, and not Parliament. Charles took no notice and retired to bed. The following morning at daybreak he was roused by soldiers under the command of Cobbett and hurried off without his breakfast. As one of the soldiers tried to follow him into his coach Charles thrust him back. 'It's not come to that yet!', he exclaimed.

He was taken across the Solent to Hurst Castle, a defensive fortress surrounded on three sides by sea, connected at low tide with the mainland by a thin strip of gravelly sand. The Governor was uncouth but not unkind; the rooms were so dark that candlelight was needed right through the day; the King's exercise was merely a daily walk along the shingle where, as usual, he outstripped his companions; the air was dank with winter mist and vapours from the marshes of the mainland. His only solace was in the passing ships that reminded him of freedom and of his own navy. While he was there Colonel Pride, on December 6, stationed himself with a body of musketeers outside the doors of the House of Commons, turning back the Presbyterian

429

Members as they arrived. He did the same the following day, excluding some 96 altogether, leaving about 56 sitting Members.

Charles was kept at Hurst Castle for a little over two weeks. On the night of December 17 he was awakened by noise and, ringing his little silver bell, sent Herbert to investigate. It was the drawbridge being let down to admit Colonel Harrison, who had been one of the most vehement in demanding the death of the Man of Blood. Charles was convinced that he was come to murder him in that bleak and desolate place, but the reality was reassuring, for on the 19th he was conducted by Cobbett to Windsor. He almost enjoyed the journey. As he was approaching Farnham he noted a fine-featured, splendidly-dressed Officer in command of the welcoming party. On enquiry he learned it was no other than Harrison. That evening after supper Charles perceived the same officer standing across the room from where he stood in his accustomed place in front of the fire. He beckoned him to him and, taking him apart, asked if he really had intended his death at Hampton Court? The answer was no doubt evasive, but the question shows that Charles had a real fear of assassination at that time.

At Bagshot Charles dined with Lord Newburgh. One more hope remained. Newburgh owned some of the fastest horses in England and one of them would be ready if the King could arrange to change his mount. Charles was prepared but again fate – or was it his captors? – had arranged that the horse should become lame shortly before his arrival. There was encouragement from the people who cheered him as he passed towards Windsor, some even crying out for God to bless him. The Castle, where he arrived on December 23, was more like a fortress than ever, for it now held many Royalist prisoners, including his kinsman, friend, and counsellor, Hamilton. Christmas was bleak and lonely. But Charles watched the river from the terrace where he took his daily walk and looked towards Eton with its memories of his first tutor and of bathing parties with Buckingham. A little of his old state was preserved in the serving of his meals, but gradually it was depressed, his attendants were dismissed. As he continued his hurried walking up and down the terrace, pausing to gaze out over the river, his hold on all that he had known throughout his life perceptibly loosened. He had no communication now with the wife who had borne him nine children in fifteen years, nor with his two eldest sons, nor with the daughter whose marriage might have helped his fortunes, nor with that baby, now a little girl of nearly five, who represented his last contact with Henrietta-Maria. Only Elizabeth and Henry, the children of his happiest years, remained near him – like himself, prisoners.

Charles was to remain at Windsor until 19 January 1649, while his opponents discussed his fate. A strong party of soldiers still urged his trial and condemnation. Fairfax shrank from such a procedure and kept outside the discussions. Lilburne and his party continued to assert that neither Parliament nor Army had the legal right to try the King and that to do so would be to open the door to further arbitrary government. Cromwell hesitated; even Ireton hung back. The Earl of Denbigh was sent with a secret message to Charles at Windsor which could have paved the way to further negotiation. Charles refused to see him. He would struggle for terms no longer; he could not consult his wife; he would no longer plague his conscience to determine what was right; there was no need to prevaricate; as he had written, they had left him with but the 'husk and shell' of life; he merely had to make his peace with himself, which meant with God, and he was helped by the wide, grey river that symbolized the best of his life. He believed that, except for the betrayal of Strafford, he had acted well; he believed his son would reign after him; he believed his captors were evil men and he knew what to expect. It was consequently easy for him to wait. As he had written: 'That I must die as a Man, is certain, that I may die a King, by the hands of My own Subjects, a violent, sudden, and barbarous death, in the strength of My years, in the midst of My Kingdoms, My Friends and loving Subjects being helpless Spectators, My Enemies insolent Revilers and Triumphers over Mee . . . is so probable in humane Reason, that God hath taught Mee not to hope otherwise.'

35

'To vindicate his helpless right'

Charles had not long to wait after his refusal to see Denbigh. On 1 January 1649 an Ordinance passed the House of Commons for the trial of the King on a charge of treason on the grounds that he had levied war against the Parliament and Kingdom of England. The Lords rejected the motion. On the 3rd the Commons passed it a second time together with an Ordinance establishing a High Court of Justice of 135 Commissioners. On the same day they refused to consider a letter from Henrietta-Maria begging permission to visit her husband. The next day they constituted themselves the sole law-making body without the concurrence of King or House of Lords and on the 6th passed what they could now call an Act, for the trial of Charles Stuart on the grounds that he

> had a wicked design totally to subvert the ancient and fundamental laws and liberties of this nation, and, in their place, to introduce an arbitrary and tyrannical government; and that, besides all other evil ways and means to bring this design to pass, he hath prosecuted it with fire and sword, levied and maintained a cruel war in the land against the Parliament and Kingdom, whereby the country hath been miserably wasted, the public treasure exhausted, trade decayed, thousands of people murdered, and infinite other mischiefs committed.

Since they could not make use of the Great Seal with its inscription in the name of Charles they had another made which was inscribed 'In the first year of freedom, by God's blessing restored'. The trial was fixed for January 20 and a Committee appointed to consider the preparation of Westminster Hall for the purpose.

The leaders of the Army, who since Pride's Purge were also the leaders of the nation and among whom Cromwell was the chief, had come to the conclusion that there could be no peace while Charles remained King. Cromwell's last, almost despairing, effort to avoid the consequences of that decision by sending Denbigh to Windsor had failed and he saw no alternative to the trial: what he expected from it is uncertain. It is likely that, as in the case of Strafford, he and his most intimate associates had come to the conclusion that 'stone dead hath no fellow'. But many supporters of Parliament and the Army shrank from either the trial itself or the consequences. The eminent and respected lawyers John Selden and Bulstrode Whitelocke were among those who retired from the capital. Equally serious were the refusals of Lord Chief Baron Wilde, Chief Justice Henry Rolle and, above all, Chief Justice Oliver St John, the kinsman of Cromwell and defender of Hampden in the ship-money case, to serve on a High Court of Justice to try the King. At its first meeting on January 8 only 52 were present out of the 135 named, and procedure at the trial could not be agreed. When Algernon Sidney made the point that the King could be tried by no court and no man by that court, Cromwell betrayed his anxiety by shouting, 'I tell you we will cut off his head with the crown upon it!' Sidney did not attend again.

Fairfax gave the first meeting of the court some substance by his presence, but he had nothing to contribute and never reappeared either at preliminary meetings or at the trial itself. Fairfax was a good and brave soldier who took and executed military decisions firmly, yet off the field he was indecisive and weak, and at this moment of crisis chose to stand aside. Another notable absentee was Philip Skippon, Commander of the London trained bands and a zealous Puritan.

But the list of appointees to the High Court of Justice was long, including soldiers, Parliament men, lawyers, civic dignitaries and local leaders, and since a quorum of only twenty had been named, even the small attendance of 45 at their next meeting on January 10 was sufficient to enable them to proceed to business and elect a Lord President to conduct the trial. The choice was difficult, and in the absence of so many powerful legal figures it fell upon Sergeant John Bradshaw of the Sheriff's court in London, who had recently been appointed Chief Justice of Chester but who was otherwise of no particular repute. Equally important was the choice of Counsel for the Prosecution. The Attorney General, Anthony Steel, withdrew at the last moment on the plea of illness, real or feigned, and the lawyer John Cook was brought in to present the charge against the King, which he immediately began to draw up with the help of Isaac Dorislaus, a Dutch lawyer who had been Professor of Law at Cambridge University.

Meanwhile on January 9 the Sergeant at Arms had made proclamation in Westminster Hall, at Cheapside and at the Old Exchange that Charles Stuart, King of England, was to be brought to trial and that the Court of Justice would be in session from January 10 in the Painted Chamber which adjoined Westminster Hall. On January 13, the report on the preparation of the Hall was received. Public trials were only occasional episodes in the life of the great timbered Hall, whose hammerbeam roof was the finest in Europe. It was 240 feet long, 67 feet wide, large enough to house several of the courts of law – Common Pleas, King's Bench, the Exchequer Court, and Chancery – which functioned in various parts of the Hall with only low, temporary partitions separating them from the citizens, courtiers and others who sauntered at will, gossiping, buying news-sheets from hawkers or patronizing the booksellers' and stationers' booths that lined the walls. Westminster Hall had now to be cleared, decisions had to be made concerning the seating of the judges, the admission of the public, the position of the King during the trial, and security: mighty subjects had stood trial in Westminster Hall but never before had a reigning monarch been brought there as a prisoner on trial for his life.

Strafford had been brought in, as was customary, by the public or great North door of the Hall and his trial had been conducted about halfway down towards the southern end. Such a dignified walk, in full view, was to be denied the King. His place of trial was brought nearer to the southern end of the Hall and he would enter from a short passage beneath the Hall that brought him, by a flight of a few steps, close to the place he would occupy. A wooden partition was to be built from wall to wall across the width of the Hall, between him and the public, behind which soldiers would stand. Security would thus be provided and, what was perhaps more important, he would be denied contact with the spectators, and they with him, for he would be effectively screened from the body of the Hall except when he was standing.

Charles was brought on January 19 from Windsor to St James's in a coach and six, escorted by soldiers and with Hugh Peters, the Puritan divine, riding in front of the entourage. When a man on horseback put off his hat to him Charles returned the courtesy but his guard threw both man and horse into a ditch. The following day Charles was taken in a closed sedan chair to Whitehall and thence in his own barge, again enclosed, to Cotton House, which was conveniently near to Westminster Hall. Spectators thronged the river and the banks and some of them cheered, but his own boat was closely followed and preceded by guards. While he was on his way Cromwell and the Commissioners were still discussing procedure in the Painted Chamber and as they heard the sounds that indicated that Charles was disembarking at Cotton steps Cromwell rushed to the window, turning deathly white: 'He is come, he is come!', he cried, 'and now we are doing that great work that the nation will be full of.' But what answer, he asked, as he asked himself and others over and over again, should be given when the King enquired by what authority he was being tried? After a pause Henry Marten spoke: 'In the name of the Commons in Parliament assembled and all the good people of England.'

At the south end of Westminster Hall benches had been erected for the men who were to be Charles's Judge and Jury. In the middle of them, and a little raised, sat John Bradshaw, the President, with a table before him. The benches, President's chair and table were covered with crimson cloth; Bradshaw wore a black gown and, considering his exposed position and the feelings the trial would evoke, he had had his hat reinforced with steel plates. At right angles to the Commissioners' seats, stretching northwards down the Hall, were two bodies of soldiers, several lines deep, and in the middle of the open space in front of Bradshaw and between the soldiers was a table bearing the mace and the sword of state at which two clerks sat ready to make their notes. Beyond the clerks and opposite the Commissioners' seats was the dock, a rectangular wooden enclosure with a crimson chair in the middle facing Bradshaw and the Commissioners. Immediately behind the dock was the high wooden partition that separated off the rest of the Hall. Soldiers lined this barrier and were stationed also down the middle of the Hall as far as the door so that the spectators were divided into two. On each side of the Hall at the South end, above the Judges' seats, galleries had been erected for privileged spectators who gained access through adjoining buildings. In view of the general security and the care taken to guard the King from sympathetic eyes there appeared to be a strange carelessness here. But whatever happened in the galleries there was no chance of escape for Charles, for all the doors to the Hall were securely guarded and troops of horse waited outside.

When all was ready it was apparent that only half of the Commissioners' chairs were occupied and, in fact, only 68 answered to their names. As the name of Fairfax was pronounced Lady Fairfax cried out

435

from the gallery that her husband was not there and never would be there. Order was restored as she hastily withdrew and the court waited.

It was a small man who walked into Westminster Hall with short steps and hurried gait under the guard of Colonel Tomlinson's men and mounted the few steps to the dock. He was dressed entirely in black with an enveloping black cloak round his shoulders on which gleamed the large embroidered star of the Order of the Garter. Apart from the deep white collar and cuffs, the only relief was a jewel at his throat and round his neck the blue ribbon of the garter, suspending the onyx and diamond George, his most precious jewel, which opened to reveal a portrait of his wife. The beard was tinged with grey, it was bushier, less finely trimmed that it had been, and there was more hair on his upper lip. Under the high-crowned black hat the dark auburn hair fell down to his shoulders and was still thick though its lustre had gone and it was streaked with grey. Those who had not seen him since the war would have noted the sunken eyes and the pouches beneath them. He looked a man who had suffered, who had faced hardship and expected more; who was disillusioned, and somewhat bitter. It was the face of one who had fought hard and perhaps knew he had lost. Yet as well as resignation there was a maturity in the face that was absent from the Court portraits of Van Dyck. Nor was his face or his figure that of an old, or of a sick man, and when he spoke people noted, as Lady Fairfax did, that his stammer had entirely gone.

Charles looked slowly round the hall and up at the galleries; he sat down on his red chair, rose, and turned to look over the barrier at the spectators and the guards behind him before resuming his seat. His head remained covered to mark his refusal to recognize the court. After Bradshaw had opened proceedings, John Cook, the Solicitor General, who was standing within the bar by the King, began the charge. Charles, wishing to speak, tapped him on the shoulder with his cane and as he did so its silver top fell off. No one stirred to pick it up so Charles stooped and put it in his pocket while Cook continued, 'I do in the name and on the behalf of the people of England exhibit and bring into this court a charge of high treason and other high crimes whereof I do accuse Charles Stuart, King of England.'

'By your favour, Hold!', exclaimed Charles, but the clerk to the court was ordered to proceed with the long indictment: 'Charles Stuart, King of England . . . trusted with a limited power to govern by and according to the laws of the land . . . obliged to use the power committed to him for the good and benefit of the people for the preservation of their rights and liberties' had nevertheless 'out of a wicked design . . . to . . . uphold in himself an unlimited and tyrannical power' conspired 'to overthrow the rights and liberties of the people . . . to take away . . . the right and power of frequent and successive Parliaments' and for the accomplishment of his design had 'trayterously and maliciously levied war against the present Parliament, and the people therein represented.'

There were then enumerated the various battles of the civil war, the attempted use of foreign troops and the renewal of the war in 1648, all the evils resulting being laid at his door. 'Charles Stuart', concluded the charge, was 'guilty of all the treasons, murders, rapines, burnings, spoils, desolations, dammages, and mischiefs to this nation, ordered and committed in the said wars, or occasioned thereby.' On behalf of the people of England, consequently, the said Charles Stuart was impeached 'as a tyrant, traytor, murderer and a publick and implacable enemy to the commonwealth of England'.

Charles sat looking sometimes at the court, sometimes up at the galleries. At one point he rose and turned again with a stern countenance to look down the long, intimidating length of the hall. When it came to the final words of the impeachment he laughed in the face of the court as he had laughed in the face of Strafford's accusers.

Charles asked over and over again, as Cromwell had foreseen, to be told by what authority he was brought there, and the answer was always basically the one upon which his judges had agreed: 'the authority of the Commons of England assembled in Parliament'. Once they added the words 'of which you are the elected King'. Charles was quick to seize the point: the English monarchy was not elective but had been hereditary for a thousand years. And, he said, though 'I will stand for the privilege of the Commons, rightly understood, as any man here whatsoever', yet a Parliament – and he looked round – 'I see no House of Lords here that may constitute a Parliament'. He might also have pointed out that the House of Commons was not at that moment a House elected by the people but a rump of what had been elected by a part of the people over eight years before. Without the King and the House of Lords, with an out-of-date and unrepresentative House of Commons, what authority remained to institute a court of justice to try a King?

Throughout the first day Charles made his point repeatedly,

refusing to acknowledge the court or to answer to the charge made against him. 'I am your King', he asserted at one time, 'I have a trust committed to me by God, by old and lawful descent. I will not betray that trust to answer to a new unlawful authority.' 'I stand more for the liberty of my people than any here that sitteth to be my judge', he declared. Bradshaw became increasingly on edge: 'You, instead of answering, interrogate this court, which doth not become you in this condition . . .' 'Well, let me tell you', said the King brightly, 'to *say* you have legal authority will satisfy no reasonable man.'

'That is your apprehension', snapped Bradshaw. Charles remarked that *apprehension* – neither his nor Bradshaw's – would decide the issue and in despair Bradshaw ordered the guard to withdraw the prisoner, but the last word on the first day of the trial rested with Charles:

'I do not fear *that*', he remarked pointing to the clerk's table upon which lay both the indictment and the sword. No one was quite sure to which object he was referring.

The court was adjourned until Monday, leaving Sunday free for prayer and meditation, and Charles was taken back to Cotton House with Herbert in attendance. A few people cried for God to bless him but others cried 'Treason!' as he passed. He was allowed the services of Dr Juxon, Bishop of London, and while the Commissioners were fasting and listening to sermons Charles heard the words of the Church of England in the fashion he desired. The soldiers guarding him were contemptuous, occupying his bedroom and puffing in his face the tobacco smoke he detested. He went to another room, where Herbert slept on a mattress by his side, but he himself slept little; sometime over that weekend he put into writing his reasons for refusing to acknowledge the jurisdiction of the court.

Monday the 22nd, the second day of the trial, was not unlike the first, but with Charles more fluent, clearly having considered his words in the interim. Upon Cook's formal request that the prisoner be called upon to plead, Bradshaw recapitulated the position, finally turning to Charles: 'the court expects that you apply yourself to the charge not to lose any more time, but to give a positive answer thereto', he concluded.

'It is not my case alone, it is the freedom and the liberty of the people of England', Charles began, 'and, do you pretend what you will, I must justly stand for their liberties. For if power, without law, may make law, may alter the fundamental laws of the kingdom – I do not know what subject he is in England can be assured of his life or anything he can call his own.'

Bradshaw was at a loss to stem the King's eloquence. But as Charles continued,

'My reasons why in conscience of that duty I owe to God first, and my people afterwards for their lives, liberties and estates, I conceive I cannot answer at this time till I be satisfied of the legality of it . . .'

Bradshaw seized his opportunity.

'Sir, I must interrupt you . . . it seems you are about the entering into arguments and disputes concerning the authority of the court . . . You may not do it!'

Since this had been Charles's point all along, Bradshaw's interjection at this point fell a little flat.

'Sir', replied the King courteously, 'by your favour . . . I do know law and reason though I am no lawyer professed. I know as much law as any gentleman in England, and therefore, Sir (by your favour), I do plead for the liberties of the people of England more than any of you do . . .'

Charles was again interrupted, but the argument continued. When pressed by the King Bradshaw said again, 'We sit here by the authority of the Commons of England, and that authority hath called your ancestors . . . to account.'

'I deny that! Show me one precedent!'

'The point is not to be debated by you!'

'The Commons of England was never a court of judicature.'

'Confess or deny the charge!', cried the clerk.

'By what authority do you sit?' reiterated the King.

'Take him away!', roared Bradshaw.

'I do require that I may give my reasons.'

' 'Tis not for a prisoner to *require* . . .'

'I am not an ordinary prisoner . . .'

At this Colonel Hewson, who was sitting as one of the Judges, rushed forward, called out 'Justice!' and spat in the King's face.

'Well Sir', remarked Charles, wiping his face, 'God hath justice in store both for you and me.'

The next day Cook pointed out that it was the third time they had met and the issue had not been joined. Charles attempted still to keep them from coming to the charge for, as he observed, the affirmative was easier to establish than the negative – it would be easier to charge him than for him to rebut the accusation. But although he managed to

439

speak at some length, Bradshaw had this time been well primed. He wasted no time on argument with the prisoner.

'Clerk, do your duty!' he commanded.

'Duty!' exclaimed Charles derisively, but the clerk read on:–

'Charles Stuart, King of England, you are accused in the behalf of the People of England of divers high crimes and treasons; which charge hath been read to you. The court now requires you to give your final and positive answer by way of confession or denial of the charge.'

Charles still refused. To acknowledge the court would be contrary to the privileges of the people of England and an alteration of the fundamental laws of the land, he said.

'Sir!' thundered Bradshaw, 'this is the third time you have publicly disowned this court and put an affront upon it.'

He was visibly agitated and he proceeded hurriedly to the attack:

'How far you have preserved the fundamental laws and freedom of the subject, your actions have spoken it. For truly, Sir, men's intentions are used to be shown by their actions. You have written your meaning in bloody characters throughout the whole kingdom . . . Clerk, record the default! And, gentlemen, you that brought the prisoner, take him back again.'

Charles was surprised by the sudden dismissal and cried in vain, 'I have one word to you . . . I find I am before a power . . .': the words were drowned in uproar as he was hustled away.

The court did not sit again in Westminster Hall until Saturday January 27. Meanwhile it continued to consult in the Painted Chamber, taking evidence from selected witnesses. But less than half the Commissioners attended; in spite of all that Cromwell could do only 63 were present on Friday 26 when, after long debate, it was ordered that the King be brought on the morrow to Westminster Hall to be sentenced.

Bradshaw appeared on that final day in scarlet. As he rose to open the court Charles, who knew that their intention was to sentence him that day, also attempted to speak. 'A hasty judgment', he was saying, 'is not so soon recalled . . .'

'You shall be heard before judgment is given,' Bradshaw promised him.

Charles required a double assurance, perhaps surprised at the ease with which he had won his point:

'I shall be heard before the judgment be given?'

'You shall.'

With that Bradshaw began his address. As he was saying that the prisoner was to answer to a charge of treason and other high crimes exhibited against him in the name of the people of England, two masked women in the gallery cried out 'It is a lie . . . Oliver Cromwell is a tyrant!' One of them was thought to be Lady Fairfax, but they slipped away in the hubbub unidentified and, as order was restored, Bradshaw was heard saying that the prisoner would be allowed to speak before sentence was passed provided he made no more attacks on the jurisdiction of the court.

This time Charles did not address the court but asked instead to be heard before the Lords and Commons in the Painted Chamber. He was, in fact, appealing over the heads of a court he refused to recognize to a political body which, however unrepresentative it had become, was nevertheless part of the constitution which he would be able to acknowledge as legal.

An uneasiness in the court, and the King's reasonable request, caused disquiet among the Commissioners and one of them, John Downes, became so agitated that Cromwell had to rebuke him. But Downes brushed Cromwell aside, crying out that he was not satisfied. The disturbance was enough to persuade Bradshaw to adjourn the court while Charles's request was being considered. But it only delayed the real issue. No concession was made, and when the court reassembled it was in order to proceed immediately to judgment and to sentence.

'I have a plan', he cried, 'to put before the Lords and Commons for a lasting peace . . .'

But it was too late. Though Ludlow thought he might have been about to propose abdicating in favour of his son, Bradshaw would hold no longer, and had begun the long indictment. Charles abandoned his attempts to speak and listened intently, only interrupting with an occasional exclamation. When he realized the charge was at an end and that verdict and sentence would be forthcoming, he hurriedly claimed his right to speak, according to Bradshaw's promise. He was refused permission unless he first acknowledged the jurisdiction of the court.

'You disavow us as a court, and therefore for you to address yourself to us, not acknowledging of us as a court to judge of what you say, it is not to be permitted.'

Amid growing tension the clerk read the sentence, ending with the words:

441

'For all which treasons and crimes this Court doth adjudge that the said Charles Stuart, as a tyrant, traytor, murtherer and publique enimy to the good people of this nation, shall be put to death by the severing of his heade from his body.'

Charles tried desperately to speak.

'Sir,' roared Bradshaw, 'you shall not be heard after the sentence!'

'No, Sir?'

'No, Sir!'

'Guards, withdraw your prisoner!'

Charles was trying to speak above the noise:

'I may speak after the sentence . . . I am not suffered to speak . . . hold! . . . Expect what justice the people will have . . .'

The broken sentences were accompanied by uncouth and brutal behaviour by Colonel Axtell and his men who were hustling the prisoner and burning grains of gunpowder to make smoke to blow in his face. At a signal from their commander they broke into cries of 'Justice!' 'Execution!'.

Charles was taken in a closed sedan chair through King Street, with troops close lining the route, to his own apartments at Whitehall. He walked between guards through his own Privy garden and even saw one of his old servants, weeping at his master's plight. The next day he was taken to St James's Palace.

He had conducted his defence virtually unaided. His claim that he knew as much law as any man in England was not far from the truth, but no amount of sophisticated legal assistance would have made the slightest difference to the verdict. His refusal to plead before a court which, by all he knew of law, was unconstitutional, was a simple and straightforward way of meeting the issue, one which John Lilburne had used several times and would use again with great effect, but without influencing the verdict, in a few months' time. Whether the King could, or should, have met the charges head on and tried to prove that he was not a tyrant and not responsible for the civil wars is another matter. He would have needed more time than they gave him, he would have required assistance and access to documents to answer the long list of charges. Perhaps he knew from the beginning what the verdict would be and shrank from the long attempt to vindicate his actions in public. Perhaps the offer which he appeared about to make – but too late – really did concern his abdication. Perhaps he was relying on the kind of offer that some of his friends had reputedly made – to

442

guarantee with their estates and their lives any terms that would reinstate him. But his accusers were not prepared for compromise or negotiation. Appeals for clemency, including one from the Netherlands, were disregarded. No notice was taken of a blank sheet of paper, signed by the Prince of Wales, on which the Prince offered to let them inscribe any terms they wished in return for his father's life.

Charles remained at St James's throughout the 29th and did not hear the sounds of the scaffold being erected outside the Banqueting Hall in Whitehall. He knew nothing of the difficulties his accusers were having in obtaining signatures for the death warrant. He no longer felt the loneliness of the last months. He burned some papers, he sent his dogs away, he refused to see his closest friends; only Herbert and Juxon stayed near him. He sent Herbert on a few errands. He received a messenger from his eldest son with a note craving his father's blessing. He was allowed a visit from Elizabeth and Henry, who had been staying at Sion House. They burst into tears at the sight of their father. Charles told Elizabeth he was about to die for the laws and liberties of the land and the true Protestant religion, he begged her not to grieve and to tell her mother that his thoughts had never strayed from her and that his love would be the same to the last. Little Henry, who was only nine, he took on his knee. 'Sweetheart,' he said, 'now they will cut off thy father's head . . . and perhaps make thee a king.' But he charged the boy never to accept the throne while his elder brother lived and never to accept it from the hands of their enemies. 'I will sooner be torn in pieces first!' cried the little boy. Charles then divided the few jewels he had between the children and retired to prayer.

On the morning of the 30th he rose early, was careful of his toilet and asked for two shirts, since the weather was cold and shivering might be mistaken for fear. Morning prayers were conducted by Bishop Juxon and shortly afterwards the soldiers arrived. As they left Jane Whorwood ran forward to greet him, their affectionate embrace reviving the rumour that she had been his mistress at Hampton Court and Carisbrooke. He walked this time, with his usual quick, lively gait, across St James's Park between Colonel Tomlinson and Bishop Juxon, with Herbert following behind and foot soldiers at front and rear with drums beating and flags flying; his spaniel, Rogue, had escaped from her confinement and joyously made to follow him but was turned back. At Whitehall Charles ate a piece of bread and drank a glass of wine before returning to prayer. Not until 2 o'clock did the call come. When he stepped out of a window of the Banqueting House on to the scaffold with Juxon by his side, Herbert being too distraught to accompany him, he found Colonel Hacker and Colonel Tomlinson already there with the masked executioner and his assistant. The scaffold ran from about the second to the sixth window of the building, large enough for the fifteen or so people who occupied it, including Puritan divines, soldiers, and some of the shorthand writers who would speed the details of the execution to the printers.

The scaffold was black, the rails round it were draped with black cloth; the low block, about eighteen inches long and six inches high, was similarly covered with black and near it, attached to four staples driven into the scaffold, were the hooks and pulleys that would be attached to the King to hold him down if he resisted execution. He made no comment except to ask if a higher block were available and was told there was no other. Round the scaffold were ranks of soldiers, horse and foot, and beyond them the crowds who had come to witness the beheading of a king: by intent they were too far away to hear anything he might say. Charles realized this but, he said, if he did not speak, it would appear he submitted to the guilt as well as to the punishment. So, speaking from the notes he had made on a little piece of paper some four inches square, he addressed himself to those about him.

He made two protestations: 'I never did begin a war with the two Houses of Parliament', he said, and 'I call God to witness . . . that I never did intend for to encroach upon their privileges.'

Then he made public repudiation of his own act in signing Strafford's death warrant: 'God forbid that I should be so ill a Christian as not to say God's judgments are just upon me. Many times he does pay justice by an unjust sentence . . . an unjust sentence that I suffered for to take effect, is punished now by an unjust sentence upon me.'

He turned then to his political testament: a society, he said, must give God his due, the King his due, the people their due. A national synod, freely called, freely debating could settle religion; the laws of the land would define the position of the king; as to the people, he said, 'truly I desire their liberty and freedom as much as anybody whatsoever; but I must tell you that their liberty and freedom consists in having government, those laws by which their lives and their goods may be most their own. It is not their having a share in the government; that is nothing appertaining unto them. A subject and a sovereign are clean different things!'

He made his profession of faith, saying that he died a Christian according to the tenets of the Church of England, he put on the white satin cap which would confine his hair, placed his George, which he had worn to the last, in the hands of the Bishop, and spoke to him one word – 'Remember'. Then he lay down, put his head upon the block, and, after a second or two, stretched out his arms. It was the signal. The axe fell and the executioner raised aloft the head of Charles Stuart. The crowd groaned. The troops immediately moved to disperse the people. Devoted followers and souvenir hunters rushed to dip their handkerchiefs in his blood; to acquire hairs from his head or beard, threads from his garment or chips from the block.

The following day the head was sewn on, the body embalmed and placed in a leaden coffin which was taken to St James's Palace where it was watched over by a few of his friends. Many tried to see him but few were admitted. Rumour said that Cromwell came by night to look at the coffin, sighing 'Cruel necessity!' as he departed. Charles was refused interment in Henry VII's chapel at Westminster, but was taken on the night of February 7 in a black coach drawn by six horses decked in black to his own bedchamber at Windsor. The following day he was brought to the Dean's Hall, which was draped with black mourning cloths. There was some confusion over the exact place of burial, which was sad for one who so liked order in his life. But on February 9 his coffin was carried to St George's Chapel by soldiers, with Richmond, Hertford, Southampton and Lindsey holding over it the four corners of the black funeral pall. The service he would have wished was denied but Juxon walked behind the coffin with the English Prayer Book in his hand and Herbert and a few other friends and household servants followed their master to the vault which had been opened towards the middle of the choir and which was found to contain the coffins of Henry VIII and Jane Seymour. The simple coffin bore nothing but the words *King Charles*, and the date. As it was brought from the Hall to the vault snow began to fall and the black pall was thickly covered with white snowflakes.

People remembered that he had dressed in white for his Coronation, and the legend of the White King grew. On the day of his interment his meditations in captivity were published as *Eikon Basilike*, and the legend of the Martyr King began. Yet his opponents had executed him as a traitor and Milton wrote *Eikonoklastes* to destroy the image that had been built up. But even Milton could not succeed in doing so and the *Eikon* was published again and again in

English, French, Dutch, German, Danish, Italian, Latin and Greek editions, most with a frontispiece showing the King at his devotions – sad, ethereal, noble. For a century the view persisted, modified but basically unchanged, until the beneficiaries of the Great Rebellion began to replace it by a constitutional interpretation of the civil wars which justified their own ascendancy and cast Charles in a role which more nearly resembled the King of the indictment. Where the truth lay depended, largely, upon the point of view.[1]

Concerning religion Charles said many times, and probably believed, that so long as a man held the basic tenets of Christianity he would have no quarrel with him; it was in this spirit that he had allowed the Roman Catholic Church to approach him. But he also believed, like his father, that Church and State were mutually supporting and that a religious toleration that extended to an unlimited and uncontrolled anarchy of belief would result in social and constitutional chaos. Cromwell believed the same, the difference between them being that Cromwell would banish the Catholics whom Charles would tolerate and would tear down Charles's Church of England in favour of the Independency which Charles proscribed. Both men were suspicious of Presbyterians, and Cromwell, like Charles but with less logic, stopped short of tolerating the extremer forms of sectarianism. Both men walked with God, Cromwell in a more hearty fashion than Charles and with a more constant awareness of the Lord's hand in every event. Yet if Charles did not express himself as forcibly as Cromwell, he was none the less aware of God's presence in his life: he needed an ordered Church to assure him of this; Cromwell did not.

Most of Charles's constitutional transgressions stemmed from the fact that he was trying to raise money in a country which employed no regular system of taxation, and where he could make use of occasional taxes only with the consent of Parliament. From the beginning of his reign he was saddled with debts not of his making, with departments of state that were riddled with graft and inefficiency, with a virtually non-existent civil service and a form of local government – if it deserved the name – that was voluntary, amateur, and self-centred. The waste of the money that was raised for war was due as much to the inherited venality of his executive as to his own inability to reform. His personal expenses, even taking into account his pictures, the Court masques, and the extravagance of his wife, were not high on any comparison with his father or with European monarchs; that

Court expenditure, which he made some effort to contain, remained an unwieldy item was due as much to some of the people who afterwards opposed him as to himself. Nor did his methods of raising money without a Parliament always deserve the censure accorded them. Though they too often included pickings for his friends, they mainly affected vested interests and, apart from some monopolies, hit the rich rather than the poor, they generally accorded a care for the underdog, and they amounted to less than the taxes imposed in most other countries.

Charles was wrong in thinking he could influence the European situation in favour of the Palatine House by means of war: the ill-judged, obsessive preoccupation with La Rochelle, the gross inefficiency and the failure of each venture he embarked upon, proved the contrary. Yet during the period of which opponents chiefly complained, and while Europe was devastated by war, his country enjoyed eleven years of prosperity. He himself never ceased to attend to the details of government – like a cobbler, he once said, going through all the papers that came before him, not originating but patching and sewing.

He had faults of character and training which made him a difficult man to deal with – splitting hairs in argument, depending upon the rigid letter of the word rather than its spirit, a tendency to discount the means if the desired end could be achieved, too obvious a reliance upon Guicciardini and his *Maxims*. He could be distressingly vindictive, as he was with Eliot, but he could also show compassion. He lacked subtlety and the lighter touch, though he was shrewd and a good judge of an argument or a character. When driven into a corner he could become obstinate and, though he himself would have shrunk from the accusation, there was a grain of justification in his opponents' belief that he could not be trusted, and that he would substitute his own interpretation for whatever agreement might be reached.

But faults in Charles do not necessarily imply virtue in his opponents. The core of opposition which began the struggle and remained to the end consisted of the men of property for whom Ireton spoke at the Putney debates. But the easy slide into opposition under the cry of 'Freedom' had brought in many people who either returned to neutrality, joined the King, or – mistakenly – remained with the opposition until it was too late. It was not the King who stood in their way, denying the universal suffrage and the toleration which the *Agreement of the People* demanded – it was those very men for whom Ireton

447

spoke. The 'poor scrubs' had been deceived certainly – not by the King but by their own superior officers. One of the few who saw the situation clearly was John Lilburne – and he was kept in prison by Parliament or by the Army throughout the greater part of the civil wars. There was truth in Cromwell's vision of revolution after revolution stretching out indefinitely as layers of dissatisfaction came to the surface. But to arrest it at the point where the underprivileged, who had joined Parliament for freedom and a decent standard of life, still stood outside his settlement could hardly be justified. When, after the King's execution, the Rump abolished the monarchy and the House of Lords and erected in their place a Council of State, Lilburne's bitter cry of 'the old cheat, the transmutation of names', rang out in the pamphlet he called *England's New Chains*. Cromwell's reply was to crush Lilburne and the Levellers shortly after the execution of the King. If honest dealing was in question, it was a case of the pot calling the kettle black.

It was three hundred years before 'the poorest hee in England' could raise his head in social and political equality. But the men of property for whom Cromwell was at first the instrument but was, in the end, too radical, achieved their ends when Charles's son ascended the throne in 1660. The irony was that the Restoration Settlement broadly restored the constitution of 1641, which Charles himself had agreed to observe and had later proposed as the basis of a settlement. The difference between 1660 and the 1640s lay in a new monarch, more pliant than his father, a man who was the grandson of Henri IV – not the grandson of Mary, Queen of Scots – who knew that if Paris was worth a mass England was worth a settlement with men whose preoccupation with their property could be made to coincide with his own interests. The crowning irony was that Charles I himself was not far removed from at least some of his opponents: Ireton's speech at Putney and Charles's on the scaffold show precisely the same attitude to the people and the uses of government.

Whether Charles I could have averted, or postponed, the civil war, whether the change could have been effected peaceably, is doubtful. Charles had all the faults of character and temperament which made negotiation difficult, while his opponents had, in Parliament, the supreme negotiating body. Charles, like Laud and Clarendon, had always feared Parliaments – particularly Parliaments that sat long, giving to their Members the advantages of self-knowledge and propinquity. And now he was brought down by the longest Parliament of all.

In the end, when the various currents of the Interregnum had settled into one stream and the men of property were securely at the helm, there seemed to be a certain inevitability about the events that brought Charles to the scaffold; wealth must be matched by influence, it had been said, economic power by political power. Since wealth, even when reinforced in other ways, still depended primarily upon land, there was no need to change the electoral system. It was merely necessary to restrict the power of the monarch and guarantee frequent Parliaments, to sweep away irksome vestiges of feudalism like the Court of Wards and Knighthood fines in a general tidying up that brought echoes of Salisbury's Great Contract and, of necessity, to make the adjustments that had become necessary through the land confiscations of the civil wars. Religion remained difficult to fit into any mould but, in a similar spirit of expediency, Bishops returned to the House of Lords and the Church of England was Established without being too strongly political, while Dissent was tolerated but skilfully excluded from effective influence.

Charles did not see all this – or only dimly. He had fought for something more simple. If he had won, as in the early stages it had seemed he could, he might well have postponed, or even averted, the Whig supremacy. But the alternative – involuntary, perhaps – might well have been, as many of his opponents feared, a royal despotism of a European kind. The ordered society, benevolently guided from above, that Charles envisaged belonged to the past rather than the future and there is no certainty that it would have prevailed.

It was Charles's misfortune that accident had placed him in the path of momentous change of one kind or another. His strength lay in preservation, in guarding his heritage. He had no aptitude for presiding over the difficult birth of a new society. He once wrote to Digby that if he could not live as a King he would chose to die like a gentleman; it was his personal tragedy that he was not allowed to *live* as a gentleman, for it was a role he would have filled impeccably.

References

Abbreviations

Am.Hist.Rev.	*American Historical Review*
Bull.I.H.R.	*Bulletin of the Institute of Historical Research*
C.H.J.	*Cambridge Historical Journal*
C.S.P.	*Calendar of Scottish Papers*
C.S.P.D.	*Calendar of State Papers Domestic*
C.S.P.V.	*Calendar of State Papers Venetian*
D.N.B.	*Dictionary of National Biography*
Econ.Hist.Rev.	*Economic History Review*
History	*History*
H.J.	*The Historical Journal*
H.M.Comm.	*Historical Manuscripts Commission Reports*
J. British Studies	*Journal of British Studies*
J.Econ.Hist.	*Journal of Economic History*
J.M.H.	*Journal of Modern History*
Law Q.Rev.	*Law Quarterly Review*
Quart.Rev.	*Quarterly Review*
Trans.R.H.S.	*Transactions of the Royal Historical Society*
P.R.O.	*Public Record Office*
Salvetti	*Despatches of Amerigo Salvetti, 1625–8*
S.P.	*State Papers in Public Record Office*
Birch, *James*	*Court and Times of James the First*
Birch	*Court and Times of Charles the First*

1 Duke of Albany

1 C.S.P. 1597–1603, Pt. II, p. 737; Chancellor, p. 2; and see *Bibl*. Charles's birth and childhood (G.1).

2 The second christening of Charles. The description given here is based
   upon the detailed account of Islay Herald, John Blinsale, first printed by
   the Rev Henry Cantrell in *The Royal Martyr, a true Christian*, in 1716. A
   copy is in the British Library. The original MS in the Herald's Office at
   Edinburgh (the Lyons Office) was copied by Carte and this copy is now
   with the Carte papers in the Bodleian Library. The authenticity of the
   original was, however, disputed by William Harris in 1758 in his *Life* of
   Charles. If the document was a forgery Charles did not receive baptism
   by a bishop into the Church of England; neither did he receive the good
   offices of such eminent Huguenots as Soubise and Rohan as
   godparents. Harris based his case largely on the assertion that Soubise
   and Rohan were not in Scotland at the time of Charles's christening.
   This, however, appears to be erroneous. The diary of Finett (the
   Master of Ceremonies) notes their presence, the English
   correspondents of Cecil in Scotland note that the Frenchmen were very
   well entertained, mention them by name, at first suggest it is likely they
   will be gossips to James's newborn son, and on November 27 assert
   that they will be; finally, on December 30, they report (George
   Nicolson to Sir Robert Cecil) that they *were* gossips. Nicolson's short
   account of the ceremony agrees with Islay Herald's. The *Voyages du
   Duc de Rohan fait en l'an 1600*, published in 1646 in Amsterdam, says
   that he was in Scotland in 1600 and there are several later references in
   Charles's life to his meeting one or the other as one of his godparents,
   for example, an audience that Prince Charles gave to the Duke of
   Soubise 'to whom he was at his christening in Scotland Godfather'
   (Finett). If additional evidence of a second christening is needed it is
   found in the repairing of Anne's litter to carry the baby from
   Dunfermline to Holyrood and the transport of other articles for the
   baby's use to Holyrood. Isaac D'Israeli discusses the evidence briefly in
   Commentaries on the Life and Reign of Charles I, I, ch. II.
   C.S.P. 1597–1603, Pt. II, *passim*.
3 Peyton, p. 22, *Bibl.* (E).
4 Chancellor, pp. 4–5, *Bibl.* (E).
5 *Letters to James*, Intro, pp. xxviii, xxxii, *Bibl.* (C).
6 *State Papers of James*, pp. 46, 55; *Accounts High Treasurers of Scotland, passim
   Bibl.* (C).
7 *Bibl.* Charles's birth and childhood (G.1).
8 Weldon, p. 216; Carey, pp. 167–8, *Bibl.* (C, G.1).
9 Carleton to Winwood, Winwood, *Memorials*, II, p. 45.

2 Duke of York

1 Arabella Stuart to the Earl of Shrewsbury, 8 Dec., 1603, *Letters to James*,
   Intro, p. xxiv; Willson, p. 227; Harleian MS 6987 (24). *Bibl.* (Q.1).
2 *Letters to James*; Ellis First S.III, pp. 92, 94, *Bibl.* (C, B).

3 *Bibl*. Prince Henry (Q.4).

4 Harington I, pp. 348–54, *Bibl*. (D).

5 *H.M.Comm. Various Collections* 3, p. 259; Winwood, III, pp. 179–81; 'Tethys Festival' in Samuel Daniel, *Works* ed. Grosart, 3. There is no foundation for the supposition made by Lucy Aikin that the little girls danced in a ring round Charles to hide his legs. On the contrary, the masque directions expressly bring him forward to present the sword.

6 No details survive.

7 'A Declaration of the Diet . . . of King Charles the First, when Duke of York', *Archaeologia* XV (1806), pp. 1 ff.

8 Chancellor, pp. 13–14 and various other sources, *Bibl*. (E).

9 Ellis First S.III, p. 96.

10 *Letters to James*.

11 Chancellor, p. 15.

3 Heir Apparent

1 *Bibl*. Prince Henry, (Q.4) Wilson, pp. 62 ff, *Bibl*. (Q.1); Chamberlain I, pp. 388, ff.

2 Chamberlain I, pp. 423 ff, *Bibl*. (D); Wilson, pp. 64 ff.; Lily, p. 3, *Bibl*. Elizabeth (Q.5).

3 Wilson, pp. 145–6, f. *Bibl*. Gondomar (Q.18).

4 There is a handwritten note signed ED at the beginning of Douce's copy of Thomas Birch's *Life of Henry Prince of Wales* (1760), now in the Bodleian Library, which says: 'Bishop Burnett says that Coll. Titus assured him that he had it from King Chas I own mouth, that he was well assured his brother, Prince Henry, was poisoned by the Earl of Somerset's means. See M. Oldmixen's critical hist of England I 175, 177. There is a tale of mystery in this transaction that I will one day or other unfold on very good evidence'.
   Charles's 'wilfulness' see Weldon, p. 218; Lily, p. 2.

5 'nicht starcker Complexion', Rye, p. 155; D'Ewes *Autobiography*, p. 49; the portrait appears as the frontispiece to Dallington's translation of Guicciardini's *Aphorisms* (1613).

6 Van der Doort's *Catalogue*, *Bibl*. (I.3).

7 This copy is in the Reading Room of the British Library.

8 C.S.P.D. 1611–18, *passim*.

4 The Heritage

1 e.g. Chamberlain to Carleton, I, p. 394.

2 Beatrice White, *Cast of Ravens*, uses much of the contemporary evidence.

3 *Rise of Villiers* – narrative of Archbishop Abbot in Rushworth, I, pp. 456–7, *Bibl*. (C), and *Bibl*. Buckingham (Q.6).

4 D.N.B.; C.S.P.D. 1611–18, p. 273.

5 C.S.P.D. 1611–18, p. 373, and *Bibl*. Wool (O.3).

5 Prince of Wales

1 Nicholls, III, pp. 207 ff, *Bibl.* (D); C.S.P.V. 1615–17, p. 328.
2 Carey *passim*; Cranfield, *Bibl.* (H.6).
3 *Bibl.* Buckingham.
4 Gardiner, *History*, III, p. 98, *Bibl.* (S).
5 Chancellor, p. 35; C.S.P.D. 1611–18, pp. 354, 370; Birch, *James*, II, pp. 78–9, *Bibl.* (D).
6 Ellis First S.III, pp. 102–4.
7 *Letters to James*.
8 *Bibl.* James (Q.1).
9 C.S.P.V. 1617–19, pp. 136–7.
10 Bacon's letter 1616, *Cabala*, p. 47, 1691, *Bibl.* (B).
11 C.S.P.V. 1621–23, pp. 450 ff.
12 Chancellor, pp. 49–50.

6 The Palatinate

1 Anne's death and funeral, Chamberlain, II, pp. 236–8; C.S.P.V. 1617–19, pp. 494–5; Strickland, *Queens*, *Bibl.* (Q.2).
2 Charles to Doncaster, *Camden Soc.* 90, p. 140.
3 Gardiner, *History*, III, pp. 333, 366, 326; C.S.P.V. 1619–21, pp. 363, 475.
4 *Traditional Memoirs*, p. 83, *Bibl.* (Q.1), *Vox Populi* (1621), *Tom Tell-Troath* (1622).
5 Green, *Elizabeth*, p. 200.
6 Chamberlain II, p. 434; Birch, *James*, II, pp. 313–14.

7 The Spanish Match

1 Weldon, pp. 217–18.
2 *Bibl.* Puritanism (J.2).
3 C.S.P.D. 1611–18 many refs., incl. pp. 232, 469, 470, 478, 484, 490.
4 *Bibl.* Cottington, Porter (Q.20, 11).
5 The Spanish Match in general, *Bibl.* (G.2).

8 The Prince's Parliament

1 Chamberlain, II, pp. 515–19; Nichols IV, pp. 907 ff.; Gardiner, *History* V, pp. 128–30.
2 Bristol and Proxy, *Bibl.* (G.2).
3 Parliament of 1624, *Bibl.* (L.2); Buckingham's Narration, L.J.III, pp. 220–33; Charles's speeches, L.J.III, particularly pp. 257–8; Buckingham's popularity, Conway Jr. to Carleton, C.S.P.D. 1623–5, pp. 197–8.
4 Charles's appearance and popularity, Kellie to Mar, H.M.Comm. Mar and Kellie MSS., Supplement, pp. 202–4; Conway to Carleton,

C.S.P.D. 1623–5, p. 91; Zouch to Zouch, *ibid.*, p. 107; Conway Jr. to Carleton, *ibid.*, pp. 197, 257; Chamberlain II, pp. 546, 550.
5 Middlesex, *Bibl.* Finance (H.6). James to Charles and Buckingham, Clarendon I, section 54 *Bibl.* (S).
6 Bristol's defence, *Bibl.* (G.2).

9 A Daughter of France

1 Clarendon MSS, 96, 97; Henrietta-Maria, *Bibl.* (Q.3).
2 Rosencrantz and Gildernstern, Gardiner, *History*, V, pp. 185 ff; *Cabala*, Chamberlain, I, pp. 556–7.
3 C.S.P.V. 1623–5, pp. 191–2, 208, 216–17; Clarendon sections 41–6.
4 Death of James, *Bibl.* (Q.1).
5 *Ho-Elianiae*, or *Familiar Letters*, *Bibl.* (D.).
6 Henrietta-Maria *Bibl* (Q.3).

10 Charles's First Parliament

1 Aylmer, *King's Servants*, p. 18, *Bibl.* (S).
2 C.S.P.D. 1625–6, Appendix.
3 C.S.P.V. 1625–7, pp. 2; 26–7; *Salvetti*, p. 4.
4 *Bibl.* Finance (H.6).
5 Parliament of 1625, *Bibl.* (L.2).

11 'Reason of the Spaniards'

1 Development of Parliament, *Bibl.* (L.1).
2 Gardiner, *History*, VI, p. 7.
3 Cadiz, *Bibl.* (G.3).

12 Charles Saves the Duke

1 Parliament of 1626, *Bibl.* (L.2).
2 Charges against Bristol, *Bibl.* (L.2).
3 Charges against Buckingham, *Bibl.* (Q.6, L.2).
4 Buckingham's defence, *Bibl.* (Q6, L2).

13 Charles Saves his Marriage

1 Clarendon I, sections 82–3; Gardiner, *History*, VI, pp. 4–5, 56–7; C.S.P.V. 1625–6, pp. 311, 320–22, 327–9, 545; Ellis First S.III, pp. 213–19.
2 Gardiner, *History,* VI, pp. 134–7; C.S.P.V. 1625–6, pp. 497–8, 545; Birch, I, pp. 119–22, 134–8.

14 La Rochelle

1 S.P.D. LXXXIV, No. 78; C.S.P.D. 1627–8 *passim*; *Bibl*. La Rochelle (G.3).
2 Charles and the Mantuan Collection, *Bibl*. (I.3).
3 C.S.P.D. 1627–8, pp. ix–x, 393, 315; Hardwick State Papers II, pp. 19, 20, *Bibl*. (B).
4 No. 9, 1627, Knowler, *Bibl*. (B); Ellis First S.III, p. 251; Birch, pp. 304, 281, 285.

15 The Assassination of the Duke

1 C.S.P.V. 1626–8, pp. 542–3.
2 *Bibl*. Parliament and Petition of Right (L2, L4).
3 Fairholt *Poems and Songs*, *Bibl*. (Q.6); Birch, I, pp. 364–5, 367–9, 373 etc.
4 Assassination and funeral of Buckingham, *Bibl*. (Q.6).
5 In a letter from Carleton, Ellis First S.III, p. 254.

16 The Last Parliament

1 C.S.P.V., 1628–9, pp. 295, 359.
2 Weston, *Bibl*. (Q.9).
3 Wentworth, *Bibl*. (Q.7).
4 Parliament of 1629, *Bibl*. (L.2).

17 Peace

1 *Acts of the Privy Council*, July 1628–April 1629, p. 203.
2 e.g. C.S.P.V. 1628–9, pp. 287, 293–4; C.S.P.D. 1628–9, p. 393.
3 Birch, II, pp. 7–8.
4 Birch, I, pp. 355–6 – the date given, May 20, 1628, is a mistake for 1629; C.S.P.D. 1628–9, p. 548; C.S.P.V. 1629–32, p. 70.
5 Gardiner, *History*, VII, pp. 106, 107.
6 C.S.P.V. 1629–32, p. 160.
7 Gardiner, *History*, VII, p. 171.
8 Rubens' *Letters*, Parts IV, V, VI, *Bibl*. (Q.12).
9 Henrietta-Maria *Letters*, pp. 17, 18, *Bibl*. (Q.3).

18 The King in Council

1 Aylmer, *King's Servants*, pp. 162–3.
2 Alexander, p. 150, *Bibl*. (H.6).
3 Burlamachi, *Bibl*. (H.6).
4 Ashton, *Money Market*, *Bibl*. (H.6).
5 Birch, II, p. 219.

6 'Reports of Cases in Star Chamber and High Commission,' Camden Soc. 1886, No. 145, pp. 280–1, 298.
7 Gardiner, *History*, VIII, p. 87; Clarendon I, Sections 208–11.

19 Modern Prince and Feudal Lord

1 *Acts of the Privy Council, passim*; Rymer, IX, *passim, Bibl.* (C).
2 C.S.P.D. 1627–8, p.491.
3 Gardiner, *History*, VIII, pp. 71–6, 284.
4 Rymer, IX, pp. 242–50.
5 *Acts of the Privy Council* Sept. 1627 – June 1628, pp. 192–3, 243.
6 *Bibl.* Finance (H.6).
7 Rymer, IX, pp. 242–3; *Bibl.* Lotteries (P.2).
8 *Bibl.* Fens drainage (O.2).
9 C.S.P.D. 1631–3, p. 215; 1633–4, pp. 490–1.
10 C.S.P.D. 1631–3, p. 501.
11 Possibly in Selwood and Roche, see C.S.P.D. 1629–31, p. 141; forest fines in general, *Bibl.* (O.2).
12 Allan, 'Rising in West', Hammersley, 'Forest Laws', *Bibl.* Agrarian affairs (O.2).
13 Knighthood fines, Alexander, Dietz, *Bibl.* (H.6).

20 The King's Great Business

1 'The sovereignty of the seas', *Bibl.* (H.3); S.P.D. vol. CCIII, Nos. 53, 54; *Bibl.* Fishing (H.2).
2 C.S.P.D. 1634–5, pp. 68–9.
3 See Needham's trans. of Selden, *Bibl.* (H.3).
4 Oppenheim, p. 253, *Bibl.* (H.1).
5 *ibid.*, p. 261.
6 Heywood; Oppenheim, pp. 257–63, *Bibl.* (H.1).
7 Aylmer, pp. 112–13.
8 Oppenheim, pp. 236 ff.
9 Ship money, *Bibl.* (H.4).
10 Alexander, pp. 218–19.
11 Charles's social policy, *Bibl.* (M, O, P).

21 The King and his Court

1 *Bibl.* (I).
2 Jan. 9, 1631, C.S.P.D. 1629/31, p. 478.
3 Rymer, XIX, pp. 120–1.
4 *Grammelogia*; C.S.P.D. 1638–9, pp. 191, 243.
5 Birch, II, p. 205.
6 C.S.P.V. 1636–9, p. 128, Dobson, *Bibl.* (F).
7 Steele, *Bibl.* (I.2).

22 The Yearly Round

1 T. H. Wilson; Ashmole, *Bibl*. (I.2).
2 C.S.P.D. 1634–5, pp. 26, 77–9.
3 *Bibl*. King's Evil (I.7).
4 C.S.P.D. 1635, p. 366.
5 C.S.P.V. 1632–6, p. 483; *Bibl*. Little Gidding (I.6).
6 C.S.P.V. 1632–6, p. 519; 1636–9, pp. 36, 40, 44–5, 53, 64; Gardiner, *History*, VIII, pp. 151–2.
7 Birch, II, p. 228.
8 *Bibl*. Little Gidding, esp. *Two Lives* (I.6).

23 The King and his Church

1 Meyer, p. 17, *Bibl*. (J.1).
2 E.354/2.
3 Birch, *Letters*, II, p. 71.
4 Clarendon I, section 167.
5 Gardiner, *History*, VII, p. 298.
6 Roe to Elizabeth, C.S.P.D. 1633–4, p. 104.
7 Gardiner, *History*, VIII, pp. 108 ff.
8 *The Declaration of Sports*, Gardiner, *Documents*, pp. 17 ff, *Bibl*. (K.).
9 Gregg, pp. 47–72 *passim*, *Bibl*. (J.2).
10 Panzani, pp. 135, 157, 196, 197, *Bibl*. (J.1).
11 Meyer, p. 23.
12 Strickland, V, p. 268, (ed. 1851).
13 Meyer, pp. 15–16, 18.

24 The King and the Scots

1 *Bibl*. (N).
2 C.S.P.V. 1636–9, pp. 435–6.
3 Gardiner, *History*, IX, p. 32.
4 Verney Papers, p. 233.
5 C.S.P.D., 1639, pp. 242–3.
6 Gardiner, *History*, IX, p. 30 and note.
7 Aiton, pp. 392–7, *Bibl*. (N.).
8 Knowler, II, p. 362.
9 Gardiner, *History*, IX, p. 46.
10 Knowler, II, pp. 372, 378.
11 e.g. Oct. 23, 1634, Knowler, I, p. 331.
12 S.P. CCCCXXXVI, No. 47, 30 Dec., 1639, in Charles's own hand.
13 e.g. Robert Reade to Thomas Windebank, C.S.P.D. 1639/40, p. 474.
14 *Two Lives. Bibl*. (I.6).

25 The King and the Opposition

1 *Bibl.* (J.2); (Q.19).
2 C.S.P.V. 1636–9, pp. 110–11, 124–5.
3 *Bibl.* (Q.16).
4 Knowler, *Bibl.* (Q.7).
5 Gardiner, *History*, IX, p. 86.
6 C.S.P.D. 1639–40, p. 321.
7 *ibid.*, p. 158.
8 *The Priviledges and Practice of Parliaments in England* (E.161/1).
9 C.S.P.D. 1639–40, pp. 581, 491–2, 608, 565, 609; 1640, p. 7.
10 Parliament, *Bibl.* (L.2).

26 The King and Parliament

1 Strafford, *Bibl.* (Q.7).
2 Gardiner, *History*, IX, pp. 129–30, 132–4, 142, 149; C.S.P.D. 1640, pp. 491, 193; Birch, II, p. 287.
3 *Life of Porter*, Townshend, p. 181.
4 C.S.P.D. 1640–1, pp. 104–5, 128–9, *Bibl.* (Q.11).
5 The Long Parliament, *Bibl.* (L.3).

27 The King and Strafford

1 Green, *Princesses*, Vol. VI, pp. 106–25, *passim.*, *Bibl.* (Q.5).
2 Evelyn, *Diary*. For most of this chapter, see *Bibl.* Strafford and Parliament, *Bibl.* (Q.7), (L.3).

28 The Last of London

1 Gardiner, *History*, IX, pp. 403–4.
2 Porter to Nicholas, *Life*, by Townshend, pp. 191–2.
3 Bray, II, private correspondence Charles and Nicholas, pp. 25, 32, 46, etc, *Bibl.* (B).
4 Warwick, *Memoirs*, pp. 201–2.
5 Various versions, see Gardiner, *History*, X, pp. 136–41.
6 Townshend, *Porter*, p. 256.
7 C.S.P.V. 1642–3, p. 5.

29 The King's Standard Unfurled

1 Rushworth, IV, p. 532.
2 *Nineteen Propositions* and King's Answer, *Bibl.* (K).
3 *Memoirs* (1888), p. 13.
4 Letters of Henrietta-Maria, *Bibl.* (Q.3).

30 Commander-in-Chief

For this chapter see *Bibl*. (G.4).
1 Young, *Civil War*; *Cavalier Army*, Chs. 1–3.
2 Ellis, First S.III, p. 291.
3 Young, *Edgehill*.
4 Young, *Cavalier Army*, Ch. IV; Wood, *Oxford*, Vol. II, pp. 438 ff.
5 Thomas, *Berkenhead*, pp. 29–55 *passim*.
6 Lake, *passim*.
7 Henrietta-Maria, *Bibl*. (Q.3).

31 The Second Campaign

1 For campaign generally see Young and *Bibl*. (G.4). For Cropredy Walker *Historical Collections*, pp. 30–35 and annotated MS in the Library of Christ Church, Oxford; and Toynbee and Young.
2 Marston Moor, see Young.
3 Lostwithiel campaign, see Young, *Civil War*.
4 Laud, *Bibl*. (Q.8).
5 Gardiner, *Civil War* II, pp. 85–6.

32 'My marching Army'

1 Symonds, *Bibl*. (G.4).
2 *Bibl*. (G.4).
3 Rupert *Bibl*. (Q.10).
4 W. D. Macray, *Annals of the Bodleian*.

33 'Never Man So Alone'

1 For Charles in captivity, *Bibl*. (G.5).

34 Dum Spiro Spero

1 For Charles in captivity, *Bibl*. (G.5).
For evidence concerning Charles's natural daughter see Hugh Ross Williamson, *Jeremy Taylor* (1952).

35 'To vindicate his helpless right'

1 For the trial and execution of Charles, *Bibl*. (G.6).

Bibliography

Index

L Parliament
    1 General
    2 Particular Parliaments
    3 The Long Parliament
    4 Particular topics
    5 General discussion

M Government
    1 At the centre
    2 In the localities
    3 Towns

N Scotland

O Economic and social development
    1 General
    2 Agrarian affairs
    3 Wool
    4 Trade etc.

P Class and society
    1 General
    2 Lotteries
    3 The Gentry

Q Biographies of people close to Charles
    1 King James I
    2 Queen Anne
    3 Queen Henrietta-Maria
    4 Prince Henry
    5 Elizabeth of Bohemia
    6 George Villiers, Duke of Buckingham
    7 Thomas Wentworth, Earl of Strafford
    8 William Laud, Archbishop of Canterbury
    9 Richard Weston, Earl of Portland
    10 Prince Rupert
    11 Endymion Porter
    12 Peter Paul Rubens
    13 Sir Benjamin Rudyerd
    14 Oliver Cromwell
    15 Sir John Eliot
    16 John Hampden
    17 John Pym
    18 The Count of Gondomar
    19 The Earl of Essex
    20 Lord Cottington

R Essay collections and discussions on the causes of the civil wars
S General works

Bibliographical note

There is no shortage of contemporary or near contemporary material dealing with the period of Charles's life. Seventeenth-century people were articulate, they enjoyed writing, and they were avid collectors. Families with official state connections, or close to the Crown, realized the importance of the letters and documents that came into their hands and either kept the originals or made copies of them. Antiquarians accumulated more artificially, buying up documents, whether originals or copies, that appeared of importance and adding them to their own libraries. In both ways private collections grew. Reports of proceedings in Parliament and in the courts, printed news-sheets, broadsides, pamphlets, masques and plays, poetry and prose proliferated. Scholars transcribed and published material relevant to their purpose; state papers were calendared and partly transcribed; the Historical Manuscripts' Commission reported on and described the monumental collections in private hands and in the House of Lords; historians built upon the material to hand, interpreting and re-interpreting.

All this has resulted in both an abundance and a duplication of evidence relating to seventeenth-century England, and the following notes do no more than offer a brief guide to, and an indication of the chief sources used for this account of the life of Charles I.

Important MSS collections are:
Ashmolean MSS., Clarendon MSS., Tanner MSS., Rawlinson MSS. in the Bodleian Library; Egerton, Harley, Lansdowne, Stowe and 'Add. MSS.' in the British Library; the MSS of the House of Lords. For other important MSS sources see guide to Historical MSS Comm. Reports in Davies and Keeler, p. 13.

A Bibliography

Davies, G. and Keeler, M. F., *Bibliography of British History, Stuart Period, 1603–1714*, 1970.

Bulletin of the Institute of Historical Research publishes periodic guides to new work.

Richardson, R. C., *The Debate on the English Revolution*, 1977, is a bibliography which reflects changing views from the seventeenth century to the present day

Catalogue of the Thomason Tracts lists in chronological order the thousands of pamphlets collected by the bookseller, Thomason, between 1640 and 1661 which are now in the British Library. The Index to the Catalogue in vol. II is helpful.

An excellent bibliography of works concerning *Charles I King of Great Britain and Ireland* is in the British Library catalogue. It covers, under subject headings, biographies, letters, speeches and proclamations, and the main events of his life. Also useful is the catalogue of the Bodleian Library under *Carolus*.

B Charles's letters, speeches and writings

a) Charles's letters exist in many places, the various publications that include them often duplicating each other. Not all the letters have been printed and there is no collected edition of those that have. The original letters are in various manuscript collections including the Clarendon MSS in the Bodleian Library, the Strafford MSS in the Central Library, Sheffield, the MSS of the Duke of Beaufort, the Domestic State Papers in the Public Record Office, and the MSS of the House of Lords. Among important printed sources are:

Cabala sive scrinia sacra, 1654 and later 1787.

Bromley, G., *Collection of Original Royal Letters*.

Letters to King James the Sixth from the Queen, Prince Henry, Prince Charles (these are facsimiles), Maitland Club, No. 35, 1835.

Halliwell, J. O., *Letter of the Kings of England*, 1846.

Ellis, H., *Original Letters Illustrative of English History*: 1st Series, vol. 3; 2nd Series, vol. 3; 3rd Series, vol. 4., 1824–6.

Petrie, C., *The Letters, Speeches and Proclamations of King Charles I*. This is a small selection, as is a later edition, 1935.

Letters concerning the Spanish Match are in the *Hardwicke Papers*, vol. I printed from the Harleian MSS; so are letters and documents concerning the Earl of Bristol printed from the State Papers.

Letters, etc. concerning the Isle of Rhé are in the *Hardwicke Papers*, vol. II, printed from the State Papers.

Kensington's (Holland's) proxy courtship letters of Henrietta-Maria are in *Cabala*.

Charles's own courtship letters to Henrietta-Maria are in the Clarendon MSS and calendared in the Clarendon *State Papers*.

Letters from Charles to Strafford are in W. Knowler, *The Earl of Strafford's Letters and Despatches*, 1739.

The correspondence of Charles and Secretary Nicholas in 1641 is in an Appendix to most editions of Evelyn's *Diary and Letters*.

Charles's letters to James, Duke of Hamilton, are in G. Burnet, *Memoirs of the Lives and Actions of James and William, Dukes of Hamilton*, 1677.

The correspondence captured by Parliament after Naseby was published in many forms, generally called *The King's Cabinet Opened*, from 1645 onwards. The original letters are among H/Lords MSS, 6, I.

Charles's letters to Henrietta-Maria from Newcastle in 1646 were published by J. Bruce as *Charles I in 1646*, Camden Society, 1856.

Charles's letters to Glamorgan (Worcester) are in MSS Duke of Beaufort, calendered in *H.M.Comm. Duke of Beaufort*, 12, IX.

Charles's letters to Ormonde are in the *Carte Papers*.

'Escape' letters of Charles to Firebrace while at Carisbrooke are in an Appendix to P. Barwick, *Life of John Barwick*, 1724.

b) Charles's Speeches and Proclamations.

Some will be found in *Petrie* (above), in the *Proceedings of Parliament* (below), in *Rushworth* (below) as well as in separate publications. Important are the

Reliquiae Sacrae Carolinae, 1649.

Bibliotheca Regia 'such of the papers . . . as have escaped the wrack and ruine of these times', 1659.

Charles's disputations with Henderson at Newcastle in 1646 are in the *Reliquiae* (above) as well as being published separately.

Unlike his father, Charles wrote very little apart from a few odd verses, a paraphrase or two, a few lists and many annotations. His chief period of composition was in captivity and resulted in the *Eikon Basilike*, published immediately after his execution. The generally accepted view now is that the *Eikon* was written jointly by Charles and John Gauden, Bishop of Worcester, see

Madan, F. F., *A New Bibliography of the Eikon Basilike*, 1950.

Roper, H. R. Trevor, *History Today*, 1951.

Herbert, however, thought that some of the sheets that Charles was handling were not in his own handwriting. It cannot be certain how far Herbert was reliable. But the sentiments of the *Eikon* so strongly accord with Charles's own, and the style so strongly resembles his, that there can be little doubt that Charles was closely involved. Perhaps his drafts were prepared for the printer by Gauden and the sheets Herbert saw Charles handling were in the nature of 'proofs'. Someone was certainly operating on the practical side to have the machinery of printing and distribution ready to operate immediately after the King's death. See also

The Last Counsel of a Martyred King, 1660.

Heylin, P., *The Works of King Charles I . . . with the Life and Reign*, 1735.

Chalmers, G., *The Poetic Remains of some of the Scottish Kings*, 1824 (includes 'Majesty in Misery' said to have been written at Carisbrooke by Charles in 1648 and 'Lines on a Quiet Conscience' from Woty's *Poetical Calendar*, vol. VIII, also attributed to Charles, though without date).

C State Papers, etc.

The official State Papers Domestic cover a vast variety of state and inter-departmental correspondence and instruction, memoranda, reports; they include reports of foreign missions, letters to and from

Ambassadors, they record official payments, they include letters and instructions from the King and petitions from ordinary people. They are calendared as *Calendar of State Papers Domestic*.

The Reports from the Venetian Ambassadors in London to the Doge and Senate at Venice cover the period. A tradition of keen observation, generally accurate, makes them enjoyable and useful reading. They are translated and calendared as *Calendar of State Papers Venetian*.

Other collections of State Papers include

Rushworth, J., *Historical Collections of Private Passages of State* etc., 7 vols, 1659 ff.; later eds. 8 vols, 1680–1701.

Nalson, J., *An Impartial Collection of the Great Affairs of State* etc., 2 vols, 1682–3.

For Scotland the *Letters and State Papers during the Reign of King James the Sixth* contain useful material concerning the baby Charles, Abbotsford Club, VI, 1838.

Letters to King James the Sixth contain early letters of Charles and his family as well as the *Accounts of the Lords High Treasurers of Scotland* published as an Appendix to the Introduction which are useful for Charles's birth and nursery years.

Statutes of the Realm

Besides the official publication there are several abridged editions:

Firth, C. H. and Rait, R. S., *Acts and Ordinances of the Interregnum 1642–1660*, cover the period when Charles was absent from Westminster, 1911.

Steele, R. R., *Bibliotheca Lindesiana* (a bibliography of royal Proclamations), 1910.

Rymer, T. and Sanderson, R., *Foedera*, includes many pronouncements made by the Privy Council during the Personal Rule, 20 vols, 1704–32.

Records of the Privy Council

The Privy Council Registers are officially published in full transcript as *Acts of the Privy Council of England, New Series, 1542–1631*, 46 vols, 1890–1964.

The Registers for 1631–1637 are reproduced photographically on micro-opaque cards, 1962.

The Registers for 1637–1645 are published as slightly reduced facsimiles in codex form, 6 vols, 1967–68.

D Various collections

Many news-letters from the State Papers in the Public Record Office have been transcribed by Thomas Birch and edited by R. F. Williams in 4 vols as *The Court and Times of James I* and *The Court and Times of Charles I*, 1849.

The Letters of John Chamberlain (many of which are in the State Papers and are included in *Birch* (above)) were edited in 2 vols by N. E. McClure, 1939.

The despatches of the agent of the Grand Duke of Tuscany are full of interest. They are calendared in Reports of the *H.M.Comm.*, 11, i (Skrine MSS).

Harleian Miscellany: or a collection of scarce, curious, and entertaining tracts . . . found in the late Earl of Oxford's library, ed. W. Oldys, 8 vols, 1744–6; ed. T. Park, 10 vols., 1808–13.

Somers Tracts . . . selected from . . . public as well as private libraries, 16 vols, 1748–51; ed. W. Scott 13 vols, 1809–15.

Howell, J., *Epistolae Ho Elianae*, 3 vols, 1645.

Whitelocke, B., *Memorials of the English Affairs*, 1682 and later.

Harington, J., *Nugae Antiquae*, 2 vols, 1769.

Nichols, J. (ed.), *The Progresses . . . etc. . . . of King James the First* (compiled from MSS and pamphlets, 4 vols), 1828.

E Biographies of Charles

Arnway, J., *The Tablet, or Moderation of Charles I, Martyr*, 1649.

Wotton, H., *A Panegyrick of King Charles*, 1649.

Anon., *The Life and Reign of King Charles or the Pseudo-Martyr Discovered*, 1651.

Gerbier, B.(?), *The Non-Such Charles his Character*, 1651.

Lilly, W., *The True History of King James the First and King Charles the First*, 1651.

Weldon, A., *The Court and Character of King James, Whereunto is now Added the Court of King Charles Continued unto the Beginning of these Unhappy Times*, 1651.

Peyton, E., *The Divine Catastrophe of the House of Stuarts*, 1652.

L'Estrange, H., *The Reign of Charles I*, 1655.

Heylin, P., *Observations upon the History* (i.e. of L'Estrange, above), 1655.

L'Estrange, H., *The Observator Observed*, 1656.

Sanderson, W., *A Compleat History of the Life and Reigne of King Charles From His Cradle to His Grave*, 1658.

Van den Bos, L., *The Life and Raigne of King Charles*, 1658.

Rider, W., new ed. of *Arnway* (above), 1661.

Perrinchief, R., *The Royal Martyr, or the Life and Death of King Charles I*, 1676.

Butler, S., *The Plagiary Exposed . . . against the Memory of King Charles I*, 1691.

Hollingworth, R., *The Character of King Charles*, 1692.

Hollingworth, R., *A Defence of King Charles*, 1692.

Perrinchief, R., *The Life and Death of King Charles I* (similar to Perrinchief, 1676), 1693.

Harris, W., *An Historical and Critical Account of the Life and Writings of Charles I*, 1758.

D'Israeli, I., *Commentaries on the Life and Reign of Charles I*, 1828–31.

Abbott, Jacob, *History of King Charles the First of England*, 1848.

Guizot, F. P. G., *History of Charles the First and the English Revolution*, 1854.

Chancellor, E. Beresford, *The Life of Charles I, 1600–1625*, 1886.

Adams, W. H. D., *The White King*, 1889.

Seton, W. W., *The Early Years of Frederick Henry, Prince of Wales and Charles, Duke of Albany*, 1916.

MacKilliam, A. H., *Charles the First*, 1917.

Coit, C. W., *The Royal Martyr*, 1924.

Higham, F. M., *Charles I*, 1932.

Belloc, H., *Charles the First*, 1933.

John, Evan, *King Charles I*, 1933.

Brookes, J., *A Vindication of Charles I*, 1934.

Pakenham, M. P., *Charles I*, 1936.

Stratford, E. Wingfield, *Charles, King of England* (3 vols), 1948–50.

French, A., *Charles I and the Puritan Upheaval*, 1955.

Wedgwood, C. V., *The King's Peace, 1637–1641*, 1955.

Wedgwood, C. V., *The King's War, 1641–1647*, 1958.

Toynbee, M. R., *Charles the First*, 1964.

Hibbert, A. R., *Charles I*, 1968.

Hibbert, C., *Charles I*, 1968.

Bowle, J., *Charles I*, 1975.

F Particular studies of Charles

Williamson, H. Ross, *Charles and Cromwell*, 1946.

Young, G. M., *Charles I and Cromwell*, 1950.

Dobson, J., *The Children of Charles I*, 1975.

G Particular episodes in Charles's life: the sources given below are a few of the most useful:

1. Birth and childhood:

Chancellor (above) is the only one who deals with the early years in any detail.

Carey, Robert, Earl of Monmouth, *Memoirs of the Life of . . .* , 1759 (*passim*)

Cantrell, Henry, *The Royal Martyr, a true Christian*, 1716 (for the baptism of Charles).

Keevil, J. J., 'The Illness of Charles, Duke of Albany from 1600–1612', *Journal of the History of Medicine and Allied Sciences*, Vol. IX, No. 4, October, 1954.

Arbuckle, W. F., 'The Gowrie Conspiracy', *Scottish Historical Review*, 36, pp. 1 ff and 89 ff, 1957.

2. *Spanish marriage*

The Hardwick State Papers vol. I are the main repository of the letters from Charles, James, Buckingham, Bristol and contain the answers of Bristol to the charges against him. Also

Wotton, H. *The Life and Death of George Villiers, Duke of Buckingham*, in *Reliquiae Wottonianae* (reasons for going).

Chamberlain, J. *Letters*, Vol. II, 480–81 (for the return from Spain).

Journals of the House of Lords, Vol. III, 220–33 for Buckingham's 'Narration'.

Proposed Spanish Marriage Treaty, and the negotiations, Clarendon MSS., Rushworth I, 76 ff; Fray Francisco de Jesus, 'Narrative of the Spanish Marriage Treaty', ed. S. R. Gardiner, *Camden Soc.*, 1869.

'The Earl of Bristol's Defence of his Negotiations in Spain', Camden Soc. Misc. *VI*, 1871.

3. *Cadiz and La Rochelle*

Glanville, J. 'The Voyage to Cadiz in 1625'; Camden Soc, 1883.

Journal of all the Proceedings of the Duke of Buckingham in the Isle of Ree, 1627.

4. *Civil war*

Manley, T., *Iter Carolium*, Jan. 1642–1649, 1660.

Walker, E., *Historical Discourses*, 1705.

Maseres, F. (ed.), *Select Tracts relating to the Civil Wars in England*, 2 vols, 1815.

Parsons, D. (ed.), *The Diary of Henry Slingsby (1638–45)*, 1836.

Cary, H. (ed.), *Memorials of the Great Civil War, 1642–52*, 2 vols. 1842.

Symonds, R., *Diary of the Marches of the Royal Army 1644–5*, Camden Soc., 1859.

Peacock, E. (ed.), *Army Lists of Roundheads and Cavaliers . . . 1642*, 1874.

Langmead, T. L. (ed.), *Sir Edward Lake's account of his Interview with Charles I*, Camden Soc., 1858.

Varley, F. J. *The Siege of Oxford . . . 1642–1646*, 1935.

Young, P., 'King Charles I's Army in 1642', *J. Soc. Army Hist. Research*, 17, pp. 102–9, 1938.

Ketton-Cremer, R. W., 'The King's Journey', in *A Norfolk Gallery*, 1948.

Burne, A. H., *The Battlefields of England*, 1950.

Burne, A. H. and Young, P., *The Great Civil War*, 1950.

Woolrych, A. H., *Battles of the Civil War*, 1961.

Roy, I., 'The Royalist Council of War, 1642–6', *B.I.H.R.*, XXXV, pp. 150–68, 1962.

Young, P., *Edgehill, the Campaign and the Battle*, 1967.

Young, P., *Marston Moor, the Campaign and the Battle*, 1967.

Smith, G. R., *Without Touch of Dishonour* (Life and death of Slingsby), 1968.

Thomas, P. W. *Sir John Berkenhead 1617–1679, a Royalist Career in Politics and Polemics*, 1969.

Toynbee, M. and Young, P., *Cropredy Bridge 1644, the Campaign and the Battle*, 1970.

Young, P. and Emberton, W., *The Cavalier Army, its Organization and Everyday Life*, 1974.

Smith, G. R. and Toynbee, M., *Leaders of the Civil Wars 1642–1648*, 1977.

Malcolm, J. L., 'A King in Search of Soldiers: Charles I in 1942', *Hist.J.*, 21, 1978.

5. Captivity

Herbert, T., *Threnodia Carolina*, being the 1st ed. of *Herbert's Memoirs of the last two years of the Reign of . . . King Charles I* (other eds 1702, 1813, *infra* Stevenson, etc.) 1678.

Peck, F. (ed.), *Desiderata Curiosa*, 2 vols, 1732–5; (contains much material on escape to the Scots), 1779.

Birch, T. (ed.), *Letters . . . Hammond . . . relating to King Charles I while he was confined in Carisbrook*, 1764.

Ashburnham, J., *Narrative . . . of his Attendance on King Charles*, 2 vols, 1830.

Berkeley, J., *Memoirs* (Appendix to above), 1830.

Montreuil, J. de, *The Diplomatic Correspondence of 1645–48*, ed. J. G. Fotheringham, 2 vols, *Scot. Hist. Soc.* (for Charles's escape to the Scots), 1898/9.

Fea, A., *Memoirs of the Martyr King, 1646–9*, 1905.

Stevenson, G. S. (ed.), *Charles I in Captivity from Contemporary Sources*. Contains Herbert's *Memoirs*, Narratives of Col. Edward Cooke, Major Huntington, Henry Firebrace, 1927.

Firebrace, C. W., *Honest Harry, being the biography of Sir Henry Firebrace, Knight, 1619–1691*, 1932.

Mackenzie, N., 'Sir Thomas Herbert of Tintern, a parliamentary royalist', *Bull.I.H.R.*, 28, pp. 23–86, 1955/56.

Jones, J., *The Royal Prisoner* (in the Isle of Wight), 1965.

6. Trial and execution

Nalson, J., *A True Copy of the Journal of the High Court of Justice for the Tryal of King Charles I*, 1684.

Herbert, T., *Memoir of the Last Years of the Reign of King Charles I to which is added a Particular Account of the Funeral of the King*, several eds, 1678.

The State Trials, vol. IV, (ed. from contemporary sources by W. Cobbett, T. B. Howell and others) 1809–28.

Halford, H., *Essays and Orations*, 'An Account of the Opening of the Tomb of King Charles I at Windsor in 1813', 1831.

Muddiman, J. C. (ed.), *The Trial of King Charles the First*, 1928.

Galwey, R. Payne, *The Scaffold George of Charles I*, 1908.

Lockyer, R., *Trial of Charles I*, 1959.

Wedgwood, C. V., *The Trial of Charles I*, 1964.

H Particular topics

1. Ships and the navy

Heywood, T., *A True Description of His Majestie's Royal Ship* [the Sovereign of the Seas], 1637.

Oppenheim, M., *A History of the Administration of the Royal Navy and of Merchant Shipping in Relation to the Navy from 1509 to 1660*, 1896.

Penn, C. D., *The Navy under the Early Stuarts*, 1913.

Pett, P., *The Autobiography of Phineas Pett*, ed. W. G. Perrin, 1918.

Davis, R., *The Rise of the English Shipping Industry*, 1962.

2. Fishing

Smith, S., *A True Narration of the Royall Fishings of Great Britaine and Ireland*, 1641.

Smith, S., *The Herring-Busse Trade*, 1641.

Elder, J. R., *The Royal Fishery Companies of the Seventeenth Century*, 1912.

3. Sovereignty of the Seas

Selden, J., *Mare Clausum* (written 1617 or '18, pub. 1635, trans. M. Nedham 1652).

Borough, J., *The Sovereignty of the British Seas*, 1633, pub. 1651.

4. Ship Money

Gordon, M. D., 'The Collection of Ship Money in the reign of Charles I', *Trans.R.H.S.*, 3rd S.4, pp. 141–62, 1910.

Keir, D. L., 'The Case of Ship-Money', *Law Quart. Rev.*, 52, pp. 546–74, 1936.

Bard, N. P., 'The Ship Money Case and William Fiennes, Viscount Saye and Sele', *Bull.I.H.R.*, 50–51, pp. 177–84, 1977.

Swales, R. J. W., 'The Ship Money Levy of 1628', *ibid.*, pp. 164–76.

5. Patents and monopolies

Price, W. H., *The English patents of monopoly*, 1906.

Rymer, Privy Council (*supra*, C.)

Leonard, H. H., 'Distraint of Knighthood: the last phase, 1625–41', *History*, No. 63, pp. 23–7, 1978.

6. The King's Finances

Dietz, F. C., *Receipts and Issues of the Exchequer during the Reigns of James I and Charles I* (Smith College Studies, Northampton, Mass), 1928.
Dietz, F. C., *English Public Finance, 1558–1641*, 1932.
Judges, A. V., 'Philip Burlamachi', *Economica 6*, 286 ff., 1926.
Ashton, R., 'The Disbursing Official Under the Early Stuarts: the Cases of Sir William Russell and Philip Burlamachi', *Bull.I.H.R.*, 30, pp. 162–74, 1957.
Ashton, R., *The Crown and the Money Market, 1603–1640*, 1960.
Tawney, R. H., *Business and Politics under James I: Lionel Cranfield as Merchant and Minister*, 1958.
Prestwich, M., *Cranfield, Politics and Profits under the Early Stuarts*, 1966.
Alexander, M. Van Cleave, *Charles I's Lord Treasurer*, 1976.

I The King and his Court

1. Whitehall and architecture

Dugdale, G., *Whitehall Through the Centuries*, 1950.
Charlton, J., *The Banqueting House*, 1964.
Millar, O., *The Whitehall Ceiling*, 1958.
Summerson, J., *Architecture in Britain 1530–1830*, 1953.
Akrig, G. P., *Jacobean Pageant or the Court of King James I*, (for Whitehall and the courtier's life), 1962.

2. The Court masque and Order of the Garter

Simpson, P. and Bell C. P., *Designs by Inigo Jones for Plays and Masques at Court* (Walpole Soc.), 1924.
Steele, M. S., *Plays and Masques at the Court during the Reigns of Elizabeth, James, and Charles*, 1926.
Welsford, E., *The Court Masque*, 1927.
Nicoll, A., *Stuart Masques and the Renaissance Stage*, 1938.
Orgel, S., *The Jonsonian Masque*, 1965.
Ashmole, E., *The Institution, Laws, and Commerce of the Most-Noble Order of the Garter*, 1672.
Ashmole, E., *A History of the Most Noble Order of the Garter*, 1715.
Wilson, T. H., *Saint George in Tudor and Stuart England – the development of the Cult of the Order of the Garter*, (London M.Phil. thesis), 1976
For both 1 and 2 (above) lives of Inigo Jones, e.g.
Gotch, A., *Inigo Jones*, 1928.
Summerson, J., *Inigo Jones*, 1966.

3. Art and the King's pictures

Waterhouse, E., *Painting in Britain 1530–1790*, 1953.

Whinney, M. and Millar, O., *English Art 1625–1714*, 1957.

Millar, O., *The Queen's Pictures* (partic. Pt. 3), 1977.

Hewlett, H. G., 'Charles I as a Picture Collector', in *The Nineteenth Century*, vol. XXVIII, Aug. 1890.

Phillips, C., *The Picture Gallery of Charles I (Portfolio Monograph* No. 25), Jan. 1896.

Pickel, M. B., *Charles I as Patron of Poetry and Drama*, 1936.

Hoff, U., *Charles I: Patron of Artists*, 1942.

Millar, O., 'Charles I', *Burlington Magazine*, Vol. XCI, p. 86, 1949.

Roper, H. Trevor-, *The Plunder of the Arts in the Seventeenth Century* (for Mantuan Collection), 1970.

Sainsbury, W. N., Appendix H (Q.12) for Mantuan Collection.

Van der Doort, A., *Catalogue of the Collections of Charles I* reproduced with an Introduction by Oliver Millar (Walpole Soc. vol. XXXVII), 1960.

Millar, O., *The Age of Charles I: Painting in England 1620–1649*, 1972.

Nuttall, W. L. F., 'King Charles's Pictures and the Commonwealth Sale', *Apollo*, Oct. 1965.

4. Literature

Knights, L. C., *Drama and Society in the Age of Jonson*, 1937.

Wedgwood, C. V., *Seventeenth-Century English Literature*, 1950, 1970.

Wedgwood, C. V., *Poetry and Politics Under the Stuarts*, 1960.

5. Portraits of Charles

Cust, L., 'The Equestrian Portraits of Charles I', *Burlington Magazine*, XVIII, pp. 207 ff. 1910–11.

Mann, J. G., 'The Charles I Statue at Charing Cross', *Country Life*, pp. 908–9, May 16, 1947.

Toynbee, M. R., 'Some Early Portraits of Charles I', *Burlington Magazine*, XCI pp. 4–9, 1949.

Esdaile, K. A., 'The Busts and Statues of Charles I', *ibid*, pp. 4–14, 1949.

Millar, O., *Age of Charles I* (above).

Strong, R., *Charles I on Horseback*, 1972.

6. Little Gidding

Mayor, J. E. B. (ed.), *Two Lives*, 1855.

Carter, T. T. (ed.), *Nicholas Ferrar, his Household and his Friends*, 1892.

Blackstone, B. (ed.), *The Ferrar Papers*, 1938.

Haycock, A .L., *Nicholas Ferrar of Little Gidding*, 1938.

Maycock, A. L., *Chronicles of Little Gidding*, 1954.

7. The King's Evil; the Occult, etc.

Browne, J., *Service used in touching for the King's Evil*, 1684.
Crawford, R., *The King's Evil*, 1911.
Toynbee, M. R. 'Charles I and the King's Evil' in *Folklore* vol. LXI, March 1950.
Thomas, K. V., *Religion and the Decline of Magic*, 1971.

J The King and his Church

1. The Church of England and the Church of Rome

Laud, biography (Q.8).
Charles's own letters and speeches, etc. (B).
Gamaches, C. de, *Memoirs of the Mission in England of the Capuchin Friars . . . 1630–1669* are printed in vol. II of Birch, *Court and Times of Charles I (supra)*.
Panzani, Con, Rossetti, transcripts of the correspondence are in the P.R.O.
Panzani, G., *The Memoirs of Gregorio Panzani, including an account of his Agencies in England 1634–1636*, ed. J. Berington, 1793.
Meyer, A. O., 'Charles I and Rome', *Am.Hist.Rev.*, 19, pp. 13–26, 1913.
Albion, G. G., *Charles I and the Court of Rome*, 1938.
Hill, J.E.C. *Economic Problems of the Church*, 1956.
Havran, M. J., *The Catholics in Caroline England*, 1962.
Tyacke, N., 'Puritanism, Arminianism and Counter-Revolution' in *Origins of the English Civil War*, ed. C. Russell, 1973.
Hibbard, C. M., 'Early Stuart Catholicism: Revisions and Re-Revisions', *J.M.H.*, vol. 52, No. 1, March 1980.

2. Puritanism and Puritan protest

Laud's speech against Bastwick, Burton, Prynne in 1637 is in *Harleian Misc.*
Prynne, W., *Canterburie's doome*, 1646.
Heath, Sir Robert, 'Speech . . . in the case of . . . Leighton in the Star Chamber', Camden Soc. Misc. VII, 1875.
'Proceedings against Prynne', Camden Soc. N.S. 18, 1877.
Ball, T. *Life of the Renowned Doctor Preston*, ed. E. W. Harcourt, 1628.
Newton, A. P., *The colonizing Activities of the Early Puritans*, 1914.
Kirby, E. W., *William Prynne: A Study in Puritanism*, 1931.
Haller, W., *Tracts on Liberty in the Puritan Revolution*, 3 vols, 1934.
Haller, W., *The Rise of Puritanism*, 1938.
Morgan, I., *Prince Charles's Puritan Chaplain*, 1957.
Hill, J. E. C., *Puritanism and Revolution*, 1958.
Hill, J. E. C. (ed.), Brailsford, *The Leveller Movement*, 1961.
Gregg, P., *Free-born John* (a biography of Lilburne), 1961.

Lamont, W., *Marginal Prynne*, 1963.
Hill, J. E. C., *Society and Puritanism in pre-Revolutionary England*, 1964.
Lamont, W., *Godly Rule*, 1969.
The Thomason Tracts, passim.

K Political theory

Until recently, theoretical discussion, principles of political obligation, etc. have attracted more attention than either the day-to-day happenings in Parliament or the development of Parliament itself. Thus:

Gardiner, S. R., *Constitutional Documents of the Puritan Revolution 1628–1660*, 1889.
Figgis, J. N., *The Theory of the Divine Right of Kings*, 1896.
Tanner, J. R., *English Constitutional Conflicts of the Seventeenth Century, 1603–1689*, 1928.
Gooch, G. P., *Political Thought in England from Bacon to Halifax*, 1914/15.
Gooch, G. P., *English Democratic Ideas in the Seventeenth Century* (2nd ed. edited Laski), 1927.
Tanner, J. R., *Constitutional Documents of the Reign of James I 1603–1625*, 1930.
Allen, J. W., *English Political Thought, 1603–1660*, 2 vols, 1938.
Sabine, G. H., *A History of Political Theory*, 1937.
Wormuth, F. D., *The Royal Prerogative 1603–1649*, 1939.
Judson, M. A., *The Crisis of the Constitution*, 1949.
Zagorin, P., *A History of Political Thought in the English Revolution*, 1954.
Kenyon, J. P., *The Stuart Constitution*, Documents and Commentary, 1966.
Daly, J., 'The Idea of Absolute Monarchy in 17th Century England', *H.J.*, 21, pp. 227–50, 1978.

L Parliament

1. General

Journals of the House of Commons
Journals of the House of Lords
These Journals contain some speeches, procedural accounts, attendances, but are scrappy and incomplete.
The Old Parliamentary History, compiled 1751–62.
The Parliamentary History of England, compiled by William Cobbett 1806–20.
Both these Parliamentary histories need supplementing and should be used with caution, but they make good use of contemporary pamphlets, etc. to fill in gaps in the *Journals*.
Firth, C. H., *The House of Lords During the Civil War, 1603–1660*, 1910.

2. Particular Parliaments

Notestein, W., Relf, F. H. and Simpson, H., *Commons Debates, 1621*, 1935.

Ruigh, R. E., *The Parliament of 1624*, 1971.

Gardiner, S. R., 'Debates in the House of Lords 1624', 1626, Camden Soc., 1879.

Gardiner, S. R., 'Debates in the House of Commons in 1625', Camden Soc., 1873.

Fuller, M. B., *Negotium Posterorum and the Parliament of 1625*, 1919.

Ball, J. N., 'Eliot in 1625', *Bull.I.H.R.*, 28, pp. 103–27, 1955.

Hulme, H., *The leadership of Sir John Eliot in the Parliament of 1626*, 1932.

Johnson, R. C., Keeler, M. F., Cole, M. J. and Bidwell, W. B., *The Commons' Debates in 1628*, 1977.

Notestein, W. and Relf, F. H., *The Commons' Debates for 1629*, 1921.

Fraser, I. H. C., 'The Agitation in the Commons 2nd March 1629', *Bull.I.H.R.*, 30, pp. 86–95, 1957.

Ball, J. N., 'Sir John Eliot and Parliament, 1624–1629' in *Faction and Parliament (infra)*, 1978.

Thompson, C., 'The Divided Leadership of the House of Commons in 1629' in *Faction and Parliament (infra)*, 1978.

3. The Long Parliament

May, T., *The History of the Parliament of England which Began November 3, 1640*, 1647.

D'Ewes, S., *The Journal of Sir Simonds D'Ewes, Nov. 1640–March 1641*, ed. Notestein; *Oct. 1641–Jan. 1642*, ed. Coates, 1923.

Verney Papers, *Notes of Proceedings in the Long Parliament*, ed. J. Bruce, Camden Soc., 1845.

Keeler, M. F., *The Long Parliament, 1640–41, a biographical study of its Members*, 1954.

Brunton, D. and Pennington, D. H., *Members of the Long Parliament*, 1954.

Hexter, H. H., *The Reign of King Pym*, 1941.

Brett, S. R., 'The Long Parliament', *Quart. Rev.*, 275, pp. 107–17, 1940.

MacCormack, J. R., *Revolutionary Politics in the Long Parliament*, 1973.

4. Particular topics

Relf, F. H., *The Petition of Right*, 1917.

Foster, E. R., 'The Printing of the Petition of Right', *Huntingdon Liby Quarterly* I, pp. 81–3, 1974.

Forster, J., *The Debates on the Grand Remonstrance*, 1860.

Schoolcraft, H. L., *The Genesis of the Grand Remonstrance*, 1902.

Coates, W. H., 'Some Observations on the Grand Remonstrance' *J.M.H.*, 4, pp. 1–17, 1932.

Forester, J., *The Arrest of the Five Members by Charles I*, 1860.

5. General discussion (see also Essay Collections)

Notestein, W., 'The Winning of the Initiative by the House of Commons', *Proc.Brit.Acad.* 11, pp. 125–75, 1924–5.

Willson, D. H. (ed.), *The Parliamentary Diary of Robert Bowyer*, 1941.

Hinton, R. M. K., 'The Decline of Parliamentary Government under Elizabeth and the Early Stuarts', *C.H.J.*, 13, pp. 116–32, 1957.

Mitchell, W. M., *The Rise of the Revolutionary Party in the English House of Commons 1603–1629*, 1957.

Johnson, R. C., 'Parliamentary Diaries of the Early Stuart Period', *Bull.I.H.R.*, 44, pp. 293–300, 1971.

Russell, C., 'Introduction' and 'Parliament and the King's Finances' in *The Origins of the English Civil War (infra)*, 1973.

Hirst, D., *The Representative of the People?*, 1975.

Russell, C., 'Parliamentary History in Perspective: 1602–1629', *History*, 61, pp. 1–27, 1976.

Sharpe, K., 'Parliamentary History 1603–1629: In or out of Perspective?' in *Faction and Parliament (infra)*, 1978.

Russell, C., *Parliaments and English Politics 1621–1629*, 1979. This is the most comprehensive study of early Stuart Parliaments to have appeared. With the work of Hirst and Sharpe it emphasizes both the new approach to Parliamentary history and the importance of day-to-day happenings as opposed to the theoretical approach represented by the works listed under K (above).

Important reviews are:

Underdown, D., *Am.Hist.Rev.*, 85, Feb. 1980.

Hirst, D., 'Parliament, Law and War in the 1620s' *H.J.*, 23, 1980.

Woolrych, A., 'Court, Country and City Revisited', *History*, June 1980.

Hexter, J. H., 'The Not-So-New-Men', *New York Review*, Dec. 18, 1980.

M Government

1. At the centre

Aylmer, G. E., *The King's Servants: the Civil Service of Charles I 1625–1642*, 1961, rev. 1974.

2. In the localities

The emphasis upon Parliament has been matched by an increasing number of studies of local affairs, which are of crucial importance to an understanding of Charles's reign:

Coate, M., *Cornwall in the Great Civil War and Interregnum 1642–1660*, 1933.

Wood, A. C., *Nottinghamshire in the Civil War*, 1937.

Barnes, T. G., *Somerset 1625–40*, 1961.

Chalkin, C. W., *Seventeenth-Century Kent*, 1965.

Everitt, A., *The Community of Kent and the Great Rebellion*, 1966.

Morrill, J. S., *The Revolt of the Provinces*, 1976.

Holmes, C., *The Eastern Association in the English Civil War*, 1974.

Fletcher, A., *A County Community in Peace and War; Sussex 1600–1660*, 1975.

3. Towns

Pearl, V., *London and the Outbreak of the Puritan Revolution 1625–42*, 1961.

Howell, R., *Newcastle-upon-Tyne and the Puritan Revolution*, 1967.

Clark, P. and Slack, P., *Crisis and Order in English Towns 1500–1700*, 1972.

N Scotland

Donaldson, G., *The Making of the Scottish Prayer Book of 1637*, 1954.

Wedgwood, C. V., 'Anglo-Scottish Relations, 1603–40', *R.H.S. Trans.*, 4th S. 32, pp. 1–15, 1960.

Donaldson, G., *Scotland: James V–James VII*, 1965.

Schwarz, M. L., 'Viscount Saye and Sele, Lord Brooke and aristocratic protest to the First Bishops' War', *Canadian J. Hist.*, vii, pp. 17–36, 1972.

Stevenson, D., *The Scottish Revolution, 1637–44*, 1973.

Kaplan, L., *Politics and Religion during the English Revolution: the Scots and the Long Parliament 1643–1645*, 1976.

O Economic and social development

1. General

State Papers Domestic for instructions to and responses from counties to particular situations.

Reports of Cases in Star Chamber and High Commission ed. Gardiner, S. R., Camden Soc., 1886.

Rushworth, Vol. II, part 2, Reports of Star Chamber cases, 1625–8.

Nef, J. U., 'The Progress of Technology and the Growth of Large Scale Industry in Great Britain 1540–1640', *Econ.Hist.Rev.*, 5, pp. 3–24, 1934.

Supple, B., *Commercial Crisis and Change in England 1600–1642*, 1959.

Barnes, T. G., *Somerset 1625–40* (for the Book of Orders and Poor Law Policy), 1961.

Wilson, C., *England's Apprenticeship 1603–1763*, 1965.

2. Agrarian affairs

Darby, H. C., *The Draining of the Fens*, 1940.

Allan, D. G. C., 'The Rising in the West, 1628–1631', *Econ.Hist.Rev.*, 5, pp. 136–61, 1952.

Harris, L. E., *Vermuyden and the Fens*, 1953.

Hammersley, G., 'The Crown Woods and their Exploitation in the Sixteenth and Seventeenth Centuries', *Bull.I.H.R.*, 30, pp. 136–51, 1957.

Hammersley, G., 'Julius Caesar: Memo. on Crown Forest Land', *Bull.I.H.R.*, 30, pp. 157–8, 1957.

Kerridge, E., 'The Revolt in Wiltshire against Charles I', *Wilts. Arch. and Natural History Mag.*, LVII, pp. 64–75, 1958.

Beresford, M. W., 'Habitation versus Improvement' in *Essays in the Economic and Social History of Tudor and Stuart Times*, ed. F. J. Fisher, 1961.

Thirsk, J., *The Agrarian History of England and Wales, IV*, 1500–1640, 1967.

Kerridge, E., *Agrarian Problems, the 16th Century and After*, 1969.

3. Wool

Friis, A., *Alderman Cockayne's Project and the Cloth Trade*, 1927.

Bowden, P. J., *The Wool Trade in Tudor and Stuart England*, 1962.

Ramsay, G. D., *The Wiltshire Woollen Industry in the Sixteenth and Seventeenth Centuries*, 1943

4. Trade etc.

Ramsay, G. D., *English Overseas Trade during the Centuries of Emergence*, 1957.

Outhwaite, R. H., *Inflation in Tudor and Early Stuart England*, 1969.

P Class and society

Peacham, H., *The Compleat Gentleman*, 1622.

Brathwaite, R., *The English Gentleman*, 1630.

Brathwaite, R., *The English Gentlewoman*, 1631.

Campbell, M., *The English Yeoman under Elizabeth and the Early Stuarts*, 1942.

The relation of economic wealth to political stability and in particular the changing fortunes of the gentry and the aristocracy have, since

Charles's own time, given rise to fruitful discussion. The most important contributions are:

Harrington, J., *Commonwealth of Oceana*, 1656.

Tawney, R. H., 'Harrington's Interpretation of his Age', *Proceedings of the British Academy*, 1941.

Tawney, R. H., 'The Rise of the Gentry 1558–1640', *Econ.Hist.Rev.*, 11, 1941.

Stone, L., 'The Anatomy of the Elizabethan Aristocracy', *Econ.Hist.Rev.*, 13, 1948.

Roper, H. R. Trevor-, 'The Elizabethan Aristocracy: An Anatomy Anatomized', *Econ.Hist.Rev.*, 2nd. S. 3, 1951.

Stone, L., 'The Elizabethan Aristocracy, a restatement', *Econ.Hist.Rev.*, 2nd S. 4, 1952.

Roper, H. R. Trevor-, 'The Gentry 1540–1640', *Econ.Hist.Rev. Supplement*, 1, 1953.

Tawney, R. H., 'The Rise of the Gentry, a Postscript', *Econ.Hist.Rev.*, 2nd. S. 7, 1954.

Cooper, J. P., 'The Counting of Manors', *Econ.Hist.Rev.*, 2nd S. 8, 1956.

Zagorin, P., 'The Social Interpretation of the English Revolution', *J.Econ.Hist.*, 19, 1959.

Hexter, J. H., 'Storm Over the Gentry', in *Re-appraisals in History*, 1961.

Simpson, A., *The Wealth of the Gentry 1540–1660*, 1961.

Stone, L., *The Crisis of the Aristocracy 1558–1641*, 1965.

Stone, L., *Social Change and Revolution in England 1540–1640*, 1965.

Coleman, D. C., 'The Gentry Controversy and the Aristocracy in Crisis', *History*, 51, 1966.

Zagorin, P., *The Court and the Country*, 1969.

Christianson, P., 'The Causes of the English Revolution: A Revaluation', *J. of British Studies*, 15, 1976.

Journal of Modern History, 49, No. 4, a special issue devoted to the English Revolution, Dec. 1977.

Commentaries on the above in *ibid.*, March 1978.

Pocock, J. G. A. (ed.), *The Political Works of James Harrington*, 1977.

For information on Lotteries, see

Ashton, J., *A History of English Lotteries*, 1893.

Ewen, C. L., *Lotteries and Sweepstakes*, 1932.

Q Biographies of people close to Charles

1a King James I

Wilson, A., *The History of Great Britain, being the Life and Reign of King James the First*, 1653.

Osborne, F., *Some Traditionall Memoyres on the Raigne of King James the First*, 1658.

Bibliography

Harris, W., *Historical and Critical Account of the Life and Writings of James I*, 1753.
Ashton, R. (ed.), *James I by his Contemporaries*, 1969.
Willson, D. H., *King James VI and I*, 1973.
Smith, A. G. R. (ed.), *The Reign of James VI and I*, 1973.

The most important of James's own works are:
Daemonologie, 1597.
Basilikon Doron, 1599.
The Trew Law of Free Monarchies, 1603.
A Counterblast of Tobacco, 1604.
A Meditation upon the Lord's Prayer, 1619.
A Meditation upon verses of St. Matthew, 1620.
His *Collected Works* were published by Bishop Montague in 1616; also ed. C. H. McIlwain in 1918.

b The death of James

See Harris (above) and
Eglisham, G., *The Forerunner of Revenge*, 1642.
Keynes, G., *The Life of William Harvey*, 1966, pp. 143–8.

2. Queen Anne

Strickland, A., *Lives of the Queens of England*, 1840–8.

3. Queen Henrietta-Maria

Green, M. A. E., *The Letters of Queen Henrietta-Maria*, 1857.
Dauncy, J., *Henrietta-Maria*, 1660.
Strickland, A., *Lives of the Queens of England*, 1840–8.
Taylor, I. A., *Henrietta-Maria*, 2 vols, 1905.
Haynes, H., *Henrietta-Maria*, 1912.
Oman, C., *Henrietta-Maria*, 1936.
Toynbee, M. R., 'The Wedding Journey of King Charles I', *Archaeologia Cantiania*, vol. LXIX, 1955.
Bone, Quentin, *Queen of the Cavaliers*, 1973.
Hamilton, Elizabeth, *Henrietta-Maria*, 1976,
Smuts, R. M., 'The Puritan followers of Henrietta Maria in the 1630s', *E.H.R.*, 93, pp. 26–45, Jan. 1978.

4. Prince Henry

Maxwell, J., *The Life and Death of Prince Henry*, 1612.
Cornwallis, C., *A Briefe Life of Henry, Prince of Wales* written 1626, pub. 1641.
Cornwallis, C., *An Account of the Baptism, Life, Death and Funeral of the most Incomparable Prince Frederick Henry, Prince of Wales*, 1751.

Birch, T., *The Life of Henry Prince of Wales*, 1760.
Wilson, E. C., *Prince Henry and English Literature*, 1946.

5. Elizabeth of Bohemia

Baker, L. M., *Letters of Elizabeth, Queen of Bohemia*, 1953.
Ward, A. W. (ed. Tout and Rait), *Elizabeth, Electress Palatine and Queen of Bohemia*, 1902.
Green, M. A. E. (revised S. C. Lomas), *Elizabeth Electress Palatine and Queen of Bohemia*, 1909.
Buchan, A., *A Stuart Portrait*, 1934.
Oman, C. M. A., *Elizabeth of Bohemia*, 1938, revised 1964.
Williams, J., *Elizabeth, the Winter Queen*, 1977.

6. George Villiers, Duke of Buckingham

Wotton, H., *Reliquiae Wottonianae*, 1651.
Fairholt, F. W. (ed.), *Poems and Songs relating to . . . Buckingham and his Assassination* (Percy Society), 1850.
Gardiner, S. R., 'Documents Illustrating the Impeachment of Buckingham in 1626', Camden Soc., 1889.
Thomson, K., *Life and Times of George Villiers, Duke of Buckingham*, 1860.
Gibbs, P., *The Romance of George Villiers, 1st Duke of Buckingham*, 1905.
Gibb, M. A., *Buckingham, 1592–1628*, 1936.
Cammell, C. R., *Buckingham*, 1939.
Williamson, H. R., *George Villiers, First Duke of Buckingham*, 1940.
Erlanger, P., trans. Smith-Gordon, L., *Life of Buckingham*, 1953.

7. Thomas Wentworth, Earl of Strafford

Knowler, W. (ed.), *The Earl of Strafford's Letters and Despatches*, 2 vols, 1739.
Cooper, J. P., 'The Fortune of Thomas Wentworth, Earl of Strafford', *Econ. Hist. Rev.*, Dec. 1958.
Wedgwood, C. V., *Thomas Wentworth, First Earl of Strafford, a Revaluation*, 1961.
Cooper, J. P., (ed.), *The Wentworth Papers*, Camden Soc., 1973.

8. Willian Laud, Archbishop of Canterbury

Scott, W. and Bliss, J., *The Works of William Laud*, 7 vols, 1847–60.
Roper, H. R. Trevor-, *Archbishop Laud, 1573–1645*, 1940 (rev. ed. 1962).
Bourne, E. C. E., *The Anglicanism of William Laud*, 1947.

9. Richard Weston, Earl of Portland

Alexander, M. Van Cleave, *Charles I's Lord Treasurer*, 1976.

10. Prince Rupert

Prince Rupert's Diary: notes preserved in the Wiltshire Record Office at Trowbridge.
Warburton, B. E. G., *Memoirs of Prince Rupert and the Cavaliers*, 3 vols, 1849.
Scott, E., *Rupert, Prince Palatine*, 1899.
Thomson, G. M., *Warrior Prince, Prince Rupert of the Rhine*, 1899, 1976.
Cleugh, J., *Prince Rupert*, 1934.
Wilkinson, C. A., *Prince Rupert the Cavalier*, 1934.
Edinger, G. A., *Rupert of the Rhine*, 1936.
Fergusson, B. E., *Rupert of the Rhine*, 1952.
Knight, F. E., *Rupert, Prince of Cavaliers*, 1967.
Ashley, M., *Rupert of the Rhine*, 1976.
Morrah, P., *Prince Rupert of the Rhine*, 1976.

11. Endymion Porter

Townshend, D., *The Life and Letters of Mr. Endymion Porter*, 1897.
Huxley, G., *Endymion Porter: the Life of a Courtier, 1587–1640*, 1959.

12. Peter Paul Rubens

Sainsbury, W. N., *Original Unpublished Papers Illustrative of the Life of Sir Peter Paul Rubens*, 1859.
Magurn, R. S., *The Letters of Peter Paul Rubens*, 1955.

13. Sir Benjamin Rudyerd

Manning, J. A. (ed.), *The Memoirs of Benjamin Rudyerd, containing his Speeches and Poems*, 1841.

14. Oliver Cromwell

Firth, C. H., *Oliver Cromwell and the Rule of the Puritans in England*, 1900.
Ashley, M. P., *The Greatness of Oliver Cromwell*, 1957.
Hill, J. E. C. *Oliver Cromwell*, 1958.
Fraser, A., *Cromwell, Our Chief of Men*, 1975.

15. Sir John Eliot

Forster, J., *Sir John Eliot: a Biography*, 2 vols, 1864.
Hulme, H., *The Life of Sir John Eliot, 1592–1632: a Struggle for Parliamentary Freedom*, 1957.

16. John Hampden

Nugent, G. G., *Memorials of John Hampden, his Party and his Times*, 2 vols, 1831.

Williamson, H. R., *John Hampden*, 1933.
Adair, J., *John Hampden the Patriot*, 1976.

17. John Pym

Wade, C. S., *John Pym*, 1912.
Brett, S. R., *John Pym: the Statesman of the Puritan Revolution*, 1940.
Hexter, J. H., *The Reign of King Pym*, 1941, 1960.
Glow, L., 'Pym and Parliament', *J.M.H.*, 36, 1964, pp. 373–97.

18. Diego Sarmiento de Acuna, Count of Gondomar

Mattingly, G., 'A Game of Chess', *Renaissance Diplomacy*, 1955.
Carter, C. H., 'Gondomar: Ambassador to James I', *H.J.*, VII, 1964.

19. The Earl of Essex

Snow, V. F., *Essex the Rebel, the Life of Robert Devereux, the third Earl of Essex 1591–1646*, 1970.

20. Lord Cottington: no biography but see DNB.

21. William Harvey

Keynes, G., *The Life of William Harvey*, 1966.

R Essay collections and discussions on the causes of the civil wars

Hill, J. E. C. *English Revolution, 1640*, 3rd. ed. 1955.
Aiken, W. A. and Henning, B. D. (eds), *Conflict in Stuart England*, 1960.
Fisher, F. J. (ed.), *Essays in the Economic and Social History of Tudor and Stuart England*, 1961.
Carter, C. H. (ed.), *From the Renaissance to the Counter-Reformation*, 1966.
Taylor, P. A. M., *The Origins of the English Civil War*, 1966.
Innes, E. W. (ed.), *The English Revolution 1600–1660*, 1968.
Parry, R. H. (ed.), *The English Civil War and After*, 1970.
Reinmuth, H. S. (ed.), *Early Stuart Studies*, 1970.
Russell, C. (ed.), *The Origins of the English Civil War*, 1973.
Stone, L., *The Causes of the English Revolution, 1529–1642*, 1973.
Manning, B. (ed.), *Politics, Religion and the English Civil War*, 1973.
Elton, G. R., *Studies in Tudor and Stuart Politics and Government* (papers and reviews), 2 vols, 1974.
Sharpe, K. (ed.), *Faction and Parliament*, 1978.
Pennington, D. and Thomas, K., *Puritans and Revolutionaries: Essays in Seventeenth Century History Presented to Christopher Hill*, 1978.
Clark, P., Smith, A. G. R. and Tyacke, N., *The English Commonwealth 1547–1640: Essays in Politics and Society Presented to Joel Hurstfield*, 1979.

S General works

Finally, the monumental histories of the period, which are indispensable:

Clarendon, Edward Hyde, Earl of, *The History of the Rebellion and Civil Wars in England*, several eds, 3 vols, 1702–4; 6 vols, 1888.

Gardiner, S. R., *History of England from the Accession of James I to the Outbreak of the Civil War 1603–42*, 10 vols, 1883–4.

Gardiner, S. R., *History of the Great Civil War, 1642–9*, 4 vols, 1893.

Also

D'Ewes, S., *The Autobiography [to 1636] and Correspondence [to 1649]*, 2 vols, 1845.

Verney Family, *Memoirs of the Verney Family from the letters . . . at Claydon House*, 2 vols, 1925.

Wedgwood, C. V., *The Thirty Years War*, 1938.

Firth, C. H., *Essays Historical and Literary*, 1938.

Wormald, B., *Clarendon, Politics, History and Religion 1640–1660*, 1951.

Ashley, M. *England in the Seventeenth Century*, 1952, 1978.

Aylmer, G., *The Struggle for the Constitution 1603–1689*, 1963.

Roots, I., *The Great Rebellion, 1642–1660*, 1966.

Pennington, D. H., *Seventeenth-Century Europe*, 1970.

Cooper, J. P., 'The Fall of the Stuart Monarchy' in *The New Cambridge Modern History*, Vol. IV, 1971.

Hill, J. E. C., *Change and Continuity in Seventeenth-Century England*, 1975.

Manning, B., *The English People and the English Revolution 1640–49*, 1976.

Ashton, R., *The English Civil War, Conservatism and Revolution 1603–1649*, 1978.

White, S. D., *Sir Edward Coke and the Grievances of the Commonwealth*, 1979.

Ashton, R., *The City and the Court*, 1979.

Woods, T. P. S., *Prelude to Civil War, 1642: Mr Justice Malet and the Kentish Petition*, 1980.

Index